THE CAMBRIDGE HISTORY OF
THE PACIFIC ISLANDERS

THE CAMBRIDGE
HISTORY OF
THE PACIFIC ISLANDERS

edited by

DONALD DENOON
with
STEWART FIRTH, JOCELYN LINNEKIN,
MALAMA MELEISEA and KAREN NERO

CAMBRIDGE
UNIVERSITY PRESS

PUBLISHED BY THE PRESS SYNDICATE OF THE UNIVERSITY OF CAMBRIDGE
The Pitt Building, Trumpington Street, Cambridge CB2 1RP, United Kingdom

CAMBRIDGE UNIVERSITY PRESS
The Edinburgh Building, Cambridge CB2 2RU, United Kingdom
40 West 20th Street, New York, NY 10011–4211, USA
10 Stamford Road, Oakleigh, Melbourne 3166, Australia

First published 1997

Printed in Singapore by Kin Keong

Typeset in Palatino 10 pt

National Library of Australia Cataloguing in Publication data

The Cambridge history of the Pacific Islanders.
Bibliography.
Includes index.
ISBN 0 521 44195 1.
1. Pacific Islanders – History. 2. Pacific Islanders –
Social life and customs – History. 3. Oceania – History.
4. Oceania – Social life and customs – History. I. Denoon,
Donald.
305.899

Library of Congress Cataloguing in Publication data

The Cambridge history of the Pacific Islanders/Donald Denoon . . . [et al.].
    p.   cm.
Includes bibliographical references and index.
ISBN 0-521-44195-1 (alk. paper)
1. Oceania – History. 2. Pacific Islanders. 3. Ethnology –
Oceania. I. Denoon, Donald.
DU28.3.C33 1997   96–52784
995–dc21

A catalogue record for this book is available from the British Library

ISBN 0 521 44195 1 hardback

CONTENTS

MAPS AND FIGURES

MAPS

FIGURES

CONTRIBUTORS

SANDRA BOWDLER's doctorate was earned at the Australian National University. She lectured at the University of New England, and was a consultant archaeologist in Sydney, before her appointment to the chair of Archaeology at the University of Western Australia. Her research focuses on early prehistory and links between Australia and South-East Asia.

PAUL D'ARCY studied in Otago and at the University of Hawai'i, has lectured in Pacific Islands History at the University of Otago, and is a doctoral student in the Australian National University; he aspires to restore and strengthen the maritime dimension of Pacific Island scholarship.

DONALD DENOON lectured at Makerere University in Uganda, after his Cambridge PhD. His African career was interrupted by Idi Amin, and he became professor of History at the University of Papua New Guinea, and is now professor of Pacific Islands History at the Australian National University; his research interests include medical history and the comparative study of settler societies.

STEWART FIRTH lectured in History at the University of Papua New Guinea, and is now associate professor of Politics at Macquarie University; he is the author of *Nuclear Playground*, and *New Guinea Under the Germans*. His research interests also include Australian politics.

VILSONI HERENIKO, author and playwright from the island of Rotuma, earned his PhD from the University of the South Pacific and is Assistant Professor at the University of Hawai'i at Manoa, teaching Pacific literature, film and video, drama and theatre, and cultural identities. His plays include *Last Virgin in Paradise* and *The Monster*. *Woven Gods: Female Clowns and Power in Rotuma*, was published by UHP in 1995 and he is general editor of *Talanoa: Contemporary Pacific Literature*.

PŌKĀ LAENUI (Hayden Burgess) is an attorney in Wai'anae, Hawai'i. He was the primary political spokesperson for the World Council of Indigenous Peoples from 1985 to 1990. He is President of the Pacific–Asia Council of Indigenous Peoples, Director of the Institute for the Advancement of Hawaiian Affairs, was elected by the native Hawaiians as a trustee to the Office of Hawaiian Affairs, and was a member of the Hawaiian Sovereignty Elections Council.

BRIJ LAL graduated from the University of the South Pacific, and was awarded his doctorate at the Australian National University. He has taught at the Universities of the South Pacific, Hawai'i and Papua New Guinea, and is a Senior Fellow at the Australian National University. He has served on the Fiji Constitutional Commission, and his other interests include the experiences of the Indian diaspora, and the modern history of Fiji.

ROBERT LANGDON's career in journalism and historical research is described in his autobiography, *Every Goose a Swan*. He has been awarded an honorary MA by the Australian National University, and a knighthood by the King of Spain. He was the first executive officer of the Pacific Manuscripts Bureau, and a Fellow of the Australian National University; his interest in Pacific Island settlement history is undiminished in retirement.

LAMONT LINDSTROM earned his PhD in Anthropology at the University of California, Berkeley. Since 1978 he has been involved in anthropological and linguistic research in Melanesia, primarily in Vanuatu. As well as cargo cults and custom, his interests range across Melanesian knowledge systems, *kava*, and Pacific War experiences. He is professor of Anthropology at Tulsa University, Oklahoma.

JOCELYN LINNEKIN studied at Columbia, and took her PhD at the University of Michigan. She was a research assistant to Marshall Sahlins, and has conducted research in Hawai'i and Samoa. She is Professor of Anthropology at the University of Hawai'i, and author of *Children of the Land: Exchange and Status in a Hawaiian Community*, and *Sacred Queens and Women of Consequence*. Her research interests include ethnography, gender relations and cultural identity.

VICKI LUKERE won History medals at both Melbourne and Sydney Universities. Her doctoral dissertation for the Australian National University analyses health and gender issues in early colonial Fiji, and she researches similar issues in other colonial contexts. She lectures in History at Victoria University in Wellington.

MALAMA MELEISEA studied at the University of Papua New Guinea, and took his doctorate at Macquarie University. He has taught at the University of the South Pacific, was Director of the Macmillan-Brown Centre in Christchurch, and now directs the Centre for Pacific Studies at Auckland University. His research interests flow outwards from Samoa.

KAREN NERO, Senior Lecturer in Anthropology at Auckland University, conducted historical research in Palau. As director of Micronesian Field Studies at the University of California at Irvine, she headed collaborative studies of Pacific migration, and contemporary transformations in Micronesian gendered food systems. She has also edited a volume on Pacific arts and politics.

RUTH SAOVANA SPRIGGS studied Education at the Universities of Papua New Guinea and Hawai'i, and co-ordinated the Language and Literature Program in Bougainville. She has been a research assistant in Linguistics at the Australian National University, and has begun her doctoral studies on changing women's power structures in Bougainville.

PENELOPE SCHOEFFEL studied at the University of Papua New Guinea, and took her doctorate in Anthropology at the Australian National University. She has lectured at the University of Canterbury, and is a frequent consultant for development projects in the Pacific Islands. She now lectures in Anthropology at the Tamaki campus of Auckland University.

MATTHEW SPRIGGS took his first degree at Cambridge, and earned his Prehistory PhD at the Australian National University. He has taught at the University of Hawai'i and was a Fellow in Prehistory at the Australian National University until his recent appointment to the chair of Archaeology in the same university. He has researched and published extensively on the recent prehistory of the Pacific Islands.

DARRELL TRYON, a linguist who has written widely on Austronesian and Oceanic languages, is Convenor of the Division of Society and Environment at the Australian National University. His research includes comparative and historical linguistics, pidgins and creoles, and language and society in the Asia-Pacific region.

TOON VAN MEIJL gained his PhD in Social Anthropology from the Australian National University, and is a Senior Fellow of the Royal Netherlands Academy of Arts and Sciences at the Centre for Pacific Studies in Nijmegen. His interests include the politics of culture and identity, and the comparative study of kingship in the Pacific Islands.

KARIN VON STROKIRCH gained her PhD in Political Science from La Trobe University, for her study of Tahitian politics, a topic on which she has several publications. She now lectures in Political Science at the University of New England, New South Wales.

GERARD WARD was foundation Professor of Geography at the University of Papua New Guinea, and became Professor of Human Geography at the Australian National University, where he was also director of the Research School of Pacific and Asian Studies. He recently edited *Land, Custom and Practice in the South Pacific,* and his research interests include the history of labour migration in Papua New Guinea.

ABBREVIATIONS

Angau	Australian New Guinea Administrative Unit
BRA	Bougainville Revolutionary Army
CEP	Centre d'Expérimentation du Pacifique (Pacific Experimentation Centre, French Polynesia)
CNMI	Commonwealth of the Northern Mariana Islands
CRA	Conzinc Riotinto Australia
CSR	Colonial Sugar Refining Company, *later* Corporation (Australia)
DHPG	Deutsche Handels- und Plantagen-Gesellschaft
FLNKS	Front de Libération Nationale Kanake et Socialiste (New Caledonia)
FSM	Federated States of Micronesia
LMS	London Missionary Society
NFP	National Federation Party (Fijian political party)
OPM	Organisasi Papua Merdeka (Free Papua Movement, Irian Jaya)
PNGDF	Papua New Guinea Defence Force
RDPT	Rassemblement Démocratique des Populations Tahitiennes (Tahitian political party)
SVT	Soqosoqo ni Vakavulewa ni Taukei (Fijian political party)
UNCLOS III	United Nations Convention of the Law of the Sea, 1982
UTD	Union Tahitienne Démocratique (Tahitian political party)

CONVERSIONS

Length
1 inch = 25.4 mm
1 foot = 30.5 cm
1 yard = 0.91 m
1 mile = 1.61 km

Mass
1 ounce = 28.3 g
1 pound = 454 g
1 ton = 1.02 t

Area
1 acre = 0.405 ha

Volume
1 gallon = 4.55 L

Currency
Sums of money are in United States dollars and pounds sterling unless otherwise specified.

PREFACE

Since *The Cambridge Modern History*, edited by Lord Acton, appeared in sixteen volumes between 1902 and 1912, multi-volume Cambridge Histories, planned and edited by historians of established reputation, with individual chapters written by leading specialists in their fields, have set the highest standards of collaborative international scholarship. The original *Modern History* has now been replaced by the fourteen-volume *New Cambridge Modern History*, and has been joined by histories of Islam, Japan, Literary Criticism, Iran, Judaism, South-East Asia, Arabic literature and Africa among others.

This history is conceived as a source of information and interpretations, for readers who seek an introduction to the experiences of the people of this vast and ill-defined region. We seek to provide clear and reliable first words, not to lay down the last word. After each chapter we suggest sources for readers who wish to pursue a topic in depth.

The book addresses the question of insularity, since continental people often imagine that island life must be insular and introspective. That intuition is reinforced if we assume that the terms Melanesia, Polynesia, Micronesia and Aboriginal Australia refer to bounded populations rather than clusters of cultural features. We show how Islanders overcame their geographical isolation, and we have designed the chapters to highlight linkages. Our geographic limits are elastic, sometimes including Aboriginal Australians in northern and eastern Australia. Similarly we include Maori, and Irianese in western New Guinea. We follow island migrants to New Zealand, Australia and North America; and we include settled immigrant communities in Fiji and New Caledonia, and in Hawai'i until the archipelago was incorporated into the United States. Wherever possible we organise our narratives by topic, at the expense of geographic and even chronological neatness.

The first chapter reveals the assumptions and approaches which inform our writing, and in chapter 2 we display several different traditions and styles of portraying Islanders' pasts. Once the outlines of settlement are established, we consider how people elaborated techniques of production and devised methods of exchange, before trying to grasp their perceptions of the Europeans who sailed across their horizons. These encounters challenged Islanders' sense of themselves, and introduced economic and political opportunities and threats, reviewed in chapter 5. Ambitious Islanders, inspired or provoked by explorers, traders and missionaries, embarked on the transformation of political structures, with effects which are discussed in chapter 6; while chapter 7 considers changes in production, and the population loss which accompanied these new linkages. As power relations shifted in favour of Europeans, colonial governments replaced the informal imperial arrangements of the nineteenth century. In the eyes of colonial officials, diverse peoples all became 'natives', with similar and limited abilities. The invention of the 'native' is treated in chapter 8, together with an account of the programs and the limitations of colonial authority.

Part Two treats the Pacific region since World War II. Chapter 9 outlines the Pacific War which swept across the region like a four-year cyclone, and explores its ideological and political consequences. Once peace was restored, Western powers used some islands to test nuclear weapons. Chapter 10 examines these episodes and their political fallout. Chapters 11 and 12 review the legacy of the colonial era, which has closed in most of the islands but which has altered the political, economic, cultural and ideological conditions in diffuse ways. We close by asking to what extent the islanders' experience has been that of isolation or insularity, and to what extent these were inventions of scholars and administrators.

Writing this book required constant balancing. Our desire to hedge our general statements is balanced against the readers' need for clarity. In an ideal history, indigenous scholars would determine the structure and dominate the writing of the text. One consequence of the region's recent history is that few Islanders enjoy the facilities for this task. Rather than wait another generation, we rely on our own largely expatriate experiences of teaching, research and island living, and ensure that the voices of Island participants and scholars are present in the narratives. In some ways these voices subvert our own arguments. The same is true when we try to encompass the often distinctive experience of women, without segregating them in separate chapters.

Ideally, we would give weight to each part of the region, in rough proportion to its population. In practice, we rely on published scholarship which is highly uneven, and is largely the work of outsiders. The literature about native Hawaiians, New Zealand Maori, Samoans and Tongans is highly developed and includes substantial contributions by island intellectuals. At the other extreme, books on Irian Jaya are distressingly scarce, and almost entirely the work of outsiders. Similar problems of uneven source material arise in balancing the immense anthropological literature and the more limited work on linguistics and literature, against the later arrival of economists, geographers, historians and political scientists. To compound the problem, each discipline approaches the region differently. Archaeologists articulate the most powerful sense of the region as an integrated entity. It may be that their emphasis on material evidence enables them to transcend boundaries marked by cultural complexes. By contrast, the work of anthropologists, political scientists and linguists is usually specific to one or a few neighbouring communities. Only international relations commentators, analysing modern regional organisations such as the South Pacific Commission and the South Pacific Forum, are thoroughly regional in their canvas. Between 'pre-history' and the 1970s, scholarship often obscures the linkages and common experiences of the region.

ACKNOWLEDGMENTS

We are grateful to Gerard Ward and Elizabeth Kingdon for allowing us to quote from *Land, Custom and Practice in the South Pacific*; to Andrew Strathern for permission to reproduce text from *Ongka: A Self-account by a New Guinea Big-man*; to Anne Salmond for quotations from *Two Worlds: First Meetings between Maori and Europeans*; to Epeli Hau'ofa for extracts from 'Our Sea of Islands', in *A New Oceania*; and to Greg Dening for quotations from *Mr Bligh's Bad Language*. Chicago University Press generously allowed us to quote extracts from Richard Parmentier's *The Sacred Remains*; and the University of Hawai'i Press did the same for sections of Martha Beckwith's edition of *The Kumulipo* and Joel Bonnemaison's *The Tree and the Canoe*; the Gunter Narr Verlag also allowed us to reproduce sections from Stephen Wurm's *Papuan Languages of Oceania*, and the University of Stanford Press was equally helpful in respect of text from Schieffelin and Crittenden, *Like People You See in a Dream*. An earlier version of Vilsoni Hereniko's 'Pacific Cultural Identities' (in chapter 12) was published by the University of Hawai'i Press in Kerry Howe, Bob Kiste and Brij Lal (eds), *Tides of History*: we are obliged to the editors for permission to publish this revised version.

Winifred Mumford prepared the maps and illustrations with characteristic care and flair; and Janet Mackenzie's exemplary editing removed many errors and ambiguities. We also acknowledge the help of the many students who contributed towards this book, discussing draft chapters in formal classes and in innumerable informal conversations.

THE PACIFIC TO 1941

CHAPTER

1

CONTENDING APPROACHES

Like eunuchs, they grace the shoreline of Waikiki. Coconut palms without coconuts. Symbols of lost identities. Exotic images as a backdrop for semi-naked tourists lounging on the beach.

Coconut palms have grown at Waikiki since the first Hawaiians arrived in their magnificent canoes some two thousand years ago . . . Coconut palms were much valued then—for the many different uses of their roots, trunks, and leaves, but mainly for their nuts, which provided a reliable source of sustenance. Coconut flesh was scraped and its cream used for cooking; coconut juice was refreshing and nourishing—ideal for a tropical climate. But all that has changed forever, at least at Waikiki, where tourists now reign. There, coconut palms are merely decorative, essential to complete the picture of Paradise—a tropical world of pleasure and personal happiness. To maintain this illusion, coconuts are removed so that dreams of Eden may remain intact.

Vilsoni Hereniko[1]

What we think about the past of Samoa (and its future) is determined by what we are.

Albert Wendt[2]

POINTS OF VIEW

In every community there are diverse points of view on past events and experiences. Clearly there can be no single, seamless history of the many peoples who inhabit the Pacific Islands. *The Cambridge History* acknowledges the diversity of Pacific voices and the particularity of their experiences, while narrating common patterns and intersections with global events. This is 'a' history, not the only possible construction of events affecting Islanders. A composite history told through indig-enous genres would consist of oral accounts, related in many languages and taking widely varying forms. Some would explain the origins of gods, humans, plants and animals; others would recount great voyages or the rivalries and conquests of great chiefs. Chanted, spoken, or sung, the narratives might not relate events in chronological order. Some

---

1 'Representations of Cultural Identities', in Howe, Kiste and Lal, *Tides of History*.
2 'Guardians and Wards', 113.

would take the form of genealogies, and crucial details might vary with the teller—and with each audience. Europeans and Americans would figure in accounts of recent times, but the Islanders' versions of events would likely hold a severely critical mirror to those Western histories which celebrate 'discovery' and the benefits of colonisation.

This volume does not attempt to compile indigenous histories in their native formats. The authors have been trained in Western universities, in history and anthropology, and the text follows many conventions of the Western narrative form which we call 'history'. Excepting direct quotations, the volume is written in a single language. Without attempting to be all-inclusive, the chapters by and large centre on events, though not always the events which Western observers considered significant. The accounts are roughly in chronological order, but this volume differs from conventional published histories in several respects. Most obviously, we focus on the experiences of peoples who did not produce written accounts before the coming of Europeans. This is but one reason why narrating Islanders' 'history' is controversial today. Some indigenous Pacific leaders and intellectuals argue that foreign scholars have neither the right nor the competence to write objectively about cultural 'others'. Anti-colonial political critiques and post-modernist moves to 'deconstruct' and 'decentre' received discourse have also undermined the implicit authority of scholarly writing. The reflexive challenge has been so effective that in some social sciences the impersonal, un-selfconscious narrator is becoming extinct.

Vilsoni Hereniko's epigram powerfully conveys the host of cultural, ethical and epistemological issues raised by 'history'. Lawyers and film makers as well as academics have documented the 'Rashomon effect' in accounts of lived experience: that witnesses to the same event produce radically different testimonies, and it may be impossible to validate one version while rejecting others. The post-colonial Pacific is marginal to the economic and strategic concerns of the major industrial nations. In this context of unequal power, whose version of history should be the authoritative text, and how will Islanders be portrayed—as effective actors or as history's victims? Is it possible to avoid constructing a Western 'master narrative' in which Islanders' stories are but a sub-plot? Moreover, is it not presumptuous to speak of 'Islanders' as if Pacific peoples spoke in a single voice? Even within the smallest Pacific societies there are wide disparities of status and authority. How can we include the stories of those who are not dominant in their own societies, such as women, lower-status men, and 'subaltern' minority groups?

In the second epigram, the Samoan historian and novelist Albert Wendt points out that history is always written from a point of view. This statement in his 1965 thesis foreshadowed the now-fashionable dictum that all knowledge is constructed rather than simply uncovered. This insight implies that Pacific history is not a set of unambiguous facts, awaiting scholarly discovery like a buried cache of adzes. Rather, our understandings are influenced by the biases of our sources and are bound up with our own context: class, ethnicity, gender, education, political persuasion and biography all influence an author's perspective. The recognition of context and point of view applies to ourselves as writers as well as to the observers on whom we depend for information. The implications for analysis are profound. How can we take into account context and still use ethnohistorical information, partial and flawed as it is? Much has been written about the effects of Eurocentrism on descriptions of non-Western cultures. In many situations the pre-conceptions of Western observers amounted to blindness. To what extent, for example, did European male explorers and traders possess a vocabulary—categories, a 'cognitive map'—for thinking about women's position and agency in Island societies?

The notion of 'interest' is important to the theory of constructed knowledge. Even without a direct material interest or a conscious political agenda, the argument runs, a writer has a 'stake' in pursuing a question and arguing a position. The contributors to this volume aspire to neutrality, if not to the chimera of objectivity, but they do not represent a unified point of view and the reader should be forewarned of disagreements, as well as differences of voice, emphasis and inter-pretation. Several chapters and sections are authored by Islanders and elsewhere we draw on statements of Islanders from a variety of sources. Using such primary material is one way to include the voices of Islanders who are subaltern (or subordinate) in their own societies.

The product of collaboration between historians and anthropologists, this volume aims to be more than a chronicle. A striking feature of Western scholarship in the Pacific Islands is the dominance of Anthro-pology since the late nineteenth century. The fieldwork methods and the intellectual concerns of academic Anthropology have also had a profound influence on other social sciences, including Linguistics, Human Geography, Political Science and Archaeology, as well as History. Anthropologists have been concerned with the past since the inception of the discipline, but their gaze tended to focus on cultural wholes and broad patterns of change rather than unpredictable events and outcomes. Until recently, anthropologists emphasised the struc-tured, routine aspects of events such as market transactions and ritual performances. They rediscovered history as a theoretical problem in the 1980s—when historians were extending their own gaze beyond par-ticular sequences of events. This conjunction has resulted in productive collaborations. Blending the insights of their disciplines, the authors of this volume elaborate the contexts and consequences of events in a com-parative framework, offering generalisations qualified by the particu-larities of culture, geography and event.

As Hereniko's reflection suggests, transformations in cultural identity, politics and economics are very much part of Islander histories. Moreover, the apparent 'insularity' of Pacific peoples appears less significant than the connections between people. Only recently have scholars begun to give full weight to the complex entanglements that have linked Pacific peoples to one another and, more recently, to Westerners. One of the pervasive effects of Western intervention and colonial administration was the decline of many maritime systems of trade and exchange. By the early twentieth century therefore, when serious academic research began in the region, inter-island connections were markedly less important than they had been—and have often been ignored as a result. Archaeologists, for example, long interpreted Hawai'i's social and demographic evolution in terms of geographic isolation. A recent iconoclastic theory suggests that voyages to Hawai'i may have been more frequent than previously supposed, and may have originated in several island groups rather than a single jumping-off place, hitherto presumed to be the Marquesas. As this example illustrates, emphasising connectedness rather than isolation has sweeping implications for the way we represent such issues as ethnicity, identity, mobility, and 'Western impact'.

Long before the appearance of square-riggers, Islanders maintained long-distance exchange and marriage relationships with one another. It is difficult to deny, however, that the most sweeping transformations followed colonisation by Western powers. From the eighteenth-century era of exploration to the cataclysm of World War II, Islander histories have been intimately linked to the actions of Westerners. With few exceptions Islanders have been the colonised rather the colonisers, and this unifying experience is perhaps the most compelling justification for a single-volume history of the region. Modern Pacific political leaders have argued that Islanders share not only common interests but, in the broadest sense, a cultural heritage which is in many ways antithetical to that of the industrial, erstwhile colonial nations.

BOUNDARIES

In the first epigram above, Vilsoni Hereniko develops a metaphor for culture change and the profound losses occasioned by Western contact. Hereniko's own background illustrates the complexities of cultural boundaries and affiliations in the modern Pacific. An author and playwright from the island of Rotuma, Hereniko earned a PhD from the University of the South Pacific in Fiji and is now on the faculty of the University of Hawai'i. Rotuma is termed a Polynesian outlier because its language and cultural institutions appear to have closer affinities with the island groups to the east; yet Rotuma belongs politically to the nation of Fiji, which is assigned to Melanesia on geographic and linguistic grounds. Several Fijian cultural institutions are considered characteristic of Polynesia, however, notably hereditary chieftainship and the *kava* ceremony. Depending on the situation, Hereniko can properly identify himself as Rotuman, Polynesian, a Fijian citizen, or as a Pacific intellectual, among other possible affiliations. One theme of this volume is that collective categories and self-ascribed identities have a history of development, and vary according to the demands of the present. Group identities and labels are not primordial or fixed, but arise and change. The categories which foreigners applied to indigenous peoples typically reveal more about outsiders' preconceptions than they do about indigenous models of group identity. Similarly, modern political boundaries are historically created rather than preordained or inevitable.

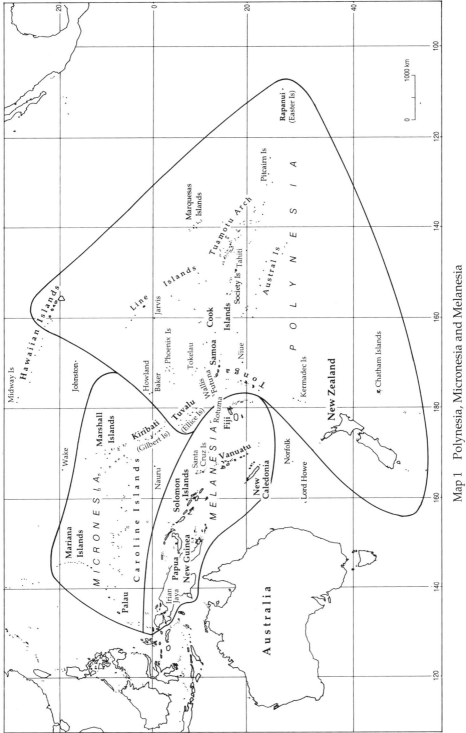

Map 1   Polynesia, Micronesia and Melanesia

The most popular paradigm for discussing the Island Pacific has been the regional division of Melanesia, Polynesia and Micronesia. Though it has long been a stock feature of scholarly writing, the scheme has a history of its own. The tripartite division is credited to the French explorer Dumont d'Urville, in an address to the Geographical Society of Paris.[3] Though defined largely through geography, the division has a basis in linguistic and cultural affinities; hence the notion of 'Polynesian outliers' in Melanesia and Micronesia. D'Urville and his contemporaries saw the three regions as coterminous with human 'races'. Melanesia means 'black islands', and nineteenth-century writers deterministically equated culture and behaviour with perceived racial categories. Polynesians were sensual and hospitable; Melanesians were typically described as savage. The tripartite division both derived from and buttressed prevailing European stereotypes about non-Western peoples.

'Race' and 'culture' were equated in Western scholarly and popular thought until the emergence of anthropology as a coherent discipline in the early twentieth century. The conceptual separation of race and culture was a central tenet in the scholarship of Franz Boas, one of American anthropology's founding figures and the mentor of Margaret Mead and many others who studied Pacific peoples. Boas is credited with articulating anthropology's guiding ethic of 'cultural relativism', the doctrine that all cultures are equally valid as human life-ways, and are not to be judged from the vantage point of Western values. Boas impressed upon his students the necessity of fieldwork, with the goal of producing detailed, ideologically neutral documentation of non-Western cultures. As the intellectual wellspring of American anthropology, Boasian 'historical particularism' had far-reaching influence on Pacific studies generally, particularly in the vehement rejection of racial determinism and the goal of value-free description.

Received categories such as Melanesia, Micronesia and Polynesia have become increasingly vulnerable. They were in their inception artificial creations by Europeans—labels to make sense of the cultural, linguistic, and phenotypic contrasts and commonalities that they encountered. Attention has been called to their origin in Orientalist and racist European thought; at least one writer has levelled the accusation that modern scholars who employ the tripartite division share the racist presuppositions of their nineteenth-century forebears.[4] Archaeologists and prehistorians find a distinction between Near Oceania and Remote Oceania more useful for describing the stepwise settlement of the Pacific Islands. There is the immediate sense that regional divisions have little relevance in the current era of transnational diasporas, global economy, and telecommunications, when Auckland is the most Polynesian city in the world and Cook Islanders watch Rambo films with the aid of generator-powered VCRs. Scholars have increasingly asserted that the 'regions' never were discrete entities, and if the labels suggest social, cultural, or racial isolation then they may be more mis-

---

3   D'Urville, *Voyage de la Corvette L'Astrolabe*, vol. 2, 614–16; Thomas, 'The Force of Ethnology', 30–1.
4   Thomas, 'The Force of Ethnology', 33–4.

leading than illuminating. Most modern scholars agree that cultural boundaries have always been dynamically changing and permeable.

Having noted the historicity and vulnerability of this scheme, however, we concede that the labels are a useful shorthand and we employ them to a limited extent. While acknowledging recent critiques, most of the writers believe that 'Melanesia' and 'Polynesia' retain some utility for describing regional cultural homologies and linguistic relationships. The cultural diversity of Micronesia makes that label useful primarily, again, as a geographic shorthand. However, we emphatically do not impute timeless, fixed, or finite boundaries to these 'regions' and we explicitly reject any equation of 'races' with the geographic labels. Similarly, we reject the premise that some island groups represent an 'authentic' or 'pure' cultural core or essence.

If we envision a historical continuum of human movements and transactions across the Pacific, then demarcating the scope of this volume becomes especially difficult. Many commonly used categories reflect the agendas of those who invented them, but for practicality's sake we must also limit the volume's range of inquiry. Aboriginal Australian peoples, for example, are not conventionally included in the category 'Pacific Islanders' although they are indigenous Pacific peoples. The rationale is that native Australian languages and customs do not appear to be closely related to those of the island Pacific, reflecting the ancient separation of Australia from the Islands. However, Aboriginal peoples in the Torres Strait and northern Australia have long had casual contacts and exchange relationships with 'Melanesians' in New Guinea and outlying islands. Rather than exclude those populations because they seem to fall into a different ethnic pigeonhole, we discuss Torres Strait Islanders and Aboriginal peoples in the north and east of Australia to the extent that they have interacted with Pacific Islanders. The indigenous peoples of West Irian (Irian Jaya) are also included, despite the paucity of scholarship concerning them. Categorised by scholars as Melanesians, the Irianese fall on the other side of a recent political boundary, and the western half of the island of New Guinea is now a province of Indonesia.

The problem of boundaries also arises in treating the predominantly European nations of the South Pacific. We do not attempt a comprehensive history of modern Australia and New Zealand, but these settler states can hardly be ignored. They have been major players in Islands history and are today the most frequent destinations of emigrating Islanders. Our purview also includes migrant communities such as the Indians of Fiji and the French colonists in New Caledonia, but our focus is the experiences of indigenous Pacific peoples.

HISTORY AND ETHNOHISTORY

A long-standing convention in Western scholarship was that historians studied events while anthropologists studied cultures. To cultural anthropologists, 'ethnohistory' meant the reconstruction of past life-ways by analysing documentary materials. The major Pacific societies have all been treated extensively in this sense, ethnohistorians often beginning with the era where archaeologists left off. Ethnohistorical reconstruction embodies an obvious paradox: the aim is to formulate inferences—informed guesses—about a society that is no longer extant, using materials from the period of European contact. Nearly all the sources are written by foreigners. Participant observation and interviewing—the anthropologist's stock-in-trade—are impossible, and the mundane features of daily life are usually the most elusive details to establish.

To the academic audience, the significance of ethnohistorical work usually hinges on its thoroughness, and originality is measured by the extent to which the scholars ferret out unpublished sources and make sense of fragmentary records. Marshall Sahlins's researches on early Hawai'i and Fiji set a standard for the comprehensive and innovative use of archival sources. Both history and ethnohistory are document-oriented: published explorers' accounts, unpublished correspondence, ships' logs, and early missionary reports are the ethnohistorian's starting-point. With luck, the researcher may find archival records which lend depth and quantitative substance to the analysis: census reports, land deeds, court testimony, wills, tax rolls, petitions and the like often throw light on local conditions and daily life. Such materials are the basis for many statements in this volume, particularly for the eighteenth and nineteenth centuries.

Anthropologists working with ethnohistorical sources face much the same dilemmas as historians. Travellers' reports are, at best, highly selective. Early visitors to the Pacific were following their own agendas —exploration, trade and missionisation, usually in that order—and these purposes influenced what they reported and the value judgements they made. Ideally, the observer's bias should be ascertained and taken into account, but there are no hard-and-fast rules for evaluating sources. The decision whether and how to use a particular source involves judgement by the researcher, assisted by received wisdom about the reliability of particular observers and by certain common-sense criteria. Was the writer present for a day, a week, or several months? Did he or she disembark, or view the island from shipboard? Are the comments based on personal observation, or on interviews with a castaway or other resident foreigner? Are specific statements corroborated by other writers? And when one finds apparent corroboration, how can we determine whether the author simply plagiarised another writer's work? Needless to say, eighteenth- and nineteenth-century standards of citation and attribution were less rigorous than today's.

Early visitors to the Islands did not think in anthropological categories, and important details about kinship, politics and other cultural matters are typically embedded in reports on other matters. Gender relations and women's status are particularly difficult to reconstruct. European explorers and traders—all men—came from a highly gender-stratified, male-dominant society. In the social classes which produced literate observers during the period of exploration, women were largely relegated to domestic duties while men dominated the public domain. This public/domestic separation is not universal in human societies, but the division with its implicit gender hierarchy prevailed among middle- and upper-class Europeans and Americans at the time. Western naval officers and merchants expected to conduct most of their dealings with their Islander counterparts, persons of authority; commonly this meant male chiefs and local leaders. Local women were often seen merely as potential sexual release for the crew. We cannot know how Hawaiian women construed their first sexual encounters with Captain Cook's crew, but the journals of the Third Voyage show clearly how the men interpreted their advances. A surgeon's mate gleefully described giving one nail for a woman's company for the night. The women may well have understood such gifts as love tokens from high-status visitors, but the seamen defined the exchange as prostitution.

Women in Island societies seldom fulfilled the European preconceptions of passivity, devaluation and dependency. But because male visitors interacted primarily with Island men, men's activities are relatively well documented while detailed information on women's lives scarcely exists. Marxist feminist scholars argue, following Friedrich Engels, that sexual asymmetry and male dominance are the artefacts of capitalism and state formation. However, most writers on gender in the Pacific believe that a male bias in public authority was not solely a European introduction, but was and is endogenous to many cultures. Particularly in Polynesia, women were significantly more autonomous, assertive, and culturally valued than women in the West. Even so, it would be difficult to argue that Pacific societies were gender-egalitarian before the coming of foreigners.

Historians and anthropologists have increasingly incorporated into their work the insight that Europeans approached the Pacific with a complex set of preconceptions—a 'vision', an interpretive paradigm, which shaped their interactions with Islanders. The state-sponsored explorers were particularly concerned to identify authorities with whom they could negotiate, and their reports focus in part on politics and governmental forms. Even these descriptions differed in emphasis, depending on national interest. 'Social organization to the Englishman was centered on kingship', Dening comments; 'for the American and Frenchman it was seen in terms of democratic republicanism.'[5]

A path-breaking work was Bernard Smith's *European Vision and the South Pacific, 1768–1850* (London, 1960). An art historian, Smith was far ahead of his time in addressing how Europeans constructed knowledge about indigenous societies during the period of exploration and colonisation. He analysed eighteenth- and nineteenth-century graphic representations of non-Western peoples, to reveal pervasive European constructs such as the 'noble savage'. Smith did not neglect diversity and change in elite European thought, showing how Edenic portrayals gave way in the early nineteenth century to less optimistic images of wildness, savagery and barbarism. He characterised the contending

5   Dening, 'Ethnohistory in Polynesia', 37.

European attitudes towards Pacific peoples as 'soft primitivism' and 'hard primitivism'. To eighteenth-century explorers such as Bougainville and Banks, the Tahitians exemplified 'the soft primitives of classical mythology . . . The land . . . was like Paradise before the Fall of Man, and the people lived in a natural state of innocence enjoying its bounty.' However, Calvinist Christians at home and evangelical missionaries in the field found this 'sentimental primitivism' repugnant: 'to most God-fearing Englishmen . . . it was only too apparent that these so-called innocents of nature were depraved and benighted savages'. Changes in representation during the early nineteenth century paralleled and revealed a transition in European thinking about humankind's natural state.

Smith presaged the current scholarly interest in Western colonial ideologies, but outside Pacific scholarship it is less well known than *Orientalism*, by the Palestinian literary critic Edward Said.[6] The concept of 'Orientalism' has had a profound impact on all scholarship, compelling non-native writers to reflect upon their own context and unconscious biases. Said argued that distancing, stereotypic visions of the exotic not only informed European colonialism but continue to pervade Western representations of colonised peoples. Representing the culture or the past of an indigenous people is implicitly a matter of political power. Said's critique thus targets contemporary scholarship as well as artistic and literary representations for abetting Western cultural domination.

Political and post-modernist critiques have led to increasing dissatisfaction with ethnohistory as previously practised. Anti-colonial writers such as Said have questioned whether it is possible or politically defensible for non-native scholars to attempt an 'objective' reconstruction of past cultures. Ethnohistory tended to portray pre-European societies as timeless, unchanging isolates, neglecting the patent fact that they had their own dynamics of development before Westerners arrived. Too often, anthropologists and historians implicitly and perhaps unwittingly conveyed the impression that culture change and 'history' begin with foreign contact. In the 1980s some anthropologists advocated reorienting ethnohistory to include the study of culturally variable models and genres of history: 'There are no culture-free historical facts', one monograph begins.[7] Native concepts of time, event and 'the past' are therefore crucial to any study of history in a non-Western society. Indigenous narrative forms and conventions of history—to the extent that such a genre exists—must be part of the inquiry. When 'ethnohistory' is defined in this way, Western understandings of history are equally open to examination.

Until recently, academic historians were less interested than anthropologists in introspection and debate over methods. In Western universities 'history' denotes a field of inquiry, a methodology for studying the past, and a narrative mode. To the general public, history has a

6   New York, 1978.
7   Schieffelin and Gewertz, 'Introduction', *History and Ethnohistory In Papua New Guinea*.

clearer identity and charter than anthropology. Through painstaking documentary research the historian ascertains 'historical fact'. At least in history textbooks, the typical product is a sequential account of events emphasising names, places, and dates. It was therefore a bold move for David Henige to entitle his 1982 book on method *Oral Historiography*. Historians of the 1960s would have seen the title as a contradiction in terms—'historiography' by definition denotes written rather than oral history. Henige signalled a broadening of history's purview in the era of decolonisation. Third World societies have become a subject for academic historical inquiry, and oral traditions are seen as valid sources. In effect, history became more anthropological while anthropology turned increasingly to historical questions.

To address the histories of non-literate peoples, historians had to take account of differences between oral and documentary sources. Anthropologists have long known that revision is common in oral accounts, and is intensified when political fortunes are at stake. A chiefly genealogy, for example, reflects the interests of the lineage or dynasty reciting it. Hawaiian chiefly genealogies could be told differently according to immediate purpose; genealogical specialists would highlight particular lines of relationship to legitimise an alliance between chiefs or to make peace possible. Genealogies also reflect historical outcomes. If in Polynesia a junior-ranking chiefly line came to dominate, contemporary genealogies would probably emphasise higher-ranking ancestors and connections to the senior line. 'Genealogists were called the washbasins of the *ali'i* [chiefs]', wrote the Hawaiian historian David Malo, 'in which to cleanse them.'[8]

Retrospective legitimation is not unique to non-literate cultures. Shakespeare portrayed Richard III as a ruthless, deformed murderer— an image that has come to be identified as the historic Richard, despite scholarly attempts to rehabilitate him. It is no coincidence that Shakespeare wrote in the reign of Elizabeth I, whose grandfather Henry defeated Richard and ensconced his own, not-too-illustrious Tudor dynasty. Recognising the contingent quality of oral narratives has spurred all scholars to acknowledge that written histories must also be examined as 'representations' and not simply accepted as accounts of 'facts'. This reflexive approach does not imply that nothing certain can be known about past events; the recognition that knowledge is contingent does mean that we must evaluate carefully all forms of historical discourse.

Oral traditions, like travellers' accounts and Western histories, are produced in a contemporary context, reflecting particular points of view. In scholarship about the Pacific Islands, issues of history and historiography have become conflated with issues of cultural identity construction. Geoffrey White, who worked in the Solomon Islands, writes that narratives about the past perform 'identity work', defining who people are at both local and national levels. In the Solomons, 'historical narratives do much of their "identity work"' in relation to

8   Malo, *Hawaiian Antiquities.*

descent, land and chiefly leadership.[9] But Islanders also produce stories of the recent past, 'narratives of colonisation and acculturation that forcefully shape the social realities of contemporary life'. Analyses such as White's illustrate the extent to which 'tradition' has been redefined in history and the social sciences. Once an objective statement by a scholarly authority, 'tradition' now means a model of the past that is symbolically constructed in the present and reflects contemporary agendas. The content of 'tradition' is politically charged, changeable, often ambiguous and hotly contested.

INDIGENOUS HISTORICAL GENRES

When Jean-Paul Latouche published genealogical and cosmological traditions of southern Kiribati (formerly the Gilbert Islands), he called the collection *mythistoire* 'myth-history', signifying that the two are inseparable in indigenous conceptualisation.[10] Westerners tend to view 'myth' as fantastic happenings in distant antiquity, in contrast to 'history' which is considered an objective account of more recent, verifiable 'facts'. Islanders did not presume such a distinction, and their histories often linked humans to gods and to the natural world (see chapter 2). Among many Island peoples, historical legends identify mountains and other features of the landscape with ancient supernatural beings who were turned into stone or otherwise transformed: Joel Bonnemaison describes this practice as Ethnogeography.[11] Hawaiian myth-history explains that the taro plant is the older brother of humankind, with all the role expectations attendant upon a senior–junior relationship. The anthropologist Reo Fortune wrote of Dobu Island in 1928: 'There is no sharp distinction between past and present in Dobuan legend.' Explaining the felt meaning of a complex narrative, Fortune's informant 'vigorously' asserted:

> This is not legend just . . . this is everyday speech absolutely verified. Some legends we hear with our ears only, but this thing we have seen. Near Sawatupa, the root lies. We have seen the place. Our canoes are under tabu not to approach it closely at peril of the root opening again, more water coming forth, and the sea rising to engulf the level land and the highest hills.[12]

Neither do modern Pacific Islanders relegate their oral histories to a backward or irrelevant past. In Kiribati genealogical traditions explain the present-day hierarchy and territorial organisation of society, and those I-Kiribati who refer to themselves as Tungaru still engage in vigorous debate about their cosmological origins. Chanted, recited, or written down in the period of literacy, genealogies and political histories remain vital social charters and precious family heritage.

9 Geoffrey White, *Identity Through History*, 15.
10 Latouche, *Mythistoire Tungaru*.
11 Bonnemaison, *The Tree and the Canoe*.
12 Fortune, *Sorcerers of Dobu*, 263–6.

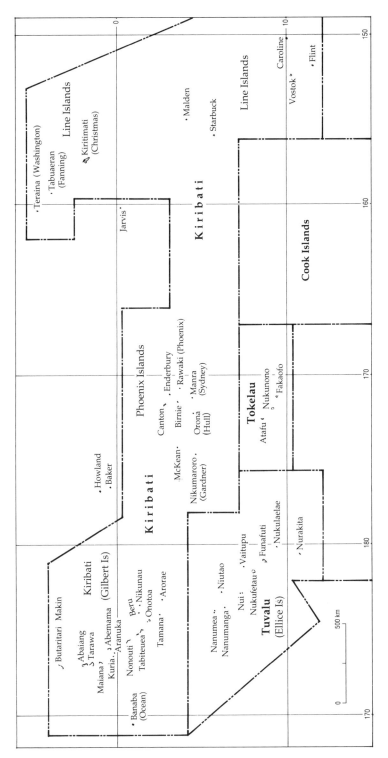

Map 2 Tuvalu and Kiribati

It is debatable whether any indigenous Pacific narrative form can be identified with the Western model of 'history'—that is, a neutral, comprehensive, chronological account of events. We can, however, find many kinds of historical discourse in Pacific narratives. A few examples illustrate the range in narrative forms and the ways in which historical understandings contrast with Western histories. Most of the earliest historical narratives collected in the Islands were first written down by missionaries. They varied widely in their intellectual capacities, and some held such a negative opinion of native society—Smith's 'hard primitivism'—that they refused to delve into cultural or historical matters. Nevertheless, many sustained a scholarly interest in the folklore and culture of their congregants and took the trouble to collect oral traditions—at least those which they deemed significant. The Reverend Charles Hardie of Samoa explained his motivation:

> The phylosophy [sic] of the manners, customs & institutions of idolatry is more satisfactory to us when derived from the very words & legends of the natives themselves. For these reasons I have been at great pains to discover & comit to writing from the recitation of the orators their original traditions & from these compositions, made beyond the memory of man & the reach of history, every reader is qualified to form opinions & receive impressions, as if he were in contact with the inhabitants of Polynesia.[13]

In the early years of missionisation, Hardie and his colleagues collected tales which they classified as 'traditional history'. The Samoans, of course, had other categories for these narratives. Around 1847, the Reverend Samuel Ella listed eleven genres of Samoan oral literature.[14] Most took the form of chants or songs, and Ella described the dancing, hand movements, and choral styling that accompanied each one. Of the genres which might have historical content, several were in praise of chiefs; other forms included war songs, popular songs on passing events, and *fāgogo*, usually translated as 'fables'. Part song, part narrative, the latter continue today as a form of family story telling. *Fāgogo* feature ancient culture heroes and heroines engaged in supernatural happenings, and Samoans today classify them as 'legends' rather than 'history'. Other narratives of distant times are called *tala fa'aanamua*, 'stories in ancient style', or *tala o le vavau*, 'old-time stories'. Some of these recount events significant to all Samoans, such as the expulsion of the Tongans, while others explain the origins of chiefly titles and the meanings of popular proverbs.

One such tale recounts the ways by which Leutogi, Samoan wife of the King of Tonga, escaped death for murdering a co-wife's infant. First the Tongans placed her up in a *fetau* tree and attempted to burn her, but bats flew over and put out the fire with their urine. The incident is told to explain the origin of the Savai'i title Tonumaipe'a, which means 'the plan from the bats'. Leutogi greeted the surprised Tongans with the words: *'Ua tatou fetaia'i i Magafetau soifua*—We meet again safely in the fork of the *fetau* tree.' As used today in Samoan formal greetings, this

13 Diary of Rev. Charles Hardie, 1835–55, Mitchell Library, Sydney, Ms. A368, 118.
14 Samuel Ella, c.1847, Mitchell Library, Sydney, Ms. B271.

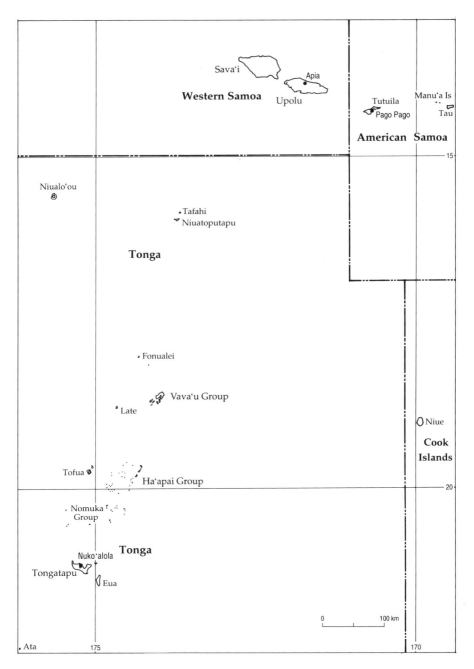

Map 3   Samoas and Tonga

proverb expresses the speaker's gratitude for being reunited with people not seen for some time.

Historical references are a requisite part of modern oratory. Every speech should mention *taeao o le atunu'u*, 'mornings of the country', or notable events. The popularity of particular *taeao* has changed over time, reflecting changes in political priorities and self-definition. Depending on the context of the speech, the 'mornings' could refer to local events, wars, or myth-historical murders. Nowadays most of the *taeao* cited are 'gospel mornings' marking the arrival of the first missionaries. Orators try to invoke events with positive connotations for almost all Samoans, and appeal to a shared sense of cultural and national identity. As in most Polynesian islands, Christianity is central to daily life. The missionary arrivals therefore evoke the unity of 'the country', particularly in contrast to the largely secularised industrialised nations. But early missionary writings suggest that the most culturally significant form of historical discourse may have been *gafa*, 'genealogies'. Missionaries, reflecting Western concerns with political centralisation, were particularly interested in narratives which appeared to be national in scope. One tale which seemed to shed light on the Samoans' origins as a people was 'The Genealogy of the Sun'. Several versions were collected, the first in 1835. Hardie, in about 1854, reported that such narratives

> form the traditional or sacred history of the islands. It is designated by the natives as *tau aitu*, belonging to the Gods, & is also considered as one of the most ancient of these legends . . . This piece is never recited at any of their public meetings, but is kept secret by the orators from every one but their own children . . . During heathenism it was impossible for any stranger to acquire the least information regarding them . . . It required the express authority of Malietoa (the greatest chief) to induce the orator to allow me to take down from his recitation.[15]

Early formal education in the Islands was almost wholly in the hands of missionaries, who taught such subjects as 'church history'. The earliest Samoan dictionary translates 'history' simply as *tala*, a word used to refer to any kind of tale or narrative. But in later publications the missionaries rendered 'history' with the phrase *tala fa'asolopito*, 'tales [of events] told in succession', that is, sequential narratives. In time, Islanders came to write their own histories in a form nearer to Western expectations. Sometimes they were directly requested by mission teachers or colonial administrators. A government translator, Te'o Tuvale, recorded what may be the first native-authored written history of Samoa in 1918, at the behest of Colonel Logan, the commander of the British Military Occupation. Tuvale introduces his text as follows:

> Although the stories and opinions from different districts differ and lack a single origin, yet they have been recorded . . . Samoan stories in the days of darkness were treasured in the heart and not written.

---

15 Hardie, 'O le Gafa o le La', Mitchell Library, Sydney, Ms. A368; Pratt, 'The Genealogy of the Sun'.

> I, Teo Tuvale, have tried to gather these stories over many years for my own use and interest. Colonel Robert Logan intimated to me that he wished me to put on record the story of happenings in Samoa from ancient times to the present day in order that they should be issued in printed form, and I attempt to obey his wish with this object in view.[16]

The first chapters take the form of genealogies—*gafa*. Parts of his history overlap with the content of 'old-time stories' explaining the origins of chiefly titles, proverbs, and place names. Peggy Dunlop, a relative of Tuvale, notes that in the early colonial period literate Samoans began to produce 'individual *a'iga* ['family'] papers recording family, community and national events . . . In these *a'iga* writings, Samoans were using the written language in the ways they had learnt it should be used.'[17] Tuvale's last chapter, 'A record of events in Samoa since 1822', is essentially a time-line: a chronological, annotated list of year-by-year events. Tuvale's history encapsulates a post-contact transformation in historical genres, beginning in the form of genealogies and later approaching 'history' in the Western sense. It would be grossly misleading, however, to suppose that all Islanders have adopted and internalised such Western models as 'history'. Tuvale's is the voice of an educated cultural interlocutor, in the same tradition as David Malo in nineteenth-century Hawai'i.[18] Many examples of historical discourse can be found in the Pacific. Michael Young's informant Kwahihi tells her life story without mentioning anyone beyond her own lineage and those of her husbands.[19] Her story cannot be set within a wider text; her frame of personal experience defies encapsulation in a generalising history.

Pacific narratives also illustrate how global events are incorporated into personal contexts and expressed in local cultural terms. In recent years scholars have collected stories about World War II from Islanders. The editors of *The Big Death: Solomon Islanders Remember World War II* caution against essentialising 'an indigenous' or even a single Solomons historical genre. To Islanders, history is lived individual experience, not the totalising synthesis we have come to expect from Western history. As an alternative to 'Eurocentric' written accounts, *The Big Death* is a collection of bilingual narratives, given first in Solomons Pijin and then in English. An example illustrates their form and content:

> *Mifala go long Shortlands. Kam baek. Sekon taem mifala go long Shortlands nao mi waka long disfala sip* Wai-ai. *An melewan long Mono an Shortlands wanfala Zero faeta blong olketa Japan kam strefem mifala long tem klok long morning. Mi herem. Mi lei daon. Mi herem enjin deferen saon. Mi sei, 'Samting hem mas rong wetem enjin.' Mi lei daon olsem bat open antop long mi. Mi luk olsem bat mi lukim eroplen long dea noa. Hemi go raon wantaem. Mektu taem hemi open faea. Mifala tufala sip go tugeta. Mektri taem hemi faea, hemi mis moa. Hemi no skrasim mifala. No hitim mifala. Lake tumas.*

---

16 Te'o Tuvale, 'An Account of Samoan History up to 1918', comp. E. Riddell, Mitchell Library, Sydney, Ms 39/C.
17 Dunlop, 'Samoan Writing', 44.
18 Malo, *Hawaiian Antiquities*.
19 Young, '"Our Name is Women"'.

We went to the Shortlands. Then we came back. The second time we went to the Shortlands I left to work on the ship *Wai-ai*. And between Mono and Shortlands a Japanese Zero fighter strafed at us at ten o'clock in the morning. I heard it. I was lying down. I heard that the engine of the *Wai-ai* suddenly sounded different. I said, 'Something must be wrong with the engine'. I was lying down like this and there was an opening above me. I looked and there was the aeroplane. It went around once. The second time it came around, it opened fire. It fired a third time, but it missed us again. Neither of our two ships, which were going together, got a scratch. It did not hit us. We were very lucky. (pp. 13, 137)

'Indigenisation' challenges orthodox history not only by exemplifying varieties of personal experience but, more radically, by interpreting that experience through alternative rationalities. Some Marshallese view the continued United States military interest in Enewetak and Kwajalein as evidence that the Pacific War did not end: 'Oh yes, perhaps Americans lost one battle [Vietnam], but they won many others; when the war settles down there, it only appears elsewhere.' This theory not only makes sense of the present, the ethnographer comments, but also draws on an indigenous model of warfare in which the concept of 'preparedness' is crucial:

the war, it still goes on. Like the fighting on Enewetak. It began on Hawaii and then grew. They moved to Kiribati and then to the Marshalls, then they came to Enewetak and ruined it, and then moved onward to that place they call Korea and afterward to Vietnam. You see that, they haven't finished fighting, they only move around from place to place . . . and all the time [the warriors] have to remain ready.[20]

COLONIAL HISTORIES

In contrast to the variety of indigenous concepts and narrative formats, academic histories of the region share the same premises about historical time, significance and perspective, and adhere to relatively consistent conventions. Until the 1960s, written Pacific history was largely about white men in the Pacific and narrated the political-economic benchmarks of Western expansion. In British universities 'Imperial History' designated a particular field, 'the history of particular empires'. 'Imperial history' can also serve as an ironic label for a historiography centred on the interests of Western states and their representatives. James Davidson, who mentored the reorientation of Pacific history in the 1960s, observed that 'the study of empire . . . has attracted those who have identified themselves with the rulers of the state'.[21]

In this chapter 'colonial history' denotes a perspective and style of historiography rather than the time of its production. Colonial history long commanded exclusive authority as a discursive model, defining

20 Laurence Carucci, 'The Source of the Force in Marshallese Cosmology', in White and Lindstrom, *The Pacific Theater*, 77.
21 Davidson, 'Problems of Pacific History', 5.

the appropriate content and narrative form of history for both Western and indigenous scholars. Recounting events significant to Western core states and affecting Westerners, colonial history situates agency, causality and effective power in the actions of the imperial nations and their citizens. Europeans are generally portrayed as actors, and Islanders as the acted upon, those who suffer impacts. In its most Euro-centric forms, colonial history is racist. At best, it represents native peoples and societies as less rational, less industrious, less capable, and less stable than their Western counterparts. Colonial histories typically begin with the first encounters between European explorers and native people, narrate events important to Westerners, and promulgate stereotypic notions about Islanders and their societies. The revisionist, 'island-oriented' history associated with Davidson and his students was in part a reaction to the Western bias of colonial historiography. Recent Pacific historians have tried to expunge the imperial point of view and exchanged heated criticisms over allegations of lurking Eurocentrism.

Two themes are particularly salient in the contrast between the two styles of history: the portrayal of Pacific peoples (their character and the nature of their society) and the treatment of indigenous agency (the ability of Islanders to affect the course of events in the encounter with the West). In the early post-contact period a conventional wis-dom emerged in historical accounts. Certain events came to be identi-fied as 'key', and early observers' characterisations of the indigenous society influenced later portrayals. It is startling to recognise the longevity of these formulations, for the same fundamental analysis of early contacts often recurs in later histories, even after the colonial period.

Colonial historiography tends to convey certain key messages about early encounters: that Islanders were naive and readily responded to crude materialist appeals, that foreign introductions were the primary agents of change, and that first encounters with famous Europeans were the most important events in Island history. The 'cargo' theory of the Samoans' conversion to Christianity, first promulgated by the mission-ary John Williams, exemplifies such received wisdom. Williams and many of his contemporaries believed that native peoples were first attracted to superior Western technology: gifts of material goods were to pave the way for more spiritual rewards. This premise is most clearly expressed in an oft-quoted speech from Williams's 1838 work, *Narrative of Missionary Enterprises in the South Seas*, which was published in many editions. (Williams was killed at Erromanga in the New Hebrides in 1839 and was widely celebrated as a martyr. His death at the hands of Islanders made him, like the explorers Captain Cook and La Pérouse, a European tragic figure whose death contributed to European scepticism about primitive man's true nature.)

Williams's entrée to Samoa—notably his introduction to the import-ant chief Mālietoa Vainu'upō—was facilitated by a Samoan named Faueā. Williams quotes Fauea promoting the adoption of Christianity in these terms:

I look . . . at the wisdom of these worshipers of Jehovah and see how superior they are to us in every respect. Their ships are like floating houses, so that they can traverse the tempest-driven ocean for months with perfect safety . . . Their axes are so hard and sharp that with them we can easily fell our trees and do our work, but with our stone axes we must dub, dub, dub, day after day . . . Their knives, too—what valuable things they are! How quickly they cut up our pigs, compared with our bamboo knives! Now, I conclude that the God who had given to his white worshipers these valuable things must be wiser than our gods . . . We all want these articles, and my proposition is that the God who gave them should be our God.[22]

The original rendering of this speech in Williams's 1832 journal is less elaborate, and the prototype of the cargo speech recorded in the 1830 journal is simpler yet.[23] Clearly, Williams promoted the 'cargo' theory because it appealed to contemporary European common sense and to the businessmen on whom the mission depended for support. Its truth seemed equally self-evident to colonial historians, and the later Williams version of Faueā's speech was cited in numerous accounts. Published histories seldom challenged the fundamental premises of Islander simple-mindedness and the irresistible appeal of Western technology.

A related presumption is that Islanders were politically incompetent, so that foreign intervention was required to put an end to chronic warfare and instability. As part of the Western received wisdom, the premise of political incompetence is implicit or explicit in most published histories. Such portrayals were not always overtly racist or unsympathetic to Islander self-rule. Sylvia Masterman's 1934 *Origins of International Rivalry in Samoa* was originally a thesis for a master's degree at London University. The work illustrates the perspective and presuppositions of colonial history although its tone is explicitly pro-Samoan. A New Zealander writing while Samoa was still a colony of that nation, Masterman was supervised by A. P. Newton, Rhodes Professor of Imperial History. In his introduction Newton praises the work for showing 'how missionary enterprise and trade went side by side . . . to extend the contacts of the white races with the savage but always attractive islanders of Polynesia'.[24] Masterman describes Western meddling as a response to the Samoans' inability to cope: 'We have seen the islands . . . pass from a state of primitive but happy disorder, to a condition of semi-civilised but unhappy confusion . . . until the bewildered Samoan chiefs, distraught by intrigues, begged that the burden of government might be lifted from them' (p. 194).

Masterman and her mentor sympathised with Samoans, but their historiography invokes racial theories to account for social and political changes. Samoans are portrayed as helpless to withstand the machinations of white men, and Masterman links their growing 'confusion' to deterioration resulting from intermarriage. Two further annotations can be made. Masterman wrote during the period of the Mau, the

22 Williams, *Missionary Enterprises*, 412.
23 Moyle, *Samoan Journals of John Williams*, 68, 237.
24 Sylvia Masterman, 'The Origins of International Rivalry in Samoa', 8.

Samoan resistance movement against colonial rule. Reports and journals by contemporary New Zealand authorities contain virulent racist statements against the *'afakasi*, the so-called 'half-castes', whom they blamed for the uprising. The premise among colonial officials was that intermarriage caused the degeneration of both the European and Samoan 'races', and echoes of this assumption are found even in Masterman's largely sympathetic history. She was also writing during the rise of Nazism; not coincidentally, she portrays the British as essentially altruistic and Germans as aggressive traders 'who, while pursuing material gain, were yet working for the honour and glory of Germany' (p. 198).

Colonial history is grounded in the Western political vision, which implies that the referent of history is a nation. Masterman's characterisation of Samoan society illustrates the belief, shared by nineteenth-century diplomats and settlers as well as by most foreign scholars, that the indigenous political system was inherently unstable and anarchic. This interpretation relates to the Great Powers' obsession with the creation of a national polity in Samoa. It suited the imperial nations to foster a centralised government with which to conduct trade and negotiate treaties. The stratified chiefdoms of Polynesia seemed to offer a prototype of kingship, and Europeans accordingly promoted the monarchical model in those islands.

Even recent Western scholars characterise indigenous Pacific polities as unstable and fissiparous. Paul Kennedy's *The Samoan Tangle* was published in 1974 but still illustrates important premises and concerns of colonial historiography. The 'tangle' is a Great Power history of diplomats, consuls, trading firms and metropolitan governments. In contrast to the wealth of detail about colonial wranglings, the accounts of Samoan politics and society are superficial. Samoan chiefly politics are described as 'rather like the Scottish clan system in some respects'.[25] To Kennedy's English audience (the book was originally an Oxford thesis) the Scottish clan system evidently represented the archetype of political decentralisation. The imperial-centre point of view is also suggested by the fact that the Samoans and the Scots of old are classed together as less civilised, peripheral peoples. Although Kennedy exposes Great Power blustering and machinations to sharp criticism and ridicule, he sees the absence of an enduring central government in Samoa as a fundamental deficiency requiring paternalist intervention.

Other invidious judgements have made their way from early observers' accounts into scholarly histories. Foreigners and colonial administrators often characterised Islanders as lazy. This charge typically sustained an argument for importing foreign labour. Nineteenth-century entrepreneurs lobbied administrations by claiming that Islanders made poor workers or refused outright to work on plantations. Most such charges were canards. Every stereotype has a history, and negative characterisations typically reflect the interests of the dominant group. Hawaiians made up the bulk of the sugar plantation

25 Kennedy, *The Samoan Tangle*, 2.

workforce for decades, but their declining numbers could not match the industry's rapid expansion in the 1870s. The lazy Hawaiian stereotype appears to have arisen in the early twentieth century, after the indigenous people had been outnumbered by immigrant Asian workers. Similarly in German New Guinea planters pestered the government to allow unrestricted labour immigration (see chapter 7). The problem was not that Tolai villagers of New Britain were lazy, but that they demanded too high a wage. Chinese, who would work for much less, were brought in as indentured field-workers, alongside Melanesians from other parts of New Guinea. German traders complained about the villagers' erratic production of copra for sale, but their apparent lack of industry was entirely rational. Given the alternative productive activities available, cutting copra at the going rate was simply not worth their while.

A less invidious variant of the lazy characterisation attributes lack of industry to Pacific communalism or to a beneficent environment. This quotation from *The Samoan Tangle* (p. 7) echoes Bernard Smith's 'soft primitivism': 'The plantations necessitated a large labour force but the Samoans themselves were not disposed to work all day when the natural produce of the islands gave them all they required in the way of food, clothing and habitation.' A similar statement about natural abundance and effortless subsistence can be found in the 1787 La Pérouse journal. Orientalist assumptions about Islanders pervade Western scholarship, even in conscientious and well-meaning histories. Whether called common sense or conventional wisdom, seemingly self-evident characterisations are formulated in a particular social context and are frequently bound to political projects. Negative appraisals of Islanders' capabilities made colonial intervention and takeover appear inevitable to the history-reading audience.

THE 'ISLAND-ORIENTED' REVISIONISTS

Though often sympathetic to Islanders, colonial historians tended to portray them as ineffectual in dealing with Westerners. Combined with the Great Power reference point, this underplaying of indigenous agency led to what Kerry Howe called 'Fatal Impact' interpretations, after the book by Alan Moorehead.[26] Howe traces the image of 'the poor benighted savage reeling under Western impact' from the early explorers' writings to the nineteenth- and twentieth-century projections of the 'Dying Savage'. 'Fatal Impact' writers engaged in a more sympathetic brand of colonial history, commiserating with Islanders while portraying them as hapless victims of Western political and technical superiority. The revisionist historians of the 1960s offered an alternative perspective—an 'island-oriented' historiography which differentiated itself from Eurocentric imperial discourse by attempting to view events from the Islanders' point of view. In practice they valorised indigenous

26 Howe, 'The Fate of the "Savage"'; Moorehead, *The Fatal Impact*.

societies, recontextualised events in native cultural terms, and asserted 'the image of an active, initiative-taking savage whose way of life was not necessarily ravaged by European contact'.[27] The writings of these post-colonial historians appeal to anthropologists because they attempt to frame events in terms of indigenous cultural values and political priorities.

James Davidson formulated the priorities and methods which distinguish the island-oriented approach. Davidson's appointment in 1954 to the world's first Chair of Pacific History at the Australian National University is a benchmark date for the new historiography. He not only exerted intellectual leadership but was involved in research and planning for the independence of Pacific nations. Davidson and his student, Richard Gilson, wrote the definitive histories of Samoa. These works begin not with the arrival of explorers but with descriptions of Samoan social structure and political institutions.

The post-colonial revisionists are, for the most part, Australian and New Zealand historians. It may be germane that as products of the British colonial periphery they are critical of Great Power actions in the Pacific. (In contrast *The Samoan Tangle*, written at Oxford, seems to represent the older imperial style of history although it postdates the 'island-oriented' move.) The post-colonial revisionists challenge colonial canards about Islander values and societies. Notably absent are statements about primitive abundance, lack of industry, and political chaos. Davidson, for example, calls the Samoans a 'politically capable people' who were unjustly treated as wards by the New Zealand administration.[28] Gilson does not attribute to the Samoans a simple materialistic motivation for conversion, but foregrounds indigenous agency in missionisation; his chapter on the fortunes of Christianity is called 'Samoan Influence upon the Church' rather than the other way around.[29]

Reviews of Kerry Howe's *Where the Waves Fall*, a popular Pacific history, reveal points of controversy among academic historians as well as politically inflected tensions between revisionists and indigenous scholars. The effectiveness of native agency and the stability of indigenous polities remain sensitive issues. In an earlier piece Howe had denounced 'Fatal Impact interpretations [as] more often than not the product of overfertile and perhaps guilt-ridden imaginations'.[30] Nevertheless the Australian historian Caroline Ralston chided Howe for smuggling in a 'fatal impact' perspective in spite of his avowed intentions. The title of his book, for example, seemed to define the Islands as the place where foreign 'waves' landed. Malama Meleisea, on the other hand, accused Howe of giving too much weight to native agency and thereby underplaying the destructive effects of Western interference: 'To underestimate the force of settler intriguing and international wrangling . . . in order to give priority of explanation to indigenous political structures is taking the argument a great deal too

27 Howe, 'The Fate of the "Savage" ', 147.
28 Davidson, *Samoa mo Samoa*, 12.
29 Gilson, *Samoa 1830–1900*, 74.
30 'The Fate of the "Savage" ', 151.

far.'[31] Meleisea also criticised Howe for portraying Samoan political authority as chronically decentralised—in effect, for replicating the colonial view. Howe was simultaneously charged with being too Eurocentric and too optimistic about Islanders' ability to withstand Western incursion.

INDIGENOUS POST-COLONIAL HISTORIANS

Western-trained Islands scholars have sought to replace Eurocentric colonial interpretations with a native political view of indigenous history. As Meleisea points out, however, a 'native point of view' is equally problematic.[32] Indigenous scholarship differentiates itself from foreign-authored historiography by valorising and recasting events and behaviour which colonial scholars represented as destructive, deficient, or irrational. In this sense Pacific scholars are engaged in a revisionist project similar to that of the 'island-oriented' historians who were their teachers. But is an anti-colonial stance sufficient to constitute a native voice? To most indigenous scholars the obvious answer is no, but few have attempted to specify the cultural credentials or social status that entitle one to speak for the group. University training and professional status have become a new source of authority, but one which articulates uneasily with indigenous bases of authority.

Whether it is possible or desirable to assert 'a' unified indigenous voice is troublesome on several levels. Long before the introduction of capitalism there were forms of inequality, notably birth rank and gender. Internal differences of class and education continue to ramify as the Islands engage with the global economy. The Pacific nations— particularly those of Melanesia—also face the daunting task of crafting a national identity to encompass groups who may share little beyond the legacy of the same colonial masters. The Bougainville insurgency against the government of Papua New Guinea (see chapter 12) demonstrates that belonging to the same nation does not automatically translate into shared political interests, much less the recognition of a common group identity.

Roger Keesing was publicly attacked in the Solomons for publishing accounts of the 1927 'massacre' of a colonial officer and his Islander police force.[33] Keesing featured the voices of the pagan Kwaio of central Malaita, who had committed the killings and who became victims of bloody reprisals, mainly by other Malaitans. Reflecting on government threats to ban the work from sale, Keesing mused that his 'sin' lay in 'articulating too forcefully the representations of the wrong indigenes'. Ironically, in the Solomons the prevailing ideology about the event features 'the Kwaio as dark savages and . . . the killing of Bell as an

---

31 *Pacific Studies* 9: 1 (1985), reviews by Caroline Ralston (150–63) and Malama Meleisea (149); *cf.* O. H. K. Spate (163–6).
32 'Preface' to Meleisea *et al.*, *Lagaga*, vii.
33 Keesing, 'Colonial History as Contested Ground'; Keesing and Corris, *Lightning Meets the West Wind*.

unthinkable outrage'—an interpretation echoing the colonial portrayal. Keesing articulated the internal divisions which made his work a 'contested ground':

> the Kwaio pagans . . . constitute both an underclass and a persecuted and marginalised cultural minority. The cultural nationalist discourse of a post-colonial elite, counterposing the indigenous and authentic to the foreign, alien, and exploitative, lays down ideological smokescreens that cover and hide the realities of class interest, neo-colonialism, and the exploitation and pauperisation of hinterlands villages.

In the Pacific as elsewhere, nationalist discourse is typically anti-colonial, yet Keesing's study shows how seemingly contradictory axioms may be articulated. When history is politicised and scholarship becomes an issue in public debate, the rhetoric about the written product may bear little relationship to the source. For indigenous scholars, the question is whether the 'native voice' should be a nationalist voice, or a voice from some 'authentic' cultural enclave. The latter position potentially creates an arena for argument over the defining of authenticity and which group most closely approaches the cultural ideal. Does training in Western universities and by foreign mentors compromise the Island scholar's right or capacity to speak in the 'native voice'?

Samoan and Tongan scholars have been prominent contributors to published Pacific history since the 1960s. Their writings illustrate the complex relationships between different genres of historiography and the dilemmas of producing 'decolonised' historical accounts. As might be expected, university-trained Island historians use the narrative format, adopt the objective authoritative voice of academic writing, and publish in English. Post-colonial indigenous historians meet all the formal criteria of Western scholarship but attempt to assert a native cultural and political point of view, particularly by critically evaluating the actions of Westerners. The Samoan historians Eteūati, Meleisea and Wendt all analysed aspects of the colonial period. Wendt and Eteūati wrote theses on the Mau rebellion against New Zealand. Meleisea's dissertation and later published book discussed the German administration and the Mau rebellion, but primarily analysed the Land and Titles Court as an agent of social change.

Albert Wendt, well-known and honoured as a novelist, first earned a graduate degree in history. His career exemplifies the provenance of indigenous post-colonial scholarship, as well as some of its conflicts. He graciously acknowledges his tutor Mary Boyd (at Victoria University) as the teacher 'who revealed, to me, how little I knew of the history of my own country'.[34] His thesis was based primarily on documents in the National Archives of New Zealand, but Wendt also used what he called 'folk history', the narratives of elderly Samoans. Describing the impact of the horrific 1918 influenza epidemic, for example, he cites his grandmother as a source for the statement that some Samoans thought the New Zealanders had introduced the disease deliberately.

---

34 'Guardians and Wards', vi; see Boyd, 'The Military Administration of Western Samoa'.

'Guardians and Wards' argues that the Mau was 'deeply-rooted' not only in the post-1900 colonial period but in the longer contact encounter 'between Samoa and Europe'. This argument extends the anti-colonial critique offered by revisionist Pacific historiography, differing from the latter in degree rather than kind. Few Pacific historians of the 1960s would have disputed Wendt's analysis. Indeed, in the thesis the antagonistic point of view is represented by the report of the Royal Commission which investigated the Mau in 1927. But in 'Guardians and Wards' Wendt departs radically from island-oriented historiography in recognising that history is an interested and subjective product, and in his self-conscious narrative attempts to deal with that paradox. The last chapter, 'A Matter of Interpretation', embarks on a highly unorthodox experiment which foreshadows Wendt's defection from academic history to fiction. He abandons the authoritative historical voice, and the narrative becomes a dialogue between the author and an unseen interlocutor, part of himself, perhaps his conscience. Cynical and flippant, the inner voice challenges the preceding (and all other) history:

> A lot of history is written as wish-fulfilment, deliberately or otherwise . . . objectivity is for astronauts and moon-flights . . . History is for mortals like you trying to finish a degree.
> We went to the past of Samoa for sympathy, for instruction.
> Call it flattery. Or justification, if you like.

The thesis ends with a critique of culture and of authoritative discourse, carried on in a final debate between Wendt and his alter ego:

> I would have thought that after plagiarising other people's ideas, views and everything else, you'd have come up with really something. An interpretation like this won't get you anything (or anywhere), much less a degree. But I am a product of our times, of our education system . . . I'm a salesman, remember? ...who's got nothing to sell but himself . . . Sell the dead (and the living) for immortality, you told me . . . I can only hope to remain true to what I am.

Wendt's later stories and novels narrate the existential anguish and personal conflicts of Samoans torn between customary and Western worlds. Although Wendt discussed the influenza epidemic in his thesis, he chose a short story to convey its human impact.[35] University education became available much later in the University of Papua New Guinea. Several of the first students, including John Waiko, wrote short stories and novels, and produced plays to dramatise their critiques of the colonial encounter. Waiko proceeded to a doctorate at the Australian National University, analysing the recent history of his Binandere people. He then arranged a ceremony at home, explicitly as a cultural counterpart to the Australian graduation ceremony.[36] Wendt, Waiko and Meleisea all acknowledge tension between the pursuit of a native historical voice and the use of Western conventions, narrative form, and the English language. 'It may be', Howe suggested, 'that straight history

35 'A Descendant of the Mountain', *Flying-Fox In a Freedom Tree*, Auckland, 1974.
36 Chris Owen, *Man Without Pigs*, documentary film.

never has a strong appeal for island writers.'[37] Several Island scholars have either turned from academic publishing to literature, or have chosen to write in both genres. The Tongan historian Epeli Hau'ofa holds a university position and his scholarly works are frequently cited, but he is more widely known for outrageous scatological novels such as *Kisses in the Nederends*,[38] satirising the follies and ironies of the post-colonial Pacific, and depicting the dilemmas of Islanders operating in the hybrid, contradictory modern world.

Not all university-trained Islanders have rejected conventional history. Augustin Kituai, like Waiko, published creative writing before he graduated in History from the University of Papua New Guinea and the Australian National University, and came home to lecture in History. Malama Meleisea, the best-known Samoan historian, graduated from the University of Papua New Guinea, received his doctorate at Macquarie University, and has held leadership positions at New Zealand universities. Some of his teachers were highly critical of the colonial powers. Meleisea's doctoral thesis—published as *The Making of Modern Samoa*—examined the Land and Titles Commission, charged with resolving disputes involving chiefly titles and authority over land. As Meleisea acknowledges, indigenous scholars face the difficulty of defining a point of view that is distinct not only from Eurocentric colonial scholarship but also from sympathetic liberal revisionism. Those intellectuals who do not categorically reject foreign-authored history tend to be even more critical of colonial actions than their mentors. The difference between their perspective and that of revisionists tends to be a matter of degree.

Meleisea is one of few historians of any ilk to offer a critical assessment of Christianity's effects on Samoan society. The German Governor Wilhelm Solf, who administered Western Samoa from 1900 to 1910, is often credited with benevolence and foresight for opposing land alienation and free immigration. Stewart Firth argued in contrast that Solf's alleged altruism reflected a particular strategy of control over small planters.[39] Working with the same documents, Meleisea analysed Solf's motivations and attitude towards the Samoans even more critically, asserting that Solf's knowledge and apparent regard for Samoan custom enabled him to effect thorough-going changes in the indigenous political system.

Collaborating with other Samoan intellectuals, Meleisea also edited *Lagaga*, a short general history of Samoa. *The Making of Modern Samoa* appeals particularly to academics, but *Lagaga* is intended as a readable introduction for Samoans and foreigners. In the preface Meleisea suggests some of the differences between Western and Samoan views of history:

> For Samoans, knowledge is power, and the most powerful knowledge is historical knowledge: treasured and guarded in people's heads, in notebooks locked in boxes and matai's briefcases or with their precious mats under mattresses. The valuable histories of families, lands, genealogies, villages and events long ago are family property . . .

37 'The Fate of the "Savage"', 153 n. 51.
38 Auckland, 1987.
39 'Governors versus Settlers'.

> Even 'common' historical knowledge such as well-known legends, are controversial. Each has many versions . . .

Modern Samoan-authored accounts resemble Western histories in their methodology and narrative form, Meleisea suggests, because they use the same sorts of written materials: 'we have little of the great, rich fund of historical information of our people locked in their heads and note books. We have relied extensively on facts from documentary sources.' Like foreign-authored history, this Samoan perspective projects—with qualifications—the cultural homogeneity and shared past of the archipelago as the basis of a common history. In this sense Wendt and Meleisea articulate a nationalist voice, like many other Pacific intellectuals. However, the degree to which nationalist discourse is deployed to mystify and disenfranchise, as Keesing argued for the Solomons, varies with local conditions. The apparent homogeneity of island groups such as Tonga and Samoa should not be taken for granted, but the proposition of a shared history is more comfortable to Samoans, Tongans and Hawaiians than it is to Malaitans and ni-Vanuatu. The notion of 'Samoa' as a cultural and political entity predates European contact, for example, and is not solely an artefact of colonial administration. The contrast between 'Melanesia' and 'Polynesia' should not be overstated, but structural and political differences between Pacific societies affect the way that history is constructed—and contested.

DECOLONISING PACIFIC HISTORY?

Sympathetic liberal academics typically believe that training Islanders to 'write their own histories' is important as intellectual decolonisation, and they derive enormous satisfaction from the publication of their students' work. But the same scholars often feel an inchoate dissatisfaction with Islander-authored histories. Perhaps such critics apply ambiguous criteria, one writer suggests, or expect epiphanies.[40] Nationalist history is the logical successor to anti-colonial, island-oriented historiography. Yet nationalist history shares many of the premises of colonial history, notably the assumption (shared until recently by most anthropologists) that Island groups represent bounded cultural essences, nations in the rough. Nationalist historiography aspires to a 'native point of view' by valorising indigenous society and narrating anti-colonial struggle, but it is itself produced in a context of interaction with and dependence on First World academic institutions. In Howe's terms, 'Even though it may be decolonized, Pacific history is still essentially a product of a Western intellectual tradition and world view.'

Keesing observed that 'the more sophisticated approaches of the best Third World scholarship have yet to wash up on Pacific shores'.[41] He saw a simplistic nationalism dominating the rhetoric of Island elites.

---

40 Routledge, 'Pacific History as Seen from the Pacific Islands', 85.
41 Keesing, 'Colonial History as Contested Ground', 279.

The implied alternative is the 'subaltern historiography' identified with a group of South Asian scholars. To put it perhaps too simply, 'subaltern' is the inverse of 'hegemonic'. Subaltern refers to people who are not in power and do not belong to the dominant group: the difference may be gender, ethnicity, political standing, or economic class. One Indian historian identifies the subaltern as the 'insurgent'.[42] The subaltern historiographers have argued that elite nationalist history tends to replicate the categories and premises of colonial discourse. A truly 'decolonised' Third World historiography must be 'anti-foundational', breaking away from the perspective of the dominant groups and classes.[43]

The notion of subalternity in the Pacific Islands rests uneasily with many Pacific intellectuals and foreign scholars. In part this is because Pacific studies were dominated by the cultural isolate model, and the homogeneity and insularity of Pacific cultures seemed self-evident. Surely an island group equals a cultural boundary; after all, we can see ocean all around. But subalternity is a class-based theory of internal difference, and Pacific scholars have been reluctant to address stratification and other forms of inequality within Island societies. Because it emphasises internal inequities, subalternity contradicts the nationalist anti-colonialism that has dominated scholarship in the Pacific. In 'Fourth World' Pacific Island groups such as Hawai'i and Tahiti, where the indigenous people are an impoverished minority in their own land, the concept of subalternity is compatible with anti-colonial analysis: in political discourse Hawaiians and Tahitians are clearly subalterns. Elsewhere, few scholars have been willing to suggest that some indigenous people may be more subaltern than others.

Apart from Keesing, foreign academics have been reluctant to raise the issue of subalternity. Most scholars support the call for native sovereignty, which in the current political context means some form of nationhood. It is easier to envision subaltern historiography in ethnically complex states such as Vanuatu, Papua New Guinea and the Solomons, where subordinate status coincides with ethnic boundaries. Material disparities between families and classes continue to intensify, however, and with mass communications the global rise of micro-nationalism affects political aspirations in the Islands. The vision of a universal authoritative history is increasingly unsupportable. As contending voices and points of view proliferate, history becomes not so much a text as an ongoing debate.

42 Ranajit Guha (ed.), *Subaltern Studies: Writings on South Asian History and Society*, vols I–VI, Delhi, 1982–9; quotation from Gayatri Spivak, 'Subaltern Studies: Deconstructing Historiography', in vol. IV (1985), 330.
43 Gyan Prakash, 'Writing Post-Orientalist Histories of the Third World: Perspectives from Indian Historiography', *Comparative Studies in Society and History* 32 (1990), 398.

INTRODUCTION TO PACIFIC ISLANDS BIBLIOGRAPHY

Significant works are listed briefly here and in the chapter notes, and in full in the bibliography at the end of the book.

From the late nineteenth century, New Zealand scholars pioneered academic research in Polynesian history, and the *Journal of the Polynesian Society (JPS)* regularly published learned articles. That scholarship was matched in Hawai'i, where the Bernice P. Bishop Museum supported anthropological and other researchers and published their monographs. From the 1950s the Research School of Pacific Studies at the Australian National University (ANU) in Canberra became the largest concentration of academic historians, geographers, anthropologists, linguists and archaeologists with Pacific interests; the *Journal of Pacific History (JPH)* the leading outlet for historical articles; and ANU Press the leading publisher. The demise of ANU Press during the 1980s created an opportunity which was grasped by the University of Hawai'i Press (UHP) which became the leading academic publisher in the field. Other leading historical journals are *The Contemporary Pacific (TCP)*, published in the University of Hawai'i, *Pacific Studies*, published by Brigham Young University in Hawai'i, and *Journal de la Société des Océanistes*, published by Musée de l'Homme in Paris. Publishing in Island universities enjoys fewer resources, and Island-based scholars have fewer opportunities. However the Institute of Pacific Studies (IPS) at the University of the South Pacific in Fiji is a prolific publisher of Islanders' research. The University of Papua New Guinea publishes *Yagl-Ambu*, as well as the proceedings of the annual *Waigani Seminar*, and the Micronesian Area Studies Center in Guam publishes *Isla*, a journal of Micronesian research. *Micronesica* publishes some social science articles, as well as contributions to the natural sciences.

Debates about Pacific historiography commonly begin with James Davidson's charter, 'Problems of Pacific History', and Greg Dening's 'Ethnohistory in Polynesia: The Value of Ethnohistorical Evidence'. Analytical issues are also raised by H. E. Maude, *Of Islands and Men: Studies in Pacific History*. These debates are developed by Kerry Howe, 'The Fate of the "Savage" in Pacific Historiography'; Geoffrey White, *Identity Through History: Living Stories in a Solomons Island Society*; Roger Keesing, 'Colonial History as Contested Ground: The Bell Massacre in the Solomons'; Klaus Neumann, *Not the Way It Really Was: Constructing the Tolai Past*; Marshall Sahlins, 'The Discovery of the True Savage', in Donna Merwick (ed.), *Dangerous Liaisons*; Albert Wendt, 'Guardians and Wards: A Study of the Origins, Causes and First Two Years of the Mau Movement in Western Samoa'; Nicholas Thomas, 'The Force of Ethnology: Origins and Significance of the Melanesia/Polynesia Division'; and 'Partial Texts: Representation, Colonialism and Agency in Pacific History'.

Gananath Obeyesekere's *The Apotheosis of Captain Cook: European Mythmaking in the Pacific* revived debate about the role of foreign scholars, as well as the methods of ethnohistorical analysis. The Book

Review Forum of *Pacific Studies* xvii: 2 in 1994 allowed leading participants to explore these issues, and Marshall Sahlins—the subject of Obeyesekere's critique—responded with *How 'Natives' Think—About Captain Cook for Example.* The classic studies of Islanders' cosmologies include Peter Lawrence, *Road Belong Cargo*; K. O. L Burridge, *Mambu*; Marshall Sahlins, 'The Stranger-King, or Dumezil among the Fijians', and *Historical Metaphors and Mythical Realities*; Greg Dening, *Islands and Beaches* and *Mr Bligh's Bad Language.* Much of the debate concerns the evidence arising from 'first contact' encounters. In this field, major research efforts have focused on particular encounters, such as Anne Salmond, *Two Worlds: First Meetings between Maori and Europeans, 1642–1772*; and Edward Schieffelin and Robert Crittenden, *Like People You See in a Dream.*

Few scholars have attempted general histories of the region. Kerry Howe, *Where the Waves Fall*, was first in the field, its value limited only by his decision to end the narrative when colonialism began. The most recent is Kerry Howe, Robert Kiste and Brij Lal, *Tides of History*. The most accomplished, in breadth and literary quality, is Oskar Spate's trilogy, *The Pacific Since Magellan.* Spate's interests are geopolitical rather than social or cultural. The most useful single-volume work is Deryck Scarr, *The History of the Pacific Islands: Kingdoms of the Reefs.* For the recent French Pacific, see Stephen Henningham, *France and the South Pacific.*

The most recent and seminal contribution to regional topics is Epeli Hau'ofa, 'Our Sea of Islands'. International relations scholars have analysed regional institutions and politics. See, for example, Ramesh Thakur (ed.), *The South Pacific: Problems, Issues and Prospects*, especially chapters on security issues (Peter King), fisheries management (David Doulman), and the politics of co-operation (Greg Fry). The major studies of regionalism and its institutions are Greg Fry, 'South Pacific Regionalism'; Richard Herr, 'Regionalism in the South Seas'; and T. R. Smith, *South Pacific Commission.*

We rely on several general histories. For Hawai'i, Gavan Daws, *Shoal of Time*, serves this purpose. On Western Samoa these include James Davidson, *Samoa mo Samoa*; Malama Meleisea *et al.*, *Lagaga*; and Meleisea, *The Making of Modern Samoa.* Fiji is well served by Brij Lal, *Broken Waves*; Deryck Scarr, *Fiji: A Short History*; Timothy Macnaught, *The Fijian Colonial Experience*; and Bruce Knapman, *Fiji's Economic History, 1874–1939.*

Papua New Guinea is the subject of several accounts, including Stewart Firth, *New Guinea under the Germans*; James Griffin, Hank Nelson and Stewart Firth, *Papua New Guinea: A Political History*; John Waiko, *A Short History of Papua New Guinea*; Hank Nelson, *Taim Bilong Masta*; and Augustin Kituai's doctoral thesis, 'My Gun, My Brother: Experiences of Papua New Guinea Policemen, 1920–1960'.

Recent summaries of Pacific prehistory are J. D. Jennings (ed.), *The Prehistory of Polynesia*; Patrick Kirch, *The Evolution of the Polynesian Chiefdoms*; Peter Bellwood, *The Polynesians*; and Peter Bellwood, James Fox and Darrell Tryon (eds), *The Austronesians.* For the Pleistocene archaeology of Australia, New Guinea and Island Melanesia, see

M. A. Smith, M. J. T. Spriggs and B. Fankhauser (eds), *Sahul in Review*. Navigation and early settlement are reconstructed in Geoffrey Irwin, *The Prehistoric Exploration and Colonisation of the Pacific*.

Gender relations have been studied mainly by ethnographers. Until the 1970s most were men and attuned to male concerns. See Denise O'Brien, 'The Portrayal of Women in Melanesian Ethnography', in D. O'Brien and S. W. Tiffany (eds), *Rethinking Women's Roles*. The most complete descriptions come from feminist scholars writing since the 1970s. See Marilyn Strathern (ed.), *Dealing with Inequality*; O'Brien and Tiffany, *Rethinking Women's Roles*; Paula Brown, 'Gender and Social Change: New Forms of Independence for Simbu Women'; Annette Weiner and J. Schneider (eds), *Cloth and Human Experience*; Annette Weiner, *Women of Value, Men of Renown*; Margaret Jolly, *Women of the Place: Kastom, Colonialism and Gender in Vanuatu*; and Julia Hecht, 'The Culture of Gender in Pukapuka: Male, Female and the *Mayakitanga* "Sacred Maid"'. Useful studies are brought together by Margaret Jolly and Martha Macintyre (eds), *Family and Gender in the Pacific*. Writing perceptively in other traditions are M. J. Meggitt, 'Male–female Relationships in the Highlands of Australian New Guinea'; Gregory Bateson, *Naven*; D. K. Feil, 'Women and Men in the Enga Tee'; and Patrick Kirch, *Feathered Gods and Fishhooks*. For gender issues broadly, Jocelyn Linnekin, *Sacred Queens and Women of Consequence*; Claudia Knapman, *White Women in Fiji, 1835–1930: The Ruin of Empire*; Chilla Bulbeck, *Australian Women in Papua New Guinea*; and Lili'uokalani, *Hawai'i's Story by Hawai'i's Queen*.

Missionary activity has generated a vast literature. Much is pious, triumphalist, and Eurocentric, such as John Williams, *Missionary Enterprises in the South-Sea Islands*; but recent works break away from that tradition. The best include W. N. Gunson, *Messengers of Grace*; Gavan Daws, *Holy Man: Father Damien of Molokai*; and James Clifford, *Person and Myth: Maurice Leenhardt in the Melanesian World*. Particular missions are covered in Diane Langmore, *Missionary Lives*; Hugh Laracy, *Marists and Melanesians*; David Wetherell, *Reluctant Mission: The Anglican Church in Papua New Guinea*; and David Hilliard, *God's Gentlemen*. Comprehensive overviews are provided in John Garrett, *Footsteps in the Sea*; and James Boutilier, Daniel Hughes and Sharon Tiffany (eds), *Mission, Church and Sect in Oceania*.

Island agriculture in general is described in F. R. Fosberg (ed.), *Man's Place in the Island Ecosystem*. Case studies include Marshall Sahlins, *Anahulu: Historical Ethnography*; Marshall Sahlins, *Moala: Culture and Nature on a Fijian Island*; Donald Denoon and Catherine Snowden (eds), *A History of Agriculture in Papua New Guinea*; D. E. Yen and J. M. J. Mummery (eds), *Pacific Production Systems*; Patrick Kirch, *The Wet and the Dry*; and M. J. T. Spriggs, 'Vegetable Kingdoms, Taro Irrigation and Pacific Prehistory'. Gerard Ward and R. G. Crocombe pioneered land tenure studies. These are brought up to date by R. Gerard Ward and Elizabeth Kingdon, *Land, Custom and Practice in the South Pacific*, which covers Vanuatu, Western Samoa, Tonga and Fiji, and includes a full bibliography.

W. H. R. Rivers (ed.), *Essays on the Depopulation of Melanesia*, expressed the alarm of officials and missionaries. The pioneer of professional demographic studies was Norma McArthur, whose work is summarised in her *Island Populations of the Pacific*. More focused studies include David Stannard, *Before the Horror*; and Andrew Bushnell, '"The Horror" Reconsidered'. The broadest and most persuasive monograph is Stephen Kunitz, *Disease and Social Diversity*. Health and health services are treated in Clive Bell (ed.), *The Diseases and Health Services of Papua New Guinea*; Donald Denoon, Kathleen Dugan and Leslie Marshall, *Public Health in Papua New Guinea*; and Margrit Davies, *Public Health and Colonialism: The Case of German New Guinea*.

Economic history is not well developed, but some excellent pioneering work has been consulted. Leading sources include Richard Salisbury, *From Stone to Steel*; Dorothy Shineberg, *They Came for Sandalwood*; Ken Buckley and Kris Klugman, *The History of Burns Philp*; Michel Panoff, 'The French Way in Plantation Systems'; Bruce Knapman, 'Capitalism's Economic Impact in Colonial Fiji, 1874–1939'; and David Lewis, *The Plantation Dream*.

The modern historiography of labour recruiting and the plantation experience begins with Peter Corris, *Passage, Port and Plantation: A History of Solomon Islands Labour Migration*; and Deryck Scarr, 'Recruits and Recruiters'. *JPH* xi (1976) is a special issue on the labour trade. These publications are self-consciously 'revisionist', ascribing a measure of agency and autonomy to the plantation workers. Doug Munro, 'Revisionism and its Enemies', reviews these interpretations; this provoked a response from Tom Brass, 'The Return of "Merrie Melanesia"'. Many episodes are described in Clive Moore, Jacqueline Leckie and Doug Munro (eds), *Labour in the South Pacific*. The best synthesis is Brij Lal, Doug Munro and Ed Beechert (eds), *Plantation Workers: Resistance and Accommodation*. Clive Moore, *Kanaka*, and Patricia Mercer, *White Australia Defied*, are excellent sources on Melanesians who remained in Australia in the twentieth century.

Pre-colonial mining has been researched by John Burton, 'Axe Makers of the Wahgi'. Phosphate mining is treated by Maslyn Williams and Barrie Macdonald, *The Phosphateers*. Gold-mining is best treated by Hank Nelson, *Black, White and Gold*; Ciaran O'Faircheallaigh, *Mining in the Papua New Guinea Economy*; and 'Atu Emberson-Bain, *Labour and Gold in Fiji*.

Hank Nelson's researches in the Pacific War are summarised in 'Taim Bilong Pait: The Impact of the Second World War on Papua New Guinea'. A broader account is Geoffrey White and Lamont Lindstrom (eds), *The Pacific Theater*. See also Neville Robinson, *Villagers at War*; Hugh Laracy (ed.), *The Maasina Rule Movement*; Geoffrey White *et al.* (eds), *The Big Death*; and Asesela Ravuvu, *Fijians at War, 1939–1945*.

Works on migration include Antony Hooper *et al.*, *Class and Culture in the South Pacific*; John Connell (ed.), *Migration and Development in the South Pacific*; Michael Lieber (ed.), *Exiles and Migrants in Oceania*; and Grant McCall and John Connell (eds), *A World Perspective on Pacific Islander Migration*.

For neighbouring regions, information on Maluku is drawn from Leonard Andaya, *The World of Maluku*. The Ryukyu Archipelago and the Okinawan state are sketched by Richard Pearson, 'Trade and the Rise of the Okinawan State'.

Since the 1970s especially, many excellent documentary films and television programs have been made, on a startling variety of topics. Many are listed in Diane Aoki, *Moving Images of the Pacific Islands* (see the end of the bibliography in this volume).

Since the 1970s the Pacific Manuscripts Bureau at ANU has microfilmed 'at risk' manuscript material, and circulates copies to the major libraries specialising in Pacific Studies.

CHAPTER

2

HUMAN SETTLEMENT

There are many traditions of explaining how the world and its people came to be where they are and how they are. In this chapter we present several samples, including oral histories in poetry, archaeology in the prose of the natural sciences, linguistics in the form of genealogies, and the more conventional language of academic history.

All people order knowledge of past events, as statements of eternal truths and guides to current choices. These folk histories are not fixed, they need not agree with each other, and they do not 'add up' to a chronology of Islanders' experiences. For many centuries Hawaiians and Palauans told variations of the following narratives, before professional folklorists recorded, published and fixed them. Two sets of conventions therefore shape these texts. The Kumulipo chant and the 'Story of Latmikaik' are not narrowly historical, but creation stories from Polynesian Hawai'i and Micronesian Palau. They describe the creation of the islands and their inhabitants; then they go on to their more important purpose when they prescribe proper relations between people and spirits and environment, between past and future, and among different groups of people within the community. The narratives must hold the audience's attention in order to instruct them, so they use every available poetic device.

In the 1940s the folklorist Martha Beckwith was concerned to record Hawaiian narratives faithfully, to capture their poetry in her translation, to establish their sources as a step towards the comparative analysis of Polynesian myths, and to publish them for an academic audience. The same procedures shape the form in which the anthropologist Richard Parmentier presents the 'Story of Latmikaik', as it was told to him in Belau (his spelling of Palau). In each case, fluid oral narratives are fixed like jewels in the utilitarian setting of literary scholarship.

CHANT FROM THE KUMULIPO[1]

At the time when the earth became hot
At the time when the heavens turned about
At the time when the sun was darkened

---

1   Beckwith (trans. and ed.), *The Kumulipo*, 58–9.

To cause the moon to shine
The time of the rise of the Pleiades
The slime, this was the source of the earth
The source of the darkness that made darkness
The source of the night that made night
The intense darkness, the deep darkness
Darkness of the sun, darkness of the night
Nothing but night.

The night gave birth
Born was Kumulipo in the night, a male
Born was Po'ele in the night, a female
Born was the coral polyp, born was the coral, came forth
Born was the grub that digs and heaps up the earth, came forth
Born was his [child] an earthworm, came forth
Born was the starfish, his child the small sea cucumber came forth
Born was the sea urchin, the sea urchin [tribe]
Born was the short-spiked sea urchin, came forth
Born was the smooth sea urchin, his child the long-spiked came forth
Born was the ring-shaped sea urchin, his child the thin-spiked came forth
Born was the barnacle, his child the pearl oyster came forth
Born was the mussel, his child the hermit crab came forth
Born was the big limpet, his child the small limpet came forth
Born was the cowry, his child the small cowry came forth
Born was the naka shellfish, the rock oyster his child came forth
Born was the drupa shellfish, his child the bitter white shellfish came forth
Born was the conch shell, his child the small conch shell came forth
Born was the nerita shellfish,
      the sand-burrowing shellfish his child came forth
Born was the fresh water shellfish,
      his child the small fresh water shellfish came forth
Born was the man for the narrow stream, the woman for the broad stream
Born was the Ekaha moss living in the sea
Guarded by the Ekahakaha fern living on land
Darkness slips into light
Earth and water are the food of the plant
The god enters, man cannot enter
Man for the narrow stream, woman for the broad stream
Born was the tough seagrass living in the sea
Guarded by the tough landgrass living on land
Refrain
Man for the narrow stream, woman for the broad stream
Born was the 'A'ala moss living in the sea
Guarded by the 'Ala'ala mint living on land
Refrain
Man for the narrow stream, woman for the broad stream
Born was the Manauea moss living in the sea
Guarded by the Manauea taro plant living on land . . .

STORY OF LATMIKAIK[2]

So you want to hear the story of Latmikaik. Belau was totally empty and had no people dwelling on it. Uchelianged (Foremost of Heaven) looked out upon it and saw the expanse of the sea, which was completely empty. Uchelianged's voice then said, 'Let a land arise. Let a land arise.' So a piece of land rose up to the surface of the sea at a place called Lukes, between Ngeaur [Angaur] and Beliliou [Peleliu] today.

And then there was a clam which came into being there. This clam grew larger and larger, and then there came into being the insides of the clam. And, like a human being, the insides of the clam grew larger and larger and became pregnant, with its belly swelling to a large size. Its belly was very large. But it was not able to give birth. Uchelianged observed this condition and said, 'Let there be a strong sea. Let there be a strong, running sea to shake it up so that it can give birth.' When it gave birth, there were many, many fish.

And then these fish in turn gave birth and gave birth, until the sea was crowded. When the sea became crowded, Uchelianged said to Latmikaik, 'Tell your children to gather together rocks and coral and pile them up to the surface of the sea.' So they cleared away the rubble beside Ngeaur and built it up until it reached the surface of the sea. Uchelianged then said, 'Build it so that you will be able to travel to the heavens.' So Latmikaik said to her children, 'Build it even taller so that we can come near to the heavens. . . .' The meaning of this expression is that this Babeldaob is the heavens, and those creatures are creatures beneath the sea.

And so when they had built it very tall it became slightly tilted. They informed Latmikaik that they could not travel to the heavens, since it had become tilted. Latmikaik then said to them, 'Bring me a measuring instrument so I can take a look at the situation.' They brought a measuring instrument, and when the measurement was made, if the [stones] fell over the end would reach Oikull [Measured] village. Latmikaik then said to them, 'Go ahead and kick it over.' They kicked it and when it fell, Beliliou and all the rock islands all the way to Oikull were created. And now the children of Latmikaik could travel to Babeldaob. As they travelled, the land of Belau became more and more crowded. Villages became crowded with people. These children of Latmikaik could live on land or in the sea. . . .

So Chuab and the Woman of Ngetelkou lived there [at Ngeaur]. And the Woman of Ngetelkou bore a child and called her Tellebuu. This Tellebuu in turn gave birth and bore her first child Kebliil, and then bore her second child Seked, a boy. She bore her third child, a girl, Dedaes. They all crossed over to Beliliou, and they went to Liull house at Beliliou. They lived there, and people started giving birth. They were fish-people who could live in the sea and could also live on land.

Chuab also gave birth and bore her first child, a girl, Chitaueiuei. She then bore her second child, Labek, and then bore another male child,

2 Parmentier, *The Sacred Remains*, 130, 138–9.

Boid, and bore another male child, Mengelechelauchach, and then bore another male [child], Omuutaidnger. They traveled, circling around Belau. Chuab lived there, and more and more people were born, and those who lived in the sea came up on land. There was no marriage, but they just mated in the sea and gave birth there.

The lawlessness of these people grew very great, and so Uchelianged said to Chuab, 'Create chiefly councils which will be the reason (*uchul*) for lawfulness at Ngeaur.' So Chuab appointed Ucherkemur el Reked and these other chiefs who were also named Ucherkemur, and they carried the responsibility for Ngeaur. When Ucherkemur came up from the sea he rapidly became out of breath in sitting [on land], so they searched near Mekaeb and brought the shell of the giant clam [Latmikaik] and placed it in front of the meeting house at the village of Rois, named Bairebech. And the waterspout at Bkulengeluul shot up into the air and filled this clamshell with water, and so the shell became the drinking vessel of Ucherkemur. There were Ucherkemur el Reked, and Ucherkemur el Bebael, Ucherkemur el Chedeng, and Ucherkemur el Chai, and Ucherkemur el Lilibangel. These became the chiefs, and they were the only ones at that time.

Uchelianged then said, 'Now travel to Belau and create chiefly councils there.' So Chuab traveled northward to Ngerechol and appointed Uchelchol to be the chief at Beliliou. Chuab traveled northward to Belau and established Secharaimul, and established Tucheremel at Ngerusar, and established Rechiungl at Ngeremid. Chuab then traveled to Ngersuul and created a council at Ngersuul, and then came to Ngeruikl and created a council at Ngeruikl. Chuab traveled northward to Ulimang and created a council at Ulimang and then established Bdelulabeluu as the chief of Mengellang. These chiefs were the eight chiefs [of Belau].

DISCIPLINES AND DATES

History became an academic discipline in the nineteenth century. Academic historians cut their teeth on written documents, and especially government archives whose interpretation became their agenda. The division of academic labour allotted early human experience not to History but to Anthropology or Archaeology. Anthropologists explored the history of pre-literate societies by comparing cultural traits, until this approach fell from favour in the 1930s. Meanwhile Archaeology was developing formidable skills in analysing physical remains of past societies, while linguists organised languages into families with genealogies describing their evolution from common ancestor languages.

Disciplines are shaped by their material and their methods. To approach the remote past through these disciplines involves some understanding of their methods and materials. To analyse physical remains of past societies, archaeologists collaborate with the natural sciences. Where few ancient artefacts survive, that material must be subjected to exact scientific analysis, so archaeologists adopt not only the procedures, but also the style of other scientists—rigorous argument and specialised technical terms, couched in the austere prose of Science and avoiding any hint of poetry.

High technology yields precise records, but has its limits. Radiocarbon dating has been the main tool in creating a chronological framework, but this method only covers the last 40,000 or 50,000 years. Radiocarbon dating fixes the time of death of the sample, so we must be clear about what is providing the date, and the event which we wish to date. If we date a sample of charcoal, for example, we must be sure that humans burned the wood, or that the fire occurred at the same time as some human activity. The new technique of thermoluminescence dating promises to expand that time-frame. Electrons are trapped in quartz crystals at a predictable rate. If quartz sand or pottery is exposed to heat or sunlight, these electrons are released. If it is then buried, electrons become trapped again. If pottery from archaeological layers is heated rapidly in a laboratory, it emits light at a strength which is proportional to the release of the trapped electrons. Measuring this light therefore tells us how long the pottery was buried. The interpretation of this evidence is, however, controversial. It is possible that this technique yields measures of time which differ from radiocarbon time.

We can never be sure of all the ways in which environment and time have spared or destroyed evidence. One factor which has biased our record in the Pacific Islands is the effect of rising sea levels. The standard deviations attached to radiocarbon dates indicate the range of time which they may represent. For example the proper radiocarbon date for human occupation of the Lachitu rock-shelter in New Guinea is 35,360 ± 1400, which indicates that the actual date falls somewhere in the range 36,760 to 33,960, or (to be 95 per cent sure by doubling the margin of error) between 38,160 and 32,560. This standard deviation embodies 7000 years of uncertainty. For these reasons archaeological judgement is always provisional. Fresh evidence or new techniques may alter the significance of old data. Archaeologists must infer large statements from small samples, and there are usually at least two credible ways to interpret the same data. The next text represents the most likely interpretation of present evidence on the basis of present technology. Every sentence should include 'probably': but most have been omitted because their reiteration would be tedious.

THE PLEISTOCENE PACIFIC

The south-west Pacific has not always had the physical shape which it has now. During the Pleistocene era, commonly known as the Ice Age (from about 2 million to 12,000 years ago), massive glaciers often covered parts of the earth. This coincides roughly with the time it took for our first human ancestors to appear in Africa, to evolve into modern humans (*Homo sapiens sapiens*) and to colonise the major land masses. Glaciers had little direct impact in the south-west Pacific, except the highest peaks of New Guinea; but there were significant indirect effects.

Large-scale freezing of the world's water made sea levels fall. Some 'continental islands' (New Guinea and Tasmania) were then part of neighbouring land masses. This did not apply to 'oceanic islands' such as New Ireland, the Solomons and the islands of East Melanesia and Polynesia. The south-west Pacific was therefore dominated by a much expanded land mass which we describe as Australasia. Many intervals between it and the smaller islands shrank, and so did gaps between the islands themselves.

Australasia (or 'Sahul land') was never linked by land to South-East Asia ('Sunda land'). Australasia has been isolated by water for at least 60 million years, since the dawn of the age of mammals. As a result, the region's mammals are in evolutionary terms primitive—marsupials and monotremes, quite distinct from the more advanced placental mammals of the 'Old World' (Africa, Asia and Europe). Since humans and other primates are placental mammals, we must seek the origin of our species outside the region. Many Aboriginal Australians believe that they have always inhabited the continent; but evolutionary scientists look towards South-East Asia for a colonising source, and note that colonisation depended on the ability to cross water barriers.

The ancestors of human beings diverged from the ancestors of chimpanzees and gorillas relatively recently, perhaps within the last 5 million years. The oldest identifiable human ancestor is probably one of the Australopithecines, dated to c.3.5 million years ago in Africa. The oldest member of the genus *Homo* appeared about 2 million years ago, along with patterned stone tools. About 1.6 million years ago *Homo erectus* appeared, again in Africa—the immediate ancestor of modern humans. *Homo erectus* appears to have been the first hominid to spread across the globe: the remains of this species have long been known from China ('Peking man') and Java ('Java man').

Scholars disagree about the emergence of modern humans. Some endorse the 'Regional Continuity' view, which proposes that *Homo erectus* evolved in different parts of the world into regionally distinctive populations of *Homo sapiens*. Others prefer the 'Replacement' theory, that modern humans evolved only once, in Africa, and then spread across the world, replacing *Homo erectus* populations within the last 100,000 years.

Adherents of regional continuity see two separate lineages in Asia and the Pacific. In China, a line of descent leads from early *Homo erectus* populations (represented at the hominid fossil sites Lantian and Yuanmou) through the more evolved Zhoukoudian specimens to more sapient forms such as Dali and Maba and eventually modern Asian ('Mongoloid') populations. In South-East Asia and Australasia another distinct lineage leads from the Javanese *Homo erectus* forms of the earliest Pucangan formations, through the younger Trinil then Ngandong fossils, to modern Australian Aboriginal ('Australoid') populations. Fossil evidence from Australia is considered by some to support this argument. Replacement theorists place a different interpretation on much the same evidence. The relatively recent colonisation of Australasia is taken to demonstrate the movement of fully modern humans out of Africa. In either case, colonisation of the south-west Pacific must be part of the wider story of Asian prehistory. We now leave this topic until we have reviewed the cultural evidence.

We can be certain that humans had reached Australasia 40,000 years ago, beginning a continuous human presence which continues to the present. Archaeologists disagree whether humans arrived any earlier. Thermoluminescence dating of sediments in the Arnhem Land (Northern Territory) rock-shelter site of Malakunanja II shows that they were deposited between 50,000 and 60,000 years ago; but it is not certain that humans were there at the time. Other sites in Arnhem Land reveal a human presence no older than 24,000 years. Elsewhere in Australasia several sites are dated to between 40,000 and 35,000 years BP (before the present). There is also evidence of human occupation on the Huon Peninsula on the north coast of New Guinea. Occupation has been proposed at 40,000 years ago. This date is disputed,[3] but people certainly occupied the Lachitu rock-shelter on the north coast of New Guinea 35,000 years ago. They also occupied the Australian mainland (as it is today) from a similar date: in the north, at Carpenters Gap 1 in the Kimberleys (39,000 BP) and Nurrabulgin Cave in Cape York Peninsula (37,000 BP); in the south-west, at Upper Swan near Perth (38,000 BP); in the south-east, at Lake Mungo and associated sites in the Murray–Darling basin (37,000 BP); and also in Tasmania, at the Warreen cave site (35,000 BP).

These dates may or may not represent the earliest occupations of these areas, given the problems mentioned above, and noting that radiocarbon dating does not cover periods much older than 40,000 BP. However, dates of such great antiquity occur only at the bottom of deep deposits, which suggests that they were indeed the earliest occupations. By contrast, in many sites in Europe, Africa and the Middle East dates of this age occur at the top of deposits, indicating a long record of earlier occupation. If we accept these dates as the earliest occupation of these areas, does this indicate rapid colonisation? This cannot be answered, since the standard deviations of radiocarbon dates allow a wide range of time. All we can say confidently is that in *archaeological* time, colonisation was extremely rapid.

We naturally look to South-East Asia for the antecedents of these colonists, and there we face a puzzling absence. The famous 'Java man' fossils are some of the furthest-flung examples of *Homo erectus*, which originated in Africa at least 1.6 million years ago. The dating of Javanese specimens is controversial. Most would agree with a date of nearly 1 million years for the oldest examples, although radiometric dates of nearly 2 million years have been obtained. Even more problematic are the Ngandong or Solo forms, a more evolved form of *Homo erectus*, or perhaps even an archaic *Homo sapiens*; their most likely dates are between 300,000 and 100,000 years ago. One aspect of the puzzle is that no cultural evidence whatever is associated with these fossils, nor is

3 Allen, 'When Did Humans First Colonise Australia?'; Bowdler '*Homo sapiens* in Southeast Asia and the Antipodes'; and her 'Sunda and Sahul'.

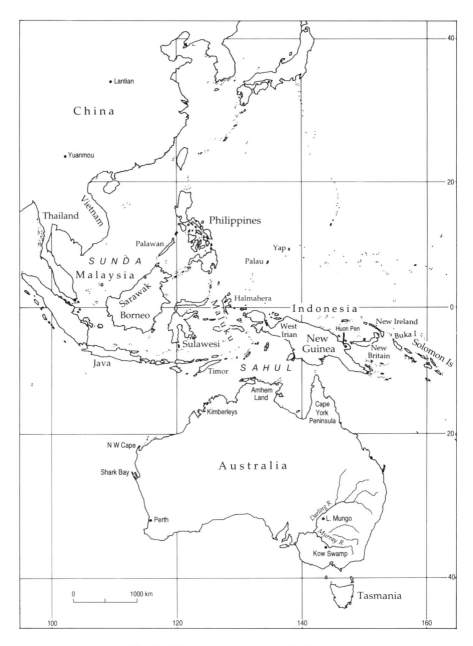

Map 4   Pleistocene archaeological sites

there any such evidence anywhere in South-East Asia which can be dated securely to that time. In fact there is no archaeological evidence from South-East Asia older than that found in Australia, that is, 40,000 years. These dates are remarkably similar to those from Australasia. In peninsular Thailand, humans occupied Lang Rong Rien cave in c.37,000 BP; in northern Vietnam, the oldest of a series of rock-shelters is dated to c.33,200; and in peninsular Malaysia, in Perak, the Kota Tampan stone workshop site is dated to c.31,000. Similar dates are found in island South-East Asia: the Niah Cave in Sarawak, in the north of Borneo, is dated to c.40,000; the rock-shelter Leang Burung 2 in southern Sulawesi is dated to c.31,000; and Tabon Cave on the Philippine island of Palawan had human occupants by 30,000 years ago.[4]

This evidence suggests that South-East Asia was colonised by modern humans at the same time as Australasia, and that colonisation was swift. It does not suggest where they came from, but the most likely source is China. In this scenario, modern humans swept out of southern China to find their way rapidly (in archaeological terms) to the mainland and islands of South-East Asia, the continent of Australia and some Pacific Islands. Colonisation took somewhere between 50 and 5000 years. There is little to suggest why it occurred at this time and no earlier. It has been ascribed to the uniquely developed capabilities of *Homo sapiens sapiens*, fully modern humans, but this suggestion begs as many questions as it answers.

The immigrants certainly needed watercraft and navigational skills, and adaptive skills to cope with new environments. Even during times of lowered sea level and expanded land masses, people always had to cross water to reach Australasia. They did not have to cross water to reach Vietnam, Thailand, peninsular Malaysia, Java, Palawan or Borneo; but the journey to Sulawesi did need watercraft for perhaps 50 kilometres of open sea. Australasia could be reached only by several crossings, of a maximum of 100 kilometres. Nor did the new colonists stop at Australasia: they went on to New Ireland by 33,000 years ago, and to Buka, the northernmost of the Solomon Islands, by 28,000 years ago.

These feats pose many questions. What craft did they use, what routes did they follow, were their voyages accidental or deliberate? No evidence sheds light on the kind of watercraft which people used. The familiar seagoing outrigger and dugout canoes of the Pacific were only developed much later, allowing the Austronesians to disperse (see next sections). We assume that the Austronesian expansion made little or no impact in Australia, so we might expect that Australian watercraft of the recent past are survivors of a Pleistocene tradition. We discount the dugouts of the north coast and the outriggers of the north-east, as these reflect recent Macassan and Papuan influences. That leaves a variety of bark canoes and log rafts which were made by Aboriginal Australians. These craft do not seem capable of long ocean voyages, and indeed some evidence suggests that none of them is very old. Aboriginal people visited offshore islands during the Holocene with such craft:

4 Bowdler, '*Homo sapiens* in Southeast Asia and the Antipodes'.

these journeys involved water crossings of less than 25 kilometres, and most were less than 10 kilometres. Furthermore, such crossings began (with perhaps two or three exceptions out of twenty-six instances) only within the last 4000 years. This suggests that the maritime technology observed in recent times in Aboriginal Australia was not the same as that which carried the first colonists to the Pacific. The original voyages of Pacific discovery may have been made with bamboo craft, perhaps rafts. Extensive stands of large bamboo did not occur in Australia, which could explain why this technology disappeared.

The possible migration routes from South-East Asia into Australasia have been canvassed by Birdsell and by Irwin.[5] These island-hopping routes assume that the shortest crossings were the most likely, and perhaps the most favoured. Birdsell suggests two main routes, one from Java through Timor to northern Australia, the other from Sulawesi through Halmahera to West Irian. He assumes that such voyages were more likely to succeed at times of low sea level, when sea distances were shorter. Irwin disputes this assumption. He argues that the different distances 'were probably all short enough for the risks to remain much the same . . . a boat that is seaworthy enough to cross 10 nautical miles can probably cross 100 or more, provided it is not of a type that becomes waterlogged and provided the weather remains the same'.[6] He also addresses the issue of accidental or deliberate voyaging. A party containing the least possible number of people was doomed to extinction, so intentional voyaging is more likely.

We can only guess at the motives for these voyages. Many ideas have been offered, including population pressures and environmental disasters driving people to seek new resources. The evidence does not lend much weight to these suggestions. The pattern of dates in geographical space may represent extremely speedy colonisation. Colonisation because of expansion under duress should leave evidence of a clear 'gradient of antiquity', with oldest dates in mainland South-East Asia, including Java and Borneo. Younger dates would be expected in Sulawesi and other non-continental islands, and even younger dates in continental Melanesia. We would then expect to find dates in northern Australia for early colonisation either at the same time as, or younger than, those in New Guinea, with even younger dates in southern Australia and oceanic Melanesia. In fact this is not the case; the evidence does not suggest a gradual settling and 'filling up' of new islands and ecological zones. There is no support for a theory of gradual population increase with ensuing pressure on resources, forcing further migrations into new regions. Some other motivation must have driven people to voyages of discovery.

The people were hunter-gatherers, dependent on wild plant and animal resources. It used to be thought that the hunter-gatherer (or 'forager') way of life was random and difficult; but it is now clear that

5   Birdsell, 'The Recalibration of a Paradigm'; and Irwin, *The Prehistoric Exploration and Colonisation of the Pacific.*
6   Irwin, *Prehistoric Exploration and Colonisation,* 27–8.

these people had sophisticated and systematic strategies, passing beyond mere subsistence. These strategies may even be the hallmark of modern humans and explain their extraordinary adaptive success.

Given their obvious maritime abilities, these colonists were well adapted to coastal environments, and were probably fishers and shell-fish gatherers as much as hunters and plant gatherers. Early sites sel-dom preserve the organic remains with which to test this assumption, but it is supported by such evidence as does exist. The remains of fish bones and shellfish are preserved in the oldest levels of the Mandu Mandu Creek rock-shelter (North-west Cape, Australia) and Matenkupkum (New Ireland), both about 33,000 years old and both located near Pleistocene coastlines. At Lake Mungo and other Willandra Lakes sites, freshwater fish and shellfish formed part of the diet from 37,000 BP. Other sites of similar age are great distances from the then coastline, so we know that the early immigrants were able to exploit a wide range of resources in unfamiliar terrain, including some which were previously unknown to them. The range of ecologies which were exploited by 35,000 BP is remarkable. The people were accustomed to tropical Asian forests and savannas, but they were soon targeting wallabies (seasonally) on the edge of the Tasmanian glaciated highlands and collecting emu eggs on the edge of the Western Australian desert.

Colonists may well have developed complex economic systems by then. Evidence in New Ireland suggests that seafaring people intro-duced mammals into new environments during the Pleistocene. Intriguing evidence from Kilu on Buka Island (north Solomon Islands) shows grains of taro on stone tools dated to c.28,000 BP. We do not know whether taro was indigenous to Buka or had been brought by people. These areas hint at the deliberate human dispersal of plants and animals during early colonisation. This in turn is open to several interpretations. On one hand, the people may have been sophisticated environmental managers (but not 'agriculturalists'). On the other hand, these dis-persals may have been by-products of providing enough food for long sea voyages.

Colonists may also have moved hard goods over great distances. In Australia, rock-shelter sites on what is now the coast of the Kimberley region contain pieces of baler shell dated to c.28,000 BP—when the coast was more than 50 kilometres away. Later, pearl-shell as well as baler is found in levels dated to c.18,000 BP, when the sea was 200 kilometres away. Further south, a site at Shark Bay contained baler shell dated to c.30,000 BP—and the coast was 100 kilometres to the west. In several areas of Australia in modern times, pearl-shell and baler shell were important items in long-distance trade. We cannot conclude that these items possessed the same significance thousands of years ago, nor can we be sure that they imply trade similar to that of recent times; but they do show that the colonists who began to exploit the resources of the interior maintained some links with the distant coast.

In south-west Tasmania, the Darwin crater was made by the impact of a meteorite. This crater contains small seams of glass produced by the collision of the meteor with local rocks. Small pieces of Darwin glass in the form of flakes and tools have been found in dated deposits up to 28,000 BP. The actual routes humans had to follow from the crater vary from 25 to over 100 kilometres. Natural glass also occurs on several Melanesian islands, as volcanic obsidian. This was an important trade item in recent times and probably much earlier. New Britain obsidian was carried to New Ireland 20,000 years ago—350 kilometres in a straight line, involving a minimum sea crossing of 30 kilometres. Small but consistent amounts of this material were deposited over a period of some 2000 years. These cases suggest that the early colonists adapted rapidly to new environments and quickly built networks to maximise the use of new resources. These were not desperate drift voyagers, accidentally beached on new lands, or even desperate explorers driven by environmental change.

It is surprisingly difficult to trace the origin of these remarkable pioneers. Two kinds of evidence might help us: cultural and biological. We would expect that colonists carried some identifiable 'baggage' which can be traced to its source: and their physiques might indicate their relationship to source populations. In both cases, the evidence is scanty and ambivalent.

At most of the early sites, the only clear cultural evidence is stone artefacts. These present many intrinsic problems, compounded by scholarly preconceptions based on Old World experience. Stone artefacts occurred in the earliest African sites of the genus *Homo*. These early assemblages make up the 'Oldowan industry' (after Olduvai Gorge). Examples of the Oldowan industry often occur as a patterned, recurrent set of types, which include pebble choppers and smaller flake tools and scrapers. In Africa, a new range of tool types (typified by a large two-faced 'hand axe') known as the Acheulian industry indicates the emergence of the immediate pre-human ancestor, *Homo erectus*. The Acheulian is also found in Europe, the Middle East and parts of India—but not in East Asia. Assemblages from China, of the same age as Acheulian sites to the west, contain a characteristic range of flake tools, with some pebble choppers. (The *Homo erectus* fossils of Java have no cultural associations.) In Europe, the Acheulian industries were followed by Mousterian industries (associated with Neanderthals) and then by Upper Palaeolithic industries associated with fully modern humans (*Homo sapiens sapiens*). These later assemblages are assumed to demonstrate increasing complexity and refinement. In China, on the other hand, the stone tool assemblages continued with few visible changes. The traditional interpretation of these differences has been judgemental. East Asian stone tool industries have been judged to lack progressive change compared with African and European sequences. It is generally implied that the Asian industries are simply a continuation of an original Oldowan industry, stagnating in an evolutionary cul-de-sac.

These traditional views are not motivated entirely by blind prejudice. Stone is inflexible, unlike pottery which is extremely plastic and lends itself to decoration. The decorations can be regarded as stylistic, so that pottery is an excellent medium for identifying cultural traits. People made stone artefacts by striking rocks to detach and reduce them, which produced a limited range of forms and little opportunity for decoration. Archaeologists face several problems in dealing with stone tools. They appear in almost all pre-agricultural sites, but we know very little about how they were used. This compounds the problem of identifying which characteristics were functional, and which were stylistic (and therefore culturally determined). Interpretation of the earliest Pacific stone industries is hampered by all these difficulties: therefore only tentative comments can be made. Early Australian stone tool industries have been grouped together as the 'Australian Core Tool and Scraper Tradition'. This entity was based mainly on artefacts from the surface of the Lake Mungo site. However, this concept implies a unity which may not exist, and perhaps masks a variety in artefact assemblages from Australasian Pleistocene sites. The artefact assemblages of early Australasia do share many features. Artefacts from the Kimberleys, Shark Bay, Cape York, Tasmania and New Ireland which are 30,000 years old or older appear to form part of a common tradition, albeit amorphous, or (more politely) *ad hoc*. The technical procedures seem to have been identical in all cases. Some types recurred, namely small steep edge scrapers and thumbnail scrapers. Stone artefact assemblages from South-East Asian sites of similar age share similar attributes. The complete lack of earlier cultural evidence from South-East Asia implies colonisation by modern humans at the same time as Australasia, c.40,000 years ago. The artefacts suggest only one possible source for this colonisation: China. Chinese Pleistocene artefact assemblages did not change much through time, and the very earliest (up to a million years old) as well as more recent assemblages (up to c.20,000 BP) bear a remarkable resemblance to those of Australasia.

Biological evidence presents quite different problems. Human remains of Pleistocene age are rare in any part of the world, and Australasia is no exception. No examples are known from Melanesia and very few from South-East Asia apart from the Javanese *Homo erectus* examples. The best-described example is the skull from the Niah Cave (Sarawak): it is usually dated from about 40,000 years ago, but this date has been questioned, as it may be a much younger intrusive burial. Several collections of human remains from Australia have been assigned a Pleistocene age. Many of these are not well dated. The best-studied are the two Lake Mungo burials dated to between 26,000 and 32,000 BP, and the large Kow Swamp collection (between 14,000 and 9000 BP). All specimens are ascribed to the fully modern human species, *Homo sapiens sapiens*. The Mungo examples, and some others, are described as extremely gracile (light-boned), and the Kow Swamp and other examples from the Murray Valley as very robust (heavily boned). One interpretation of these differences is that the gracile specimens derived from the Chinese Mongoloid lineage, whereas the Kow Swamp group derived from the Javanese Australoid lineage. (This raises problems, not least the implication that the Kow Swamp group is much more archaic than the other group, and yet its antiquity is less.) In this view, at least two separate groups of people colonised Australia, one from Java and one direct from China. An alternative interpretation is that the two forms do not represent extreme differences, but that both fall within the range of variation of modern Aboriginal populations. It has also been suggested that the characteristics of the Kow Swamp group developed only after late Pleistocene times. This view infers only one colonising population.

The view favoured here is that Australia and the south-west Pacific were colonised within the last 40,000 (or perhaps 50,000) years by modern humans, *Homo sapiens sapiens*, who emerged from China and moved swiftly across South-East Asia and Australasia. The *Homo erectus* populations of Java were not part of this colonising population: by then they were probably extinct. If we endorse this view, one more problem remains: it does not explain the origin of the physical characteristics thought to distinguish the 'Mongoloids' of East and South-East Asia and Polynesia from the 'Australoids' of Australia and much of Melanesia. To put this simply, Australian Aboriginal people of recent times, Melanesians, Polynesians, South-East Asians and Han Chinese are all descendants of one ancestral group within the last 40,000 years. This does not satisfy those who see these differentiating features in different *Homo erectus* populations, and consider that they needed more than 40,000 years to become so distinct. It seems, however, that most of the features used to define these groups are soft tissue differences which have not been preserved from great antiquity. There is also debate on how significant such differences are adaptively, and how rapidly they may have altered under changing environmental circumstances. We do not know how long it takes such characteristics to become distinctive.

To summarise, some 40,000 years ago, fully modern humans embarked on a series of voyages out of China, across South-East Asia into new lands in Australia and Melanesia. They probably reached the southern end of the Solomon Islands chain, but not beyond. They adapted quickly to an extreme range of environments, and soon set up sophisticated economic networks. The archaeological record shows continuous occupation from the earliest times until the end of the Pleistocene. This is not to deny that people made further voyages—and perhaps return voyages. In Australia, certain populations were dislocated during the height of the last glaciation c.18,000 years ago: increased aridity made previously comfortable environments marginal for humans. We do not know if this, or other effects, occurred in Melanesia; but clearly all such problems were overcome, because populations survived, expanded, and responded to new challenges described below.

LINGUISTIC EVIDENCE

One of the most useful historical disciplines which developed during the past hundred years is Linguistics. Whereas Pleistocene archaeologists co-operate most closely with the natural sciences, linguists rely on Anthropology, Archaeology and Genetics to test evident connections between languages and the people who spoke them. The study of

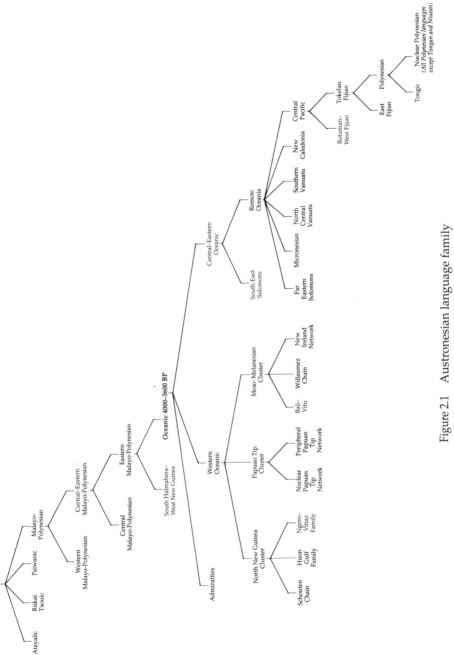

Figure 2.1   Austronesian language family

grammatical structure and vocabulary reveals language relationships which are typically represented as genealogies which diverge with the passage of time and exposure to new influences.

Austronesian languages are so closely related that linguists choose to represent them as members of a family, whose relationships can be expressed like a genealogy in which recent languages are the offspring of older ones, no longer spoken. Linguists are confident about the sequence of separations of a single language into a cluster of closely related ones, which are treated as if they were siblings. However, it is impossible to offer absolute dates for these developments, since languages do not change at a regular or predictable pace. In the genealogy in Figure 2.1, for example, the proposed date for the break-up of 'Oceanic' is estimated on the basis of archaeological rather than linguistic evidence.

Slightly fewer than half of all Pacific Islanders speak Austronesian languages. The great majority of other languages are spoken in New Guinea and the Solomon Islands. Linguists classify these either negatively as 'Non-Austronesian' or (more positively, but confusingly) as Papuan. There are about 750 Papuan languages, making the New Guinea area one of the most complex language areas in the world. The broadest classification was proposed by Stephen Wurm,[7] whose schema is summarised in Figure 2.2. To express the great distances between these languages, he uses broader terms than 'family': a loose affiliation of families is described as a 'stock', some stocks are grouped together even more loosely as 'super-stocks', and faintly related stocks are termed a 'phylum'. This classification implies a sequence of relative dates, but at present it would be foolish even to estimate the absolute dates of their separations. Commenting on Wurm's broad and bold classification, Foley observes that Papuan languages are organised into upwards of sixty distinct language families, with wider relations not yet conclusively demonstrated.[8]

RECENT PREHISTORY (THE HOLOCENE)

For the more recent (Holocene) period, covering the past 10,000 years, archaeologists can integrate evidence from the social sciences, especially Linguistics and Anthropology, and written accounts of societies in the very recent past. Rather than simplifying the archaeologist's task, diversity of evidence compounds the difficulty of interpretation: once again every statement should be read as if 'probably' were inscribed in it.

The dominant event of the Holocene (or Recent) period was the evolution of a distinctive cultural complex (Lapita) in the Bismarck and Solomon Archipelagos. The Lapita complex was first defined by its pottery, but is now known to have included stone adzes, ornaments,

7   Wurm, *Papuan Languages of Oceania*.
8   Foley, *The Papuan Languages of New Guinea*, 13.

1 TRANS-NEW GUINEA PHYLUM
Number: 507
Area: *Most of New Guinea mainland
except:*
a *greater part of Vogelkop Peninsula*
b *NW part of Irian Jaya*
c *NW Papua New Guinea*

Stocks:
Finisterre–Huon Stock
East New Guinea Highlands Stock
Central–South New Guinea
    Kutubuan Super Stock
Angan Family
Gogodala–Suku Stock
Marind Stock
Kayagar Family
Sentani Stock
Dani–Dwerba Stock
Wissel Lakes–Kemandoga Stock
Mairasi–Tanah Merah Stock
West Bomberai Stock   .
Binandere Stock
Rai Coast–Mabuso Super Stock
Adelbert Range Super Stock
Teberan–Pawaian Super Stock
Turama–Kikorian Stock
Inland Gulf Family
Eleman Stock
Trans–Fly–Yelmek–Maklew Super
    Stock
Mek Family
Senagi Family
Pauwasi Stock
Northern Super Stock
Kaure Stock
Kolopom Family
South Bird's Head–Timor–Alor–
    Pantar Super Stock

2 WEST PAPUAN PHYLUM
Number: 24
Area: *Northern part of Vogekop and
northern Halmahera*

Stocks:
Bird's Head Super Stock
Borai–Hattam Family
Northern Halmahera Family

3 SEPIK–RAMU PHYLUM
Number: 98
Area: *Sepik Provinces and western
Madang Province*

Stocks:
Sepik Super Stock
Leonard Schultze Stock
Nor–Pondo (Lower Sepik) Stock
Ramu Super Stock
Yuat Super Stock

4 TORRICELLI PHYLUM
Number: 48
Area: *Northern part of Sepik Provinces
and NW Madang Province*

Stocks:
West Wapei Family
Wapei–Palei Stock
Maimai Stock
Kombio Stock
Marienberg Family
Monumbo Family

5 EAST PAPUAN PHYLUM
Number: 27
Area: *Some parts of Island Melanesia
adjoining New Guinea mainland in
north-east and east*

Stocks:
Yele–Solomons–New Britain Super
    Stock
Bougainville Super Stock
Reef Islands–Santa Cruz Family

Figure 2.2   The major phyla of Papuan languages, 741 in number.
Adapted from S. A. Wurm, *Papuan Languages of Oceania*, Gunter Narr Verlag
Tübingen, 1982.

stilt houses in villages, and domestic animals including the pig. This technology then provided the skills and resources which enabled people to colonise Remote Oceania. Quite independently, the 9000-year record of swamp gardening at Kuk in the New Guinea Highlands reveals changes in garden type and area of cultivation, in response to environmental and social changes. If this uneven evidence is supplemented by historical linguistics and human biology, the outline of recent prehistory becomes clear. Using an arbitrary starting date of 10,000 years before the present, this section examines the settlement of the Islands, using time slices of 10,000 BP, 5000 BP, 3000 BP, 2000 BP, 1000 BP and 500 BP (or AD 1500).

The Pacific World at 10,000 BP

As described above, hunter-gatherers reached the end of the main Solomons chain well before 10,000 BP. Beyond the main Solomons the only land mammals (except bats) have been imported by humans. Thirty genera of land birds and 162 genera of seed plants find their eastern limits here, and major breaks occur in the distribution of other fauna and flora. This implies a boundary between Near and Remote Oceania, restraining human dispersal beyond the Bismarck Archipelago and the Solomon Islands. It may have barred settlement, not so much because of sea gaps but because of the paucity of naturally occurring foods.

Until 8000 BP New Guinea and Australia were joined by a neck of land near Cape York, but the prevalence of malaria may have limited the use of this corridor. Few sites of this period are known from lowland New Guinea, and our picture comes largely from the Highlands and the Bismarck Archipelago and the Solomons. Highlanders engaged in some form of cultivation from about 9000 BP, maintaining a system of drains in swamp margins at Kuk. A later, more extensive system is dated to 6000 BP. Other Highland sites at about 10,000 BP contain marine shell ornaments, showing that Highlanders enjoyed indirect contact and exchange with coastal regions.

Island Melanesian sites of a similar age show that people produced wild plant food in the form of *Canarium indicum* (a native almond and tree crop), which they may have brought from New Guinea during the late Pleistocene. They also ate wild or cultivated taro (*Colocasia esculenta*). There is evidence too that colonists deliberately introduced New Guinea wild animals, such as bandicoots and large rats, to Manus, and possums and rats to New Ireland. They may also have introduced a small wallaby to New Ireland during the early Holocene. The movement of obsidian from Talasea in New Britain across to New Ireland is attested in several sites from 20,000 BP onwards. Neither obsidian nor the introduced animals were carried to the Solomon Islands, which suggests that there was little contact between archipelagos. Manus also has sources of obsidian which was moving within that archipelago but not beyond, by the early Holocene. This distribution again implies the partial isolation of each archipelago.

In brief, after the original push into the Bismarcks and Solomons, people's horizons contracted as they settled into varying environments. They lived in hamlets of up to thirty people and often shifted their residence. Exchange networks at the beginning of the Holocene did not bridge the major ocean gaps (Manus to New Guinea or the Bismarcks, or New Ireland to the Solomons) already traversed by the first colonists.

Near Oceania at 5000 BP

Evidence from the early Holocene suggests small-scale cultivation or wild plant food production, combined with hunting and gathering. Some scholars argue that local developments then set the stage for the settlement of Remote Oceania. This view (the continuity argument) regards Lapita as a local development and sees no need to invoke migrations into the region from further west. Some pre-Lapita sites throw light on this question. Talasea obsidian was exchanged widely by 5000 BP to other parts of New Britain, New Ireland and Nissan to the east, and as far west as the Sepik area, but there is no evidence that it was used in the Solomons before the Lapita era. People at Talasea developed an industry of stemmed obsidian tools before the Lapita period, but comparable assemblages have not been found in later (Lapita) levels. In the same area there are sites which were continuously occupied before and during Lapita times, but most Lapita sites are in places which were not previously occupied. Some continuity is also apparent in the working of shell, with *Tridacna* shell adzes (albeit stylistically different), *Trochus* shell arm-rings, shell beads and *Trochus* one-piece fishhooks, as well as ground or flaked shell pieces found in both types of sites. Bone points occur in pre-Lapita levels on New Ireland and are also known from Lapita sites. The continuity argument would be stronger if the main domesticated animal, the pig, and the most common Lapita artefact, pottery, were definitely present before the Lapita era. However, neither has been claimed for Island Melanesia. Both have been claimed for New Guinea, but research has not confirmed the pre-Lapita dates for New Guinea pottery, whose forms are also very different. It would not be surprising if pigs were present before Lapita in New Guinea, but the evidence is tenuous.

Meanwhile, after 6000 BP New Guinea Highlanders cleared more forest for agriculture. Near the north coast, the Dongan site in the Sepik–Ramu area yields fruit and nut species dating to about 6500 BP. New Guinea pollen evidence points to forest clearance, and this may represent intensification of production through increasing reliance on cultivated food as a result of population increase. We should be cautious, however, before imposing this evolutionary scenario on our limited information. Evidence of forest clearance might, for example, represent the inability of the forest to regenerate after initial clearance. Over time, the forest would tend to shrink even without human population growth. In Island Melanesia, pollen sequences beginning about 5000 BP show some human interference through fire from the start of the record, but this level of impact on the vegetation is very different from a later major phase of rapid forest clearance (see below), representing a classic pattern of 'pioneer' farming.

Lapita and the Colonisation of Remote Oceania, 3000 BP

The Lapita cultural complex was first defined by its distinctive decorated pottery, which used toothed stamps to impress designs on the pot before firing. Other artefacts have been added—stone adze forms, ornament types, rectangular stilt houses in sedentary villages, and introduced domestic animals, so the complex is no longer 'just pots'. The span of Lapita is from Manus and the Vitiaz Straits (between New Guinea and New Britain) in the west to Tonga and Samoa in the east. On New Guinea itself shards have been found (at Aitape) from only one pot. The eastward spread of the Lapita complex from the Bismarck Archipelago into West Polynesia seems to be linked to the spread of Austronesian languages. Their mainly coastal distribution in Near Oceania suggests that they intruded into a Non-Austronesian area. Lapita culture dates from about 3500 BP to 2500–2000 BP, when it began to lose its more widespread and distinctive features.

The most widespread archaeological phenomenon and the most widespread language group in the same area must surely be linked. Austronesian languages derived from South-East Asia and ultimately Taiwan (see previous sections). The immediate Lapita 'homeland' lay in the Bismarck Archipelago. Polynesian languages and cultures developed later, at the eastern extension of Lapita, in a region previously uninhabited. Speakers of these languages could hardly have come from Taiwan to Island Melanesia and Polynesia without leaving any trace, and the obvious trace at the appropriate time (no later than 3000 BP) is Lapita. Island South-East Asian radiocarbon chronology shows the spread of Neolithic cultures from Taiwan through the Philippines to eastern Indonesia, and the same pattern of dates extends east into Polynesia.

This view of a movement of language and culture from the west has its critics, who see Lapita as a local development from pre-Lapita cultures in the Bismarcks, with little western influence. The evidence, however, supports a South-East Asian origin. Lapita elements of South-East Asian origin include particular kinds of pottery, pigs, dogs and chickens, quadrangular stone adzes, polished stone chisels, various shell ornament types, rectangular houses (some on stilts), large villages, language, and probably aspects of boat technology, tattoo chisels, pearl-shell knives, trolling hooks and various stone artefact classes. On the other hand some cultural elements were widespread before Lapita in South-East Asia and parts of Melanesia (and cannot be new integrations or intrusions in the Bismarcks). These pre-Lapita features include oval/lenticular polished stone adzes, grindstones, hinge-region *Tridacna* shell adzes, pierced shell pendants, shell beads, *Trochus* shell armbands, one-piece shell fishhooks, bone points or awls, vegetation clearance by fire

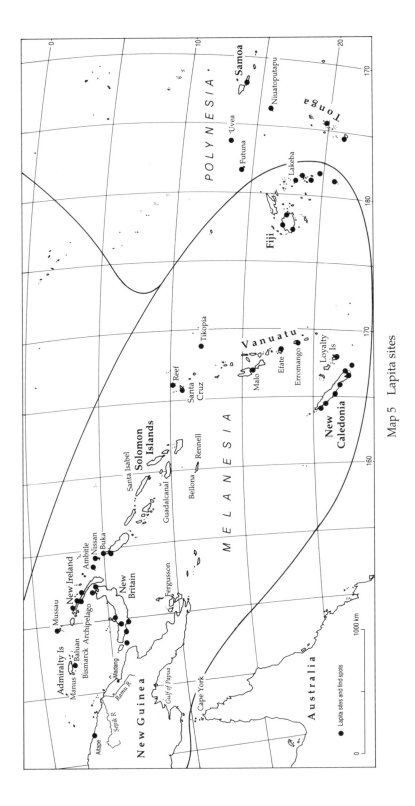

Map 5 Lapita sites

and some form of cultivation, movement of wild animals and plants, most of the Oceanic domesticated crop complex, shell-fishing and reef fishing, possibly earth ovens, and some long-distance exchange. By contrast, very few elements were unique to Melanesia: some crops, obsidian stemmed tools and dorsal-region *Tridacna* adzes (of a very different style to Lapita) and perhaps the earth oven. In brief, Lapita is basically of South-East Asian Austronesian origin, although some elements were invented and added in the Bismarcks, and some pre-Lapita Melanesian elements were integrated into it.

The complementary distribution of Austronesian languages and the Island South-East Asian Neolithic and Lapita cultural complexes suggests dates for the spread of both. Proto-Austronesian split into Formosan and Malayo-Polynesian groups around 5000 BP when some people moved south to the Philippines and Sulawesi. Malayo-Polynesian broke up when people moved from Sulawesi to north Maluku at about 4500 BP. The next split occurred with a move to the east, probably centred in Cenderawasih Bay in north-western Irian Jaya, perhaps around 4000 BP. A further spread east resulted in Austronesian and Lapita settlement in the Bismarcks by 3500 BP and the fragmentation of Oceanic as Lapita settlements spread south and east through the main Solomons and into Vanuatu and New Caledonia at about 3200 BP. The next move was from northern Vanuatu to Fiji, Tonga and Samoa by 3000 BP. In brief, first settlement of Polynesia by the Lapita culture and the absence of any but Polynesian languages there suggest that Polynesians are direct descendants of the bearers of Lapita culture. An origin in Island South-East Asia for the 'pre-Polynesians' now seems certain, with evidence of some genetic admixture with populations in northern Island Melanesia.

The connection between South-East Asia and Melanesia is not absolutely certain, because of a gap in sites of the relevant period in northern New Guinea and islands to the west. Language distribution implies cultural connections on Japen and Biak Islands in Cenderawasih Bay or on the shores of the bay. The integration of Melanesian elements into an intrusive culture occurred either in this region or in the Bismarcks, but it is at present an archaeological blank. So is the rest of northern New Guinea for the relevant period. Possible evidence for early Austronesian settlement along this coast or on offshore islands has been obscured by a later back-migration of Oceanic Austronesian speakers from east to west within the last 2000 years.

In northern New Guinea, some Non-Austronesians borrowed words from Austronesian languages. 'Pig' in many Non-Austronesian languages is an Austronesian loan-word even in inland areas, a hint of the late introduction of this animal. The Wañelek pottery and polished quadrangular adzes may represent a diffusion of Austronesian material culture inland before 3750 BP. Taken together, this evidence implies an early spread of material culture from west to east. Similarly, many crops which were carried into the Pacific during the Lapita period have also been found in pre-Lapita South-East Asia, and the words which describe many of them can be traced to Malayo-Polynesian (spoken about

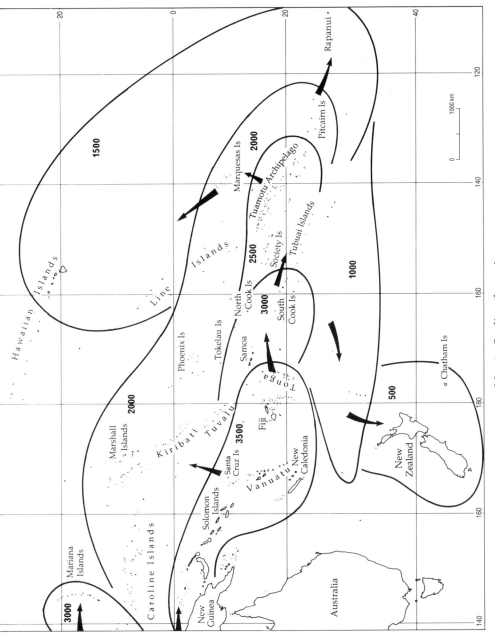

Map 6   Settling the region

5000 years ago). This evidence makes it difficult to accept a New Guinea origin, and South-East Asia is much more likely.

Whatever the origins of the Lapita crop complex, the combined package of crops and the three Pacific domesticates—pigs, dogs and chickens—formed a systematic agricultural complex. Perhaps this is what enabled the first permanent settlers to cross the Remote Oceania barrier and colonise islands beyond. The distribution of Talasea obsidian reached its greatest extension at the same time, from Borneo to Fiji, a span of 7000 kilometres.

On the issue of voyaging technology, Green argues that: 'An effective voyaging system based on dugout canoes or rafts was already in place in Near Oceania, but to it was added the outrigger canoe, the double canoe, new developments in 2-boom triangular sail technology as well as an ability to navigate these improved sailing vessels in return voyages over distances independent of having land in sight.'[9] No Lapita or pre-Lapita boats have been found. Technology and navigation skills were refined at the time of Lapita, as is evident by expansion into Remote Oceania. There is no pre-Lapita evidence of extension of voyaging range (and developments in boat technology) in Near Oceania during the Holocene: all the island groups reached before Lapita (the Bismarcks, Solomons and Admiralties) were settled in Pleistocene times. Reconstructions of Malayo-Polynesian terms include those for boat, sail, outrigger, rollers to beach a canoe, cross-seat or boat ribs, paddle, to steer or rudder, and boat/sea travel. These features were therefore known in Island South-East Asia before the Lapita period. We do not know if they were also present in Melanesia. Cognates of these terms were inherited by Oceanic speakers in Lapita times, with the addition of a new term and new technology, that of the double-hulled canoe.

Not all bearers of Lapita culture moved to Polynesia. The genes of the 'stay-at-homes' can be found in coastal and island groups in Melanesia who are descendants both of local pre-Lapita populations and of intrusive South-East Asian populations who also gave rise to the Poly-nesians. Genetic evidence suggests that Fijians mixed with Island Melanesians after first settlement by Lapita groups. The original Fijian population would have been more Polynesian in appearance. This might also have been true of the first settlers of Vanuatu and New Caledonia. The genetic evidence down-plays any direct link between Polynesians and Micronesians. Micronesian populations are diverse but in general are a distinct Island South-East Asian population with varying genetic input from Melanesia. At the same time as the spread of Lapita into Remote Oceania, for example, the first colonisers reached the Mariana Islands in northern Remote Oceania, about 3200–3000 BP. There are specific parallels in pottery style with the Philippines and Sulawesi at this time. The languages of the Marianas and Palau are related most closely to those of the Philippines and eastern Indonesia in a separate Austronesian migration contemporary with Lapita. Poly-nesians cannot therefore be descendants from populations in Micro-

9   Green, 'Near and Remote Oceania—Disestablishing "Melanesia" '.

nesia. There may have been a moment in the Bismarcks when a single people using Lapita pottery were genetically, linguistically and culturally distinct from their neighbours. But this unity and distinctiveness would have been brief. Lapita-using populations who spread to Polynesia and those in Island Melanesia then had divergent genetic, cultural and linguistic histories.

Lapita society was probably hierarchical, given the demands of voyaging and colonising far-flung islands, but its structure cannot be established from archaeological evidence. This was not the only cultural complex in Near Oceania, but it is by far the most visible, and few non-Lapita contemporary sites have been identified. To what extent pre-Lapita groups were committed to agriculture is unclear. They did not have the full Lapita complex of plants and animals, which presumably gave Lapita the demographic advantage and ability to settle rapidly across a large area. Lapita groups, however, must initially have been small—one or two canoe-loads in one locale, perhaps less than a hundred people, who gained numbers by natural increase and recruitment from their neighbours. Nearly all Island Melanesian and New Guinea societies were fully agricultural by the time of European contact. Some agricultural techniques, therefore, may have spread from Lapita centres to non-Lapita groups by various processes. Adoption of agriculture by hunter-gatherers or small-scale cultivators could have allowed population growth. They might then have adopted Lapita culture and produced Lapita sites, preventing any easy 'ethnic' classification for later Lapita settlements. The Lapita move into Remote Oceania, however, brought colonists into an uninhabited area, where local recruitment was not possible.

In the eastern Solomons, Vanuatu and New Caledonia, we first see evidence of a recurrent colonisation pattern. This consisted of 'pioneering' agriculture and rapid extirpation of many birds and other fauna. Where faunal records are available—in the small island of Tikopia in the Solomon Islands and in New Caledonia—human settlement meant the rapid extinction of many species. In New Caledonia these included a giant megapode, at least ten other birds, a terrestrial crocodile, a turtle and a large land snail. In Tikopia bones of three of the five extirpated bird species are found only in the earliest deposits, with a great reduction in turtle numbers and declining numbers (and sizes) of shellfish. This pattern reflects a deliberate targeting of pristine fauna while plant and domestic animal stocks were being established. Large-scale clearance for agriculture also led to environmental degradation. People responded by moving elsewhere and repeating the process. As population grew, such profligacy was no longer possible, and people developed conservation practices, such as terracing, to allow continuous agriculture in one location.

The Post-Lapita World: Near and Remote Oceania at 2000 BP

At least a thousand years elapsed after 3000 BP, between Lapita settlement in Tonga and Samoa, and the colonisation of East Polynesia. Perhaps this interval was needed to develop a new voyaging strategy which operated mainly upwind across the great distances of East Polynesia.

Several Micronesian archipelagos were settled at about 2000 BP. Related, generally plain pottery styles are found in the lowest levels of the earliest sites, arguably derived from late Lapita or from the plain-wares which followed it in parts of Island Melanesia. Apart from Palau (settled from Island South-East Asia), the Marianas (Chamorro) and Yap and Nauru (whose linguistic affiliations are unclear), all Micronesians spoke languages belonging to the 'Nuclear Micronesian' group, whose nearest relatives were in the region of the south-east Solomons and northern Vanuatu, or in Manus. Nuclear Micronesian was a late off-shoot from Lapita, while West Micronesia seems to have been settled by different colonists from island South-East Asia. Evidence from Fais—a raised coral island 180 kilometres east of Yap—suggests that present linguistic boundaries have shifted from earlier patterns. The people now speak a Nuclear Micronesian language but the earliest site, dating to about 1900 BP, implies first settlement from Yap to the west.

The Lapita complex ended about 2500–2000 BP. In Polynesia the dentate-stamped pottery was succeeded by plain-wares and a distinctively Polynesian material culture. By 2800 BP Lapita decoration had given way to a plain-ware in Samoa, rather earlier than in Tonga and Fiji, and in relative isolation. When Lapita decoration disappeared in Island Melanesia and Fiji, different pottery styles derivable from the non-dentate stamped 'domestic ware' of Lapita appeared from Manus to Fiji. Vanuatu obsidian and pottery types appeared in Fiji, evidence of renewed contacts to the west. Changes in pottery style might represent further population movements, or continuity of groups who continued to interact over the previous range of Lapita. The genetic evidence suggests population movement for Fiji and possibly New Caledonia and Vanuatu. A secondary movement of Austronesian speakers of a Meso-Melanesian Cluster from New Britain to New Ireland and the western Solomons would fit this time-frame, and a sharp language boundary at the southern end of Santa Isabel may be the point where we lose the linguistic signal of a spread of genes and culture which continued further south.

Archaeological and pollen evidence from Guadalcanal is interesting in this context. No evidence for Lapita settlement has been found here, and a basic culture persisted from the earliest trace of settlement at about 6000 through to about 2300 BP. A dramatic change in the pollen and cultural sequences then occurred, representing major forest clearance in the 'pioneering' pattern, a shift in exchange networks, and the introduction of pigs. It is tempting to view this as the movement of South-east Solomonic speakers, bringing the full Lapita-derived agricultural suite into a sparsely settled, Non-Austronesian, non-agricultural area. Events further north may have aided this movement: if the Nuclear Micronesian languages are indeed related to South-east Solomonic, then the agricultural expansion postulated here may coincide with settlement expansion from the same area into East Micronesia. It is significant that the only group of Non-Austronesian languages in Remote Oceania, in the Reef Santa Cruz area, has been described as a secondary movement from further north at about 2000 BP.

The need for Lapita groups to establish peaceful relations with earlier settlers probably eroded preference for marrying their own kin, and technological transfer allowed these other groups to 'catch up'. Lapita lost its distinctiveness and a variety of creole cultures developed. The earlier advantages of Lapita would ensure that the higher-status Austronesian language prevailed. In many cases in Island Melanesia, Non-Austronesian had important influences on Austronesian languages, which would fit this model. Continued exchange, though attenuated, could have ensured continuing changes in pottery style, in step over much of Island Melanesia (the 'Mangaasi' or 'Incised and Applied Relief' styles). Effects on social organisation would vary, and the reassertion (or continuity) of pre-Lapita social forms cannot be discounted. Secondary migration is one possible process of cultural change towards the end of Lapita. Other scenarios include the collapse of the exchange network, because it was onerous or redundant; transformation of a system where hierarchy had been maintained by control of a prestige-goods exchange network and perhaps a shared symbolic and religious system; or absorption by non-Lapita groups.

On the island of New Guinea just after 2000 BP, the Papuan red-slipped pottery style spread rapidly east to west along the south coast of Papua. The spread is associated with a distinctive settlement pattern, long-distance movement of obsidian (from Fergusson Island in Milne Bay) and other items of material culture derived from the Lapita culture of the Bismarcks. Slightly later, pottery appeared along the north coast and on islands offshore from Madang, also related to the Bismarcks material. These pottery distributions are matched almost exactly with east-to-west spreads of Austronesian languages out of New Britain. The coincidence suggests that post-Lapita populations moved from the Bismarcks along the New Guinea coasts and (in the Markham valley) inland as well.

In the New Guinea Highlands at this time, Phase IV of use of the Kuk Swamp (2000–1200 BP) is the first to show the rectangular grid of ditched beds linked by major drains. This has been interpreted as a 'Colocasian Revolution', in which swamps became productive centres for taro. This system enabled people to produce a significant surplus, which generated inequalities in an economy based on pig exchanges. Degradation of dryland environments into grassland areas gave the swamps a new salience in agriculture, while stone axe production began at specialised quarries, to supply intensifying exchanges.

A single piece of bronze from Lou Island, near Manus, dating to 2100 BP bears tantalising witness to the end of the Lapita connections to west and east. It is exactly contemporary with the earliest spread of metal through island South-East Asia. Afterwards the orientations of the archipelagos either side of New Guinea diverged rapidly. Island South-East Asia became integrated into the 'world system' through the Hinduised states and Chinese and Arab influences. These touched western New Guinea (for instance Vietnamese Dongson bronze drums were there, dating to about 2000 BP) but evidently had no influence further east.

After Lapita, exchange systems contracted sharply. Obsidian was never again carried so far, and from about 2000 BP diversification seems stronger than cultural unity in Island Melanesia. The region's famous diversity may be a product of the immediate post-Lapita era. In some areas of Island Melanesia (unlike the northern Pacific, where trade continued to link high islands with atolls), people stopped making or trading pottery after 2000 BP: everywhere the number of pottery-making centres declined.

The Pacific at 1000 BP (AD 1000)

Settlement of the Pacific was certainly punctuated: colonists reached Near Oceania in the late Pleistocene, parts of Island Melanesia and West Polynesia across the Remote Oceania barrier at about 3200–3000 BP, West Micronesia at the same time (with a later burst into Micronesia from Island Melanesia at about 2000 BP). They settled East Polynesia rapidly, starting around 1600–1300 BP. Most of East Polynesia was first settled between 2000 and 1000 BP: the Marquesas in AD 300–600, Hawai'i at about AD 650, the Cooks and Tahiti at about AD 750–800 and Rapanui (Easter Island) towards the end of the first millennium. New Zealand was first settled even later, in the period AD 1000–1200.

Developments in voyaging and navigation were doubtless important, but a fully agricultural subsistence base was critical in settlement. East Polynesia was harder to colonise than West Polynesia: there were greater distances, smaller islands, fewer stone resources, less variety of plants and animals, and (in the south) environmental limits to some crops. Pressure on resources must have been felt quickly, leading to a continuous search for new islands. Colonisation may have been spurred by the depletion of fauna. Each island would have had large colonies of birds (many of them flightless) and turtles, shell and reef fish. As these were depleted, some people were provoked to seek new reserves, as an easier alternative to greater concentration on agriculture. The evidence for agriculture also suggests a 'pioneer' pattern, with major erosion and other landscape degradation, requiring the abandonment of some areas for centuries. The return to such areas and greater efforts at soil conservation occurred when no more 'new' lands were available.

In this period of initial settlement of East Polynesia, we must place the contact with South America which led to diffusion of the Andean sweet potato (*Ipomoea batatas*) and its Quechua-language term *kumar* (in Polynesian, *kumara* and related terms). Despite Heyerdahl's celebrated raft trip from South America to the Tuamotus, it is more likely that the contact was made by Polynesians seeking new islands to colonise, than by South Americans. The sweet potato spread throughout East Polynesia, but not to West Polynesia or Island Melanesia. Heyerdahl and others have claimed a significant South American input in the formation of East Polynesian cultures, particularly that of Rapanui, but the case is overstated. Claims that Rapanui's original population was South

American rather than Polynesian cannot be accepted (but see the next section of this chapter).

Between 2000 and 1000 BP, Western Polynesians stopped making pottery and began to develop the settlement patterns which Europeans saw in the seventeenth century. In Fiji the outlines of a continuous cultural sequence (with pottery) have been established. Fortifications became widespread at about 1000 BP, suggesting increased warfare. In Island Melanesia important realignments of exchange networks occurred between 2000 and 1000 BP. In the Vitiaz Straits a forerunner of the more recent exchange system developed about 1500 BP. The post-Lapita trade links of the Mussau group north of the Bismarck Archipelago also differed from those before. At around 1000 BP pottery imports to Nissan switched from a northern supplier (probably on New Ireland) to a southern source (Buka) and thereafter the historic patterns of settlement and material culture can be recognised. People stopped making pots on New Ireland and/or islands off its east coast. The exchange connections of Tikopia switched at about 1950 BP, from north-western materials (obsidian, stone adzes, chert) to materials from the south and east (particularly pottery).

We know much less about this period than we do about earlier or later periods: it is too late for the distinctive pottery of the Lapita period and too soon for oral history. Cultural sequences are difficult to establish in areas without pottery. In part this is due to a lack of distinctive material culture innovation before about 750 BP: many sites are known but little is certain. However, there is evidence of forest clearance. For example at several places on Aneityum (southern Vanuatu) by about 1600 BP there was increased sedimentation, valley infilling and coastal progradation. By about 1000 BP people began to use the newly created valley flats for settlement and agriculture: at first dryland, and later irrigated cultivation.

On New Guinea detailed cultural sequences for the last 2000 years are available only for the south Papuan coast and the Massim. Between 2000 and 1000 BP these cultures were progressively 'Melanesianised', similar to processes in Island Melanesia during the Lapita period. Just after 1000 BP settlement patterns were disrupted and there were major changes in pottery and other artefacts.

Kuk Swamp in the Highlands of New Guinea yields the fullest record of human occupation and land use. Phase IV of that long history ended about 1200 BP. People developed a fallowing system using the nitrogen-fixing casuarina tree. That innovation made it possible to abandon swamp irrigation. This became a Highlands-wide trend, which occurred a few centuries later on the margins of the main valleys. Kuk Swamp was abandoned until about 400 years ago. From about 1100 BP comes the first direct evidence of sustained occupation of the islands of Torres Strait, created when rising sea levels breached the land bridge connecting Australia and New Guinea. Influences and items travelled both ways, and exchange networks operated across the strait in the nineteenth century. The contrast persisted, however, between agricultural groups at the northern end of the strait and in New Guinea, and hunter-gatherers in the south and in Australia. Throughout prehistory the islands formed a barrier rather than a bridge.

In Micronesia at about 1000 BP construction began at Nan Madol, Pohnpei, in the eastern Carolines, of low platforms and islet fills, precursors to the complex described below. Settlement at Nan Madol began on sand beaches, bars or possibly in stilt houses over the reef from about 1900 BP. Local subsidence and flooding may have encouraged people to build their artificial islets. The similar site of Lelu on Kosrae also has an early pottery phase beneath its artificial fill, dating to about 2000 BP, but the phase of pottery use on Kosrae was probably brief. Ceramic and stone material on Lamotrek Island in the Carolines suggests that voyaging and trading long connected Lamotrek with Yap, Palau and Chuuk. Ties to all these volcanic islands appear to date to at least 800 BP. Lamotrek was probably first settled between 1000 and 900 BP, although it might have been occupied 500 to 700 years earlier. The population gradually increased, with fluctuations, until it reached a maximum between 700 and 500 BP.

The Pacific Islands on the Eve of European Contact, about 500 BP

Between 1000 and 800 BP first settlement occurred of the North and South Islands of New Zealand. Occupation of the more remote Chatham Islands at about 500 BP completed the settlement of the Pacific Islands. Some islands such as Henderson, Pitcairn and Fanning (the 'mystery islands' of Polynesia) had been settled or visited but abandoned. Settlement stopped when there were no more islands to find and the eastern edge, the Americas, had been located and briefly contacted.

Between 1000 and 500 BP Polynesia achieved rapid population growth, agricultural expansion and intensification. Hawaiians cleared thousands of square kilometres of leeward forest and developed intensive dryland field systems with altitudinal zoning of crops such as sweet potato, breadfruit and taro on the big island of Hawai'i and in parts of Maui. Whether population expansion reached environmental limits before European contact and the population levelled off or declined, are debated questions. For Hawai'i the evidence is equivocal, but on Rapanui the people probably did provoke an environmental crisis and the same may be true in the Marquesas.

The environmental limits to growth have also been invoked to explain the highly stratified chiefdoms of Hawai'i and other islands. Older ideas stressed war for land, and chiefs as war leaders, as a corollary of population pressure in a circumscribed environment. More recent theories propose that people were active agents in shaping social systems, and competition among chiefs was the developmental dynamic. Hawai'i has often been invoked in discussions on the rise of stratified chiefdoms and the state, but its place as exemplar in general schemes of state formation is by no means certain. As with other Island 'archetypes', the specificities of the situation are important. The Hawaiian archipelago is the most isolated set of inhabited islands in the world. No other societies developed states beyond regular contact with other 'proto-states' or other societies with which they traded or from which they exacted tribute. On the other hand, the Tongan and Samoan archipelagos were in exactly such contact, and their developments from an ancestral chiefly system after 1000 BP should be seen in a regional perspective which includes the eastern islands of the Fijian archipelago as a 'world system'. Its effects were widely felt, with the establishment of Polynesian communities on the eastern borders of Island Melanesia, the so-called 'outliers', and in some Micronesian islands. They were more probably refugees from dynastic conflicts in West Polynesia, than lucky drift voyagers who met a friendly reception.

In some areas of New Guinea and Island Melanesia material culture and settlement patterns between 1000 and 500 BP seem broadly similar to those observed at European contact, but in parts of the Solomons and Vanuatu, major changes occurred during this interval. At about 750 BP significant changes occurred in some 'Polynesian outliers' like Tikopia or on islands adjacent to them. On Tikopia a Polynesian element became prominent in the material culture. Some architecture took on Western Polynesian forms, there were direct imports of Western Polynesian stone adzes, and some new artefact types appeared, while pottery imports from Vanuatu ceased. On Efate Island in Vanuatu at the same period is the grave of Roy Mata, a chief who—according to oral traditions—came from 'the south', set up Efate's chiefly titles, and was buried with human sacrifices and 'voluntary' immolations by representatives of the many clans under his control. Roy Mata has been portrayed as a Polynesian immigrant, and his burial recalls chiefly burials in West Polynesia. New elements of material culture came in at this time with a greater reliance on shell tools such as *Terebra* and *Lambis* adzes, and pottery manufacture probably ceased. Two chiefly graves on Aneityum display a similar assemblage of ornaments and fit with oral traditions of chiefly burial rites. One has been dated to 300–400 BP and skeletal analysis suggests a Polynesian affiliation. Several other cemetery sites of this period are known from Efate and from Polynesian outliers in Vanuatu and the Solomons with similar material culture.

Polynesian-speaking peoples on the outliers, Polynesian loan-words in New Caledonian and Vanuatu languages, local myths involving Polynesian culture heroes such as Mauitikitiki and Tangaroa, and oral traditions of 'Tongan' contact all point to Polynesian influences in the last 700 years. The nature of the contact and its effects varied. On Rennell and Bellona (in the Solomon Islands), the current Polynesian inhabitants have traditions of an earlier, darker-skinned population called Hiti whom they found when they arrived from 'Ubea' (possibly West 'Uvea in New Caledonia). After a period of coexistence, conflict erupted and the Hiti were massacred. The story seems confirmed by a 'Hiti substratum' in the languages of the two islands, pointing to the former existence of a group related to the South-east Solomonic speakers of the main Solomon Islands.

Archaeological evidence suggests that exchange systems such as the Kula Ring of the Massim, the Hiri of the Gulf of Papua, and Carolinian exchange systems were not static. The Kula involved a much stronger mainland New Guinea component 500 years ago. Although oral tradition suggests that the Hiri started about 200 years ago, settlement patterns consistent with intensive coastal trade occurred at about 1200–1500 BP and again from about 300 years ago. The eastern islands of the Carolinian exchange systems had dropped out by about 300 BP.

Direct European contact with the New Guinea Highlands only started in the 1930s, but the indirect effects began perhaps 200–400 years earlier with the introduction of the sweet potato. This allowed agriculture at higher altitude, and more productively as a dryland crop at altitudes where agriculture was already practised. Its source was transplantation of the sweet potato by Spanish colonists from South America to the Philippines, and thence through exchange routes to Maluku and west New Guinea. It was never of major importance in Lowland New Guinea, but it became the staple in much of the Highlands and was still spreading into marginal Highland areas during this century. Phase V of drainage in the Kuk Swamp (400–250 BP) may be an adjustment to the sweet potato, the size and pattern of ditches being the same as in modern western Highlands sweet potato gardens. Golson, however, has interpreted this phase as the development of raised-bed cultivation, and sees Phase VI (250–100 BP) as representing the arrival of sweet potato.[10] Spatial adjustments followed the adoption of the new crop, and two-thirds of the area under cultivation at Kuk in Phase V was abandoned in Phase VI. The major advantage of swamp gardening from Phase IV onwards had by then disappeared. Sweet potato allowed a major expansion of pig herds, underpinning the pig-killing and exchange cycles of the Highlands such as the Enga *tee* and the Hagen *moka*.

The well-endowed high islands of the Carolines were connected to each other by trade, and to the low-lying atolls by patron–client relationships. In Micronesia generally there was significant social stratification in the period 1000–500 BP. The stone pillar latte structures of the Mariana Islands, foundations for high-status residences, date from about 1000 BP, and the megalithic architecture of Nan Madol on Pohnpei from 750 BP onwards. Nan Madol consists of about ninety-two artificial islets, separated by narrow watercourses. The total area is 80 hectares, while the islet area is just over 30 hectares including residential, ceremonial and funerary structures in high-walled compounds. Oral traditions record it as the capital of the Saudeleur dynasty, who ruled Pohnpei as a centralised polity until a revolt of lower-ranking chiefs about 1350 BP led to restructuring of power into five polities. Nan Madol was then largely abandoned. The beginning of megalithic architecture at Nan Madol coincided with the end of pottery-making on Pohnpei.

A similar 'urban' complex existed at Lelu, 480 kilometres from Pohnpei. Lelu, off the coast of the main island of Kosrae, is a small volcanic island which has been artificially extended. Like Nan Madol it formed a 'disembedded elite centre' in a neutral location, consisting of similar high-walled residential and ceremonial compounds which also

10 Golson, 'New Guinea Agricultural History: A Case Study'.

have a network of canals. Its population in the early nineteenth century was about 1000–1500, consisting of the paramount chief and the other high-ranking chiefs of Kosrae. Michael Graves sees the paramount as 'chief among chiefs', rather than an absolute ruler in the way in which Pohnpei's Saudeleur dynasty has been interpreted. He also notes that Lelu's megalithic architecture is later than that at Nan Madol, beginning about 1600 AD and rapidly completed.

CASTAWAYS

Large-scale movements of people were accomplished by the sixteenth century. The consequent distribution of 'Polynesia', 'Melanesia' and 'Micronesia' is often described as if these culture areas were distinct from each other and from neighbouring Australia, East and South-East Asia, or the Americas. The histories and usages of these terms are considered in chapter 1. Here we seek to dispel two impressions: that island populations severed all connection with each other, and that the whole region was isolated from the rest of the world until the age of Cook. Insularity and isolation were partly real, but were exaggerated by eighteenth-century publicists and philosophers, for whom island societies exemplified distinct (and preferably pure) archetypes. The final section traces smaller-scale movements of people and ideas, usually more recent than those considered above, providing evidence of inter-action as a corrective to illusions of insularity and isolation.

Castaways from South-East Asia, from South America, and from Portuguese and Spanish ships of the sixteenth century appear to have been significant actors in the last 2000 years of Pacific Island prehistory. Large groups of castaways on any island were likely to leave detectable traces, especially if the strangers were physically or culturally distinct. Some Europeans in the eighteenth century were struck by the physical diversity of the Islanders, and speculated that South-East Asian cast-aways or colonists must be responsible. In 1787, for example, La Pérouse was convinced that South-East Asians had sailed as far east as Samoa:

> these different nations [in Polynesia] are derived from Malay colonies who conquered these islands at different periods. I am convinced that the race of woolly-haired men still found in the interior part of the islands of Luzon and Taiwan were the aborigines of the Philippines, Taiwan, New Guinea, New Britain, Vanuatu, Tonga, &c. in the southern hemisphere and of the Caroline, Mariana and Hawaiian islands in the northern. In New Guinea, New Britain and Vanuatu, they were not to be subdued; but, vanquished in the islands farther east, which were too small to afford them a retreat in their centres, they intermingled with their conquerors . . . These two very distinct races appeared striking to our eyes at the Samoan Islands, and I can ascribe to them no other origin.[11]

11 Author's translation of the journal of Jean-François de Galaup de *la Pérouse*. For a complete English translation, see Dunmore, *The Journal of la Pérouse*.

La Pérouse's view was long held to explain differences in the physical features, culture and language of Polynesians as opposed to Fijians and other Melanesians. More recently, scholarly fashion has swung against cultural diffusion with its emphasis on essentialised racial categories and its sometimes racist elaboration. Modern scholars prefer to explain diversity in terms of local adaptation and indigenous agency, but historical babies may have been thrown out with the diffusionist bath-water. If we revisit that scholarship in a more critical spirit than its protagonists employed, we may recover an appropriate sense of the mobility and the cultural diversity of Islanders' experience. Trans-Pacific voyages may have been rare between the settlement of East Polynesia and the irruption of Europeans in the sixteenth century, but for several centuries people sailed around the rim of the ocean. It would be extraordinary if they were never cast away on unexpected beaches. Modern genetic research, which describes wide human variety, revives interest in mobility.

Seamen and merchants from India and China were increasingly involved in South-East Asian trade by the start of the Christian era. As ships became larger and more seaworthy, they were likely to survive being carried out of their way in abnormal weather (such as occurs during the El Niño phenomenon). A Chinese source of the third century AD speaks of foreign ships more than 50 metres long that stood 4–5 metres out of the water. They could carry 600 to 700 people and 250 to 1000 tons of cargo. A Chinese source of the eighth century describes even larger ships, while a sixth-century cave painting at Ajanta, India, depicts a ship with three high masts, a bowsprit rigged with sails, intricate steering gear, and no outrigger. The scale of some voyages is suggested by the fact that people from Kalimantan eventually crossed the Indian Ocean to settle in Madagascar.

Asian mariners were also active in the Pacific. The evidence suggests at least three shiploads of South-East Asian castaways in prehistoric times. On Futuna, a well-known tradition concerns people called *Tsiaina*, the local word for China. *Tsiaina* is certainly a post-European interpolation, but there seems no reason to doubt the principal elements in the tradition. Six versions are on record. Elements common to two versions or more are: (1) the immigrants landed at Alofi, Futuna's sister island; (2) they dug wells on their arrival; (3) they intermarried with the islanders and multiplied; (4) they altered place names; (5) they travelled about beating a wooden gong called *lali* to determine, by its resonance, where they would settle; (6) they introduced better agricultural practices; (7) they introduced improved methods of making and marking bark cloth; and (8) they were finally overthrown and massacred. An additional innovation is ascribed to them in the Futunan dictionary of the missionary Isidore Grezel[12] who arrived in 1843: the word *moo* is defined as 'a kind of squat pig, said to have come from China'.

Many features of Futuna's tradition can be authenticated. Squat pigs called *moo* are confined to Futuna and its immediate neighbours. The

---

12 *Dictionnaire Futunien–Français*.

arrival point on Alofi is called Sa'avaka which translates in some Polynesian languages as 'sacred ship'. The digging of wells suggests that Futuna was in the grip of drought, so that the voyage may have resulted from El Niño conditions. A well attributed to them still exists at Sa'avaka: it is 6 metres deep and 2.4 metres wide. Gongs called *lali*, in use in 'Uvea and Fiji in early European times, were unknown in Tonga and Samoa until recently—suggesting their novel status in the central Pacific. Irrigated taro cultivation, an innovation attributed to the 'Chinese', is unknown in most of the rest of Polynesia. Likewise, one of Futuna's two ways of making bark cloth and one of its two ways of decorating it are unknown in East Polynesia. The unknown methods are those attributed to the 'Chinese'.

Futunan tradition says that the 'Chinese' were overthrown because their rule became oppressive. This was apparently after the Dutch explorers Schouten and LeMaire visited Futuna in 1616 (see chapter 4), for an artist with their expedition depicted the island's chiefs with long, straight, plaited hair—among people with frizzy hair. The Dutch also recorded a term for chief—one which fell out of use by missionary times. This was *latou* (correctly: *latu*) which is cognate with *datu* 'king, prince, ruler' in many South-East Asian languages and still preserved in Samoan *latu*, 'head builder', Fijian *ratu*, 'chief', and some Tongan surnames. Futuna's honorific vocabulary was also obsolete by missionary times. However, some traces are detectable, while the honorific vocabularies still used in Tonga, 'Uvea and Samoa obviously had a common origin and links with Futunan.

Futuna's *Tsiaina* may have been the same people who introduced the Tangaloa cult to West Polynesia where, in the opinion of E. S. Handy, a researcher in the 1920s,[13] it overlaid that of the Indo-Polynesians. Handy speculated that the Tangaloa religion originated in southern China; but, as Tangaloa was known in Polynesia as 'Lord of the Ocean', it seems more likely that the cult came with people from the Sangir Islands north of Sulawesi, where *tagaloang* signifies 'open sea, ocean'. Other Polynesian words, including *lali*, 'gong', also seem traceable to Sangir. Moreover, honorifics are important in those languages; the Sangirese were outstanding boat-builders and seamen; and the division of their society into nobles, free people and slaves is reminiscent of those parts of Polynesia that came under the influence of the Tangaloa people.

The earliest radiocarbon date so far for human settlement in East Polynesia is AD 300 for a site on Nuku Hiva, Marquesas Islands. The site yielded shards from pots evidently made in the Rewa Delta of Fiji. The first Polynesian settlers of the Marquesas were apparently Tongans because certain Marquesan words could not have come from anywhere else: *mei*, 'breadfruit'; *maa*, 'breadfruit paste'; *puou*, 'variety of breadfruit'; *too*, 'sugarcane'; *tokave*, 'variety of small coconut'; *hoho'e 'Kuhliidae*, a fish species; and *kumaa*, 'rat'. The Polynesians of non-Tongan origin also settled in the Marquesas—and settlers of ultimate American origin appear to have arrived there from Rapanui (Easter Island).

13 Handy, *Polynesian Religion*.

Rapanui was probably settled as early as the middle of the first Christian millennium. Pacific scholars long believed that its first human inhabitants were Polynesians. (Linguists divide the languages of East Polynesia into Marquesic and Tahitic, while Rapanui is regarded as an isolate.) It is more likely, however, that the first inhabitants were American Indians from Ecuador or Peru because of the array of cultivated American plants on Rapanui and other Eastern Polynesian islands at the time of European contact: notably the sweet potato, pineapple, capsicum, 26-chromosome cotton, soapberry and manioc. The gourd, banana and blue-egg chicken, introduced to South America from Asia, must also have reached East Polynesia from the east. Over the centuries, castaways from Rapanui evidently drifted to the Marquesas, Pitcairn, Mangareva, the Tuamotu Archipelago and Society Islands with some plants and chickens. At first these were important items in Eastern Polynesian economies, but as Polynesians from the west introduced such plants as taro, yam, sugarcane, breadfruit and paper mulberry, the capsicum, pineapple and cotton were virtually abandoned in those islands that had them, although the sweet potato, gourd and banana remained important. Both the fighting cock and a heavy breed of domestic fowl were also introduced to East Polynesia from the west, along with the dog and razor-backed pig. Many Eastern Polynesian words, including several relating to bananas and chickens, are unknown in West Polynesia. This suggests that the region's early culture was an amalgam of features from both east and west. One feature seems to have been entirely due to American influence: the building of massive stone structures, such as the *marae* or religious courtyards of the Tuamotu Archipelago and Society Islands. However, the term *marae* (cf. *mala'e*, 'public place', in Futunan) certainly came from the west.

Rapanui became the home of a second band of American Indians in about AD 1100. They belonged to the Tiahuanaco culture centred in the high Andes. They and their descendants built the famous statues, or *moai*, of Rapanui as well as a small, tower-like structure called *tupa*, similar in name, appearance and function to Andean structures called *chullpa*. All surviving *tupa* are built as corbelled vaults: the stones of the interior wall overlap from bottom to top, so that the diameter becomes smaller towards the top until a dome-like ceiling is formed. Small, low entrances surmounted by large lintel stones are another distinctive feature. In the Andes, the building of *chullpa* was confined to the period from about AD 1100 to the time of the Spanish conquest. The Rapanui *tupa* most closely resemble those of the earliest period. The structures in both places are assumed to have been for the display of the bones of the dead. On Temoe Atoll, near Mangareva, there is a *tupa*-like *marae* called Otupa. Otherwise, Rapanui's *moai* and *tupa*-builders appear to have had no significant impact in Polynesia.

Society Islands tradition tells of a 'prince from Rotuma' who settled on Bora Bora nine to fourteen generations before the mid-nineteenth century and married into the royal family. Other outsiders in Society Islands prehistory were castaways from the Spanish caravel *San Lesmes*, one of four ships that passed into the Pacific from the Strait of Magellan on 26 May 1526. Six days later, the ships were separated in a storm and the *San Lesmes*, with a complement of about fifty-three Galicians, Basques, other Spaniards, Italians, Germans and Flemings, was never seen again. In 1929 four ancient cannon were found on the reef of Amanu Atoll in the Tuamotu Archipelago. Two have been linked firmly to the *San Lesmes*. The caravel ran aground at Amanu by night, the crew jettisoned their cannon, and they proceeded on a westerly course, seeking a haven to make repairs. Their first stopping place was Anaa Atoll, 400 kilometres east of Tahiti, where some men left the ship. The rest reached Opoa at the south-eastern corner of Ra'iatea, some 200 kilometres north-west of Tahiti, where they began to repair the caravel or to build another. When this work was finished, they headed for Spain by sailing south-westward for the Cape of Good Hope, leaving some Spaniards behind and carrying some Polynesian men, women and children.

Cultural diffusionists speculated that castaways from one of the lost Spanish galleons of the Manila–Acapulco run were influential in the Hawaiian Islands. The theory originated soon after Cook. Three material items convinced several of his officers that Spaniards had preceded them. These were the crested helmets and feather cloaks of the Hawaiian chiefs, and several iron daggers. One officer, James King, saw the helmets and cloaks as 'a singular deviation' from Polynesian styles, and asserted 'an exact resemblance' to those of Spain of former times. Hawaiian traditions recorded in the early nineteenth century supported King's supposition. One version told how seven white men landed at Kealakekua Bay several generations before Cook. Their descendants, it was said, were 'distinguished by a lighter colour in the skin' and 'corresponding brown curly hair'. Doubts about the Spanish connection grew in the twentieth century. One critic pointed out that the chiefly Hawaiian helmets were quite unlike Spanish helmets of the sixteenth and seventeenth centuries. Nevertheless three Spanish galleons are known to have been lost between Manila and Acapulco (in 1576, 1578 and 1586), and in the late 1950s two strikingly non-Polynesian items were found in the burial casket of a deified chief that had once been deposited in a cave at Kealakekua Bay. One was a piece of iron embedded in a wooden handle like a chisel. The other was a length of woven sailcloth. It has also been suggested that the Hawaiian helmets were modelled on those worn by actors portraying Roman soldiers of Biblical times in the passion plays of the Philippines.[14]

Another lost Spanish ship of the same period seems to have ended its days on Ontong Java, a Polynesian outlier of the Solomon Islands. This was the *Santa Isabel*, one of the four ships of the Mendaña expedition that left Peru in 1595, bound for the Solomons. The *Santa Isabel* became separated from its companion vessels as they neared their destination and was never seen again. In 1971 some shards of alien pottery and other distinctive items were found at Pamua on San Cristobal, indicat-

14 These issues are developed in Langdon, *Lost Caravel*.

ing that the crew and passengers had camped there. The presence of
many European-looking Islanders on low-lying Ontong Java has since
suggested that the *Santa Isabel* later ran aground there. Other Ontong
Java people of similar appearance have migrated to Honiara and to
Santa Isabel.[15]

Three other lost Spanish ships, and a body of mutinous men
marooned in the Marshall Islands, may have played similar roles in
Micronesia. In 1527, the *Santiago* and *Espiritu Santo* were lost on a
voyage from Mexico to the Moluccas. With a combined complement of
sixty, they appear to have ended their days on Fais Island and Ulithi
Atoll in the western Carolines. Almost seventy years later, the *Santa
Catalina*, a second ship of the Mendaña expedition of 1595, probably
fetched up at Pohnpei in the eastern Carolines: leaking badly, the ship
was last seen near that island. Earlier, in 1566, twenty-seven men from
the *San Jeronimo* were marooned on Ujelang Atoll, the westernmost of
the Marshall Islands, after an unsuccessful mutiny.

The full nature and extent of castaway influence will never be known
with certainty. This account allows for many more (and more varied)
castaways than most prehistorians do. Besides external castaways,
Melanesians drifted from one island to another; Polynesians and
Micronesians did likewise. Further research may reconstruct some of
these 'invisible' mariners: but such revelations would still represent a
mere fraction of the story of castaway involvement in the settlement
and peopling of the Pacific Islands.

THE PEOPLE OF THE SEA

Little research has been done on the maritime dimension of the region's
history. Most works with a maritime theme address the initial
exploration and colonisation of Oceania.[16] They focus on the nautical
and navigational technology of Oceania's cultures at the time of first
encounters with outsiders, or isolated cultures of the present century. A
host of studies also consider the sea as a food resource. Recent enthusiasm for cultural mind-sets and world-views has enriched Pacific
history, but tends to obscure other approaches. In particular, human–
environmental interactions, a focus of archaeology and human geography, have attracted little attention from historians. Resource use has
a social and political context, while the environment imposes constraints on social and political orders, and influences world-views.
Europe's Atlantic and Mediterranean seaboards, the Indian Ocean's
Swahili, Arabian and Indian coasts, island South-East Asia and south-
east China have all generated rich literatures, but the Pacific Ocean has
not received such detailed attention.

The Pacific Ocean can be envisaged as two distinct zones. Where the
lighter oceanic plates of the earth's crust collide with the heavier

15 *Ibid.*
16 An important and recent exception is Hviding, *Guardians of Marovo Lagoon.*

continental plates of the western Pacific rim, the underlying molten magma bursts through the fractures as dramatic volcanic activity. The result is a host of volcanic islands, and atolls formed from the coral remains of the living organisms that establish themselves in the shallow waters above subsided volcanoes. About 80 per cent of the world's islands lie within a triangle formed by Tokyo, Jakarta and Pitcairn. Outside this area the plates of the seabed tend to drift apart rather than collide, so that the magma oozes out under much less pressure, creating basins and gentle ridges. They do not break the surface or disturb a huge area of 'empty ocean' in the northern and eastern Pacific.

Most historians present the sea as a uniform void between landfalls, whose most significant features are surface conditions and wind patterns which hinder or encourage voyaging. The sea has an equally important vertical dimension, which influences marine life, and varies in time and space. Historians have been slow to use scientific data on oceanic food chains to supplement archaeological and historical data on the marine resources available to Islanders. The range of species known to have been exploited needs to be compared with the full range of potentially useful species, in order to measure people's reliance on marine food and their ability to use it.

Use of the sea as a means of communication and as a food source depends largely on people's knowledge and perceptions. Many sea cultures perceived a close affinity between humans and dolphins, dugongs, seals and sharks, so that people neither feared nor hunted those species.[17] Attitudes and activities, rather than coastal residence alone, distinguish sea cultures. Sea communities are not at all uniform. Scholars of Oceania, among others, note the distinction in all sea cultures between the restricted group of sailors and navigators who go to sea, and the land-based majority who do not. Outside Oceania, many communities became sea people because of military or environmental constraints on land. Sea-oriented cultures are seldom self-sufficient, and require relationships with larger, land-oriented communities to supply their deficiencies. Trade, raiding or political subordination were the usual mediums for such relationships, and piracy and residential mobility were common side-effects. Archaeological theory in Oceania emphasises the influence of environmental constraints on small islands, but the notion of marginalised sea peoples relative to land-based polities is notably lacking. The relatively small size of many islands and polities should not blind us to the possibility of distinctions and tensions between land-based and sea-oriented communities, such as the seemingly symbiotic relationship between seagoing Motu and land-based Koita on the Papuan south coast.

Living on a coast exposes a community to influences from across the sea. Pacific history has led the way in examining the cultural logic behind the exchange of items and ideas when cultures meet. Island beaches are portrayed as transformative processes where objects, ideas and individuals move between cultures, mediated by power relations

17 See, for example, Sahlins, 'The Stranger-King, or Dumezil'.

and acculturation.[18] This approach has much to offer the utilitarian explanations which pervade much writing elsewhere, but we should not ignore the economic utility which underlay many such exchanges. Explanations for claims of external origin for ruling groups show a similar dichotomy. In Oceania such scenarios are explained as social constructions to rationalise the relationship between the raw violence of power and the controlled violence of authority. Power is always usurping and external, while authority is always legitimate and local. Outside Oceania more emphasis is given to seeking historical bases for such claims.

In general, Pacific scholarship portrays external contacts as having limited significance in the development of island societies from initial colonisation until European contact. Scholars focus more closely on population growth and the resulting pressure on the environment, and competition for status through warfare, or the intensification of production for redistribution to forge social or political obligation. Recent scholars criticise the tendency to focus on single island groups or even single islands, pointing out that island communities were connected 'in a wider social world of moving items and ideas'.[19] Local traditions, the distribution of cultural traits, and observations by literate outsiders all attest to inter-island voyaging within most archipelagos. Long-distance voyaging between archipelagos was also still apparent in the eighteenth and nineteenth centuries in central East Polynesia (centred on Tahiti), West Polynesia and Fiji (centred on Tonga), the coasts of south-east Papua, and in much of Micronesia. Perhaps the most extensive and coherent of all the long-distance networks was a tributary and exchange system of 1100 kilometres linking many of the atolls of the western Carolines to the high island of Yap in West Micronesia.[20] External contacts probably waxed and waned according to circumstances, and so did their impact. For example Ian Campbell observes that available evidence suggests that the period from about AD 1100 to 1500 was one of significant upheaval and inter-island movement in much of Oceania.[21]

Not all exchanges were peaceful. In essence, sea-power is the ability to ensure free movement on the sea for oneself and to inhibit a similar capacity in others. Such power is rarely achieved, and the massive resources needed to build and maintain a battle fleet have exceeded the means of all but a few polities. Even when they were raised, these fleets conducted most of their operations near to shore because of technical and logistical limitations. Naval battles have been rare for the same reasons. Most naval operations have been lower-level harassment of enemy shipping or raids on coastlines. In both cases the seaborne aggressors enjoyed the advantage of surprise and mobility, but their actions rarely resulted in political dominion. Without clear naval

18 For example Dening, *The Death of William Gooch*.
19 Irwin, *Prehistoric Exploration and Colonisation*, 204.
20 Lewthwaite, 'Geographical Knowledge of the Pacific Peoples'; and Parsonson, 'The Settlement of Oceania'.
21 Campbell, *A History of the Pacific Islands*, 36.

hegemony, the ease of such operations has made the sea world dangerous. These characteristics may not, of course, apply in Oceania. The Pacific environment of islands with relatively small populations and resource bases, often separated by open ocean, may well have generated quite different configurations of power. A number of islands merit further investigation in this regard. Small island polities with limited populations—such as Bau in Fiji, Manono in Samoa, the Ha'apai group in Tonga, and the Roviana Lagoon in the Solomons—exercised political influence on their archipelagos because of their naval strength. On a larger scale the 'Yapese Empire', the influence of Tonga after unification, and Tahiti under the Pomare dynasty rested, in part, on seapower. All deserve investigation as possible thalassocracies, a concept hitherto neglected in Pacific studies.

BIBLIOGRAPHIC ESSAY

Archaeological research has been pursued since the late nineteenth century, with current centres at the Australian National University, University of Auckland and University of Otago in New Zealand, and University of Hawai'i. Most archaeological work is published in regional journals such as *Archaeology in New Zealand, Archaeology in Oceania, Asian Perspectives, Bulletin of the Indo-Pacific Prehistory Association, Hawaiian Archaeology, JPS*, and *New Zealand Journal of Archaeology. Antiquity* also reports Pacific discoveries. Other relevant journals include *Australian Archaeology, Journal de la Société des Océanistes, Man and Culture in Oceania, Micronesica, Oceanic Linguistics* and *Pacific Linguistics*. Monograph series include three from the Bernice P. Bishop Museum: *B. P. Bishop Museum Bulletins, Pacific Anthropological Records*, and *Department of Anthropology, Departmental Report Series*. UHP publishes the *Asian and Pacific Archaeology Series* and the Department of Prehistory at ANU publishes two series: *Terra Australis* and *Occasional Papers in Prehistory*.

There is a vast literature on the emergence of modern humans. The main opposing viewpoints are represented by M. Wolpoff (regional continuity) and C. B. Stringer (replacement). Both have papers in Mellars and Stringer (eds), *The Human Revolution: Behavioural and Biological Perspectives*; and in Brauer and Smith (eds), *Continuity or Replacement*. For the Pleistocene archaeology of Australia, New Guinea and Island Melanesia, see Smith, Spriggs and Fankhauser (eds), *Sahul in Review*. An older but useful review is Allen, 'When Did Humans First Colonise Australia?'. Specific topics are addressed by Allen, Gosden and Peter White, 'Human Pleistocene Adaptations in the Tropic Island Pacific: Recent Evidence from New Ireland'; Bowdler, '*Homo sapiens* in Southeast Asia and the Antipodes: Archaeological vs Biological Interpretations'; Bowdler, 'Sunda and Sahul: A 30K yr Culture Area?' in Smith, Spriggs and Fankhauser, *Sahul in Review*; and Groube *et al.*, 'A 40,000-year-old Human Occupation Site at Huon Peninsula, Papua New Guinea'.

Radiocarbon and thermoluminescence dating techniques are discussed by Roberts *et al.*, 'Thermoluminescence Dating of a 50,000-year-old Human Occupation Site in Northern Australia'; Hiscock, 'How Old are the Artefacts in Malakunanja II?'; Bowdler, '50,000-year-old Site in Australia—Is It Really that Old?'; and 'Some Sort of Dates at Malakunanja II: A Reply to Roberts *et al.*'.

Navigation and early settlement are reconstructed in Irwin, *The Prehistoric Exploration and Colonisation of the Pacific*. Specialist studies include Davidson, 'The Chronology of Australian Watercraft'; Rowland, 'The Distribution of Aboriginal Watercraft on the East Coast of Queensland'; Bowdler, 'Offshore Islands and Maritime Explorations in Australian Prehistory'; and Birdsell, 'The Recalibration of a Paradigm for the First Peopling of Greater Australia', in Allen *et al.* (eds), *Sunda and Sahul*.

Recent summaries of Pacific prehistory are contained in Jennings (ed.), *The Prehistory of Polynesia*; Kirch, *The Evolution of the Polynesian Chiefdoms*; Bellwood, *The Polynesians*; and Bellwood, Fox and Tryon (eds), *The Austronesians*, which is also relevant for linguistics. The distinction between Near and Remote Oceania is made in most detail by Green, 'Near and Remote Oceania—Disestablishing "Melanesia" in Culture History'.

For Austronesian languages, see Tryon (ed.), *Comparative Austronesian Dictionary*; and Pawley and Ross, 'Austronesian Historical Linguistics and Culture History'. For Non-Austronesian languages, see Wurm, *Papuan Languages of Oceania*, and Foley, *The Papuan Languages of New Guinea*.

Golson offers a clear overview of New Guinea agriculture in three chapters of Denoon and Snowden (eds), *A History of Agriculture in Papua New Guinea* (Boroko, n.d. [1981]): 'Agriculture in New Guinea: The Long view', 'Agriculture Technology in New Guinea', and 'New Guinea Agriculture History: A Case Study'. Prehistoric plant use and the question of New Guinea as an early centre of plant domestication are covered by Yen, 'The Development of Sahul Agriculture with Australia as Bystander'. The classic 9000-year sequence from Kuk Swamp in the New Guinea Highlands is explained in Golson and Gardner, 'Agriculture and Sociopolitical Organisation in New Guinea Highlands Prehistory'; and Hope and Golson, 'Late Quaternary Change in the Mountains of New Guinea'. For prehistoric human impacts see Dodson (ed.), *The Naive Lands*. Agriculture in Polynesia is analysed by Kirch, *The Wet and the Dry*.

On the Lapita cultural complex see Kirch and Hunt (eds), *Archaeology of the Lapita Cultural Complex: A Critical Review*; and Spriggs, 'What is Southeast Asian about Lapita?'. For Pre-Lapita and Lapita archaeology of Near Oceania since 1985, see Allen and Gosden, *Report of the Lapita Homeland Project*. Lapita pottery design is considered in Spriggs, 'Dating Lapita: Another View'.

The later settlement of East Polynesia is discussed by Kirch, 'Rethinking East Polynesian Prehistory'; and Spriggs and Anderson, 'Late Colonization of East Polynesia'. There is no available synthesis of

Micronesian prehistory, but recent archaeological work is summarised in a special issue of the journal *Micronesica* (1990). The field of genetic evidence is changing so rapidly that a perusal of recent journals is necessary, but Hill and Serjeantson (eds), *The Colonization of the Pacific: A Genetic Trail*, summarise the evidence to 1989.

Langdon's sources are as diverse as his interests, traversing linguistic, botanical and genetic evidence as well as a close study of early written sources. The analysis of Polynesian religious systems was pioneered by E. S. Handy, *Polynesian Religion*. Langdon's own iconoclastic publications include *The Lost Caravel*, *The Lost Caravel Re-explored*, 'When the Blue-egg Chickens Come Home to Roost', and 'The Banana as a Key to Early American and Polynesian History'.

The physical nature of Oceania is described by Thomas, 'The Variety of Physical Environments among Pacific Islands', in Fosberg (ed.), *Man's Place in the Island Ecosystem*. Its exploration and settlement are detailed in Lewthwaite, 'Geographical Knowledge of the Pacific Peoples'; and Parsonson, 'The Settlement of Oceania: An Examination of the Accidental Voyage Theory'. Anderson (ed.), *Traditional Fishing in the Pacific*, describes its exploitation. The analysis of the beach is developed by Sahlins, 'The Stranger-King, or Dumezil among the Fijians'; and by Dening, *The Death of William Gooch*.

CHAPTER
3

PACIFIC EDENS? MYTHS AND REALITIES OF PRIMITIVE AFFLUENCE

PRIMITIVE AFFLUENCE

What is loosely described as 'subsistence' production has a poor reputation among economic planners, and so has stone technology. In 1975, for example, a World Bank mission to Papua New Guinea tied both concepts together to dismiss the whole pre-colonial record:

> the original stone-age tribes have lived unto themselves in conditions of primitive isolation . . . [Modernisation] began among a people who had no alphabet and hence no writing, knew neither the knife nor axe nor any form of metal, used only stones for cutting, hunted and killed with bows and arrows and clubs, knew neither wool nor cotton, used only pounded bark as cloth, and used no bullock, ox, horse or cow in their subsistence agriculture. Subsistence agriculture is relatively easy and has bred an agricultural labor force that has not had to acquire disciplined work habits . . .

This critique is unusually crude, but its elements are widely accepted—stages of development, the stagnation of isolated communities, denigration of stone technology, a sharp dichotomy between subsistence and market production, and subsistence as a school of idleness. These assumptions impede appreciation of the systems of production which Islanders refined over centuries, the strategic alliances they created and maintained, the environmental imperatives they accommodated, and the threats they averted. Many planners assume that all pre-colonial production and consumption can be described as subsistence, and that trade and exchange were incidental. They also imagine that subsistence has not been modified to meet changing needs, and that it demands little labour, expertise or planning. ('Primitive affluence' or 'subsistence affluence' was a popular colonial explanation for Islanders' irritating refusal to work for low wages.) There are many objections to this argument, but here it is sufficient to describe the environmental constraints and the production systems which Islanders developed, and to assess how far they created reliable ways of surviving and prospering.

Natural hazards abounded. Bennett quotes the opinion of South Malaitans about infertile Uki Island:[1]

---

1   Bennett, *Wealth of the Solomons*, 11.

Uki with its oily yam mash
Its flying sands
Uki of the sandy shore
Disappear in the coconuts
Net fish with yells
Uki where yam sets die.

Better-favoured spots were attended by other risks. The New Guinea Highlands and most of New Zealand suffer frost today, and lower altitudes were affected at the end of the Ice Age. At the other extreme, low-lying tropical islands endure such heat that labour is possible only in the early morning and late afternoon. There is little protection from other hazards. Aneityum in the New Hebrides endured thirty-one hurricanes in sixty years from 1848. For people who relied on taro and breadfruit, the effects could be devastating. During a hurricane in January 1858 (in the Coral Sea hurricane season) the winds 'laid fences everywhere prostrate, blew down houses, and broke and uprooted trees; and as only about half of the breadfruit crop was collected, the remaining half was completely destroyed'.[2]

Consequences were especially severe for atolls. Lamotrek's population, for example, increased until about AD 1400. Thereafter there was a general decline, possibly related to warfare, but more likely to typhoon damage and food shortages. Contrarily, late wet seasons quickly depleted food reserves in the dry parts of western Fiji, the west coast of New Caledonia and the Papuan south coast. Even the lush islands of Hawai'i were sometimes evacuated when drought struck, although such high islands created their own rainfall. In islets too small to affect cloud formation, drought was frequent, especially close to the equator. The southernmost of the Gilbert Islands (now Kiribati) endured thirteen over 120 years, compounding the problems of a marginal environment. During the 1938 drought, it seemed to Harry Maude that

> the lagoon ecosystem was determined to combine with the terrestrial in ousting man from the scene; for at the height of the drought, when the flora was dead or dying, the prolific fish population deserted the lagoon ... Gilbertese felt ... that the food of the fish was no longer there ... even in normal times many of the human inhabitants of such islands as Nonouti and Tabiteuea were habitually hungry, despite the efficient use of the ecosystem and often drastic population controls, the resources of the island being insufficient to maintain the density of population.[3]

Earthquakes and tidal waves were common in the western islands near the unstable junction of tectonic plates. Aneityum experienced three in seventy years following 1848. During one (in 1875) 'large blocks of overhanging rock were rent off, and precipitated to the valleys below. On other parts where large boulders were lying half buried on the surface, they were upheaved and shaken out of the earth.'[4] Kosrae, a high island in the eastern Carolines, suffered massive depopulation late

---

2 Inglis, 9 April 1858, cited in Spriggs, 'Vegetable Kingdoms'.
3 Harry Maude, in Fosberg, *Man's Place in the Island Ecosystem*, 174.
4 Inglis, 1887, cited in Spriggs, 'Vegetable Kingdoms'.

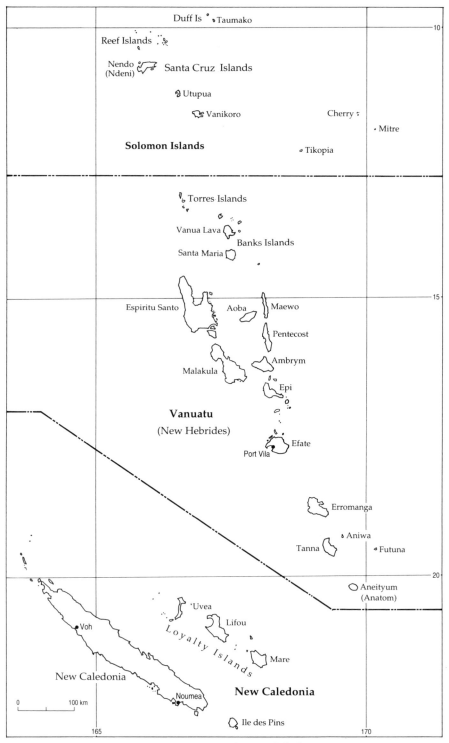

Map 7   Vanuatu and New Caledonia

in the eighteenth century, despite a salubrious climate and high fertility. Outsiders thought that Kosrae could easily support many more than the 3000 people they found—something like the 40,000 inhabitants of Yap, roughly the same size. The decline was evidently due to civil war and a typhoon. A survivor explained that 'their houses were swept away, their breadfruit and coconut trees were broken down, and consequently a famine followed which swept away thousands of people. The stores of breadfruit that they had underground were soon exhausted and those that survived lived on fish.'[5] Such eventful environments made food security imperative.

PRODUCTION

The pioneers who colonised the western Pacific found immense forests and rivers fed by copious rain. Bone and shell were readily available for tools and useful stone cropped up widely, so that trees could be felled for canoes, drums and shields, and for houses, thatched with palm. Catching fish and marine animals and collecting shellfish presented no problem to people already skilled in these arts, but hunting was complicated by the absence of pig and buffalo which abounded in South-East Asia, so birds, bats and rats were consumed. Outside a few rain-shadows, vegetation was dense, diverse—and some of it edible, including pandanus, *nipa*, *galip* and *okari* nuts, and a range of green vegetables. Along the coasts, mangrove could be processed in emergencies, coconuts flourished, and sago offered a staple in swampy sub-coastal regions. Agricultural systems were created partly around these cultigens, but South-East Asian plants were added. The distinction between 'hunting and gathering' and 'agriculture' is a matter of emphasis. Even when people adopted cultivation, they also collected vegetables from the bush, caught fish, collected shellfish, and hunted birds or animals. Natural stands of sago may have fostered the earliest 'wild plant management'. Weeding and thinning increased yields and—where population mounted—shoots were planted beyond their natural habitat.

The pioneers developed systematic agriculture first in coastal New Guinea, then in the Highlands and later on smaller islands where natural resources would not sustain hunters and gatherers. The commonest system which developed in large islands was swidden, often based on dryland taro. Vegetation was slashed, allowed to dry and usually burned. The ashes nourished crops for about a year until they leached away. Gardens were therefore cultivated for one to two years until grass and pests invaded. The plot might lie fallow for over twenty years. A short growing period and selective weeding of the fallow promoted woody regrowth. Yams were often grown in a similar manner, but some farmers devised a different system for growing 'long' yam (*Dioscorea alata* from South-East Asia), digging a hole up to 3 metres

---

5 L. H. Gulick, 'A Visit to King George of Kusaie [1852]', quoted in Ritter, 'The Population of Kosrae at Contact'.

deep and filling it with topsoil. Most yams respond badly to flooding, but water-tolerant varieties were selected for the flood plains north of the Sepik River. Throughout the Sepik region, in the Trobriand Islands, and wherever else yams were a staple, people composed incantations as the core of rituals to ensure a great harvest. Given the effort required to fell the forest, farmers usually cleared gardens from secondary re-growth. The system is not without risk. Too brief a fallow allowed open grassland—where swidden is difficult—to displace forest. The same hazard attended the hunting of animals with fire.

Some coastal New Guineans were committed to agriculture more than 9000 years ago, probably growing taro, yam, sago, bananas and coconuts. Only taro flourished at higher altitudes. Highland settlers cleared forests, and embarked on large-scale drainage and irrigation in wetlands where, over several thousand years with digging sticks and paddle-spades, they devised systems of continuous cultivation. What began as water control then revealed the advantages of subsoil to increase fertility between ditches, and this mounding technique per-mitted the farming of grassland. A common consequence was the domestication of pigs, since shrinking forests could no longer sustain feral pigs or other fauna to complement a starchy diet. Since these prac-tices produced substantial surpluses, and as pigs sustained exchange systems, these centres of intense production were probably the sources of the spectacular public exchanges described below.

By 5000 years ago the forest was being cleared apace, and this invasion continued for a thousand years more, until people developed farming methods which allowed the forest to stabilise and regenerate. Fast-growing casuarina trees were introduced into the grasslands as fallow and for timber. Continuous agriculture was well established when, three or four centuries ago, the laborious farming of wetlands abruptly ceased. The arrival of sweet potato (*Ipomea batatas*) from the Americas had profound effects across the region. In Okinawa (the Ryukyu Islands) it eased a transition to agriculture from fishing and regional trade. From the Philippines tubers passed through innumerable hands to New Guinea, then inland, to transform production and social organisation.

At first *kaukau* was popular in proportion to altitude, where it had decided advantages over taro. In parts of the Highlands, for example, although taro retained ritual importance, sweet potato became the staple. In the Balem valley of Irian Jaya, people developed subtle and spectacular production, recognising over seventy varieties of sweet potato. The dense populations of the alluvial plains dug irrigation ditches with fire-hardened wooden paddles: 'From time to time a man will set his paddle aside and reach into the ditch for smaller lumps of mud which he plasters against the side of the reshaped canal. This soon bakes dry in the sun and gives to these gardens a look of permanence and tidiness which lasts until they are abandoned to fallow.'[6]

On the hill slopes, sweet potato cuttings were planted in prepared beds, while minor crops grew in odd corners. A Dutch scientist judged

6   Gardner and Heider, *Gardens of War.*

that 'The Balim native exhibits a sound understanding of the problems of slope cultivation and the principles of soil conservation through erosion control. In the sweet potato, on which his agriculture is based, he has a most efficient erosion-resistant crop, which forms a ground cover within a few weeks after planting.'[7] The crop was not, of course, 'his'. Men dug ditches, but women planted, tended and harvested crops. When sweet potato was adopted, land could support more people or more pigs—or both. Since it yields more food than taro for the same labour, and especially in poor soil, it continues to expand to the present day.

Lowland farmers also intensified their cultivation. Kolepom Islanders (off the south coast of Irian Jaya) elaborated a system to cope with such heavy rain that most of the land is inundated each wet season. They built islands in the swamp, with layers of reeds and clay from ditches. Mud was used for manuring and (with drift grass) as compost. Island beds, 2–3 metres wide, stretched to hundreds of metres. Islands built to different heights (to regulate moisture) were devoted to coconut and sago, to moisture-sensitive yam, to taro, and more recently to sweet potato.

When they tackled the remoter islands a thousand years ago, Lapita colonists combined very different plants, animals and skills. Their domestic animals were pigs, dogs and chickens; their crops presumably included taro, breadfruit, bananas and yams; and their sustainable practices (see chapter 2) included irrigated fields of taro on the larger islands and taro pits down to the water table on atolls. Agriculture could then support dense populations wherever water was abundant and controllable. The Rewa and other Fijian deltas probably sustained the greatest productivity and the densest populations of the region. Continuous cultivation of taro supported stratified societies centred on fortified towns. By the nineteenth century Rewa was probably the wealthiest and most powerful town in Fiji, its alleys intersecting several hundred houses within elaborate fortifications, attracting ambitious people from Tonga as well as Viti Levu, and deploying twenty large double-hulled canoes for its defence. Equally intensive farming developed in other islands of the central Pacific, and in New Caledonia, where (again by the nineteenth century) the whole *grande terre* was cultivated, except the mountainous and arid south and west.

Between AD 1000 and 1500 East Polynesia was transformed by population growth and agricultural expansion and intensification, increasing the variety of cultivation. In Hawai'i, whole forests were cleared for dryland fields of sweet potato, taro and breadfruit. On O'ahu, the traveller Archibald Campbell described Ewa as 'an extensive and fertile plain, the whole of which is in the highest state of cultivation. Every stream was carefully embanked, to supply water for the taro beds. Where there was no water, the land was under crops of yams and sweet potatoes.'[8]

7   L. J. Brass, 'Stone Age Agriculture in New Guinea', in Whittaker *et al.* (eds), *Documents and Readings in New Guinea History.*
8   Campbell, *A Voyage round the World from 1806 to 1812.*

Europeans often became lyrical about continuous cultivation. Maori horticulture in the 1830s was extolled, not for its ingenuity or productivity, but because it looked rather like European practice. An English observer rejoiced that: 'The ground is compleatly cleared of all weeds—the mold broke with as much care as that of our best gardens . . . In one Plott I observed these hillocks, at their base, surrounded with dried grass. The Arum is planted in little circular concaves, exactly in the manner our Gard'ners plant Melons.'[9] Such correspondence was accidental. It was also rare, and Europeans were often baffled. When Magellan's expedition reached Guam, for example, one of his crew was struck by a sense that 'these people live in freedom': 'They do not go to work in the fields nor stir from their houses, but make cloth and baskets of palm leaves.'[10] Breadfruit—from the Solomon Islands eastward—amazed foreigners with its easy abundance. Its long harvest period provides year-long sustenance—if people select varieties with different harvesting periods, cook it and store the surplus. It was especially important in Micronesia, which possessed even fewer natural resources than other groups. On Pohnpei, Yap and Kosrae, yams were grown with intense care; elsewhere they were harder to grow, and bananas, coconut and taro varieties, together with breadfruit, were the essentials of survival.

Europeans imagined primitive simplicity. Unable to speak with Islanders, they could be impressed only by visual evidence. In swidden agriculture, however, tubers grew amid tangled vegetation. Apparent disorder belied the siting and excavation of atoll taro pits, the selection of yam varieties, the inter-planting of species, or the mulching and irrigation which suited particular environments. Bafflement arose also from differences between temperate and tropical practices. European farming was typically bound by defined seasons and relied on grain and pasture, whereas Islanders relied on tree and root crops, in seasons demarcated by wet and dry. Dependable transport and money allowed European farmers to specialise. Reliance on a single crop in the Islands would have been dangerous, since crops were difficult to store and emergency supplies unreliable. Strategies were developed instead, which involved inter-planting (untidy to Western eyes) or exchange relations with people in other environments (invisible to casual observers). Pigs and cassowaries made different demands from cattle or sheep. Compounding the enigma, Islanders amassed skills in their heads, not in their tools; and they expressed that knowledge in the language of magic, observing that correct spells were as vital as appropriate soils.

Tools—the repository of European competence—were not visually impressive, but this did not inhibit their innovative use nor the manufacture of artefacts on a large scale. On the atolls, tools were made from calcified shell; cowries were used to scour breadfruit; and lime-

9 Peter Adams, *Fatal Necessity: British Intervention in New Zealand, 1830–1846*, cited by Janet M. Davidson, 'The Polynesian Foundation', in Oliver and Williams (eds), *The Oxford History of New Zealand*, 21.
10 Antonio Pigafette, *Magellan's Voyage: A Narrative Account of the First Circumnavigation*, in Hezel and Berg, *Micronesia: Winds of Change*.

stone was often used as mortars. Islanders on Rapanui, with very few resources, contrived the immense stone figures which still astound observers. Marquesans, like other Polynesians, created stone-paved *me'ae* to support elaborate wooden spiritual centres, and the feather cloaks of Hawaiian *ali'i* found their way into countless museums. The great double-hulled canoes which carried Islanders across the ocean evolved into a variety of designs, different again from the cargo vessels carrying bulky goods around New Guinea. Spades and gardening paddles were wooden, as were the towering *haus tambaran* and other sacred structures, so that carpenters were the most respected artisans in the towns of Viti Levu. Almost all buildings, and shell and bone decorations, were made by stone tools, which underpinned most production systems.

New Guinea Highlanders, including the Rungi, worked quarries for axes.

> Two old people went into the forest, hunting for marsupials. [Afterwards they had intercourse.] The old woman felt something stick into her back . . . So they looked and found that the blade of a kumbamon axe was just showing above the ground. [They found many others.] When they reached home they said that every man, old and young, should assemble . . . Then the two old people showed them the axe blades and said 'Let's now go into the forest and hunt marsupials for the axes. When we've killed some, we shall make sacrifice to the spirit of the axes.'
>
> When the present people go to make axes, so do they first hunt marsupials and sacrifice them to the two old people . . . Then they climb down into the pit and burn torches, which they impregnate with resin. With these torches they light the way. When they have found the veins they drive in wedges and make axes.[11]

Technical ingenuity, religious awe and social relations were so intertwined that it is misleading to isolate the 'economic' meaning of multidimensional experience.

From the late nineteenth century, shell flooded in from the coast and exchanges proliferated, provoking well-placed communities to intensify quarrying. All adult Tungei men, for example, were mobilised whenever stocks of axes ran down and peace prevailed. They secluded themselves from women, to be ritually pure when they confronted the female spirits of the quarry. There they worked for three to five months. Unlike other Highland masons, they did not use fire: hammer stones were smashed against the rock-face. Later, individuals shaped the blanks into axe blanks. In 1933 an early colonial patrol observed this scene north of the Sepik–Wahgi divide:

> This district seems to be neutral ground, the axe-makers being left in peace by all their warlike neighbours to pursue the useful art. We saw many natives engaged in working the axes, sitting by waterholes and patiently grinding away at them with sandstones, stopping every few moments to dip the stones in water and to sight with a craftsman's eye along the tapering blades, so slowly taking shape. Each beautiful axe must have required many days of patient work.[12]

11 Burton, 'Axe Makers of the Wahgi', 255.
12 *Ibid.*, 164.

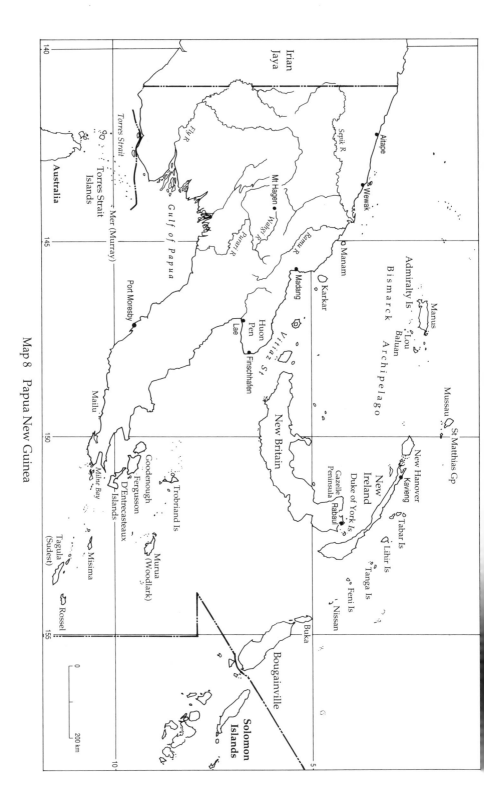

Map 8   Papua New Guinea

Most production was local, since stone was widely available, and warfare and sorcery discouraged travel. Formal trade links were seldom
required, and few axes travelled further than 20 kilometres through the
mountains. However, some niche processes evolved: tree oil for body
decoration, palm for bows, mineral oil and vegetable salt, string bags,
tobacco, bone daggers, decorative feathers, coloured ochres—and even
edible earth tonics for pigs.

Stone working was not always sophisticated. In the Bismarck Archipelago, Lou Island obsidian may have been quarried by 'day-trippers'
with little skill. It is likely that whole blocks were exchanged, whose
owners engaged masons elsewhere. Techniques and labour relations
varied immensely, but Burton's analysis of Highland quarries per-
suades him that:

> non-ranked, non-hierarchical societies can organise themselves for large-
> scale productive ventures when a range of conditions are met . . . [This
> organisation is] very cheap, but also very volatile—liable to disappear or be
> unusable if the conditions change . . . By comparison, the bureaucratic
> structures needed by hierarchical or industrialised societies . . . are very
> costly, but they are less dependent on serendipitous circumstances and have
> the capacity to reorganise themselves to fit different conditions.[13]

This dichotomy may be overstated. Women built pots to precise
patterns in such places as Mailu Island off the Papuan coast, where they
had suitable clays, trade routes intersected, and men enforced a regional
monopoly. Mailu women produced for export, and refined their production through an early period of diverse patterns and shapes, to a
more recent period in which pots were mass-produced and virtually
uniform.[14] Further north-west, Motu potters enforced a similar
monopoly through the *hiri* trading network to the Papuan Gulf. Shell
valuables were also mass-produced in many Islands. Commonly these
were small shells ground to a standard size and linked in strands of
standard value. In quality, quantity and consistency, some production
was at least equal to the later quarrying of minerals under foreign
direction, which Europeans treated as development.

Hierarchical societies sustained a greater division of labour. Some
men became masons and carpenters. Demand for mats (commonly
produced by women) was almost infinite, from the simple mats which
sufficed for Hawaiian commoners, to the stacks of thirty or forty fine
mats on which high chiefs walked and slept. Most work was 'gendered'.
In Samoa, for example, *'ie toga* (fine mats) were the principal form of
woman-made wealth, complementing *'oloa*, the food, canoes and tools
produced by men. Women beat pandanus leaves into wafer-thin strips,
which were plaited together into mats. This was mass production, yet
the finest mats acquired a silky sheen over generations of exposure to
dew—and their own names and genealogies. It was not only their
intrinsic qualities which gave them value, but the social meanings

13 *Ibid.*, 88.
14 Irwin, 'The Emergence of Mailu'.

invested in them. Pottery was always a female craft, and weaving (with back-looms) was almost always women's work in Micronesia.

LAND TENURE

Land tenure arrangements are often described as 'traditional' or 'customary', but tenure practices on 'customary' land often differ greatly from practices described by early observers, land commissions, or in recorded oral history. Today's 'traditional' arrangements are often greatly simplified or modified versions of what was customary in the nineteenth century or earlier. Early accounts yield evidence of many features of land tenure which are broadly common to many parts of the region, to specific environments, to particular agricultural systems, or to particular social structures. Many traits stem from the needs which all tenure arrangements must meet. The users of land need security, at least long enough to harvest their crops. For tree crops, this period may span decades; for other crops, only a few months. Some means are also needed to transfer ownership or usufruct rights as needs change, such as the relative size and power of social groups. Different interests in one piece of ground must be accommodated. People may require rights of way across the land of others, to reach their own. All members of a community may need access to a resource such as a fresh-water spring. Different individuals or groups may hold rights to the one area for different purposes such as cultivation, hunting, or gathering wild produce. One person or group may own the trees on a plot while another owns the root crops growing beneath them. 'Almost invariably there are many different rights in any one parcel of land and they are often held by different parties.'[15]

In most Pacific Islands, fulfilment of a community's needs required access to several ecological sites, scattered throughout the island or even across several islands. Most families produced most of their regular needs, and few specialised in a narrow range of produce. They also had to provide for times of hardship. Land tenure arrangements within the territory of each community usually reflected every household's need to hunt, gather food and collect building materials, and to have access to different types of soils for a variety of crops, to fresh-water sources and areas of lagoon and reef for fishing and gathering shellfish. Access was controlled by rules governing the use and retention and disposal of the land or resources, and how and to whom land might be transferred.

On many high (volcanic) islands the sequence of ecological zones extends from the reef and lagoon, inland across a beach and sandy area backed by swamp, to fertile soils at the base of steeper slopes rising to the central and often forested ridges of the island. Access to the range of sites by each lineage could be achieved by tenure patterns like those

15 R. G. Crocombe, 'Land Tenure in the South Pacific', in R. Gerard Ward (ed.), *Man in the Pacific Islands*, Oxford, 1972, 220.

in Lakeba, Fiji, where groups hold wedge-shaped portions of land from the coast to the highest part of the interior. Many other high islands exhibit similar divisions, including Moala in Fiji, O'ahu in Hawai'i and Rarotonga in the Cook Islands. Similarly, the raised almost-atoll of Atiu, in the Cook Islands, with its encircling ring of rough coralline limestone (*makatea*), inner circle of swamps and fertile soils, and core of central ridges, was divided into seven wedge-shaped districts with boundaries radiating from the centre to the outer edge of the fringing reef. Districts were further subdivided, again with boundaries running from the centre to the coast, and highly valued land was further subdivided among much smaller groups. In Tahiti, each valley system includes a coastal strip at the valley mouth, fronting lagoon, reef and offshore waters, all backed by a wedge-shaped segment containing the island's major resources. 'It appears all Tahitians had access to the valley, coastal and marine resource zones contained in the particular valley system in which they lived' and 'there is . . . some evidence that each system, and its inhabitants formed a single political unit within large tribal groups'.[16] In Samoa the land of each village normally extends from the reef to the central ridge, again giving the community a cross-section of resources. On larger islands with more interior settlements, this pattern was not practical, but communities still tried to incorporate ecological variety into their lands. Social networks and exchange arrangements provided other ways of obtaining essential products.

In atolls where land areas are small and elongated and where the balance between resources and people is delicate, land-holdings generally take the form of a slice across the island from lagoon to ocean. On the islets of an atoll, the ocean shore provides different resources from those of the lagoon. Each household needs access to dry sites for housing and for coconuts and other tree crops, to wells which tap the freshwater lens below the centre of the islet, and to those areas where the water table lies close enough to the surface to be reached by pits in which swamp taro can grow. Thus throughout the Marshalls, 'each parcel of land is a transverse section of the islet' which provides the land-holding unit with access to most of the resources, including marine life, coconut and pandanus trees and living site on the lagoon strand, and a strip of the interior for breadfruit trees. In Kiribati, boundaries generally ran straight from lagoon to reef. The same was true in the three atolls of Tokelau. Tokelau kin groups, like those in the Marshalls and the Carolines, also had rights to lots dispersed on different islets around the atoll, which increased the chance of access to at least one productive area at any time.

Each household or kin group grew most of their own food, gathered their own firewood and caught their own fish. To grow all the crops necessary for a satisfactory diet and to cover the risks of pest damage and drought or storm, most households had a number of scattered food gardens and tree-crop plots using different soils. They commonly included a grove of coconuts near the shore, some breadfruit trees and

16 Finney, *Polynesian Peasants and Proletarians*, 16.

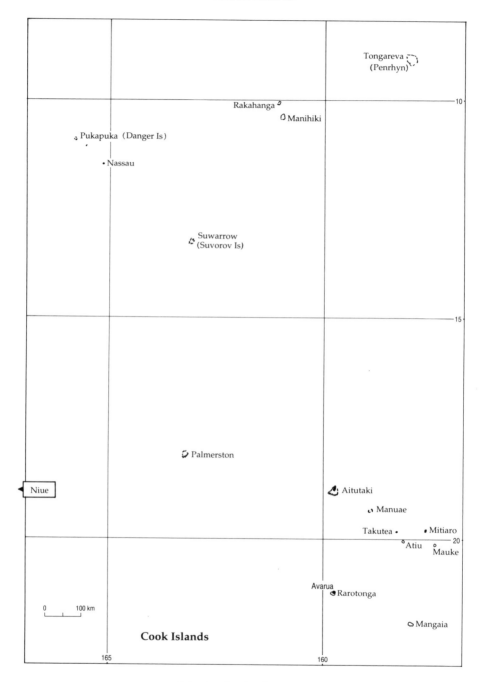

Map 9   Cook Islands

bananas in a more sheltered site with moister soils, a patch of swamp land reshaped for beds of taro, and yam gardens on fertile and drier soils. These plots were often interspersed among those of other households. Each household also needed the right to use, but not exclusive ownership of, the forest or savanna land for firewood and building materials, hunting and collecting wild foods.

Tenure arrangements generally involved some control by the maximal lineage or the residential community over a broad territory. All member groups could gather produce in uncultivated parts of this territory. Such land, held in the name of the whole community, was a form of commons. When land was cleared and cultivated, its crops were generally recognised as the property of the planter or their immediate kin group, and the land remained under their control so long as the crops stood. With inter-cropping of root crops, bananas, and shrubs such as kava (*Piper nethysticum*), this period might last for several years. Once yields declined, under the swidden system the gardens reverted to fallow for some years. Previous cultivators' rights would gradually 'grow cold' as the fallow period lengthened. Once the former users had ceased to express an interest, moved away, or been forgotten, others could clear and take the land into gardens. Thus changes in the relative size and needs of lineages were accommodated with clearly sanctioned transfer of usufruct rights. Tree crops might remain in production and under the control of the original planter long after the ground-level crops had disappeared and an understorey of shrubs had regrown. In time, the land below the coconuts might be cleared and planted by someone else. Thus a food-crop garden might have a different owner from that of the coconuts sharing the same land.

A great deal of labour was needed for some improvements, constructing pond fields or irrigated terraces or mounded gardens. With such wetland cultivation the soil could be used almost permanently, with nutrients supplied by irrigation water, and top dressing with mud or mulching. In places as far apart as the southern Highlands of New Guinea, southern Irian Jaya, and the Rewa delta of Fiji; and in the taro terraces or pond fields of Aneityum, southern Vanuatu, and Vanua Levu and Moala in Fiji, the long-term use and high investment of labour often resulted in such plots being regarded almost as the permanent property of those responsible for construction. Similarly, in many societies house sites were also considered the property of the specific family.

Apart from the transfer of control of usufruct (or eventually ownership) which could result from a new planter clearing and cultivating fallow, landowners could alienate their land by customary practices in virtually all communities. In some societies people with certain kinship relationships to a landholder had strong grounds for seeking a gift of land. People marrying into and coming to reside in a community might be given land (and assigned a communal affiliation) which could eventually grow into clear ownership (and community membership). Land might be given to reward service to a chief or landholder, or group. Refugees might be given protection, shelter and land, and eventually

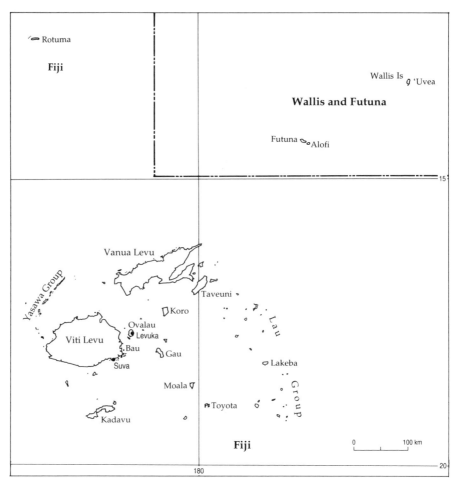

Map 10   Fiji and Wallis and Futuna

absorbed into the community. Land and other property could be seized
or surrendered in warfare, or as punishment for transgressing rules.
Above all, communities could divide after internal dispute and either
divide their land or occupy new territory.

All land tenure arrangements were flexible and pragmatic. Since they
were never codified, 'customary rules are subject, to a marked degree,
to pressure of circumstances and dominant interests'.[17] Authority to
exercise those interests ranged from societies in which hereditary chiefs
or elected leaders were responsible for acting on behalf of their community (and could sometimes turn that role into personal fiefdom), to
those in which control, and the authority to dispose of particular areas,
was clearly acknowledged to be in the hands of specific individuals.

17 T. G. Harding, 'Land Tenure', in P. Ryan (ed.), *Encyclopaedia of Papua New Guinea*,
   Melbourne, 1972.

Communalism and reciprocity were core principles. Farming operations which had to be performed quickly required more labour than one family could provide. For example, forest clearance was laborious, but co-operation in a work group made the task feasible. Working on the margins of the community, a group was also safer than an individual, as well as more congenial. House building was commonly handled in the same way. Although the immediate kinship group was usually the basic production unit, the help of others could be obtained on the basis of reciprocal obligations. Group work could also be an expression of common community interests even when it was not a technical necessity. Communal garden work did not make the produce communal property. Conversely, the control by individuals and their immediate families of the fruits of their work did not enable them to reside outside the community or to ignore the obligations of membership. Apart from labour, special services or needs—such as canoe building, herbal or spiritual intervention—had to be reciprocated. Most important was the need for protection. Neighbouring communities, often hostile, were organised in the same way. Inevitably the individual's interests were best served by participation.

Since social and economic organisation, the control of land, spiritual beliefs, and the hierarchy of authority were interlaced, land was pivotal for the society's well-being. Land was and remains a vital component of the cosmology of most Islanders, and respect for ancestors or their spirits may require care, attention or acknowledgment to the land they occupied. Land and people were often said to be two parts of the same entity.

Marshall Sahlins, adapting Marx, describes land as 'the inorganic body of the people . . . Hawaiians could refer to their ancestral lands as *kula iwi*, the "plain of one's bones", just as they knew themselves as *kama'āina*, "children of the land" which had nurtured them.'[18] A wealth of proverbs conveys these ideas, and words for 'land' have wide and rich resonances. As Ravuvu points out: 'the Fijian term, *vanua* [land], has physical, social and cultural dimensions which are interrelated. It includes . . . the people, their traditions and customs, beliefs and values, and the various other institutions established for the sake of achieving harmony, solidarity and prosperity . . . It provides a sense of identity and belonging.' The concept of *vanua* is therefore 'the totality of a Fijian community'.[19] In this wider sense it appears in the name Vanuatu, given to that country on independence. 'Cultural identity in Melanesia [and Polynesia] is a geographical identity that flows from the memories and values attached to places. Membership in a clan or social group, individual or collective identity, is inherited through a network of places, the sum total of which constitutes a territory.'[20] Individual, as well as collective, identity is bound up in land in ways which are sometimes very explicit, as in Yap, and in Tanna, where a child's first name is also the name of its land. Land use

---

18 Sahlins, *Anahulu*, 31.
19 Ravuvu, *Vaka i Taukei*, 70; and Ravuvu, *The Fijian Ethos*, 15.
20 Bonnemaison, 'The Tree and the Canoe', 117; see also his *The Tree and the Canoe*.

involved not only secular activities but also sacred rituals. Practices for land control and allocation, therefore, are often core elements of social identity. In recent years they have been used as symbols of national identity. In Papua New Guinea, the Solomon Islands and Vanuatu, clarification of land issues was a prerequisite to adopting modern constitutions. In Vanuatu, the constitution is an instrument of land tenure reform, bringing all land back into the realm of custom.

TRADE AND EXCHANGE

Complementing most people's attachment to particular pieces of land was an equally profound commitment to social relations which rested on (and reinforced) trade and exchange. It is tempting—but mis-leading—to interpret trade, bride price, mortuary payments and com-pensation simply as ecological adaptations to maximise material benefits. In the New Guinea Highlands 'exchange is so fundamental a feature of Huli cosmology and society that it resists abstraction. The Huli universe is itself constructed upon a notion of exchange between living humans and ancestral and non-ancestral spirits.' Knowledge and skill were valued just as highly as material items, and exchanged just as eagerly. Seeps of mineral oil were 'critical nodes within Huli sacred geography, in which the oil itself represented a substance crucial to the survival of the Huli universe'. The oil had scant intrinsic value (pearl-shells were equally 'unnecessary' to the Highlanders who treasured them) but the Huli made it central to the logic of their trading relations. People did not foster relations merely to facilitate exchanges, nor did they exchange merely to build alliances, since they drew no such dis-tinctions between 'economic' and 'social', profane and sacred. Huli trade can only be understood in terms of their sacred geography.[21]

Once committed to agriculture, every society aspired not merely to survive but to produce a surplus with which to sustain exchange partnerships. Typically these relationships were intensely competitive: gifts imposed obligations, which must be acknowledged at almost any cost. A party of missionaries on Murua Island in Milne Bay observed a drought in 1849 and 1850, which reduced the Muruans to walking skeletons. When their trading partners arrived, Muruans rationed themselves. They received pigs' teeth, whale bones and cassowaries, which might seem a poor exchange for food, but to do otherwise would brand them as ungenerous and break the bonds: so starving Muruans welcomed their partners with a feast. The inhabitants of several resource-poor islands in Milne Bay often enjoyed higher standards of living than their better-resourced neighbours, so long as their trading partners maintained the flow of food and material in a system of 'trading subsistence'.[22]

21 Ballard, ' "The Centre Cannot Hold" '. Bonnemaison, *The Tree and the Canoe*, describes
     similar 'sacred geography' in Tanna.
22 Martha Macintyre and Jim Allen, 'Trading for Subsistence: The Case from the Southern
     Massim', in Yen and Mummery, *Pacific Production Systems*.

The rhetoric of giving was often profoundly aggressive: Michael Young describes such contests as 'fighting with food'.[23] On Tanga Island in 1933, for example, Buktom of Tenkuien village organised a twelve-day feast. The first presentations passed smoothly, but required Buktom's constant attention, for example when Sumsuma, from a rival clan, swaggered in and proclaimed that he was returning with interest a pig which Buktom had presented on a previous occasion. Tension mounted as gifts accumulated. When the chieftain Tambau arrived with twenty-two animals and was welcomed, he responded, 'I chew you up, as the victor eats his victim!' Tambau's unexpected intervention posed an appalling dilemma. Buktom could repay pigs or provide a feast—but not both. Fortunately 'Buktom's close friend and "brother" Kospui came to the rescue with a present of thirty well-matured pigs which he had been reserving for an important series of rites which he planned to celebrate at the conclusion of the next planting season.' Buktom probably had a hundred pigs owing to him and owed almost as many. Nobody was ever allowed to forget a debt, and 'the matter of debits and credits . . . occupies hours of argument and discussion'.[24]

Ceremonial exchanges reached their most lavish expression in the New Guinea Highlands—*moka* among the Melpa, and *tee* among the Enga. By the late nineteenth century at latest, surpluses of sweet potato sustained massive production of pigs, the main exchange items. These exchanges continued throughout the brief colonial era, but the approach of independence made some Big Men wonder whether they would continue. Confronted by changing political structures and social mores, the Melpa Big Man Ongka made his final *moka*, and took the trouble to explain its dynamics and rationale to Andrew Strathern, quoted here at length.

Ongka's Last *Moka*[25]

Now let me talk again about how I make *moka*. On ceremonial ground after ceremonial ground I have done this. I have given war-compensation payments to many different clans, starting a long time ago, in the days when we did it all with pearl shells, laying them out on rows of fern and banana leaves. I have given them *kng enda*, too: this is when we give a number of pigs without calling out the names of individual exchange partners and without receiving big solicitory gifts in advance; we give it to all the men of a group together as a payment for a killing we have inflicted on them or they have incurred in fighting for us as allies . . . On these occasions I wore special decorations—the big plaque of multi-coloured feathers set on a backing (*Koi wal*), and the pale-blue crest feathers of the King of Saxony bird (*Koi ketepa*). I made these *moka* gifts along with the men of my own clan, the Mandembo, at different times and in different years. Sometimes we did the dance in which we bend our knees and make our long aprons sway out in front of us (the

23 Young, *Fighting With Food*.
24 F. L. S. Bell, 'The Place of Food in the Social Life of the Tanga', *Oceania* xviii (1947), in Whittaker *et al.*, *Documents and Readings in New Guinea History*.
25 *Ongka: A Self-account by a New Guinea Big-man*.

morl dance); sometimes we did the stamping dance in which we move round the ceremonial ground in a procession (the *nde mbo kenan* dance). We did all this many times, until it was all completed, and I was tired of it. On ceremonial ground after ceremonial ground I had done this again and again, and on these same sites the cordylines planted at their edges grew old and grey, the special round houses at the head of the grounds tumbled down, weeds grew up ... It was close to the time of self-government, and Parua had become, since 1972, our Member for the national House of Assembly. The times had changed, and I thought to myself that I would take off my bark belt, my cordyline sprig rear-covering, and my apron, and I would follow the new ways.

It seemed to me that we no longer had men of the old style who could do the hard work of rearing pigs or the women to make the strong netbags for harvesting the sweet potatoes, or to make the pig ropes and fasten them on the pigs, and so, if I waited much longer, we would not be able to make another *moka* in the good old way. We used to speak of those women of the old times as wearing long straw-coloured aprons with short pig-ropes tucked into them. Over their hair, which they wore in ringlets, they placed a piece of barkcloth, and on top of this they carried their large working netbags. These were the kind of women who could do the work to raise pigs, and now there were none like that left. Such women could raise many, many pigs, sows and barrows. The pig herd would cluster at her house door in the early morning, squealing for their feed of sweet potatoes. There were enough pigs to use for many different things ...

I decided, 'Well, if the old ways must go, let's at any rate do something as our last big show.' So I called on all the men from each small group inside our three clans to come to my place at Mbukl, and I said to them:

> Our fathers were true big-men, but their sons are wearing long trousers and drinking beer and are really rubbish men now. Our mothers were strong women, but their daughters have gone light-headed. The edges of the big gardens we used to make are covered with weeds. Self-government and Independence are here, and the old ways will disappear, but let us do one thing before that happens, so that all the groups around and all the white men too will say 'The Kawelka put on a little show, we saw it.' Now the old ways will be shaken off as we shake clods of earth from a stump of a tree, and we will take on the new ways. Everything's crazy now, so let us just do this one thing before it all happens. Listen to what I say and go ...
>
> Go to all your relatives and friends and ask for gifts, make the initiatory gifts to them and prepare to pull in the returns in order to make a big *moka*. We will give all the things which are customary, cassowaries, decorating oil, all kinds of valuable shells, cattle and special farm-raised pigs (which have become available since the white men came). We will also give some things that others have never given before, in order to make our name. In the old days, when our fathers gave *moka*, they made their name by giving large cassowaries from the place Kora in the Jimmi Valley where stone axe blades were manufactured in the past; or by giving *kum kokop*, special little pearl shells with magical power which they hung from the back of their heads. We Kawelka made our name in the past too by giving away a woman in *maka* as

a wife for the Kitepi clan leader, Kuri, father of Parua. People spoke of our doing this and asked others 'Have you done that?' Now, so that our sons in turn may be able to say that their fathers did something notable, let us give now what others have not given.

I spoke like this to them without revealing exactly what I meant.

Parua was elected as our Member of the national House of Assembly. However, because of a car accident and the death of a driver from the Nengka tribe, Parua was attacked ... Parua was very sick in Port Moresby hospital for a long time. When he returned to our area, he ... gave us four sets of eight pigs, to be distributed among all the Kawelka, because we had cried for him and had felt pain on his behalf when he was wounded. He added a cassowary, which we cooked and ate. So I called all our people together and said to them

> See, these gifts have come to us. We do not have women now who will raise pigs for us the way women used to do. Our women used to rear pigs for us men, I built men's houses, I paid death compensations, I gave away pigs in *moka*. But now what do they do? The modern girl goes off to the stream with her towel, soap, and comb, she washes herself and powders her neck, and then she goes out to smile at men and look for money. Those women of the old times, they put on girdles at their waist, covered their hair with a head-net, carried sweet potatoes in huge netbags. Today's girl walks out and about and lets the weeds grow over the sweet potato garden, she won't rear pigs any more. Self-government is close at hand, and the whole place is turning silly. I am calling this meeting for all of you men of our different clans; each man should go back home and think about it. Go back to your places and rear pigs, talk to your exchange partners from other clans, and prepare yourselves. Let your women put on the old-fashioned working clothes and tend their pigs. I am a man who built men's houses and lit the ritual fire in them, who laid out new ceremonial grounds, who paid compensation for killings, who cooked pigs, who gave live pigs away. Now I have paid for the government tractor to come and expand our ceremonial ground, and straighten it out, to pull out tree stumps and level its surface ... Remember this was not done to make a private garden for me, it was for our *moka*.
>
> Look what is happening to our men nowadays too. It is not only our women who are going crazy. In the old days a man grasped his spade and dug the ground, he cut down the tall stands of wild canegrass, he turned the soil and made tall bananas and sugarcane grow from it, tending and binding them till they came to maturity. Then he had food for his family and enough for his wife to cook for visitors as well; but men don't do that kind of thing now. Our young men wear long trousers and sun-glasses, drink beer ... In the old days young men would shoulder netbags of sweet potatoes to help the women, but now they walk around idle, fancy free and easy. In the old days they would do the work to make ceremonial grounds and to dig out the pits for earth ovens, but now they refuse to do all that ... Now self-government is close, let us just do this one thing before it all goes quite crazy. Before, when we Kawelka gave *moka* to the Tipuka we did something which made our name for us. The usual gifts are pigs, cassowaries, shells, pork, decorating oil; but no-one had ever given what we gave, a woman, the Kawelka woman Nomane, at the Mbukl ceremonial ground. We gave her as a wife for the leader Kuri, and so we 'won' and increased our prestige. She became the mother of Parua, and now in turn he has brought four sets of pigs and a cassowary to us. What shall we do? Each one of our clans has its place

in the *moka*. We plant our stakes to which the pigs are tied in separate rows on the ceremonial ground, we plant these again and again until they reach well out beyond the ceremonial ground. But these are for the gifts which everyone knows. What new thing can we give now? Let us give a car.

. . . At our big *moka* we [also] gave away as many as 20 cattle as extra gifts. We purchased 20 commercially raised pigs and added these to our own home-reared ones. We gave 40 cassowaries. As for our own pigs, how could you possibly count them?

At the head of the row of pigs I put my own pigs . . . As extra gifts I myself bought two cows and gave them away. The car too was purchased as a result of my persuasion: we all contributed to its price. They spoke of me and said, 'He should have stayed at home and made his own gardens so as to eat food, but instead of that it's as if he's burning up his money in a fire, what is he doing?' It was all done as my last big show. . . .

[I said,] 'See how many things we have given, pigs which are our own and ones we have bought with money; cassowaries; decorating oil; cattle, a motorbike, a car, and money as well. If anyone thinks he can match all of these things, let him take the knotted cordyline leaf from me as a sign now.'[26] No-one took up the challenge. So I finished my show after very many years of planning, after holding several small *moka* in preparation, after saying so many times that I would do it. In the end I did bring it off, I wrapped all the strong things of men and women from the past and laid them in their grave with my last big *moka*.

Other Exchanges

Mervyn Meggitt, observing the Enga *tee* exchanges, concluded that Big Men kept the system going

> by paying off those supporters whose aid is essential to them but also retaining for themselves whatever resources they can abstract at the expense of the weaker and poorer members of the group . . .
>   Now, this tempered rapacity is not simply a casual attribute of individual Big Men. Indeed . . . many Big Men regard it as both a diacritical mark and a privilege of Big Men as a category, and frequently they overtly or covertly manipulated exchanges . . . to their mutual advantage.[27]

By hectoring their clients, they sustained heroic production of crops to fatten the pigs which were, in effect, the store of harvest surplus. The great ceremonies not only sharpened rivalries: they brought communities into frequent relations. On the surface there is little value in forever exchanging the same pigs, but good managers prospered and inspired productive efforts, and everyone's chances of survival increased.

More obviously functional were exchanges of specialist goods. In the Torres Strait at the end of the nineteenth century some Islanders depended confidently on canoe-borne trade to supplement their

26 As a sign that his group would be the next to make a *moka* and it would be comparable to Ongka's.
27 Meggitt, ' "Pigs Are Our Hearts" '.

agriculture: items from the Papuan mainland included stone and bone tools, bows, arrows and stone weapons. According to an early colonial report, canoes were the most important items, 'and some of the tribes engaged in the traffic did not even regard each other as friends'.[28] Nor was this an isolated cluster. Mailu and Motu villagers exchanged pots for basic foods which grew scantily on their own arid land. By the 1880s Motu villages were despatching twenty multi-hulled *lakatoi* on each year's *hiri* expedition to the Gulf of Papua, carrying about 26,000 pots and returning with perhaps 500 tons of sago. By then New Guinea was surrounded by inter-linking trade routes, at many points drawing in the produce of inland people, usually in exchange for shell—which was then traded through countless hands to the distant Highlands. At the western tip of New Guinea, trade had a more sinister element: the sultanate of Tidore, in Maluku, was the focal point of trade in Papuan slaves as well as birds of paradise and baked sago, which served as a South-East Asian equivalent of ships' biscuits.

Long-distance trade and exchange relationships were, according to Hau'ofa, fundamental to Islanders' way of life:

> Fiji, Samoa, Tonga, Niue, Rotuma, Tokelau, Tuvalu, Futuna and 'Uvea formed a large exchange community in which wealth and people with their skills and arts circulated endlessly. From this community people ventured to the north and west, into Kiribati, the Solomon Islands, Vanuatu and New Caledonia, which formed an outer arc of less intensive exchange . . . Cook Islands and French Polynesia formed a community similar to that of their cousins to the west; hardy spirits from this community ventured southward and founded settlements in Aotearoa [New Zealand], while others went in the opposite direction to discover and inhabit the islands of Hawai'i. And up north of the equator one may mention the community that was centred on Yap.
>
> Evidence of the conglomerations of islands with their economies and cultures is readily available in the oral traditions of the islands concerned, and in blood ties that are retained today. The highest chiefs of Fiji, Samoa and Tonga, for example, still maintain kin connections that were forged centuries before Europeans entered the Pacific, in the days when boundaries were not imaginary lines in the ocean, but rather points of entry . . . The sea was open to anyone who could navigate his way through.[29]

Exchanges were central between—and within—stratified societies, where obligations to chiefs validated the extraction of products from commoners. Samoan *ali'i* (chiefs), who depended on powerful *tulāfale* (orators) for the acquisition of paramount titles, had to present fine mats to secure their support, to reward them at installation, and to reinforce possession. To the early missionaries, it seemed as if chiefs were forever on circuit, presenting food and exacting fine mats and bark cloth. Underpinning these courtly exchanges were innumerable men growing food and women beating bark and weaving pandanus, far beyond the amounts required for mere survival.

---

28 Appendix to *British New Guinea Annual Report*, 1905.
29 Hau'ofa, 'Our Sea of Islands', 9.

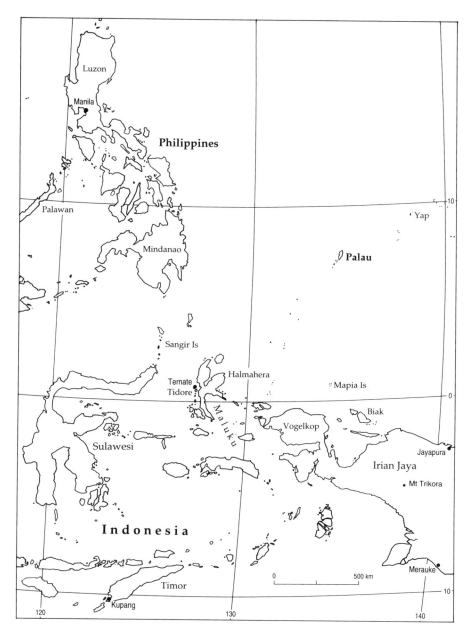

Map 11   Palau, Philippines and eastern Indonesia

Similar structures of value and authority also sustained clientage between Pacific Islands. Atoll populations relied on the patronage of high islands. Having few resources except shell, atoll-dwellers depended on high islands for many items of daily use. High island patrons could succour their clients in the event of drought, cyclones or other calamities decimating an atoll's trees—or even its people—while the high islands were less affected. The nexus included intercession by high island priests to avert disaster, such as the hegemony of Yapese priests over atolls in the central Carolines. 'Each year dozens of canoes streamed into Yap from other islands to present what looked like tributary gifts to certain chiefs, even though Yapese warriors never ventured out to these places to assert their overlordship.'[30] Carolinian ocean-going canoes travelled along named sea-lanes, relying on sailing instructions memorised by one generation after another. In the 1720s, one crew from Woleai Atoll was cast away on Guam, where they described and located a host of islands which had eluded Spanish ships. Such encyclopaedic knowledge was essential to survive natural or human disasters.

The most important form of tribute was banana-cloth textiles made by women. More widely known today, however, are *gau* (strings of shell crafted from *Spondylus*). Interdependence also connected high islands. Yap's relations with Palau evolved through the trade in *raay* (calcium carbonate discs), half a metre in diameter, with a central hole. (The better-known and colossal discs, several metres across, were quarried only from the nineteenth century when larger vessels could carry them.) From about the seventeenth century, Yapese from south-western districts of the island sailed regularly to Koror in Palau. Payment for quarrying rights was made by the chiefs of the two Yapese villages to the chiefs of Koror and Melekeok, and chiefly control helped to solidify the power bases of chiefs in both island groups. There they offered their labour for the privilege of quarrying. Mining absorbed immense labour, before the Yapese ferried *raay* home on frail rafts across hundreds of kilometres of ocean.

Many exchanges amounted to tribute or barter, in the absence of an agreed 'currency'; but Langalanga, the artificial islands to the north of Malaita in the Solomons, were one of several centres for manufacturing shell. Mass-produced by women (here, gardening was the province of men), they found their way throughout and beyond the Solomon Islands.[31] Among the best-known forms of wealth were the great looping fathoms of *tambu* shell which represented wealth for the Tolai in New Britain. Whale's teeth performed much the same function in other islands. In Fiji, for example, the little island of Bau projected its power far beyond its horizons, across the islands to the densely populated Rewa delta of Vanua Levu, through its chiefs' access to *tabua* (whale's teeth) (see chapter 5).

Like other shells, *raay* were a store of value, more highly esteemed than *gau*. Rates of exchange fluctuated. Ownership passed from village

---

30 Hezel, *First Taint of Civilization*, 264.
31 Cooper, 'Economic Context of Shell Money Production in Malaita'.

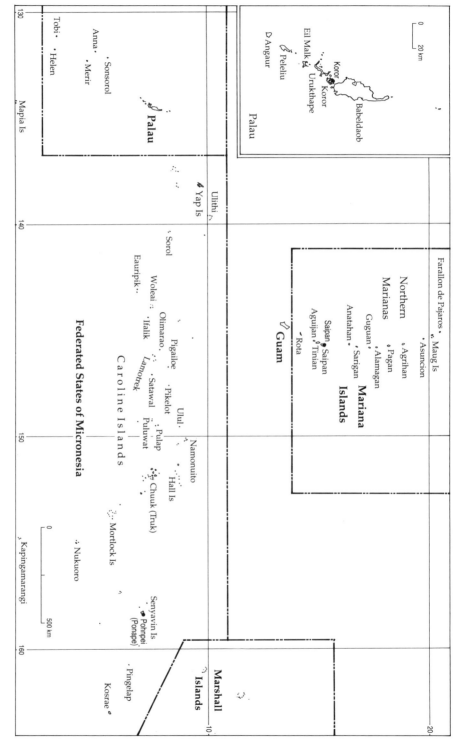

Map 12   Northern Marianas and Federated States of Micronesia

to village even when *raay* were irretrievably sunk. Like any other currency, *raay* provoked political contest, attempts at monopoly and much ingenuity—while accumulated wealth buttressed the holders of political power. Unlike Western currency, however, *raay* was not anonymous: the discs retained the personality of those who quarried, ferried and owned them, in the form of stories told about them. The same distinction applies to other forms of wealth, including the *'ie toga* fine mats of Samoa, with individual qualities and narratives. It follows that wealth could be amassed only in a social and political context. People possessed wealth—but not capital. *Tambu* represented wealth for the Tolai: but *tambu* became 'capital' only when relations were commercialised in the nineteenth century. Until then the convention which distinguishes the (economic) production of wealth from the (political) accumulation of power makes no sense of Island experience. Wealth and authority were two sides of the same *raay*.

These exchanges are often described as 'traditional', but they were not as inflexible as that term implies. As demand changed, so did production and the exchange networks. Palau aragonite production languished until about AD 1400 when Yapese settled near the quarry: export trade evolved much later. Sweet potato transformed production and exchange in the New Guinea Highlands. The later expansion of quarrying responded to a flood of goods from the coast, though neither the masons nor traders recognised the connections. Polynesian exchanges quickly accommodated European commodities, just as the *moka* embraced manufactured imports.

GENDER DIVISION OF LABOUR

Underpinning all other relations were a host of relationships between women and men, in production, consumption and exchanges. Throughout this book we warn against the conventional division of the Pacific into three 'culture areas', to explain commonalities and differences. On a purely descriptive level, however, some regional generalisations can be offered about male–female relations and the gender division of labour. In most Melanesian societies women played a greater role in agriculture and food production than did women in Polynesia. Polynesian women's primary work was to manufacture mats and cloth for domestic and ceremonial use. In most of Melanesia, male dominance was more explicit and more extreme than in Polynesia, and was often buttressed by ideologies warning of female danger and pollution. Polynesian cultures varied widely in the content and force of their ritual prohibitions, but most associated women to some degree with notions of taboo and sacred spiritual power. Yet Polynesian women were the equals of men in genealogical status and social rank. They not only produced cultural valuables, but wielded formidable personal and political authority as kinswomen and chiefesses.

By contrast, Micronesia presents a wide range of environments. The social and political range was equally diverse, from stratified chiefdoms to localised extended-family organisation. Cultural solutions did not necessarily correlate with environmental conditions, and even within the same sector of islands the division of labour could vary radically. The men of Chuuk Lagoon, for example, gardened while men in the western isles of Chuuk District believed that gardening was women's work. Regional patterns are of course relative, and there are always exceptions. While in Highland New Guinea women did most of the productive work, in the matrilineal societies of Island Melanesia women owned and passed on the land, and both sexes worked in the gardens. But matrilineal descent did not ensure that men respected women, nor that women were equal decision-makers. There is no apparent relation between the rule of descent, the division of labour, and the esteem accorded to women.

Statements about the division of labour should also be nuanced by a distinction between production and exchange. In some societies women contributed little to subsistence, but produced domestic necessities and valued exchange goods, and played active roles in exchanges. Further, women's contributions to subsistence did not correlate with high public esteem: witness the extreme male dominance and denigration of women in certain New Guinea societies where women produced most of the staple foods and, in contrast, the high cultural valuation of Polynesian women, who primarily manufactured cloth and mats. Age differences were another source of variation: boys and girls often had quite different work expectations from adults, whose duties differed in turn from those of elderly men and women. Samoan girls in the 1920s weeded and gathered plant foods, as well as helping to prepare family meals. In the Trobriands, men were the primary yam producers and women produced cloth goods, but women might plant and tend their own yam gardens on lands of their matrilineage. The distinction between men's work and women's work should not, in other words, be viewed as a categorical exclusion. In most societies there were no ritual prohibitions restricting economic tasks and, particularly in agriculture, men and women often helped each other when needed. Highland New Guinea was a notable exception, however, with its ritualised sexual segregation and pollution beliefs.

This brief reconstruction begins with societies in which women contributed significantly to food production. The discussion proceeds to women's manufacture of domestic necessities and ceremonial valuables, as well as women's roles in exchange. These descriptions are only as sound as the sources on which they are based. In many areas of Melanesia and Micronesia, pre-European activities persisted well into the era of modern ethnography and may still be practised today in modified form. In Samoa, Tonga, and many smaller Polynesian islands, the subsistence economy has been well documented, and inferences about the pre-European division of labour can be substantiated with first-hand observations. For most of these societies, twentieth-century monographs contain data on gender roles. Such material is not always easily accessible or consolidated, however, and female activities are rarely given equal treatment. For highly 'acculturated' societies, conclusions must rely on ethnohistorical sources. Nearly all were Western men whose biases led them to ignore or denigrate Island women and their activities.

Our focus is not so much the proportion of women's contribution as the question of male dominance: did women work *for* men? Did men have decision-making authority over the products of women's labour? In most of Highland New Guinea they did, and this asymmetry is part of a larger gender complex that has been called 'sexual antagonism'. Sexual asymmetry varied, but most Highland societies had institutions that vaunted male superiority, notably male cults revolving around men's houses, arcane knowledge, and secret men-only rituals. A central function of the men's cults was to conduct initiation rites to mould boys into warriors. Though this function has been abridged, male initiation rituals continue in many societies. In these rites and in daily life men explicitly and publicly denigrate women, and in some cases routinely abuse them physically. Highland economies centred on sweet potatoes and pigs. Many societies also emphasised the ceremonial exchange of shell valuables. The sweet potato is considered a 'female' crop, in contrast to 'male' plants such as taro, ginger and sugarcane, which are cared for by men. Pigs are also categorically 'female' in contrast to dogs and cassowaries, which are 'male'. Since pigs eat sweet potatoes, men's ceremonies intrinsically depend on women's work, and if men like Ongka hold more feasts, women must work much harder.

It is difficult to compare the effort that women expend on cultivation in different parts of Melanesia. Jill Nash calls the matrilineal Nagovisi of Bougainville a relatively 'low production' society, especially by comparison with the Highlands. Until the taro blight of the 1940s, the Nagovisi grew taro as their staple crop, raised pigs, and supplemented their diet with hunting and gathering. (After the taro blight, sweet potato supplanted taro.) As an indicator of cross-cultural differences in women's work, Nagovisi informants told Nash that a Highland woman who had married into the area worked much harder at gardening than they did. By comparison with the Highlands, Nagovisi pig feasts tended to be smaller and the Nagovisi placed much less emphasis on winning competitive advantage in exchanges. Rather, they valued 'reciprocity and balance' in relationships. Though Nash rejects the notion that women in matrilineal societies universally enjoy 'higher status' than women in patrilineal systems, she reports that Nagovisi men and women have relative equality in rights and control over resources. She also vividly conveys the meaning of 'work' for women:

> Though active, Nagovisi women do not give the impression of being over-worked, and rarely go to the garden more than three times a week . . . To count 'hours in the garden' is misleading, for women by no means get down to their tasks in a businesslike manner—they stop at villages en route to chat and chew betel, and once in the garden, they cook snacks, tend to small children, bathe, and so on. In other words, 'work' is not well differentiated into a separate category.[32]

32 Jill Nash, 'Gender Attributes and Equality', in Strathern (ed.), *Dealing with Inequality*, 152, 155.

Rather different arrangements prevail in the 'sago complex' of the Sepik River area. In some Sepik societies men do most of the planting and gardening, while women catch fish. Paddling out in canoes to set fish traps, women supply most of the protein food. They also prepare sago, cook, and have their own markets where they barter foodstuffs with other women. Here as elsewhere, the division of labour is buttressed by beliefs in the intrinsic qualities of each sex. Iatmul men believed that they could not learn to cook sago pancakes, but among the sago-pro-ducing societies of the Sepik there was much flexibility in performance: few tasks were strictly reserved for one sex, and men and women helped each other as needed. Both sexes worked sago, but men and women customarily performed different phases of the process.

Sepik women also tended the pigs upon which men's ceremonies depend, and Bateson observed that 'wives hold the purse strings very tight'.[33] Most of the literature on New Guinea emphasises female subordination, ritual separation and male misogyny, but most ethno-graphers have been male. Since the 1970s, some scholars have sug-gested that women may have a different perspective, and even their own alternative cosmology and gender ideology. We have few intensive studies of female perspectives, but in the early 1960s, when the Highlands were still minimally affected by Western contact, Paula Brown recorded these contrasting statements from a Simbu (Chimbu) woman and man:

> What we women do is very difficult. 1) We cook for our family every day in our life. Never rest. 2) Go to the garden every day of our life. 3) Clean the grass in the garden and plant the food crops. 4) Look after pigs every day of our life. 5) Look after our babies while we are doing the other jobs. So it is very very hard. Men never help us . . . The work that men do is very simple. It's not very hard to them. They break firewood, cut grass or clear the bush, dig the garden drains, build houses only. They do not do it every day. Men spend most of their time doing nothing and talking. They just sit in the men's house discussing buying wives for young boys and about feasts and ceremonies.

> We men worked hard for our own satisfaction and to serve our family. We worked harder than the women because we thought we had more strength and we worked extra hours. We show our strength by making fences, building new houses, making new gardens, breaking firewood, helping our wives to plant. Our wives worked the same as we husbands worked but they worked a bit fewer hours than us men. They woke up early in the morning to set the pigs free to look for their food. After that the women went to their work and returned when the sun is about to set. When they prepare food for the family it is extra work but it is the job of the women to serve the family.[34]

Women's production of goods for men's ceremonial exchanges is becoming more widely acknowledged. In Pohnpei and Palau, women are recognised as the key figures in family ceremonies, exchanges, and

33 Bateson, *Naven*, 148–9.
34 Brown, 'Gender and Social Change', 128.

public feasts—events in which men are vitally concerned. In most descriptions of New Guinea Highland exchanges, however, women are largely absent. Since women are the gardeners, they also provide the food for men's gatherings. Among the Tombema Enga, women influence their husbands' political ambitions by virtue of their role as providers. Women participate in negotiations over acquiring pigs. If a woman left her husband, the result would be disastrous for his pig herd—and his aspirations. Moreover, male exchange partners in the *tee* are related through women: 'Enga would not consider giving pigs to persons without a female tie for there would be no guarantee of return.' A man's wife has direct say over distribution to exchange partners who are not related to her, and the would-be recipients must ask her for the pigs: 'women are essential in shaping and defining the partnerships that nominally belong to men'.[35] Women's roles in ostensibly male-centred exchanges offer a new perspective on sexual polarity. Ideology is not the be-all and end-all of women's social position. Even where male dominance appears absolute, the division of labour may temper the conventional portrayal of unremitting female subordination.

In many societies women manufactured cultural valuables—things that are stored as heirlooms, rarely displayed, and transferred only on ceremonial occasions. Early ethnographers typically ignored the significance of these articles. This neglect was an artefact of male bias, but it also derived from the Western expectation that primitive peoples were crudely materialist, largely concerned with filling their bellies. They therefore tended to undervalue non-subsistence exchange goods, even though Islanders viewed these as treasures. Annette Weiner, working in the Trobriand Islands, calls these items 'cloth wealth', because in many societies women's ceremonial manufactures take the form of cloth or mats. In Polynesia, bark cloth (*tapa* or *kapa*) and pandanus mats are the highest cultural valuables. They were appropriate gifts for gods and chiefs, and in some societies particular items embodied the history of families and dynasties. In Pohnpei, women also made cloth goods for exchange—skirts of hibiscus fibre, belts, headdresses, and mats. In the Trobriands, women still produce banana-leaf bundles and fibre skirts which are exchanged in funeral ceremonies. Weiner judges that: 'Oceanic societies with cloth traditions value such wealth not only as a form of currency, but also as a major exchange object, presented to others at births, marriages, deaths, and the inauguration of chiefs.'[36] Items of cloth wealth are never really alienated from the families that produced them, and they embody kin group identity as well as political authority.

The Trobriand Islands are best known in academic circles for the inter-island *kula* exchange network, described by Malinowski in *Argonauts of the Western Pacific*. Men travelled long distances in elaborately decorated canoes to exchange armshells and necklaces with their

---

35 Feil, 'Women and Men in the Enga Tee'.
36 Annette Weiner, 'Why Cloth?', in Weiner and Schneider, *Cloth and Human Experience*, 35.

trading partners. Malinowski largely ignored women and their activities, including women's mortuary exchanges which Weiner describes in *Women of Value, Men of Renown*. Although women produce and own the cloth wealth—banana-leaf bundles and skirts—and conduct the mortuary ceremonies, their husbands have an abiding interest in proceedings. When a ceremony is pending, a man 'will work for months from morning until late at night trying to accumulate as much women's wealth as possible for his wife'. At such times he will say publicly that he is working for his wife, although he may denigrate women in other contexts. 'Behind every big-woman who distributes more women's wealth than anyone else during a mortuary ceremony stands a man.'[37]

Early European visitors failed to comprehend the value of Samoan fine mats and *siapo* (bark cloth); missionaries and administrators discouraged, regulated, and even prohibited fine mat exchanges on the grounds that they distracted people from productive work. Samoans repeatedly explained that their fine mats were the 'gold and diamonds' of their society. Large distributions were essential in public ceremonies, and those who aspired to the highest titles had to garner certain old and sacred mats that symbolised overarching authority. Importantly, Samoan women participate equally in discussions with male chiefs over which mats to give at a ceremony, and how many. Women may call on their own extended family when their marital household needs more mats for an exchange.

The role of cloth wealth in ancient Hawaiian society has been overlooked, in part because the fine-quality mats and *tapa* were quickly superseded by European items. Formal, public exchanges of cloth wealth appear in any case to have been less prominent than in Samoa. Even with voluminous ethnohistorical materials, the pre-European division of labour can remain uncertain: few foreign visitors recorded details of who was working in the taro patches, and when. The nineteenth-century writer David Malo summarised the division of labour with the formula that outdoor work was done by men, indoor work by women.[38] Men did most of the agricultural tasks, as well as woodwork, stonework, and deep-sea fishing. Men felled trees, built houses, made canoes, bowls and adzes, and fished from canoes at sea. In Polynesia men also did the cooking; according to Malo, under the gender taboos (the '*kapu* system') Hawaiian men and women could not eat from the same animal, the same dish, or the same oven. A man must therefore prepare two ovens (*imu*), one for the men of the family and one for the women.

Hawaiian women were occupied with making pandanus mats, bark cloth, and feather ornaments, as well as reef fishing and marine gathering close to shore. Observers noted that most of the mats and cloth were made by older women, however. If contemporary Polynesian societies are any guide, girls and younger women would have been responsible for child-care, domestic duties, and assisting older

37 Weiner, *Women of Value, Men of Renown*, 14.
38 Malo, *Hawaiian Antiquities*.

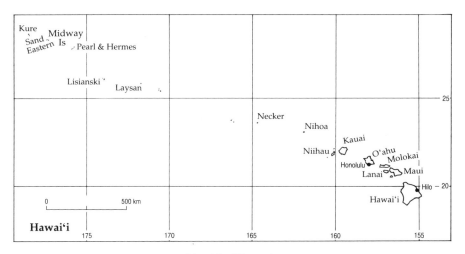

Map 13   Hawai'i

women, effectively as apprentices. Hawaiian men were also the bird-catchers, camping in the upland forests and harvesting the brilliant feathers that went into chiefly cloaks and standards; their wives accompanied them, however, and sorted the feathers. Early sources attest that women made the feathered cloaks, insignia of high-ranking male chiefs. Modern scholars tend to impute this task to men, largely because the prevailing interpretation of the taboo system has been one of categorical female-pollution and devaluation. Hawaiian gender taboos, which mandated separation of males and females during eating, religious rituals, and menstruation, have led some scholars to presume that women were ritually prohibited from growing certain crops, such as taro. While men performed most of the work with taro, there is no evidence of a categorical exclusion. There are times in the growth cycle when wetland taro requires frequent weeding, and it is likely that women and children participated. A visitor to Hawai'i in 1798, when the *kapu* system was still in effect, wrote that 'the young women never work in the field, but the old ones sometimes do'.[39] The historian Samuel Kamakau left us a curious summary:

> All the work outside the house was performed by the men, such as tilling the ground, fishing, cooking in the *imu* . . . This was the common rule on Kauai, Oahu, and Molokai, but on Maui or Hawaii the women worked outside as hard as the men . . . it was not uncommon to see the women of Hawaii packing food on their backs, cooking it in the *imu*, and cultivating the land or even going fishing with the men.[40]

In light of other sources associating women with sweet potato cultivation, an archaeologist has suggested an explanation for Kamakau's

---

39 'Extract from the Diary of Ebenezer Townsend, Jr., Supercargo of the Sealing Ship *Neptune* on Her Voyage to the South Pacific and Canton', Hawaiian Historical Society Reprints, 4 (1921), 25.
40 Kamakau, *Ruling Chiefs*, 238–9.

description: that dryland field systems, with sweet potato the dominant crop, were more prevalent on Maui and Hawai'i islands. Dryland cultivation required more constant and intensive labour for weeding and mulching, and in these areas women's labour would have been particularly important.[41]

Still, women were busy enough with their primary duties. Bark cloth is perishable and its manufacture labour-intensive—tending the shrub, preparing the raw material, beating the bark with mallets to the desired thinness, and stamping or painting designs on the cloth. Fine *tapa* cloth and pandanus mats were also part of tributary offerings to the chiefs; their delicacy and quantity indexed chiefly rank, and Hawaiian women would have been fully occupied producing these valuables as well as domestic items. The fine varieties of mats and *tapa* made their way into chiefly gift exchange and religious rituals. Wrapping signified the containment of divine power; offerings and images of the gods were customarily wrapped in fine *tapa* and/or mats.

Recent ethnographers have explored the cultural logic of the gender division of labour. In Polynesia, one typically finds thorough-going complementarity, in economics, cultural symbolism and ritual status. Men and women supplied categorically different, complementary goods. In Pukapuka, in the Cook Islands, 'men work on the periphery and women work in the centre'.[42] Women work taro fields in the atoll's swampy interior, while men tend coconuts on the encircling dry land. In other contexts too, Pukapuka women are symbolically 'wet' where men are said to be 'dry'. Both sexes may fish within the reef but, as in Hawai'i and Samoa, only men venture onto the ocean. In marriage exchanges, men contribute the products of their gender—coconuts, fish, and sennit fibre—while women give women's things—taro and pandanus mats. There is ample evidence for such complementarity in other Polynesian societies, and in Pohnpei and Palau. A missionary in Hawai'i described a tributary procession wherein a column of men presented foods to a chiefess, followed by a column of women bearing mats and *tapas*. Polynesian marriage exchanges typically entail gifts of food and other men's products by the man's family, and cloth wealth by the woman's side.

Complementarity may be the one feature common to the gender division of labour in Pacific societies, and perhaps in all societies. The diverse cultural elaborations that characterise Island economies defy simple explanations. Men may fish and women garden—as in Yap, Palau, and Pohnpei—or vice versa, as in the Sepik. In Polynesia, men typically produced most of the food, while women manufactured cloth wealth. Where both men and women garden, there is a division of labour by crop, and where both sexes fish, there is usually a distinction between inshore and open-ocean fishing and/or a gender division by marine species. While taro farming was largely the job of Hawaiian men, some sources associate Hawaiian women with sweet potato. In

41 Kirch, *Feathered Gods and Fishhooks*, 224–5.
42 Hecht, 'The Culture of Gender in Pukapuka', 186.

matrilineal Palau, women were categorically associated with taro patches and men with fishing; men were also associated with crops that require little regular care—tree crops, sugarcane and arrowroot—as well as tobacco and pepper vines. In Pohnpei, male wealth included giant yams, pigs and *kava*, while women's wealth consisted of cloth goods and agricultural items such as sugarcane, sennit and coconut oil. Because productive tasks can readily be divided into stages and phases of preparation, tending, collecting, processing, and so forth, the division of labour facilitates the enactment of perceived differences between social categories—high/low, young/old, and male/female. Although usually portrayed in broad strokes, the gender division of labour is highly nuanced; it both derives from and continues to communicate fine cultural distinctions between men and women.

LIVES AND DEATHS

We glimpse the population levels of the remote past only through emotive debates about the depopulation which almost always followed interaction with Europeans. For more than a century after white settlement in Australia, the pre-contact Aboriginal population was taken to have been about 150,000. White and Mulvaney now judge that 750,000 is more accurate. Later population decline in tropical Australia may have been relatively slight: sustained contacts with Indonesian fishing crews 'may have produced greater immunity from some diseases, but may also have acted to keep populations lower than they might otherwise have been'.[43] At the other end of the region, a similar revaluation is being made. The first published estimate of Hawai'i's population—400,000—was by James King who sailed with Cook. King's peers proposed figures closer to 250,000, which was generally accepted until 1989 when David Stannard proposed at least 800,000. On the other hand the observations of early European visitors persuade Andrew Bushnell that some lethal infections were not immediately available in Hawai'i, that the decline was slower, and the original population smaller than Stannard proposes.[44]

In New Zealand, Maori numbers have been estimated between about 110,000, and five times that total. Similar uncertainty crops up across Polynesia. A missionary census estimated 56,000 Samoans in 1839, after seven decades of contact with Europeans; though the pioneer demographer Norma McArthur preferred significantly lower figures. As for Tahiti, estimates run from an implausible 8000 to 200,000: 66,000 may be a fair estimate. Scholars differ most in Tonga, depending on the credence they attach to a missionary estimate in 1847 of 'about 50,000', declining to an agreed 19,000 by the end of the century. Similar disagreements mark accounts of populations in the Marquesas and Cook

43 White and Mulvaney, 'How Many People?', in Mulvaney and White (eds), *Australians to 1788*.
44 Bushnell, ' "The Horror" Reconsidered'; and the responses of Eleanor Nordyke and Robert Schmitt, in Stannard, *Before the Horror*.

Islands, where McArthur reckoned there were 20,000 each. Micronesian estimates pose equally acute problems, since so many disasters and epidemics occurred before any recorded estimates. Kosrae in the 1820s may have been recovering from typhoon and civil strife and beginning to regain its earlier population levels. If so, the recovery was aborted by new diseases. Hezel estimates 3000 people on Kosrae, 10,000 on Pohnpei and a similar number in Palau, 15,000 in the Marshall Islands and 30,000 to 40,000 in the Marianas.[45] The islands of today's Kiribati had a population of perhaps 30,000.

In Vanuatu and the Solomon Islands (as in most of Melanesia) colonial record-keeping began only after a couple of generations of interaction. Even painstaking research therefore offers only approximations. Spriggs is fairly sure that there were 3500 to 4000 people on Aneityum in 1854 when missionaries counted them. Numbers had certainly fallen since 1830, but he cannot estimate that decline more narrowly than a range of 17 to 33 per cent.[46] Vanuatu as a whole experienced at least 50 per cent depopulation in the nineteenth century, and in some islands much more. In mid-century there were 3500 people in Aneityum, 15,000 to 20,000 in Tanna, and 5000 in Erromanga.

McArthur reckoned that the Fijian population had been about 135,000 in the early 1870s, but by the 1879 census, only about 110,000 were counted. In the previous century some Fijians had survived a pulmonary infection in 1791–2, acute dysentery in 1802–3, and a measles epidemic of 1875, besides other episodes which left neither oral nor documentary traces. Roux's reconstruction of pre-contact agriculture in the *grande terre* of New Caledonia leads to a persuasive estimate of at least 90,000 people. For the Solomon Islands, reports estimated between 100,000 and 150,000 people. Until the 1930s, neither the Dutch New Guinea administration nor those of Papua or the Mandated Territory of New Guinea was aware of Highland populations. None pretended to know for how many people they were responsible, but each suspected that depopulation was occurring. Some New Guinea islands did experience decline—Ontong Java, a Polynesian outlier, much of New Ireland, and the western islands in Manus province. The first censuses were attempted in Papua New Guinea only in the 1960s, suggesting fewer than 2 million people. In Irian Jaya, no full census had been taken before the Dutch departed in the 1960s, leaving a guesstimated 750,000 people.

Today Melanesians far outnumber Polynesians, and Micronesians are many fewer than either. These numbers were probably closer to equality in the fifteenth century, since (for reasons explained below) many Melanesians were shielded from the worst effects of exotic infections, and large islands were probably less exposed than small ones. In a global perspective, however, even the most generous estimates are remarkably low. Since New Guinea has been inhabited for 30,000 years, and most of Polynesia for at least a millennium (chapter 2),

45 Hezel, *First Taint of Civilization*, 317–18.
46 Spriggs, 'Vegetable Kingdoms'.

eighteenth-century populations were arrestingly sparse. Either there were stringent constraints on population growth, or there had been several episodes of drastic population loss. It is likely that both scenarios were played out in different parts of the region.

More discoverable than quantity is the quality of people's lives. Europeans admired the health of Polynesians when they first met: Bougainville likened Tahitians to Greek gods. There was much for sailors to envy in the Islanders on the beach. All societies were protected by the fact that many diseases require a population mass before they can become endemic. Oceania had long been isolated from dense populations and their infections. However, the closer to Asia, the weaker the *cordon sanitaire*. Coastal New Guinea, like northern Australia, was exposed to infections through South-East Asian traders: there was no sharp microbiological break like that which separated Polynesia from the Americas, although infections may have been limited by quarantine systems.[47] Distance and small scale protected most Islands from influenza, leprosy, measles, mumps, smallpox, tuberculosis, cholera, plague, typhoid, whooping cough and venereal diseases. Judging by the later effects of pulmonary diseases, many of these may have been absent in earlier times.

Malaria (including *falciparum*, the most deadly variety) and filariasis were endemic in coastal Melanesia. In the Solomon Islands, Bennett estimates that coastal populations suffered from reduced fertility through malaria and yaws, so that 40 per cent of babies died. Altitude offered some protection, but that had to be weighed against the inconvenience of food supplies. Although some people did reach old age, few could expect to live beyond about thirty years.[48] Yet there were significant pockets throughout Melanesia where malaria did not prevail. The New Guinea Highlands were the most significant, but many smaller areas were also secure, if people drained or avoided the swampy breeding grounds of anopheles mosquitoes. Over several generations, exposed populations could acquire some resistance, but European and Polynesian missionaries who moved into malarial regions suffered acutely (which helps to explain the contrast between Europeans' lyrical accounts of Polynesia and their dread of Melanesia). In a fresh population, malaria was lethal. It also depressed immune systems, laying victims open to other infections. Malaria may have been the most important barrier to the movement of people and technology across Torres Strait. Few Aborigines who crossed the barrier to New Guinea would survive, while any who settled in Cape York, and began to cultivate, would have endured at least a generation of high mortality, with no reasonable prospect of improvement.[49] The New Guinea Highlands may be conceived as a refuge, where population could increase briskly. Any community driven from this refuge would be unable— through sickness—to fight their way back. Mid-altitude societies were

47 Allen, 'A Bomb or a Bullet or the Bloody Flux?'
48 Bennett, *Wealth of the Solomons*, 9.
49 Groube, 'Contradictions and Malaria in Melanesian and Australian Prehistory'.

therefore smaller, and less healthy, than their neighbours at higher altitudes. Since Highlanders attributed illness to lower altitudes and had little need for marriage partners from these parts, they enjoyed de facto quarantine.

The evident well-being of most Islanders at first encounters can support a sinister interpretation. In the Aitape area of New Guinea, for example: 'The village environment favoured the reproduction and spread of pathogens which selectively killed children and weaker adults. Village populations appeared "healthy" to outsiders because those who survived childhood were largely immune to the most common infections to which they were exposed, and those who aged or weakened, quickly sickened and died.'[50] It is reassuring that Cook's expedition observed deformed Hawaiians; and similar deformities were observed elsewhere after the first euphoria. But the absence of degenerative diseases was largely due to the fact that few people lived long enough to develop them.

Little is known of indigenous therapies. Many communities developed surgical skills to treat war wounds, but nowhere in New Guinea has evidence been found of expertise in childbirth, and a woman in labour fended for herself or relied on kinswomen. Father Rougeyron in New Caledonia in the 1840s scorned the Kanaks' reliance on divination, but applauded their surgical skills and their use of bleeding, purging and poultices;[51] which suggests that Melanesian therapies were no worse—but no better—than the folk-remedies on which most Europeans relied. Well-being owed more to nutrition and isolation. Commentators refer more commonly to spiritual than to 'clinical' healers. Individual misfortune was widely read as evidence of social disharmony, and efforts to identify ill-wishers were often more ingenious than the treatment of the sick. In 1968 Raymond Kelly observed this in a Highland fringe population in Papua New Guinea: 'The Etoro themselves say that they are dying out. They attribute this to internal witchcraft. For each death a witch is named and a demand for compensation (or execution) follows. In an epidemic year the level of social conflict that is generated by this severely tests the social bonds which hold the society together.'[52] Melanesian witches tend to be older women, and a society in which every grandmother may prove to be a witch must endure acute anxiety, especially in times of epidemics.

Health was unequally enjoyed by Melanesian women and men: women aged faster and died younger than their brothers. Although men and women were roughly equal numerically in other islands, Melanesian men outnumbered women by perhaps 110:100, and even more in some communities. A Dutch colonial administrator in Irian Jaya was surprised by this disequilibrium in the Marindanim population during the 1930s. There were so many more boys and men than girls and women that it was difficult to see how the community could

50 Allen, 'A Bomb or a Bullet or the Bloody Flux?', 228.
51 Douglas, 'Discourses on Death in a Melanesian World'.
52 Kelly, *Etoro Social Structure*, 31.

reproduce itself. Like some anthropologists in Papua in the 1920s, he wondered if this was a short-term consequence of colonial attacks on cultural practices; but whatever the cause, boys outnumbered girls in every age group, including the new-born. Other scholars in New Guinea noticed a tendency either to abandon or to neglect baby girls. Although the sex ratio was fairly equal at birth, boys outnumbered girls thereafter. During the 1980s a scholar in the Highlands of Irian Jaya noticed that the population was increasing rapidly, but so was masculinity, so that 'the sex ratio may be rising even among an expanding population'.[53] This common Melanesian pattern may be explained partly by differences in diet, whereby some (especially high-protein) foods were either reserved for men or forbidden to women in pregnancy or lactation, or after menopause; these restrictions expressed pervasive evaluations of male and female lives. Women also risked death in childbirth, in the absence of birth attendants.

One critical variable cuts across all others. Most Islanders practised shifting cultivation, but in Hawai'i, in the river deltas of Fiji, in New Caledonia and in the New Guinea Highlands, dense populations built up around continuous cultivation. Natural hazards provoked many Island peoples to limit population by abstinence, abortion, or selective infanticide. Only in Hawai'i and some other parts of Polynesia could the pressure of population be ignored. For these and other reasons, the quality (and length) of lives varied immensely and often, and depopulation was not unknown, from natural and human causes. Men's diets varied with rank, so that Big Men and chiefs ate much better (and oftener) than 'rubbish men' or commoners. Living standards also varied with climate. Coastal people enjoyed access to fish and shellfish. Highlanders were isolated from sea resources—and from malaria. Least fortunate were inland people on the highland fringes, who had access to malaria but not to fish. Away from the coast, diets centred upon taro or sweet potato, which must be eaten in bulk to yield adequate protein. Even within these broad categories, well-being was uneven. Motu and Mailu villages on the Papuan coast were sited in marginal environments, but by producing pottery and controlling trade they could usually ensure a flow of shells from Milne Bay, fairly fresh meat from the mainland, and sago from the Gulf of Papua. Their greatest risk was any interruption—natural or human—to trade.

Like other populations of the eighteenth century, Melanesians endured high infant death rates—possibly approaching 50 per cent. Mortality rates were especially high in the first year of life, and weaning onto the high-carbohydrate diets of adults was the most dangerous transition in anyone's lifetime. Life expectancy was short, although we cannot say how short. So widespread were practices of fertility control that we may infer a common anxiety about food resources, long after the environmental crises of the pioneering generations. Three conditions permitted some communities to sustain dense populations. One was plentiful arable land with reliable water—impossible in the atolls.

53 Gotschalk, 'Sela Valley', Appendix D.

A second was the development of cultigens and farming techniques which permitted continuous (or long-term) cultivation. A third was the absence of malaria. Where all these conditions were met, life expectancy could have been among the highest in the eighteenth-century world.

Magellan's companions were mistaken in assuming natural abundance and free consumption. Production always required intelligent management, most environments demanded strenuous labour, and natural hazards were compounded by competition which often spilled over into hostilities. Survival was a significant achievement, and affluence was both rare and precarious. By the ingenuity of their agriculture, the determination of cultivators and quarrymen, the mass production of pottery, mats and shell valuables, the confidence of their navigators, and the maintenance of networks, Islanders struggled to contain dangers and to transcend the limitations of their crops and tools. Over time, land management improved, and disasters were endured and mainly survived.

BIBLIOGRAPHIC ESSAY

The sources on land tenure, production and exchange are listed in the Introduction to Pacific Islands Bibliography at the end of chapter 1. So are the leading sources on the gender division of labour, but see also McDowell, 'Complementarity: The Relationship between Female and Male in the East Sepik Village of Bun, Papua New Guinea', in O'Brien and Tiffany, *Rethinking Women's Roles*.

To estimate pre-contact populations is difficult and politically delicate. Norma McArthur, *Island Populations of the Pacific*, is the essential starting point. A recent regional summary is Denoon, 'Pacific Island Depopulation'. For Hawai'i, see Stannard, *Before the Horror*, and Bushnell, '"The Horror" Reconsidered'. For Australia, see White and Mulvaney, 'How Many People?', in Mulvaney and White (eds), *Australians to 1788*. For New Zealand, see Pool, *Te Iwi Maori*; for French dependencies, Rallu, 'Population of the French Overseas Territories in the Pacific'; for Vanuatu generally, Bonnemaison, *The Tree and the Canoe*; for Aneityum, Spriggs, 'Vegetable Kingdoms'; and for New Caledonia, Roux, 'Traditional Melanesian Agriculture in New Caledonia'. For other islands, estimates are little more than guesses.

CHAPTER

4

DISCOVERING OUTSIDERS

Since at least the eighteenth century, European explorers and scholars have been reporting their 'discoveries' in the Pacific Islands. Descriptions of very different ways of organising social relations had a profound influence on European intellectuals, broadening their sense of social, political, cultural and economic possibilities. They assumed that the discovery of Europeans had equally profound effects among the Pacific Islanders who were simultaneously 'discovering' new ways of living and thinking. This chapter examines a sample of early cross-cultural encounters, from the sixteenth to the twentieth centuries, to try to grasp the ways in which some Islanders understood both the events and their implications for their own lives and ideas.

DISCOVERING?

Samoans and Tongans conceived of their islands as a complete universe of sea and lands, contained by the dome of the sky and divided into invisible layers containing the living places of gods. Below the sea was the realm of Pulotu, entered by the spirits of the aristocratic dead through an entrance under the sea, off the westernmost shore of the islands. They called the strangers *papālagi*, meaning 'sky bursters': when the strange ships sailed across the horizon, their utter unfamiliarity caused Islanders to suppose that they must have burst through the dome of heaven. The modern equivalent of Islanders discovering outsiders would be encounters with extra-terrestrials. The explorers' ships, appearance, clothing and manners suggested that they had come from another world.

The idea that the horizon delineated the edge of the world, beyond which lived spirits and gods, was also widespread in Melanesia. Some of this cosmology can be inferred from an encounter in 1930, when a party of gold prospectors passed westward through the Goroka valley in the eastern Highlands of New Guinea. Sole Sole and his fellow villagers of Gorohonota knew that their ancestors were often in their midst, and that dead people departed in that direction. Tearfully they welcomed back their ancestors and the recently dead, and spread the news in all directions:

we gave them a pig and also one of our men stole a knife from them. We all gathered around to look, we were pointing at them, and we were saying 'Aah, that one—that must be . . .' and we named one of our people who had died before. 'That must be him.' And we'd point to another one and say that that must be this other dead person . . . and we were naming them.

Gopie, from Gama village, was certain that one of the New Guinean carriers was his cousin Ulaline:

My cousin had been killed in a tribal fight. When he came towards me I saw half his finger missing, and I recognised him as my dead cousin. The reason his finger was cut off was that [when alive] he'd had too many children with his wife. His people had punished him by cutting off his little finger. When he came towards me I said to him, 'Cousin!' And he raised his eyebrows. So I knew it was definitely him.[1]

When Europeans and Islanders 'discovered' each other, the self-conscious European explorers were fully expecting to grapple with strange languages, customs and modes of living and thinking. Exploration was a familiar European process, backed by centuries of African, Mediterranean and American episodes. Islanders had many fewer such experiences to guide them. This seeming absence of precedents has gripped the imagination of many Western scholars, eager to reconstruct the ways in which Islanders imagined their universe, and how they conceived the extra-terrestrials who appeared, so to speak, out of the blue.

Some research produces disconcerting observations. Some first-contact events, reconstructed from the records of ships' logs, prove to have left no durable impression.[2] In other incidents the people were at least equally impressed by other Islanders who played supporting roles as servants and carriers for European expedition leaders. From the nineteenth century onwards, most first-contact encounters involved Polynesian missionaries, rather than the handful of Europeans who organised the evangelising programs. The scholarly emphasis on the very first cross-cultural encounters also tends to mask the fact that 'contact' was an extended process rather than a discrete incident. It is possible that that process was already old before the celebrated voyages by Cook, Bougainville, Vancouver and La Pérouse in the late eighteenth century. In chapter 2 and elsewhere Robert Langdon canvasses the possibility of South-East Asian, Spanish and other strangers being cast away on beaches throughout the northern and eastern Pacific. Similar misadventures must have involved Islanders themselves. 'First-contact' encounters are so called not because they were certainly the first cross-cultural meetings, but because they occurred in an era of purposeful European exploration by navigators, philosophers and scientists who defined the events as historic.

Some encounters clearly deserve the attention lavished on them. In Dening's terms, they were ethnographic moments, when both parties

1   Quoted in Connolly and Anderson, *First Contact*, 36–7.
2   e.g. Ron Adams, 'Nokwai—Sacrifice to Empire', in Merwick (ed.), *Dangerous Liaisons*, 23–40.

found that their social and philosophical categories were inadequate, and had to be expanded to comprehend new realities.[3] The strangers were usually invulnerable so long as they remained in their vessels, and Islanders were relatively secure on land; but the beach was a dangerous 'liminal' space where new concepts as well as new people and baffling behaviour had to be negotiated. And in trying to understand the Other, each experienced painful new understandings of Self.

The scale of the Islanders' known worlds varied. For some it was a few valleys whose inhabitants considered themselves the only humans. In the New Guinea Highlands, Huli people were unusually extensive traders, who conceived of their closest neighbours as sharing a remote but real common ancestor, whereas more distant people, albeit human, were not related to them. For others, the world comprised a number of nations living in different localities or on different islands made up of people similar to themselves, but with different languages and customs. The high islands of Polynesia and Micronesia were divided into often mutually hostile chiefdoms, where common culture and language created only precarious unity. The islands of Melanesia were a mosaic of tiny, warring polities. Outsiders—whether kin or unrelated—were divided into allies and enemies, with often only a fine dividing line between the two. Throughout the Islands, interactions with outsiders were mediated by careful protocol; alliances were usually made by gifts of women and valuables. The creation of kinship through strategic marriage alliances might offer some assurance of peace, but only expediency separated enemy from friend.

The possibility of mysterious super-humans was widely entertained. On the northern seaboard of New Guinea the legends of origin of many people told of a roaming god who came from the sea. Fijians and many Polynesian societies believed that, while common people belonged to the land, their chiefs were demi-gods from the sea. The religions of most Islanders contained beliefs about ancestors who became spirits after death and manifested themselves in strange forms. Thus, just as people today would interpret the sudden appearance of humanoids possessed of remarkable technology as 'extra-terrestrials' in the light of contemporary popular culture and imagining, so did Islanders construe outsiders in terms of their own ideas. So too did they construct appropriate ways to deal with them.

There are detailed accounts of how outsiders perceived Islanders as savages noble and ignoble, of the impact of Tahiti on Western humanist philosophy, and on the criteria by which Islanders were ranked in the stratified order of humanity imagined by European intellectuals (see chapter 1). But there is little evidence of Islanders' perceptions, other than the often baffled observations of the outsiders themselves. Except for testimony contained in a handful of recent studies, we can only speculate. What is clear from the written record, however, is that first encounters from the sixteenth to the twentieth century were generally tragic; they were fraught with misunderstanding born of different

3 Dening, *Islands and Beaches* and *Mr Bligh's Bad Language*.

perceptions, conflicting motives and mutual fears. Regardless of the behaviour and intentions of the outsiders, or how their motives were inferred by Islanders, or the assumptions of Islanders about the origin of the outsiders and the context of their existence, the dominant pattern was a 'sickening cycle of friendly welcome, misunderstanding, sullen retreats, occasional reconciliations, robberies and killings'.[4] Oskar Spate's words apply not only to encounters involving Spaniards, but to many later collisions.

EARLIEST ENCOUNTERS

In 1567 the Spaniards extended their quest for gold and souls from the Americas to the Pacific Ocean when Alvaro de Mendaña was despatched with two ships to find rich islands. The Spaniards had in mind the Biblical King Solomon's mines of Ophir. Agreements between Spain and Portugal blocked the expansion of the Spanish empire from the Americas to the Spice Islands (centred on the sultanates of Ternate and Tidore, based on islets off the coast of Halmahera, now eastern Indonesia), which were claimed by Portugal and were acquiring a separate colonial identity. Expansionist ambitions turned to the Pacific and hopes of finding Terra Australis. Mendaña's expedition of two ships with a crew of about 100 men, including Franciscan friars, set out to search for gold while conducting God's business of winning the souls of 'indians'. As Spate observed of conquistador ethics, 'the Indians were to mediate the gold to the Spaniards, the Spaniards to mediate the true God to the Indians'.

After months at sea, Mendaña's expedition sighted a small island in January 1568 (probably one of the islands of Tuvalu), but they sailed on for three weeks until they came upon a large island which they named Santa Isabel. Soon they found other large islands, naming them Guadalcanal, Florida, New Georgia and San Cristobal. The archipelago was named, optimistically, the Solomon Islands. The people of Santa Isabel came out to greet Mendaña's ships and initially friendly relations ensued; but what could the Islanders have thought of the songs and rituals of possession, and the instructions in making the sign of the cross and reciting the Lord's Prayer? Were they returning ancestors or spirits? What explanations did they propose for the strangers and their motives? How did they try to verify their theories? People of the New Guinea Highlands who first thought that white men and coastal people were ancestral spirits soon discovered that these beings defecated like men and that 'their shit smelled as ours did'.[5]

After initial politeness, an exchange of entertainments in which Islanders played their pan-pipes and Spaniards their guitars and fifes, and Mendaña and a chief exchanged names, relations soured. Islanders began to hide from their inquisitive visitors, and to alternate harass-

4   Spate, *The Spanish Lake*, 129.
5   In Connolly and Anderson's film, *First Contact*.

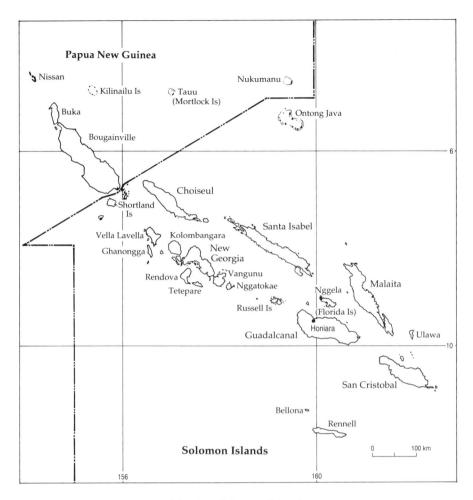

Map 14   Solomon Islands

ment with gestures of reconciliation, including gifts of human flesh. The issue was food, which the visitors demanded insatiably, taxing resources to the limit. On Guadalcanal the Spaniards' quest for pigs—among the greatest and scarcest treasures—led one man to ransack a village and take hostages. The Islanders killed and ate nine Spaniards in retaliation. In a counter massacre, the Spaniards mutilated the corpses of Islanders they had killed, to balance the atrocity of cannibalism. This cycle soon extended to San Cristobal. By August, five months after their arrival, Mendaña's expedition departed; lack of food impeded the search for gold. On their way home they came upon Namu in the Marshall Islands but—famished and diseased—they did not linger.

Similar encounters involved Portuguese navigators, from their East Indian bases of Ternate and Tidore. Since most of the Pacific was deemed a Spanish domain, Portuguese exploration concentrated on the westernmost islands, including some of the Carolines. They, too, sought for gold or other precious metals. Typical of the frustrating search was an expedition from Maluku to Sulawesi in 1525. It was blown off course to an atoll which was probably Ulithi in the western Carolines. The Islanders seemed delighted. 'And, in truth, as shown by the assured manner in which they went near the Portuguese, it appeared that they were a people who had never received any harsh treatment or harm whatsoever because they openly approached the strangers.' The Portuguese showed them metal samples:

> The inhabitants only recognized gold; by gesturing with their hands, they informed the Portuguese that this metal was found in a high mountain to the west of the island (possibly the Philippines).
> They had large proas. But since the Portuguese did not see the islanders use iron, they asked them how the proas were made. The islanders showed them fish spines that they used for cutting and that were such that the Portuguese were able to use them just like iron.[6]

The first recorded confrontation between Polynesians and Europeans was briefer but no less tragic than the experience of Melanesians. It occurred when Mendaña and his lieutenant Pedro de Quiros set off for the Solomon Islands again in 1595, undeterred by their experiences and aiming to establish a Christian colony. Mendaña took four ships and 378 men and women, including six friars. Their first landfall was a group of islands which they named Las Marquesas de Mendoza. The Polynesian inhabitants were much admired by Quiros, who regretted that such attractive people were destined for an eternity in hell. The Islanders welcomed them with celebration, but when they were invited aboard they rushed about grabbing everything they could lift, and cutting slices from sides of bacon and pieces of meat. The commander's lady fondled the heads of children on her visits ashore—the most sacred and untouchable part of the Polynesian body—and no doubt other acts of mutual cultural outrage occurred. The event quickly lost its friendly character; guns were fired and an Islander who refused to leave was wounded with a sword. His companions made threatening gestures and tried to beach the ship. Shooting followed. By the time the fleet left the archipelago two weeks later, Quiros estimated that about 200 Islanders had been killed.[7]

As the fleet crossed the Pacific, other islands were sighted, but luckily for their inhabitants, Mendaña did not anchor. Reaching the Solomon Islands again, he landed on an island which he named Santa Cruz. Some of its inhabitants greeted the strangers with arrows and received bullets in return, but friendlier relations were struck with another group, whose chief received them ashore and allowed them to begin work on their settlement. These friendly relations deteriorated when

---

6 Barros, *Terceira decada da Asia* (1563), quoted in Lessa, 'The Portuguese Discovery of the Isles of Sequeira', and reproduced in Hezel and Berg (eds), *Micronesia: Winds of Change*, 9–11.
7 Dening, *Islands and Beaches*, 9–10.

disillusioned colonists began to kill Islanders. Quiros suspected that they hoped to wreck the colony and force its abandonment. A bloody struggle erupted and disease broke out among the settlers. Mendaña and other leaders died, and after two months the colonists withdrew.

Passing New Guinea, the fleet arrived starving in Manila in early 1596. Quiros was still determined to create Mendaña's Christian colony, and to find Terra Australis—a land mass which European philosophers assumed must exist somewhere in the far south. In 1603 he won royal authorisation, two ships, 200 to 300 people with provisions for a year, and seed and animals to establish a colony. The fleet sailed in 1605. Its first brief but friendly landfall was Hao Atoll in the Tuamotus. The next was probably in the northern Cook Islands, where they were received with hostility, although Quiros reported some amorous encounters between his men and Island women. They reached Taumako Island, north-east of Santa Cruz, where they were received kindly with water and provisions, but Quiros kidnapped four young men in order to save their souls and to use them as interpreters—of whom three escaped overboard as the ship rounded the island of Tikopia. In May 1606 the ships reached a mountainous island in what is now Vanuatu. This Quiros named La Australia del Espiritu Santo. Here he determined to establish his New Jerusalem, but the people resisted from the first moment. A reconnaissance party was met by a great crowd who drew a line on the ground and indicated that both sides should lay down their arms—but the settlers advanced and a battle broke out. After some weeks, Quiros assessed the situation as hopeless and withdrew. The ships sailed north past Butaritari in Kiribati and on to Acapulco in Mexico.

This ill-fated venture had one more chapter when Luis Vaez de Torres's ship, separated from Quiros's expedition, sailed to southern New Guinea and the Philippines, through the strait between Australia and Papua which now bears his name. Before entering the strait, the expedition paused at Mailu, on St Bartholomew's Day. They landed the next day, and made signs of peace.

> They responded by brandishing their arms namely lances and shields, which was a sign of battle; notwithstanding this, we again made them signs of peace and they replied with shouts brandishing their arms. Seeing that we were losing time by treating them with further consideration we knelt down and saying a Pater Noster and an Ave Maria, Cierra España [a war-cry], we gave them a Santiago [an invocation to St James] and in that skirmish some fell dead, and we seized their gate and pressed on, shooting them as they fled. [After more skirmishing] we sacked the fortress and found a quantity of cocoanuts and mats on which they sleep and fishing nets and very large pearl shells; the pearls, because they are round and have no handles, they throw into the sea.

These meagre spoils were supplemented by fourteen youngsters who were captured, transported to Manila, baptised, and entrusted to the church. The Spaniards compounded senseless violence by an equally vacuous assumption of sovereignty over an island which they would never again locate.[8] Torres's voyage ended contacts between Spaniards and Melanesians. No doubt the apparent absence of gold, the prevalence of malaria, the belligerence of the people and their resistance to evangelism convinced the Spaniards to look elsewhere for gold and converts. They had found no resource to justify Melanesian exploration, and the prospects for settlement were grim. We cannot know what Melanesians thought when these violent, avaricious strangers disappeared across the horizon, but we can assume that they were mightily relieved. With hindsight it is clear that Melanesians were delivered (by the anopheles mosquito) from a particularly rapacious era of colonialism, allowing them to come into contact with Europe of the gentler late-nineteenth century, when the rights of indigenous peoples were gaining at least some recognition. A few communities had been invaded, harangued in a foreign language, and pressed into curious rituals. Some young people had been kidnapped, and no convincing explanation could account for this harassment. It had been impossible to predict the strangers' behaviour from day to day.

It was not, however, the end of a Spanish presence. Spanish authorities concentrated on the more realistic project of exploiting the trade of East Asia. As Spanish interest shifted north to the shipping routes connecting Mexico to the Philippines, Japan and China, Micronesians were involved in a long era of interaction, beginning in 1676. Guam had been claimed as part of the Viceroyalty of Mexico in 1565, but a century passed before an administration was established there, to victual galleons for the annual expedition between Manila and Mexico. These little islands had no intrinsic value to Spain, but regular supplies were ensured by subjecting the Islanders to the same discipline which was imposed in the Philippines—Christian conversion and iron control by religious authorities. Encounters with the Chamorro were first peaceful and based on the mutual desire for trade, but from 1668 an alliance between Spanish Jesuit missionaries and soldiers and Chamorro chiefs and leading landowners led to the creation of an oppressive hierarchy, which then provoked wars between sections of Chamorro and Spanish soldiers throughout the 1670s and 1680s. The Spaniards could not always impose their will, but in the Marianas the weight of Spanish numbers overwhelmed the Chamorros.

By 1695 the Spaniards had crushed resistance on Guam and on other islands of the Marianas, and the population was greatly reduced by 'pacification' campaigns, resettlement from scattered settlements to crowded villages where they were vulnerable to new infections—including smallpox. For Islanders on the galleon route, foreign contacts involved not only compulsory conversion and resettlement, but also exposure to the ruthless exactions of governors who sought to recoup the cost of purchasing their offices. Soldiers were seldom paid, and survived mainly by looting. Once the Chamorro rebellions failed, even conversion to Christianity offered no protection against institutional rapacity.

8   *Relacion Sumaria of Captain Don Diego de Prado y Tovar . . .*, cited by Barwick, *New Light on the Discovery of Australia*, 154–7.

Most Islanders quickly discovered that the strangers brought disease and death. An especially gruesome narrative concerns the impact of strangers on Yap. In 1843 the trader Andrew Cheyne, anchored off Yap awaiting permission to land, put ashore a feverish sailor. He soon recovered—but 'the Influenza has broken out among the natives at Tomal, and they are very much alarmed, never having had any disease like it before'. As Yapese died, their priests advised the chiefs that the strangers were responsible, and as the Islanders prepared to attack his ship, Cheyne decamped.[9] The full extent of Yapese casualties, from this and other introduced infections, cannot be known; but the population shrank from about 30,000 or even 50,000 to 7500 by the end of the century, and to 2500 by the 1940s. Similarly, the Islanders of Tanna drew the obvious conclusion from the fact that dysentery followed the first missionaries and smallpox the second.[10] In the eighteenth century many sailors carried tuberculosis, which was endemic to Western Europe but absent in the Islands, whose inhabitants were therefore highly vulnerable. Ships' captains were more alert to the risk of venereal infections, and sometimes tried to prevent infected sailors from contacting Island women; but some captains were casual, their inspections were inconclusive, and the sailors had usually spent many months yearning for female company. Some unfortunate Islanders learned that Spanish settlers did not possess enough food and provisions to sustain themselves, so that they resorted to pillage. Many Islanders also discovered that sailors would exchange almost anything for sex, and organised themselves accordingly. The circumstances of the first interactions— with both sides wary—limited these risks but did not eliminate them.

During the seventeenth century Spain's dominance of the Pacific began to be eroded by English and Dutch assaults. In particular the Dutch began to explore the Pacific from their trading bases in what is now Indonesia, seeking not gold and souls but new lands. Like the Spaniards, they sought Terra Australis, hoping to expand their East Indian realms. When Jan Carstensz (1623) found the arid west coast of Australia, it was not what he had hoped. Generally the Dutch had briefer contacts than the Spaniards and were less likely to interfere, since they wanted neither to evangelise nor to colonise islands with scant resources. However, violent incidents still occurred. Isaac LeMaire and Willem Schouten and their men were attacked by Islanders in the Tuamotus, who tried to disarm a party of sailors. They were attacked again by Tongans of Niuatoputapu, when a visit from a chief turned into a skirmish: LeMaire offended his hosts by refusing to take *kava* with a welcoming party.[11]

Most of these meetings took place on shipping routes. It was only in 1642 that the Dutch captain Abel Tasman called at Taitapu (Golden Bay), at the north end of the South Island of New Zealand. Sighting the ships, the Ngaati Tumatakokiri conferred anxiously on what sort of *waka* (canoes) these were, and what sort of beings were on board. Two canoes

9 Shineberg (ed.), *The Trading Voyages of Andrew Cheyne*.
10 Bonnemaison, *The Tree and the Canoe*, 53.
11 Howe, *Where the Waves Fall*, 79–80.

approached the vessels that evening, carrying (Salmond suggests) some of their bravest warriors, to 'inspect the ships more closely and to challenge them with incantations and ritual blasts of their shell trumpets. It is possible that they have decided that these were spirits of some sort, since . . . they commonly blew trumpets and shouted to frighten them away.' The Dutch drove them away with cannon fire. The next morning, a canoe returned and the Dutch offered them gifts and tried to persuade them aboard. An old man called out to the visitors in what was probably a *haka* (war chant) provoked by the exchange of challenges the night before. The Dutch tried to interpret the message, using a vocabulary given to them in Batavia, but since this contained Tongan rather than Maori, it was of little use. More canoes gathered. The Dutch held a council, sending a small boat between the ships for this purpose. On its return trip, a canoe rammed the boat at high speed, then attacked the occupants, killing four. The Dutch fired on the canoes while they rescued survivors, then sailed away.[12]

If Tasman expected other meetings to proceed in the same violent fashion, he was disabused. He was welcomed by Tongans on Tongatapu and observed that no one carried weapons. His barber and surgeon observed that some women 'felt the sailors shamelessly in the trouser front' and clearly 'desire fleshly intercourse'. A similar encounter to that of Tasman at Taitapu occurred between Jacob Roggeveen and Samoans in 1722. Roggeveen's first contact in the western islands of the archipelago was civil, but when he called in at Tutuila in the east, a party of his men was ambushed and murdered. The killers had apparently come to Tutuila from the western islands and their actions may have been acts of revenge for some earlier insult.[13] In view of the radically different expectations which strangers and Islanders brought to the same encounters, such violence was only too common, and impossible for either party to predict.

The image of the South Seas as islands of ferocious savages was transformed by accounts of Tahiti by the French explorer Louis-Antoine de Bougainville.[14] His rhapsodic depiction of an island paradise was quickly taken up by philosophers, influencing European ideas about the condition of humankind in a 'state of nature'. Polynesians must have perceived Europeans as equally exotic, and their views of human nature were similarly challenged by the strangers on their shores. Tahitians (like other Polynesians) were fastidious about cleanliness and personal hygiene, and abhorred hairiness, carefully shaving and plucking unwanted facial and bodily hair. Stunted, bearded sailors stinking of sweat and infested with lice must have revolted them, provoking them to wonder how such uncouth beings came to possess such enviable technology and materials. The strangers had no women, and—judging by their lust—felt that deficiency acutely. While many Polynesian women were barred from open-sea fishing, women obviously must have travelled on voyaging canoes. Tahitians must have been perplexed

12 Salmond, *Two Worlds*, 77–82.
13 Gilson, *Samoa, 1830–1900*.
14 Thomas, 'The Force of Ethnology', 30–1.

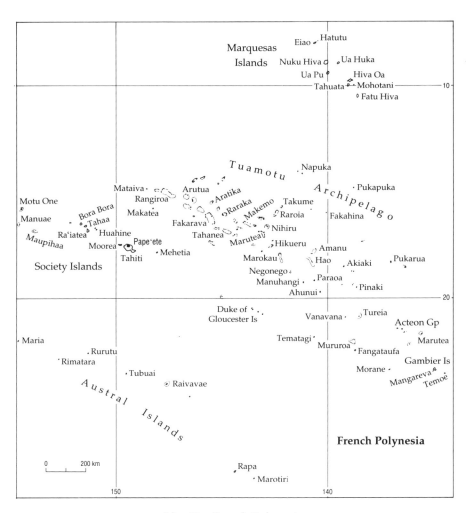

Map 15   French Polynesia

by the all-male complements of these expeditions. Indeed the absence of women might have reinforced the misconception that the strangers were supernatural. Polynesian gods were not always virtuous or heroic: many looked and behaved strangely, malignantly and lasciviously.

Tahitians first met Europeans when the English naval captain Samuel Wallis (1767) moored off the east coast and he was greeted by a hundred canoes filled with men waving banana-leaves and orating. Some of those in the canoes went on board after further speeches and throwing their leaves. The sailors gestured that they wanted pigs and chickens, offering beads, knives and ribbons. On board ship, the Tahitians responded in much the same way as the Marquesans in 1595, helping themselves to everything they could find, and removing nails from the ship's structure—adding weight to Howe's contention that the accepted protocol for strangers was to hand over their possessions:

castaways or weary travellers could usually expect a welcome, provided that they posed no obvious threat. They would be met with long speeches and other customary greetings. The newcomers then surrendered what possessions they held, such as their canoe, fishing gear, and any remaining food to their hosts as a sign of humble acceptance of and token compensation for the food and shelter they would be offered. If later they wished to leave, they might be supplied with a canoe and provisions, and given a send off. Such rites of reciprocity and the guests' acknowledgments of their hosts' authority were never understood by European explorers.[15]

The sailors repelled the Tahitians with gunfire. According to Howe, 'from the Tahitian point of view, this was an outrage. Their welcome had been abused, and the newcomers were acting as enemies rather than submissive friends.' The conventions of greeting in Polynesia were certainly conditioned by common understandings, and encounters with markedly different cultures were rare. Most greeting rituals were designed to assure hosts that the visitors came in peace, acknowledged by the giving and receiving of gifts, the exchange of speeches of introduction, and the removal of alien spirits which might have accompanied the visitors. Hosts assumed an obligation to treat guests honourably. It is likely that first encounters with European explorers produced anomie, in which conventions were quickly suspended or abandoned due to mutual incomprehension. In any event expectations may not have been as clear, or as universal, as Howe's description of them, and it is unlikely that all Islanders in all circumstances observed all rules. Until European ships anchored in island bays, however, most chance arrivals would indeed have been powerless castaways, with little choice but to throw themselves on their hosts' mercy.

Wallis's vessel anchored off Matavai Bay, and tense trading ensued. On several occasions his crew opened fire on Tahitians who came too close. A few days later, groups of naked young women were displayed in what appears to have been a ploy to distract the crew, because as soon as the sailors began looking at the women, men threw stones, provoking musket fire and cannon balls. This was followed a day later by gestures of apparent submission by the Tahitians who once again gathered in hundreds, again bearing banana-leaves, which the English construed as emblems of peace. The Tahitians later attempted another attack, to which the British retaliated with further cannon fire, causing many deaths. The Tahitians then began to offer women. Howe explains: 'Tahitian chiefs, intimidated by British firepower, had discovered an effective way of placating the strangers . . . some women of low birth were ordered to prostitute themselves as a political strategy. Not only did this ensure the goodwill of the English, it also brought considerable economic advantage to the chiefs.'[16] When Bougainville called nine months later, his ship was immediately surrounded by canoe-loads of young women, most of them naked, and by the gestures of the men the French understood that the women were being offered for sex. Cook, arriving soon afterwards, received much the same welcome, as he did in

15 Howe, *Where the Waves Fall*, 85.
16 *Ibid.*, 88.

Hawai'i. The alacrity, indeed determination, with which Polynesian women offered themselves to seamen has made a major contribution to the legend of the South Seas as a libertarian paradise. While some observers interpreted their actions as evidence of the exploitation of females by their menfolk, others commented on the apparent independence of Polynesian women in trading their services.[17] Not at once apparent were some inevitable consequences; not only venereal infections, but the stealthier progress of tuberculosis. In the extreme case of the Marquesas, the population fell to less than 5 per cent of its eighteenth-century levels in the first hundred years of interaction.

Material considerations undoubtedly influenced women to offer themselves and men to abet them. The strangers seemed to possess everything except women, and at once exhibited sexual enthusiasm and willingness to exchange the objects coveted by their hosts. But at first there may have been other motives. It is likely that the strangers were believed to be supernatural. Polynesians believed that aristocrats were distinguished from common people by the divine *mana* of the gods from whom they traced descent. Accordingly, chiefs often exercised a kind of *droit de seigneur* with women of lesser rank. Sahlins points to the Hawaiian custom of *wawahi* (to break open) by which virgin daughters of commoners were offered to a ranking chief in the hope of bearing his child. Such children were welcomed by the woman's eventual husband and accorded the status of a *punahele* (favourite child). Such connections were useful to commoner families. Sahlins points to:

> an incident that took place when the British left Kauai for the second time, in March 1779, some thirteen months after the original visit. A number of men and women came out to the ships in canoes; and while the women remained alongside, the men, following their instructions, went on board and deposited the navel cords of new-born children into cracks of the decks. Commenting on the incident, a modern Hawai'ian authority on traditional customs observed: 'Cook was first thought to be the god Lono, and the ship his "floating island". What woman wouldn't want her baby's *piko* [umbilical cord] there?'[18]

Maori recollections of Cook's visits also suggest that the first explanation was supernatural. Horeta Te Taniwha described his childhood encounter:

> when I was a very little boy, a vessel came to Whitianga (Mercury Bay). . . . We . . . were there according to our custom of living for some time on each of our blocks of land, to keep our claim to each, and that our fire might be kept alight on each block, so that it might not be taken from us by some other tribe. We lived at Whitianga, and a vessel came there, and when our old men saw the ship they said it was an *atua*, a god, and the people on board were *tupua*, strange beings or goblins . . . As our old men looked at the manner in which they came on shore, the rowers pulling with their backs to the bows of the boat, the old people said, 'Yes, it is so: these people are goblins; their eyes are at the back of their heads . . .' When these goblins came

17 Chappell, 'Shipboard Relations', 131–48.
18 Sahlins, *Historical Metaphors and Mythical Realities*, 40–1.

on shore we (the children and women) took notice of them, but we ran away from them into the forest, and the warriors alone stayed . . .; but, as the goblins stayed sometime, and did not do any evil to our braves, we came back one by one, and gazed at them, and we stroked their garments with our hands, and we were pleased with the whiteness of their skins and the blue of the eyes of some of them.

These goblins began to gather oysters, and we gave some *kumara*, fish and fern root to them. These they accepted, and we (the women and children) began to roast cockles for them; and as we saw these goblins were eating *kumara*, fish and cockles, we were startled, and said, 'Perhaps they are not goblins like the Maori goblins.' These goblins went into the forest, and also climbed up the hill to our *pa* [fort] at Whitianga. They collected grasses from the cliffs, and kept knocking at the stones on the beach, and we said 'Why are these acts done by these goblins?' We and the women gathered stones and grass of all sorts and gave to these goblins. Some of the stones they liked, and put them into their bags, the rest they threw away! and when we gave them the grass and the branches of trees they stood and talked to us, or they uttered the words of their language. Perhaps they were asking questions, and, as we did not know their language, we laughed, and these goblins also laughed, so we were pleased.

. . . There was one supreme man in that ship. We knew that he was the lord of the whole by his perfect gentlemanly and noble demeanour. He seldom spoke but some of the goblins spoke much. But this man did not utter many words: all that he did was to handle our mats and hold our *mere*, spears, and *waha-ika* [fish-mouth spears], and touched the hair of our heads. He was a very good man, and came to us—the children—and patted our cheeks, and gently touched our heads. His language was a hissing sound, and the words he spoke were not understood by us in the least. We had not been long on board of the ship before this lord of these goblins made a speech, and took some charcoal and made marks on the deck of the ship, and pointed to the shore and looked at our warriors. One of our aged men said to our people, 'He is asking for an outline of this land'; and that old man stood up, took the charcoal, and marked the outline of the Ika-a-Maui [the North Island].[19]

Te Taniwha's account described events in November 1769, when the *Endeavour* sailed into Whitianga harbour and stayed for twelve days, while Cook visited settlements and Joseph Banks and Daniel Solander searched for new species of plants and useful minerals. Salmond points out that the term *tupua* (translated as goblins) refers to 'visible beings or objects of supernatural origin, regarded with a mixture of terror and awe and placated with *karakia* (ritual chants) or offerings. If they took a human-like shape, it was thought that they could not eat human foods.'[20]

Much of the debate about Islanders' perceptions concerns the character of Cook. During his lifetime he was highly regarded as a navigator and explorer, not only in his native England, but also among Europeans and North Americans, who guaranteed safe passage to his expeditions even when war prevailed. In death, he assumed legendary status among Europeans. 'In every corner of the earth there are wayside

19 Salmond, *Two Worlds*, 87–8.
20 *Ibid.*

shrines to Captain Cook—cairns to say he was here, plaques to remember the remembering of him there. His relics are in glass cases on shelves, in safes of five continents.'[21] The difficult question is whether Hawaiians saw him in the same light. According to the now-dominant scholarly interpretation, in Hawai'i Cook was seen and treated as a god. Both of his arrivals in 1778 and 1779 coincided with the *makahiki* festival which celebrated the symbolic return of one of the principal gods, Lono. During the annual festival, images representing Lono were paraded round the islands. Taxes were collected by the highest chiefs and the people celebrated the arrival of the god as a sign of the renewal of the earth's fertility in a period of leisure, feasting, sports and other amusements. Cook's first voyage approximated the ritual progress of Lono, so that when he reappeared the following year during the *makahiki*, he seemed to confirm the suspicion that he was the incarnation of Lono:

> Cook came from the sea, as Lono had promised he would, and Cook's ships had tall masts and white sails, shaped very like the upright sticks and swaths of kapa cloth that were carried in the *makahiki* procession to announce the presence of Lono. Cook's course followed that of the main procession, which always went around the islands in a clockwise direction, and he chose to put in for a long stay at Kealakekua, the home of the chief whose exploits had become part of the Lono myth and the site of an important *heiau* dedicated to Lono.[22]

On this view, that misapprehension probably led to Cook's death. A cutter from one of Cook's ships had been appropriated at Kealakekua, and Cook went ashore with an armed party, intending to take the chief Kalaniopuu hostage to secure its return. A hostile crowd gathered and, after an altercation, Cook's party was attacked and Cook was slain. Gavan Daws, following Sahlins, describes the event as predictable in terms of prevailing beliefs. The islands were divided into opposed secular and sacred factions, and in the culminating phase of the *makahiki* it was the practice for a challenge to occur between the warriors escorting the priests of Lono and god's effigy, and the warriors of the ruling chief of the island, thus ending the period of the god's ascendancy.

Howard and Borofsky propose another perspective—that Cook's reluctance to make liberal use of firearms contributed to his death. 'A less humanistic man, a person more concerned in demonstrating Western weaponry, might have left the island alive, independent of whatever ritual identity Hawaiians sought to place on him.'[23] From a Polynesian point of view, Cook, his ships and his men may have seemed supernatural, but they were greatly outnumbered and presented tempting targets. The attribution of supernatural powers did not necessarily deny the possibility of attack and expropriation.

A more radical revision has been developed by Gananath Obeyesekere, who argues that Hawaiians could not have mistaken

21 Dening, *Mr Bligh's Bad Language*, 172.
22 Daws, *Shoal of Time*, 26.
23 Howard and Borofsky, *Developments in Polynesian Ethnology*, ch. 8.

Cook for a god, in view of the many human failings exhibited by him and his crew, and that his apotheosis as a *European* legend was an intrinsic element of the justification of European imperialism. This iconoclastic assault delighted the Hawaiian scholar Lilikala Kame'eleihiwa, who grasped the rhetorical opportunity with both hands:

> The noted Hawaiian scholar Haunani-Kay Trask often dismisses Cook as 'a syphilitic, tubercular racist', and when I teach that part of Hawaiian history I relate to my students that he brought venereal disease, violence, and, eventually, an unrelenting wave of foreigners, once his journals had been published in Europe.
>
> From the Hawaiian perspective, however, the best part about Cook's visit is that we killed him, as the *mana* (spiritual power) of his death accrues to us. [Also] we can defend our honor by declaring that at least *we* killed Cook, and having done so we rid the world of another evil *haole* (white man).[24]

Kame'eleihiwa's review is more explicitly political than most, and the argument is by no means resolved. Sahlins's original analysis enjoys support among those most familiar with the evidence. The debate has since been revived by the publication of Sahlins's book-length response. Recapitulating the extensive historical evidence that the Hawaiians believed Cook to be Lono, he offers a trenchant critique of the application of politically expedient interpretations of the past, shaped by 'bourgeois practical rationality', which ignores the culturally specific world-view of eighteenth-century Hawaiians.[25] The waves caused by this interchange do suggest the hazards of reconstructing Hawaiian perceptions after two eventful centuries.

Dening's study of the mutiny on the *Bounty* has generated one of the most suggestive reconstructions of Islander perceptions. Tahitians had to deal with Captain Bligh and his crew collecting breadfruit plants; then, after they had sent Bligh and his loyalists on their way by open boat, with Fletcher Christian and the mutineers; and eventually with the Royal Navy hunting down the mutineers. Tahitian cosmology made provision for receiving and domesticating powerful strangers from the sea. From Wallis's arrival onwards, Tahitians tried with varying success to make the strangers conform to these rituals, whereby their alarming power was rendered understandable, predictable—and to an extent manageable. In this light we may perhaps grasp the significance of the ritually powerful feather girdles, signs of the god 'Oro, which were 'the currency of authority. They conferred title and rank.' One such girdle worn by Pomare of Tahiti (see below) transformed his raw power into authority, and when Captain Bligh returned to Matavai Bay, in pursuit of the *Bounty* mutineers, he saw this girdle and made a rough drawing of it.

> The Tahitians had sewn into the feather girdle a thatch of auburn hair belonging to Richard Skinner, one of the Bounty mutineers ... [and Bligh]

---

24 Lilikala Kame'eleihiwa's review in *Pacific Studies* xvii: 2 (1994), 111–18.
25 Sahlins, *How 'Natives' Think*.

was mystified that somebody as insignificant as Skinner should be remembered in so sacred an object . . . Skinner was the ship's barber. He had astounded the Tahitians . . . by producing a barber's model head and wigs styled in the latest fashion from London. In Tahitian eyes, Skinner was somebody special. As a barber, he had a special power to touch *tapu* places. And his own head was red—*tapu*, as special as a parakeet's feather. One could wave a red feather to catch 'Oro's attention in prayer: one could sacrifice it to Pomare's sovereignty: one could do it with a lock of a stranger's auburn hair as well . . .

Bligh saw something else . . . a British red pennant sewn into the body of the girdle, as a lappet or fold of its own . . . It was the pennant that [Wallis's crew] had erected on a pole on June 26, 1767, when he took possession of Tahiti for King George III. The Tahitians had taken down the symbol of English sovereignty and incorporated it into a symbol of sovereignty of their own.[26]

Tahitians around Matavai Bay observed strangers intermittently from 1767 onwards, and were alert to the divisions which led to the *Bounty* mutiny and to the ruthless hunt for mutineers. Over a generation they learned about the strangers' sexual enthusiasms, and must have noticed the disease and death which so often accompanied their visits. They were awed by the military power which foreign ships deployed, and Pomare tried with some success to harness that power to his ambitions. The ritual incorporation of foreign symbols of authority is suggestive: in the generation of random contacts, Tahitians saw no need to overthrow their social and ideological categories. Both the collective *mana* of Britain expressed in the red pennant, and that of individuals like Skinner, could be accommodated within existing conceptions.

One of the most persuasive attempts at making general sense of Polynesian perceptions was developed by Pearson,[27] who proposed that responses conformed to three phases: outright hostility, then a caution born of fear and perplexity, and finally ceremonial welcoming. Pearson was less convincing in proposing that Polynesians shared expectations about responsibilities between strangers and hosts. In his view, boats and property should be handed over; hosts should sustain and protect visitors, and equip them with boats and victuals for the next leg of their voyage. Implicit in his argument is the assumption that Islanders either had nothing like a European concept of private property, or operated in terms of radically different beliefs about ownership. Campbell points out several flaws in this explanation for the accusations of theft which so often soured European accounts.[28] Neither Islanders nor Europeans regarded their first meetings as normal, and often behaved with unusual restraint. Again, many (possibly all) Island societies had very clear ideas about property: thieves were often severely punished, which demonstrates that their actions were understood as theft, whether from other Islanders or from strangers. Individuals who tried to appropriate iron or clothing from visiting ships often exhibited signs of guilt or

26 Dening, *Mr Bligh's Bad Language*, Act 2, 207–8.
27 'The Reception of European Voyagers'.
28 'European Polynesian Encounters: A Critique of the Pearson Thesis'.

embarrassment. These episodes are better understood as the breaking of rules, than as culturally legitimate expropriations. Above all, there were many instances when Polynesians made no attempt to appropriate the foreign ships or their exotic cargo.

FIRST ENCOUNTERS IN THE TWENTIETH CENTURY

The sharpest insights come from studies of recent episodes in Papua New Guinea, where mutual discoveries still occurred in the 1930s, and where scholars have recorded the recollections of Papua New Guineans. Schieffelin and Crittenden, who reconstructed these experiences in an account of the Hides–O'Malley expedition in 1935, comment that

> The arrival of the first outsiders is usually recalled as an exciting but deeply unsettling event of apparently cosmological import. Strange Beings broke into their world from outside its known horizons. Sometimes these Beings were thought to be mythical heroes coming back to their lands of their origins; sometimes they were thought to be ancestral beings returning. The people were filled with astonishment, fear and wonder at these creatures and sometimes feared that their arrival was the portent of dire world upheaval.[29]

The Hides–O'Malley expedition of forty-two men made a six-month journey into the interior, passing through 1800 kilometres of country unknown to Europeans and supporting large populations quite unlike those of the coast. Hides and O'Malley were Australian officials leading native police from coastal regions with long contact with outsiders. They had peaceful intentions, yet about fifty people were shot, fending off aggression, real or perceived.

On the Great Papuan Plateau, three peoples had not previously sighted Europeans, but had been receiving steel tools through their trading networks. These were accepted with mixed feelings. While some welcomed their remarkable efficiency, other groups such as the Onabasulu were disconcerted:

> They suspected that these strange objects were things of Malaiya [a legendary Origin place] . . . They were things that should not be touched or used by mortal men. Now they were moving back towards their origin point and many Onabasulu feared their owners . . . would soon follow.
>
> In the anxious discussion during the days preceding the days of the patrol's arrival, one of the leaders . . . proposed a course of action. 'Axes and bushknives are their children,' he said! 'They are coming to reclaim them.' He told all those who owned these implements to bring them . . . [and] they could be gathered and returned to the Beings when they arrived. Then perhaps they would go away quickly, and disaster would be averted. Otherwise they would search for them. 'Do not try and hide these things in the forest', he warned, 'for they will cry out, and their parents will hear them and come after them. Gather and return them all at the same time.' As the patrol drew nearer, even people who had ignored or scoffed at the idea . . . brought their axes and bushknives in . . . [and] laid them out in the main hall of the long house. [pp. 68, 81]

29 Schieffelin and Crittenden, *Like People You See in a Dream*, 3.

Hides was puzzled by the refusal to accept gifts, and by their hostility and fear. The reaction of one elder was typical:

> the patrol had emerged out of the forest virtually without any warning. 'We jumped [with surprise]', he said. 'No one had seen anything like this before or knew what it was. When they saw the clothes on [the Europeans] and the others, they thought they were like people you see in a dream; these must be spirit people (*kesame*) coming openly, in plain sight.

When the expedition moved on to the Tari basin, it entered from the direction of the enemies of the Tari, who feared the people of the plateau as cannibals and witches. The Tari explained the strangers in terms of their beliefs in ambiguous spirit beings called *dama*. According to one man,

> On the afternoon of April 21, 1935, he was weeding his garden. Glancing up he saw a group of 'strange' men standing at the edge of the bush about 150m away. Most of them had dark skins but their bodies were covered with unknown material. A number of them held what appeared to be wooden staves. Others carried regularly-shaped burdens, some on their shoulders and others slung on poles . . . The most frightening feature of the group was the two creatures who stood at the front. Their skins were so pale they seemed to glow, and their feet and their lower legs were covered with something. The only creatures Telenge knew of who was said to have pale skins, were ghosts or powerful spirits. These creatures then must be *Dama*, a conclusion also reached by other men who gazed in amazement from other parts of the garden.
>
> Telenge was so frightened by the apparition that had appeared at the garden's edge that he took his bow and arrows which Huli men carried at all times, and hid them in some long grass. *Dama* should not be provoked.[30]

A prominent Huli leader sought to assert his authority over the *dama*, bravely confronting them and making speeches apparently telling them that their gifts of axes, beads and cloth were not wanted, and trying to advise them which route they should take. His motive was apparently to show leadership and win renown, by deflecting the patrol from populated areas where they might bring disaster. In contrast, a younger aspiring leader sought to befriend the patrol leaders, perhaps to win status and spiritual gifts.[31]

Elderly Wola people also recalled their encounter with the expedition, believing that its members were ghosts or ancestor spirits.

> [Some] people, seeing the blackened teeth of the carriers and police (the result of chewing betel nuts) thought they were confronted with malevolent forest spirits; grotesque walking heaps of vegetation, with human-like limbs and features, that lurk in dark regions of the forest to kill and eat the unwary: 'We said there are bush spirits coming! their teeth are black like pyt berries. Bush spirits are coming, their teeth like pong fruits, black, real black like pyt fruits, they're coming.' Man-eating things, we said they were. We'd seen nothing like it before.[32]

---

30 Bryant Allen and Stephen Frankel, 'Across the Tari Furoro', in *ibid.*, 101.
31 *Ibid.*
32 Paul Sillitoe, 'From the Waga Furari to the Wen', in *ibid.*, 150.

Not all Wola agreed. One man believed that the spirit of his ancestors had returned to seek revenge for past wrongs. Another thought that the white men were deities who had fallen from the sky and were bringing pearl-shells to share. And other explanations were offered, such as a legend involving a dark-skinned and a fair-skinned brother, suggesting that one of the white strangers might be the white brother returning to the world. Many of the difficulties and violent incidents had to do with the fact that the patrol became increasingly dependent on local food supplies and, like Mendaña before them, overtaxed the resources of their hosts. When people refused to trade, the hungry police helped themselves, raiding gardens and killing pigs.

Western New Guineans discovered outsiders even later, and in even more baffling circumstances. Until the twentieth century, Dutch authorities made no move to interrupt the trade in sago, birds of paradise and slaves from New Guinea to Maluku, and the traders had no cause to travel beyond the coast. Dutch scientific expeditions between 1907 and 1913 tried to climb snow-covered Mount Trikora. With the resources of the Dutch East Indies, these expeditions were much larger than Australian patrols, and involved Dayak carriers and Dutch East Indian troops, led by European scientists. The East Indian soldiers, as good Muslims, were appalled when they were smeared with pig blood in a friendship ceremony. Similar expeditions were mounted by British scientists, from 1909, to scale Puncak Jaya. The leaders had some interest in physical anthropology. Once they reached the mountains therefore, they wanted to measure heads, 'an operation so appalling that large strips of cloth had to be offered before they could be tempted to surrender their bodies to the Inquisitors. Some of the older men, indeed, trembled so violently during the process that they were hardly capable of remaining on their feet.' During the second British expedition, some mountain families came to meet the strangers, and begged for food. The expedition could not feed them all, and sent them home; but before they arrived home, thirty or forty died. Whether they were killed by hunger or an epidemic, their confidence in the strangers was remarkable—and misplaced.[33]

West New Guinea was a matter of indifference to the Dutch until the end of World War II, when Indonesian nationalists seized most of Indonesia, leaving only some eastern provinces under Dutch control. During the 1950s a massive effort was mounted to explore, control and 'develop' the province, but the effort was much too late to detach it from the rest of Indonesia. When the Dutch departed in 1962, they left behind them an estimated 717,055 people, of whom a quarter had not been brought under any administration. When West New Guinea became the Indonesian province of Irian Jaya, it was closed to most research, and the last episodes of first contact have probably not been studied.

Further east, in what is now Papua New Guinea, mountains and heavy rainfall also delayed the advance of colonial frontiers until very

33 C. G. Rawlings, *The Land of the New Guinea Pygmies*, and A. F. R. Wollaston, 'An Expedition to Dutch New Guinea', quoted by Ploeg, 'First Contact in the Highlands of Irian Jaya'.

recent times. Telefolmin people's first impressions of Australian *kiaps* (patrol officers) could hardly have been worse. A patrol post opened in 1948, and a mission station two years later. In 1953 some men took exception to sexual offences against Telefolmin women, and killed *kiaps* and New Guinean policemen. Their first sustained exposure to the intrusive culture was a ten-year prison term. Their Wopkaimin neighbours—even less accessible by patrols—learned much from these encounters. In 1957 a *kiap* reached Tumgunabip, and

> everyone fled except our *kamokim* (leader). The kiap was accompanied by policemen, carriers, and a Telefolmin interpreter. The interpreter told the *kamokim* we had to build a rest house . . . Then the policemen demanded that the *kamokim* kill his pig and arrange for other food to be brought to Tumgunabip. They killed the *kamokim*'s hunting dog to demonstrate their guns. The *kamokim* was frightened and angry and reluctantly gave away his pig for some soap, matches, salt and cloth. Women brought taro while the men fully armed themselves and secretly surrounded Tumgunabip. One brave man joined the *kamokim* but they were unsuccessful in negotiating for some steel knives for the food they presented to the kiap. Although the men felt they had been treated unfairly, they in the end, hid their weapons and peacefully returned to Tumgunabip because they were afraid that if they attacked the patrol, the government would retaliate against them as harshly as they had against the Telefolmin . . .[34]

Wopkaimin were 'discovering' very different outsiders than (say) the Tahitians of the 1770s. These modern strangers enjoyed a vast predominance in weaponry, and behaved as if they exercised legitimate authority. A body of knowledge (the experience of the Telefolmin, no doubt reinforced by the interpreter) informed their perceptions and guided their actions. So different were the circumstances, and so different were the participants, that they can scarcely be compared. In one respect however the parallels are arresting. Within a generation of this incident, the Wopkaimin world was transformed by the arrival of gold-mining, just as surely as the Hawaiian world was reconstructed by traders and permanent settlers.

In general, the self-conscious explorers and scientific investigators were more baffling than their more mundane successors. They expected Islanders to be exotic, so they were seldom disappointed; and they were acting out dramas scripted by Europeans, for quite specific audiences. Joseph Banks and the other naturalists wanted to be understood (and acclaimed) by the Royal Society and other scientists. Nearly two centuries later, the Leahy brothers—Australian gold prospectors in the New Guinea Highlands—had the foresight to take colour film and movie cameras, recording the expected puzzlement of Highlanders for the entertainment of Australians. Whether the explorers measured skulls or filmed New Guineans 'discovering' mirrors, they expected to defy Islanders' comprehension.

As often and as much as possible, Islanders tried to squeeze these strangers, their commodities and technologies, and their bizarre be-

---

34 Hyndman, 'A Sacred Mountain of Gold'.

haviour, into pre-existing categories. One of the least understood encounters is also one of the most revealing. A prospecting expedition led
by twin brothers with sixteen carriers marched through Huli country in
the southern Highlands of Papua in 1934. Unlike other explorers, these
adventurers resolutely deterred human contact. Their method was 'to
come in like a brass band. You don't beg your pardon at all. You walk in
as if you have been in the country for a hundred years.' The party
camped in a fresh spot every night and flatly refused to engage local
carriers. They stole pigs and other foodstuffs, made no attempt to
exchange goods, and shot any owners who resisted. Huli witnesses
remember in great detail the killing of at least fifty of their kin.

How, then, did Huli understand these tragedies? At least three
categories might accommodate the killers. Huli and their neighbours
were construed as descendants of a common ancestor. Huli also
acknowledged distant peoples to whom they claimed no relationship.
Then there were *dama* spirits, related and unrelated, benevolent or
malign. At first sight the strangers fitted best into the *dama* category: the
wood which they cut down did not bear the marks of proper stone axes,
and their killing power was awesome:

> I was at Pimbano when I heard that *dama* were coming. We had never heard
> people actually saying this before . . . I went with a kinsman down to
> Biangoanda. We were coming down a stream, near a house, when we noticed
> a man standing in a ditch. His heart was hanging out of his chest . . . What
> had killed him? We looked down and we could see footprints, but they had
> no toes.

For a variety of reasons the strangers did not conform to any *dama*
stereotypes, any more than they conformed to human ones. Neither
then, nor now, could Huli reach agreement on explaining these
strangers. Almost all other strangers of the same vintage were quickly
classified—because they entered into relationships of exchange which
definitively made them humans. These homicidal visitors, who refused
all human relationships, created a riddle which was impossible to
solve.[35]

In all these mystifying encounters, the first step was to accommodate
strangers into categories of kinship, social status, alliance or enmity, or
supernatural conditions which were the language of all human relationships in the Islands. Only when strangers failed or refused to conform to these categories were new forms of explanation required.
Missionaries, following in the footsteps of explorers, were often the
apostles of these forms of understanding the world.

MATERIAL RELATIONS

Once Europeans had encompassed Pacific Islands in their maps, and
Islanders in their categories of humanity, rather different kinds of

---

35 Chris Ballard, work in progress.

interaction followed. With the establishment of mutually beneficial material relations during the eighteenth and early nineteenth centuries, Islanders came into contact with strangers whose interests were simpler and more comprehensible. These were no less threatening. Whaling ships found their way into the rich waters of the South Seas from distant ports in the Atlantic, and later from Sydney. The great distances and long periods at sea required these ships to seek provisions in the Islands, so they carried trade goods. At first these were lengths of flattened iron (used to fasten casks and barrels), fishhooks and nails, axes and knives. Shineberg quotes the captain of a whaler in the Ellice Islands (now Tuvalu): 'It is astonishing to see in what weather these poor unenlightened people will venture five or six miles from the land, in their light canoes, to obtain a few pieces of iron hoop, a fishhook or, the ultimatum of their riches, a knife.'[36] Later, Islanders also sought cloth, beads, mirrors, scissors and firearms. People were prepared to give in exchange their highly prized pigs, and yams, taro, breadfruit and bananas, as well as the right to collect fresh water and to take leave ashore. Coins were of no interest at first, although some chiefs wore them as ornaments. Mariner, an English youth captured by Tongans in 1806, recorded his attempts to convince his chiefly captor Finau of the uses of money. Finau was unimpressed:

'If', said he, 'it were made of iron, and could be converted into knives, axes, and chisels, there would be some sense in placing a value on it; but as it is, I see none. If a man', he added, 'has more yams than he wants, let him exchange some of it away . . . Certainly money is much handier, and more convenient, but then, as it will not spoil by being kept, people will store it up, instead of sharing it out, as a chief ought to do, and thus become selfish; whereas, if provisions were the principal property of a man, and it ought to be, as being the most useful and the most necessary, he could not store it up, for it would spoil, and so he would be obliged either to exchange it away for something else useful, or share it out to his neighbours, and inferior chiefs and dependents for nothing.' He concluded by saying; 'I understand now very well what it is that makes the Papālagis so selfish—it is this money!'[37]

However, learning how money was used, Finau regretted that he had not collected the dollars aboard the *Port au Prince* (Mariner's ill-fated ship) before burning it.

The prayer of a Rarotongan chief illustrates his desire to obtain the new materials and marine technology: 'O, great Tangaroa, send your large ship to our land; let us see the Cookees. Great Tangiia, send us a dead sea, send us a propitious gale, to bring the far-famed Cookees to our island, to give us nails and iron, and axes; let us see those out-riggerless canoes'.[38]

Material considerations encouraged Pomare of Tahiti to accept responsibility for the first missionaries. In 1797 the *Duff* brought the first London Missionary Society party, comprising four ordained ministers

---

36 Shineberg, *They Came for Sandalwood*, 15.
37 Martin, *Tonga Islands: William Mariner's Account*, 155.
38 Cited in Shineberg, *They Came for Sandalwood*, 14

and twenty-five former servants, artisans and craftsmen, of whom five brought wives and children. Three missions were planned: in Tahiti, the Marquesas and Tonga. The party in Tahiti were received auspiciously by 'Oro's high priest, and when the ship's captain put his cannon on deck, the unarmed party of Arioi (a special class of servants of the god) who attended the priest assisted the captain to put them in position. It being the Sabbath, no barter was permitted, to the astonishment of the Islanders. A service was held and the Tahitians seemed charmed and amazed by the singing. In the following days the missionaries were received by leading chiefs and their consorts. However, missionary advice on manners and morals (such as remonstrances against infanticide and the transsexual *mahu*) were poorly received. After the *Duff* departed, relations deteriorated further when the missionaries failed to provide Pomare with goods and firearms, or to lend moral support for his war and political ambitions. In the worsening climate, eleven men, several with families, left for Sydney. In all these respects, the missionaries were a grave disappointment. Unlike all previous Europeans, they offered little material benefit and much unwelcome moral exhortation.

The two missionaries sent to the Marquesas also fell out with their hosts when they rejected the gifts of bedmates, and were robbed. One refused to stay, and the other left after a year. The small party in Tonga also floundered. Their efforts to settle and preach were opposed by chiefs and by beachcombers whom some chiefs had adopted. One missionary, George Vason, 'went native'. He was adopted by a chief and incorporated into the chiefly class through marriage, and took to all aspects of Tongan life, even becoming a warrior. Some unfortunate missionaries were killed in the war which then raged, but the remainder escaped to Sydney. The Tahiti mission limped along and relations with Pomare gradually improved so that by 1808 he had promised to banish 'Oro, and to 'cast off evil customs'. New missionaries arrived and the 'Society Islands' became a Christian epicentre from which missions evangelised the Cook Islands, Samoa and Niue.

Material considerations also influenced the decision of leaders and followers to adopt the Christian faith. The missionary John Williams, on his second voyage to Samoa in 1832, described the reasoning of Samoan chiefs on the issue. The deciding consideration was that Jehovah was the source of the superior technology and goods of the Europeans whom they were meeting in increasing numbers. Jehovah was thought to possess greater powers than the old gods.

> The Chiefs of the different settlements held meeting after meeting to consult upon the propriety of changing the religion of their ancestors & the case was argued on both sides with a calmness that seldom characterises debates in more civilised countries & with an acuteness that does credit to their senses. On one of the occasions a chief of superior rank stated his wish that Christianity should be embraced, saying Only look at the English people. They have noble ships while we have only canoes. They have strong beautiful clothes of various colours while we have only *ti* leaves. They have sharp knives while we have only a bamboo to cut with. They have Iron Axes while we use stones. They have scissors while we use the shark's teeth. What

beautiful beads they have, looking glasses & all that is valuable. I therefore think that the God who gave them all things must be good & that his religion must be superior to ours. If we receive and worship him he will in time give us all these things as well as them.[39]

In chapter 1, Linnekin argues that Williams's commentaries were influenced by the need to appeal to the businessmen who funded the mission. However, if Williams exaggerated the materialist element of Polynesian perceptions, he did not invent it, and his considered opinion must carry some weight. Trade was an essential aspect of missionary operations. Missionaries had to maintain some economic independence from Islanders and to maintain their mystique as emissaries of a more powerful God in their manner of living, in order to earn respect. There was considerable debate among early missionaries about the proper material style of living for missionary settlers. Living in poverty and humility in the manner of Christ made a poor impression on rank-conscious Polynesians. There was also criticism by missionary leaders of their brethren who did not try to stimulate interest in the amenities of 'civilisation', and for failing to influence converts to build houses in the new, mission style with coral lime walls. Most of the Protestant missionaries of this period were, in Gunson's terms, 'godly mechanics' with middle-class aspirations; as the church became established they exerted increasing influence on the technology and dress as well as the religious practices of the Islanders. Many engaged in trade and some left the church to set up in business on their own account. Tithes were paid in coconut oil and arrowroot starch, which were exported to England to defray operating costs.[40]

The islands of Melanesia also began to attract foreigners' interest. The trade with China led to a quest for commodities to exchange for tea. Enterprising traders from the new entrepôt of Sydney found two such items in the Islands—sandalwood and *bêche-de-mer*. Fiji offered both, while Hawai'i, the southern New Hebrides, New Caledonia and the Loyalty Islands were found to contain stands of sandalwood. In Fiji trade was fairly orderly under the patronage of chiefs who provided labour and safe passage in return for whale's teeth, trade goods and firearms (see chapters 5 and 6). The trade was far less orderly in the New Hebrides and New Caledonia, where political authority was limited to smaller areas, making it more difficult for sandalwood-getters to organise systematic relations. The trade was therefore associated with violence on both sides.

Shineberg notes that Melanesians bargained acutely, being eager for trade and foreign goods and well aware of the value of the wood to the Europeans. As in Polynesia, the initial demand was for metal and metal tools, broadening into cloth, beads, tobacco and pipes, muskets and powder. In some Islands, people demanded indigenous forms of wealth such as pigs and shells, which traders were obliged to find and import. The veneration or fear with which Europeans were first greeted was soon displaced by hard-headed attitudes based on the calculations of

39 Moyle, *The Samoan Journals of John Williams*, 234.
40 Gunson, *Messengers of Grace*, 132–46.

material advantage. Traders who established sound economic relations were generally tolerated and assisted in the quest for sandalwood, but those who failed to do so were likely to be killed. Where traders defrauded or antagonised Islanders, the people might exact revenge on the next party. It is believed, for example, that the murder of John Williams on Erromanga in 1839 was an act of revenge towards foreigners generally. However, Shineberg is sceptical of historical interpretations which explain all massacres in terms of revenge for European atrocities. She acknowledges that 'vengeance was a concept firmly rooted in most Melanesian cultures; among some peoples it was an obligation placed upon life itself'. But many conflicts arose from the desire to plunder.

> Cutting and carrying sandalwood was hard work; when occasions arose on which trade goods could be much more plentifully acquired simply by killing a boat's crew, it must have been an attractive alternative. A successful attack brought, relatively speaking, vast wealth to its authors. A ship itself is not a useful prize, and after everything removable had been carried off it was usually burnt . . . A ship's boat, on the other hand, even without its cargo, was in itself an extremely valuable piece of property and one that the islanders could not hope to obtain by barter.[41]

Shineberg also suggests that 'the suspicion of sorcery' motivated attacks on traders as the early visits of the Europeans often led to strange epidemics. It was undoubtedly believed that Europeans possessed malign powers to cause disease and death, for which revenge would have been sought.

In the early contact period, Islanders not only sought the goods of outsiders but also their technical skills and knowledge. By the 1820s a process was firmly established, by which chiefs recruited outsiders to live with and serve them. Dozens of foreign men lived among the people of Fiji, Tonga and Samoa. They were mainly British, other Europeans, and Americans, but some were Islanders who had joined foreign ships, and a few Chinese, Lascars and Black Americans. These men were mainly sailors who had jumped ship, but some were escaped convicts from New South Wales and Norfolk Island. Many joined the households of important chiefs, and were considered useful because of their skills in using and repairing firearms and their command of the technology for building single-hulled boats and other woodworking techniques. They could also tell stories of the strange lands from which they had come, and their religions. Some were desperadoes who clearly inspired fear among their hosts, but since fierce warriors were highly esteemed in some Islands, they were tolerated; however, those whose violent ways became tiresome were killed. Most were of humble origin but some were relatively well-educated men, such as the ship's surgeon Stevens, who interpreted for John Williams on his first voyage to Samoa, or the young clerk Mariner, who was adopted by Tongan chiefs after his ship-mates were murdered. Some beachcombers were the first

41 Shineberg, *They Came for Sandalwood*, 200–1.

Christian 'missionaries' in some Islands, although their teachings and influence were later strongly opposed by the missionaries who arrived under the formal sponsorship of Christian churches. Most eventually left the Islands, but some spent the rest of their lives among their adopted people.

Some beachcombers lessened their dependence on Islanders by establishing themselves as traders, who could act as middlemen between ships and Islanders. However, foreigners who chose to live among Islanders or trade with them did so on terms dictated by Islanders, and at their own risk. Traders who were killed by their hosts or who were attacked and plundered generally had no redress. But in the 1830s British and United States warships began to patrol, albeit infrequently, and to defend or promote the interests of their citizens. A US naval commander sought to arrest and try a Samoan chief for an attack on US citizens. The Wilkes expedition had been sent by the US government to conduct scientific research. Among Wilkes's instructions was to promote 'commerce and civilization', with special reference to the interests of the New England whaling industry. Calling at Samoa, Wilkes was asked to investigate an occurrence in 1834 in which the village of Palauli had attacked the Nantucket whaler *William Penn*, killing three sailors and stealing two boats. The chief held responsible was Tualau Tonumaipe'a Popotunu, who held extremely high rank. Wilkes decided to arrest and try him, but in vain. The chief took refuge beyond his polity and his fellow chiefs declined to surrender him. This experience led Wilkes to endorse British efforts to appoint consuls and establish a code of laws wherever foreigners were active, to regulate interactions with Islanders and thereby protect the interests of outsiders.[42] This was the first step towards changing the balance of power, a transition which is taken up in the following two chapters.

CONCLUSIONS

There are several perspectives on contact between Islanders and Europeans. Perhaps the most widely held view is the theory of 'the fatal impact' popularised by Alan Moorehead's book of that name (chapter 1). This view dwells on the first Europeans in the Pacific, who arrogantly believed themselves to be the lords of humankind. Convinced of the superiority of their religion and culture, they nonetheless committed iniquitous deeds and brought infectious diseases, resulting in violent confrontations, epidemics, a loss of innocence and the destruction of cultures. This apocalyptic view has distant resonances with the social Darwinism which was gaining currency in the late nineteenth century, and which assumed that native cultures—and the natives themselves—must inevitably perish in the path of Western culture and technology. Epidemics of influenza, venereal diseases, tuberculosis and other afflictions did cause population decline and sometimes collapse:

42 Gilson, *Samoa, 1830–1900*, 147–55.

in extreme cases, such as Kosrae or Rapanui, populations of several thousands fell to a few hundred. Many European observers interpreted these tragedies in somewhat mystical terms, as if they were witnessing an accelerated manifestation of a natural law of the survival of the fittest, rather than the physical consequences of micro-organisms on non-immune populations.

The most sophisticated and erudite version of this approach is presented by Dening, and it is well justified in the case of Te Henua, the Marquesas Islands, where the culture and most of the populace were obliterated between 1774 and 1880. Dening observes how little light theories of imperialism throw in explaining why a remote archipelago—with little to offer Europeans—should have been exploited so destructively.

> There was no conscious conspiracy to exploit the Land [Te Henua], no explicit philosophy of a superior culture's right to destroy. The Men [the Marquesans] were dispossessed nonetheless. The discrepancy between cost and consequence in 'a life for a nail' in Cook's day was constant in all the cross-cultural history of Te Henua . . . Where there was no contract to understand one another, there was death. Where there was no instrument of government, men lived in a 'brutish manner'. The beach itself was a savage place, made so by the mutual contempt of those who stood across it from one another. The savage was always the 'other', presumed to be lesser, known to be without order to which he could be called. The winner made an island or he made a desert. In the Land the winner made a desert. The Men were totally dispossessed.[43]

Although outcomes were less catastrophic for most Islands, Dening makes an important point about the early contact period and relations on the beach—the absence of a 'contract to understand one another', and the fateful consequences. In Island societies trade—the mundane exchange of useful commodities—always took place in the guise of social relations. For many centuries Tonga, where natural resources were few, acted as a 'middleman' between Samoa and Fiji, the sources of red feathers, timber for boat building, adze blades and fine pandanus cloth. Tongan seafaring was far more extensive than that of Samoa or Fiji throughout the last pre-European millennium. But this trade was never conducted in the impersonal terms of the marketplace. Instead, marriage alliances between chiefly dynasties provided intermittent opportunities for ceremonial exchanges of valuables. Another celebrated example, the *kula* centred on the Trobriand Islands, was described by Malinowski in the 1910s, when he likened the Islanders to adventurous Argonauts.[44] Islanders embarked on perilous ocean voyages to visit partners with whom they exchanged shell armbands and necklaces. This exchange of items which were imbued with deep symbolic and aesthetic significance but were strictly speaking 'non-utilitarian' was couched in the idiom of personal friendships, and

---

43 Dening, *Islands and Beaches*.
44 Malinowski, *Argonauts of the Western Pacific*.

ceremoniously masked the exchange of essential things such as pottery, salt and adze blades.

Rights to interact with outsiders were sometimes inherited. The island of Tanna was divided into polities whose inhabitants treated each other as strangers and potential enemies. The right to communicate across boundaries was inherited by individual men, and attached to the names they were given by their fathers. These privileges were jealously guarded, so that proper interaction might occur only through hereditary spokesmen and messengers. Throughout the Pacific, contractual arrangements prevailed between all groups who were known to each other, whether as friends or as enemies, and these arrangements prescribed how to interact and how to signal intentions. This style of interaction stands in stark contrast to eighteenth-century Europe, where impersonal trade was the norm and the driving force between communities and nations. European trade did not require kinship, nor fraternal partnerships between men, nor did their material interests require ceremonies of affinity and friendship. These radically different understandings of how material interests should be mediated underlay the bizarre and tragic character of many early encounters.

In *Two Worlds* Anne Salmond explores contact between Westerners and Maori, and places their actions, interests and perceptions in the context of their cultures and mores. The brutal social inequalities of Europe, and European practices such as witch-hunting and public executions, are set beside the endemic warfare and cannibalism of seventeenth-century Maori. From one perspective, their encounters were merely 'puzzling interludes':

> The ships—floating islands, mythological 'birds' or canoes full of *tupua* or 'goblins'—came into this bay or that, shot local people or presented them with strange gifts, were welcomed or pelted with rocks, and after a short while went away again and were largely forgotten . . . [From the vantage point of] seventeenth and eighteenth century European chroniclers, the same encounters were simply episodes in the story of Europe's 'discovery' of the world—more voyages to add to the great collection of 'voyages' that had already been made. The genre of discovery tales was an ancient one in Europe, with a well-worn narrative line—explorers ventured into unknown seas, found new lands and named their coastal features, described exotic plants, animals and inhabitants, and survived attacks by tattooed savages (or worse still, cannibals) with spears. The stories . . . defined Europeans as 'civilised' in contrast with 'savages' and 'barbarians' to be found elsewhere . . .

Today the myths of Indians and savages have been superseded by new fables. Beautiful Polynesian girls and handsome youths wearing flowers and grass skirts innocently practise free love on silver beaches beside a turquoise sea under swaying palms. These myths are celebrated in Western culture through songs, novels, poetry, films, advertising and tourist promotions, so that they have permeated the Western cultural subconscious. The images can be traced to romantic interpretations of the sexual exchanges of the early contact period, and are manifestly remote from realities. The Islanders' motives in the earliest encounters may have been based on religious preconceptions, or a desire to create affinities with powerful strangers, or as tricks to distract the strangers so that they could be overcome; but by the 1860s, in many Islands, trafficking in women had become part of a flourishing commodity trade. Whaling ships calling at Te Henua (the Marquesas) had well-established rates for whoring:

> captains like J. J. Fisher were willing to pay eight jaws of whale with three hundred and fifty teeth and a gun, for a girl 'eleven and a half years and soft', but the less fastidious had less costly pleasures . . . The vast profits of the whaling industry to persons and nations was dependent on subordinate and disadvantaged savages. It was a long chain linking coconut, sperm-oil candle and whalebone corset but there was interconnection all the same.

The image of drunken, poxed European sailors debauching Island maidens and introducing innocent Islanders to guns, rum and tobacco has also become part of the Island legend, along with censorious black-coated missionaries forcing nubile maidens into Mother Hubbard dresses, and prohibiting dancing. Such stereotypes are rooted in the assumption that at least some Islands were in some sense a paradise; that there was an innocence to be lost, and that islanders were always victims in contacts with outsiders. This was seldom the case. Some Islanders (assisted by the anopheles mosquito and rugged terrain) terrified and repelled foreigners. Niueans, who earned their island the foreigners' name of Savage Island, sent men aboard visiting ships with their faces blackened, their bodies smeared with ash, their hair tangled and matted, shouting and gesticulating wildly. This strategy brought about the speedy departure of many ships. At the other extreme, Tongans adapted themselves rapidly to an influx of foreigners: the remarkable Tāufa'āhau Tupou I used the ideological confusion and political instability of the era to conquer the archipelago and establish himself as its monarch. The outcome of contact with Europe was tragedy in the Marquesas, Hawai'i and many parts of New Zealand, but in most Island groups the populace not only survived, but responded in markedly different ways, and elaborated their cultures into the robust and unique forms which they retain to the present day.

APPENDIX:
FOREIGN VOYAGES AND THE WIDER REGIONAL CONTEXT

1405–31   Chinese expeditions, under Zheng He, through Pacific and Indian oceans.

1494   Treaty of Tordesillas divides 'New World' between Spain and Portugal.

1519–21   (Spanish) Ferdinand de Magellan (Magalhāis), westward to Guam and the Philippines and Maluku.

1515   Portuguese reach the Spice Islands, volcanic islets near Halmahera in Maluku, the largest source of spices for export to Europe.

1526   'The Lost Caravel'.

1527–29   (Spanish) Alvaro de Saavedra Ceron, westward through the Marshall Islands, Guam, to Spice Islands, then via Manus, Guam, the Caroline Islands, probably Pohnpei, Ujelang and Enewetak, returning westward.

1560s   Philippines trade from Manila under Spanish control; Maluku spice trade under Portuguese control.

1565   Beginning of regular galleon trade between Mexico and the Philippines.

1567–68   (Spanish) Alvaro de Mendaña, westward to Santa Isabel, Florida, Guadalcanal, Malaita, San Cristobal.

1578   The first of many English and Dutch buccaneer assaults on Spanish settlements and shipping.

1595   (Spanish) Mendaña and Pedro de Quiros, westward through the Marquesas, Pukapuka, Niulakita, Espiritu Santo, to Guam and the Philippines.

1602   Formation of Dutch East India Company, but the company was not securely based in Java (with its centre of operations at Batavia) until the 1670s.

1605–06   (Spanish) Quiros and Luis Vaez de Torres, westward through the Tuamotus, Santa Cruz, Espiritu Santo: Quiros sailed back to America; Torres through Torres Strait and southern New Guinea to Maluku.

1615–16   (Dutch) Isaac LeMaire and Willem Schouten, westward through the Tuamotus, northern Tonga, Futuna, Alofi, New Ireland, New Guinea to Maluku.

1623   (Dutch) Jan Carstensz, west coast of Australia.

1636   Ban on Japanese ships trading overseas; increasingly stringent *sakoku* (seclusion) policy.

1642   (Dutch) Abel Tasman, from Mauritius to Tasmania, New Zealand, Tonga, Fiji, New Britain, returning to Mauritius.

1644   (Dutch) Abel Tasman, from Batavia to West New Guinea, north-western Australia.

from 1668   (Spanish) Jesuit Father Diego Luis Sanvitores in Guam and Marianas.

1699–1700   (English) William Dampier, via Cape of Good Hope, Mussau, Emirau, New Britain, returning to the Cape.

1722   (Dutch) Jacob Roggeveen, Rapanui, Bora Bora, Samoa, New Guinea to Batavia.

1767–68   (English) Samuel Wallis, westward to Tuamotus, Tahiti, Tinian and Batavia.

1766–69   (French) Louis-Antoine de Bougainville, westward to Tuamotus, Tahiti, Samoa, Pentecost, Aoba, Malakula, Louisiade Archipelago, Choiseul, Bougainville to Batavia.

1768–71   (English) James Cook (with Joseph Banks and other naturalists), Tahiti, New Zealand, New South Wales, Great Barrier Reef.

1772–75   (English) James Cook (with J. R. and G. Forster and others), New Zealand, Tahiti, Tonga, Rapanui, Marquesas, Tahiti, Tonga, Vanuatu, New Caledonia.

1776–80   (English) James Cook (with Charles Clerke and James King), Tasmania, New Zealand, Tonga, Hawai'i, North-west Passage, Kamchatka, Kealakekua Bay.
   1788   'First Fleet' at Botany Bay: foundation of Sydney.
1786–88   (French) Jean-François Galaup de La Pérouse, Hawai'i, North-west Passage, Ryukyu Archipelago, Kuril Archipelago, Samoa, Tonga, Botany Bay, New Caledonia, Vanikoro.
   1789   (English) William Bligh, Tahiti, Tonga, 'mutiny on the *Bounty*'. Mutineers pursued by *Pandora*, returned to England 1792.
1791–95   (English) George Vancouver, New Zealand, Chatham Islands, Tahiti, Hawai'i, North-west Passage, Hawai'i.
   1797   London Missionary Society sends the *Duff* with four ministers and 25 other men (five with families) to Tahiti, the Marquesas and Tonga.
   1815   The last galleon from Acapulco to Manila.

Later Expeditions in New Guinea

1907–13   Dutch expeditions to Mount Trikora in West New Guinea.
   1926   Gold found at Edie Creek in New Guinea.
1927–28   Charles Karius and Ivan Champion cross New Guinea from south to north.
   1933   Prospectors Mick, Dan and Jim Leahy, and Jim Taylor, enter the Wahgi valley.
   1935   Jack Hides and Jim O'Malley cross the Papuan Plateau.
1938–39   Jim Taylor and John Black, from Mount Hagen to the Sepik.

BIBLIOGRAPHIC ESSAY

The exploration of the Pacific was first described from the perspective of the explorers. Leading works in this tradition include Beaglehole (ed.), *The Journals of Captain James Cook* and *The Exploration of the Pacific*; and Andrew Sharp, *The Discovery of Australia* and *The Voyages of Abel Janszoon Tasman*.

Since European missionaries were prominent in early cross-cultural encounters, there is much to be learned from Gunson, *Messengers of Grace*, and Garrett, *To Live Among the Stars*. Spate's three-volume work, *The Pacific Since Magellan*, is a comprehensive synthesis of these sources, analysing the strategic issues at stake for the major powers from the sixteenth century until the eighteenth.

The techniques of anthropology were later applied to reconstruct Islanders' world-views and perceptions. Melanesian cosmologies are analysed by Lawrence, *Road Belong Cargo*; Burridge, *Mambu: A Melanesian Millennium*; and Worsley, *The Trumpet Shall Sound*. Oliver reconstructed *Ancient Tahitian Society* in three volumes. Sahlins and

Dening pioneered ethnohistorical approaches in much of the Pacific. The more important works in this tradition include Sahlins, 'The Stranger-King, or Dumezil among the Fijians', *Historical Metaphors and Mythical Realities*, and 'The Discovery of the True Savage'; Dening, *Islands and Beaches*, and *Mr Bligh's Bad Language*; Pearson, 'The Reception of European Voyagers on Polynesian Islands, 1568–1797'; Campbell, 'European Polynesian Encounters: A Critique of the Pearson Thesis'; Salmond, *Two Worlds*; Schieffelin and Crittenden, *Like People You See in a Dream*; and Ballard, research in progress.

The methods and assumptions of ethnohistorical reconstruction have been criticised by Obeyesekere, *The Apotheosis of Captain Cook*. For responses to this critique, see e.g. Kame'eleihiwa's review in *Pacific Studies* xvii: 2 (1994), other reviews in the same volume by David Hanlon, Nicholas Thomas and Valerio Valeri, and Obeyesekere's response. The controversy also gave rise to a series of contributions to *Social Analysis* 24 (December 1993) by Bruce Knoft, Deborah Bird Rose, Anne Salmond, Jonathan Lamb, Bernard Smith, Tom Ernst and Richard Parmentier, together with a further response by Obeyesekere.

In a more empirical tradition, contact encounters are described by Shineberg, *They Came for Sandalwood*; Bonnemaison, *The Tree and the Canoe*; Chappell, 'Secret Sharers: Indigenous Beachcombers in the Pacific Islands'; Bargatsky, 'Beachcombers and Castaways as Innovators'; Campbell, 'European Transculturalists in Polynesia'; Maude, *Of Islands and Men*; Connolly and Anderson, *First Contact*, and their documentary film of the same name; Lessa, 'The Portuguese Discovery of the Isles of Sequeira'; Langdon, *The Lost Caravel*; Jaarsma, '"Your Work Is of No Use to Us . . ."'; Hezel and Berg (eds), *Micronesia: Winds of Change*; and Hezel, *The First Taint of Civilization*.

The European obsession with the Islands of Solomon is anatomised by Jack-Hinton, *The Search for the Islands of Solomon*, and the debate is summarised by Frost, 'Towards Australia: The Coming of the Europeans 1400 to 1788', in Mulvaney and White (eds), *Australians to 1788*.

CHAPTER

5

LAND, LABOUR AND INDEPENDENT DEVELOPMENT

DEVELOPMENT?

Throughout the nineteenth century, ambitious Pacific Islanders saw a variety of chances to transform their lives and their production and exchange. Several formed alliances with foreign adventurers, to extract or exploit resources. As the balance of political power tilted against the chiefs, however, it became increasingly difficult to retain land, labour, and autonomy.

The economic sense of the term *development*, now widely used, is surprisingly recent. It was coined in twentieth-century Australia when hopes of economic progress had been dashed, and it retains currency mainly in regions where economic performance lags behind expectations. If the term is new, the underlying idea of progress is as old as Western civilisation, and in one guise or another it has inspired Westerners to transform the world according to a seemingly preordained schedule. John Locke, the leading English philosopher of the seventeenth century,[1] asserted a stage theory of development when he argued that 'in the beginning all the world was America, and more so than it is now'. He also advanced a justification for empire: 'God gave the world to men in Common, but since He gave it them for their benefit and the greatest conveniencies of life they were capable to draw from it, it cannot be supposed He meant it should always remain common and uncultivated. He gave it to the use of the industrious and rational . . .'. Adam Smith, the founder of modern economic theory, refined this vision in *An Inquiry into the Nature and Causes of the Wealth of Nations* (1776), describing progress as a set of stages from hunting and gathering, through pastoralism and farming, to metal-working and mechanisation. The problem, as Europeans saw it, was to mobilise laggard societies whose lives were mired in obsolete phases, whose technology was crude, and whose vision failed to encompass new possibilities.

In this century, Rostow's *Stages of Economic Growth: A Non-communist Manifesto*[2] restated the classic assumption that an economy should develop through logical stages. Despite criticism by radical theorists

1 Locke is chiefly remembered for his *Essay Concerning Human Understanding* and *Two Treatises of Government*, both published in 1690.
2 Cambridge, 1959.

and amendments by orthodox scholars, some form of Rostow's teleology still underpins most economic planning. Planners aspire to be free of cultural bias, but the idea of development is culturally inflected, and gross prejudice often informs analyses. In 1975, for example, when Papua New Guinea became independent, the World Bank mission cited in chapter 3 spelt out the stages. The country

> starts from a considerably earlier stage of human history than many better-known developing countries. . . . Some 700 local languages, mostly mutually unintelligible and none of them written, have been identified. Cut off from each other by mountains, forests, major rivers, and the sea, the original stone-age tribes have lived unto themselves in conditions of primitive isolation until very recently . . . the indigenous culture of the region was a more primitive one than the Western world was to discover anywhere . . . [Modernisation] began among a people who had no alphabet and hence no writing, knew neither the knife nor axe nor any form of metal, used only stones for cutting, hunted and killed with bows and arrows and clubs, knew neither wool nor cotton, used only pounded bark as cloth, and used no bullock, ox, horse or cow . . .

Many planners assume that the pre-colonial condition of Islanders, revolving around finite needs, cannot develop through its own dynamics. Increased production requires foreign capital, technology and management, linking the Islands to wider networks, displacing subsistence with market production by monetising transactions. These processes then generate diffuse and durable benefits.

Radical scholars argue that development can be destructive, especially in societies remote from metropolitan centres and lacking political leverage. However, radical pessimism is not the antithesis of optimistic orthodoxy, but a variation on it. Both views assume that 'under-development' encompasses much of the world, that development can be measured, and that an evolving global economy is the engine of change. Development is conceived in material terms and its agents are individuals and corporations, who impact upon island societies which cannot control or deflect them. Islanders are either beneficiaries or victims of forces beyond their control.

In reality, the entry of foreign interests was a disorderly mixture of trading, strategic and ideological pursuits (see chapter 4). Islanders' experiences were therefore less orderly than either scenario, and cannot be measured by statistics alone. Previous chapters show that abstracting 'the economy' from its social context distorts Islanders' experiences. Their production systems did not function like European institutions past or present, and they were relegated to a condition of 'under-development' mainly because Europeans did not grasp them. Since white men were reluctant to change their views, transactions continued to generate conflicting expectations. Islanders saw these exchanges in a moral context which Europeans could not—or would not—acknowledge. Burridge observed this impasse in the 1950s:

> [Tangu people think that white men] cannot be pleased, importuned, or even corrupted directly . . . accepting the gift is to accept the man; and repayment of the gift is of paramount importance. Tangu and Manam islanders accept

European goods and ideas but they are unable to accept men who have brought them because these same men will not allow themselves to be accepted except exclusively on their own terms. When Kanakas try to repay the gifts of goods and ideas they are either patronised or laughed at.[3]

Conflicts persisted, between Island societies built on the giving and receiving of gifts, and Westerners who fixed the prices of inanimate commodities. There are other reasons for doubting the role of Europeans as agents of orderly progress. Their earliest ventures amounted to resource raiding. Their colonies in Australia and New Zealand disrupted Aboriginal and Maori societies profoundly, using every device to appropriate land. Traders and planters were not apostles of a free market, but manipulators of political power. In their responses, Islanders deployed whatever political and cultural weapons came to hand. It was often difficult to endure the social costs of 'development'. It needed ingenuity to turn great forces to advantage, yet Islanders endured the costs and some found benefits in imaginative ways and unexpected forms.

RESOURCE RAIDING: WHALES, *BÊCHE-DE-MER* AND SANDALWOOD

Until the sixteenth century, webs of maritime trade connected China, Korea, Japan and South-East Asia, often under the guise of tribute to China. The Indian Ocean journeys of the great explorer Zheng He reveal that China had the potential to create global networks in the fifteenth century, linking the Pacific Islands to East Asia. The frequency of shipwrecks even in the seventeenth century implies that many earlier vessels, seeking sandalwood or *bêche-de-mer*, struck the western Carolines (though fewer sailed home). In the only regular trading link, however, western New Guinea supplied slaves, birds of paradise and sago to the sultanate of Tidore (Indonesia).

The irruption of armed European merchants during the sixteenth century coincided with (and probably provoked) a contraction of East Asian trade. Chinese exploration lapsed as the Ming dynasty collapsed and their Qing successors rebuilt a land-based regime suspicious of seaborne trade. The Tokugawa shoguns in Japan became increasingly introverted. Alarmed by the impact of Christian missionaries and merchants, they first restricted, then throttled, the overseas trade of feudal daimyos. The non-evangelising Dutch were allowed to trade at Deshima Island in Nagasaki harbour, and the door of the Okinawa kingdom remained ajar. Europeans aspired to deal directly with China or Japan, but their settlements—Macao, Ternate and Tidore in Maluku, Kupang in Timor, and Manila—were peripheral. As late as 1788, when the *Bounty* mutineers cast Bligh adrift near Tonga, the Dutch port of Kupang was his nearest refuge—5000 kilometres away in Timor.

---

3 Burridge, *Mambu*, 39–40.

European explorers imported images of isolation into European consciousness. Within the region, however, Europeans' main role was to ferry island produce into Asian markets. For three centuries after Magellan, most European trade in the Islands responded to Asian demand. Only after 1788, as settlers dispossessed Aboriginal Australians and built an export economy, was it possible to link the Islands into Atlantic markets. Until then Europeans had minimal interest in the Islands. New production required control over land and labour, regular shipping, secure markets and venture capital: none was available until the nineteenth century. So long as shipping was dear and slow, only high-value goods could repay their costs—spices, gems or precious metals. Neither gemstones nor spices occurred in the Islands. Gold and silver were present, but elusive. When the Islands were found to yield few cargoes, they sank to the category of navigation hazards. The Spaniards were content to exploit the ores of America, with which to command the attention of Chinese merchants, and their galleons clove to safe latitudes with few uncharted reefs. Buccaneers therefore scoured only the narrow latitudes where galleons might be captured.

During the 1790s that view was modified when merchants developed a trade in furs from America to China. The trans-Pacific trade made insistent demands for fresh water, food and sexual services. Honolulu, Pape'ete and Koror became ports of call, specialising in 'rest and recreation', and the region's first towns. From the 1800s the commonest foreign vessels were whalers which loaded water and food at Island anchorages, and sometimes replenished crews. Europeans also pursued opportunist ventures in older networks, carrying smoked *bêche-de-mer* (trepang, or sea slugs) to China. Sandalwood (for incense) provided other cargoes from Polynesia and Fiji from the early nineteenth century, and from Melanesia during the 1840s. Seal skins and New Zealand timber also found their way to China, while turtle-shell shaped the headdresses of ladies in Manila. Some trading vessels improved inter-island links. The trader Andrew Cheyne, visiting Pohnpei in 1842, found beachcombers collecting and selling turtle-shell as agents for the chiefs. On Yap, the chiefs permitted no such liberties and Cheyne was inveigled to transport Palauan aragonite discs instead. Thirty years later the Irish castaway Daniel O'Keefe also began by shipping discs. He recruited Yapese to quarry them in Koror, and shipped them home: his rewards included labour for plantations, and his example inspired other traders.

Precious metals became important surprisingly late, considering their actual distribution. Only after the 1840s, when gold was found in Australia and New Zealand, did adventurers see the Islands in a new, golden light. Meanwhile foreign shipping increased. British trade with China was consolidated by the cession of Hong Kong in 1842. Shipping routes then linked South China through Singapore, Australia and Honolulu to the rest of the world. Spain's control of the Philippines was eroded by British and American traders. Even more dramatic was the transformation of Japan from insularity to vigorous participation in regional trade and warfare. When the United States Navy breached Japan's defences in the 1850s, there was every prospect that it would share the melancholy fate of China. A feudal society had neither modern arms for defence nor capital for industry. Unequal treaties gave foreigners economic and legal privileges until—after rebellion and civil war—Matsuhito reclaimed imperial authority in 1867 as the Meiji emperor and presided over a program of revolutionary modernisation.

By the 1870s Japan controlled Sakhalin and the Kuril Islands to the north, and the Ryukyu Islands to the south. Okinawa kingdom in the Ryukyu Archipelago had been Perry's staging-post for the assault on Japan, so it felt the full impact of Japan's anxiety. It had suited Japan for Okinawa to be nominally independent, trading through East and South-East Asia. The lords of Satsuma treated Okinawa like a trained cormorant which regurgitated trade profits as tribute. This illusory independence was trampled in 1879. Since the Islanders were similar to Japan in culture and language, Meiji policy was to assimilate them: the monarchy was abolished, the gentry pensioned off, and feudal relations dismantled in favour of Meiji modernity. Assimilation had already been imposed on the Bonin (Ogasarawa) Islanders to the south-east in 1875, though these descendants of Honolulu adventurers were not easily absorbed. These sub-tropical islands provided forward bases for merchants who began to compete for the trade of the Marianas and Carolines.

The Spanish–American War consolidated United States maritime power in the Pacific. New England vessels had dominated whaling, American planters already enjoyed massive influence over the Hawaiian monarchy, and American companies had helped to open the Philippines to international trade. The conquest of the Philippines in 1898 did, however, transform power relations. The Spanish empire was finally extinguished, and the United States was committed to an imperial role—inaugurating its 'Pacific Century'. The war also led to the transfer of Guam to the United States, while Germany acquired most of Spain's other islands. The United States, already compromised by a settler revolt against the Hawaiian monarchy, took the final step of annexation (chapter 7). All these developments promoted regular sailing routes, threading through seas which the galleons had avoided.

Islanders quickly found ways on board foreign ships. Many of the earliest were kidnapped to reinforce ships' crews. During the era of scientific exploration, a few celebrities travelled to London, China and North America, but many more enlisted as workers. When whaling waxed, kidnapping waned. Some Islanders volunteered: others were conscripted. Kamehameha I of Hawai'i, aspiring to create a modern navy, offered crewmen to fur traders bound for North America. By the 1830s Hawaiian sailors were so reliably available that whalers often embarked short-handed from New England, recruiting their full complement at Honolulu. Soon there were perhaps 3000 Hawaiians on whalers. Together with Maori and Tahitians in Australian vessels, they comprised perhaps one-fifth of all whaling and sealing crews. Maori were as likely as Englishmen to become beachcombers, and Pomare of

Tahiti employed Hawaiians just as Kamehameha engaged Tahitians. Once on board ship, Islanders joined the polyglot society of sailors, sharing their risks, profits, and traditions. Some spent the rest of their lives afloat, and others settled far from home, commonly in other Islands, although some Hawaiians formed colonies in North America where their cultural identity has endured for two centuries. Most returned home, however, and when they distributed their earnings they shed their worker status.

This floating population was mainly masculine—but not entirely. Since almost all the foreigners were men, women often mediated as cultural interpreters. Some women were clearly the victims of Island men's avarice and sailors' carnality, but a few shipped out as passengers and more as workers. Brief sexual encounters predominated, but a few women formed permanent relations, such as the young Maori woman who became a captain's consort and conformed to 'our rules of table etiquette, in a style that would do credit to many persons laying claim to a greater share of refinement'.[4] As this patronising judgement implies, the women's status was contingent on their protectors' whims. Commonly they identified with their new companions, even against their own kin. Through close association with one sailor or many, they often acquired fuller knowledge than their brothers.

Bêche-de-mer was the commonest marine resource. Slugs were gutted, boiled, washed, and the soft body sun-dried or smoked to survive the slow boat to China. These processes were best carried out by Islanders. Islander divers also collected pearl-shell and turtle-shell. At first the beach workers were mobilised by chiefs and merely overseen by trading vessels. By 1830 *bêche-de-mer* was Fiji's leading export, and after a few years stocks were so depleted that vessels had to spend many weeks at anchor, and employed scores of Europeans, Fijians and other Islanders. On this scale, the camps made great demands on food and fuel, with significant political consequences. One beneficiary was the Vunivalu (war king) of Bau, who exercised wide influence in eastern Viti Levu and Vanua Levu and attracted much of the trade. Vessels commonly called at Bau *en route* to the fishing grounds; and among the benefits to the Vunivalu were huge quantities of whale's teeth, which consolidated his regional influence.

Sandalwood was a different proposition, since stands were inland and scattered, and much labour was needed to fell and transport logs to anchorage. Sandalwood became a significant export from Hawai'i by about 1790, inspiring Kamehameha I to grant himself a monopoly. Observing the traders' profits, he bought ships and engaged in the China trade directly. When those ventures lost money, he fell back on revenue from pilot and port fees. It fell to the common people to provide the labour for timber-getting, and to the chiefs to squander the profits, which were very high in the first decade until over-supply undermined prices. Chiefs—most famously, Boki (see chapter 6)—

4   Peter Dillon, *Narrative and Successful Result of a Voyage*, London, 1829, quoted in Chappell, 'Shipboard Relations'.

persisted in the trade, but always in vain. Sandalwood was also the focus of trade in Fiji, New Caledonia and the New Hebrides. Most traders in these islands were based in Sydney, and at first they could buy sandalwood for trivial amounts of iron, beads and glass, but Islanders soon acquired better knowledge of comparative values. As knowledge grew, so did the quantity, quality and variety of trade goods. Merchants grew anxious, as profits were squeezed between declining prices in China and increasing rewards for chiefs; then irritated, as Tannese and others, sated by European goods, demanded pigs, dogs and turtle-shell from other islands. Sandalwood made some traders middlemen in inter-island trading.

Traders devised ingenious rewards and penalties to secure co-operation. Islanders were introduced to the stock in trade of the market—cloth and nails, then tobacco (sometimes through 'smoking schools'), alcohol, and firearms. The whole population of Pohnpei were addicted smokers by the 1840s, and tobacco was the most common measure of value. Shineberg elegantly summarised the nexus as a matter of teaching Islanders to smoke tobacco so that Chinese could burn incense—so that Australians could drink Chinese tea.[5] These new needs inclined Islanders to spells of employment, and ships' masters employed Islanders directly, built shore stations, and visited every few months to bring supplies and ship out the shell.

Exceptional natural resources presented wide opportunities in New Zealand, displacing the gruesome trade in heads for which these islands were briefly famous. From the 1790s, whalers called at the Bay of Islands for water, food, rest and recreation. They also enlisted men and women as ships' crews. More consequential were sealing and onshore bay whaling which (unlike deep-sea whaling) required little capital and attracted Australian adventurers from the 1800s. Sealers and bay-whalers employed Maori and bought Maori food. The stimulus of the New South Wales market also fostered flax production in the 1820s, and timber-getting and wheat from the 1830s. Maori farmers swiftly adopted potatoes and wheat, and a few began herding cattle and sheep. At one level they were embracing the logic of Western commerce, but at another level they were pursuing old ambitions. An early British Governor of New Zealand, FitzRoy, was invited to a feast near Auckland in 1844, and found that he was less a guest of honour than a prize of the Waikato chiefs, paraded to humble their rivals. Just as impressive as a Governor in uniform was a bank of potatoes 7 feet wide, 4 feet high and 400 yards long, overhung by thousands of dried fish and mirrored by a lattice-work trestle draped with hundreds of blankets. These were not amassed for consumption, but to be given away as evidence of Waikato's supremacy in 'traditional' terms.

The first of the Islands' mineral exports was guano, shovelled out of Peruvian islands. Micronesian nitrates followed, enabling Australian and New Zealand farmers to feed a world-wide hunger for grain. These exports reflected the integration of markets in agrarian produce. Sugar

5   Shineberg, *They Came for Sandalwood*.

was already a global commodity, followed by tea, tobacco, coffee and cocoa. Bulk shipping widened the range. In the early nineteenth century the Philippines exported some sugar and more indigo, birds'-nests, ebony and *bêche-de-mer*: fifty years later these exotica were displaced by tobacco, hemp and coffee, grown as field crops. This trend from natural resources to agricultural exports was slower in the Islands, but the logic was the same.

SETTLERS

Across the temperate South, British settlers flowed with increasing strength and turbulence. Within a hundred years of the penal settlement at Botany Bay, free settlers had expanded by leaps and stumbles through the continent to Torres Strait. No treaties were made: during the nineteenth century colonists elaborated a doctrine of *terra nullius* which asserted that British settlement extinguished native rights to land. That doctrine had no basis in British legal traditions, but reflected the power relations of the frontier. It would take over a hundred years to unravel that self-serving error, and meanwhile the colonists came to see themselves as the sole legitimate inhabitants.

Settler self-government prevailed in New South Wales and Queensland from mid-century, but the Torres Strait islands lingered in a constitutional limbo for another generation. In 1872 the British government extended Queensland's borders to include some of them, but baulked at New Guinea. The Western Pacific High Commission, created in 1877, supervised British interests in the islands but was starved of resources to discharge that trust except through the co-operation of Islanders on land and the Royal Navy at sea. The High Commissioner (fully occupied as Governor of Fiji) was authorised to regulate British subjects only. This cheap device collapsed after 1884, when the Berlin Congress prescribed occupation and effective administration as criteria for recognising colonies. Queensland's unilateral annexation of New Guinea in 1883 was disavowed, but the Protectorate of British New Guinea (i.e. Papua) was declared in 1884, on condition that the settler colonies covered its costs. The Solomon Islands Protectorate (declared in 1893 and implemented in 1896) was also conceived as a holding operation pending Australian federation.

The Australian colonies debated federation for ten years, then conceded limited powers to a federal Commonwealth in 1901. The Commonwealth's agenda was to provide for national defence, to create a national identity distinct from 'Asia', to clarify borders, and to foster economic development. The Commonwealth was notable for its prohibitions. The first Parliament, addressing national defence in an imperial framework, enacted the so-called White Australia policy which asserted that the national character was non-Asian and its orientation British. Six years later Australia assumed grudging responsibility for Papua. Each of these policies clarified social boundaries, and reordered relations with neighbouring societies.

Far north Queensland, interacting with Asia and the Islands more intimately than the rest of Australia, posed distinct policy issues. Cattle pastures, gold, sugar and *bêche-de-mer* attracted restless and ruthless men to Cape York. Pastoralists with huge appetites for land swept through Queensland by the 1860s, shattering Aboriginal communities whose survivors were deployed as domestic workers and stockmen, or as Native Police. A population of perhaps 120,000 in 1788 declined to perhaps 32,000 a century later. Aboriginal resistance was general, but the effective limits to pastoral settlement were the mountains and coastal plains in Cape York which could not be turned to pasture. The Queensland government, empowered by the *Aboriginals Protection and Restriction of the Sale of Opium Act* of 1897, segregated the races and created reserves in the far north. As its title implies, the law was designed to segregate black from white Australians—and to isolate both from 'Asia'.

An even more violent frontier followed the gold rushes of the 1840s. Armed prospectors reached the tropical north in the 1870s. Many men with prospectors' eyes, gamblers' anxieties, and little capital then crossed the Coral Sea. Their traditions included hostility towards Aborigines and Chinese, reliance on each other on fields remote from police and provisions, and suspicion of each other's propensity to conceal ores. Missionaries of the London Missionary Society (LMS) in Papua, knowing the prospectors' reputation, appealed in vain to Britain to intervene. The diggers were not altruistic, but neither were they suicidal. In 1878 the first party from Cooktown arrived in Port Moresby, an enclave of Motu people familiar with missionaries. They elected a mining warden, then agreed to try any miner who harassed local women, and vowed to oppose any Chinese who tried to land. (None came, but the ban was later ratified by the British New Guinea government.) One hundred diggers struggled inland and learned to restrain themselves lest the Koiari landowners attack them. Peace prevailed while the Koiari estimated costs and benefits, whereupon fighting broke out and (eight months after arrival) the remnants of the band fled, defeated by malaria as much as Koiari. The next expeditions descended on small islands in Milne Bay, and mainland prospecting awaited the protection offered by a government.[6]

In New Zealand and Australia, pastoral properties required few workers, and grain and dairy farms were mainly family operations. However, after a few seasons of cotton, sugar became an export staple in north Queensland during the 1860s—a plantation crop hungry for labour. The western Pacific Islands became a 'labour reserve' in the perception of planters. From 1863 until 1904, more than 62,000 Islanders worked in Queensland, most from Vanuatu and the Solomons, and mainly on sugar plantations. This Melanesian frontier offended the White Australia sentiment of the new Commonwealth, and the *Pacific Island Labourers Act* of the first Parliament determined that Islanders be repatriated. Sugar producers were forewarned. During the 1890s

6   Nelson, *Black, White and Gold*, ch. 5.

plantations yielded to family farms, while the Colonial Sugar Refining Company (CSR) processed cane in central mills. Since the Commonwealth also paid a bounty on sugar produced by white workers, the industry survived the repatriation crisis.

Islanders were less fortunate. There had been nearly 10,000 in Queensland in 1901. By 1906 there were only about 4500. Some deportees at Cairns harbour shouted 'Good-bye Queensland, good-bye, White Australia; good-bye, Christians.' Those whose long residence entitled them to stay found most jobs closed by white labour preference. They continued to practise Christianity and to assimilate culturally to settler society: for example, the use of the distinctive Kanaka pidgin English declined. Yet they were largely excluded from that society, with lower standards of living and education, pressed always closer to the even more marginal Aboriginal population. Some resettled in the Torres Strait islands, a location which underlined their unsettled status between White and Aboriginal Australia and Melanesia. During the following decades their descendants laid increasing emphasis on the blackbirding tradition, which portrayed them as victims of kidnapping. The legend had little basis in fact, but 'cultural kidnapping' was an enduring truth in their lives.

The Commonwealth also turned its baleful attention to Torres Strait and Cape York, a meeting point for Aborigines, Papuans, and Makassans who fished for *bêche-de-mer*—a fleet of sixty ships and a thousand crew had been surprised to see Matthew Flinders in 1803. Trading quickened when whalers arrived, and again when Pacific traders found pearl, trochus and turtle-shell in the 1840s. In the 1850s they were joined by sandalwooders. *Bêche-de-mer* was plentiful, and the first curing station was established in 1868. By 1877 more than a hundred pearling vessels were drawn in from Sydney, Japan and further afield, most of them carrying diving gear, since the shallow beds were soon exhausted. European goods were carried beyond Torres Strait along trade routes which encircled New Guinea, and more goods were scavenged from shipwrecks. Some order was imposed from Queensland's port of Somerset (from 1866)—and the trade attracted canoe-borne raids by Tugeri from south-west New Guinea, levying tribute in heads. The islands themselves resembled other Pacific beach communities: Thursday Island was the 'sink of the Pacific' in reference to its variety of Islanders, Europeans, Japanese, South-East Asians, black and white Americans, and even Africans. Aborigines and Islanders engaged in relations inconceivable further south:

> Aborigines provided the raw labour and local knowledge; foreigners provided the artefacts, food and narcotics . . . What the newcomers demanded from the local people was free on their part to give. It did not apparently threaten their lives or their land. Despite population reductions, and new but largely unenforceable laws, these Aborigines were relatively free to pursue their own ends in their own ways.[7]

7 A. Chase, 'Which Way Now?'

The re-emergence of Japan was an urgent spur to Australian consolidation. The Meiji program shared many elements with the Australian Commonwealth, but was pursued more vigorously. The program set Japanese apart from—and above—their neighbours, emphasising national unity under the emperor, military strength, the revival of maritime trade, and the clarification of boundaries. Incorporation into Japan meant acute distress for Okinawans. The resource-poor islands could not attract Japanese capital; manufactured goods displaced local crafts; and talented Islanders became employees of the state or metropolitan companies. Okinawa's sugar found a niche in the Japanese market, but the planting of land to cane eroded what remained of self-sufficiency and exposed farmers to a fickle market. The islands became—by 1900—merely a poor prefecture of Japan. Land was converted to individual title, and by 1903 the basis was laid for capitalist agriculture. As in the rest of the country, land reform created a mass of people who lacked enough land to sustain a family. In 1903 the first party of 941 sailed for Hawai'i: by 1907 more than 10,000 were working abroad—a great proportion of a population under half a million.[8] In Japan itself, the peasantry yielded capital for industry and armaments, through swingeing taxation. Japanese peasants, like Okinawans, were indentured to work in Hawai'i, New Caledonia and Banaba.

Most alarming to a racially sensitive Australian government was the arrival of Japanese entrepreneurs in Australia's north. Women bore the brunt of Japan's southward expansion. In the southern provinces, many peasants and rural workers were obliged to sell their daughters to procurers, to work overseas. The procurer Muraoka Iheiji embellished his autobiography with a patriotic gloss:

> The women write letters home and send money every month . . . Put a whorehouse anywhere in the wilds of the South Pacific, and pretty soon you've got a general store there to go with it. Then clerks come from Japan. They grow independent, and go into business. A company will open up a branch office. Even the master of the whorehouse will open up a business . . . Before long, the place is thriving.

The recollections of Osaki confirm some of Iheiji's observations:

> It was impossible for us [orphaned] children alone to work rented land. [My brother] Funazo had finally come of age; without land he would not be able to take a bride . . . I had seen some of the neighbouring girls make a lot of money by going abroad, and . . . I thought that if I went, my brother would be able to buy land, build a large house, marry well, and become a man in the best fashion.[9]

In effect Japan sent out 'prostitutes in large numbers, with the idea of bringing to fruition the [Meiji] slogan "Enrich the Nation: Strengthen the Army" through use of the foreign currency'. By the 1890s, more than thirty women were working in Thursday Island, and many others were scattered throughout northern Australia. They may have provided the

8   Pearson, 'Trade and the Rise of the Okinawan State'.
9   'The Story of Osaki' in Yamakazi, 'Sandakan No. 8 Brothel'.

capital with which other Japanese bought pearling vessels. These entrepreneurs arrived from the 1880s, and achieved a virtual monopoly of diving and crewing the luggers. To the dismay of legislators, they bought or built their own vessels. Only racially restrictive licensing laws prevented them from acquiring the whole fleet: even so, they often controlled vessels through white 'dummy' owners.

Some order was imposed by the pearl-shell and *bêche-de-mer* industries. Trading companies such as Robert Towns and Burns Philp advanced the money with which captains bought luggers. The masters brought crews and shore parties already employed in Pacific pearling; and luggers relied on the skills of 'dress-divers' at the end of air pumps. There was compelling reason for the (mainly Japanese) divers to demand trusted tenders—preferably their kin. The Queensland government, 2000 kilometres away in Brisbane, appreciated the revenue and merely codified the industries' conventions into regulations. More surprising was the tolerance of the Commonwealth, which exempted Japanese pearlers from the provisions of White Australia, in an enclave of nineteenth-century labour practices. From the 1870s colonial order was reinforced by mission stations. On Cape York, missions administered Aboriginal reserves. The paradoxical outcome was that many Aborigines continued to work on luggers, but most of their earnings were appropriated to subsidise reserve management, so they had no incentive to gain skills. As swimming-diving became obsolete and the industry demanded long-term commitment, Aborigines sank to the lowest ranks of employment.

Some Torres Strait Islanders—especially in the eastern islands—relied mainly on agriculture and scorned the 'lazy' exploitation of marine resources. Their knowledge of luggers and *bêche-de-mer* expanded when sailors settled among them, and again when they embraced Christianity. Their local knowledge enabled them to work in pearling, and soon after the turn of the century both missionaries and Queensland officials resolved to transform them into independent entrepreneurs. Their trajectory exempted them from the *Aboriginals Protection Act*, and earned a civil status like that of the Kanakas—neither white nor Aboriginal. Many kin-groups took up loans to buy luggers. Once the boats were clear of debt, their masters used them as passenger vessels as well as for pearling or fishing, enhancing the quality of their lives but eschewing the profit-maximising behaviour which the government favoured. Officials imposed increasingly onerous obligations, partly to promote working habits and partly to raise revenue; and relations became vexed. Islanders who might have managed resources on a sustainable basis were excluded, in favour of captains who merely ransacked pearl and *bêche-de-mer*. The regional economy entered a slow decline, and government became ever more paternal. The Islanders' legal status survived, however, and their lands were not expropriated. In the 1990s it was the Mer (Murray) Islanders who at last overturned the *terra nullius* doctrine, and began the unravelling of colonial institutions throughout Australia.

From the perspective of the new Commonwealth, the great achievement was order on a remote frontier: the missions preserved order cheaply and the racial hierarchy was durable. The protectorate over Papua in 1884, and a Dutch administrative centre established at Merauke on the northern shores of the strait in 1893, closed the circle of colonial authority in a notably anarchic region. The long-term effect of the White Australia immigration policy was to restrict Japanese to prescribed jobs, while Chinese immigration was brought to a halt. Together with the repatriation of Kanakas, these measures created an ethnic hierarchy.

Inspired by British methods in Australia, French colonisation was markedly less successful. La Pérouse set the pattern when he reached Botany Bay a week after the First Fleet; later exploration of the Australian coast was not pressed forward to annexation. In a burst of colonising enthusiasm, French settlers were landed in the South Island of New Zealand at Akaroa in 1840—again slightly too late to sustain possession. Instead, the French Navy focused its attention on East Polynesia, where claims rested on Catholic mission complaints against Protestant missionaries and converts. The Navy's annexation of the Marquesas in 1841 and the protectorate over Tahiti the next year made little difference to daily life, since Protestant missionaries were deeply entrenched in Tahiti and large-scale settlement was impossible in either group. The annexation of New Caledonia ten years later provided the only prospect for settlement and—precisely when the transportation of convicts to eastern Australia was ending—a penal colony modelled on convict-built Australia. New Caledonia was also the only French dependency which confined indigenous people to *cantonnements* (reserves), to make room for settlers. Wallis and Futuna, taken in the 1880s, were strategically marginal and offered no prospect of settlement.

Unlike the French dependencies, Australia and New Zealand became far more than imperial outposts. They exported wool, wheat, gold and meat to Europe, and attracted British capital and entrepreneurs. As self-governing states they achieved regional dominance in shipping and trade, as markets in their own right, and as the principal suppliers of goods to the Islands. In time they became colonial powers. In 1901 Britain ceded to New Zealand the administration of the Cook Islands, and in 1906 Papua passed to Australia. In the redistribution of German colonies after World War I, Australia seized New Guinea, and New Zealand Western Samoa, while Japan was rewarded in Micronesia.

New Zealand's political leaders attended the federal negotiations, recognising many interests in common with the Australian colonies; but in the end they chose to stand aloof. Their intimate and complex encounters with Maori had created, by the end of the nineteenth century, a quite distinct pattern of social relations, political institutions, and proto-national identity.

THE NEW ZEALAND WARS AND
THE MAORI KING MOVEMENT

In the early nineteenth century the New Zealand Maori had earned a reputation as brutal yet intelligent natives. On the basis of their settlement patterns and agriculture, their stratified social organisation and their art, matched by sturdy physique and copper skin colour, they were distinguished from other 'savages' and placed on the border between savagery and barbarism, which implied that they could graduate to civilisation. For that reason too, missionaries, who began arriving from 1814, instructed the Maori in European farming methods and encouraged barter with visitors from New South Wales. Trade intensified as settlers increased. Large-scale economic activities soon affected Maori work patterns and village life, which, in turn, generated a need for new forms of leadership. Many chiefs became literate as the principal means to negotiate changes. From 1830 Maori interest in Western goods was displaced by a quest for the knowledge behind European authority.

In the early 1820s Maori acquired muskets in great numbers, and inter-tribal wars for such reasons as *utu* ('return' for anything; revenge) soon got out of control. The most renowned warrior was the chief of the northern Ngapuhi tribe, Hongi Hika, who led more than two thousand warriors in campaigns as far south as Taranaki, beginning a seemingly endless cycle of attack and revenge. Conflict erupted also in the southern half of the North Island. The wars did not end until—in the north in the 1830s, and in the south in the early 1840s—European arms were equally distributed across all tribal regions. The results of warfare were dramatic: new diseases and increased enslavement caused a drastic population decline. Since traditional methods failed to solve these problems, many Maori tried radical solutions. In the 1830s conversion took place on a massive scale, particularly in Northland (the far north of the North Island). Conversion was not simply the result of cultural disruption. The Thames–Waikato tribes were prospering in trade, but they also responded positively to Christianity. It seemed to be associated with the wealth and strength of European culture, and conversion must be seen in the wider context of Maori receptivity for European settlement and trade, agriculture, literacy, muskets, and so on. Enthusiasm for foreign influences was soon qualified. The results of contacts with European explorers and traders were manageable, but social changes flowing from European settlement soon passed beyond Maori control.

Soon Maori were exposed to a new world, in which settlers outnumbered missionaries. Most were from New South Wales and intended to exploit the growing market economy, beginning in the Bay of Islands but soon spreading across the entire country. Observing the anarchy from across the Tasman Sea, the Governor of New South Wales suggested that a British Resident be appointed to protect the Europeans and Maori from each other. James Busby arrived in May 1833, and arranged for thirty-four chiefs to declare their independence as the 'United Tribes of New Zealand', but as sole administrator he lacked the power to impose law and order on this imperial frontier. By 1839 some 1300 British subjects had settled permanently on the North Island, and 700 on the South Island.

British policy, formulated in the Colonial Office, was reluctant to intervene, but obliged to support British emigrants as well as to control their excesses and to protect the Maori from the consequences of uncontrolled settlement. Actions of the mastermind behind the New Zealand Association (later Company), Edward Gibbon Wakefield, who aimed to establish a colony by purchasing land, prompted the Colonial Office to act. On 29 January 1840 the first governor, William Hobson, landed at the Bay of Islands with instructions to secure sovereignty, preferably by treaty. Hobson invited chiefs to Waitangi and presented them with a treaty, which was signed by more than forty. The compact, later known as the Treaty of Waitangi, was eventually signed by over 530 chiefs. British sovereignty was proclaimed by May 1840.

The modern debate on the Treaty of Waitangi is voluminous. There are at least four versions of it, with significant differences between English and Maori translations. It seems certain that signatories had different understandings of key aspects. The treaty contains three articles. In the first, the English version states that the chiefs ceded 'all rights and powers of Sovereignty' over their territories. However, the Maori version does not use the nearest equivalent to sovereignty—*mana*—but *kawanatanga*, a translation of 'governorship' improvised by the missionaries, which to the Maori might have meant no more than the coming of the Governor. In the second article, the English version guarantees to the Maori 'the full exclusive and undisturbed possession of their Lands and Estates Forests Fisheries and other properties'. The Maori version is less specific but confirms 'the unqualified exercise of their chieftainship over their lands over their villages and over their treasures all'.[10] The third article, conferring 'royal protection (to the Natives of New Zealand)' and 'imparting to them all the Rights and Privileges of British Subject', appears less contentious, but was compromised by the ultimate goal of British colonisation—the assimilation of the Maori people.

Dissension about European settlement surfaced during the debate at Waitangi and thereafter. Potatoes and guns symbolised irrevocable changes to some chiefs, particularly from the coastal tribes in Northland. They valued the prospect of increased trade, and signed the treaty in part because of their desire for inter-tribal peace brought about by Christianity. However, some great interior chiefs, such as Te Heuheu of Taupo and Te Wherowhero of Waikato, declined to sign, for reasons that can only be inferred. They may have valued their past more than the uncertain European-influenced future, but the evidence of prosperity in their areas suggests that they possessed sufficient resources to dispense with European support.

Maori society had changed significantly by the time of the Treaty of Waitangi, although historians differ on how profound that change was. Some contend that by 1840 Maori society was on the verge of collapse, while others take a more cautious view. Radical changes were taking place before 1840, but they were channelled according to traditional tribal patterns. Moreover, Maori tribes retained control of the situation throughout New Zealand for at least fifteen years after the treaty. From the 1820s huge areas were turned to cultivation, and trade in food

10 Kawharu (ed.), *Waitangi*, 319–20.

flourished. In the 1840s many areas had thriving cultivations and flour mills. So much wheat was grown that steel hand-mills no longer sufficed to grind it, and water-mills were built. The money for community mills was often subscribed by local people. The expanding economy demanded new implements and created new needs, but while crops and agricultural methods were European, the organisation of production seemed more Maori. Before long the European markets were supplied and Maori producers were trading far afield. Coastal tribes took to shipping. By the 1850s tribes owned and operated most of the coastal shipping in the North Island. By 1858, fifty-three Maori vessels of more than 14 tons were registered in Auckland alone. They supplied the local market with almost all its produce and maintained a large trade to Australia and the Pacific with Maori-grown cargoes. At least until the late 1840s, the British depended on Maori enterprises for food. However, this dependency was not acknowledged by all settlers, most of whom could not envision the Maori as their competitors. Moreover, settlers lacked productive land on which labour could be employed.

At first many Maori had been willing to sell vast tracts to settlers. It is debatable whether they had any inkling before 1840 that settlers were seeking permanent title. After the Treaty of Waitangi they realised that settlers believed they had permanent title. Despite this growing awareness the sales did not altogether stop, in part because plenty of land lay fallow. Many communities wanted settlers to live among them as they wished to procure the wealth which they brought. In the 1840s the desire for immigrants in or near Maori settlements had spread throughout the North Island, including the areas thriving on trade. However, interest in trade did not necessarily imply a willingness to sell land. In the mid-1850s the problem of Maori resistance to the sale of land became acute in prosperous areas, particularly Waikato. Partly due to the end of the gold rush and the expansion of agriculture in Australia, the market slumped in 1856. Maori had to compete more often with settlers, and the advantage of communally organised labour was increasingly outweighed by the individual tenure of their European rivals. In addition, the latter responded to the slump by switching to extensive pastoralism, which compounded the land pressure caused by recession. Competition shifted from the land's products to land itself.

In the 1850s groups of settlers began lobbying the government to press the Maori to sell more land—while more Maori voices were raised against sales. Resistance to land alienation caused various tribes to disavow inter-tribal rivalries and discuss common interests. Meetings of Maori were held across the North Island, which caused great concern in the Land Purchase Department, set up to provide land for the settlers. Officers spread the rumour that an anti-land-selling league had been formed in Taranaki in 1854. The term *league* implies more agreement and organisation than existed: it has even been argued that the notion of a league was a European construction to justify political pressure on the Maori to dispose of land.

To protect themselves from European interference and to enforce a ban on land sales, a more coherent political organisation was required. Maori united into inter-tribal councils (*ruunanga*) to devise a common strategy. Meetings of what became known as the movement for *kotahitanga* (oneness) were at first geared to put a *tapu* on land sales within certain boundaries, but soon the Maori kingship crystallised as a political goal. The idea of a unifying kingship was not entirely new. Samuel Marsden, the first missionary, had urged chiefs to make Hongi Hika king in order to halt inter-tribal disputes. (It has often been suggested that Hongi Hika had mapped out a plan to become king after he visited London, where he was intrigued by stories about Napoléon Bonaparte.)

In 1852 the Ngaati Raukawa chief Matene Te Whiwhi led a chiefly deputation around the North Island, touting the idea of a king. Their principal motivation was to *whakakotahitanga* (make unity), to create order from the chaos which followed European settlement. They proposed a tribal confederation with one chief in charge as governor or king. The kingship was offered to several paramount chiefs, but many deferred to Potatau Te Wherowhero of the Waikato tribe. Potatau's line of descent was believed to be linked with the senior lines of all 'canoes'. He was also attached to historically important and fertile lands, and he controlled abundant food-supplies and fisheries. Potatau declined until another Waikato leader, Wiremu Tamihana, put his weight behind the movement. Wiremu Tamihana was concerned about law and order, and was disillusioned with ineffective government policies: he had become convinced that inter-tribal peace was more likely to result from some Maori initiative. In 1856 several influential chiefs agreed to make Potatau the King. He did not accept until 1858, when he was crowned. The charter of the first Maori King was: 'to hold the *mana* or prestige over the land; secondly, *mana* over man; thirdly, to stop the flow of blood [inter-tribal wars]; fourthly, the Maori King and the Queen of England to be joined in concord and God to be above them both'.[11] At first the King was supported by twenty-three tribes, mainly of the Waikato and Taupo districts. Other tribes were reluctant to cede control over their lands and refused to pledge allegiance, but they supported the movement's land policy. The coronation of Potatau and the un-furling of the flag of the Kingitanga (kingship) could only reduce, rather than resolve, tribal rivalries. Maori populations were split into three segments of opinion. The loyalists opposed the Kingitanga for fear of racial disharmony and exclusion from the benefits of the European economy. They wished to make their own laws, but proposed to have them sanctioned by the Governor and administered by a European magistrate. Extremists and moderates both favoured a king. Extremists opposed the selling of land in any circumstances, whereas moderates were willing to yield certain disputed blocks for the sake of peace. The latter emphasised the preservation of Maori autonomy without neces-sarily intending to thwart European settlement. The speaker for the

11 Jones, *King Potatau*, 196, 223.

moderates, Wiremu Tamihana, repeatedly pointed out that he aimed to protect the *mana* and lands of the people, but also to live on friendly terms with the government.

Tamihana was profoundly inspired by the Bible, and quoted the Old Testament to justify a monarchy. The government was well aware of the Christian connotations of 'king' to moderate Kingites, but the Colonial Office could not accept a semi-autonomous movement since all Maori were deemed to have ceded sovereignty by signing the Treaty of Waitangi. For that reason too, the Governor was instructed to persuade the Maori to give up their determination to elect a king. Since Potatau had the authority to withhold land and the right to forbid sales, the Kingitanga appeared to be substantially a land league. This formed the real objection of settlers, who gradually gained the government's sympathy.

Governor Grey tried a new policy before resorting to force, setting up 'new institutions' in a system of indirect rule. The scheme intended to involve Maori tribes in the European polity by building on tribal *ruunanga* which would recommend to the Governor the laws they required. Although guided by Civil Commissioners and Resident Magistrates, authority over land remained with corporate tribal groups, a provision fiercely opposed by most settlers, who advocated individual titles. They criticised the Governor for deceiving the Maori—and hoped that he was preparing for war. The new institutions seemed, however, a genuine attempt to find a peaceful way through conflicting interests. The government hoped it would clarify Maori land titles, and eventually facilitate alienation, thus meeting both the settlers' demand for land and the goal of assimilation.

The 'new institutions' were introduced in a profoundly hostile environment. The government was desperate to gain control over the Kingites without offending the humanitarian lobby, but Maori were deeply disillusioned with the effects of the aggressive policies of, particularly, the Land Purchase Department. Hence most tribes made only selective use of the institutions, and the Kingites simply refused to accept them. In the Waikato area the tribal council was never dissolved and Grey's District Ruunanga never assembled. Extreme Kingites even expelled the Resident Magistrate and later Civil Commissioner in the upper Waikato.

Despite the Kingitanga's early successes, the tribes failed to achieve unity. In some areas feuds erupted between sellers and non-sellers. Some chiefs refused to recognise Potatau as King in the belief that Maori social organisation did not allow for such difference in status, while many northern chiefs argued that a Maori kingship was incompatible with the Treaty of Waitangi. The Kingites themselves remained divided on strategy. Nevertheless the mere existence of a king influenced inter-ethnic relations throughout New Zealand, whether or not the local tribe paid homage to Potatau. Maoridom was more centrally organised than it had been.

The wars of the 1860s were not caused simply by conflict over land, but were the outcome of a multi-dimensional colonial encounter.

Neither European aggression nor a fierce reaction to the advance of settlement was the simple cause. More significant was rivalry over control of the economic infrastructure and its political management. After twelve years of skirmishing between land-sellers and land-holders, war broke out in Taranaki in March 1860. Belligerent manoeuvring was first confined to Taranaki, but it was apparent that the government considered these battles a dress rehearsal for the invasion of the Waikato. As soon as a substantial victory was achieved, all troops were transferred to Auckland. The critical question was how the government would respond to the Maori King since some of his adherents had interfered in Taranaki.

Potatau died in June 1860, and his son Maatutaera (a transliteration of Methuselah) was enthroned. Some people had argued that he was not competent to replace his father, but he won the allegiance of increasing numbers who became convinced that the settlers were planning to seize their lands. The Waikato was finally invaded on 12 July 1863. General Cameron's troops crossed the Mangatawhiri River, demarcating Kingitanga territory within which no land was to be sold. The wars lasted until the end of 1864, and consisted largely of pitched battles in which each tribe made a final stand on its domain. The battle against Waikato was fought at Rangiriri, after which Cameron captured the Maori King's capital at Ngaruawahia without a fight. The Kingites made their last stand under Maniapoto's chief Rewi at Orakau. In the legend of Orakau the Maori have been made heroic to inflate Cameron's victory. Three hundred Maori refused to surrender for three days, it is said. Their slogan 'Ka whawhai tonu ake! Ake! Ake!' (We shall fight on forever! Forever! Forever!) has become a rallying cry in Maori protest movements.

The government immediately confiscated 3 million acres of the most arable areas. As early as June 1863 the Grey government indicated its intention to confiscate and redistribute 'the lands of the hostile Natives'.[12] In December the *New Zealand Settlements Act* authorised the Governor to take land for the purpose of settlement. Under this law the Kingitanga tribes lost 1,202,172 acres, mainly in the Waikato area. Their allies in Taranaki lost 1,275,000 acres, while 290,000 acres were confiscated in the Tauranga area and 448,000 acres in the Bay of Plenty. Most of the forested hill country and steep limestone valleys of the more extreme Maniapoto tribes were untouched. Punishing rebels was a pretext; confiscations were plainly for the purpose of settlement. Military settlements were established, and an ambitious Immigration Scheme recruited settlers. Outside the confiscated areas the sale of land was facilitated by establishing a Native Land Court in 1865. Its aim was first to determine land titles on a sub-tribal basis, and then to individualise titles by allotting shares to a maximum of ten owners of each block. As a result, many people were dispossessed.

The confiscations obviously violated the Treaty of Waitangi, which guaranteed Maori proprietary rights. In the 1870s Maori sought justice

12 Premier Domett to Governor Grey, 24 June 1863, Appendices to the *Journals of the House of Representatives of New Zealand*, 1863, E–7: 8.

in many cases, but found that the treaty offered no protection. A leading case in 1877 involved Wi Parata, the Western Maori Representative in Parliament, who in the Supreme Court requested that land issued to Bishop Selwyn of Wellington be returned to his tribe Ngati Toa. Chief Judge James Prendergast described the Treaty of Waitangi as 'a simple nullity' for 'No body politic existed capable of making cession of sovereignty, nor could the thing itself exist.'[13] This ruling dismissed Maori rights on the basis of the treaty and set a precedent for all cases until 1987. For 110 years the treaty was ignored by the government, despite an unceasing Maori quest for acknowledgment. In 1884 the then Maori King, Taawhiao, led a deputation to England to petition the Queen, because he believed she had an obligation under the treaty. He asked her to return all the confiscated lands and to approve an independent Maori government, although he qualified this request by explaining that: 'I am called a king, not for the purpose of separation, but in order that the natives might be united under one race, ever acknowledging the supremacy of the Queen, and claiming her protection.'[14] The petitioners did not see the Queen, because in terms of responsible government (from 1852) Maori matters were the responsibility of the New Zealand government. In 1886 Taawhiao appealed to the New Zealand government to recognise him as king in the form of head of an annual Maori Council which would administer the provisions of the Treaty of Waitangi. The Minister for Native Affairs refused. Taawhiao then simply claimed the right of governmental authority for himself and in 1894 promulgated the constitution of the Great Council—but many tribes could not accept his claim to rule over the entire North Island. Taawhiao had managed to keep united only those tribes which had been most affected by confiscations. *Raupatu*, or 'conquest', as his Waikato tribe branded the loss of their land, had provided the King Movement with the purpose of seeking redress. This focus, however, was primarily for the benefit of the Waikato people. Most of the movement's founding supporters who had retained some land were ambivalent about the King's policies.

Towards the end of the century it was commonly believed that the Maori were on the verge of extinction. Their number reached its nadir in 1896, when only 41,993 people were censused. Some co-operation between tribes was seen as imperative to avert total assimilation, but not everyone was prepared to unite behind King Taawhiao. The Maori had been granted four seats in Parliament in 1867. In 1892 the Maori members revived the *kotahitanga* movement of the 1850s and set up a Maori Parliament to present grievances to the government. Unlike Taawhiao's Great Council, which claimed traditional sovereignty, the Maori Parliament accepted the European Parliament and sought control over a limited range of affairs. The Maori Parliament was not a success.

---

13 *Wi Parata v. The Bishop of Wellington and the Attorney-General* (1877) 3 NZ Jur. (NS) SC 72.
14 Quoted in Pei Te Hurinui Jones, 'Maori Kings', in Schwimmer (ed.), *The Maori People in the Nineteen-Sixties*, 137–8.

European society was so well entrenched that it could afford to neglect it. Many Maori were uninterested. Kingites still argued for unity behind Taawhiao, while others shunned the Maori Parliament because they accepted European society. Large sections refused to join because they were seeking other approaches than the protest meetings of the Maori Parliament that often stalled in tribal bickering. In part, the lack of enthusiasm resulted from a large-scale movement of Maori into the money economy. Eventually the division of Maoridom proved fatal. Several young leaders who had opposed the Parliament's constitutional proposals made a positive stand for the government. Unlike the conservative 'home-rule' party of elderly leaders, who distrusted the government outright, they no longer resisted some governmental protection. In 1898 the old guard refused to co-operate further with the younger leaders, and walked out. The Maori Parliament was disbanded in 1902.

VISIONARIES AND ENTREPRENEURS

Outside the settler colonies, economic intrusions and innovations were much more erratic. Until the mid-nineteenth century, the leading exports were natural resources harvested on moving frontiers. Beginning in the northern and central Pacific, luggers and schooners prospected south and east until the industries settled on the last and richest frontier, Australia's tropical coasts. By then conditions began to favour new production, if middlemen linked land, labour and markets. The settler colonies spawned many such adventurers. Few had much knowledge of production and none understood the societies whose resources they coveted. Their ventures relied heavily on luck: Nauru's phosphates were revealed when an office-boy chanced to analyse a curio serving as a Sydney office door-stopper.

Some entrepreneurs were latter-day buccaneers—Benjamin Pease and Bully Hayes cut bloody swathes through Micronesia in the 1860s and 1870s, kidnapping labourers, cheating customers and agents alike. Others had benign intentions. In 1834 Captain Eagleston of the *Emerald* took Cokonauto, a leading chief of Rewa, to Tahiti. On their return he gave him two cattle—the first in Fiji. Asked what they were, Eagleston 'classed the two in one and called them "Bula ma Cow" which was very readily taken up by the natives . . .'.[15] This may be the first use of the pidgin word *bulamakau*. Some men's visions were lofty but fanciful. John Dunmore Lang, passionate Presbyterian and Sydney politician, inspired a gold-prospecting association in 1871 which proposed this romantic plan for Papua:

> [The Association should] conciliate the natives as much as possible; and stringent rules will be made to prevent members from spoiling the success of the Expedition by any unjust interference with the aborigines, or violation of their rights. By promoting and sustaining friendly relations with them, a

15 Quoted in Ward and Kingdon, *Land, Custom and Practice in the South Pacific.*

constitution may be formed similar to that which has been so successfully initiated in the Fiji Islands, and by the purchase of large tracts of land from the natives a sure source of immense future profit will accrue to the Association.[16]

Optimism was tempered by advice that each venturer provide his own tools, tents, and firearms, and when the ambivalent expedition struck a reef off Queensland, the miners found more use for guns than tools. Charles du Breil, Marquis de Rays, proposed an equally preposterous settlement to farm, fish and mine at Nouvelle-France, assuring colonists that 'The natives do not share our idea of ownership and do not argue about the land with the new occupants.' Eight hundred people landed on the southern tip of New Ireland between 1879 and 1881. 'The natives' did not have long to wait for the invasion to implode through illness and starvation. Bad faith and poor management were not always fatal. In 1862 Joseph Byrne resolved to recruit Melanesian workers for Peruvian guano-quarrying. Poor navigation brought him to Tongareva, 'the one island in all Polynesia where the people were only too eager to be recruited' as their coconut trees were diseased and their missionaries encouraged them to work abroad.[17] Byrne's profits provoked Peruvians to charter any ship which might float. When volunteers were few, Islanders were kidnapped. Most vulnerable were small islands (such as Rapanui, which lost a third of its people). Mercifully the venture lasted only two years. A total of 3634 people had left the islands: one in ten returned, since repatriation was just as haphazard as recruitment.

These ventures aimed not to invest but to amass capital. A rare entrepreneur (like Daniel O'Keefe in the Carolines) could mobilise the Islanders' own wealth, but the parties seldom understood each other well enough to allow this. Like the pearling captains before them, de Rays, Lang and Byrne sought windfalls. Lacking capital, they were just as likely to defraud investors and colonists as to exploit Islanders. Once resources were proven, most speculators yielded to company promoters to raise capital. One exceptional businessman with a flair for exciting investors did float his own companies. John Higginson, born in Britain and migrating to Australia, came to New Caledonia in 1859. He cornered the colony's Australian supplies and was one of few settlers who won the Governor's confidence. When prospectors discovered gold at Fern Hill in 1870, Higginson was the conduit for capital and acquired the mine outright. With help from the Australian William Morgan, he floated a copper-mining company and—when Morgan's capital was spent—persuaded the Rothschilds to invest. When gold and copper lost their glister, nickel came to the colony's rescue. In 1880 with further support from Rothschilds, Higginson launched Société le Nickel. The Rothschilds took over Le Nickel in 1890 and nursed it through depressed prices until a cartel raised price levels in 1895.

Recruiting labour for the nickel mines, Higginson observed with dismay that Protestant missionaries were well established in the New Hebrides, and that Australians were urging Britain to annex the group.

16 Whittaker et al., Documents and Readings in New Guinea History, 386–9.
17 Maude, Slavers in Paradise.

To forestall that outcome, Higginson created the Caledonian Company of the New Hebrides and in 1882 set out with piles of trade goods and the heroic vision of buying the islands piecemeal. By 1886 the company had paper claims to 780,000 hectares—about half the entire land area—and had begun to plant French settlers. Some land was purchased from existing planters (such as Donald MacLeod, who became a company agent); much was 'bought' from Melanesians who had no conception that they were 'selling', and were outraged when settlers arrived to dispossess them. Purchase prices reflect this distinction. MacLeod sold at 263 francs per hectare: Melanesians in eastern Efate 'sold' for 0.07 francs.[18] When Higginson died in 1904, even the Caledonian Company had failed, along with much else. More investors than Islanders had been fleeced, and it fell to the colonists who bought company land to try to dispossess Melanesians.

Expanding trade attracted shipping companies with sufficient ballast to survive natural disasters and erratic prices. Godeffroy & Sohn of Hamburg flowed in from South America in the 1860s, to place agents through the central Pacific, whose trade they dominated in the 1870s. To escape dependence on Islander-grown copra, they bought land in Samoa and laid out plantations tended by indentured workers. The house of Ballande, wine-shippers in Bordeaux, built another string of retail outlets. Their interests led them, by the same business logic, to recruit labourers (and carry their rations) from Vietnam to New Caledonia. Meanwhile the English company J. T. Arundel diversified out of Peruvian guano into island trading and nitrate mining; while Burns Philp stretched its Queensland coastal trade into the islands and (briefly) the labour trade. Henderson & MacFarlane of Auckland, Crawford & Co. of Honolulu, and several German companies swelled the ranks.

Some beachcombers made the transition to company agents, but their work habits disqualified most of them. Throughout the New Hebrides in mid-century, several survived by trading tobacco and other goods for coconuts or *bêche-de-mer*. An intrigued observer thought that 'This career only tempts former sailors, half-castes, [men] who have lost their social position, and adventurers who have encountered all dangers and all diseases.'[19] Godeffroy's agents were required to speak the local language, live peacefully and monogamously, and be discreet about company business. One of the most successful—Adolph Capelle—possessed all these skills. The first trader to settle in the Marshalls, as agent for a German firm, he placated his hosts and their missionaries, married an Ebon woman (most beachcombers took mistresses) and became a pillar of the mission. In the 1860s he built his own company and began coconut planting. In 1873 he relocated to Jaluit and soon had a fleet of schooners and a network of agents throughout the southern Marshalls and Carolines.

Anywhere there was a missionary, white or brown, an agent for Capelle was almost invariably to be found . . . The commoners who did the actual work of

18 Bonnemaison, *The Tree and the Canoe*, ch. 3.
19 E. N. Imhaus, *Les Nouvelles-Hebrides*, Paris, 1890, cited in *ibid.*, 45.

cutting and drying the copra before handing it over to the chiefs, in keeping with the traditional tribute system, were rewarded or not with a share of the trade goods as the chiefs saw fit . . . Every three or four months a Capelle vessel would visit the agents to pick up the copra and pay them off . . .[20]

Capelle and O'Keefe understood that the support of power-holders was vital. Missionaries often bridged the chasm between companies and Islanders. Alliances were sometimes sought by missionaries seeking co-religionists as business partners (see chapter 6). Choosing— or being chosen by—missionaries, many companies had a sectarian tinge. Burns Philp favoured Presbyterian missionaries in Vanuatu, and offered them discounts, hoping to recoup that cost through access to copra. The pious André Ballande invoked St Anthony to bless ventures which bore few marks of piety. The young J. T. Arundel toyed with a missionary vocation until the LMS assured him that a devout businessman could also please God. He and Lord Stanmore (like Ballande) liked to think that Christianity and commerce were compatible: when these interests clashed, God's agents redefined His wishes to accommodate sound business practice in much the same manner as sinners.

Swindlers and saints alike depended on island power-holders. The Hawaiian monarchy gave missionaries' sons their start in business. The Pomares in Tahiti, intermarrying with Salmons and Branders, created an Anglo-Polynesian, Protestant commercial ascendancy, which survived French annexation. A colonial state would serve just as well as a monarchy. Higginson started his career as a government contractor; André Ballande aligned himself with the church, reinforced by his influence as deputy for Bordeaux, and weathered the bitter dispute between church and state at the turn of the century. Higginson's commercial empire faltered only when he lost the Governor's confidence: Ballande survived even that crisis, and had his debts cancelled by a friendly government. Conversely, many German companies were wound up when other powers annexed their Island markets. Distinctions between economics, religion and politics may have seemed clear to outsiders but had little real significance. Most ventures were financially marginal and politically vulnerable. Since small traders relied absolutely on chiefs for security, labour and land for stores or stations, chiefs often negotiated on strong terms. That leverage shrank as small traders were either displaced or (like Capelle) co-opted by companies with enough capital to plant their own crops on their own land, and recruit workers from other Islands.

PEASANTS AND PLANTATIONS

As traders sought reliable supplies, the first issue was to identify a crop. In Hawai'i, where *haole* (white) entrepreneurs acquired land, they grew pineapples and sugar. In Samoa in the 1850s, Godeffroy acquired 25,000

---

20 Hezel, *The First Taint of Civilization*, 216.

acres, and raised cotton. When the American Civil War disrupted the largest cotton producer, Godeffroy was poised to benefit. Australian and New Zealand adventurers took up land in Fiji under the patronage of chiefs who mobilised labourers to harvest cotton for a few boom years before Appomattox restored American cotton production. When the cotton bubble burst, coconuts stood alone. During the 1850s technical advances made copra a feasible substitute for whale oil and turned coconuts into an industrial material. They were split open and dried in the sun (or, later, smoke-dried). A planter reflected that 'we were always short of labour. And as copra is the least labour-intensive of all the tropical products, that was why we were forced back willy-nilly into copra production.'[21]

Copra need not be grown on plantations, if chiefs would command commoners to produce it. Missionaries were busily forging links between production and piety, and astute traders aligned themselves with missions and mission-minded chiefs. The Tongan economy, for example, evolved into something like peasant production, with German traders purchasing the crop. Fledgling state systems in Fiji fostered a similar nexus. The Tongan adventurer Enele Ma'afu (Ma'afu'otu'itonga) dominated the Lau group in mid-century, buttressed by Tongan Methodists, and by the trader William Henning who bought the copra. In these regimes, chiefs could retain control over both land and labour; parts of the economy were monetised, political power centralised, and the populace Christianised; yet the resulting society was not animated by orthodox capitalist dynamics. Nobody depended entirely on market goods or the sale of labour. When copra prices fell, therefore, people turned back to food crops. The planters who endorsed Cakobau's claims to Fijian supremacy (chapter 6) enabled him to repeat the pattern even where the state was frail. Something similar emerged even where there was no recognisable state. In the nineteenth century Tolai from southern New Ireland began to colonise the Gazelle Peninsula of New Britain. Power rested on markets, and the flow of goods was smoothed by *tambu* shell. *Tambu* also enabled market masters to collect fees, and fathoms of *tambu* strengthened the authority of ToRigaragunan, the *lualua* (or king, as some Europeans glossed it). Traders and evangelists reinforced Tolai colonisation by introducing new commodities, and buying as much copra as people could grow.

On Aoba (now Ambae) Island in the New Hebrides, young men returning from Queensland became initiators. The old spur to production was a graded hierarchy of positions for which men competed, mainly by sacrificing pigs. Some Islanders had become Christians in Queensland or when they came home. They built their own churches and opposed many practices including pig-killing. Opposition to 'paganism' implied other production—notably copra. When trader-missionaries arrived in 1907, rivalry began between Christian copra-growers and pagan pig-keepers. Compromise was difficult, if only

---

21 Quoted in Doug Munro and Stewart Firth, 'Company Strategies—Colonial Policies', in Moore, Leckie and Munro (eds), *Labour in the South Pacific*, 6.

because pigs destroyed young trees. The forces of Christ protected the coconut groves but (possibly because of fresh strains of pig) the pig population burgeoned. As late as 1932 one man killed 1000 pigs in a single ceremony. Protestants (and British officials) were firmly on the side of copra. French traders and officials were ambivalent, but Anglo-French rivalry neutralised colonial intervention, and the struggle slowly resolved itself into a victory for Christianity and copra.[22]

Islanders often had to make sacrifices to retain autonomy. The Vaitupu Company in Tuvalu (Ellice Islands) made heroic attempts at self-reliant development. The creator of the company, Thomas Williams, came from a family of missionaries, consuls and traders. This lent credibility to his scheme for a co-operative society, among Islanders frustrated by unequal relations with foreigners and humiliation by H. M. Ruge & Co.; and he had the sense to veil his commercial ambitions. The Vaitupu Company was created in 1877. Its shareholders bought a schooner—on credit from Ruge & Co.—and created a coconut plantation. Failure was swift. The company storekeeper had a stronger sense of kinship than of accounts, the LMS pastor alienated potential allies, local politics impeded business methods, and nearby islands declined to merge their interests with those of Vaitupu. By 1883 the company had debts of $13,000, which the Islanders (unlike Williams) discharged with honour, banning tobacco, rationing food and refraining from buying clothes. The debt was repaid just in time for Ruge & Co. to declare itself bankrupt. One choke-point, as Vaitupuans recognised, was the ownership of schooners. Other Islanders also bought ships but quickly fell into debt, or found that schooners were diverted and schedules disrupted. There are particular reasons for each 'failure', but beyond the specifics it is easy to discern the determination of traders to thwart any innovation which threatened their livelihood.

From the traders' point of view, autonomous development was frustrating. Production was vulnerable to chiefly whims, the elastic deference of their followers, and even civil war. Loiak and Kabua, rivals for paramountcy of the southern Ralik Islands in the Marshalls, halted production on Ebon in 1876. When peace returned, the chiefs bid up the copra price by fanning competition between traders. From one cent per pound (and a commission of $2 per thousand pounds to the chiefs) the price jumped to two and a half cents (and a $3 commission). Equally alarming was the demand for muskets, which implied more warfare. Even without political hazards there was structural 'economic' risk. As prices fell, producers stayed at home; and if prices soared, they were content to meet income targets. Traders who contracted to provide regular cargoes fretted, and tried to tie down chiefs through promises, threats—and debt.

Not surprisingly, they bent their minds to land: at the very least, traders and missionaries needed land for churches, homes and stores. Some received permissive residence rights, but others sought freehold

22 Allen, 'The Establishment of Christianity and Cash-Cropping in a New Hebridean Community'.

title. Not all donors or sellers realised that they were transferring land in perpetuity. On the other hand some chiefs who sold land claimed greater rights than their followers would acknowledge, or 'sold' land which did not belong to their kin group. Few whites or Islanders had clean hands or pure hearts. Island leaders, as in the Solomons, found that the sale of land gave them quick wealth and status. Emerging governments often banned or controlled land sales. In Tahiti, Queen Pomare's government asserted inalienability in 1842, as did King Tāufa'āhau Tupou I of Tonga. In any case, governments had to clarify the claims of earlier settlers. Often they uncovered disconcerting evidence. Higginson was not unique: a San Francisco syndicate claimed nearly half of Samoa, and total claims amounted to more than double the area of the country.

Once land was secured, plantations developed. O'Keefe set the Pacific precedent, with a plantation on uninhabited Mapia, a Palauan outlier far removed from Yap, where he recruited workers who could travel only on his vessels. The essence of a plantation was insularity. Planters commonly chose clearly defined parcels of land—often islets— where workers could not grow their own food nor respond to clan obligations. Hawaiians in the 1850s were the first islanders to discover the consequences of plantations. Commoners expected to remain under the protection of local chiefs, retaining rights of access. Chiefs expected to retain authority even as they sold their new rights to extinguish old debts. Both were grievously disappointed. One planter spoke for many: 'I understood at the time, that with the exception of squatter titles, which a few natives, having grass houses, pretended to have, I received a perfect title . . . And whereas very anxious to have a clear title to all the real estate I own, I took immediate steps to get rid of those natives.'[23] Plantation societies were built on sharp distinctions between managers and workers, and between both and the host community.

By mid-century planters employed half of all adult male Hawaiians —and demanded to import indentured workers. The monarchy sought workers who could assimilate into the declining native population. Those efforts were abandoned only when the difficulty of recruiting and repatriating Islanders outweighed any advantage, and planters turned to the Philippines, Japan, China, India and even Europe. As in Hawai'i, so everywhere: planters wanted cheaper, more regular and plentiful labour than local sources provided. The ideal workers were employed under indenture for fixed periods at set wages. Housing was provided, and the plantation store was usually the only point of sale. Managers could then predict and control costs. Reliance on powerless workers reinforced reliance on primitive technology. Plantations generated fewer technical advances than any other form of market production, since managers had no need to save labour. Using crude methods of production, managers stuck grimly to a labour force with little skill, much muscle and low wages. This commitment created a determined demand for indenture.

23 Joel Turrill, quoted by Jocelyn Linnekin, 'Statistical Analysis of the Great *Mahele*'.

The late nineteenth century was the heyday of Asian indentured labour—first from India, then Japan and especially China. Planters recruited haphazardly until they learned to work through labour-trading firms. Asians were preferred on the assumption that they were inured to work. When Islanders were also conscripted, managers often divided the workforce by juxtaposing workers from different backgrounds. Only in Hawai'i did planters employ Europeans alongside Asians and Islanders: elsewhere they preferred workers with lower status and fewer rights. The ethnic mix also reflected international relations. Japanese travelled to Hawai'i, New Caledonia and Banaba until World War I, when they were directed to Micronesia. Vietnamese embarked only for French dependencies. A few Indians were shipped to New Caledonia in the 1860s but the only large number went to Fiji as *girmitiyas* (workers under indenture): more than 60,000 were introduced between 1879 and 1916. The Raj gradually imposed conditions which made Indian workers less attractive to employers, and that brought the system to an end. The cumulative effect of recruiting so many ethnic categories, and exploiting them in proportion to their political powerlessness, was workers sharply differentiated by ethnicity, such that people doing the same task received very different wages.

From the 1850s until the 1920s, most recruits signed on in southern China and the Chinese diaspora. Eventually that supply also evaporated. During a decade of negotiations with German authorities in Samoa, China demanded increasing concessions, narrowing the gap between the civil rights of Chinese and Europeans. In a tight corner, German officials would concede these demands—perhaps with their fingers crossed—but increasing employees' rights dismayed employers. By default, Islanders were drafted into production. Perversely, since all employers preferred tractable foreigners, Islanders were embarking for Queensland, Fiji, Samoa and New Caledonia precisely when Asians were arriving in the Islands. By the 1860s, when many Tannese men worked on whaling and trading vessels and on plantations in Australia and Fiji, local planters had to recruit from other Islands.

The first recruits were poorly informed, and often kidnapped. Recruiters had no language in which to explain conditions of work, the short life expectancy, or the value of wages, so no recruit could envision the three years ahead. Violence was also likely. A massacre on board the *Carl* in 1871 was widely reported. Like some other recruiters, the men lured Malaitan canoes alongside and then sank them, grappling survivors on board and confining them below deck. There was an affray and the crew fired into the hold, killing or wounding seventy people—who were thrown overboard. Twenty-five survivors were transhipped in Fiji to the *Peri*, which they captured. The vessel drifted for a month until it struck the Queensland coast, by which time provisions were exhausted and some non-Malaitans had been eaten. The murder of the Anglican missionary Bishop Patteson north of Santa Cruz was thought to be an act of revenge, and seemed to imply that 'blackbirding' must be curbed, if only to protect Europeans from payback.

Kidnapping became rare after 1872 when the British government passed the *Pacific Islanders Protection Act* and Queensland enacted complementary legislation. The Royal Navy policed minimum standards for recruiting, and Queensland vessels carried Government Agents. The proliferation of missionaries—likely to report malpractice—reinforced these restrictions. An important loophole was the refusal of French authorities to act in concert. French recruiters could therefore perpetuate coercion, but kidnapping soon became superfluous. The same pressure which drove Gilbertese to recruit for Peru in the 1860s—drought—continued to drive them to Fiji and Samoa and as far afield as Guatemala. Even when they heard that a recruiting vessel had been lost with all hands, more volunteered. An incredulous Royal Navy commander inspected the recruits and reluctantly concluded that coercion was not involved.

In much of the 'Melanesian labour reserve', migration became an institution. Tobacco and alcohol were powerful inducements, and returning workers persuasive:

> When the men were first stolen they thought the white men had taken them and killed them . . . Then the men came back with guns and knives and axes and showed the people how these could be used in the garden and to kill birds and men. And then the people wanted to go, and the fathers encouraged their sons to go.[24]

A censorious missionary complained that: 'Queensland was a veritable refuge for wrong-doers in the islands; murderers, sorcerers, adulterers, wife-stealers, thieves, discontented wives, rebellious children, all hailed the coming of a labour-vessel as a chance to be freed from the likelihood of punishment or from the irksomeness of home restrictions.'[25]

Where a flow of recruits was established, power-holders such as Kwaisulia and Foulanga on Malaita began to organise recruitment, taking commissions, and dominating large parts of the island. These passage masters were *'wane baita*, the important pivotal position in traditional Malaitan society. But in negotiating with Europeans around the entrances to the Malaitan cultural fortress they used traditional reciprocal relationships and established cosmological cycles to provide human capital for the Queensland sugar industry.'[26]

There is much debate about the nature of the Melanesian labour trade.[27] Despite the decline of physical violence, a variety of legal constraints at work, and social pressures at home, severely circumscribed workers' lives. Not only did they endure dreadful living and working conditions and high rates of death and illness. The pioneer anthropologist W. H. R. Rivers pointed to the broader societal effects, to sustain his judgement that the Queensland labour trade was

24 Moore, *Kanaka*, 46, quoting Ishmael Itea, interview, 1976.
25 *Ibid.*, 63, quoting W. G. Ivens, *Dictionary and Grammar of the Language of Sa'a and Ulawa, Solomon Islands*, London, 1930.
26 *Ibid.*, 92–3.
27 The points of view are summed up by Munro, 'Revisionism and its Enemies' (which emphasises Islander agency), and Brass, 'The Return of "Merrie Melanesia"' (which restates the structural constraints).

one of the blackest of civilisation's crimes. Not least among its evils was the manner of its ending, when large numbers of people who had learnt by many years' experience to adapt themselves to civilised ways were, in the process of so-called repatriation, thrust back into savagery without help of any kind. The misery thus caused and the resulting disaffection . . . underlie most of the open troubles in the recent history of Melanesia . . .[28]

Negotiations between employers, recruiters and Islanders were very unequal, but average wages rose over the fifty years of the Queensland phase. Employers could well afford these costs, since seasoned workers were more productive than fresh recruits and likelier to survive. But wages did not rise through altruism: passage masters and recruits took some marginal advantage from persistent competition between employers in New Caledonia, Queensland and Fiji. The terms of trade moved against them when Indians arrived in Fiji, and after 1900 when Queensland was closed. Thousands of New Hebrideans continued to sign on for New Caledonia, where crass treatment and working conditions continued, and even deteriorated.[29]

AUTONOMOUS DEVELOPMENT?

It is a matter of enduring significance that Islanders failed to gain control over new networks. One element of that failure is so obvious that it often escapes notice: wherever European traders and missionaries established themselves, canoe-travel declined. In the New Hebrides, Islanders may have made less use of canoes for fear of being blackbirded;[30] but maritime trade-routes withered even where there was no such risk. Possibly the size, convenience and security of foreign ships encouraged dependence upon them. Trade goods may have had the same effect. At any rate, only in New Zealand did Islanders master the new technology, build their own vessels, and (briefly) make profits at sea. Trade depended on credit, contacts in the markets, and familiarity with harbours for supplies and crews. Traders were loath to share this information. Given the structure of most Island societies, only great chiefs could command the labour and resources for such ventures, and the qualities of great chiefs were not easily reconciled with commerce. The Hawaiian monarchy and Fijian chiefs alike lost capital through rash borrowing and poor planning.

The costs of 'development' are manifest—disease, depopulation, and often dispossession. On the other hand, Islanders learned to handle ships, and to hunt, process and sell whales, seals and furs. Less tangible was the benefit of dining with philosophers or working abroad. Many individuals were transformed abroad, but their societies were not remade in the image of outsiders. New techniques and ideas were often

28 Rivers, *Essays on the Depopulation of Melanesia*, 105.
29 Shineberg, ' "The New Hebridean is Everywhere" '.
30 Bonnemaison, *The Tree and the Canoe*.

assimilated into old relations of production and ideologies, modifying rather than shattering them. Some brought home goods to distribute among kin and chiefs: very few sailed home in their own schooners.

Radically different dynamics of wage-labour and village work limited the influence of each on the other. Islanders abroad behaved like foreigners, but mainly rebuilt older relationships when they returned (like beachcombers who reverted to being ordinary sailors with vivid memories and tedious boasts). Tannese cheerfully worked abroad, but at home their relations with Europeans were tense and often violent. After they drove out missionaries, they endured naval bombardment and an invasion by sailors who destroyed crops and houses. Missionaries were less often resisted than ignored, and traders and planters suffered the same indifference, inflected by the wariness of people who knew strangers to be unpredictable.[31] Cosmopolitan abroad, Tannese men were parochial at home and declined to become either workers or peasants.

Yet cultural spheres were not watertight. Many Islanders in Queensland made their own houses on Island patterns, grew their food, hunted at weekends, and insisted on their distinctness from others. Those who chose not to return home retained—and bequeathed—memories of their Island homes. To be sure, even cultural conservatism implied psychic and social change as peoples from a hundred islands merged into one community. They were made over, not as white Australians but in an image which they helped to construct. Men and women who came home cherished ambivalent hopes, implicit in the baggage of some Malaitans:

> tobacco was the most important item . . . Parcels of pipes . . . and a gross or two of matches were the natural corollaries. Assortments of axes, hatchets, cutlery, calico and coloured handkerchiefs were common to all. Saucepans and billycans were also in evidence. Among the uncommon articles were musical boxes, a bundle of score music, bathing pants, ginghams, pomatum, fancy soap, and some shells being taken back to where they had been gathered.[32]

These acquisitions tell us only about aspirations. The tobacco, the alcohol, and the Christianity which some brought home foreshadow tales of physical and spiritual addiction, which are pursued in the next chapter.

Men and women could cross the psychic beach individually, but that beach continued to encircle 'cultural fortresses'. Some had been transformed by their guardians, others were infiltrated by subversive people and values, and a few had become indefensible. The beach protected economy and polity as well as culture. The preservation of the Hawaiian and Tongan monarchies required dramatic economic restructuring, with all the risks attending revolutions from the top. New

---

31 *Ibid.*
32 J. D. Melvin, *The Cruise of the Helena* (ed. Peter Corris), Melbourne, 1977, 7, quoted in Moore, *Kanaka*, 74.

political structures in Fiji could be created only by harnessing economic and religious forces to chiefs' ambitions. The transformation of Maori production generated new forums for political contest and required the assimilation of alarming cultural values.

Some changes were less dramatic. The introduction of metal tools, for example, has been seen as a sort of Industrial Revolution, and far-reaching effects did flow into the division of domestic labour and the ventures which villagers attempted. Steel tools made labour more efficient, but the extent of that advantage is unclear. Salisbury estimated that among the Siane in New Guinea, clearing and fencing gardens took three to four times as long with stone tools in 1933 as with steel in 1953. Other tasks were less affected.[33] The advantage was seldom so great as in gardening work, in part because the tasks changed. Certainly many communities found their workloads reduced, and new crops required less labour. Savings of time allowed people to manage larger holdings without assistance. Some innovations were self-limiting: as people became accustomed to novelties, their demand for tools dwindled and tobacco became attractive. When stands of sandalwood and beds of *bêche-de-mer* were exhausted, therefore, and the frontiers shifted, older patterns of production and exchange were reasserted, modified mainly by the efficiency of the tools left behind.

These new forces were uneven, and the responses stochastic. Only a few Islands bore the full brunt of mines, plantations, or depopulation; but at the other extremity, few retained control over their own land and labour. And the chances for independent restructuring were passing. The initiative was seized by colonial powers, seeking to reorder affairs in different ways to those which Islanders themselves developed during the century of autonomous interaction.

BIBLIOGRAPHIC ESSAY

Leading sources in economic history include Salisbury, *From Stone to Steel*; and Shineberg, *They Came for Sandalwood*. Islanders' conceptions of 'development' are analysed in Burridge, *Mambu*; Lawrence, *Road Belong Cargo*; and in chapter 12 of this volume. Introductions to Maori history include Sinclair, *The Origins of the Maori Wars*; Williams, *Politics of the New Zealand Maori*; Ward, *A Show of Justice*; and Kawharu, *Waitangi: Maaori and Paakehaa Perspectives of the Treaty of Waitangi*.

Chappell has combed the archives to reconstruct the lives of Islanders afloat. See his 'Secret Sharers' and 'Shipboard Relations between Pacific Island Women and Euroamerican Men, 1767–1887'. Torres Strait Islanders' lives are analysed by Becket, 'Politics in the Torres Strait Islands'. Sections on land tenure again derive from Ward and Kingdon, *Land, Custom and Practice in the South Pacific*; Shineberg, '"The New Hebridean is Everywhere"'. On the Melanesian labour

33 Salisbury, *From Stone to Steel*, 109.

trade, see Corris, *Passage, Port and Plantation*; Scarr, 'Recruits and Recruiters'; *JPH* xi (1976), a special issue on the labour trade; Moore, Leckie and Munro (eds), *Labour in the South Pacific*; Munro, 'Revisionism and its Enemies'; and Brass, 'The Return of "Merrie Melanesia"'. On the lives of Melanesians in Australia, see Moore, *Kanaka*; and Mercer, *White Australia Defied*.

CHAPTER

6

NEW POLITICAL ORDERS

NEW POSSIBILITIES

For much of the nineteenth century, especially in the central and eastern Pacific, political openings matched the material opportunities discussed in chapter 5. The institutions and traditions of chiefly societies were often modified in the light of new perceptions of power and sometimes at the instigation of foreigners. Some ambitious chiefs created central-ised polities: but these structures often yielded more advantage to foreign adventurers than to the common people of the Islands.

Political destinies were shaped mainly by patterns of European trade and migration interacting with indigenous political structures. Two models of foreign settlement crystallised in the nineteenth century, with very different long-term implications. In Australia and New Zealand, indigenous people were outnumbered by European settlers who gained power through settler states and controlled the political agenda. Abo-riginal Australians were decimated by introduced diseases, massacred, expelled from arable lands and pastures, and marginalised by force of numbers. Intermarriage, rape, cohabitation and compulsory adoption threatened cultural continuity. New Zealand Maori were also out-numbered, but were better able to engage in European-style economic and political contest. Because indigenous people become in effect an internal colony of the immigrant society, they were subjected to regimes which have been called 'domestic colonialism'.

The second model is more familiar: a minority of foreigners exerted increasing influence, or fomented chaos, until the Island group was taken as a colony by one of the imperial nations. This situation, exempli-fied in Fiji, Pohnpei, Samoa and Tahiti, provoked rivalry among the Great Powers and the bullying of Island regimes. After colonisation the people retained their numerical majority and much of their land, but were ruled by a colonial administration. A foreign elite shaped market transactions, and local production was skewed by land alienation, cash cropping, plantation labour, and taxation. Hawai'i combined the fea-tures of the settler state and the colony. Though decimated, Hawaiians did not become a minority in their own land until late in the nineteenth century. They were then outnumbered not by Europeans but by Asian labourers brought in by the *haole* (white) economic elite. Less than a decade after a clique of *haole* businessmen overthrew the monarchy, Hawai'i was annexed as a United States territory. Hawaiians have lived the classic Fourth World scenario: depopulation, land alienation, loss of sovereignty, and repression of culture.

While we abjure 'fatal impact' analyses (see chapter 1), the coming of Europeans did alter irrevocably the directions in which Island societies developed. The foreigners were impossible to ignore, because of their military organisation and technology, the deadliness of their diseases, and the allure of their goods. Christianity, capitalism, and the nation-state were aggressively promoted. Agents of the Great Powers pursued imperial visions and economic ambitions on an unprecedented scale, and some were committed to thorough religious, economic or political change. The different ways in which Island societies were organised critically affected their transactions with foreigners and their destinies, and Western institutions were not simply replicated but transformed into a host of variants, shaped by local circumstances.

Political outcomes are inseparable from other projects. Thus explorers, missionaries and merchants reappear in this chapter, along with the more obviously political chiefs, consuls and colonial administrators. The sequence of Western arrivals was usually much the same: explorers, then beachcombers, traders, and missionaries, followed by representatives of Western governments. Great Power political architects arrived relatively late to craft colonial solutions to problems which threatened the new economic and political orders. Meanwhile Islanders had been introduced to Western institutions by a chequered cast of libertines and martyrs, egomaniacs and do-gooders, bullies and dreamers. At first trade was far more important than strategic concerns, and the *laissez-faire* ethos of merchant capital prevailed for several decades. The imperial nations promoted political centralisation largely to ensure orderly commerce and to protect their citizens' businesses.

In this chapter Polynesia and Micronesia receive more attention than Melanesia, where intensive interactions came later. Climate, terrain, malaria, Islanders' resistance and Western racism all deterred foreigners, and early altercations tended to perpetuate the 'savage' stereotype. In 1839 the famous missionary John Williams was killed at Erromanga, and missionaries avoided the island for several years. On Santa Isabel in the Solomons, a Marist bishop was killed in 1845 with an axe he had presented as a gift, because the killers suspected him to be an ally of a rival group. Two years later, decimated by attacks and malaria, the Marists abandoned the mission. British missionaries in Samoa sent Polynesians to missionise the 'savage' isles to the west. Westerners often saw Melanesians and Polynesians as fundamentally different because of racist associations with 'blackness'. Europeans therefore ensconced themselves on the beach earlier in Polynesia. The death of Captain Cook and the La Pérouse 'massacre' shocked Europeans, who suspended contacts with Hawai'i and Samoa; but Hawaiians and Samoans were quickly rehabilitated in European eyes as trade increased.

Polynesia and some Micronesian islands also seemed more hospitable. In much of Melanesia Big Men achieved local leadership through public gift-giving, oratory, marriages and recruiting followers: the out-come was a myriad small-scale societies with opaque political struc-tures. By contrast, in chiefdoms social status was largely a matter of rank, which was a function of genealogical seniority. Chiefs were chiefs because they were born to be so, and their authority was typically reinforced by religious rituals. Europeans viewed chiefdoms as nascent monarchies, which with judicious guidance might be stabilised to the great convenience of trade.

CHIEFLY AMBITIONS AND FOREIGN MEDDLING

It was through the aid of muskets and of foreigners to instruct in their use that Kamehameha was able in so short a time to bring all the islands under his rule . . . Young and Davis, became favorites (*aikane punahele*) of Kamehameha and leaders in his wars, and from them are descended chiefs and commoners of Hawai'i.[1]

In retrospect the colonisation of Island societies seems inevitable, but early relations between foreigners and indigenous elites were far more contested than colonial histories suggest. The first Westerners had no grasp of Pacific languages, and no sense of the dynamics of politics, so they were often enlisted unwittingly in the projects of ambitious lead-ers. As they began to understand something of the societies, they still lacked dependable military force to tip the scales. Foreign ships occa-sionally carried out executions and bombardments as revenge for acts of violence against foreign vessels, but most 'warship justice' had little lasting effect. Only after beach communities were firmly established, well into the nineteenth century, did Europeans deploy enough force to determine or deter Islander action. In the latter nineteenth century, foreigners and Islanders contended for control: to author the laws governing land, labour, trade and crime, and then to enforce them. In mid-century, warship justice gave way to more systematic gunboat diplomacy. The contention was many-sided, and often allowed curious alliances; Westerners were divided by nationality, religion, economic interests and personal allegiance, and Islanders' factions also pursued diverse agendas.

Westerners tried to influence politics by tipping the scales in indigen-ous conflicts. As they became stronger and bolder, some began pres-suring Islanders to adopt new governmental forms. Several Island leaders used foreigners to their own advantage. Such was the case when the British merchant ship *Antelope* was wrecked on the reefs of Palau in 1783. Hoping to build a new ship, Captain Henry Wilson ingratiated himself with the high chief (*Ibedul*) of Koror with gifts. The *Ibedul* was more impressed with firearms, and borrowed five musketeers for an attack on his principal rival. The shooting death of a single warrior routed the opponents of the *Ibedul*, and Wilson's men accompanied their allies on another, bloodier incursion. When Wilson's getaway ship was

---

1   Kamakau, *Ruling Chiefs of Hawaii*, 146–7.

nearly completed, the *Ibedul* borrowed an armed contingent for one last display of force, and his rivals formally acknowledged his supremacy. After an exchange of gifts expressing sincere mutual gratitude, Wilson and his crew sailed away, leaving all the muskets and cannon that could be spared, and a seaman who asked to stay. For many years thereafter, Palauan chiefs solicited military support from British captains.[2]

Matavai Bay in Tahiti was the most frequent spot for rest and recreation from the 1780s. Sailors were well received, and Tahiti usually enjoyed a surplus of pigs and other food, cheerfully exchanged for iron, then for firearms, and later for European clothing. The closest Tahitian authority—the *arii nui* of one of the island's three political divisions—encouraged the trade and cultivated the friendship of the sailors. For their part, visitors accepted his specious claim to hegemony over the whole island, gave him firearms, and sometimes helped in his battles. Before his death in 1803 he was acknowledged by visitors as Pomare I, and during the next dozen critical years successive visitors continued to endorse the ambitions of Pomare II, as the best guarantor of the pork trade and rest and recreation. From the 1790s the London Missionary Society (LMS) also pinned its faith to the Pomare dynasty. The civil wars reached their climax in the battle of Feipi in November 1815, when Pomare's enemies were vanquished by sea-power (in which an English gunner made a significant contribution), his own supporters, and Christian converts using muskets. Maude perhaps over-simplifies when he concludes that 'the battle of Feipi was won through the over-whelming power of muskets provided by the merchants of Sydney in return for pigs. The Pomare dynasty was now firmly set on the throne of Tahiti: thanks to the pork traders of New South Wales.'[3] Whatever the most important contributions, the outcome was a unified archipelago, in which power was wielded by the Pomare dynasty with bureaucratic support from LMS personnel and the endorsement of foreign seamen.

Other notable beachcomber retainers were the castaways John Young and Isaac Davis, who were accorded the prerogatives of Hawaiian chiefs and whose expertise in armaments is counted a decisive factor in Kamehameha's unification of the Hawaiian Islands. After the Battle of Nu'uanu in 1795, Kamehameha instituted stable centralised rule over all the islands save Kaua'i, inaugurating the Hawaiian kingdom and the Kamehameha dynasty. The political potential of the pre-contact Hawaiian chieftainship has been much debated. Kamehameha was an astute politician and general, and some argue that he—or some other chief—would have achieved this unifying conquest in much the same period. The point is moot, however: he did win his decisive battles with the aid of Western military technology and advisers. His opponents—chiefs of Maui and O'ahu lines—also had foreign allies.

Though Captain Cook was Hawai'i's most famous early visitor, the English explorer George Vancouver probably had a more lasting influence on the monarchy. Vancouver visited the islands three times

2 Hezel, *The First Taint of Civilization*, 73.
3 Maude, *Of Islands and Men*, ch. 5, 213.

between 1792 and 1794, and had extensive contacts with Kamehameha. Some reports claim that he tried, in vain, to persuade him to embrace Christianity. Others have argued that Vancouver's description of the British monarchy influenced Kamehameha's design of the Hawaiian government. Vancouver was something of a do-gooder, concerned to promote peace by exhorting chiefs to negotiation and acting as a go-between. He introduced cattle and sheep to the big island of Hawai'i (with dire ecological consequences) but refused to give or trade weapons. Kamehameha bargained for material and help to build a Western-style ship, the *Britannia*. In turn, he 'ceded' the island of Hawai'i to Britain. It is not difficult to deduce motives: Vancouver doing his duty to God and King by expanding the influence of the Empire; Kamehameha contracting an alliance with a source of muskets, cannon, artisans and large armed ships. Though the British government never accepted the offer, Kamehameha described himself as 'subject to' the English King George in an 1810 letter. His son and successor Liholiho also considered the kingdom to be under the protection of Great Britain.

Explorers and missionaries set out with fairly clear charters. Beach-combers—whites and Islanders alike—were more heterogeneous. Many were fleeing Western justice or unpleasant employers. Most whites (and some Islanders) were seeking personal glory and a quality of life that they could not achieve at home. Some appear emotionally unbalanced. Traders and entrepreneurs also became political actors on the beach. Arms traders and planters seeking land exacerbated Samoan factional strife for decades. Andrew Cheyne—the 'would-be emperor of Palau'—dreamed of a trading empire and a fortune with plantations. In the 1860s he executed a 'Treaty of Commerce' with the chiefs of Koror, authored a constitution, and drafted a petition for the chiefs to request a British protectorate. Like the Hawaiians, the Palauan chiefs inter-preted certain encounters as creating a special relationship with Britain, but the Koror chiefs eventually rebelled against Cheyne's threats and arrogance and assassinated him.

Bau, an islet on the east coast of Viti Levu, was a magnet for beach-combers in the 1800s—Europeans, Chinese, Indians and Islanders who were shipwrecked or discharged, or jumped ship. From 1808 until his death in 1813, Charlie Savage led them through physical courage and other personal qualities. The only beachcomber who spoke Fijian fluently, he became the trusted lieutenant of Naulivou, the Vunivalu (war king) of Bau. In warfare and skirmishing against other towns, the new mercenaries eclipsed the Tongan retainers of the Vunivalu. Savage was richly rewarded. During his life he received a title, money, and high-born wives; in death he became a legend with an English geneal-ogy to match his heroism. Colonialist writers have made even bolder claims, attributing to Savage and his friends not only a determining influence on warfare, but also the concept of a Fijian kingdom united by conquest. Similar claims have been made for beachcombers in other monarchies including Tahiti, the Marquesas, Hawai'i and Tonga. The relationship between Naulivou and Savage may therefore be an appropriate test of this general argument.

Bau often waged war on chiefdoms in the Rewa delta and the windward (eastern) coast of Viti Levu. Guns were clearly important, but
Shineberg has described the technical limitations of inaccurate and
slowly primed muzzle-loaders in a humid climate, poorly maintained
and used by untrained warriors.[4] Clunie shows that very few were
available, and that Fijians usually preferred the more reliable and
ritually sanctioned war-club.[5] The importance of guns was neither their
numbers (few) nor their accuracy (poor), but the use made of them by
foreigners. Fijian warriors were not squeamish, but they were impressed by the foreigners' 'wildness'. Even more than the Tongans,
Savage's beachcombers ignored taboos. Naulivou gained a decisive
advantage 'through the sacrilegious and brilliant deployment of
Charles Savage and a spearhead of several dozen beachcombers armed
with muskets and rifles. These foreign mercenaries, in worldly contrast
to the tradition-bound Fijian warriors . . . cared naught for the divinity
of chiefs, and less for their sacred immunity in battle, potting them first
on principle.'[6] It was their wildness which commended them to
Naulivou. As Sahlins observes, Bau was unlike other Fijian polities and
the Vunivalu unlike other chiefs. The ritual head of Bau was not the
Vunivalu but the Roko Tui Bau, responsible for the land and its people.
Successive Vunivalu—ritually responsible for maritime trade and
war—eclipsed the Roko Tui, making Bau more combative than its
neighbours and better prepared for warfare with immense seagoing
canoes. Long before the arrival of beachcombers, Bau warriors raided
their neighbours, and every victory won fresh allies. Military victories
allowed Bau to lead a confederacy, but leadership could not develop
into a legitimate, centralised polity, since every defeated chiefdom
survived the death of every chief.

In Europe at this time, Napoléon Bonaparte's battles did lead to the
creation of new states. His contests with King George and the Duke of
Wellington were eagerly followed by many Island leaders, who read
them in terms of their own ambitions. Hongi Hika has been mentioned
(in chapter 5), and Pomare I was equally eager for news from Europe. A
Tongan tradition suggests how European narratives could be indigenised, claiming Napoleoni as the son of an American mother and a
Tongan father: 'From our stock has sprung the race of warriors—men
whose names are known—some whose mighty deeds have been done
among our own people, and others who have lived and fought among
foreign nations. Thus Napoleoni was a son of Tonga.'[7] But Island
circumstances would not permit Napoleonic outcomes. The political
culture of Fiji favoured the military ambitions of the Vunivalu, but
constrained their political consequences. Whatever their ambitions,
Charlie Savage and his colleagues could not replicate European history.
They were actors in Fijian history, specialists in violence in the service of
the strategist Naulivou, who could not transcend the limitations of

4   Shineberg, 'Guns and Men in Melanesia'.
5   Clunie, *Fijian Weapons and Warfare*.
6   Sahlins, 'The Discovery of the True Savage'; *cf.* Clunie, 'Manila Brig', 51–2.
7   Vave of Kolonga, quoted in Fison, *Tales from Old Fiji*, 135.

being Vunivalu. Conversely, in Palau (see above), no *Ibedul* ever unified the island group under the rule of Koror: they may have possessed the means, but they lacked interest in doing so.[8]

There were choleric and litigious types on the beach, who harassed the chiefs with complaints and elaborated grievances to their home governments. Other foreigners' agendas are less clear. More middle-class than the typical beachcomber, less easy to stereotype than missionaries, their interests appear personal and egocentric. Some were do-gooders, at least in their own minds. Others were self-aggrandising adventurers. All relished the role of chiefly adviser and political architect. In this category fall Walter Murray Gibson in Hawai'i, A. L. Steinberger in Samoa, John Bates Thurston in Fiji—and Williams and Pritchards everywhere. Many foreign advisers took their responsibility very seriously, casting themselves as native tribunes, even when that role outraged the other foreigners. However, they usually believed that they knew better than the leaders whom they served, and this arrogance brought some of them down. In the 1840s Hawaiians petitioned in droves against the '*haole* rulers' in their government. The historian David Malo repeatedly warned against the evils befalling his people through Western influence.[9]

Scholars have dwelt on the entertaining excesses of Gerrit Judd and Walter Murray Gibson. A Puritan with a taste for pomp and trappings, Judd left the American mission to become factotum of Kamehameha III's cabinet, but he alienated so many foreigners that he had to leave office. Gibson's public career was longer and more bizarre. He arrived in Hawai'i in 1861 and took over leadership of the Mormon settlement on Lana'i Island, calling himself 'Chief President of the Islands of the Sea and of the Hawaiian Islands'. The Mormons excommunicated him when they discovered that he had registered the land on Lana'i in his own name, but the scandal did not dampen his self-regard or his ambitions. Fluent in Hawaiian, Gibson cast himself as the people's tribune. Hawaiians elected him to the legislature in 1878, and in 1882 he accepted a post in King Kalākaua's cabinet. Over the next five years he served as 'Minister of Everything', in the words of Daws.[10] Kalākaua and Gibson hatched a plan for a confederation of islands and sent a delegation to Malietoa, the most credible candidate for king of Samoa. Notions of regional leadership and Island alliances seemed laughable to the foreigners, but in retrospect they appear almost visionary. Gibson weathered many crises in Kalākaua's cabinet, but not the revolution of 1887 when a cabal of *haole* businessmen coerced Kalākaua to disband his cabinet and accept a new constitution which severely curtailed his authority and disenfranchised most Hawaiians. This 'Bayonet Constitution' effectively ended native Hawaiian political sovereignty.

In Samoa the 'Steinberger affair' occurred during a period of prolonged political disorder: by the 1870s Samoans had endured three decades of warfare. Mālietoa Vainu'upō was the last chief to hold the

8 Hezel, *The First Taint of Civilization*, 73.
9 Malo, 'Decrease of Population', and *Hawaiian Antiquities*.
10 Daws, *Shoal of Time*.

four paramount titles which made up the position of Tafa'ifā. Though foreigners tended to gloss Tafa'ifā as 'king', the status appears to have conferred ceremonial precedence rather than centralised rule. Mālietoa decreed that at his death the four titles must be 'scattered', and the 1840s and 1850s were scarred by conflict. Firearms became significant in the war of 1848–57, and thereafter foreigners increasingly interfered. Meleisea argues that foreign intervention made it impossible for any Samoan faction to achieve a decisive victory and establish rule by conquest, a customary mode of legitimation.[11] While some foreigners tried to act as peacemakers and political architects, the arms merchants and land grabbers had much to gain from war. Samoans mortgaged lands to buy arms, and when agriculture was disrupted the people had to buy food. Missionaries counselled peace and expelled combatants from the church. Representatives of the Great Powers—mostly military men—exhorted the Samoans to form a national government. In the 1860s most Europeans were advocating a confederation, because the question of a single head of state invariably provoked contention. The Mālietoa title itself had been split, and the two holders set up rival governments on opposite sides of Apia Bay. Though foreigners spoke of the two Malietoas as kings, the immediate goal of the struggle was the paramount chieftainship of Tuamasaga, the middle district of Upolu. Kingship remained the focus of foreign machinations and became the goal of Samoan politics for the rest of the century.

A bicameral government was formed in 1873, including none of the principal chiefly contenders, and lasted for about fifteen months. A dual kingship was then attempted, with two kings selected by the legislature from the Malietoa and Tupua families. This arrangement lasted only a few months. Steinberger, an American claiming to be a diplomat, won the trust of the chiefs and in 1875 proposed a new constitution. His solution was an alternating kingship, with scions of the Mālietoa and Tupua families taking turns in four-year terms. The solution appealed to Samoans in part because the king was to be largely ceremonial; effective power was vested in the office of premier, to which the Samoans named Steinberger. But ten months after Mālietoa Laupepa took office as the first king, Steinberger was ousted at the instigation of the foreign community and deported on an American warship. The more foreigners attempted to promote central government, the more violently the society was divided.

In Fiji by 1861 Bau's writ ran further than ever, but not as far as centralised power over the rest of Fiji, and not far enough to convince British officials that it was a monarchy,

> though the Island of Bau unquestionably has full right to be regarded as the native Metropolis of Fiji; though the people of Bau have a recognized superiority throughout the group,—though the Chief of Bau receives . . . tribute from various districts of Fiji,—though every district, every town has a Mata-ki-Bau (or ambassador)—the Chief of Bau [is] little more than the most powerful, the most influential, the most dignified Chieftain of his race.[12]

11 Meleisea, *The Making of Modern Samoa*.
12 Consul Pritchard to Commissioner Smythe, 14 January 1861, cited in Scarr, *I, The Very Bayonet*, 23–4.

William Pritchard, who wrote the letter, was the latest in a long line of foreign advisers, and one of many missionary-trader-diplomats whose careers are described below. Naulivou's brother's son Cakobau was now Vunivalu. He and other leading chiefs were Christian, and so were some of their followers. The foreign community was approaching 3000 by 1870, including Australians and New Zealanders who responded to Pritchard's invitation to take up land to plant cotton.

Bau's eminence was matched by its problems. Defeated chieftaincies awaited their chances to cast off Bau's hegemony, and some were courted by Enele Ma'afu, leader of a flourishing Tongan community based in Lakeba and expanding under the auspices of Methodism. Planters and traders were reluctant to recognise any indigenous authority, and some aspired to a white men's republic. Ma'afu, leader of the Lau confederacy and a credible candidate to unify Fiji, was threatened by a white man and reflected that many 'are evil disposed and opposed to law: . . . and because we have dark skins they think we are wild beasts and that they can carry out any iniquity without being called to account'.[13] Some aspired to a settler republic, but most favoured British annexation; almost all expected indigenous authority to lapse. It was impossible to pay an inflated American claim for compensation, so Cakobau was persuaded in 1870 by an Australian syndicate (the Polynesia Company) to grant it ill-defined privileges in exchange for paying the debt. Cakobau—on Pritchard's advice—had requested a British protectorate. This had been denied, leaving Bau's problems annually compounding. In June 1871 he declared himself King of a united Fiji, co-opting Ma'afu as his Viceroy and other chiefs and traders as ministers. The next year he brought in John Bates Thurston as Chief Secretary.

The English merchant seaman Thurston had been cast away on Rotuma in 1865, aged twenty-nine. Making his way to Levuka, the commercial centre on the island of Ovalau, he became master of a Methodist schooner, collecting the coconut oil which financed the mission; then he invested in cotton plantations. Acting briefly as British Consul, he joined one of Cakobau's campaigns into Colo in the Viti Levu interior. Unlike most settlers, he studied Fijian politics and language. As Chief Secretary, his competence drew to him most of the work of the cabinet, and his loyalty to the monarchy outraged other settlers. The chief business of the government was to preserve a peace threatened by chiefs and planters, to remain solvent, and to secure recognition from foreign powers. When British officials changed their strategy and demanded the cession of Fiji, Cakobau had little choice but to acquiesce. Defiance would risk war and guarantee the secession or open hostility of Ma'afu and many others. Thurston helped to negotiate the eventual cession of Fiji to the British Crown in 1874.

What distinguished Thurston from other advisers was his durability. When Sir Arthur Gordon (later Lord Stanmore) arrived as Governor, Thurston became his lieutenant and eventually his successor, partly inspiring and implementing the paternalist policy for which Gordon enjoyed the credit. What distinguishes Cakobau from other centralisers was not the unstable monarchy which survived just long enough to negotiate cession, but the relatively favourable terms of annexation. Ma'afu's challenge was blunted, the brawling planters were curbed, Fijian lands were largely protected, the islands were brought under one government, and an aristocracy was entrenched, albeit without a monarch at its apex.

CHIEFS AND CONVERSION

In these highly political circumstances the missionary charter was to teach the word of Christ, not to meddle in politics. Most of the 'messengers of grace' adhered to that precept, but their religious goals intersected with indigenous politics and sometimes became attempts at wholesale social reform. Even the minimal scenario for imbuing Islanders with Christian values implied sweeping changes in modes of justice and dispute resolution. Missionaries first targeted chiefs for conversion, reasoning that the people would follow them.

Mission societies varied in conversion styles and attitudes toward indigenous practices. The American Board (centred in Hawai'i and expanding into Micronesia) tended to be more judgemental than the LMS (whose first focus was Tahiti), and more convinced that profound social change was imperative. To Hiram Bingham, leader of the first company, Hawaiian culture was irredeemably depraved. The Americans therefore viewed their mandate more broadly than religious conversion: Hawaiians were to be scolded, threatened and instructed, and the chiefs educated in the ways of civilisation. The young Kamehameha II (Liholiho) was indifferent at best, and it took five years—and Liholiho's death from measles in London—for the Americans to win over several high-ranking ali'i. Their first major success was the powerful widow of Kamehameha I, the chiefess Ka'ahumanu, who became a dutiful pupil and made a circuit of Hawai'i Island burning images of the old gods. The indigenous religion had been overthrown after Kamehameha's death in 1819, before missionaries even arrived. In more ways than one, Ka'ahumanu's tour heralded the end of the old taboos and the instating of new ones; her circuit mimicked rituals that had once legitimised chiefly authority—but she travelled in the ritually incorrect direction.

The American Board had no prior experience when the first company was sent to Hawai'i. Two decades earlier the LMS had learned hard lessons in Tahiti and Tonga (chapter 4), where they were embroiled in disputes beyond their comprehension, and were briefly forced to retreat to Sydney. In Tahiti the Pomare dynasty chose to protect them and deploy their skills in centralising and administering the kingdom. The ten missionary artisans who landed in Tonga in 1797 were civilly treated until their supplies were exhausted and civil war resumed. The survivors who withdrew in 1800 could not yet speak Tongan nor comprehend Tongan affairs. Sorties over the next three decades fell foul of the interest of chiefs and priests, the hostility of traders and beach-combers, and their own inability to communicate. The impasse was broken in 1826, when two Tahitian teachers were sent to Nuku'alofa on the main island of Tongatapu, and built a church and a congregation before British missionaries joined them in 1827.

The decisive initiative was taken by Tongan chiefs of the Tu'i Kanokupolu family, and especially Tāufa'āhau, for dynastic reasons. Lātūkefu explains that Tāufa'āhau's conversion was the missionaries' greatest asset:

> Tāufa'āhau had become sceptical of the Tongan gods and the traditional religious practices. He had reason to doubt his family gods, for they had failed to come to his father's aid . . . Nor had they assisted him in his initial struggle against Laufilitonga . . . Increasing contact with Europeans and the superiority of their weapons also helped to undermine his beliefs in the traditional gods . . .
>
> After several trips to Tongatapu in 1827 and early in 1828, where he met the missionaries and some of his [Christian] relatives . . . he began to imitate some of the ways of the Christians. He also tried to make his people learn them . . . [14]

Reversing the outcome in Samoa, Tāufa'āhau fought and negotiated successfully to combine the essential dynastic titles. As George Tupou (a name reflecting his respect for the British monarchy) he ruled a united Tonga. Hitched to his rising star, Methodism became almost the state religion. The normal relations between monarch and missionaries was reversed: the mission depended so massively on the King's patronage that he, rather than any missionary, was both the temporal ruler and the real head of the church.

Conversion was seldom so simple, and in most mission fields fresh tactics had to be devised. By 1830, when John Williams arrived in Samoa, the British missionaries were avoiding wholesale condemnation and focusing on long-term strategies. They were perhaps more practical than the Americans, and several became amateur scholars of indigenous cultures. Williams took advice from a Samoan guide who suggested a gradual approach. In his 1832 journal Williams recounted the reasoning underlying his instructions to mission teachers:

> there were many things among them that were Sa ['sacred' or 'forbidden'] or bad but we thought that force or authority to put them away at present would not be judicious. When they were a little more enlightened in the doctrines of Christian Religion they themselves would see the evil of many things . . . My advice was that those dances which were manifestly obscene such as dancing naked, singing their filthy songs & such like they should advise the Chiefs . . . to prohibit in their settlements but an entire prohibition of them at present I did not think advisable . . . where no immorality is connected I thought best not to notice . . . being a people much given to amusements they would lament the loss of them greatly & perhaps take a total dislike to a religion which prohibited that in which their whole life & comfort consisted.

14 Lātūkefu, *Church and State in Tonga*, 62.

Islanders are largely silent in the historical record. At best, their voices are related second-hand by missionaries who interpreted their words according to their own aims. The early missionaries in Hawai'i, frustrated by the young King's inattention and drinking bouts, recorded with disgust his many flippant remarks and farcical antics. Williams enjoyed greater initial success in Samoa, where the people knew of Christianity through other Islanders, and Tongan teachers had already made some converts. Williams's access to the victorious chief Mālietoa Vainu'upō was facilitated by Faueā Samoan who had lived in Tonga for some years and helped to present Christianity to elite Samoans. In his 1830 journal Williams paraphrased Faueā: 'He told them also of the number of Islands which has become lotu [Christian] . . . and he said they are all much better . . . Wars have ceased among them. Ships visited them without fear and anchored in their harbours and brought them an abundance of Property . . . On hearing Faueas speech they all exclaimed It would be good to lotu too.'[15]

The missionaries' motives and trials are well documented. Less accessible are the motives and interests of Islanders in embracing or rejecting Christianity. Wherever they landed, missionaries became unwitting players in power struggles. Christian teachings—identified with writing and books—and the missionaries themselves became tokens in factional rivalries. Williams was amazed at his reception in Samoa, where chiefs entreated him to send teachers. On his 1830 visit he put Malietoa Vai'inupō in charge of the fledgling mission and gave him eight teachers to place where he chose. Despite this new sphere of authority and prestige, however, Malietoa was slow to forsake his gods. Chiefs who welcomed missionaries hoped for more immediate benefits than a state of grace: tools, clients and skills such as literacy among them. Rejection of indigenous gods could also subvert the authority which the gods legitimised; such factional advantage was a factor in the overthrow of the Hawaiian *kapu* (taboo) system by Kamehameha II, in Tāufa'āhau's initial interest in Christianity, and in the speedy conversion of junior chiefly lines of Tokelau.

Pohnpei also had a chiefdom organisation based on senior and junior genealogical lines. When the first American Board company arrived in 1852, they were adopted by the paramount chief (*Nahnmwarki*) of Madolenihmw, the highest-ranking chiefdom. Military superiority belonged to the neighbouring chiefdom of Kiti, however, and there the missionaries found a more powerful ally in the paramount chief's junior relative, the *Nahnken*. The normative role of the *Nahnken* was similar to that of the Samoan 'talking chief'. Though of lesser formal rank, the *Nahnken* was the effective administrator of the chiefdom and the paramount's intermediary. The paramount chief of Kiti was feeble, but his *Nahnken* was a formidable leader who had defeated Madolenihmw and attracted much foreign trade. The missionaries accepted his invitation to settle in Kiti, and began a mutually beneficial relationship. The *Nahnken* gave them land, protection, and access to the

15 Moyle, *Samoan Journals of John Williams*, 124, 142 and 68.

people; in Pohnpei such patronage meant that a chief 'owned' the client individuals. The missionaries instructed the *Nahnken* in literacy and arithmetic, which helped him to deal with traders, and at least once warned him against an exploitative contract. Often the *Nahnken* seemed tantalisingly close to conversion, but he adroitly prolonged the arrangement. In ten years the Protestants won no converts.

Mission societies usually agreed on a geographical division of labour, at least at first. Where missions competed, as in Samoa, Islanders used affiliation as a lever to extract goods, relaxed rules, or other inducements. Sectarianism became simply another dimension of factionalism. For their part, missionaries imported all their suspicions of other denominations. Methodists and LMS Congregationalists hurled accusations at one another, and the Protestants' attitude towards Catholics verged on bigotry. Many observers noted that Islanders saw no doctrinal differences between denominations, and could not comprehend the vicious rivalries among people who espoused brotherhood. But they did know that one is counted strong by the number of one's followers. What were the missionaries prepared to do in return for their allegiance? Aaron Buzacott's 1836 journal is revealing: 'a number of their little villages are split into factions where they contend as violently as the Corinthians ever did for Paul & Apolos. In many instances they seem to talk as though we were under obligation to them because they have become of our party instead of feeling thankful for our instruction.'[16]

Sectarianism was particularly bitter in Samoa because of a disputed 'agreement' between the Wesleyan and London societies. In 1836 John Williams claimed that the Wesleyan missionaries in Tonga had agreed to leave Samoa to the LMS. The status of this agreement occasioned decades of recriminations. Peter Turner, the Methodist missionary in Samoa, adamantly refused to leave until 1839, when he received personal instructions from the Wesleyan Society. In a Samoan village in the 1830s, therefore, one might find followers of the '*lotu* Tonga' (Methodist), the '*lotu* Taiti' (LMS), the syncretic Sio Vili movement, charismatic cults centred on beachcombers, as well as the 'devil party'—the unconverted. The groups used hair-styles or apparel as markers of affiliation. A chief's pursuit of distinction, or displeasure with a missionary, could cause an entire village suddenly to switch denominations. Even without resident missionaries, some Samoans—particularly on Savai'i and Manono—refused to abandon the 'Misi Tana [Mr Turner] party'. Much to the irritation of the LMS missionaries, they maintained their distinctiveness with the aid of Tongan teachers who continued to enjoy a privileged position. The LMS was outraged when the Methodists resumed the mission in the 1850s, after a lapse of almost two decades.

Missionisation gave new form to factionalism, and Samoa's example shows that mission rivalries exacerbated communal divisions. Pre-European relationships and cultural associations also inflected

16 LMS papers, 14 July, 1836, Mitchell Library, Sydney, microfilm.

sectarianism. To understand Samoans' allegiance to Wesleyanism, for example, we must look to the significance of Tonga in Samoan history. Tonga once ruled Samoa, oral traditions say, and Tongan kings took wives from Samoan chiefly families. Tongans had greater mastery over long-distance ocean travel, so that the contacts were unequal. Turner's adherents claimed that he had promised them that missionaries would one day come again from Tonga. In the event King George of Tonga did send messengers and teachers, and promised more. In 1842 the King himself came to Samoa where, in Turner's words, he and the chiefs 'entered into a solemn covenant never to abandon each other, but to cleave more and more to each other'.[17] The Tongan King and chiefs vowed, again according to Turner, 'that *they* will never abandon Samoa the land of their relatives and the birth-place of some of their fathers'. There are regional and personal interests behind such an alliance, and historical and cultural dimensions that have nothing to do with Christianity.

The political perceptions of converts often worsened the rivalries between missionaries. Rotuma Island, for example, received Samoan, Tongan and Fijian mission teachers and pastors from 1839. European Catholic missionaries followed in 1846, but inspired so little enthusiasm that they withdrew in 1853. In their absence an English Wesleyan consolidated the work of his Polynesian forerunners, so that French Catholics—who returned in 1868—found themselves at a great disadvantage. Conversion was complicated by the dynastic ambitions of regional chiefs, and the 1870s were marked by sporadic warfare between traditionalists, Protestants and Catholics. Eventually in 1879 Marafu, a chief who saw no other way to resolve the impasse, petitioned the Governor of Fiji for incorporation. Rotuma was added to Fiji two years later. Whether the wars were religious (as the missionaries believed) or both dynastic and religious (as Rotuman traditions describe them), secular and sacred issues reinforced each other, confirming the mutual hostility of Catholic and Protestant mission workers.[18]

Almost every theme described so far can be illustrated in Vanuatu (formerly New Hebrides), thanks to Joel Bonnemaison's reconstruction.[19] The sandalwood rush reached its climax here in the 1840s, when Tanna, Erromanga and Aneityum received perhaps 150 expeditions in ten years. Violent incidents were not uncommon, although an honest trader (such as Paddon, who married a Tannese woman and spent the rest of his life based on the island) was welcome as a reliable source of trade goods. Although sandalwood prices collapsed and timber-getting declined, the labour trade peaked towards the end of the century.

After the martyrdom of John Williams in Erromanga in 1839, and several other failed LMS ventures, it fell to fundamentalist Presbyterians to evangelise the southern islands, when John Geddie arrived in Aneityum in 1848. Ferociously hostile to all cultures but

---

17 LMS South Seas Letters 14/5/A, Thomas Heath, 30 April 1841, and 15/6/B, Peter Turner to the Samoan Mission, 1 December 1842, Mitchell Library, Sydney, microfilm.
18 Howard and Kjellgren, 'Martyrs, Progress and Political Ambition'.
19 Bonnemaison, *The Tree and the Canoe*.

their own, and to other Christian denominations (not to mention pagans), they also rejected any distinction between spiritual and temporal authority. It would be difficult to find a mission society with less cultural sensitivity, yet within twelve years Presbyterianism had conquered, and there was not one avowed pagan on Aneityum. Beginning on the coast, among men familiar with Europeans through working on ships or in Queensland, the mission created a Christian village and a seminary school trained evangelists, who then confronted the inland pagans (and Paddon, whom Geddie treated as an accomplice of paganism) and created a network of schools and churches throughout the island.

Aneityum became practically a Presbyterian theocracy. The church was the real centre of each village, and its Samoan or Aneityumese teacher the real political leader. Local courts comprising zealous Christians enforced Biblical injunctions, with the aid of a private police force. Coconut plantations yielded commodities to supplement the first cash crop of arrowroot, and the proceeds financed the mission. A new missionary wife was astounded in 1869:

> There is a Church, a Training Institution, and a dwelling house with many appendages such as a carpenter's shop, smith's shop, store-room etc. . . . In the morning we were awakened by the church bell ringing the people to school, which we all attend from six to seven, before going to their planta-tions. The Bible is the sole book. It is a real national Scriptural education the natives here receive. There are schools all over the island, within ten minutes' walk of each home, and these are presided over by native teachers. These teachers are of great value, and, I may say, give their labour free, for they only receive £1 per annum for their services. The natives are well behaved; in each house family worship is held morning and evening.

The only fly in this ointment was the fact that the Islanders were fast dying out.

Neighbouring Tanna resisted vigorously. A measles epidemic which swept the islands in 1860 provoked the Tannese to expel the Presby-terian missionaries, John Paton and his wife. Five years later Paton returned with a Royal Navy vessel which—at Paton's inciting—shelled the island, burned villages and smashed canoes. Paton then persuaded some Tannese to sign a document confessing a host of crimes and sins, and asking the captain to 'inform your good Queen Victoria that we will kill no more of her people but in future be good, and learn to obey the word of Jehovah'. The episode did nothing to endear missionaries to Tannese. Tannese wanted the wealth, not the evangelists, of the outside world, but missionaries proved more able to attract it. Paton's auto-biography[20] raised such international interest—and opened so many purses and sporrans—that the mission prospered. Not for another generation did Tannese embrace Christianity. When they did, the mission imposed a theocratic regime—Tanna Law—which became a byword for cultural intolerance and repressiveness.

20 *John G. Paton, Missionary to the New Hebrides.*

By good fortune the northernmost islands of Vanuatu attracted New Zealand Anglicans, who operated on two principles: never to compete with any other Christian denomination, and to avoid imposing English cultural values 'except insofar as they are part of morality and godliness'. Their tactics were also unusual. Missionaries merely visited Christian communities and recruited students, who sailed to Norfolk Island to train as priests or teachers. Mota Islanders responded as eagerly to liberal Anglicanism as Aneityumese embraced illiberal Presbyterianism. In the liberal spirit articulated by the New Zealand mission strategist Bishop Selwyn, the Anglican mission became an independent diocese as early as 1861 and within a decade its success seemed just as comprehensive as that of Aneityum.

Unluckiest of all missionaries to Vanuatu were Marists, despatched from New Caledonia at the behest of Higginson, to redeem the archipelago from Protestantism and to forestall British annexation (chapter 5). A veteran Marist missionary wrote resignedly:

> What pains me is the thought that we're going there accompanied by the military and at the behest of political agitators. I'm convinced that the Protestants will shout from the rooftops that our presence was imposed by force, with the backing of gun-boats. I'm convinced too that before long we'll be at loggerheads with the Company, whose purpose is clear anyway: they just want to make use of us as an advance guard in places they're finding it difficult to get into. God help us!

The prophecy was accurate. Predictably, Protestant missionaries treated them with hostility; inspired by the Protestants' bigotry, Islanders were contemptuous of the poverty of the priests (who travelled by canoe while Protestants sailed their own vessels); and they did fall out with Higginson. Taking these extraordinary episodes together, it is clear that conversion was not the direct consequence of 'liberal' or 'illiberal' missionary tactics, so much as the outcome of Islanders' choices. It is now impossible to know what inspired either conversion or rejection, but some circumstances can be conjectured. In Vanuatu the key decision-makers included coastal men who had travelled abroad, while the interior communities put up the most protracted resistance. And in Vanuatu especially, evangelisation coincided with appalling depopulation, such that many Islanders could readily imagine the extinction of their cultures—and even of their whole societies.

WORDS AND THE WORD

> As soon as the chiefs saw what a good thing it was to know how to read and write, each chief took teachers into his home to teach the chiefs of his household.[21]

In most Pacific cultures words have power: to cure, to curse, to provoke wars, to invoke the divine. Once uttered, their effects cannot be undone.

21 Kamakau, *Ruling Chiefs of Hawaii*, 248.

Islanders were at first more attracted to words—the power of reading and writing—than The Word as abstraction. Education was part of the missionaries' mandate. Early mission companies included printers such as Elisha Loomis in Hawai'i, William Woon in Tonga, and Samuel Ella in Samoa, to publish the scriptures and tracts in the native tongue. Tongans became literate so quickly, and made such demands that the Methodists brought in a press and a printer, who published 3000 copies of a school primer within ten days of his arrival. They produced remarkable volumes. Kamakau reported that between 1824 and 1846 the mission published eighty books, totalling 65,444 pages. Christian villages in Aneityum were termed *skul*, and Bible study was a mandatory daily activity.

Some missionaries were poorly educated, but most taught literacy and arithmetic as well as doctrine. Often the bulk of the teaching fell to missionary women, who were expected to be specialists in domestic skills and family values. Mission education was the first system of public education. Islanders were typically eager for literacy, even while indifferent to church membership. In the early years of the Micronesian mission seven schools operated on Pohnpei, enrolling from eight to thirty-four students, although there were no converts.[22] Maori in New Zealand proved equally keen to learn to read and write, expecting this technology to reveal the dynamics of European society and economy. In Hawai'i the American Board was slow to admit converts to church membership, suspecting Hawaiians of 'formalism' and discerning a fundamental 'lack of awe'. Yet, once the chiefs were won over, the mission schools' success was astounding.

In Hawai'i when Liholiho died in 1824 his successor Kauikeaouli (Kamehameha III) was a boy, and through the 1830s the kingdom was effectively ruled by two 'queens', Kamehameha's widows Ka'ahumanu and Kina'u. In most Polynesian societies, women's social standing and personal autonomy ran counter to Western assumptions about gender roles. Chiefly women ranked as high as their brothers, and high-ranking women were seen as vessels of sacred power. 'Marrying up' was a common strategy for ambitious male chiefs. Hawaiian chiefly women had their own lands, retainers and personal property, and commoner women were important figures locally. The earliest foreigners assumed that the important people—those empowered to make agreements and ensure personal safety—were men. Some revised their opinion, but most Westerners found women's position unnatural, and in need of radical change. Missionaries attempted to instil Western gender roles by example and by education. Most foreign political advisers learned to respect chiefly women. Other foreigners resented prominent women: some in Honolulu dubbed the chiefess Kina'u 'the Big-Mouthed Queen'. Ka'ahumanu and her brothers comprised a powerful pro-missionary faction. The young chief Boki, Governor of O'ahu, resisted their dominance and allied himself with Catholic missionaries in Honolulu. Boki once threatened rebellion against the government and

22 Hanlon, *Upon a Stone Altar*, 102.

later counselled Kamehameha III to marry his sister, which would have
been an exalted union in the indigenous cultural system. Boki's
opposition ended with an echo of an old recourse for dissatisfied junior
chiefs. He sailed towards Erromanga in search of sandalwood, and was
never heard from again. With Boki out of the way, the pro-Protestant
chiefs expelled the French priests and gaoled some Hawaiian Catholics.
The American Board mission then enjoyed a virtual monopoly and the
common schools thrived. In the early 1830s there were 1100 schools
with 50,000 students, mostly adults.

Missions also founded seminary schools to train (male) teachers and
missionaries. Only the Anglicans (see above) trained workers outside
their home community. The LMS created Malua College in Samoa for
these purposes. Tupou College opened in Tonga in 1866, to educate
'choice young men who would ultimately fill important positions both
in the Church and the State'.[23] The mission school complex at Ohwa, on
Pohnpei, included a boys' and girls' boarding-school as well as the
Caroline Islands Training School for mission workers. The curriculum
for (male) missionary candidates entailed three years of study in subjects ranging from Biblical geography to anatomy. Candidates' wives
pursued a parallel course in literacy and domestic skills. Despite this
impressive structure, the Training School produced few teachers. However, as in Hawai'i, the 'higher education' produced a generation of
Islanders who were bilingual and to a degree 'bicultural'—possessing a
native cultural understanding but adept at dealing with foreigners.
Some gifted Islanders of lesser birth used their education to achieve
prominence. The analogous institution in Hawai'i was the Chiefs'
Children's School, founded in 1839 to educate the highest-ranking
young *ali'i*. All of Hawai'i's future monarchs attended the school, where
they studied in English and were expected to learn through example to
be members of a Christian 'family'. The historian Kamakau, a devout
Christian, described the curriculum:

> The first lesson taught was belief in righteousness and in God, the second
> was instruction in the English language. Instruction was given in surveying
> and electricity, chemistry and other natural sciences, mathematics, astro-
> nomy, and the history of foreign lands. The pupils were bright and delighted
> their teachers. They grew up to be dignified and god-fearing so that the
> kingdom did not lack what it greatly needed, wise and virtuous chiefs.[24]

In 1846, however, as the Protestant mission lost influence, it also lost
control over public education. The Chiefs' Children's School was
renamed the Royal School and placed under the Minister of Public
Instruction. Ironically, although church membership boomed during the
'great revival' of the late 1830s, the Congregationalists never claimed
more than a quarter of the people. And despite Kamakau's optimism,
the careers of Royal School graduates illustrated the general decline of
the *ali'i* in the latter nineteenth century.

23 Quoted in Lātūkefu, *Church and State in Tonga*, 76.
24 Kamakau, *Ruling Chiefs of Hawaii*, 405.

Missionaries have been accused of many sins, among them suppressing native cultural ways and paving the way for capitalism. On the
first charge, missionaries did see some interference in custom as necessary for inculcating Christian values, although mission societies and
individuals varied in the degree and aggressiveness of their intrusion.
On the second point, many writers have noted that missionisation made
it easier for traders to deal with Islanders. Facilitating trade was seldom
a conscious goal of missions. But, if missionaries themselves were
enjoined against capitalistic activity, their offspring were not. George
Pritchard, an early LMS missionary in Tahiti, became an adviser to
Pomare until he was gaoled and deported by the French. Appointed the
first British Consul to Samoa, he was keenly interested in trade as well
as hostile to all things Catholic. His son William, as British Consul in
Fiji, extended the family tradition into land speculation. The first
commercial business in Samoa was founded in 1839 by John Chauner
Williams, British Consul and son of the martyred missionary. In
Hawai'i, many missionary descendants became wealthy and powerful
in the *haole* elite who controlled politics and the economy until the 1950s.

Did the early missionaries promote capitalism in less direct ways?
From the Islanders' perspective, missionaries and traders were sources
of Western goods and technology. The *Missionary Magazine* of March
1838 remarked that with the Gospel came a demand for British hard-
ware. But the tenor of relations between missionaries and traders
varied. Missionaries typically denounced the 'immoral' beachcombers
and traders who preceded them. Some traders accused missionaries of
teaching Islanders the value of foreign goods, causing inflation in
prices. Such tensions were nowhere as rancorous as in Hawai'i.
Honolulu was already a busy port when missionaries arrived in 1820,
and initiated a prolonged feud with mariners and merchants. Sailors
rioted when the chiefs promulgated puritanical 'blue laws' authored
largely by missionaries. However, where missionaries established
themselves before traders, as in Samoa, relations were often neutral or
even supportive, justifying the metaphor of Christianity paving the way
for trade. On Pohnpei, missionaries encouraged congregants to produce
commodities for sale, arguing that 'commerce would facilitate the
civilising process by engendering in Pohnpeians a healthy respect for
the proper forms of exchange and profit'.[25]

Despite Max Weber's famous theory linking 'the Protestant ethic' and
'the spirit of capitalism', it is difficult to find evidence that Islanders
internalised the missionaries' values—industry, individualism, frugality,
self-denial—or became harder-working or more receptive to capitalist
development. Thirty years of missionary teaching did nothing to prepare
Hawaiians for the privatisation of land in mid-century (see below). Yet
missionaries did impart lessons of capitalism by their fund-raising.
Church contributions were paid in commodities, and Islanders were
continually exhorted to produce more for the mission and the glory of
God. Protestant missionaries, normally supporting large families on

25 Hanlon, *Upon a Stone Altar*, 131.

small allowances, were particularly energetic in urging productivity and liberality towards the church. The Presbyterian theocracy in Aneityum was also a copra-producing economy, whose profits were church contributions. Catholic missionaries tended to be less demanding and more generous. Spanish priests in Pohnpei even accused their Protestant rivals of 'mercantilism'.[26] In Micronesia and in Fiji, Protestant missions collected and sold copra, and used mission boats to conduct trade.

Protestant missionaries in Rotuma were delighted by the visible effects of conversion. One missionary wrote in 1865: 'The contrast between the skins and garments, stained with turmeric and the clean shirts and dresses, was too marked to be overlooked. The young men of the [converted] district appeared in a sort of uniform, clean white shirts, and clean cloth wrapped around them in place of trousers. The idea was their own: the effect was good.' As historians of Rotuma observe, Protestant reports were replete with cost accounting. Another missionary summed up a generation of evangelisation:

> What have we got for the labour and money expended? . . . there are other fields in these seas which for the same amounts of labor and money would have yielded [many more converts]. Here we have one of the richest Islands in the South Pacific, & yet from the outset she has not anything like defrayed the current expenses. She has been a dead loss financially from the first.[27]

The early LMS missionaries may have been the first agents in Samoa to spur production for an external market. In 1842 the mission began to collect donations of coconut oil, which they sold to John Chauner Williams. The missionaries enthused that they could collect much more oil if only they had casks, and one suggested that each station be supplied with a storage tank. Through the 1840s and 1850s, their letters chart increasing amounts—a thousand gallons in 1850. The missionaries also sold books for coconut oil: one gallon would buy 'a portion of Scripture' in 1843. Attentive to the tastes of their customers, they requested good cloth for binding: 'I trust the Directors will attend to our request for cloth &c.', one wrote, 'especially as the people are far from being indifferent to the appearance of a book they purchase.'[28]

Samoan chiefs contributed with typical politeness, as in this 1843 letter:

> we shew to you certain things which have begun to grow up in Samoa here; these are the things, the arrow root and the cocoa nut oil to assist in the work of God. Behold, [it is not for us your loving kindness, but for these lands.] *nisi mea ua faatoa tupu l Samoa nei. O mea ia o masoa ma Mali e faafesoasoani i le galuega ale Atua faauta e la iate i matou lou tou alolofa mai i nei atu nuu.*[29]

Throughout Polynesia, lineages—and congregations—competed to give the largest contributions (*vakamisioneri*) to the church, and the practice

26 *Ibid.*, 180.
27 Wesleyan Missionary Notes, April 1866, cited by Howard and Kjellgren, 'Martyrs, Progress and Political Ambition'.
28 LMS papers South Seas Letters 16/7/A, John Stair, 12 September 1843, Mitchell Library, Sydney, microfilm.
29 South Seas Letters 16/6/C, Mitchell Library, Sydney, microfilm.

was carried into Melanesia by Samoan, Tongan and Fijian evangelists. This might suggest that converts had internalised capitalist values, but *vakamisioneri* also belongs to a much older tradition of creating obligations through competitive gift-giving.

THE NEW LAWS

The Hawaiian race live like wanderers on the earth and dwell in all lands surrounded by the sea. Why have they wandered to strange lands and other kingdoms of earth? They say because they were burdened by the law of the land. The time when all these people went away was that in which the chiefs took up learning letters, and made the new laws for governing the land which is called the missionary law. The foreigners were benefited and they have stayed here because they like new lands, but the people of Hawai'i waited for the benefits of the government under the law from strange lands . . . There was no powerful chief to stand back of the people and put together the parts that were broken to pieces. It is a wonder that the land survives at all as a so-called independent kingdom when the rock that forms its anchor is shattered by the storm.[30]

The demands of merchants and developers inspired many legal systems and constitutions. Andrew Cheyne of Palau was one of many who tried to reinvent political systems for their own benefit. Many peoples were first introduced to legalistic agreements and contracts through treaties, instigated by mariners for the convenience of trade. The naval officers who dispensed 'warship justice' often pressured Island leaders to sign treaties guaranteeing the safety of foreigners and their property. Thus in 1870 an American captain assembled the chiefs of Pohnpei to sign a treaty protecting foreigners. The agreement went on to mandate a radical change: the right of foreigners to buy land in permanent ownership. Pohnpeian chiefs saw the treaty as largely a temporary expedient however, and Pohnpei never experienced wholesale land alienation. Reflecting a common aim of such documents, the constitution of Cakobau's Fijian kingdom included in its purposes 'to preserve the perfect harmony which should exist between the two races, [and] to facilitate the increasing European commerce'.[31]

Foreign entrepreneurs were irresistibly attracted to lands apparently under-used (see chapter 5). They did not understand that Islanders needed bush and forests for essential products, and they tended to define uncultivated lands as 'waste'. The fact that Pacific economies were oriented towards self-sufficiency was seen as a problem in need of solution. For their own good, as well as the benefit of foreigners, Islanders must be encouraged to produce regularly for external markets. Foreigners saw commodity production as an obvious remedy to the 'problem'. If Islanders would not change their modes of land use, then means must be found for removing the land from them. Land

---

30 Kamakau, *Ruling Chiefs of Hawaii*, 404–5.
31 Scarr, *Fiji: A Short History*, 56.

alienation became a key variable in shaping destinies. Large-scale alienation was often followed by loss of sovereignty as well as cultural loss, whereas Islanders living on the land had some chance to retain familiar practices and local solidarity. Once dispossessed, they suffered the attenuation of custom and cultural knowledge and often lost some ability to resist colonial scenarios.

Missionaries were responsible for crafting the early law codes governing civil and domestic behaviour. Many missionaries, unalterably opposed to sexual licence, prostitution, gun peddling and alcohol sales, had bitter conflicts with traders and beachcombers who had come to the Pacific partly to escape such restraints. In Fiji in mid-century, zealous missionaries over-stepped the truth, accusing the whole beach community of buying and selling Fijian women. Naval officers and colonial officials in Australia found the charges credible, until closer investigation revealed that relations between white men and Fijian women were governed by chiefly authority and provided some elements of choice for the women.[32] Wherever chiefs wielded centralised control, as in Tahiti and Hawai'i, missionaries could act out their principles and prejudices, and outlaw practices once they won over the chiefs. However, the customs of capitalism gradually became as evident in law codes and government policies as Protestant morality. The most far-reaching provisions of law codes governed land tenure, taxation, and the rights of foreigners. Among the foreign advisers to chiefs, former missionaries and other devout Christians believed strongly in commerce and private property. Privatising lands, they argued in Hawai'i, would spur the common people to industry and encourage 'improvement' of the land by entrepreneurs. Mission-educated intellectuals and government officials facing massive debts and angry creditors often agreed.

In Hawai'i, a set of laws passed in 1850 had devastating ramifications for rural Hawaiians and set the stage for the loss of sovereignty. The *Kuleana Act* allowed 'native tenants' to be awarded their lands in fee simple. Another 1850 law gave foreigners the right to own land, so that commoners were enabled to sell just when foreigners were allowed to buy. The ports of Hilo, Kawaihae and Kealakekua were opened to commerce, previously restricted to Honolulu and Lahaina, while a law abolishing the payment of taxes in kind impelled Hawaiians into the market economy. Land taxes had been payable in currency since 1846; now poll taxes too had to be paid in coin. Cultivators who had managed to remain self-sufficient were now thrust into cash cropping, selling produce, wage labour, or prostitution. Missionaries wrote plaintively that the new tax law was driving people away from rural lands.

The Māhele—ostensibly a land reform, in reality a strategy for the sale of communal land to individuals—made for large-scale and rapid dispossession. The legal framework of the land division was designed by foreigners according to the individualistic ethos of entrepreneurial capitalism. Kamehameha III and some foreign advisers were first

32 Vicki Lukere, 'Mothers of the Taukei'.

concerned to protect the rights of commoners, but other Westerners and most of the highest chiefs were more concerned to maximise their own interests. In the end commoners—the 'native tenants' of no rank who had always fed the chiefs—received short shrift. The distribution was grossly skewed; less than 30,000 acres were distributed to the mass of the people (who numbered close to 80,000), compared to 1,500,000 acres awarded to a few hundred chiefs. The government received 1,500,000 acres, and 915,000 acres were set aside as Crown lands, the monarch's share. Portions of the government and Crown lands were then sold cheaply to *haole* planters and ranchers. The developers sought to augment their holdings by buying commoners' lands or by making life intolerable for small farmers. And by a cruel conjunction, measles and smallpox struck between 1848 and 1854, while the Māhele process was in full swing. Many claimants who had registered their lands in 1848 were dead before the Land Commission representatives arrived two or five years later to verify claims; and if no heirs were alive and present, deceased claimants' lands fell to the government. Observers elsewhere pointed to Hawai'i as a worst-case example of native land alienation. Cakobau and Thurston in Fiji understood it as a scenario to avoid, whereas entrepreneurs were inspired by the prospect.

The Kingdom of Tonga's laws and constitution were elements of a strategy to retain independence by securing recognition from foreign powers. Missionaries were a source of ideas and precedents—but their influence was diffuse. King George was no puppet, and his ideas were broader than those of the missionaries. The first essay in law-giving (the Vava'u Code of 1839) committed Tonga to Christianity, prohibited 'Murder, Theft, Adultery, Fornication and the retailing of Ardent spirits', and was mainly concerned with social and political order. In 1850 this structure was extended. The sale of land to foreigners was, for example, explicitly forbidden (XXIX); the Law referring to Men (XXXVI) stated that 'You shall work and persevere in labouring for the support of your family, as well as yourself, and in order to trade and contribute to the cause of God, and the Chief of the land', and the Law referring to Women (XXXVII) made a similar point: 'You must work, women, and persevere in labouring to clothe your husband and children; unmarried women shall work to be useful to their relatives and parents.'

A revision in 1862 was so extensive that it could be read as a constitution. The influence of Christianity persisted, but the bans on dancing and some other customs disappeared, and economic issues were seriously addressed, reflecting the breadth of King George's experience. 'Serfdom' and 'vassalage' were explicitly abolished, the ban on the sale of land to foreigners was restated, and land tenure was tackled.

[In Sydney the King] saw many poorly dressed people, obviously ill-fed, sleeping in the parks . . . [He] could not understand how there could be homeless and poverty-stricken people in a land as large and obviously rich as Australia . . . [and] determined that such an appalling situation should never be allowed to arise in Tonga. The King was also very impressed with the leasehold system . . . which he saw in Sydney, and he made up his mind that the land in Tonga should be distributed among his own people along similar lines.

This appears to have been the origin of King George's idea of legislating for the individual ownership of land—a revolutionary change in the system of land tenure in Tonga. The prohibition of the sale of land which appeared in Clause II of the 1862 Code was only a legislation of customary land tenure, but the notion of individual ownership of land by leasehold was something quite new.[33]

Access to land still depended on kinship, clientage to particular chiefs and relations with the church, including *misinale* contributions towards overseas missions. With land securely in Tongan hands, the economy evolved through something like peasant production and larger-scale production on nobles' estates.

Four decades after the Māhele, Samoa too had a land division, but with a very different outcome. In the wars of the 1860s and 1870s Europeans engaged in a speculative land rush, exchanging guns and supplies for land. But Samoans sometimes 'sold' land without the authority, or *pule*, to do so; some lands were sold more than once, and overlapping claims abounded (chapter 5). In 1889 Germany, Great Britain and the United States conferred to craft a solution to the Samoa problem. Though the conference and its major product—the *Berlin Act* of 1889— failed to end Samoan strife, the treaty mandated a review and adjudication of land claims. An international Land Commission met from 1892 to 1894. In Hawai'i's Māhele, the burden of proof was on the native claimant. In Samoa, the onus was on foreigners. Westerners claimed more than two and a half times the entire area of Samoa. In the end, about one-fifth of the land was confirmed in foreign hands, but the *Berlin Act* forbade further alienation, and later colonial governments upheld that principle. In Western Samoa today, the proportion of land held in freehold is less than the 20 per cent figure for alienated land in 1894.

Civil and domestic laws reflected Western cultural and class biases that we loosely identify as 'Victorian'. Family law tried to institutionalise Western gender norms from the top down, and defined men and women as intrinsically different. In Hawai'i an 1845 law established the principle that a married woman was legally assimilated by her husband and became 'civilly dead', with no right to dispose of property. This notion was profoundly at odds with the autonomy, cultural value and personal authority of Polynesian women, and it is unlikely that these legal disabilities had much impact outside the towns. When Hawaiians flocked to the ports after the Māhele, many older women stayed on the land as household heads and place-holders. Women became focal in rural communities because they wielded local authority and because they were structurally central in the family—despite their legal inferiority at the national level.

The new laws often expressed a convergence between missionaries' enthusiasms and the ambitions of power-holders. Often the missionaries' literacy and wider experience are reflected in the language of the laws, but occasionally (as in Tonga) missionary ideas were clearly subordinated to chiefly interests. A revealing code of laws survives from

33 Lātūkefu, *Church and State in Tonga*, 162–3.

an area where missionaries had no direct role in drafting them. During the struggle between Christians and 'pagans' in Aoba (now Ambae, see chapter 5), a Church of Christ elder recorded the rules of the congregation, revealing the Protestant ethic, the masculinism and the moral and hygienist values which reinforced each other:

> 1 Do not loved other women. 2 Do not given too much wine. 3 Do not steal money or animals. 4 Do not mock a man who watches over you. 5 Do not sell your wife to someone. 6 Do not write a paper to say sin. 7 Do not spoil a young girls. 8 Do not fight someone. 9 Do not touch your sisters. 10 Do not bring false witness. 11 Do not speak lie to your teacher. 12 Do not see any animal spoil some garden. 13 Do not angry against your missionary. 14 Do not fight your wife. 15 Do not playing dice. 16 Do not fight for some land. 17 Do not shoot a man with gun. 18 Do not cut any man with knife. 19 Do not rob any man. 20 Do not take long time with your account. 21 Do not run away from sending your account.

These instructions targeted men. Others instructed families how 'to change from old life to the new in each home':

> 1 Do not make bed on the wet ground. 2 Do not have rubbish [in] house sleep. 3 Do not live without having tank water. 4 Do not have rubbish kitchen for house cook. 5 Do not live without [water] closet at home. 6 Do not go without washing face or teeth. 7 Do not let any pigs come close to your home. 8 Do not eat with the dirty hands. 9 Do not see the small children do also. 10 Do not have any dirty clothes for wear. 11 Do not eat in the wrong time of hour. 12 Do not let your children go without asking you. 13 Do not let your children go you no say, you pray [don't let children leave the church without your permission].

The debt to the Ten Commandments is obvious, and so are the circumstances of the crusade against paganism. Equally clear is the influence of Queensland plantation rules, with their emphasis on regularity, punctuality and personal hygiene. The condemnation of male violence goes beyond any of these codes; nor can the explicit masculinism be a casual borrowing. The thirty-four commandments do not foreshadow a centralised polity, but one constituted by adult men, heading stable and sober family households, worshipping in a congregation united under one preacher, sending their children to the village school, and bound together in an economy lubricated by credit and cash. No coercive state imposed these values on this society working through the interlinked dimensions of modernisation: production, exchange, age, gender, and social cohesion.

POLITICAL TRANSFORMATION AND RESISTANCE

The effectiveness of 'native agency' in colonial encounters has occasioned much debate. Granted, Islanders first saw foreigners as a resource to be directed towards their own agendas. Western nations had the military and organisational advantage, however, and foreign meddling provoked profound changes. If colonisation was the bottom line for most peoples, is it at all useful to highlight the motives, actions and interests of the Islanders? Clearly, Islander agendas affected the course of Western contact, but often not in ways that Islanders intended. The same can be said for Western scenarios: the interaction of peoples and plans had unintended consequences for both sides. Beyond the level of individual agency, the organisation of Pacific societies caused foreigners to alter their plans and significantly affected outcomes.

Such apparently precipitous religious changes as the Hawaiian *kapu* abolition of 1819 must be explained by reference to local political conflicts and the agendas of particular chiefs. In Tahiti, Protestant missionaries laboured for years with little success, only to witness mass conversions when Pomare II adopted Christianity and unified Tahiti. Missionaries in Tahiti went far beyond moral and spiritual guidance. They were not only advisers, but architects and managers of a new governmental structure. Henry Nott, Pomare's teacher, was the principal author of the 1824 constitution which established a parliament of male chiefs and elected district representatives. Chosen as the Parliament's first president, Nott presided over the drafting of laws governing taxation and courts as well as civil behaviour.

On Kosrae too, an American missionary shaped transformation. Depopulation combined with missionisation set chiefs against Christian converts. Faced with declining tribute and an erosion of their authority, the leaders tried to revive pre-Christian rituals and forbade observance of the Sabbath. The sudden death of the adamantly anti-mission paramount chief shook the chiefs' confidence and the Christian community grew in numbers and in political power. Seizing the advantage, the missionary Benjamin Snow pressured the new paramount to accept a new government structure in 1869. A council was formed, of seven elected regional representatives and the seven surviving chiefs of the island's original eighteen titles, along with the paramount chief. In 1874 the council ousted the paramount, however, and installed the first Christian 'king' of Kosrae.

Missionary influence on Tongan legislation is clear, but the question of agency is less so. In 1875 King George proposed a new constitution to Parliament. It was quickly endorsed.

> The form of our Government in the days past was that my rule was absolute, and that my wish was law and that I could choose who should belong to the Parliament and that I could please myself to create chiefs and alter titles. But that, it appears to me, was a sign of darkness and now a new era has come to Tonga—an era of light—and it is my wish to grant a Constitution and to carry on my duties in accordance with it and those that come after me shall do the same and the Constitution shall be a firm rock in Tonga for ever.[34]

The constitution won recognition from Britain, Germany and the United States, but it was not the last word in securing Tonga's independence. British authorities intervened even during King George's lifetime, and a

34 Lātūkefu, *Church and State in Tonga.*

crisis arose early in the next century when Tonga only narrowly averted an interventionist protectorate. It is nevertheless a remarkable document which, with few modifications, still serves the kingdom. Whose was it? On King George's instruction, it was drafted by the missionary Shirley Baker, who consulted the Premier of New South Wales and the Hawaiian Consul-General in Sydney, who provided copies of their laws. However, Baker was in bad odour with the Methodist mission, and worked secretly on a project which did not commend itself to his peers. Baker was the agent of the King, not the missionaries; and the King was nobody's agent.

Samoa and Pohnpei were the foci of bitter inter-imperial rivalry. The destinies of both were adjudicated by Westerners in conferences in Berlin. The British were briefly interested in Pohnpei in the 1870s, but most foreigners on the island were German traders. In 1885 a German warship landed a company of marines and the captain demanded that the five high chiefs sign a treaty of annexation. The chiefs signed, but the warship left without establishing a credible presence. After political manoeuvres which brought Spain and Germany close to war, an international conference decided that Spain had rightful possession of the Carolines. The Spanish arrived in 1886, provoking twelve years of violent resistance. An American missionary, Edward Doane, became the Spanish Governor's political antagonist and was arrested and deported, in part because of charges brought by German traders. In 1887 Pohnpeians achieved a very rare feat for a Pacific Island people: they assassinated the Spanish Governor and forced out the colonists. The Spanish returned four months later, but spent the remainder of their colonial tenure behind a high wall protecting them from their subjects. After Spain lost the Spanish–American War, Germany acquired Pohnpei by agreement in 1898.

No imperial nation was anxious to annex the Samoan archipelago— as long as no other power did. The Great Powers preferred that Samoans form a government capable of maintaining peace and order. Dynastic competition, shifting territorial alliances, inter-imperial rivalry and the machinations of foreign nationals generated a political saga of mind-boggling complexity. In Steinberger's time, the principal contenders for the 'kingship' were from the Malietoa family. After his removal, two more rivals emerged from the Tupua family—Mata'afa and Tupua Tamasese. At various times would-be kings (*tupu*) set up competing governments and appealed to the audience of resident foreigners. One tactic was to proclaim laws and circulate them to the consuls. All contenders invoked history and custom to justify their claims. In the 1880s letters and editorials in the *Samoa Times* pursued a public debate over the genealogical credentials of the chiefly rivals and other matters of Samoan custom. But agents of the major German trading firm worked to undermine the already limited authority of the Malietoa Laupepa government. When Tupua Tamasese set up a rival government, he too sent letters and proclamations as 'King of Samoa'. Tamasese's supporters wrote to educate the British Consul on 'the beliefs and customs of our country'. Malietoa went one better, writing to

Queen Victoria to explain 'the customs of our country beginning from ancient times'.[35]

In 1887 the German faction made customary legitimation moot by installing Tupua Tamasese as king and sending Eugen Brandeis to serve as his premier. For a year and a half the government was run by and for German interests. Onerous taxes were levied, to be raised by mortgaging lands and copra to the German firm. Samoans could be prosecuted and gaoled for trading with other companies. Organised opposition was met with bombardment and arrests. The Brandeis–Tamasese regime was the first time that a Western power established a monopoly of force in Samoa and, moreover, used coercive power to enforce the laws of a national government. The government's tyranny provoked a revolt and almost led to war between the Great Powers. The famous Apia hurricane of 1889, in which several warships were destroyed, ended the confrontation, but factional conflict and imperial intervention continued through the 1890s. In a bizarre climax to decades of strife, an American judge presided over a court case to determine who would be King. The two candidates were Mata'afa and Malietoa Tanumafili, the son of Laupepa. Both sides presented evidence from history and custom: Tanumafili won on a technicality—causing an immediate return to warfare. The next and final international commission concluded that the kingship was a foreign concept and abolished the position. The Great Powers struck a deal whereby Western Samoa became a German colony and the eastern isles, including Tutuila with Pago Pago harbour, came under the administration of the United States Navy.

Samoan tactics were seldom systematic. Samoans had leverage with traders because home producers, not plantations, produced the bulk of the copra. The main hindrance to agricultural development was the availability of labour, not land. Copra traders used land mortgages primarily as a threat to prod the Samoans to produce. There was no advantage to widespread foreclosures, which would only decrease production and cause a crash in the Samoan consumer trade. The excesses of the Brandeis–Tamasese regime flowed in part from the fact that traders competed intensely with one another for Samoan copra. Samoan debts and communal mortgages ballooned beyond the point where they could possibly be recovered, and this situation paralysed foreign coercion, though it was probably not the outcome of a conscious strategy.

In many Islands colonialism was contested and its impact uneven. European plans were often frustrated without apparent organisation and without an explicit ideology of resistance. Samoans refused to work or produce copra below a certain price, and practised many small subversive acts of theft and vandalism against the plantations. They used unripe nuts or supplied inadequately dried copra, which was heavier and more likely to spoil. They added rocks, coral and salt water to increase the weight of their loads—while traders doctored their scales in the other direction. Traders had to grant credit against the promise of future copra, but Samoans were adept at postponing payment, and

35 Letter, 18 August 1885, British Consular Series, National Archives of New Zealand.

were seldom dupes or victims suffering under the burden of debt. Despite foreigners' dreams, profits on tropical agriculture and trade were by no means assured. In Samoa and Hawai'i the profitability of commodity agriculture hinged on governmental measures in support of planters. Given the uncertainties of commercial ventures, unsystematic resistance had significant impacts on foreign plans.

Similarly, pre-colonial resistance in other Island societies rarely took the form of organised movements targeting foreign institutions. In retrospect, however, the cultural revivals and nativistic rebellions that occurred from Kosrae to Hawai'i appear directed at Western encroachment into custom and politics. The *mamaia* movement in Tahiti, from 1826 into the 1840s, combined Christian and pagan elements and its prophets predicted a coming millennium. Missionaries saw the cult as a direct threat to the mission and to the government's authority. The overthrow of the Hawaiian religion was, at one level, a struggle between pro-foreign and traditionalist factions among the high chiefs. However, the *kapu* abolition also followed a Hawaiian cultural logic which defined the roles of older and younger brothers. Authority over the land normatively went to the senior sibling; to the younger brother devolved the care of the gods, illustrating the common Polynesian pattern whereby genealogical juniors serve as the 'priestly line' to ruling chiefs. Despite this ideal division, power struggles between older and younger brothers were endemic in Hawai'i. The 'fatal flaw' in chiefly authority was that younger brothers could use the *mana* of the gods to overthrow their genealogical seniors. Kamehameha himself lived out this scenario of usurpation and, not coincidentally, was a staunch traditionalist devoted to his patron deity, the war god Kūka'ilimoku.

When Liholiho succeeded Kamehameha I, Kekuaokalani, his junior collateral or 'younger brother' (the kinship term is the same), a favourite nephew of Kamehameha, inherited care of the god Kū. By most accounts Kekuaokalani was more capable than Liholiho. He also had the status of sister's son to Kamehameha, a relationship of affection and privileged familiarity. Liholiho and his chiefly 'mothers', the widows of Kamehameha, supported social change and foreign influence, while Kekuaokalani led the traditionalist faction. Given the cultural scenario of usurpation, what better way to undercut the ritual potency of a junior collateral than to declare that the gods no longer have *mana*? Kekuaokalani led an armed rebellion against the overthrow of the *kapu*, but he died in battle, with his wife fighting at his side. The *kapu* abolition illustrates how a complex conjuncture of indigenous precedents and introduced ideas spurred social and political transformation.

In the 1820s Christianity became the new state religion. Later rulers suffered bouts of anguish and dissipation, or played out cultural conflicts in anti-missionary and nativistic episodes. Hawaiians refer to the period from 1833 to 1835 as the 'troubles of Kaomi'. Encouraged by his Tahitian companion Kaomi, the teenaged Kamehameha III rebelled against puritanical strictures by throwing himself into drink, gambling and debauchery. At one point he sent a crier into the streets to announce the repeal of all laws save those against theft and murder. Many chiefs and commoners followed his example, reviving the hula and other prohibited customs. According to the custom of sibling marriages among the highest chiefs, Kamehameha III would have been destined to perpetuate the dynasty by wedding his sister, Nāhi'ena'ena. To the missionaries, of course, 'royal incest' was an abomination. The princess vacillated between pious obedience and open rebellion, at great personal cost. The two consummated their love and Nāhi'ena'ena bore a child, but infant and mother died soon afterwards. Whether because of culture shock, venereal disease, or some combination of psychic and biological factors, the high chiefs thereafter failed to reproduce themselves.

In some parts of the world, divide and conquer was the strategy for imperial expansion. In most of Polynesia, however, 'unify and conquer' was the mechanism for gaining colonial control. In Hawai'i, Fiji and Tahiti, the creation of centralised governments preceded the loss of sovereignty. The project failed in Samoa, where the Great Powers saw partition as a solution to the strife which their own citizens had exacerbated. By the beginning of the twentieth century all the major Polynesian societies, save Tonga, were colonies. Tonga was also unified, and the monarchy remained independent, although its political system and culture had an increasingly British flavour. Only in New Zealand did Maori attempt to build a monarchy with which to co-ordinate the defence of their land after sovereignty was already lost (chapter 5).

In the early colonial period the internal divisions of Island societies were eclipsed by the divide between native and foreigner. Political inequality was grounded in economic stratification and rationalised by Western racial ideologies. Island colonies became two-tiered societies, with an intermediate (and mediating) class formed of descendants of mixed marriages. Called 'half-castes' by the British, 'afakasi in Samoa, demi in Tahiti, and hapa-haole in Hawai'i, they became merchants, intelligentsia, government officials—and anti-colonial leaders. White expatriates tended to classify them with 'natives' or revile them as degenerate agitators. Islanders who were lumped together by colonial administrators came to see themselves as unified peoples and to act accordingly, and in the early twentieth century responses to foreign rule began to resemble systematic resistance and organised rebellion.

In both Pohnpei and Samoa, German interference in political custom provoked organised resistance. In Pohnpei the trigger was the administration's move to remove the land from chiefly control and issue private titles. The Germans had also interfered in the chiefly tribute system and sent Pohnpeians to road projects as forced labourers. The 1910 Sokehs Rebellion was an armed resistance movement in which Pohnpeians assassinated the German Governor and several other officials. The rebellion was crushed in six months and its leaders executed, but as David Hanlon points out: 'the Sokehs Rebellion did not mark the end of all Pohnpeian resistance to foreign domination, only the end of all armed resistance ... Resistance to foreign intrusion became part of their culture.'[36]

In Samoa, Governor Solf abolished the status of king and outlawed the two leading orator groups, who had long been Samoa's 'king-makers'. Resistance did not become well organised until the Mau Rebellion under New Zealand rule (chapter 8). But early in the German period, Samoans tried to wrest some control over copra prices by forming a national trading company, to be supported by contributions from villages. The administration suppressed the 'Oloa' company, but a nascent independence movement then emerged. The new opposition movement articulated a general critique of German policies and came to be called the 'Mau a Pule' (the Opinion of Pule). Its primary spokes-man was a celebrated orator of Savai'i, Namulau'ulu Lauaki Mamoe. The Germans deported him to Saipan in 1909. He was pardoned by the New Zealanders in 1915 but died on the return voyage. The Lauaki Mau does not even merit a footnote in many Pacific histories, but it marks a transition from unsystematic local resistance to a more unified opposition.

Most Islanders lost their political independence, but other important issues had also to be resolved: language, cultural integrity, the priority of local custom, the persistence of concepts and practices of kinship and exchange. Certain factors appear crucial for the destiny of Island cultures under foreign rule, notably demography, land alienation, and language. Simply put, Islanders fared worst where they were out-numbered by settlers and/or immigrant workers, and where they were dispossessed of their lands. These characteristics often went together. Australian Aborigines and Hawaiians represent the worst-case scenario on both counts, and in both cases there has been severe attrition in indigenous languages. Few colonial powers were as aggressive in suppressing the language as was the United States in Hawai'i, where public schooling was seen as a tool for Americanisation. Language loss resulted in a profound sense of cultural loss. As in Australia, geography and disease were also significant in Hawai'i's post-contact history: the population declined by at least three-quarters between 1778 and 1854.

Samoa, in contrast, survived sixty-two years of colonial rule while preserving cultural knowledge and practice to a great extent. Western Samoa now appears more 'traditional' in its reliance on native house-building materials and the subsistence economy, but even American Samoans continue to speak Samoan, select family *matai*, hold land communally, and conduct ceremonial exchanges. Samoans were never outnumbered, and escaped large-scale dispossession. Chinese and Melanesian indentured labourers were imported, but not in large numbers, and both the German and New Zealand administrations en-couraged their repatriation. Both administrations were also committed to preventing land alienation—and the fate of the Hawaiians served as a cautionary tale.

36 Hanlon, *Upon a Stone Altar*, 406.

The degree of indigenous political centralisation may also have been significant in 'cultural survival'. In Hawai'i and Tahiti, centralisation was followed by increasing foreign influence and takeover. The more some chiefdoms resembled European monarchies, the more vulnerable they appear to have become to foreign cultural influences. Local-level organisation was much stronger in Samoa than in Hawai'i or Tahiti. Few would describe Samoan strife as productive, but the chronic conflicts may have delayed foreign hegemony. Even after colonisation local chiefs were a force to contend with, and administrative edicts were mediated to some extent by the Samoan emphasis on public debate and negotiation. Some (but by no means all) of the atomised polities of the western Pacific proved more difficult for imperial nations to assimilate than the weak native states; but in every instance Islander initiatives either deflected or arrested the scenarios of colonial authorities. Nowhere did they despair.

BIBLIOGRAPHIC ESSAY

On European perceptions of Polynesia and Melanesia, see Linnekin, 'Ignoble Savages and other European Visions'; Thomas, 'The Force of Ethnology'.

This chapter relies partly on unpublished archival material for Protestant missionary societies. The most complete collection is that of the London Missionary Society, in the School of Oriental and African Studies, London University. Microfilm copies have been made available in several other libraries, including the Mitchell Library in Sydney. The Mitchell Library also holds the bulk of Methodist missionary archival material. Anglican archives are held in Lambeth Palace, London, in the Library of the University of Papua New Guinea, and in several depositories in New Zealand and the Solomon Islands. These collections are described in the bibliographies of Langmore, *Missionary Lives*; and Hilliard, *God's Gentlemen*.

Catholic mission archives are less accessible to researchers who are not members of the relevant congregations. However, the Pacific Manuscripts Bureau has microfilmed most of the Pacific material of the Missionaries of the Sacred Heart. For Marist sources, see Laracy, *Marists and Melanesians*.

Lātūkefu, *Church and State in Tonga*, is the leading source on constitutional change in Tonga. Kamakau, *Ruling Chiefs*, is the starting point for Hawaiian politics, followed by Kuykendall, *The Hawaiian Kingdom*. Hezel, *First Taint of Civilization*, and Hanlon, *Upon a Stone Altar*, introduce political change in Micronesia. Meleisea, *The Making of Modern Samoa*, analyses the political history of Samoa; Scarr, *I, The Very Bayonet*, does the same service for Fiji; and Howard and Kjellgren, 'Martyrs, Progress and Political Ambition', accounts for parallel developments in Rotuma. For Vanuatu, see Bonnemaison, *The Tree and the Canoe*; for the Marquesas, Dening, *Islands and Beaches*; for the Loyalty Islands, Howe, *The Loyalty Islands*; and for Tahiti, Newbury, *Tahiti Nui*.

On Savage and related matters of warfare, see Sahlins, 'The Discovery of the True Savage'; Campbell, 'The Historiography of Charlie Savage'; Shineberg, 'Guns and Men in Melanesia'; Clunie, *Fijian Weapons and Warfare* and also his 'The Fijian Flintlock' and 'The Manila Brig'; and Fison, *Tales from Old Fiji*.

NEW ECONOMIC ORDERS:
LAND, LABOUR AND DEPENDENCY

NEW SOURCES OF INSTABILITY

During most of the nineteenth century, the British Navy was the main over-arching authority in the Pacific, exercising 'informal empire' at a time when Britain was committed to free trade and reluctant to incur the costs of colonial administration. Frail kingdoms and mission theocracies flourished under that umbrella, and Protestant mission families provided consular services which hinged the Navy's maritime power to island-based authorities. Three kinds of instability challenged this informal empire. In the Islands the expansion of commerce un-settled social relations and attracted the opportunists and empire-builders described in chapters 5 and 6. Other industrial powers were also drawn into the region. The French Navy from the 1840s projected French power. American naval power provoked the re-emergence of Japan, and then extinguished the decaying Spanish Empire, to initiate America's Pacific Century. The new German Empire, under Chancellor Bismarck, was the least of Britain's anxieties. Island produce generated only a fraction of Germany's imports, and Bismarck (like Britain but unlike France) resisted tariff protection and colonial acquisitions.

The greatest sources of instability were British settlers in Australia and New Zealand, and French settlers (*caldoches*) in New Caledonia. They competed with Samoan-based German recruiters for the labour of the western Islands, and all demanded that their metropolitan govern-ments annex every island which either was inhabited or might possess minerals. European governments were understandably reluctant to risk global conflicts for the sake of remote islands and obscure propagand-ists. They could not ignore the increasing disorder, nor simply rebuff their importunate subjects, but their responses were minimalist and cheap. The (British) Western Pacific High Commission, for example, was appended to the tasks of the Governor of Fiji, and its authority was largely to advise the Royal Navy which continued to patrol the Islands, protecting the interests of British subjects. When Bismarck determined, in 1884, to move from informal empire to a system of protectorates, he tried to operate through chartered companies rather than assuming direct responsibility for administration. When the Western Pacific High Commission proved inadequate to its task, Britain declared protectorates over Papua and the Solomon Islands—on condition that Australian and New Zealand colonies foot the bill. And the rivalry of Australian settlers, British missionaries and Higginson's Caledonian Company for the New Hebrides led to the tardy, ineffectual—but cheap—mechanism of the Anglo-French Condominium.

The earliest traders needed the support of local power-holders, for ventures which made slight demands on land and labour. During the century power-relations shifted markedly through the intervention of states which permitted much larger-scale production. Whether they were created by Islanders or by foreigners, all governments took anxious steps to promote export production. Their interests complemented those of the traders, planters and miners who offered coherent (if self-serving) advice. Entrepreneurs who crossed the beach from resource raiding to production needed at least three services from governments. Plantations and mines needed secure land title. Capital was a serious bottleneck, and investors put a premium on government oversight. Most insistently, employers yearned for governments to force Islanders to work.

German traders dominated the commerce of the central Pacific by the 1870s. By far the most powerful was Godeffroy, based in Samoa, where it acquired plantations, bought Samoan-grown copra, and handled most business. It cornered Tongan copra by a treaty with the Methodist mission, and pursued trade and labour west into Micronesia, New Guinea and Torres Strait. Smaller Samoan-based companies, such as H. M. Ruge & Co., struggled to compete. Fred Hennings concentrated on Fiji, and smaller companies ranged further north in the Marianas. In the Marshalls, Adolph Capelle engorged the copra trade until he was co-opted by Godeffroys. Other small operators remained independent, like Eduard Hernsheim who traded from Palau and then from the Duke of York Islands, and his brother Franz in Jaluit. These interests were not matched by political power, so that German firms were badly affected when other Europeans annexed islands and patronised compatriots. Once Fiji became a British colony, for example, Hennings wilted, and even Godeffroy suffered losses.

Wise in the Pacific, Godeffroy was rash in Europe. It was declared bankrupt in 1879 and the Deutsche Handels- und Plantagen-Gesellschaft (DHPG) was created to buy its assets. Enduring depressed copra prices through the 1880s and 1890s and competition from other labour recruiters in Melanesia, they implored Berlin to intervene to protect their land, labour and trade. Pressure was co-ordinated by the Colonial Society, which might not have persuaded Bismarck to declare protectorates in 1884, but companies willing to act as governments reassured the Chancellor that he might annex islands without incurring the cost of administration.

Chartered companies (like the device of making Eugen Brandeis premier of Samoa, see chapter 6) were designed to avert formal colonialism, but as matters turned out they merely delayed that outcome. A frail state was created in Jaluit in 1878 when Kabua and some lesser chiefs signed a treaty on behalf of the Ralik Islands, declaring

Germany the most favoured nation, allowing its citizens protection and its navy free access to Jaluit and other ports, including the right to establish a coaling station. This treaty fell short of annexation, but real power—reflected in the Ralik Islands' black, white and red banner with its uncanny resemblance to the German flag—lay with Germany. An unpaid German Commissioner arrived in 1885 but in 1888 the Jaluit Company was chartered to rule on behalf of the German government.

The largest force unleashed by arm's-length colonialism was the New Guinea Company, capitalised in Hamburg by Adolph Hansemann, a banker and dabbler in colonial projects. In 1884 the company was commissioned to govern New Guinea—the north-eastern quarter, and the Bismarck Archipelago. Hansemann studied the Dutch East Indies, which inspired an elaborate scheme of plantations. Land was acquired after perfunctory negotiations, but Hansemann did not count on malaria, which cut down company officers and forced the evacuation of one settlement. Nor did he anticipate the impact of tropical micro-organisms on exotic field crops. Nor did he expect the fevers and dysentery which struck down Melanesian and Chinese labourers. Only in the Gazelle Peninsula and the Duke of Yorks, where planters were already established, did plantations flourish, while large tracts on the mainland failed to attract colonists. This woeful planning was a consequence of conventional commercial calculations in Hamburg, applied to a task which required painstaking negotiations in New Guinea. The effects included massive loss of life, as well as the dissipation of capital. In 1899 the company surrendered its mandate, and New Guinea became an orthodox colony, where Governor Hahl struggled to promote the collective interests of planters, to restrain their appetites for New Guinean labour, and to bring down the mortality rates of Chinese workers. By 1914 a fairly prosperous plantation colony had been created in the Bismarck Archipelago.

French annexations in the 1840s were essentially strategic in purpose, though the consequences were much broader. The annexation of New Caledonia in 1853 provided the only prospect for a settler society, and it was developed as a penal colony during the 1860s. Unlike other French dependencies, land was appropriated on a large scale, and Kanaks confined to reserves. Physical conditions made commercial ranching more lucrative than cropping, and towards the end of the century minerals eclipsed all other production. From New Caledonia naval squadrons patrolled the New Hebrides, labour recruiters sought workers, and Higginson spun financial fantasies. Wallis and Futuna, annexed in the 1880s, offered neither strategic advantage nor prospects for settlement.

The Australian periphery

As settler states expanded and confronted German and French authority, the Western Pacific High Commission was replaced piecemeal by protectorates over Papua (the south-eastern quarter, briefly known as British New Guinea) and the Solomon Islands, and by an Anglo-French

Condominium in the New Hebrides. At the perimeter of French, British and Australian strategic and commercial interests, the protectorates were declared without enthusiasm or resources. In Papua from 1888 to 1898, Lieutenant-Governor MacGregor pinned his hopes on gold. After his departure the administration merely marked time until 1906, when the new Australian Commonwealth grudgingly assumed responsibility. A Royal Commission proposed to replace British officials with Australians, and drafted a development policy. That strategy—development through plantations—was easier to formulate than to realise, since it was hedged by constraints which applied nowhere else. Large-scale investment was desired in principle but discouraged in practice: the British New Guinea Syndicate, assembled in London in 1897, was denied the land on which its plans depended. Papuan officials reflected the Australian public's suspicion of private British capital, yet few Australians had the resources or experience for plantation development. Again, the White Australia policy barred the entry of Asian labour or Japanese entrepreneurs. Third, cargo could only be carried by ships manned by Australian crews, so that costs crippled export production. By default, policy switched towards coerced production by Papuans. Government was hampered at every point by Australian interests, and never escaped dependence on subsidies. By 1914 only one-third of the territory was under any control.

As the Australian Parliament observed: 'The form of [British] rule has been what best suited the occasion and the moment.' Forms of rule were certainly *ad hoc*, but there was a pattern in proconsuls' choices. Everywhere head taxes and import duties were convenient imposts. At least three strategies might yield more revenue: mining, plantations, and village production. It is not obvious why the latter strategy was so seldom adopted, but the approach of Resident Commissioner Woodford in the Solomon Islands is suggestive. The Solomon Islands Protectorate was created in 1893, on condition that the Resident Commissioner generate his own revenue. That implied support for anyone with a plausible scheme. When Woodford arrived in 1896, money was circulating alongside shell and other valuables. Passage masters had accumulated European clothing and furniture as well as boats. Dependence on foreign goods was general: ordinary people used imported axes and fishhooks, an alarming number of men had guns, and many adults drank alcohol and smoked tobacco (though some grew their own). These could be acquired by selling *bêche-de-mer*, curios and copra. Commerce was often matched by an increase in political scale, not only by passage masters extending their networks but also (on Nggela Island) by what Bennett calls an embryonic proto-state with written rules, and a blend of chiefly and Christian authority. In many Islands, then, people were committed to regional commerce.

Woodford acknowledged that villagers could generate revenue—but not soon enough. He assumed that Melanesians were dying out, so that their production should not be relied upon: plantations must be established instead. To secure land, labour and peace, he believed that Islanders must be made to acknowledge the authority of the state. He could never achieve such control with his handful of Fijian police, who cadged lifts to travel through the islands. The outcome was a series of punitive expeditions in which traders and 'friendly tribes' were enlisted as a militia. These campaigns degenerated into vendettas, moderated only by the intervention of missionaries. Christians were placed in an invidious position, but continued to act on behalf of the new regime:

> As early as 1902, Woodford's former police sergeant, William Buruku, after twenty-three years in Fiji, returned to his home at Wanderer Bay, Guadalcanal, where he became the means by which the new law was introduced to the area. Further east at Talise . . . David Sango returned in 1907 from twenty years in Queensland. As a Christian he worked with the [South Seas Evangelical Mission] to evangelize the district [and] reinforcing the government's pacification policy.[1]

Within ten years, results seemed to vindicate Woodford. Revenue matched expenditure, and the budget was balanced almost every year after 1905. By the 1920s the government had modified many people's behaviour—though changes in belief depended more on evangelical Islanders. Its power was widely acknowledged, and warfare and head-hunting were rare. As late as 1927 some Kwaio on Malaita, resisting tax collection, murdered a District Commissioner and incurred ferocious reprisals (see chapter 1); but disorder was remote from the centres of production. Woodford assumed that the state knew better than its subjects, that Islanders were less rational than Europeans, that they would disappear anyway, and that planters could transform Islanders into productive subjects of the empire. We can only speculate that village production might have surpassed that target, that fewer people might have been killed, and that the proceeds might have been more creatively distributed.

The New Hebrides remained in constitutional limbo into the twentieth century. Higginson's grandiose Caledonian Company promised commerce, industry and agriculture, and acquired dubious title to lands, but had to be rescued by the French government and reconstructed in 1894 and in 1904. When the Condominium was created in 1906, the archipelago's regional role was still a labour reserve. Since migration to Queensland had ended, and to Fiji had dwindled, New Caledonia was the main destination. British interest faded to little more than ritual criticism of French practice. There was much to criticise: 'French authorities seem to have taken less care than their German and British counterparts to prevent the most serious malpractices' in registering title to land. British planters tried to come under French jurisdiction, to enjoy the 'collusion between French officials and planters to tolerate any brutality towards labourers and then to prevent them from lodging complaints and securing redress'.[2] Panoff doubts whether the lives of labourers were very different under one or another colonial

1 Bennett, *Wealth of the Solomons*, 111.
2 Panoff, 'The French Way in Plantation Systems', 210.

power, but he isolates a significant difference in approach: 'where the French government was implicitly colluding with planters . . ., its German counterpart [in New Guinea] in all good conscience was declaring and trying to implement a system geared to reducing the New Guinean to powerlessness and exploiting his work in the extreme'.[3]

Sluggish in peace-time, the Australian government was galvanised by war in 1914, despatching troops to capture New Guinea. Under military oversight Germans continued to manage their estates and extended their plantings, but when the war ended they were expropriated and replaced by 'British' ex-servicemen. Despite some war-time rhetoric about brutish German administration, the League of Nations Mandated Territory of New Guinea remained a plantation colony. 'No More um-Kaiser' proclaimed the military occupation in a first essay in New Guinea pidgin: 'God Save um-King.' The distinction was minimal. Not until the 1930s did control extend beyond the limits of German occupation. Chinese immigration was halted, Japanese immigration restricted, and urban segregation enforced. Missions continued their work, though German nationals were usually replaced. Copra remained the staple export; wage levels remained low (half that of Papua); for a few children, schooling was nasty, brutish and short; and the law discriminated between the races.

Most New Guineans did not notice a colonial state until the 1930s, when the dense Highland populations were revealed by prospectors and evangelists. Meanwhile settlers took up expropriated plantations just in time for the collapse of copra prices in the Great Depression. Papua and New Guinea were the largest blocks of land in the Pacific, with the richest resources. The stagnation of their colonial economies owed much to their proximity to Australia, which barred Asian labour, inhibited capital investment, and imposed high shipping costs. These obstacles stifled developments until the discovery of gold in the Highlands. In the 1930s, fifty years after most other colonies, enough capital arrived to animate a lethargic colonial economy.

New Zealand

The most promising New Zealand export from the 1860s was sheep. By 1880 there were 13 million. As they multiplied, pastures were enclosed, forests cut, natural grasses replaced by imported varieties, and close management of flocks and pastures allowed productivity to leap ahead. Merinos (bred for wool) were replaced by cross-bred varieties which also yielded mutton. Mechanised shearing (in the 1880s) added to profits, and refrigeration allowed farmers to ship dairy products and mutton to the prime British market. New Zealand, like Australia, prospered through extreme dependence on British capital, technology and immigrants. In fifty years after the Treaty of Waitangi the *pakeha* (white) population surpassed 600,000 while Maori sank towards 42,000. New Zealanders attended the negotiations for Australian federation,

3 *Ibid.*

but felt no need to join, having already developed something like a national identity. As a by-product of registering Maori lands, the settler intelligentsia tidied up Maori history and—in the Polynesian Society and its journal—recast Maori as precocious Aryan settlers. On that view New Zealand was not an Australian frontier but a blend of pioneering populations, with unique talents for race relations.

That genial legend glossed over dispossession. With the demise of the Maori Parliament, Maori people were becoming less concerned with political autonomy and more with the development of their remaining land. They also increasingly recognised that social welfare could be improved only by obtaining equal rights within European society. Yet recognition of European power was not expected to entail complete assimilation. Thus Maori ideology came to serve two objectives. 'Inclusion' into European society was advocated as a plea for socio-economic equality, a demand for equal rights in agriculture, politics and education; but the people retained a distinctive culture, and pleaded to be excluded from some dimensions of New Zealand society to protect their identity. This aim has been described as the policy of biculturalism.

This dual policy was most effectively advocated by members of the students' association of a Maori Anglican boys' college, the Te Aute College Students' Association. The 'Young Maori Party' never became a political party. It was more a group of Western-educated men who operated politically, some of whom won parliamentary seats. Most advocated complete integration into the frameworks of European society. They simply believed that 'Maori society was degraded, demoralised, irreligious, beset with antiquated, depressing, and pernicious customs'. Their motto was expressed by Maui Pomare: *'Kua kotia te tai-tapu ki Hawaiki'* (There is no returning to Hawaiki [the mythical homeland]).[4]

Young Maori campaigned for better hygiene and education. More importantly, they advocated European technology to develop land still in Maori ownership. Several tribes attempted to overcome the fragmentation of ownership in blocks of Maori freehold land, with reference to the *Natives Land Court Act* of 1894 opening up the avenue to incorporation. Under the auspices of Apirana Ngata, several landowners of the Ngaati Porou tribe vested land in a committee of management and became, in effect, shareholders. The company could negotiate loans and develop their land as a unit. In this manner, the Ngaati Porou tribe began dairying, and founded the first co-operative Maori dairy at Ruatoria in 1924.

The Young Maori Party campaigns were at a peak when Parliament passed a number of acts granting limited self-government to Maori. Meanwhile the population started to revive; in 1921 it regained the level of the 1850s and its growth rate exceeded that of the Europeans in 1928. The early twentieth century has been thought of as the dawn of a Maori renaissance, but the impact of the Young Maori Party on welfare may have been exaggerated. It was respected by Europeans, but its influence

4   Quoted in Fitzgerald, *Education and Identity*, 29–30.

on the mass of Maori people was not obvious. Its campaigns to improve Maori welfare simply aimed to bring Maori social practice into a degree of conformity with European values, which caused many people to suspect its intentions. It advocated European, middle-class, respectable conventions, evidently derived from its members' education. As a result, its political program was widely contested, and some elders grieved that the boys at Te Aute College were lost for the Maori cause.

Maori fought for the British Empire in the Boer War, then at Gallipoli and on the Western Front in France (where Peter Buck—Te Rangi Hiroa—was an officer). Their sacrifices reinforced New Zealand's claims to the Cook Islands, and to the mandate over Western Samoa; and letters between Buck and Ngata document their pride in Maoritanga—and the Empire. They criticised New Zealand administrators in Samoa, for example, but not New Zealand's mandate: replacing the administrator Richardson with Sir Maui Pomare would, they felt, resolve most of the vexatious issues. Perhaps their years of accommodation blinkered their vision of possibilities. However, in circumstances as they found them, it is difficult to see what more they could have achieved. A measure of rural prosperity did result from this strategy, implemented by local government and progress associations attending to mundane matters of pasture improvement, sanitation and water, primary schools and roads. Living standards and life expectancy lagged behind those of *pakeha*, but depopulation was reversed and life expectancy was greater than that of any other Polynesians in the 1920s. Many retained access to land, and Maoritanga had a future.

Fiji

The administration of Fiji was anomalous. Unlike other British acquisitions, its Governor was not beholden to the Australian colonies and his legitimacy (if not his formal authority) rested on the cession of the islands by chiefs organised by Cakobau and advised by John Thurston (chapter 5). The Governor was also anomalous. Sir Arthur Gordon was a confident and experienced governor, with excellent political connections through his aristocratic birth. Thurston, his right hand, was uniquely experienced and reinforced his general policy direction. Addressing the assembled planters, Gordon explained his purposes: 'We want capital invested . . . We want a cheap, abundant, and certain supply of labour; we want means of communication; we want justice to be readily and speedily administered; we want facilities for education; and . . . we want revenue.'[5] The Colonial Sugar Refining Company (CSR) provided the first; indentured Indian labour the second; but it was the approach to land which was most distinctive. Although Gordon was keen to release land for commercial purposes, he was determined to avoid the dispossession which had occurred in Australia, New Zealand and Hawai'i. The solution was to formalise the Bose levu Vakaturaga (Great Council of Chiefs) to advise the Governor on Fijian

5 Cited in Lal, *Broken Waves*, 13.

affairs, to enlist the chiefs in rural administration and tax collection, and to guarantee to Fijians the possession of most of their land. A Native Lands Commission was created, first to assess settlers' claims, and then to demarcate the land which remained under communal control. The structure was not as benign as it appeared, and its impact is discussed further below, and in chapter 8; but it did reconcile the needs of the sugar industry with the authority of the chiefs, and both with British imperial interests.

PLANTATIONS AND PLANTATION WORKERS

For colonial governments keen to promote plantations, land was essential—but sometimes unattainable, as French officials discovered in Tahiti. During the 1830s the Pomare government legislated to prevent foreigners from buying land or gaining access through marriage. As the Pomares subordinated the local chiefs, traditional land titles were eroded, and the French protectorate (1842 until 1880) compounded confusion by promoting villages instead of scattered and intermingled clans. However, the government could not alienate land on a large scale, except in the aftermath of the war of the 1840s when rebellious Tahitians were expropriated. Estates did form, but the owners were members of the overlapping royalty, nobility, *'afa tahiti* and Protestant establishment. By 1880 when Tahiti was formally annexed, it was too late to subvert these property rights.

> Instead of trying to understand the native principles and to adjust them to new conditions, Protectorate policy denied their existence. [As a result] French metropolitan law has been enforced by French courts for a hundred years without having the intended effect. What the Tahitians in fact do about their land and what rights they recognise in it, are very different from the legal situation.[6]

Two tenure traditions operated, often manipulated to individual advantage. A few colonists gained parcels of land, but there was no scope for large companies. Copra became the staple export, and only a fraction was grown on plantations.

This outcome was avoided in New Caledonia. Following Australian precedents, the government in 1855 acquired, as 'vacant', all lands which were not under cultivation, and placed them in the hands of planters and ranchers. Here the usual pattern of colonial relationships was briefly interrupted by a bizarre interlude. Governor Guillain, taking office in 1862, and required to create a convict settlement, was inspired by the anti-clerical sentiments of many French people of that era. Accordingly he preferred to negotiate with 'pagan' Kanaks than with missionaries and their converts. With his departure, more conventional alignments developed. Throughout this era, the government

---

6   Michel Panoff, 'The Society Islands: Confusion from Compulsive Logic', in Crocombe, *Land Tenure in the Atolls*.

and its various Kanak allies possessed enough force to dispossess Kanak communities, and to put down the ill-coordinated revolts of the dispossessed, even the largest and best-supported rising of 1878–79, led by the chief Atai. A convict settlement was the foundation for a society of *libérés* and free settlers, creating a capitalist economy on the bases of mining and pastoralism. The Kanaks were not so much integrated into this economy as evicted from it, to offshore islands and reserves on the main island. Free settlers shared the official view of the country. For the 150 who settled in Voh during the 1890s, for example, 'there was nothing':

> The New Caledonian bush was like a blank page on which they had to write their own words . . . They organised space according to what they knew, they took possession of the soil by imprinting on it their own land-marks . . . The world of the Kanaks made no sense to the Europeans and they did not even try to make sense of it . . . since they considered themselves the pioneers of an empire, the representatives of civilisation.[7]

The Voh settlers depended on a nearby nickel mine, whose Asian workers ate their vegetables, and whose management employed their sons until their coffee farms matured.

Even when land was acquired, labour did not flow. German intrusion into New Guinea was essentially maritime, reaching only the coasts or the banks of the Sepik—the one navigable river. The Tolai of the Gazelle Peninsula were exposed to plantations and the New Guinea Company. They were already familiar with traders, they owned volcanic land well-suited to tree crops, they welcomed the chance to buy commodities, and throughout the 1870s they could repel any traders who threatened to intrude upon Tolai life. On their own terms they became reconciled to missionaries. *Tabu* shell continued to be the most acceptable medium of exchange, more widely used than company currency or even tobacco. Settlers had to acquire *tabu* to trade with Tolai, and its circulation increased sharply. The company was irked by its persistence, even when it was 'demonetised' in 1900, and when head tax was introduced in 1905 and made payable only in coin. They were right to be annoyed: *tabu* enabled Tolai to blend productive work with social relations, which were reinforced by *tabu* contributions to marriage settlements, mortuary rites and other exchanges. Tolai insulated themselves from the full logic of capitalist production while enjoying some of its benefits.

New Guinea was bigger and Micronesia more lucrative, but Samoa remained the focal point of German enterprise. The Deutsche Handels-und Plantagen-Gesellschaft (DHPG) had land, but could not mobilise enough labour to dispense with Samoan-grown copra. Samoans would not work on plantations and Gilbertese (I-Kiribati, who recruited readily) were too few. By the 1880s Germany had a consul in Apia, who regulated affairs to suit DHPG. He endorsed DHPG's appeals for the annexation of New Guinea to ensure labour; and when the New Guinea

---

7 Merle, 'The Foundation of Voh, 1892–1895'.

Company tried to reserve New Guinean labour for its own needs, Berlin intervened again to guarantee DHPG's access. Formal annexation of Western Samoa by Germany in 1900 made little difference to DHPG dominance in framing and interpreting land and labour policies. Its plantations were bearing, they had a virtual monopoly of alienated land and exclusive rights to recruit in New Guinea. Small settlers received much less support from Governor Solf. Like other governors, he preferred the reliable revenue and coherent demands of corporations, to the erratic profits and turbulent politics of settlers. The Samoan case strengthens the argument of Munro and Firth that lack of revenue led all administrators to encourage development by Europeans, 'for only a vigorous export trade [offered] a dependable source of taxation. Traders and shipowners of small means and the individual planter on a pocket-sized holding could never generate sufficient revenue to run a colony . . . [Companies] were better equipped to ride out hard times.'[8]

The first dividend was paid only five years after operations began. Four years later—when its rivals Ruge & Co. collapsed—the company was reconstructed again, halving its nominal capital. Workers paid a high price for DHPG's financial crises. A commission of inquiry was provoked in 1875 by workers who walked 50 kilometres to petition the government at Mulinu'u. The mainly Gilbertese labourers complained of being recruited by misrepresentation, corporal punishment, Sunday labour, the arbitrary reduction of wages, withholding of wages, inadequate rations and miserable medical treatment. Such was the influence of DHPG that the commission attributed the strike to agitators. The Gilbertese did not again protest until the Gilbert Islands became a British protectorate, whereupon they could complain to the British Consul with slightly better prospects of redress.

In the Solomon Islands, plantations also ran up against labour shortages, despite the Islanders' tradition of working abroad. The power of passage masters was eroded by the elimination of warfare and overseas recruiting, and the presence of missionaries, traders and Christians. Deep-seated habits of consumption encouraged them—and men back from Queensland—to sell land, yielding money faster than wage labour or copra. Woodford was delighted when planters took up land, and his prospects improved in 1898 when the Pacific Islands Company began to negotiate for Chartered Company rights and the (seemingly limitless) 'unoccupied' land. As matters turned out, the company became a stalking-horse for Sir William Lever, who accumulated 400,000 acres. The Australian firm Burns Philp was also keen to secure plantations, and smaller Australian investors were also attracted. Leases of 999 years compensated for the fact that Woodford could issue only Certificates of Occupation which fell short of clear title.

On the new plantations, Islanders familiar with Queensland or Fiji were offered lower wages and worse conditions. The law favoured employers, and the government had few supervisors and little incentive to harass employers. Violence was common. Black perpetrators were

8 Doug Munro and Stewart Firth, 'Company Strategies—Colonial Policies', in Moore, Leckie and Munro (eds), *Labour in the South Pacific*, 25.

severely punished, whereas whites were quietly deported. Wages were depressed artificially, and the labour force climbed only to 7000 (in 1921) before numbers fell below 4000 over the next decade. The government might have coerced more men if it had possessed enough power, but head taxes could not be imposed until 1921 and were resisted strenuously for several more years. In another ill-considered attempt to depress labour costs, the government tried in 1923 to replace the capitation fee by an advance on wages, mainly to bar passage masters from recruiting. The passage masters were depressed, but so was the labour supply.

In New Caledonia, demand for labour also outstripped supply as free settlers became employers. When convicts' sentences expired they could not leave, but must fend for themselves as *libérés*. Employers preferred New Hebrideans. Beginning in the 1850s as a state venture, recruitment continued as a private business from 1865 until the Great Depression in 1929, with interruptions in the 1880s (when importation continued clandestinely). No fewer than 14,000 recruits arrived in that period, the great majority before 1900. From then onwards they were gradually displaced by South-East Asian workers; and by that time the French administration was successfully imposing head taxes in the Loyalty Islands, so that these Islanders were entering the *grande terre* under indenture.

A visitor to Noumea in the 1880s observed a party of New Hebrideans who were

> marched in gangs to the verandah of the owner's store, and there left for the inspection of intending purchasers . . . I say 'purchasers' and 'sale' advisedly, for the transaction was as openly and avowedly a sale as anything to be seen in the old days 'down South'. [An Australian arrived in search of a 'house-boy'.] 'That lot up there ain't sold' said the good-natured factotum; 'there's one little fellow can speak English.' Then my friend examined the 'little fellow' as a veterinary surgeon would a horse . . . [I]n the end 100 francs was given for the boy of fourteen, who thenceforward became the slave for three years of his purchaser.

Recruits were commonly engaged for three to five years, not only by planters and mine managers, but by the government. Islanders suffered from pneumonia in underground mining, and employers reckoned that Vietnamese were hardier, but Islanders were employed in surface work: one nickel mine was known as 'La Mine des Sans-Culottes' on account of its under-dressed Islanders. A report of 1883 recorded that 'the New Hebridean is everywhere and few households manage without them'. Employers could pay them as little and as late as they chose, and made arbitrary deductions from wages. There was another advantage. Precisely because New Hebrideans were as 'foreign' as the settlers, they were more trusted than Kanaks or convicts or *libérés*. They were a 'natural gendarmerie', whose commitment to their 'owners' implies at least some measure of choice and autonomy.

Most encounters were between men and other men, but the minority of female workers was larger than in other Islands. From the 1880s they comprised 10 or 20 per cent of many passenger lists. By law, a woman could recruit only with the consent of her husband or father, but sly recruiters conducted 'marriages' themselves. A few women worked as miners and field hands, but most entered domestic service. Their work is implicit in the prices they fetched. An opponent of recruitment was appalled that 'girls paraded in the yards and under the verandahs of our estimable merchants: 500 francs, the young ones of fifteen years, 400 francs, those approaching 20 years and 300, those unfortunates whose charms have faded'. Among free settlers, men outnumbered women by a wide margin: the imbalance was perhaps ten to one among New Hebrideans, rising to thirty to one among convicts and *libérés*. Many women became concubines. Others were made available to male workers. These prospects seem discouraging, and repatriates certainly described their lives under indenture, yet some women clearly volunteered. Administrative records suggest that some were escaping from domestic crises, and went to great trouble to attract cruising vessels. Others were exercising acknowledged rights, so that particular anchorages were well known for women volunteers. Many chose not to go home after their first contract, taking their chances as concubines, prostitutes, or laundresses.[9]

In Fiji as well, Gordon preferred one corporation, CSR, to the small planters who had flocked to the islands from the 1860s. CSR's Queensland operations relied on up-to-date technology, a bounty, and white labour. In Fiji the same ingenuity produced a radically different pattern. Between 1879 and 1916, 60,000 Indians were recruited under five-year contracts (*girmit*), replacing the smaller labour force of Islanders. At the end of the indenture, *girmitiyas* could remain or (at their own expense) return to India. Indian and Fijian government requirements provide a detailed statistical portrait of working conditions. (Samoan statistics reflect minimal accountability.) Despite legal limits to the powers of employers, *girmitiyas'* lives were misshapen in immense detail at the discretion of employers. Minimum wages were prescribed, for example, but CSR insisted on piece-work, and a generation passed before men and women attained the legal minima. Employers levied deductions for incomplete tasks: their obligation to provide medical care and shelter was elastic. The Indian government prescribed a proportion of 100:40 for men and women, but few *girmitiyas* could afford permanent unions, women were harassed by supervisors and other men, and prostitution or concubinage were the only survival strategies available to many. Workers had a right to sue defaulting employers, but unequal resources mocked that entitlement. *Girmitiyas* experienced their indenture as hellish. When their contracts expired, however, and they chose to stay in Fiji, they usually remained under the control of the company, in new forms. CSR dictated to its tenant-farmers what crops they grew, and in what combinations—and set the price for their cane.

Many general features of plantation life are manifest in Fiji. The

9 Shineberg, ' "The New Hebridean Is Everywhere" ', quoting Julian Thomas [James Stanley], *Cannibals and Convicts*, London, 1886; settlers' petition in *Neo-Calédonien*, 4 July 1882; and Eugene Mourot, in *Le Progrès de la Nouvelle-Calédonie*.

government regulated recruitment, wages and conditions, but delegated enforcement to employers. Workers were discouraged from invoking the rules and rarely did so. The plantation therefore became a self-contained autocracy. Work was governed by the clock and the siren, and its quality governed by company rules which defined tasks and by managers who judged whether they were complete. Overseers often imposed a reign of terror. In these unpromising circumstances, labourers struggled for self-respect. Rigid production targets, for example, perversely helped to create a working culture in which over-achievement was disparaged. Culture itself expressed a solidarity which protected individuals from some excesses. Where no common language united labourers, pidgins evolved, simple enough to permit workers to deal with each other, and elusive enough to baffle overseers. The barracks, too, allowed some solidarity among residents who discussed the affairs of the day and anticipated the harshness of tomorrow.

Formal strikes were rare. They made little sense when labourers could be replaced, when management could withhold pay, when the government supported employers, and when workers had no other sustenance. The exceptional 'Rabaul Strike' (chapter 8) proves the rule: its organisers were not plantation workers, and the log of claims was more an indictment of colonialism than a demand for wages. More common were physical tussles. In Solomon Islands plantations:

> The 'new chum' overseer was always 'tried out' by plantation laborers. Men would openly defy the overseer and expect him to hit them or lose face. Sometimes they would try to get him down to the labor lines at night when he would be an easy target. Everyone involved in plantations, including the government, knew that fisticuffs, or a brawl, were a standard and acceptable way of enforcing discipline—provided the laborer was in the wrong, knew it, and was not caused serious physical harm. If, however, the laborers felt they had been wronged they would frequently gang up on an overseer and beat him.[10]

This moral economy was inequitable, but it allowed some predictability, and labourers had some marginal influence on it.

The social controls over Fijians were very different from those which governed *girmitiyas*, since chiefly structures mediated the force of capitalist logic. Fijians were required for public works, for cash crop production, and for stevedoring and mining, but the culture of the plantation infected all managements. As the leader of a Fijian work party put it in 1942: 'We know that Fiji is dependent on the Company and the Government pays a good deal of attention to the Company's wishes. We Fijians believe that the Company is at the bottom of low wages.'[11] The suspicion was well founded. All employers conspired to offer comparable wages and refrained from bidding them up.

Plantations made such demands on land, and depended so completely on cheap labour, that they were inimical to the autonomy of Islanders. Such conflicts are perfectly illustrated in Hawai'i. The

10 Bennett, *Wealth of the Solomons*, 169–70.
11 Quoted by Jacqueline Leckie, 'Workers in Colonial Fiji: 1870–1970', in Moore, Leckie and Munro (eds), *Labour in the South Pacific*, 47–66.

rhetoric of American settlers (as in Australia and New Zealand) espoused equality and equal opportunity. These universal values were in practice tinged with racism. Settlers doubted or denied the equal worth of Islanders, and were neither surprised nor concerned when Hawaiians did not take equal advantage of an expanding economy. The effect of a 'free' market was to release land for *haole* developers, and the attack on hereditary power targeted the monarchy. Immigration left the forms of the monarchy intact, but by mid-century plantation interests predominated in public policy, and by the 1890s the kingdom had been largely 'pre-adapted' as a settler society. Only the monarchy itself remained. In the century since Cook, the indigenous population had withered; Hawaiians still owned about 14 per cent of the land, by no means the best; most had quit—or been driven from—the countryside, to survive on plantations or in town. How did they cope?

It is commonly supposed that the elimination of cloth-making by textile imports depressed the status of the women who made the cloth and were ritually linked to it. Numbers of women declined faster than numbers of men. Yet an increasing proportion of women inherited land after the Māhele—when fewer Hawaiians were inheriting at all:

> Hawaiian women were favored in land inheritance during the period of the Māhele *because* women were symbolically associated with land, *because* women were valued as producers of high cultural goods . . ., *because* an ideology of male interpersonal dominance and superiority was weakly developed in Hawai'i, *because* the gender tabus of the native religion founded a separate domain of female ritual and social power, *because* women were seen as powerful, autonomous beings in the indigenous society, *because* from the male perspective women were points of access to rank, land, and political power, *because* women could assume positions of the highest jural authority though men were favored in such roles, and *because* depopulation and economic events disrupted normal chains of inheritance in local communities. With the accelerated dislocation of the commoners, alternate jural figures—women—emerged as landholders and household authorities, though they saw themselves as temporary guardians of the family destiny.[12]

Hawaiians did not submit passively to a malign destiny, buttressing the integrity of family and lineage, the oldest, most durable, and only surviving shield against dispossession. The political superstructure proved much less resilient.

THE OVERTHROW OF THE HAWAIIAN MONARCHY

As early as the reign of Kamehameha I, Hawai'i was recognised as a sovereign nation. By 1887 Hawai'i had treaties and conventions with a score of nations, at least five treaties or conventions with the United States, and about a hundred diplomatic and consular posts. In 1843 Britain and France joined in a declaration recognising Hawai'i's independence and pledging never to take possession. When the United States was invited to join this declaration, J. C. Calhoun, the Secre-

12 Linnekin, *Sacred Queens and Women of Consequence*, 238.

tary of State, replied that the President adhered completely to the disinterested spirit which breathed in it. Immigrants came from all parts of the world, many renouncing their former allegiance and taking up Hawaiian citizenship. By 1892, Hawai'i was a multi-racial, multi-cultural nation engaged in intellectual and economic commerce with the world. Literacy rates were among the highest of any nation and multi-lingual citizens abounded. Hawai'i had telephones and electricity in its Iolani Palace before the American White House.

The 'missionary party'—an alliance of missionary descendants and businessmen—had implemented radical legal, economic and social changes. The sugar plantations were made possible and profitable by the privatisation of land, immigration and labour laws, and the Reciprocity Treaty which opened the United States market. During Kalākaua's reign it became clear that profoundly influencing government policies was not enough for the sugar interests. The missionary party gave rise to a cabal intent on overthrowing the monarch and securing annexation by the United States. Two leading members were Lorrin Thurston, grandson of one early missionary, and Sanford Dole, son of another. As early as 1882, Thurston exchanged confidences with American officials on the matter of the takeover of Hawai'i. The Secretary of the Navy assured him that the administration of Chester Arthur would favour annexation. In 1892 Thurston received the same assurance from the administration of Benjamin Harrison. American interests were primarily strategic, focused on Pearl Harbor. After Kalākaua signed the 1887 'Bayonet Constitution', the United States was given the exclusive right to use Pearl Harbor in exchange for a seven-year extension of the Reciprocity Treaty.

Kalākaua died in 1891 in San Francisco. Rumours persist in Hawai'i that his death was caused by the missionary party's agents. Soon after her accession, his sister Queen Lili'uokalani received a petition of two-thirds of the voters imploring her to do away with the Bayonet Constitution and return the powers of government to the Hawaiian people. By 14 January 1893, she completed a draft constitution and informed her cabinet of her intention to institute change immediately. Under the Bayonet Constitution her cabinet was controlled by the missionary party, and Thurston claimed that she had no business attempting to institute a new constitution by fiat. He and twelve others formed a 'Committee of Public Safety' and visited the American Minister in Hawai'i, John L. Stevens.

Stevens had arrived in 1889, convinced that his mission was annexation. His letters to Secretary of State James Blaine document this passion. In March 1892 he requested instructions on how far he might deviate from rules and precedents, should an orderly and peaceful revolutionary movement emerge. He later wrote:

> the golden hour is near at hand . . . So long as the islands retain their own independent government there remains the possibility that England or the Canadian Dominion might secure one of the Hawaiian harbors for a coaling station. Annexation excludes all dangers of this kind.[13]

13 Kuykendall, *The Hawaiian Kingdom*, vol. 3, 648.

When Thurston met Stevens on 15 January 1893, the 'golden hour' had come. They agreed that Marines would land on the pretext of protecting American lives. The revolutionary party would declare themselves the provisional government and turn Hawai'i over to the United States in an annexation treaty.

On 16 January the Marines landed in Honolulu without warning, and marched along the streets, rifles facing Iolani Palace. The following day, eighteen conspirators, mostly Americans, sneaked into a government building a few yards from the American bivouac. There an American lawyer, Henry Cooper (resident in Hawai'i for less than a year), proclaimed that he and seventeen others were now the government. Calling themselves the 'provisional government' and selecting Sanford Dole as president, their explicit purpose was annexation to the United States. Stevens immediately recognised the 'provisional government' and joined their demand that the Queen surrender under threat of war with the United States. Lili'uokalani capitulated under protest. The United States has consistently denied responsibility, but the Queen's words indicate that American force was the determining factor, and that she expected the American government to undo Stevens's actions:

> I, Liliuokalani, by the grace of God and under the constitution of the Hawaiian Kingdom, Queen, do hereby solemnly protest against any and all acts done . . . by certain persons claiming to have established a Provisional Government of and for this Kingdom.
> . . . I yield to the superior force of the United States of America, whose minister plenipotentiary, his excellency John L. Stevens, has caused United States troops to be landed at Honolulu . . .
> Now, to avoid any collision of armed forces and perhaps the loss of life, I do, under this protest, and impelled by said force, yield my authority until such time as the Government of the United States shall, upon the facts being presented to it, undo the action of its representative and reinstate me and the authority which I claim as the constitutional sovereign of the Hawaiian Islands.[14]

By February a treaty of annexation was negotiated, signed and presented for ratification by President Harrison. However, Cleveland replaced Harrison before the Senate voted. The Queen's emissaries managed to enter the United States and pleaded with Cleveland to withdraw the treaty and conduct an investigation. Congressman James Blount was appointed special investigator. He arrived in Honolulu to find the American flag flying in front of Iolani Palace. He had it taken down and ordered the Marines back to their ships. After several months of collecting testimony, he returned to the United States. His report denounced the revolution and recommended that the 'legitimate Government' be restored. In an address to Congress, Cleveland used passionate and unambiguous terms to describe the 'act of war' against Hawai'i:

14 Lili'uokalani's protest was published in *Blount's Report* (*House Executive Documents*, 53rd Congress, 2nd Session, No. 47) 120, and in the Honolulu *Daily Bulletin*, 18 January 1893. It has been republished in many places.

the Government of a feeble but friendly and confiding people has been overthrown . . .

The lawful Government of Hawaii was overthrown without the drawing of a sword or the firing of a shot by a process every step of which, it may be safely asserted, is directly traceable to, and dependent for its success upon the agency of the United States acting through its diplomatic and naval representatives. But for the notorious predilections of the United States Minister for annexation, the Committee of Safety, which should be called the Committee of Annexation, would never have existed. But for the landing of the United States forces upon false pretexts respecting the danger to life and property the committee would never have exposed themselves to the pains and penalties of treason by undertaking the subversion of the Queen's Government. But for the presence of the United States forces in the immediate vicinity and in position to afford all needed protection and support the committee would not have proclaimed the provisional government from the steps of the Government building. And finally, but for the lawless occupation of Honolulu under false pretexts by the United States forces, and but for Minister Stevens' recognition of the provisional government when the United States forces were its sole support and constituted its only military strength, the Queen and her Government would never have yielded to the provisional government, even for a time and for the sole purpose of submitting her case to the enlightened justice of the United States.[15]

Cleveland added that the revolution was a 'disgrace' under international law, and refused to forward the treaty to the Senate. Lili'uokalani was advised of the President's desire to aid her restoration, if this could be effected on terms of clemency as well as justice to all parties. In short, the past should be buried and the restored government should resume its authority as if it had not been interrupted. The Queen protested that such a promise would be unconstitutional, but later acceded to a general amnesty upon the restoration of her government. The Provisional Government was informed of this decision and asked to abide by Cleveland's decision and yield to the Queen her constitutional authority. They refused, brazenly protesting Cleveland's attempt to 'interfere in the internal affairs' of their nation and declaring themselves now citizens of the Provisional Government and beyond the President's authority (despite having invoked their United States citizenship to justify the landing of Marines).

Cleveland spoke principled words but left United States troops in Hawai'i and handed the matter to Congress for further investigation. However, the Senate Foreign Relations Committee was headed by an ardent annexationist, John Morgan. His committee issued its own report, absolving everyone except the Queen! The result was a stalemate between the executive and legislative branches. The revolutionaries therefore devised a fresh plan to restructure their government to appear permanent. Hopefully, when a new president was elected, the 'permanent' government could cede Hawai'i to the United States.

15 United States Executive Document 47, 53rd Congress, 2nd Session, House of Representatives.

A constitution had to be drafted to legitimise the conspirators. Sanford Dole, acting as President, announced a Constitutional Convention of thirty-seven delegates, with nineteen selected by him and the remaining eighteen elected. Leaving nothing to chance, the candidates and voters were required to renounce Queen Lili'uokalani and swear allegiance to the provisional government. Less than 20 per cent of the qualified voters participated: the vast majority refused to dignify this sham by participation. The convention adopted a 'Constitution' for the 'Republic of Hawai'i', substantially as submitted by Dole and Thurston. Foreigners who supported the new regime could vote; citizens loyal to the Queen could not. Only those could vote who could speak, read and write in English or Hawaiian and explain the Constitution, *written in English*, to the satisfaction of Dole's supporters. Japanese and Chinese, who supported Lili'uokalani, were therefore also disenfranchised.

On 4 July 1894, Dole simply proclaimed the Constitution with himself as President. Lili'uokalani, remembering Blount's warning not to take up arms lest the Marines land and forever quash the hopes of the Hawaiians, waited patiently, still believing in the justice of the United States. When William McKinley replaced Cleveland as President, Dole's group rushed to Washington to complete the conspiracy. With a Constitution declaring that they governed Hawai'i, the 'Republic of Hawai'i' ceded sovereignty. Realising that the treaty would not get the two-thirds Senate vote required for approval, the revolutionaries settled for a joint resolution of Congress—the Newlands Resolution of 1898. The United States set up a territorial government, changing Dole's title from President to Governor. The Organic Act of 1900 declared that all citizens of the Republic of Hawai'i were automatically United States citizens and subject to United States law. The Hawaiian people were given no voice in these changes. As the revolution reached its culmination, Lili'uokalani addressed the American people:

> Oh, honest Americans, as Christians hear me for my downtrodden people! Their form of government is as dear to them as yours is precious to you. Quite as warmly as you love your country, so they love theirs. [D]o not covet the little vineyards of Naboth's so far from your shores, lest the punishment of Ahab fall upon you, if not in your day in that of your children, for 'be not deceived, God is not mocked'. The people to whom your fathers told of the living God, and taught to call 'Father', and whom the sons now seek to despoil and destroy, are crying aloud to Him in their time of trouble; and He will keep His promise, and will listen to the voices of His Hawaiian children lamenting for their homes.[16]

The plea fell on deaf American ears. Thurston, Dole and their associates founded the *haole* oligarchy that controlled the politics and economy of Hawai'i until the 1950s. The families of missionary descendants and sugar planters became a distinct social stratum. Economically, sugar was king. Politically, Hawaiians could not be barred from voting but were outnumbered. Vast areas—defined as Crown and

16 Lili'uokalani, *Hawai'i's Story by Hawai'i's Queen*, 373–4.

government lands in the Māhele—were transferred to the control of the United States. Most of these 'Ceded Lands' were transferred to the State of Hawai'i in 1959, but the federal government retains substantial holdings, especially on O'ahu, as military reservations.

MINING COLONIES

Distinctive relationships evolved around mining. Some precedents were set in guano quarries in the Peruvian Chincha Islands (chapter 5). Micronesian nitrates began to be exploited soon after, for farmers in Australia, New Zealand and Japan. The Pacific Islands Company, incorporated in 1897, combined J. T. Arundel's guano interests and those of the Auckland traders Henderson and MacFarlane, with Lord Stanmore (formerly Sir Arthur Gordon, Governor of Fiji) as chairman. The company languished until Albert Ellis identified phosphates on Banaba (Ocean Island) and in 1900 induced two Banabans to sign an exceptionally generous 999-year concession. Stanmore provided influence at Westminster, and William Lever gave a capital injection when he bought out the company's Solomon Islands land claims. They persuaded the Royal Navy to annex the island in 1901, adding it to the Gilbert and Ellice group. On the strength of the Banaban concessions, the company was restructured in 1902 as the Pacific Phosphate Company, and achieved economies of scale (and market leverage) in 1907 by securing similar mining rights in German Nauru.

Makatea, an islet 200 kilometres north-east of Tahiti, was inhabited by 160 to 200 Polynesians who had the misfortune to live above phosphates. Several entrepreneurs claimed mining rights, and these claims were consolidated by the Compagnie française des phosphates de l'Océanie in 1908. This syndicate of traders and the ex-Queen joined forces with the Pacific Phosphate Company, which handled shipping and sales as an integrated operation spanning Nauru and Banaba. The highest hurdle was to gain legal title, in the absence of legislation. During years of litigation and negotiation, the inhabitants were almost forgotten and, deprived of their land, drifted away, making room for labourers. The company now controlled almost all Pacific nitrate production.

The company found few local labourers, and introduced Japanese and Chinese. Banabans not only lost their chance of royalties: in 1927 they were exiled to Rabi Island in Fiji. Equally brisk dispossession followed in the German sphere. In 1906 the Jaluit-Gesellschaft leased to the Pacific Phosphate Company a 94-year concession in Nauru. Nauruans were involved only to reinforce German authority over mutinous Chinese workers, and were marginalised until they had the good fortune to gain independence before mining had finished. The present distinction between affluent Nauruans and homeless Banabans seems mainly a matter of luck.

Another mine began work in 1909 on Angaur in the Palau group, and followed the same trajectory. The island was bought for £60 (from two men, when women refused to negotiate), restricting the inhabitants to a

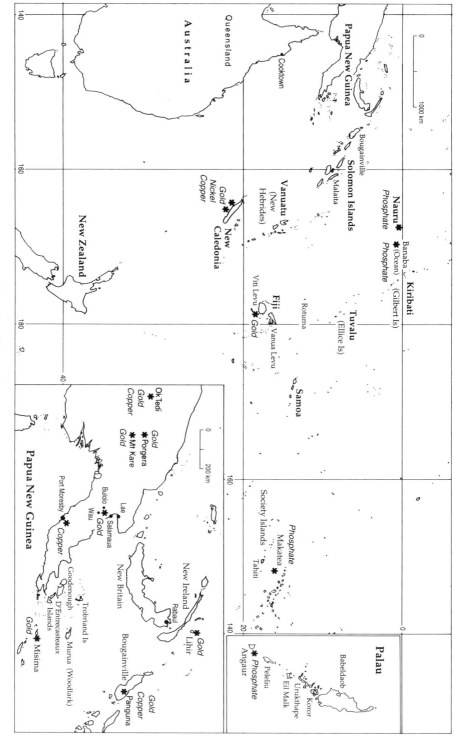

Map 16   Colonial mining sites

150-hectare reservation. Chinese were recruited until Chinese officials banned recruitment, when the company resorted to Pohnpeian prisoners of war, then nearly a thousand other Islanders, mainly atoll men 'volunteered' by Yapese patrons who confiscated their earnings. The inter-changeability of prisoners and 'free' labourers speaks volumes for industrial relations. While this coercion was extreme, Angaur mine was typical in its racially stratified workforce. By 1914 the company employed ten Germans, 100 Chinese and 500 Islanders, paid in proportion to civil status.

Angaur became a Japanese prize of war after 1914. Following German precedents, most workers were Islanders, coerced if necessary. Japanese displaced Chinese artisans. In the 1930s Willard Price found conditions little changed from the German period:

> The workmen come on contract for about six months, alone—no wives or children allowed because the island is too small . . . The laborers live on shelves in a long wooden shed like a loggers' bunkhouse but not so comfortable—, yet, much more airy, light and sanitary than the average hut in the islands. The men may enjoy pool, ping-pong and table games in a dingy clubhouse. But their lives are dreary, womanless and homeless.
>
> Angaur has always had an unhappy reputation among the Micronesians. It has been known as the 'Village of the Dead' . . . Angaur is a sort of purgatory. When a person is mortally distressed, it is said that he is suffering Angaur. Such beliefs do not make employment on the island any more agreeable.[17]

Of all the catastrophes which befell Islanders, phosphates were the worst. Rights were quickly and cheaply alienated. There was no need to involve them in production, nor even to provide space. Those who lived near gold had at least a sporting chance to benefit.

The frontier of gold prospecting flowed from tropical Australia across the Coral Sea. Australians discovered gold in New Caledonia in 1870, and persisted through the short life of Fern Hill mine until copper was discovered nearby. The most significant discovery was nickel. Rothschilds put Société le Nickel on a sound footing and, during the 1890s when European armies hardened their steel, nickel production boomed. The colonial economy exhibited the paradox of a large population, convicts—and a chronic labour shortage. From the 1860s the gap was filled by New Hebrideans and later by Vietnamese. There was little scope for Australians, except as technicians or supervisors. Papua, by contrast, became an extension of the Queensland industry. Cooktown was the base from which prospectors rushed new strikes and shipped provisions. Early mining was alluvial: the exploitation of lodes demanded more capital than local storekeepers could lend. Investment was inhibited until the administration offered protection for life and property. Lieutenant-Governor MacGregor introduced the Queensland mining laws, appointed a mining warden, provided sea transport for

17 Willard Price, *Japan's Islands of Mystery*, New York 1944, cited in Hezel and Berg (eds), *Micronesia: Winds of Change*.

prospectors, and spent much time on expeditions to smooth their paths or avenge their deaths.

Prospectors focused on the islands of Milne Bay, beginning on Tagula (Sudest) in 1888 when 400 miners descended on a population of about 1000. They scattered through the gullies where heavy rain, rough ground, thick scrub, humidity, malaria and dysentery underlined their dependence on Tagula labour, provisions—and tolerance. When the economy was saturated by trade goods, the people demanded shell valuables instead. Miners had to procure these from Langalanga lagoon in Malaita, which enjoyed an unexpected boom in shell manufacturing. The mining fraternity shrank to forty in two years. By then Islanders were washing gold, and for several years some men earned higher incomes than in formal employment. The Islanders had welcomed miners as allies to fend off raids. These raids had been provoked by a punitive expedition which was triggered by a Tagula attack on Europeans—which might have arisen from disputes with labour recruiters. The Islanders sometimes fell foul of their visitors: a suspected thief was shot, a miner was killed in revenge, and one Islander was executed in public and another gaoled for ten years. This tragedy, as well as increased mortality from the unsanitary practices of prospectors and labourers, dysentery and other infections, must be reckoned against the benefits gained during the rush and from the residual technology.

Rushes to other Islands led to similar accommodations and benefits, until the discovery of lodes changed the balance of advantage. Misima and Murua (Woodlark) attracted Australian capital, and promoters in Sydney exploited the unusual provision for no-liability companies. Thus Kulumadau (on Murua) was promoted by

> stock market manipulation, insider trading, exaggeration (if not falsification) of assays, romantic reserve estimates, bounteous vendor considerations and, ultimately, mismanagement . . . [A]s much as half of the authorised shares were issued free, and fully-paid, to the promoters. The Sydney company paid £20,000 to vendors on floating, almost three times more than it retained for its own use.[18]

The consequences in Murua were therefore more limited than the volumes of capital. Perversely, gold-mining stimulated stone axe making. Muruan axes had been made obsolete by iron tools in the 1870s. After 1900 however, miners and traders would pay £5 to £10 for each blade, to exchange for shell and copra from other Islands.

Gold was Papua's main export, although copper was extracted near Port Moresby from 1906. Until then, the colonial state strengthened the tradition of alluvial mining, curbed violence in Papua—and allowed killings in Australian share markets. In Misima the discovery of the mother-lode led to large-scale quartz-mining from 1914 when the big Australian company, Broken Hill Proprietary, took over and sustained production until the 1920s. The company employed men from other Islands—at 10 shillings per month—but few from Misima. This host

18 McGee and Henning, 'Investment in Lode Mining, Papua 1878–1920'.

society enjoyed more benefit than the workers, who ate yams which the management bought from other Islands, in exchange for betel-nut which Misimans sold to the company.

Matters turned out very differently on the mainland. Prospectors could raise only limited funds from storekeepers and scant military support from the fledgling government, so they could not assure safe passage. The Binandere on the upper reaches of the Mambare River could defend themselves, and prospectors were fair game. One was killed in 1895 in retaliation for an earlier fight. Prospectors and government officers combined in a punitive expedition, and the next chance for vengeance focused on a party led by John Green, a government officer. Green rashly handed his revolver to a Binandere policeman—who gave the signal for a massacre of the government party:

> They took the bodies to the village, and lined them up to make sure that they equalled the number of Binandere who had been killed. Then they cut the bodies, cooked them and ate them. . . . [A] warrior thought that Green's boots were part of the white man's leg. He started eating them, and when he found the small nails, he thought these were bones—until somebody told him about his mistake.[19]

Violence was by no means one-sided. In 1905 Joe O'Brien was convicted of assault, sentenced to two months' hard labour, and forewarned of charges of robbery, attempted murder, arson, rape, and killing Papuans' pigs and dogs. Set to work under a Papuan constable, he killed him and fled. He was sheltered and fed by some miners, a score of whom protested to the government of Australia, denouncing the acceptance of evidence from Papuans and the supervision of white men by black police: 'it acts like a dagger in the heart of a white man when he knows that the poor ignorant savage is placed in authority over him by his own fellow white man'. Miners were evenly split between intransigent supremacists and the others ('the better class', the Administrator called them) who felt that O'Brien had been treated justly.

After World War I, Australians scoured inland New Guinea. Inland fields demanded large numbers of carriers and each sluice needed twenty-four labourers. At the height of the 1926 rush, recruiters charged £20 for a one-year recruit (twice as much as the wage). Prospectors found alluvial gold at Koranga in 1923 and in Edie Creek in 1926, on the shoulder of Mount Kaindi. By the end of the year more than 200 miners and 1300 labourers had endured the six-day climb to Edie Creek, and in 1927 more than 110,000 ounces of gold were declared. Soon claims were consolidated and companies absorbed the small operations.

Gold drew the Leahy brothers, Mick, Dan and Jim, from Queensland in 1932, in the last wave of European exploration. In the tradition of suspicious co-operation, other prospectors subsidised their expeditions, and the government later lent them material support, but it was prospecting which drew government into 'discovering' a million souls. The Leahys did find gold, though not the colossal deposits which they

19 John Waiko, quoted in Nelson, *Taim Bilong Masta*, 139.

expected: these were not identified for another fifty years—by which time the Highlanders were citizens of an independent Papua New Guinea which the Leahys could not have imagined.

Prospectors relied heavily on their carriers:

> You bought, as we used to call them, slaves . . . at about ten pounds a head . . . [S]ome of the more unscrupulous recruiters used dog chains and padlocks. Every night they'd chain the boys up because the further they got from home, the more homesick they'd get, and they'd try to break back . . . Once they got across the water they couldn't break back, they were trapped.[20]

Carriers were protected by armed men, and the mining camps formed a garrison with extended lines of communication. When master and man were equally alien, human feelings might glitter through the veil of paternalism. Jack O'Neill recollected the 1930s:

> We white men treated our boys as inferiors; some with tolerance, some with unadmitted affection, some few with hatred bred of fear, but it was impossible to harbour such attitudes towards these wild free people [of the Dunantina valley]. They were just men; most very likeable, a few nasty bastards; just like our own kind. A few were very real friends . . . I fear we gave these people much less than they gave us.[21]

In the long run, most white men were squeezed out of mining. When a major deposit was proved, a mine needed only a few artisans to supervise many unskilled men. Australians were especially feared by employers, after maritime and shearers' strikes in the 1890s. The strikes were broken, but workers created powerful unions, and the Commonwealth, on their behalf, enacted White Australia labour policies. Employers paled at the prospect of Australian influence. Arundel, for example, confided: 'This would be the worst possible thing for our interests, particularly in regard to their ideas as to White Australia . . . We would move heaven and earth with the Imperial Government to avert such a dire catastrophe.' Telfer Campbell, Resident Commissioner of the Gilbert and Ellice Group, agreed: 'A "White Australia" including a "White Ocean Island" and "White Pacific" would be the ruin of everything.'[22]

Most spectacular of the mining giants was Bulolo Gold Dredging Ltd, which built an airstrip to fly in the components of dredges to assemble on site. Lae was the busiest airport in the world, despatching purpose-built aeroplanes on the fifty-minute flight to Wau. The company employed 350 foreigners. Such companies might have trained New Guineans and reduced their wage bills, but Australian trade unions and the colonial administration barred this approach, so New Guineans worked with picks and shovels for 5 to 10 shillings per month, alongside high-technology machines and unionised artisans.

The administration was a ruthless employer, which always needed carriers for patrolling. Organisers of the Rabaul strike, for example,

20 Bert Weston and Bob Franklin, quoted in *ibid.*, 143.
21 Jack O'Neill, quoted in Nelson, *Black, White and Gold*, 268.
22 Williams and Macdonald, *The Phosphateers*, 70.

were condemned to work in the Highland mines and some men were convicted on slender evidence merely to conscript them. Bulolo was a classic enclave development, the company spending most of its working costs on capital goods and supplies, remitting most earnings abroad, and employing New Guineans who saved little or foreigners who repatriated their savings. Apart from royalty payments and import taxes, little money stayed in the country.

The Great Depression, which launched desperate prospectors into the Highlands, raised the comparative value of gold and released capital for mining, thus helping to create a gold industry in Fiji. In 1932 gold was identified in the Tavua district of Vanua Levu. The government acted swiftly to manage this resource. Small prospectors and speculators were deterred by high fees on claims; Fijian claims to ownership were finessed by legislation; and claims to three major deposits—two in Colo province of Viti Levu—were consolidated by Australian investors. Frank Packer was already wealthy in journalism: Edward Theodore and John Wren were prominent in Labor Party politics. Between them they created a complex of companies which controlled the three mines, and formed alliances with merchants who enjoyed access to government policy-making. The sugar giant CSR was conciliated by agreeing that few Indians would be employed in mining, and the government allowed the companies to recruit Fijians. By 1938 the mines produced more than a quarter of the colony's exports. Typically the industry employed white managers and artisans, and mixed-race and Rotuman workers who were rewarded rather better than the mass of Fijians. Rotumans—too far from home to abscond easily—relished an intermediate status. Since each *buli* was rewarded for the recruits he sent to work, Fijians had little choice but to endure the heat and dust, wretched barracks, and miserable rations.

The treatment of mining and quarrying illustrates a general feature of the early colonial states. Officials assumed that any production was desirable. To promote phosphate mining, therefore, they allowed companies to acquire rights cheaply and import Asian labour, and waived regulations which protected workers. To promote gold-mining, Papuan officials exempted machinery from import duties, and set royalties and licence fees at risible levels. Fijian companies routinely manipulated working costs to minimise taxes, and persistently lobbied in Suva and in London to lower royalty payments. Little capital and scant technology were introduced before the 1930s, and no attempt was made to retain benefits. Meanwhile the state regulated labour (sometimes providing convicts), kept the peace, built infrastructure, and provided transport.

DEPOPULATION

The extent and pace of depopulation are difficult to quantify because census figures were first collected long after contact, as part of the colonial stock-taking. Thus in 1907 Governor Hahl reported of New

Guinea: 'the population is sparse, of inferior quality and diminishing: malaria and dysentery are present everywhere; high freight rates have to be paid'.[23] Census-takers believed that numbers had declined and were still falling. The earliest recorded disaster struck the Chamorros of the Marianas in the 1680s, when Spanish troops and Jesuits concentrated people from scattered hamlets into Guam, Rota and Saipan, to live within the sound of church bells. Officials could correlate epidemics with the arrival of the trans-Pacific galleons, but the obvious remedies—dispersing the people or barring the galleons—were unthinkable. The population fell by about 70 per cent over thirty years. Conversely, one of the Islands which suffered least was Chuuk, whose people consistently repelled outsiders.

Collapse was seldom as dramatic as that of Aboriginal Australians who declined by perhaps 90 per cent to 70,000 in the 1930s, 150 years after the First Fleet; or the scything down of the Hawaiian population: 'this demographic collapse . . . is the most important "fact" in Hawaiian history. As disease destroyed their numbers, it destroyed the people's confidence and their culture; finally, it was the most important factor in their dispossession: the loss of their land and ultimately of their independence.'[24] In many Island groups, the consequences were almost as severe. During the era of resource raiding and the labour trade, many islands in the Solomons and the New Hebrides were decimated by chicken-pox, whooping cough, measles, influenza, gonorrhoea, tuberculosis and leprosy. Interaction was uneven, and some Islands were little affected, while others were driven close to extinction. Aneityum, the southernmost of the New Hebrides and the most devastated, had about 4000 people in 1848, collapsing by two-thirds in a generation, then to 680 in 1895 and 186 in 1940. The New Hebrides as a whole lost about half its population. The *grande terre* of New Caledonia sustained a population of at least 100,000. Only 34,218 Kanaks saw in the new century. The Murua population of Woodlark Island fell by about two-thirds, from 2200 in 1850 to about 800 from 1910 onwards. Almost all Polynesian populations fell by at least half, and Micronesian societies risked complete extinction when new diseases compounded the effects of natural disasters. The 3000 people living on Kosrae in the 1820s, when European ships began to call there, had been reduced to one-tenth of that number by the 1880s before they began to recover. On islets, decline could be irreversible. In the 1830s Ngatik society was destroyed by pirates and rebuilt on a new biological basis. Similar consequences followed in the Tokelaus, from slave raiding, diseases, famine and voluntary emigration. There, too, immigrants rebuilt the population. Colonial administrators were not fantasising when they feared extinction.

Many new infections had dramatic impacts. Smallpox proved lethal in Australia and elsewhere, outrunning the people who brought it. Venereal diseases commonly accompanied sailors, although yaws conferred some cross-immunity against syphilis and some captains tried to

23 Quoted in Firth, *New Guinea under the Germans*, 113.
24 Bushnell, ' "The Horror" Reconsidered', 162.

isolate diseased sailors. Crowd infections could be almost as savage in 'virgin field' conditions; the epidemic which swept the Papuan coast shortly before the 1870s may have been smallpox, but chicken-pox would have been equally lethal. The impact of measles in Fiji in 1875, in perfect conditions for its introduction, was described by a government commission, which also tried to allocate responsibility:

> Introduced by H.M.S. 'Dido' in the persons of the Vunivalu's own son, Ratu Timothe, and his servant, measles spread with unexampled rapidity owing to its dissemination throughout the country on the return to their various districts of the members of a great native meeting . . . [The population of about 150,000 sustained losses of about 40,000. High mortality] was partly the consequence of the suddenness with which it befell the people, village by village, every individual being susceptible . . . Whole communities were stricken at one time, and there was no one left to gather food or carry water, to attend to the necessary wants of their fellows, or even, in many cases, to bury the dead.

The colonial authorities blamed the victims for their ignorance and apathy: Fijians were 'overwhelmed, dismayed, cowed, abandoning all hope of self-preservation, and becoming incapable of any effort to save themselves or others'.[25]

Similarly the Etoro society of the Papuan Plateau, even in 1968, had only slight exposure to colonial authority, but had endured severe population loss due to: 'extremely high mortality from introduced diseases and a traditionally low birthrate. The decline in numbers probably began in the late 1930s, during the period of exploratory patrols, and accelerated in the 1940s . . . [with] influenza and measles in about 1948 and 1949'.[26] Kelly reckons at least 50-per-cent depopulation over thirty years.

Large populations, enjoying good nutrition, suffered less and recovered faster. A bacillary dysentery epidemic in the Wahgi valley of New Guinea, in 1943, produced mortality of about 2.5 per cent, and recovery was swift. The same dysentery in the Dreikikir area caused localised losses of 30 per cent. These sub-coastal villagers were under severe stress from war and other infections, whereas Highlanders were isolated from most of the effects of war. Losses of 50 per cent may have been normal in the first exposure to exotic disease, reinforced by other threats; but we must go beyond microbiology to explain continuing depopulation in some Islands long after first exposure.

So much attention has been drawn to epidemic infections that other patterns of illness and mortality have been obscured. To account for life and death in their social context, Stephen Kunitz focuses on Polynesia, and observes that depopulation was uneven. There were huge losses in Hawai'i and New Zealand. Tahitians also fell in number—but not for so long as the nearby Marquesan population which fell precipitously and carried on falling in 1930 to a nadir of about 4 per cent of the original

25 B. G. Corney, J. Stewart and B. H. Thomson, *Report of the Commission appointed to Inquire into the Decrease of the Native Population*, quoted in McArthur, *Island Populations*, 8–9.
26 Kelly, *Etoro Social Structure*, 29–30.

population. Samoan and Tongan numbers declined by much less (unless depopulation occurred before Europeans recorded it). An obvious scapegoat is firearms—but guns were widely available and warfare common. A better correlation links morbidity to the frequency and intensity of early contact. Tahiti, Hawai'i and New Zealand received frequent visits, and New Zealand Maori were partially protected by their sparse distribution across a large land mass. Kunitz proposes that the variation mainly reflects different colonial experiences: those who suffered most were dispossessed and demographically overwhelmed by settlers, while others escaped the large-scale dispossession which created poverty, crowding and poor nutrition—the perfect conditions for respiratory and gastric diseases. 'Moreover, the expropriation of land resulted in removal and very likely in the disruption of social networks which provided both instrumental and emotional support in times of need.'[27]

Following French annexation of the Marquesas in 1842:

> Chiefs were displaced by colonial officials, and . . . the indigenous political system seems essentially to have been fractured. While some depopulation took place between 1800 and 1840, the 1840–80 period was one of appalling decline. Abel Dupetit-Thouars . . . gave an overall figure of 20,200 which was probably more accurate than any earlier estimate. The population fell to about 5,000 during the 1880s and reached a low point of less than 2,000 during the 1920s.[28]

The colonial context is at least as salient as disease. If we broaden our vision, a second insidious threat can be observed. The lessons of concentration were not learned. Missionaries generally encouraged people to resettle in village-congregations, and in Aneityum and elsewhere converts suffered the predictable consequences.

Since the arrival of Europeans often coincided with lethal infections, many Islanders attributed to foreigners the ability not only to transmit diseases but also to cure them. In New Caledonia in the 1840s, when missionaries and catechists visited the sick and baptised those who were likely to die, Kanaks drew the inference that Christian rites—or perhaps visits—were responsible for deaths.[29] The missionaries' claim to the secret of eternal life reinforced suspicions. Some missionaries saw in the misfortunes of pagans evidence of divine retribution—analyses which they regretted when converts proved equally susceptible. The outcome of these misunderstandings was often a readiness to resort to missionaries as therapists. Mission remedies were limited in the days before germ theory or quinine, and Islanders received more consolation than therapy.

Depending on circumstances, some populations recovered quickly even from dreadful epidemics. Measles in Fiji is a case in point. Population seems to have increased in the next few years. Numbers

27 Kunitz, *Disease and Social Diversity*.
28 Thomas, *Marquesan Societies*, 4.
29 Bronwen Douglas, 'Discourses on Death in a Melanesian World', in Merwick (ed.), *Dangerous Liaisons*.

then declined for twenty years, a slower decline than the epidemic, but equally significant. Influenza in 1918–19 offers even clearer evidence of the importance of political context. The pandemic travelled along the shipping routes to Australia and New Zealand. Australian authorities largely prevented its further spread. New Zealanders were less well prepared, so that flu reached Tonga (where it carried off 8 per cent of the people) and Nauru (16 per cent). The steamship *Talune* carried flu to Fiji where 9000 (or 5 per cent) died, then to Western Samoa, where 90 per cent of the people were infected, bringing life to a standstill. When it burned out, 30 per cent of adult men were dead, 22 per cent of adult women and 10 per cent of the children. The flu was excluded from American Samoa by a commander who imposed a blockade. In the aftermath the New Zealand authorities pointed to accidental causes, and contrasted the selfless work of their compatriots with the moral failings of Samoans. Samoans were not persuaded, nor forgiving. They were not only resentful—they were also fecund. Numbers increased at 2.5 per cent per annum in the five years following the epidemic, and in the following ten years it averaged 3.3 per cent.

Poverty and social dislocation are not merely the outcome of disease: they also cause avoidable illness. Colonial doctors commonly attributed mortality simply to infections—and to the behaviour of victims. Some responses did compound the problem. Maddocks points out, for example, that the sexual rites with which Marind (in Irian Jaya) responded to crises were not the best way to counter sexually trans- mitted diseases.[30] Equally, when Fijian parents cooled their fevered children in cold water, they did more harm than good. But the doctors' analyses obscure the role of governments, shifting responsibility to the realm of accident, acts of God, or the non-negotiable cost of linkage to the outside world.

Human agency is particularly clear in the labour trade, partly because the records are better. The havoc in Fiji and Queensland is documented by Shlomowitz: 'The annual average death rate declined from about 80 per thousand (1879–1887), to about 60 per thousand (1888–1892), to about 35 per thousand (1893–1910s), to about 10 to 30 per thousand (1920s–30s) . . . The main causes of death were bacillary dysentery, pneumonia . . ., and tuberculosis.'[31]

New recruits always suffered acutely, and mortality rates declined as workers became inured to working conditions. The same profile probably typified labourers within a single colony. In the first years of this century, less than 80 per cent of labourers returned to Buka after contracts elsewhere in New Guinea.[32] Shlomowitz singles out tuber- culosis. Its transmission requires close association—of precisely the kind which occurred in plantation barracks, which also nurtured dysentery and pulmonary infections. But kindness could be as lethal as negligence, and mission schools were probably as dangerous as

30 Maddocks, 'Venereal Diseases'.
31 Ralph Shlomowitz, 'Mortality and Workers', in Moore, Leckie and Munro (eds), *Labour in the South Pacific*, 124–7.
32 Scragg, 'Lemankoa: 1920–1980'.

plantations. Kunitz refers to diseases of poverty. In the Islands tuberculosis was a disease of development, becoming almost an exact
indicator of Christianity and other introduced institutions. In New
Caledonia, Kanaks called it *christiano*, 'the disease of the Christians'.[33]
But it is not *exactly* an indicator of development, because Papua New
Guinea Highlanders were a virgin field population in the 1950s, yet the
Labour Scheme which brought them to coastal plantations did not
produce a catastrophe, because the Public Health Department enforced
immunisation before recruitment.

Probably Polynesia was worse affected than Melanesia, and small
populations suffered more than large populations. It is difficult to
believe that the New Guinea Highlanders, fighting fit in the 1930s, were
only half the men and women they had been a generation earlier. Some
circumstances suggest that New Guinea experienced less loss of life
than isolated Islands, and perhaps explain why. First, New Guinea was
less attractive to European whalers and explorers. Europeans found
Polynesia therapeutic, but Melanesia sickening. The earliest resident
missionaries—mainly Polynesians—died like flies.[34] These hazards
were not offset by the attractions of rest and recreation. Stannard
attributes much of the depopulation of Hawai'i to venereal diseases in
a society whose mores favoured dissemination. Conditions were less
favourable in most of Melanesia. Further, the frontier of labour
recruiting, moving north through the Solomon Islands, reached Milne
Bay and the Bismarck Archipelago only in the 1870s. The frontier of
gold prospecting was similarly late—and ransacked the islands before
the mainland. Once colonial authority was asserted (in 1884), restraints
continued to operate. One German settlement in New Guinea had to be
abandoned, leaving the doctor to lament that 'Malaria has conquered.'
After several years in Papua, the Chief Medical Officer advised settlers
to live at least a quarter of a mile away from Papuans.

Epidemics erupted in all communities whose *cordons sanitaires* were
breached. The effects of contact varied with particular infections, and
with the well-being of the people and their circumstances. It may not be
possible (or useful) to discover how a particular microbe found its
target. Their impact is less a matter of accident, since that depends
largely on living conditions and counter-measures. In the earliest phase
of contact, infections and contagions touched societies whose structures
remained intact, so there is no reason to expect new patterns of non-
infectious illness. Once foreigners took control, they assumed responsibility for public health—and for living conditions which influenced
morbidity.

Many societies rebuilt their numbers, but some did not. Micronesians
and Hawaiians were exposed to European contact at the worst possible
time—when venereal diseases and tuberculosis were hyperendemic in
Europe. Highlanders, at the other extreme, encountered Europeans
when tuberculosis was controllable by BCG and venereal diseases

33 Douglas, 'Discourses on Death'.
34 Lātūkefu, 'Oral History and Pacific Island Missionaries'.

curable by penicillin. So long as venereal diseases were widespread—as they were in Hawai'i, Tahiti, the Marquesas and some islands in Melanesia—populations could not recover. Thus some populations continued to decline after the epidemic era, especially those who were dispossessed and whose social networks were shattered. To put the point simply, Islanders' struggles to retain access to their land and control over their labour were not merely economic calculations. They were literally matters of life and death.

LAND, LABOUR AND THE STATES

The uneven impact of governments on lives, land and labour defies summary, but one outcome was so general that it often escapes attention: Islanders' mobility was severely restricted. Many Islanders travelled as evangelists under mission auspices, as carriers for government patrols, and as indentured workers on plantations and mines, but the demands of wage labour and cash crop production inhibited independent travel. Wherever a colonial economy was established, old maritime networks either lapsed or shrank. Trade stores in Port Moresby made redundant the *hiri* expeditions to fetch sago; and the trade routes which had encircled New Guinea either lapsed or (like the *kula* centred on the Trobriand Islands) became limited to the carriage of valuables which trade stores did not stock. Foreigners dominated the seas, few Islanders could buy or maintain schooners, and many ocean-going canoes rotted on the beach or survived in museums. For many Islanders, horizons shrank and lives became more insular.

The new economy was peculiarly political. The settler who described the trading firm of Hennings as 'coeval . . . with the calling of Fiji into existence'[35] may have been a shallow scholar but he understood the traders' role in building a colony. The economy was political in other ways too. Traders bought copra and sold goods at prices calibrated to the skin colour of the customer. Pigment rather than skill also determined rates of pay. The presumed effects of a free market failed to materialise: merchants did not want competition, and pursued local monopoly, ideally through a government to register title, to license some traders and exclude others, to mobilise local labour or authorise its importation, and to protect property.

Australia and New Zealand were spectacular borrowers of capital, but island governments had no capacity to borrow, nor did they have Japan's ability to extract capital from peasants. They relied, perforce, on private investors. Almost any concession would be made to attract a major investor—'in Fiji the CSR, in German Samoa the DHPG, in the British Solomons Lever Brothers and Burns Philp, in the Marshalls the Jaluit Company, in German New Guinea the New Guinea Company, in New Caledonia Société le Nickel'.[36] Their ventures could not be allowed

---

35 Scarr, 'Creditors and the House of Hennings'.
36 Munro and Firth, 'Company Strategies', in Moore, Leckie and Munro (eds), *Labour in the South Pacific*, 25.

to fail. The French government rescued Higginson's companies and salvaged Ballande's investments, just as the New Guinea Company's liabilities were cancelled by the German government: these interventions 'exemplify the sort of action taken by the State when grand political interests . . . appeared to be at risk'. On the other hand, 'it was a commercial or an economic logic which probably lay behind most operations of takeover, merger or joint venture affecting British plantations'.[37] Even when they wished to do so, colonial governments were poorly equipped to regulate big corporations. Fiji had a better bureaucracy than most colonies, yet—as the merchant Morris Hedstrom explained in 1911—'the people who profit by the prosperity of the colony are the landowners and the merchants and capitalists, and these are the people who escape almost scot free under our present [taxation] system'. CSR enjoyed privileged treatment as the generator of wealth. Revenue was raised instead by head taxes, income and import taxes, and the government did not raise enough revenue to transform living standards.

> Had government been more aggressive early in the 20th century, it would have captured a share of sugar export income. Had it been better supplied with tax accountants, it would have acquired a larger share of repatriated profits through income taxation. Had Imperial government not required investment of monetary reserves . . . in British or colonial securities, the reserves could have contributed to Fiji's development . . . But Fiji's was a dependent colonial economy in which monetary development had not proceeded far. [38]

Deference to large companies contrasts with the harassment of indigenous businesses. Some Islanders, outraged by price discrimination, formed co-operatives to market their produce or import goods. One was the Tonga Ma'a Tonga Kautaha (Tonga for the Tongans Association) formed in 1909. Several thousand members enjoyed better prices than the traders offered. This was intolerable to the traders; they protested to the British Consul, who found pretexts for winding up the Kautaha, although its assets massively outweighed its debts. Even in independent Tonga, indigenous capital was treated as anomalous and subversive.

Although every government pandered to foreign capital, the ramifications varied. Some governments prohibited or controlled sales of land, or decreed that foreigners could obtain it only under lease. Others assumed control of 'waste and vacant' tracts and released them to settlers. Some also sought to demarcate the lands of Islanders. The general result was to produce legal models which diverged from or misinterpreted old tenure systems. Simplified and codified, these systems often came to be regarded as 'traditional'. The colonial systems had a number of new features. Where land was 'waste and vacant', it was reclassified as state land. Whereas cultivated land was usually held

37 Panoff, 'The French Way in Plantation Systems', 211.
38 Fiji, *Legislative Council Debates*, 1911, quoted by Knapman, 'Capitalism's Economic Impact in Colonial Fiji'.

by family groups, or individuals, ownership was sometimes registered in the name of larger groups, such as the 'tribe' in New Caledonia or the *mataqali* (descent group) in Fiji. Flexibility ended because boundaries were recorded as permanent and owners registered. Practices for transfer were often banned by oversight or intent. These conditions allowed increasing divergence between the needs of owning groups and the area they held.

Changes also flowed from new technologies, crops and animals. By adopting steel tools, many communities reduced their workloads. New crop varieties with lower labour demands also contributed. The enforcement of colonial peace made the use of distant lands safer. Peace also reduced the time required for warfare, and removed an imperative for co-operation. Land held in common could now be cultivated by individuals or families, increasingly for commercial crops. When missions and traders encouraged the production of copra, land-use patterns changed dramatically. The area planted to coconuts expanded immensely. The new areas were usually near the coast and villages to minimise carriage, so that new food gardens had to be located further inland on newly cleared land. The period lengthened during which land remained under the control of individuals or households before returning to fallow and eventually to community land. The life of a coconut plantation could far exceed a generation, so that land might now lie in the control of a family or an individual for as long as living memory. Other tree crops extended these effects. The new forms of value which land acquired when Europeans sought to buy it were reinforced by the potential earnings from cash cropping. Land became a commodity, even if its sale was constrained.

The state was equally critical in shaping forms of labour. The government of Fiji provided *girmitiyas* for plantations and reserved the labour of Fijians for service to the chiefs. Hawaiian planters prospected half of the world to mobilise labour. By contrast, White Australian policies ruled out the employment of Asians at home or in Papua or New Guinea. New Caledonia was (in Australian eyes) promiscuous in importing New Hebrideans, Wallisians, Vietnamese and Chinese— while the Tongan monarchy was just as restrictive as Australia. It follows that the experiences of labour differed dramatically. At one extreme were Island populations with so few resources and such exposure to natural disaster that labour migration was always welcome. I-Kiribati were not discouraged by degrading conditions or even ship-wrecks, but eagerly recruited for Peru in the 1860s, for Guatemala a generation later, and for Samoa at all times. At the other end of the spectrum, Tongans were too prosperous to consider indentured labour abroad—though many couples endured harsher environments in strange societies, earning a pittance as evangelists. Polynesians were less likely than others to enlist, probably because chiefs preferred to retain the service of commoners.

There is variety too, in the gender distribution of recruitment. In most societies women did not recruit, either because they did not want to or because their fathers and husbands forbade them; but in the

Trobriand Islands as well as some islands of Vanuatu, women chose to depart, and some chose not to return. These variations owe something to the vagaries of colonial policies, but societal values and personal preferences were also important, and this variation reflects the autonomy which individuals and communities cherished in the face of massive economic and political pressure.

Allocation of land and labour were obviously affected by the strength and needs of foreign capital, but each arrangement was the outcome of Islanders' interests and the idiosyncratic manner in which officials reconciled conflicting demands. Some conflicts took the classic form of foreigners imposing capitalist relations on reluctant Islanders; but these roles were often blurred, and in Queensland and the New Hebrides they were reversed. The diverse outcomes reflect not only the variety of interests, but also the different ways in which Islanders read the risks and opportunities, and devised strategies for survival and even prosperity.

BIBLIOGRAPHIC ESSAY

Most of the sources for this chapter have been listed in the essay following chapter 5. Bennett, *Wealth of the Solomons*, is the leading source on the impact of commerce and colonialism in the Soloman Islands. For New Caledonia, see Merle, 'The Foundation of Voh, 1892–1895', and *Expériences coloniales*. For German New Guinea, see Firth, *New Guinea under the Germans*. Much of the evidence for labour conditions in New Caledonia derives from Shineberg, '"The New Hebridean is Everywhere"'; and Panoff, 'The French Way in Plantation Systems'. Conditions in Papua New Guinea are described by Nelson, *Taim Bilong Masta*, and *Black, White and Gold*. Williams and Macdonald, *The Phosphateers*, is the essential source for nitrate mining, while Emberson-Bain, *Labour and Gold in Fiji*, is a thorough analysis of gold-mining in Fiji. Other dimensions of Fiji's colonial experience are treated by Lal, *Broken Waves*; Lal, *Girmitiyas*; Scarr, *Fiji: A Short History*; and Macnaught, *The Fijian Colonial Experience*. The plantation experience is addressed by Lal, Munro and Beechert, *Plantation Workers*. Population history is reconstructed from sources cited in chapter 3, supplemented by the researches of Ralph Shlomowitz, condensed in his 'Mortality and Workers', in Moore, Leckie and Munro (eds), *Labour in the South Pacific*.

CHAPTER 8

COLONIAL ADMINISTRATION AND THE INVENTION OF THE NATIVE

THE AGENCIES AND IDEOLOGIES OF COLONIALISM

The accepted European view of colonial rule in the 1920s and 1930s, contested only by a few dissident anthropologists and missionaries, was that it brought immense benefits to Islanders. Colonial officials believed that they had a duty to take control of Islanders' affairs for their own good. 'The suppression of intertribal warfare, vendettas and retaliatory homicide and the establishment of law and order are obligatory on all Governments', the High Commissioner for the Western Pacific said of the Solomon Islands in 1928. To replace endemic warfare with 'law and order', he thought, was self-evidently good. Missionaries had no doubt that to free villagers from fear of spirits and open their hearts to Christ was desirable, just as planters believed that they were improving the lot of the people by employing them. As decolonisation began, a contrary view became popular. By this account—the old view inverted—colonialism was a disaster for Islanders, destroying vigorous cultural traditions, imposing alien work disciplines, replacing traditional beliefs with a puritanical and oppressive Christianity, and incorporating Islanders into a global economy in which they were inevitably marginal and exploited. Both interpretations put Europeans centre-stage. Two decades after most colonial flags were lowered, the interpretation shifted again, to a more balanced appreciation of the place of outsiders, greater sensitivity to the pitfalls of language, and a more considered understanding of which outsiders mattered most.

Before we turn to these insights, let us recall the Pacific as the world defined it in 1921. Britain, France, the United States, Australia, New Zealand and the Netherlands were still there, with Japan incorporating Okinawa and the Bonin Islands and Chile including tiny Rapanui. During World War I Japan took the German islands north of the equator. Australia was rewarded with New Guinea, and with supervision (for the British Empire) of Nauru. New Zealand administered Western Samoa. In theory the former German territories were supervised by the League of Nations, but the mandate governments submitted annual reports and then acted much as they pleased.

In international law the South Seas consisted of territories under a variety of foreign jurisdictions. Those whose people were least familiar with the outside world—Dutch New Guinea, Australian New Guinea and Papua—dwarfed the others in size and population and were still being explored by Europeans. Two—or perhaps three—million people lived there. The next biggest indigenous populations were in the British Solomons (93,000 in 1931) and Fiji (84,475 in 1921, together with 60,634 people of Indian descent) followed by island groups with populations ranging from 24,000 to 47,000—Tonga, Western Samoa, the Gilbert and Ellice Islands, Japanese Micronesia, the New Hebrides, New Caledonia and the 'French Establishments' in Tahiti and its archipelagos. Some island groups had fewer than 15,000 inhabitants—Guam, American Samoa, the Cook Islands, Niue, Wallis and Futuna, Nauru and (with just 469 people in 1934) Rapanui.

To understand Islands colonialism we must recognise the limitations of colonial power. More than one-third of the region's population remained effectively independent or only lightly touched by colonial control until after World War II. The Highlanders of New Guinea had a contact history but not a colonial one. In the most famous of the exploratory journeys, in 1933, Mick and Dan Leahy travelled with the government officer Jim Taylor and sixty New Guinean carriers from Bena Bena in the eastern Highlands over the mountain range into the Wahgi valley and west to Mount Hagen and the Jimmi valley. They found hundreds of thousands of people whose existence was previously known only to themselves, and whose lives revolved around intensive agriculture and exchanges. The Australian administration used its Uncontrolled Areas Ordinance to limit the influx of prospectors and missionaries.

Often the most important foreigners were other Islanders. Between the world wars, for example, Samoans dominated the atoll people of Tuvalu through the London Missionary Society. The church language of Tuvalu was Samoan, Samoan pastors held positions of the highest authority, their houses were the biggest, and they enforced a morality founded not only in Congregational Christianity but also in Samoan tradition. In 1941 the church blocked a movement led by a local pastor called Lusia for an independent church using the Tuvaluan language.[1] Again, the first foreigners who explored the edges of the eastern Highlands in the 1920s were coastal New Guineans, converted by Lutherans and mobilised as evangelists. 'Mount Hagen is enormous', the evangelist Saki Halingkeo wrote in 1938: 'The mission station Ogelbeng lies at its foot . . . Sometimes hail falls here. It is often terribly cold, so that I freeze. I would be very glad if missionary Vicedom, who is coming from Germany soon, could bring me a coat. It is perhaps not right for me to beg like this, but I am so cold I am afraid I will not survive.' Lutheranism reached the Simbu and Hagen peoples through a coastal Melanesian cultural prism.

The terms we use to describe Islanders are the product of colonialism, and distort our understanding of identities. We call the diverse peoples of eastern New Guinea Papuans and New Guineans as if they

1   Garrett, *Footsteps in the Sea*, 410–12.

shared a common identity in the 1920s, yet they were as foreign to each other as Europeans were. Language also warps our sense of proportion. Looking back from independence, we acknowledge small groups of Islanders who achieved statehood, such as I-Kiribati and Tuvaluans, while neglecting more populous communities who have been absorbed into larger states. Colonial history becomes a story of Fijians, Cook Islanders and Tuvaluans, precursors of modern nationalities, but not—for example—of Motu, Binandere, Tolai or Trobriand Islanders, all of whom tend to be lumped together ahistorically as Papua New Guineans. There is a place for a history organised on the basis of colonial territories, but there should also be a place for a history of self-identifying groups.

Most colonial governments were skimpy, under-financed affairs which cannot be compared with the instruments of control of our own time. Most territories were run on a shoestring, expected to pay for themselves and confined to creating a limited order. Only Japanese Micronesia, Papua and the Cook Islands were receiving subsidies in the 1930s. Until World War II people in much of Melanesia experienced colonial rule as intermittent and sometimes mysterious demands made on occasional visits by *kiaps* (patrol officers), native police and recruiters. On a visit to the Gilbert and Ellice Islands in 1939, Britain's leading colonial official in the Pacific was struck by 'the appalling penury that immobilises both administrative and medical officers in a Colony where transport facilities are of paramount importance' and where district officers had to cadge lifts from trading or mission vessels.[2]

Conversely, Christian missions were strong and influential, often exercising quasi-governmental powers. That was especially common throughout the New Hebrides, where missionaries had established theocracies half a century before the Condominium (chapter 6). Pentecost Island, in the central New Hebrides, remained divided almost until 1940, between a Catholic coastal belt and the interior dominated by *kastom* or pagan beliefs, and civil war was not uncommon. Missions were far more significant mediators of modernisation than most governments. In many places the outside world was embodied not in government but in the mission station with its plantations, workshops, schools and gardens, and with missionaries who came to stay, and learned the language of their congregations. In much of Polynesia, Islanders had long since adapted Christianity to their own conceptions of rank, status, gender relations and good order, and employed its prescriptions as the ideological basis of chiefly rule. In some places men and women sat apart in church, while in others chiefs sat above commoners. Descent groups used *vakamisioneri* collections to demonstrate their wealth and compete against each other.

Neither Buddhism nor Shintoism had such enduring impact. Outside Koror, the capital of Japanese Micronesia, the government built the Kampei Taisha Nan'yo Jinja in 1940 and dedicated it to the Amaterasu

2   Macdonald, *Cinderellas of the Empire*, 124.

Omikami or sun goddess from whom the imperial family claimed descent. This Shinto shrine of great status was inaugurated in three days of celebrations, and Palauan students were induced to pray there for imperial Japan in its battles in China. Smaller shrines could be found on Saipan, Chuuk and Lamotrek Atoll and the authorities made energetic efforts to imbue Micronesians with the ideals and rituals of Shinto, but the effect on Islanders' beliefs was negligible.

The political responses of Islanders to colonial rule defy easy categorisation. There was no equivalent to the thirty-year war of resistance fought against the Dutch by the Achehnese of Sumatra, or to the rebellions against German rule in Tanganyika and South-West Africa. Nor did mass nationalist movements develop like that of Gandhi in India, or class politics that might have given rise to industrial action. For decades—in a kind of 'primary resistance'—Melanesian communities contested colonial rule by force as the frontier of contact advanced in New Guinea and the Solomons, engaging the foreigners with spears, arrows and axes in skirmishes usually followed by punitive expeditions. On Malaita in 1927, Kwaio warriors led by Basiana killed a district officer, a cadet and thirteen police who were collecting tax, and provoked a large punitive expedition. Sokehs district in Pohnpei was a centre of violent resistance to both the Spanish and the Germans before World War I (chapter 6), and sporadic guerrilla attacks by Kanaks on French settlers in New Caledonia in 1917 met with swift retribution.

'Resistance' of different kinds was not unknown. The Fijian Apolosi Nawai spent much of the interwar period exiled on Rotuma for his anti-British activities. The British confronted a widespread anti-colonial movement in the Solomons after World War II, and millenarian movements throughout Melanesia expressed a desire for autonomy and equality. But 'resistance' suggests greater organisation and more widespread dissatisfaction than was common. In the mosaic of small communities that constituted colonial Melanesia, conflict more often erupted among Melanesians than between them and colonial governments. Relations between Island societies and governments were more often characterised by alliances, accommodations and co-operation than by confrontation and protest, and protest movements themselves could be surprisingly peaceful, as in Western Samoa in the 1920s and 1930s.

The Rabaul Strike of 1929 was a rare example of 'industrial' action. Rabaul was the centre of New Guinea administration, and of plantation production. On the evening of 2 January, police and workers withdrew from Rabaul to the Methodist and Catholic missions. Most returned next morning once the missionaries advised a return to work and agreed to appeal to the government for clemency. The organisers (in colonial terms, ringleaders) were Sumsuma, a ship's captain and labour recruiter, and several senior policemen, broadly familiar with the structures of authority which denied them their worth. Ordinary workers were worse paid, and more likely to be involved in inter-ethnic feuds. Nearby Tolai villagers were not involved. Some grievances were industrial (such as the demand for a minimum wage of £12, nearly fifty times the prevailing rate), but the protest also expressed a simmering rage against paternalism. The fact that strikers were drawn from the gamut of employment underlines the political and racial dimensions of the episode, which incurred the wrath of the government—itself a large employer. Charges were discovered or invented, prison terms imposed, and prisoners drafted to carry cargo on the goldfield track, or to labour there, and most were savagely beaten while awaiting trial or during their sentences. Sumsuma abandoned 'modern' politics. For his later career in 'traditional' gift-giving, see chapter 3.

New Zealand's military occupation of Western Samoa, which lasted until 1920 when civilian government took over, produced few significant changes in law or policy. Samoans drew strength from the conviction that *fa'aSamoa*—Samoan tradition—reflected their superiority, and that their system of government was better than that imposed by New Zealanders. New Zealanders thought the Samoans a 'splendid but backward race . . . who had no thought for tomorrow and no vision as to the future of their islands'. An orator chief from the important village of Lufilufi reminded the administrator in 1919 that 'you are ruling Samoa by authority of the Samoans but you have not ruled these islands with love', an assertion which the administrator denied: 'I am not ruling Samoa by the authority of the Samoans. The allied nations which won the war gave the control of Samoa to New Zealand under King George of Great Britain and I am governing for New Zealand.'[3]

New Zealand administrators were less experienced and much less competent than their German predecessors, and they failed their first major test. The influenza epidemic of November 1918, perhaps the most horrific event of modern Samoan history, seared the memories of survivors (chapter 7). Afterwards an official inquiry exposed several acts of administrative neglect and poor judgement. The administrator was replaced, but not before he publicly vented his anger and unfairly castigated some prominent Samoans and Europeans. Given Samoan values of self-control and dignified demeanour, this alone may have crippled New Zealanders' ability to address Samoan concerns. The territory was administered by civil servants on limited-term assignments, who seldom stayed long enough to learn cultural subtleties.

The major problem was that New Zealand treated Samoans as political incompetents. The New Zealand Parliament legislated the terms of control, which amounted to an autocratic paternalism. The assembly, the Fono of Faipule, met as a customary body but had no role in decision-making, nor even a recognised advisory capacity. New Zealand acknowledged Samoan 'custom' but wholly excluded it from government. As early as 1920 the Fono and a 'Citizens' Committee' composed of Europeans and part-Europeans requested legislative authority for the Fono and representation in the New Zealand Parliament. Resident Europeans were particularly angered by measures such as prohibition of alcohol. By the 1920s the ethnic and class divide between natives and foreigners had narrowed. Marriage ties linked the

3 Meleisea, *The Making of Modern Samoa*, 124–8.

European community to prominent Samoan families. Influenza had taken a heavy toll on older *matai*, making way for new leaders familiar with Western ways. Some had worked for the colonial administrations. Others, like the merchants O. F. Nelson and S. H. Meredith, were sons of European men who had married Samoan women. By law these *'afakasi* were counted as Europeans, but their frame of reference and aspirations were 'bicultural', and they became active in the Mau Rebellion.

The administration took an activist turn with the arrival of General George Richardson in 1923. He was initially well received because he tried to learn the language and attended to local opinion. The Fono of Faipule was legally recognised, and Richardson established a hierarchical governing structure in which it played a central role. Committees of Faipule advised him on various matters, and all correspondence from the districts was to be funnelled through it. The Fono was also empowered to make regulations which would be upheld by the government. The Faipule presided over district councils which regulated a range of village activities, from sanitation to coconut planting—and could punish villagers who did not comply. This militarist structure gave the Faipule unprecedented importance, and they quickly became Richardson's willing partners in imposing measures which intruded into daily life and custom.

Richardson began to practise social engineering on a grand scale. To increase productivity he set precise requirements for planting trees and food crops, restricted cricket, initiated agricultural competitions, and attempted to prohibit *malaga*, 'travelling parties' who exchanged fine mats at ceremonial events: Westerners had long viewed *malaga* as a hindrance to industry. Richardson also proposed to individualise land tenure. The Fono unanimously adopted his scheme, whereby *matai* would subdivide and distribute their lands to untitled men. Though the government later claimed that the plan was wholly 'optional', at least some Samoans understood it as law. The most oppressive measure was the Samoan Offenders Ordinance of 1922, which gave the government the right to banish chiefs and even to revoke their titles. Governor Solf had set such a precedent in 1901, but Richardson imposed penalties more often and arbitrarily, to humiliate leading chiefs and punish dissent. His style is exemplified by this account of banishing a chief for manufacturing and selling liquor:

> Afamasaga is a High Chief who wears trousers, speaks English well and trades as a merchant in Apia. I imposed an additional penalty upon him . . . and deprived him of his titles and sent him to his Native Village where he has never lived before but where he can wear a lava lava and get time to reflect on the seriousness of this offence.[4]

Organised opposition emerged when the administration interfered in the most central institutions of social life—*matai* titles and ceremonial exchange. In 1926 Richardson proposed that *matai* should choose their own successors, replacing family selection. Even the Faipule baulked.

---

4   Island Territories 88/3 part 1, 1924, Interim Report No. 2 on Native Affairs, National Archives of New Zealand.

When a Royal Commission on the Mau held hearings in 1927, Samoans complained most often about the 'dictatorial' use of banishment and title revocation. Interference in *malaga* was the second most frequent grievance.

The organisation 'O le Mau' was founded in 1926, taking as its motto a slogan first proposed by Richardson, '*Samoa mo Samoa*' (Samoa for Samoans). Richardson banished two leaders, Afamasaga and Faumuina, to Apolima Island. Samoans then began systematic passive resistance and non-compliance with government institutions and regulations. New Zealand appointed a Royal Commission to hear grievances. Despite voluminous and heartfelt testimony on arbitrary banishments, Faipule corruption and other issues, the Royal Commission supported Richardson's position that the Mau had been instigated by a few '*afakasi* and Europeans. O. F. Nelson and two Europeans were deported, and popular support for the Mau grew. Richardson was humiliated when he arrested 400 'Mau leaders', only to have to turn away hundreds more who asked to be gaoled with them. At the Royal Commission, Tupua Tamasese Lealofi, one of Samoa's highest-ranking chiefs, was asked whether the aim of the Mau was self-government:

—Yes, that is a true object of the Mau.
Did the Mau desire to have New Zealand removed from the government of the country?
—Yes; it is the wish of the Mau that Samoa should be controlled by the Samoans.

By 1928, when Richardson was replaced by Stephen Allen, the Mau was performing many governmental functions, such as encouraging copra production and overseeing education. Nelson presented a petition summarising Samoan grievances to the League of Nations, but the Mandates Commission refused to hear it. The Mau's popularity is indicated by the fact that, of 9300 adult Samoan men, 8000 signed the petition. The Mau was also winning support in New Zealand, and in 1929 a new government ordered the Fono of Faipule suspended. For a time the Mau seemed to be stalled, and some prominent members resigned. Demonstrations continued, however, as Mau chiefs and European supporters returned from prison and exile. On 28 December 1929, a day remembered by Samoans as 'Black Saturday', a large procession marched through Apia, and police attempted to arrest some participants for non-payment of taxes. A European policeman fell, and the other officers opened fire. From a nearby police station machine-guns joined the attack. Eleven Samoans were killed, almost all of them high-ranking *matai*. The three highest-ranking—Tamasese, Tuimaleali'ifano, and Faumuina—were all seriously wounded, and Tupua Tamasese Lealofi later died. Since they wore distinctive dress and were trying to quiet the crowd when they were shot, Samoans were convinced that the police had targeted them.

The tragedy was compounded by the administration's arrogance. Allen blamed the Mau for bringing on the violence, declared it a seditious organisation, and called in troops to hunt down supporters.

Men fled to the mountains and forests, while soldiers terrorised the villages. During the early 1930s women carried on the work. Notable among them were Tamasese's widow Alaisala, Losa Taisi (the wife of O. F. Nelson), and the wives of Tuimaleali'ifano and Faumuina. The 'Women's Mau' travelled around Samoa to rally supporters and continued to stage demonstrations. Wellington maintained even stricter control over Samoa's administration and imposed even sterner punishments. In 1933 Allen was replaced by another soldier. Nelson returned to Samoa but the Mau remained an outlaw organisation, and he was arrested and sentenced to eight months' imprisonment in New Zealand and ten years of exile. A stand-off lasted until 1936, when a Labour government was elected in New Zealand. Members of the Labour Party had long sympathised with the Mau, and the change resulted in an immediate policy shift. Nelson was freed, returning to a tumultuous welcome, and the Mau was recognised as a legitimate organisation. The Samoan Offenders Ordinance was repealed and a new Fono of Faipule was elected, composed largely of members of the Mau. Moreover, the new Fono had the right to select members of the Legislative Council, giving Samoans—and particularly Mau supporters—a direct role in governance.

ETHNOCENTRISM

Let us define ethnocentrism broadly as a prejudiced attachment to one's own linguistic or cultural group. Western historians, dismayed by the racial prejudices of their forebears and with a rich literature of such views to cite, have dwelt on racial dominance by Europeans over Islanders. While colonialism was certainly that, it also offered Islanders opportunities to rearrange the ways in which they dominated each other. Colonialism is perhaps better seen as the interaction of many competing ethnocentrisms, with European racial prejudice forming an overlay.

Old traditions, persisting into the colonial period in New Guinea, were characterised by suspicion of those who did not belong to one's own kin group, contempt for their customs, and determination to avenge past wrongs. In the uncontrolled areas, most villagers dared not move more than a few kilometres from home for fear of being killed by enemies, as Australians discovered when they tried to recruit scouts and interpreters in the 1930s. Men of the Highlands valued physical courage above all other virtues. A Big Man from the Mount Hagen area, Ongka (see chapter 3), quoted the speeches given by men of his village when enemies surrounded his people:

> Let us stand here and face them, let us take the wounds in our fronts and not in our backs fleeing, let our women escape with their small sons at the breast, and later bring them back to show them the place where we, the men of Kawelka, fought and died to the last man, so they will know who their fathers were and who it was that killed them.[5]

5 *Ongka: A Self-account by a New Guinea Big-man*, 58.

Of his people's relationship with others, Ongka said:

> We of Mandembo clan in Kawelka tribe fought with the Membo clan in this way, we pushed each other to and fro back into each other's territory. We did the same with the neighbouring Tipuka clans, chasing them as far as the banks of the Moka river in the valley, and then they raced back at us and chased us back up the hill to home.

This martial rhetoric echoed the rhetoric of empire being taught to school-children in Britain, France and Japan. As the Kawelka clans pushed each other back and forth across the Highland hillsides, the Germans and the Allied forces were doing the same in Flanders and attributing their victories to the courage of their soldiers. Why was it, asked Toia, the Papuan servant of an Australian planter's wife, that white people were not put in prison for fighting as Papuans were? Europeans saw a vast cultural gulf separating them from the colonial peoples, but they had more in common than they realised. Both were ethnocentric, materialist, jealous of territory, and bellicose. The difference was not intelligence or character, as most Europeans imagined, but technology and organisation, accidents of history which conferred immense advantages on one side. The same was true of the Japanese in Micronesia, and of many Europeans in Polynesia, though their judgement of Polynesians was generally more favourable.

Like Europeans, Melanesian villagers believed that their own kind and their own customs were superior to others', but their 'own kind' usually numbered only a few thousand. In a typical encounter, a group of inland New Guinea villagers warned the prospector Jack O'Neill that some of their neighbours were 'really bad, mean bastards, who would shoot us and then eat us'.[6] Since the number of languages amounted to several hundred, the potential for prejudice was considerable. In 1918, the Lutheran evangelist Ngezinu, a Kotte speaker from the Huon Peninsula, described his Hube neighbours as

> really bad people. We Kotte were not as bad when we were heathens. Now, as they turn to Christianity, they are telling us about all their past deeds. Missionary, you yourself have seen that they sometimes grabbed hold of the sexual parts even of us Christians and that we beat their hands away. But there are yet worse things among them.

Agajo, in 1929, reported 'a disgusting custom' of the villagers he was trying to convert, and insisted that his own people had never indulged in such things: 'A feast is organised for the young men and girls. The people build a special house for it. At a certain time the young people come together and practise immorality for five or even ten days. Only later do they marry. Here there is a general immorality which is very great and there is pederasty.'[7]

Ethnocentrism provided fertile ground for divide-and-conquer tactics as *kiaps* extended the reach of government and 'friendly tribes' threw in their lot with Europeans against old enemies. Similarly,

---

6   O'Neill, *Up from South*, 60.
7   The letters of Ngezinu and Agajo survive in the Keysser Papers, Neuendettelsau.

planters commonly mixed recruits from different language groups in order to forestall agitation. 'We never had more than two boys from one district (say, one dialect)', a labour recruiter in New Guinea explained. 'Our gunboys came from villages from the south of Madang to the plains north of the Sepik River, three hundred miles away. To have boys all or most of whom spoke the same dialect was to court disaster. With ease they could desert their master.'[8]

Ethnocentrism was compounded by the fact that Samoan and Tongan missionaries commonly thought of themselves as bringing the Christian message to inferior peoples who desperately needed uplifting.

The colonisers' most significant ideological achievement was the invention of the Native, a category embracing all non-Europeans. The Native—singular and masculine—lacked European virtues such as application and foresight. His mind—the Native Mind—worked in mysterious ways. The Methodist mission chairman in Fiji in 1923 cautioned a colleague to 'take the NATIVE MIND into consideration' when attempting to give responsibility to Fijians.[9] 'It goes without saying', Australia's *Official Handbook of the Territory of New Guinea* commented in 1937, 'that the natives have no expressions for ideas quite unknown to them, such as gratitude, chastity, modesty, humility, &c.' In missions which depended on Islander evangelists, Europeans were missionaries but Islanders were 'native teachers' or 'native evangelists', barred from positions of ultimate responsibility. Pride in one's own kind was a source of solidarity for Europeans. Whites expected each other to keep social distance from the Native and to uphold 'white prestige'. Almost all Europeans believed themselves superior in intelligence, character and ability, and thought nothing was worse than Going Native. An Australian child in New Guinea in the 1930s recalled her horror of the idea:

> I remember this fellow called Norris who used to tramp around Tabar, Lihir, round there and he had a little cutter. He put into Bolagila one day . . . His hair was scraggy and his clothes were scraggy and he had great big open ulcers without bandages on his legs and no shoes on, and just nobody got around like that. We said, 'Who is he, who is he, Mummy? He's a white man and he looks terrible.' She said, 'He's a man named Norris.' We said, 'What does he do?' 'He doesn't do anything, he just lives with the kanakas.' We were horrified.[10]

The American anthropologist Hortense Powdermaker, in New Ireland in 1929, was asked by an Australian woman at a dinner party:

> 'Don't you think that the natives are just like human beings?' I replied in the affirmative. She continued, 'Have you noticed that they really appreciate kindness?' Again, I nodded affirmatively. 'Oh, I think it is so good of you, so kind, to live among the natives', she said, and pressed my hand.[11]

8 Papers of Reginald A. Beasley, Fryer Library, University of Queensland, 'New Guinea Adventure', c.1960, 194.
9 Macnaught, *The Fijian Colonial Experience*, 109.
10 Quoted in Bulbeck, *Australian Women in Papua New Guinea*, 196–7.
11 Powdermaker, *Stranger and Friend*, 103.

Where large areas were still beyond European control, white men feared that the Native would kill them or take their women or, worse, that their women were secretly attracted to the Native, as some were. A Governor of New Guinea put his fears on paper in 1919 in defence of corporal punishment. His despatch may be read as a summary of prejudices held by Australian settlers of the time:

> 1. The Native is a primitive being, with no well developed sense of duty or responsibility. A full belly and comfortable bed are his two chief desiderata. 2. This colony is sparsely settled by white people who are compelled in the circumstances of their vocations to rely upon natives for labour, and to live in close proximity to them. 3. On most plantations and centres of native labour, there is an enormous preponderance of males who are on the whole well fed and in robust health. Where there are white women and children this is a danger. 4. The native frequently mistakes kindness for weakness . . . 5. Corporal punishment does not have any brutalising effect on natives, any more than on the average school boy. With a native as with an animal—correction must be of deterrent nature. Would a man imprison his horse for offering to bite him? 6. Calaboose [gaol] is the natives' paradise, especially the calaboose run by humane officials.[12]

Japanese designated Micronesians as a 'third-class people' (*santo kokumin*), above whom were immigrant Koreans and Okinawans, as second-class people, and beyond them the Japanese themselves. Micronesians, wrote a naval officer, had no 'concept of progress' and 'no sense of industry or diligence. Theirs is a life of dissipation: eating, dancing, and carnal pleasure absorb their waking hours. For these reasons they have not escaped the common traits of tropic peoples: lewd customs, barbarity, laziness and debauchery.'[13]

A mishmash of ideas about evolution, eugenics and racial extinction served to justify foreign dominance. The first Resident Commissioner of the Solomon Islands was convinced that Melanesians were doomed. In the Solomons this view persisted. A representative of Lever Brothers was certain in 1923 that 'it would . . . tend towards perpetuating the breed, if it becomes associated and intermingled with another race'.[14] For fifty years, British governors had been arguing that Island populations could recover. This had inspired the British attempt to preserve Fijian communal life and sustained the first halting steps of governments to improve Islanders' health (see below). The influenza pandemic of 1918 was not encouraging. As we saw in chapter 7, it killed 4 per cent of Fiji Indians, 5.7 per cent of Fijians and no fewer than 20 per cent of Samoans. Nor was the 1931 census of the Solomons reassuring, revealing 93,000 Islanders instead of the expected 150,000. Evidence from Japanese Micronesia gave a mixed picture: increases in Saipan, Pohnpei and Palau between 1923 and 1933, no change in Chuuk and Jaluit, and a sharp fall in Yap. Overall, the Micronesian population remained almost static between the world wars, as did the Kanak population of

12 Johnston to Secretary, Department of Defence, 14 March 1919, Australian War Memorial, Ex German New Guinea Miscellaneous Reports, January–February 1920.
13 Peattie, *Nan'yo*, 113.
14 Quoted in Keesing and Corris, *Lightning Meets the West Wind*, 33.

New Caledonia. The first clear evidence of recovery came in the 1930s. A census of the Gilbert and Ellice Islands showed that the Islanders were increasing on almost every atoll, justifying a resettlement scheme which later took about 700 people to the empty Phoenix group. Another count established that the Cook Islander population of Rarotonga had more than doubled since 1895. Growth between 1921 and 1936 was considerable in several territories: the Western Samoans recovered quickly from 33,336 to 51,094; their kin in American Samoa grew from 7776 to 11,474; the Tongan population rose from 23,759 to 31,604; Guamanians increased from 14,090 to 20,047; and even the Fijian population jumped from 84,475 to 97,961. It became increasingly plausible to argue that administrations could improve the health of the population, and by 1950 the recovery had consigned extinctionism to the dustbin of discredited ideas.

THE ECONOMICS OF COLONIALISM

Colonialism regulated and promoted incorporation into the global economy, and fostered the exports on which governments depended for revenue. Village economies sustained the vast majority of Islanders, but the demands of the export economy increased in villages which were required to supply labour and cash crops, and the central issue of colonial policy was to decide how these sectors should interact.

The extent and form of incorporation depended, in the first place, on the extent of exposure to the West. Generally speaking, villagers in the east and north and on the coasts encountered outsiders far earlier than those in the west and in the mountains. The people of the Cook Islands and northern Marianas had become enthusiastic cash croppers and consumers of imports by the early twentieth century. Rarotonga had four cinemas in 1911 and, prefiguring trends elsewhere, migration to the centre from the outer islands began before World War I. In the 1920s Rarotongans were producing most of the bananas, oranges and tomatoes exported to New Zealand. Over the short period of German rule, many Carolinians abandoned their huts of woven matting for wooden dwellings, and Chamorros graduated from wooden to stone ones. So much food was being imported that the Germans intervened to prevent food dependency, a problem which did not affect most Islands until the 1980s. In order to 'limit the unjustifiably excessive importing of rice, meal and other kinds of food, to boost the industry of the natives and the production of the colony, and to make it independent of the outside world', the Germans required every household to plant a quarter of a hectare with food crops.[15] By the time Japan replaced Germany in the northern Marianas in 1914, its people were, in Western terms, the most sophisticated in the Pacific. The frontier of contact was still advancing into New Guinea in the 1930s.

15 Hardach, *König Kopra: Die Marianen unter deutscher Herrschaft, 1899–1914*, Stuttgart, 1990, 123, 164.

The extent and form of incorporation were determined, in the second place, by the general direction of policy. Colonial policy had to strike a balance between economic development and protecting the integrity of village life. The balance differed from power to power, from governor to governor, and over time. We focus for the moment on the colonisers, although policy could never be imposed without some regard to Islanders. Every colonial power had to decide: who was to own the land? who was to do the work? who was to supply the capital? what was to be the balance between the interests of Islanders and settlers? were the villages to be sources of wage labour or places of direct export production? how far was tradition to be preserved? These questions arose because colonialism was not merely the imposition of foreign rule but also the expansion of a capitalist economic order.

Japan saw the South Seas as a strategic asset where government and private enterprise should work together. Nowhere else was there such a close conjunction of state and private interests, nor such a confident relegation of Islanders to marginal status. The man who did most to develop Japanese Micronesia was Matsue Haruji, the founder of the Nan'yo Kohatsu or South Seas Development Company (Nanko). During the 1920s thousands of tenant farmers, mostly Okinawans, cleared the land and planted it with sugar. On Saipan and Tinian cane fields, sugar mills, railways, and distilleries manifested a prosperous industry which produced almost two-thirds as much sugar as Fiji in the late 1930s. By then the Chamorros and Carolinians, two-thirds of the population in 1920, had been swept aside by the flood of settlers to become a residual group of less than 10 per cent of the islands' inhabitants. The reasons for Matsue's success point to the conditions that all plantation companies needed: the government backed him to the hilt, giving cheap land, subsidies for planting, and low taxes. He had almost no competitors, and his Okinawan labour force were accustomed to working sugar.

More fitfully, the French also applied a policy of *mise en valeur*. In the hands of an energetic governor such as Georges Guyon in New Caledonia (1925–32), that meant roads and wharves in the interests of a settler economy. But Guyon was only one of twelve governors between the wars, and as governors came and went settlers complained of neglect. Apart from a few missionaries, no European doubted that the colony existed for the settlers. 'By what monstrous aberration do we continue to let the natives have more land than they can cultivate and than they need to live on?', a settler asked in 1928, expressing attitudes typical of his community.[16] Melanesians had become a minority and, especially after the 1917 rebellion, *cantonnement* confined them to reserves on the main island.

Australia was responsible for more subjects than all other powers put together. Still engaged in opening up their own country to whites, most Australians brought the same mentality to Papua and New Guinea. The golden years for planters in Papua came before World War I when the

16 Connell, *New Caledonia or Kanaky?*, 102.

territory beckoned settlers to a frontier where labour was cheap and prospects bright. Between 1906 and 1914 the acreage under cultivation by Europeans grew from 1500 to 44,447, jumping again to 62,162 by 1920. But the colonial economy stagnated and the area of plantations remained much the same twenty years later. The lieutenant-governor throughout was Hubert Murray. A keen proponent of European development at first, he came to see himself as a governor in the British mould with primary responsibilities to Papuans. The 'unpopularity of a Governor' with settlers, he said of himself, might be 'in direct proportion to his performance of his duty' towards the native people.[17] Australian domestic politics also hobbled Papua. Under the *Navigation Act*, copra for Europe or Asia had to travel via Sydney, nearly 2000 miles in the wrong direction.

The other territory, New Guinea, flourished far more than Papua—not as a result of policy but because of gold, discovered on Mount Kaindi in 1926. The discovery attracted hundreds of Australian prospectors and thousands of New Guinean labourers. In their wake came the companies which transformed a rush into an industry, the mainstay of the territory's revenues during the 1930s. Murray's style differed from that of his counterparts in New Guinea. He liked to think that 'the attitude of residents to natives is much more friendly and cordial in Papua'[18] and that his was a more humanitarian administration with a greater interest in welfare. Murray exaggerated the differences, but they did exist. Australians in New Guinea, according to a careful observer, saw ' "bashing the coons" as the only sound basis of race relations' and regarded the approach in Papua as namby-pambyism.[19]

Uniquely, New Zealanders made the colonial state the principal owner of the productive assets of the modern economy. Rather than selling German plantations to their own nationals, as the Australians did in New Guinea, the administration retained them as 'Reparation Estates' and used the proceeds to defray the costs of government. Any contribution this system might have made to Samoans' welfare was lost in conflict. From the purely economic point of view, nationalisation did nothing for Western Samoa because it was not accompanied by a strong push for development of the Japanese kind.

British colonial governments desperately needed tax revenue from plantations and mines, and the accepted wisdom was that colonies should provide investment opportunities for whites and 'civilise natives' in the process. Yet development was always to be balanced against the interests of Islanders. British Pacific colonies, by contrast with the Japanese, were remote outposts. Here, where little was at stake, principles of trusteeship were allowed a place in calculations, rapacious settlers kept in check and attempts made to protect villagers through paternal legislation. In the Gilbert and Ellice Islands, a colony once described as 'unique in its isolation and lack of potentialities',

17 J. H. P. Murray, *Review of Australian Administration in Papua from 1907 to 1920*, Port Moresby, 1920, xi.
18 West (ed.), *Selected Letters of Hubert Murray*, 162.
19 Mair, *Australia in New Guinea*, 15.

paternalism ran riot in regulations addressing every minute of the Islanders' day and every aspect of behaviour. British officials thought that progress was what all Islanders needed in the long term, but they also belonged to an intellectual tradition which alerted them to the pitfalls of 'progress' in a colonial situation. Nowhere was this more so than in Fiji.

Fiji

The system had been modified by the 1920s but was essentially unaltered from the formula devised by Governor Gordon and Thurston fifty years before, subscribing to the paramountcy of Fijian interests. Fijians retained 83 per cent of Fiji's land. Under the Governor as the Supreme Chief there were initially thirteen or fourteen Fijian *Roko Tui* or governors of provinces, all receiving salaries at European levels, and under them were *buli* or local chiefs with rights to levy their people for food and labour, and at the base of the pyramid of indirect rule were the *turaga ni koro* or village headmen responsible for good order. The British invented a somewhat arbitrary version of Fijian tradition. The 'traditional' landowning unit, the *mataqali*, was a Bauan idea applied to the rest of Fiji, for example. But only by establishing a consistent 'tradition' could indirect rule and Fijian landownership become legally enforceable. While it appeared to be merely preserving tradition, the native administration was in fact a form of modernisation.

The British settlement in Fiji prompted sharply different assessments. Some saw the separate Fijian administration and Fijian control of land as impediments to progress. The settlers were disgusted to discover that Fiji was not to be a white man's country. After the turn of the century a reforming governor, Everard im Thurn, thought that the social and political status of Fijians was 'extraordinary and anomalous' and that the scales must be tipped in favour of settlers. For a few years he released Fijian lands and more than 100,000 acres were sold. He was the hero of those Europeans who 'despaired of Fijians ever being accorded the full personal liberty of British subjects, the liberty above all else to sell their lands and become a free-floating pool of labour'.[20] But the Colonial Office blocked further changes to landownership after a campaign led by Gordon himself. Fijians would retain most of the land. They would be saved from themselves and from the meretricious attractions of life outside the obligations and restrictions of the village. With Indian immigrants in the modern sector and Fijians in villages, colonial society split along ethnic lines, an arrangement applauded by the British and the chiefs as protecting Fijian tradition from destructive individualism.

Successive administrators responded to the need for labour and eroded the Gordon–Thurston system piecemeal. From 1912 a Fijian married man whose employer could convince a magistrate that his dependants were provided for could leave his village and enter waged

20 Macnaught, *Fijian Colonial Experience*.

employment. Recruiters were then free to enter the villages and inaugurate a variant of the circular labour migration found in the colonies to the west. Some Fijian women simply ignored their chiefs; they departed to work in saloons, and found European and Chinese lovers and protectors. The exodus was limited, with fewer than one in ten Fijians employed as wage labourers in the 1920s, but it contributed to the decline in village housing as the 'substantial, high-built heavily thatched houses of old Fiji' yielded to 'uninsulated, ill-drained ovens of wood and iron'. Another deviation released villagers from communal obligations, to become individual farmers like the Indians, growing sugar for the Colonial Sugar Refining Company (CSR) and other cash crops. Governor Sir Murchison Fletcher saw 'no reason why, with sympathetic guidance, the Fijian should not make as good a peasant proprietor as the Indian'. A variety of exemption schemes produced about 700 Fijian cane farmers by the end of the 1930s. Hundreds became successful producers on their own account.

Taken as a whole, however, the experiment in individualism failed. Chiefs opposed it because it weakened their authority. On some Fijian cane farms the hidden workforce consisted of Indian sharecroppers. On others, crops were left in the field when Fijians could endure the isolation no longer or when—as in Nadi in 1934—villages were consumed by football fever. According to Ratu Lala Sukuna, the articulate defender of Fijian neo-traditionalism,

> some natives do well as individual growers when a market is assured; others succeed for a time and then, finding regular work irksome, either return to their villages or become rolling stones; some again stay on to escape social obligations, producing barely enough for their own requirements while living in hovels. In sickness and in old age all return for aid to the village community.[21]

The crux of the issue from the conservative point of view was put by Governor Philip Mitchell, who argued that 'Even if the exempted man . . . earned more money for himself with less obligations to his fellows, nothing would be proved which has not already been proved by the melancholy condition to which the same philosophy has brought Europe.' Like Gordon before him, Mitchell saw individualism not as the path to liberty but as a new bondage where Fijians would lose the security, community and sense of identity provided by the village. He hoped he had 'heard the last of this lunacy and that it is generally recognised that the village community is the basis of Fijian society and that for the Government to intervene to destroy it is stupid, if not indeed wicked'.[22]

Meantime Indians were grasping opportunities. Sugar production was transformed in the 1920s as the CSR converted its plantations into 10-acre farms which were leased to Indian tenants. The company made the change because indentured labour stopped in 1920, and in order to shift risks to the Indians, who now had an urgent personal interest in

21 Macnaught, *Fijian Colonial Experience*, 102–3, 138, 152–3.
22 Quoted in Lal, *Broken Waves*, 71.

working from dawn to dusk. Company and growers signed contracts covering production, price and delivery, but the advantage was all on the company's side. Indians went on strike in 1920 and again the following year. On the second occasion the government mobilised 250 Fijian special constables to suppress strikers in western Viti Levu. The government of India commented that this practice 'has tended to increase their contempt for the Indians whom they were called upon to repress. At the same time, the Indians have been irritated against the Fijians.'[23] And as Indians became more assertive, the Fijians would look to the British for protection, seeing the Deed of Cession as a guarantee of their immemorial rights to the land.

By 1936 seven out of every ten Indians had been born in Fiji, and their numbers—85,000—had risen by 25,000 since 1921. They constituted almost 43 per cent of Fiji's population and the percentage was rising. Indians rose early, laboured long, ate simply, and achieved a modest prosperity on rented land, all the while resenting the fact that Europeans would not grant them equal status. Gujarati free immigrants worked as tailors, launderers, jewellers, merchants and moneylenders to other Indians. To the alarm of chiefs, Indians sought political representation and opposed the communal franchise which organised representation, such as it was, on a racial basis. They called for a non-racial common roll for all British subjects as the basis for progress towards representative democracy. The Indian leader S. B. Patel saw an offence to his people in the denial of political rights and in liberal democracy he saw a charter of freedom for all British subjects. If there were a common roll, 'there would not be much friction between the races in the political field and we should be pulling together for the good and welfare of Fiji as a whole, instead of pulling against each other'.[24] Ratu Sukuna thought there could be 'nothing spiritually very wrong with a system that maintains the old and sick without resort to homes for the aged and schemes of social security'.[25] Some colonial officials defended Fijian tradition, others said it hindered the progress of Fijians, but all opposed a common roll or democracy. Politics became three-cornered, with an alliance between the British and Fijians made inevitable by Fijian fears of the newcomers. As one community advanced more quickly in the modern sector than the other, tensions grew in the circumstances of racial separation which the Gordon system inevitably fostered.

Historians differ in evaluating colonial Fiji. On one side are those who see the Gordon–Thurston system, for all its imperfections, as a triumph of trusteeship which saved the Fijians from marginalisation. By this account the village was a haven, ensuring that all would be cared for in sickness and old age, and providing a framework for the feasts, songs, exchanges and pageantry that gave meaning to Fijians' lives; if this security cost personal freedom in the Western sense, that was a price worth paying and part of Fijian tradition anyway. On the other side are those who argue that the communal system benefited chiefs

23 Quoted in Gillion, *The Fiji Indians*, 60.
24 *Ibid.*, 136.
25 Macnaught, *Fijian Colonial Experience*, 70.

rather than commoners, and that to protect Fijians from modernity was also to deprive them of its opportunities. On this view, the system left Fijians radically under-prepared to compete. Posing as protectors of Fijians, the British—it is argued—were mainly concerned to protect themselves against multi-racial democracy, and encouraged the sense of racial difference.

LABOUR

The Fiji system was devised to solve the problem of labour without sacrificing economic development or Fijians themselves. Elsewhere the labour problem proved less tractable and the solutions showed less concern for villagers. More than anything else, the shortage of labour limited economic development. By the 1920s the development of the Islands—the form in which each would become a tiny part of the global economy—had set into a clear pattern. Pre-war fantasies about a wide variety of crops dissolved into the sober recognition that, because of labour shortages, most planters could harvest only copra. Copra was exported from every colony and most labourers were employed in producing it. In that sense copra was king, but plantations alone could not build successful export economies. Phosphate, gold and nickel came to the rescue of several economies (chapter 7). Colonial authorities treated their phosphate islands as jewels in the crown where they could make exceptions and overlook the finer points of the law in the interests of revenue. By the mid-1930s Angaur phosphate had overtaken copra as the second most important export of Japanese Micronesia, after sugar. Nickel was the foundation of the colonial economy of New Caledonia, while gold mines boosted New Guinea and Fiji. Sugar underpinned Fiji's colonial economy but gold grew in importance and overtook sugar in value during World War II.

In most places labour was scarce because land was plentiful and remained in the hands of its owners. In these circumstances only two solutions to the labour problem ever existed: employers could either recruit labourers locally or import them from Asia. The diversity and prosperity of Japanese Micronesia rested squarely on the labour of Okinawan and Japanese workers, but employers in most other colonies had lost the Asian option. The British government, not wishing to antagonise Indian nationalists, blocked labour migration to Fiji or anywhere else and disallowed the recruiting of Chinese for most of its colonies as well. The White Australia policy barred most Asians from Papua and New Guinea. The benefits of cheap fertilisers prompted exceptions for Banaba and Nauru, where the British Phosphate Commission imported Chinese labourers from Hong Kong. Phosphate workforces were all variations on the theme of Asian and Islander labour: Chinese and Gilbertese on Ocean Island, Chinese alone on Nauru, Micronesians on Angaur, Polynesians and Vietnamese on Makatea. In Western Samoa, too, Chinese indentured labourers on six-year contracts, forbidden to marry Samoan women, continued to do most of the work on the 'reparation estates'. The 14,535 Asians of New Caledonia—Javanese, Vietnamese, Japanese and Chinese—briefly outnumbered the Europeans before leaving in large numbers during the Great Depression.

The only remaining option in British and Australian colonies was to recruit young men from the villages. The 'labour trade', which brought Islanders to Queensland, Fiji, New Caledonia and Samoa, had given way to controlled systems within the borders of colonies. These 'internal' labour trades in Papua, New Guinea, the Solomons and the New Hebrides accounted for much larger numbers than the classic labour trade, with an estimated 280,000 indentures being signed in New Guinea alone between the world wars. Recruiting and indenture became central institutions, and government officers spent much of their time supervising labour regulations, reading contracts to recruits in Tok Pisin or through an interpreter, showing them how to sign by making marks, ensuring that the contract included the names of the village, district and sub-district, checking for tropical ulcers, and so on. At the end of a three-year indenture the recruit would collect his deferred pay, usually at the rate of 3 shillings a month or 60 per cent of total pay, and spend it on the leather belts, shorts, laplaps, combs, talcum powder, razor blades, matches and tobacco that went into the tradebox which he carried triumphantly home.

The government in New Guinea did what it could to stimulate the flow of young men. Its annual head tax of 10 shillings levied on able-bodied men was designed to muster labour, and indentured labourers were exempted. Tax patrols gave *kiaps* the opportunity to check that villages were sending young men to plantations. Policy and practice were invariably different, however, and in many places villagers supplied labourers on their own terms, rather as they had done during the old labour trade. Recruiters had to cultivate local Big Men,

> as they were completely dependent on the cooperation of the local natives— and that meant the headmen, who were intelligent and could be resentful and jealous of the interloper because he usurped their position as 'number one bigpela men'. If they were not 'in' with the headmen, by domination, or grease, or payment, or a combination of all three, they would not get anywhere—or anything. It was just like politics, and just as dirty. In addition to any local methods of pressure the natives could bring against the interloper, there was always the *gauman* to complain to. And the *gauman* was usually on their side, and often with good reason.[26]

In explaining why men signed on, Europeans usually attributed familiar and individual motives to recruits, who were said to 'need the poll-tax, or to have a nagging woman to get away from for a while, or be too mixed up with someone else's, or to accept the direction of one of the big men'.[27] Motives are better understood in cultural terms. While villagers signed on to earn trade, they also wanted to discover the love

26 O'Neill, *Up From South*, 56.
27 *Ibid.*, 58.

magic of other villagers, or assist their kin group, or they saw their name on a piece of paper and thought they had no choice. In the New Hebrides, Christian villagers on west Aoba, encouraged by missionaries, decided in 1911 'to abandon the *road belong kastom* in favour of the *road belong money*' and to grow copra on their own plantations rather than offer themselves as labourers. Plantation labour by the 1920s was something that only inland *kastom* people did, defending their traditions and interests against their Christian enemies on the coasts by creating 'roads of alliance' with plantations.[28]

The distinguishing feature of labour migration was circularity. Villagers left home for the period of indenture, usually three years, and returned—sometimes to stay and sometimes to 'make paper' (sign on) for another three years. Most were men, although a few women accompanied their husbands. The plantation system never stabilised workforces in permanent settlements. Villagers did not become dependent on wages, and the colonial era did not bequeath a politics of class. Instead, the village remained intact, a hidden subsidy for wages which were far too meagre to maintain labourers' wives and children. In effect, the labour of women in gardening and tending pigs paid for the reproduction of the labour force.

Most Islanders became wage labourers only temporarily. Many also participated in the cash economy as village producers. Islanders produced more than half the copra from Fiji, three-quarters of it from Western Samoa and French Polynesia, and almost all of it from Tonga, the Gilbert and Ellice Islands, the Cook Islands, Niue, American Samoa and Guam, where the site of production was the village grove of palms rather than the ordered lines of the plantation. South Seas copra had a poor reputation because so much of it came from villages which lacked the knowledge, incentive and facilities to improve its quality.

Ownership of land and circular labour migration gave Islanders choices. They could cut copra when prices were high, they could work on plantations and mines when cash was needed for tax or the church, and they could depend on their gardens and fishing at other times. When copra prices plummeted with the Great Depression, Solomon Islanders ceased producing copra and grew more food. 'We find to our astonishment', a trader said, 'that the native can and is doing without our wares and to a much larger extent, and in a much shorter time than we thought possible, in view of the years it took to educate him up to buying what he did.'[29] To many Europeans this independence was evidence of inferiority. An official in Fiji, observing the people of Lau, thought that even two generations would not suffice to 'see a nation of careless children changed to a nation of workers. And they will have to be quick, for the child-like races cannot survive the stress of modern competition.'[30] But Islanders did not want to become permanently

---

28 Ron Adams, 'Plantation Labour in Vanuatu', in Moore, Leckie and Munro (eds), *Labour in the South Pacific*, 142; and Bonnemaison, *The Tree and the Canoe*.
29 Bennett, *Wealth of the Solomons*, 243.
30 Young, 'Lau: A Windward Perspective', 173–4.

bound to a job. The manager of a plantation on the Witu Islands in New Guinea reported in 1934 that he had failed to persuade twenty-two 'boys' to re-sign. 'I have noticed previously that it is always hard to persuade labour to make the third contract.'[31] The best sources of labourers were in the bush where people were less sophisticated and had no other means of earning cash or trade. Villagers with options were a nightmare for recruiters.

Europeans had no desire to assist Islanders to compete in the cash economy. Settlers in New Caledonia complained bitterly when officials encouraged Kanaks to grow coffee, but the coastal communities persisted and were producing over 500 tonnes by the end of the 1930s, enough to earn higher cash incomes than any other Melanesians. To the consternation of settlers in New Britain, Tolai entrepreneurs began building and operating copra driers in the 1930s to handle their own produce. The Planters' Association complained of the 'undue haste with which the economic independence of the natives . . . has been encouraged by Administrative activity'. As a result it had become 'practically impossible to obtain local indentured labour for work in those areas'.[32] On Karkar Island in New Guinea, two Lutheran mission teachers, Mileng and Yas, planted coconuts, recruited schoolboys to work in the plantation and tried their hands at cash cropping European-style in the 1930s.[33] A few Solomon Islanders, on the Langalanga and Lau lagoons, were lent money by Burns Philp to buy boats. Most such attempts were blocked by Europeans who saw no place for the villager as a planter, trader or storekeeper. Colonial ideology and regulation alike conspired to keep 'the native' in his place—as a labourer.

The heart of the policy dilemma in Melanesia, except in New Caledonia, was that village production would flourish only at the expense of plantations. Hubert Murray said it was no part of his policy to convert Papuans from 'peasant producers into a landless proletariat', and his Native Plantations Ordinance of 1918 compelled villagers to plant coconut palms and develop cash crops, with the government taking half the produce. Murray envisaged Papuan plantations flourishing alongside European ones, but the logic of plantation colonies dependent on internal labour—even where the Governor put himself on the side of the colonised people—was that village production would be short of labour. Papuans tended to see Murray's plantation ordinance as just another imposition, a view encouraged by the fact that they could exempt themselves from tax by working on village plantations. Murray's scheme did not transform Papua into a village-based export economy.

31 R. P. Mills to Manager, Islands Agencies Department, 20 December 1934, 'Reports Meto Estate Witu Group 1931–41', Burns Philp Archives, Sydney.
32 Planters' Association, Report, 30 June 1938, Australian Archives, A 1782 C 86: Information supplied by Colin Newbury.
33 McSwain, *The Past and Future People*, 67.

THE POLITICS OF COLONIALISM

Two kinds of politics characterised Island territories. Settlers every-where assumed that they alone deserved a say in affairs, since they, not the Islanders, were doing the developing and taking the risks. Settler politics took the form of endless disputes with governors over labour and taxes. Settlers in New Caledonia could elect representatives to a General Council which advised the Governor, but chafed at having no deputy of their own in the National Assembly in Paris: New Caledonia 'is vegetating under the dictatorship of the Ministry of Colonies . . . Will we have a député?', a settler complained in the 1930s. Settlers in Papua were so dissatisfied with their Governor that a group telegrammed King George V warning of a 'serious and dangerous uprising' of whites against him. Most British or British-derived dependencies had Legis-lative Councils which offered limited representation to the tiny Euro-pean communities. In all cases the government members retained the majority. In Fiji, for example, the Legislative Council initially had token representation of the 'native' communities, two Fijian members from 1904 and one Indian from 1916. By 1937, after Indian campaigns for democracy, an enlarged Legislative Council of thirty-one included five Fijians, all nominated by the Governor, and five Indians, two nominated and three elected. In the Japanese Mandate the Governor's word was absolute and unaffected by any representation.

The second kind of politics centred on foreign rule of Islands societies. In broad terms, colonial rule could be indirect or direct, though these concepts should be understood as two ends of a con-tinuum. If it was indirect, as in Fiji, the administration ruled through existing forms of government and depended on traditional elites who received the backing of the government. The Kingdom of Tonga preserved an indigenous government under British supervision. The Privy Council had a Tongan majority, and Tongans elected their own Parliament under their own constitution. The Samoans' elaborate system of government not only survived the coming of New Zealanders but successfully competed with them. The *ariki* or chiefs of the Cook Islands played an influential role in the Island Councils. In the Gilbert and Ellice Islands the Native Governments—a blend of traditional and mission governments—became the enforcers of British regulations. Indirect rule was the outcome of accommodations.

Direct rule was the colonial response to weaker indigenous govern-ments, sometimes hierarchical but typically not. It was characteristic of Japanese rule in Micronesia and of all colonial rule in Melanesia. Colonial authorities appointed agents but gave them little or no responsibility to act on their own initiative. The administration of justice typically extended metropolitan laws and court procedures for cases involving settlers, but subjected Islanders to arbitrary 'Native Regula-tions' administered brusquely by administrative officers. Almost all Kanaks, for example, were subjects rather than citizens of France and fell under the provisions of regulations known as the *Indigènat*. Kanaks were confined to reservations unless they had permission to leave, compelled to perform forced labour and, in town, subjected to strict curfews.

Designations differed—'village headmen' in the Solomons were 'village constables' in Papua and '*luluais*' in New Guinea—but everywhere their task was to enforce regulations. Colonial governments wanted villagers to dig latrines, build pig fences, maintain bush tracks and the government rest-house, pay tax, offer young men as recruits, and bury the dead rather than leaving them, as was the custom in some places, to decompose on platforms. A paramount *luluai*, Josef Selembe, explained in 1934 that the *kiap* had given him the task of meting out punishment to the boys and labourers on the mission stations; he had to report bad cases to the *kiap*, and he also had to arrange things with labour recruiters. *Luluais* in Australian New Guinea were responsible for the 'village book', where the *kiap* recorded births, deaths, absences and tax payments. A typical village book entry (from New Britain in 1935) noted that head tax had been collected, 'four defaulters but tax paid for them by other Natives. Village surroundings clean, but majority of housing the worst seen so far. Much instruction issued re housing.'[34] The new hierarchy elevated some men over others in untraditional ways. Some appointed chiefs became despots, knowing that they could call on the district officer and his police for support. Jonathan Fifi'i, from Malaita, recalled that the 'Headmen taunted and insulted the people, with the power the government had given to them. The government gave rifles to all the Headmen, gave them handcuffs . . . They beat and whipped people.'[35] Other chiefs were mere figureheads, put forward for appointment so as to inhibit the interference of government in village affairs.

Japanese rule paralleled British and Australian rule in the Solomons, Papua and New Guinea. The *sosoncho* or village chief was a traditional leader, with legitimacy in the ranked societies of those islands, and in theory his task was to give orders to the *soncho* or village headman. The Japanese appointed both, and in practice both did what they were told by the nearest policeman: collect taxes, report breaches of regulations, and assist with census-taking. 'The Japanese policeman gave the orders', a Pohnpeian chief recalled, 'I was forced to see that they were carried out.'[36] *Junkei* or 'native constables' were the equivalents of the Melanesian police, though with greater responsibilities. What distinguished Japanese rule was its intensity. Where British or Australian colonial officers were counted in scores, Japanese came in hundreds.

People on the frontier submitted through the power of the gun, the chance to enlist allies, the advantages of being at peace. The *kiap* with his line of police was open to manipulation as one village incited him against the next. A *kiap* explained in 1917 why he had taken his police to raid a village in Manus, New Guinea:

34 Village book for Kainiaua (Laubori) in the Talasea District, New Britain, entry for 14 June 1935 by George Ellis, New Guinea Collection, University of Papua New Guinea.
35 Keesing and Corris, *Lightning Meets the West Wind*, 119.
36 Peattie, *Nan'yo*, 76.

> For the past three weeks the Natives of Nandra on the North Western end of Manus have been complaining of the Inland Natives raiding and destroying their crops, and last Monday the Tultul Sinabaro, an ex Police Boy from Kokopo, reported that they had threatened to kill him and the Kiap also if he came that way.
>
> Seeing that this end of the Island is seldom visited except by an occasional recruiter . . . I felt bound for the purpose of retaining their limited confidence to take action and accordingly started on an Expedition on Wednesday last.

The *kiap* 'rushed the place' before dawn and dispensed rough-and-ready justice:

> In a few minutes police boys were in possession of each house, but some of the Kanakas made a rush for their spears. I had previously instructed the interpreter to call out as soon as we reach the place and pacify them. This he did and I am thankful to say saved any bloodshed. To my agreeable astonishment we had taken them entirely unawares and succeeded in capturing the whole village. They were soon mustered into one large house where there were no spears and a police boy put on guard at each door till daylight enabled me to hold Court.
>
> At about 6.30 a.m. they were lined up, 29 men in all and the Tultul of Nandra picked out the three leading culprits whom, with the aid of the interpreter, I tried there and then.
>
> Two were found guilty and sentenced to six months' imprisonment whilst a third was acquitted.
>
> . . . My chief object in the undertaking was to bring in sufficient of the tribe to eventually leaven the district with boys who could speak pidgin, but with justice I could only rake in two prisoners and seeing that it was the first time that Europeans had visited the place, and that it would in all probability be some time before it was again visited I decided to call for recruits. Five promptly came forward and were taken on for two years. I then dismissed the line and allowed them to intermingle with the Police boys while I had a conversation with the Chief, an intelligent old warrior as kanakas go, shortly afterwards five more came forward to recruit, but I did not feel disposed to take them on . . .[37]

These themes recurred: the *kiap* imprisoned two villagers, relying on an interpreter and the advice of Sinabaro, the man who had prompted the raid; he saw himself as 'capturing' the village; his authority rested on the gun; and, in this intimidating atmosphere, he asked young men to recruit. From the Melanesians' point of view the Europeans were a powerful language-group who could be attracted as allies; from the Europeans' point of view, 'friendly natives' offered the chance to extend control. The political setting was the mosaic of language-groups and rivalries, systems of international relations in microcosm. The physical setting was one of the most rugged in the world. As a consequence, colonial government came slowly.

Commonly, the real authority in a patrol was the most senior New Guinean policeman. He taught young patrol officers how to command, and discovered how much latitude each would tolerate. In 1938, for

---

37 H. S. Foulkes, D.O., to Pethebridge, 17 March 1917, Australian War Memorial, Ex German New Guinea Correspondence, April 1917.

example, *kiap* John Black, twelve police and sixty carriers walked through much of New Guinea towards Telefolmin on the Dutch border.[38] They were attacked by villagers, struck down by disease, and could find no way through the mountains and gorges of the far western Highlands; so they pitched camp to allow themselves to recover. In the sick camp, the police debated whether to abandon the *kiap*. One of the two experienced policemen advocated staying with him. Another was a notable sorcerer, on whose magic the others relied. He proposed to Black that they abandon the carriers and return to Mount Hagen. Black refused—but for several nights slept with a loaded revolver, fearing that the police might shoot him. The issue was resolved only when the carriers recovered and the patrol limped into Telefolmin. Such men as these joined the police 'to get on in life'. Usually the sons or grandsons of fight-leaders, but denied the chance of emulating them, they enlisted to escape from the poverty, ignominy and celibacy which might be their lot in the pacified villages.[39] A career in uniform promised power, marriage and security. When a police post was manned by a single policeman (common practice throughout the New Guinea Highlands during the process of 'pacification'), he must necessarily involve himself in local politics, usually forming an alliance by marrying into a leading clan. In these circumstances, visiting *kiaps* understood the local situation only in terms of the policeman's own perceptions and interests.

Some Islands were isolated places where individuals imposed their authority through sheer force of personality and are still remembered for their idiosyncrasies. Particular missionaries and officers built little empires. Arthur Grimble, a District Commissioner and then Resident Commissioner in the Gilbert and Ellice Islands from 1916 to 1932, was a renowned ethnographer but also a paternalist. The Gilbertese, he thought, were 'children, and at bottom very well-disposed children'. He governed like the headmaster of a boarding-school. Under his *Regulations for the Good Order and Cleanliness of the Gilbert and Ellice Islands* of 1930, a bell was sounded at 9 o'clock every evening in the villages, 'and all persons visiting the latrines after that time were obliged to carry lamps':

> Public dancing was permitted only on Wednesdays, Saturdays and public holidays between 6 p.m. and 9 p.m. All males attending dances were to carry lamps; children could not attend; 'shameful gestures and movements of the body', magic rituals, and 'unclean games' were prohibited. Private dancing practice, with a maximum of four participants, was permitted only on Mondays and Thursdays between 6 p.m. and 9 p.m. Eating in a sleeping house, or sleeping in an eating house, was forbidden.

Feasts to mark every rite of passage, from birth and betrothal to death, required the permission of the Native Governments who were responsible to Grimble, and competitive feasting was prohibited. The Islanders complained, and the regulations were changed some years after Grimble departed.[40]

38 Gammage, 'Police and Power'.
39 Kituai, 'Innovation and Intrusion'.
40 Grimble, *Tungaru Traditions*, xxii–xxiii; Faaniu *et al.*, *Tuvalu*, 133; and Macdonald, *Cinderellas of the Empire*, 127.

HEALTH AND EDUCATION

As colonial governments built revenues, they evolved beyond the supervision of village-based societies, taking responsibility for the health and the schooling of the Native and his Wife. In both spheres they were preceded by missionaries, who continued to provide services under government supervision.

To avert the Islanders' extinction demanded more than the untrained attention of religious. Foreigners flourished in most Islands, but throughout Melanesia they suffered so acutely from malaria that the colonial project was threatened. Together with the calamitous mortality rates of indentured labourers everywhere, and the fact that doctors and nurses died, health became the first priority of colonial administration. Robert Koch himself, the creator of germ theory, was despatched to the German colonies to bring the good news of quinine to embattled settlers.

Governments adopted widely divergent strategies. In New Zealand, Australia and Hawai'i, doctors organised themselves into professional associations which gained legal monopolies in care-giving, while government measures ensured clean water, pure food, sanitation—and quarantine to repel plague and other infections. Maori doctors and nurses helped to extend hygienist measures into the countryside, such that Maori were probably the healthiest Islanders by the 1920s. Public health measures and rising standards of living permitted settlers to live longer and healthier lives. As native Hawaiians became urbanised—almost half were urban in 1920—they derived a small share of these benefits. By 1940 they enjoyed a higher life expectancy (over 50 years) than any other Islanders.[41] In sharp contrast, Aboriginal Australians, in squatter camps outside the towns, or in remote rural settings, endured the health costs of dispossessed peoples everywhere.

In the settler colonies, immigrants consulted fee-for-service doctors, nurses in private hospitals, pharmacists and midwives, while the government supervised therapeutic practices and provided for indigents. Many fewer options were available to sick people in the Islands. Neither governments nor missionaries approved of folk-medicine or the 'sorcerers' who embodied folk-wisdom. The first government doctor in Fiji—William MacGregor—arrived in the aftermath of measles. Much of his attention was devoted to quarantine measures, but there and later in Papua he recognised that clean water and sanitation were essential. Having no resources other than his own skills and injunctions, however, he made little impact. Dr S. M. Lambert in 1920 described the Papuan medical service as:

> an excellent Chief Medical Officer with nothing to work with, a Judgment Day prophet in charge of the local hospital, and one physician for each of three far-flung districts. These five, with a couple of nurses and two European dispensers, were supposed to service the 90,000 square miles . . . This was typical of the medical situation over the South Pacific.[42]

41 Kunitz, *Disease and Social Diversity*, ch. 3.
42 Lambert, *A Yankee Doctor in Paradise*, 17.

Doctors were supplemented by European Medical Assistants in many colonies: usually ex-servicemen who had learned military first aid. Until the creation of penicillin and sulfa drugs in the 1940s, sick people recovered not because they were doctored but because they were nursed. The most glaring shortage therefore was not doctors but nurses. They worked mainly on mission stations, since governments were often reluctant to allow white women to work with Island men.

The formalisation of 'tropical health' in the 1890s gave colonial doctors a clearer sense of purpose. Institutes of tropical medicine in Western Europe, the United States and Australia circulated scientific information and policy advice. In the colonies, the homes and offices of colonial personnel and planters were located away from stagnant water, which was drained whenever possible; but the main thrust of policy was to impose international quarantines and racial segregation, protecting each 'race' from the diseases of the others. Medical science therefore reinforced the racism which informed colonisers and infused their policy prescriptions.

For colonial governments, the highest priority was to protect colonists and invigorate labourers. Small hospitals sprang up for white patients, tended by white nurses and visited by the doctor. Lock-hospitals incarcerated Islanders afflicted with venereal diseases. Labourers were inspected before and after indenture. Early in the century European researchers identified polished rice as the immediate cause of beri-beri, and devised diets which plantation managers were urged to adopt. Otherwise medical science offered little hope to Islanders, who sensibly avoided the patrols seeking carriers of leprosy or venereal diseases. Medical services failed to arrest depopulation from introduced infections, from the expansion of malaria, and from (for example) tobacco and polished rice. Mercifully, doctors had largely abandoned the practice of bleeding. The commonest treatment was purging, used in many circumstances including the widespread colonial disease of malingering, and in cases of dysentery, where it was almost certainly counterproductive.

Targets of opportunity cropped up. Arsenical injections proved effective in curing yaws, and the injections—easily administered by paramedics—became immensely popular. During the 1910s a curious campaign followed the arrival of the Rockefeller Foundation, seeking to induce governments to create departments of public health, by funding campaigns against hookworm. Hookworm was hardly a serious problem, yet Rockefeller subsidies persuaded several colonies to embark on campaigns. After several years of administering nauseating chenopodium, Dr Lambert concluded that it was ineffective. Happily for his crusade, carbon tetrachloride proved more effective. In these ways much of the limited resources of colonial medicine was committed to marginal activities. The real benefit was, as the foundation had hoped, the development of coherent health plans by permanent public health workers.

One reason for staff shortages was the cost of white professionals. The problem was overcome partly by the dedication of mission personnel, who usually learned the language of their patients, and acquired some knowledge of living conditions. Missions were the only source of nursing care, and (unlike governments) they attended to obstetrics and to women generally. As missionaries caught up with Western medicine they became increasingly effective. Colonial governments also trained Islanders, at first casually, such as the few days' training given to *heil tultuls* in German New Guinea, before they returned to their villages to report epidemics. However, from 1889 the Fiji administration gave formal training and certification for Native Medical Practitioners, and from 1929 most Pacific colonial governments collaborated to fund a Central Medical School in Suva teaching forty students at a time. The Great Depression made it increasingly necessary to train islanders as cheap therapists, and the school was well supplied with young men. (New Guinea's military administrator wanted to send students, but was vetoed by doctors in Australia who insisted that New Guineans were intellectually incapable.) The Papuan Chief Medical Officer trained boys himself, in Motu and English, then arranged a special course at the University of Sydney. Like the Native Medical Practitioners, they were ancillary staff, making rural patrols for hookworm or yaws and seeking out lepers and venereal carriers, or working in base hospitals under supervision. In no case were indigenous health workers accounted the equals of white therapists, even when their training entitled them to recognition. All Medical Assistants and most other Islanders employed in public health were men, although Fijian women were trained as midwives and nurses (see below). This pattern mirrored white therapies, whereby male doctors supervised female nurses in circumscribed roles with wide responsibilities but no formal power.

THE NATIVE MOTHER

Like the Native himself, the Native Mother was an invention of the colonial imagination. Some colonial administrations, worried by Islander birthrates and infant mortality, concluded that the survival of the Native depended essentially on the Native's Mother. This line of argument was best developed in Fiji where Fijians' numbers continued to fall even after twenty years under a system which was supposed to ensure their survival. In 1896 a commission of inquiry published its detailed report on this perplexing question (the Decrease Report). Birthrates were high, but official figures suggested that nearly half of all Fijian infants died before their first birthdays. A central thesis of the report—which the Governor and his commissioners stated more starkly in other contexts—was that the decrease was due to bad mothering. The Native Mother was born.

This colonial conception formed the basis for many measures over the next fifty years. The Native Mother was racially theorised as lacking maternal instinct, which led supposedly to abortion, infanticide and neglect of children. Christianity and British rule were believed to have swept away customs which had evolved to ensure that she cared for her offspring in the absence of any instinctual imperative. She was also described as ignorant, superstitious, in the thrall of traditional mid-wives, and dirty. In some respects her creators adapted the stereotype of the Working-class Mother, held responsible for racial decay in England and elsewhere at the time.

One of the first measures, Native Regulation 5 of 1892, introduced while the commission of inquiry was sitting, required Fijian magistrates to investigate all stillbirths (a category which in practice included mis-carriages) and the deaths of all infants under the age of one. The stated object was to discover grounds on which the mother could be prose-cuted for abortion, infanticide or neglect; and it was hoped that the prospect of a magisterial inquiry would deter mothers from harming their children.

This testimony by Maramanitabua reveals many typical features. She was brought before the Native Stipendiary Magistrate in Colo East following the death of her infant son:

> My child Lewadau was five months old when he came down with whooping cough last month and died on 2/3/93. When he was sick I took great care of him and made the right Fijian medicines but they were no use. In the time when he was suckling he suckled well. When I was pregnant I took great care of my pregnancy and I didn't carry heavy loads or do a lot of weeding. I always rested from some of the women's work when I was pregnant. My husband and I have a loving marriage, we don't get angry with each other. Then my first child died in the epidemic—the epidemic last month. I have had four children, three are dead and one boy still lives.

Any fault of the mother is hard to detect in the vast majority of inquiries and (not surprisingly) prosecutions rarely followed. Most demonstrate the destructiveness of introduced diseases like whooping cough, influenza or dysentery, which Fijian mothers could do little to counter. Nonetheless the original argument for the regulation remained un-shaken, and infant death inquiries continued to be a legal requirement into the 1920s.

Further measures were taken at the turn of the century when Governor O'Brien secured funds and set about implementing recom-mendations of the Decrease Report. Water pipes were laid, provincial hospitals built, and more doctors employed, while provincial inspectors were appointed to improve village sanitary and domestic conditions.

A Hygiene Mission of European Women to Fijian Women—a pivotal recommendation of the report—commenced in 1899. It was largely carried out by the minority Catholic mission, through its little band of European and Fijian sisters. A few wives of Wesleyan missionaries also contributed, but their mission responded coolly to the government's appeal to help. Laura Spence, married to a provincial inspector, also applied herself to the task. These hygienists visited Fijian women in the villages, inspected their houses, and gave all manner of instruction on baby-care, cleanliness and nursing.

The undoing of the Hygiene Mission sprang mainly from tensions between the hygienists and Fijian mothers—though the project was always impeded by sectarian and administrative discord. The hygienists subscribed to the archetype of the Native Mother, and their approach was often domineering and counterproductive. Recurring issues of conflict included the Fijian custom of pre-masticating food for infants, inoculating children with *coko* (yaws), and the retention of old mats for everyday use. Many a hygiene visit involved a game of hide and seek: the village women hid their mats, the hygienists searched them out and had them burned. With the possible exception of Mrs Heighway's idiosyncratic campaign in Kadavu, where she organised the wives and widows of Fijian ministers to work among their own people, the Hygiene Mission failed to enlist the support of Fijian women, and dissolved with little trace in 1903.

Attempts were also made to teach Fijian mothers through the government's Fijian-language newspaper. *Na Mata* ran articles on every imaginable aspect of decrease, many of which had a special message for women—on the evils of abortion, the importance of not fishing while pregnant, proper infant feeding, and so forth. Articles like 'A Child Reared in the European Fashion' (1897, pp. 45–6) taught that traditional child-rearing was benighted and promoted decrease. It is doubtful whether *Na Mata* communicated effectively to Fijian women, since it was sent only to Fijian officials, who were men, and its teachings must have seemed absurd.

Official teachings on infant feeding certainly fall into this category. Milk was a vexed issue. Many Europeans lamented the absence in the native diet of a suitable substitute for the breast-milk of Fijian mothers, which was also believed to be mysteriously lacking in nutrients. So O'Brien promoted milch-cows and baby bottles. Fijians had no tradition of raising cattle or drinking milk, and some who tried it vomited. The assertion that cows' milk was best for babies also accorded ill with Fijian thinking, in which breast-milk was the prime determinant of infant health, and food taboos and postpartum sexual abstinence were understood to preserve its quality. Mostly Fijian women ridiculed these new ideas. Some babies fed on cows' milk by 'enlightened' parents died. Even certain hygiene workers disagreed, arguing that milk deteriorated so quickly in Fiji's climate that its use would do more harm than good. These were among the first of many confused and misinformed efforts to change the way the Native Mother fed her child.

Special schools to train Fijian girls for motherhood were seen as more promising. Matavelo, which the Wesleyan Mission opened in Ba in 1899, was represented as a response to the Fijian decrease, and became a model for later Methodist girls' schools. In addition to the usual subjects, Matavelo girls learned germ theory, laundry work, child-care and sanitation. When asked how the lives of infants could be saved, in a 1910 examination, Elena wrote 'They should not eat, they should only drink good milk'; Mere declared 'They should be better taken care of, and kept clean'; and Titila stated 'If a child be ill let it be taken at once to the doctor'. Graduates of Matavelo were a minority, but often influential. The school provided many native ministers with wives, and many candidates for the new profession of nursing.

In 1908 six girls were sent to the Colonial Hospital in Suva and graduated after a short course as the colony's first Native Obstetric Nurses (NONs). Their task was to lower infant mortality and undermine traditional midwives by delivering babies and teaching infant care. The government hoped that these nurses would succeed where the Hygiene Mission and the provincial hospitals had failed. Fijian women seldom used the hospitals, and parents were reluctant to take their children there for treatment. Village midwives and 'wise women' were consulted instead.

The pioneer nurses found it difficult to compete with traditional midwives. In a typical report, a doctor wrote that NON Elana 'complains much of the ignorance and the obstinacy of the women . . . Many women prefer the services of old village "hags".' The early nurses often encountered wariness and scepticism, and they lacked the credentials which traditional midwives enjoyed—age, personal experience of childbearing, and years of tending others. With time, however, they acquired these attributes and broke down many of the barriers between colonial medicine and the village world of healing. In their own work they combined elements from both, and in their lives they moved from one domain to the other—for nurses commonly resigned a few years after graduation, nursed in a voluntary capacity while they raised their own families, and then rejoined the service. They did not displace 'wise women', but found a place alongside them.

The NONs had no significant impact on Fijian infant mortality rates, which had already declined from the levels described in the Decrease Report, and hovered below 200 per thousand until the mid-1920s. For a country of 1200 villages, the NONs were too few, and too limited in what they could do. By the 1920s Fijian infant mortality was no longer such a vivid governmental concern. From the 1900s, when the Fijian population was actually beginning to stabilise, sections of administrative and mission opinion were more convinced than ever that little could be done to save Fijians from extinction. Furthermore the immigrant Indian population was growing, and in international campaigns to end indenture and improve the conditions of the free Indian community, the plight of the colony's Indian women was salient.

The Native Mother emerged again between the world wars. Though Fijians were increasing, Indians were increasing faster, and the political consequences of an Indian majority were feared by Europeans and Fijians alike. Fijian and Indian birthrates were roughly comparable in the 1920s, but infant mortality rates revealed a disturbing contrast. In 1926 the figures for the previous year were scrutinised: the Indian rate had been 46 per thousand while the Fijian rate was over three times as great, at 172.2. Again the Native Mother was declared to hold the future of the native population in her hands, and the 1890s archetype was recycled. The Hygiene Mission was also reincarnated in the Child-welfare Scheme, which commenced in 1927.

The Child-welfare Scheme did enlist the co-operation of Fijian mothers. Women's committees were established throughout Fiji. Most of them worked under the oversight of other Fijian women and interacted with Fijian nurses, who comprised the bulk of the child-welfare staff. Though a handful of European nurses had been appointed, and a number of villages around Suva were visited by Dr Regina Flood-Keyes Roberts who brought relevant experience from Samoa, generally the European presence was at some remove. Reports from the Native Medical Practitioner in Lau show how the women's committees gained momentum. In Ra, Adi Litia Tawake, wife of the *Roko Tui*, initiated and supervised the scheme. In Colo East one of Matavelo's graduates, Lolohea Waqairaiwai, a legend for her work among women, fostered the work, walking from village to village, often carrying one of her own babies. The Methodist women's association, the Ruve, founded in the 1920s, also gave support. Baby shows were introduced (and remain popular today) while the Secretary of Native Affairs astutely instituted child-welfare medals. These often went to ladies of rank, but also honoured ordinary women. A success in so many ways, the effectiveness of the Child-welfare Scheme in lowering infant mortality rates during the 1930s is debatable. Great improvements occurred only after the Pacific War, by which time Indians had outnumbered Fijians, and the politics of population and the culture of colonialism had shifted so that the Native Mother, as a type, lost her earlier significance.

In general, colonial interventions which were premised on the Native Mother's lack of maternal instinct generated a great deal of contrary evidence—which nevertheless failed to demolish the stereotype. Many measures were ineffectual or harmful. Yet Matavelo, the nursing profession, child-welfare and committee work gave Fijian women opportunities for education, endeavour, leadership and recognition which many used to their own ends and put to the service of their community. The Fijian administration was unusual for its stated commitment to the paramountcy of indigenous interests, and was better resourced than many Pacific colonies to provide services. Its invention of the Native Mother, though a travesty, arose from a real concern for the continuance and survival of her people and confirmed Fijian women in their reproductive role. In other contexts colonial attitudes opposite to these prevailed, to the greater detriment of subject populations and the women among them.

In every Island group depopulation was arrested, but the reasons are not obvious. Quarantine and racial segregation may have limited epidemics. Dysentery lost its bite, presumably because people built resistance. Indentured workers became 'seasoned' by repeated exposures, dietary controls began to apply, and mortality rates on plantations declined to 'normal' (though still high) levels. As in Fiji, women's committees in Western Samoa took responsibility for village hygiene, and Queen Sālote of Tonga also enforced hygienic measures. It is not clear that health services had much influence, since there were so few health workers and they had severely limited medications, a clear brief to protect foreigners and to strengthen labourers rather than intervene in the conditions of Islanders, and little understanding of their patients. But they were happy enough to take the credit.

The varying degrees of commitment by colonial powers to their Pacific possessions was mirrored in colonial education. Japan, whose administration was the most rigorous, established an extensive network of public schools in Micronesia and made schooling compulsory on the larger islands. By the 1930s almost all Palauan children were at school and more than half of all Micronesians of school age were being exposed for two or three years to a relentless diet of patriotic and moral education designed to instil loyalty to Japan, devotion to the Emperor, and gratitude to the Japanese rulers. Nothing on this scale was attempted anywhere else, though the British in Fiji came closest. In the British, Dutch, French, Australian and New Zealand possessions most schools were run by missions, sometimes with small government subsidies. Typically, colonial administrations made token efforts in the direction of state schooling and left the bulk of the task to the missions.

'School' encompassed a wide range of institutions. It could be an elaborate mission boarding institution set among lawns, gardens and ovals where pupils laboured long and hard to mend clothes, grow vegetables and cut grass with strips of iron. Life in the Pacific's best mission boarding-schools had the rhythm and discipline of the monastery, with pupils rising at dawn, attending morning and evening services every day, singing hymns, and working in gardens. Sport was the one relief from a routine of prayer and learning. The most remarkable of these theocratic communities was at Kwato Island in eastern Papua, where the evangelical Protestant missionary Charles Abel removed Papuan children from paganism when they were young and taught them to be Christian in a distinctly British way. The boys became cricketers in flannels, and the girls housekeepers. Throughout the Pacific some of the best schools were seminaries run by the missions to produce new generations of pastors, priests and mission assistants.

At the other extreme, village schools could be little more than thatched huts with dirt floors. Here instruction was as brief as an hour a day and writing as rudimentary as drawing letters in a patch of sand. The missions extended their influence into the villages of Melanesia by employing Melanesian catechists and teachers who oversaw village schools. The teachers were converts with a smattering of Western knowledge. They offered a little rote learning for an hour or two in the morning and then let the children go free. One of their most important roles, a French missionary wrote in 1927, was 'bringing everybody to mass on Sunday, and if one can judge by the crowds that usually fill the churches it seems that they are succeeding'.[43]

For the colonial administrations, forever short of resources, education was there to instil loyalty to the government and secure skilled labour. As one official in the Solomons said, the administration needed a 'steady and regular supply of young native men who could be employed as sanitary officers, dispensers, nurses, vaccinators, etcetera'.[44] The small copra, sugar and gold economies of the Pacific had no need of

---

43 Smith, *Education and Colonial Control in Papua New Guinea*, 115.
44 James A. Boutilier, 'Missions, Administration, and Education in the Solomon Islands, 1893–1942', in Boutilier, Hughes and Tiffany (eds), *Mission, Church and Sect in Oceania*, 151.

the sophisticated skills that drove the government of the Netherlands Indies to build an entire system of Dutch-language native schools, but they needed at least some Islanders competent in the ways of the modern world. The best-educated Islanders became base-grade clerks, carpenters, plumbers, drivers and telephone operators. Others learnt enough in a year or two at school to weigh copra accurately, record the results and fill in order forms. That was all most settlers wanted them to be able to do.

European settlers were inclined to see education for Islanders as a waste of money, if not politically dangerous. 'The coloured man in his own country with a little but insufficient education is a great menace to the well being of that country', according to the *Rabaul Times* in 1929, which joined with settlers in campaigning successfully to prevent seven New Guineans from being sent to Australia to train as teachers. But all over the Pacific Islanders valued education, especially in English. In New Guinea villagers near Rabaul persuaded the government in the 1930s to establish state schools teaching in English, and in Fiji Governor Fletcher noted the clamour from Fijians and Indians alike to be taught in English. It arose, he thought, 'from mistaken ideas of the economic advantage to be derived therefrom'.[45] Most schools in Fiji were racially segregated but the Marist Brothers' St Felix School in Suva, to take one example, took students regardless of background. Schools like this became training grounds of the future elite.

Schools in the colonial Pacific were modelled on the schools in metropolitan countries and attempted to inculcate a colonial version of national patriotism. The colonisers emphasised loyalty to the British Empire, French civilisation, the Emperor of Japan, or American democracy, though the authority of their governments stemmed from more practical considerations. The Australian occupiers of German New Guinea quickly replaced the celebration of the Kaiser's birthday with that of the King. They handed out one mark to each policeman and government labourer, and held sports. 'Tug of War (Whites) Tug of War (Native) . . . 4.10 Marys Race . . . 4.40 Monkeys Race', said the 1915 program. Recalling the government primary school at Nodup in New Britain, established in 1932, an early pupil, Albert Toburua, emphasised the assembly of children in the morning, the singing of 'God Save the King' and the playing of the school band while children marched into class. These rituals came unchanged from Australia. Like their counterparts throughout the British Empire, Fijian and Indian children in Fiji celebrated Empire Day and learnt a history that focused on British military victories and imperial glory.

Before World War II little was achieved in the schools beyond the training of pastors and Islander missionaries and the dissemination of rudimentary secular knowledge to a minority of children. As the Resident Commissioner in the Solomons said in 1930 of one of the most backward British colonies, there was very little education of any kind. Only after World War II did colonial administrations accept responsi-

45 Lal, *Broken Waves*, 85.

bility for organising school systems on a large scale, and only then did they truly become passports to participation in the wider world.

CONCLUSION

From the perspective of the late twentieth century, colonialism can be seen as the first stage in creating nation-states founded on a new principle of legitimacy—a sense of nationhood—in place of older principles, such as rank, descent and titles or deference to achievements, in distributing wealth. Nothing like modern states had existed in the western islands. Elsewhere, the colonial state supplanted or worked around earlier polities or mission kingdoms, forged workable states out of embryonic ones, entered into competition with existing forms of the state which endured throughout the colonial period (as in Western Samoa) or, as in Tonga, was resisted by an indigenous kingdom which had modernised early and could claim sovereignty. The relative weakness of colonial administrations and the variety of Islander initiatives severely limited the effectiveness of the agenda of political modernisation.

Colonialism was also an economic moderniser, regulating—and sometimes restraining—the incorporation of the Islands into the money economy. The abstraction of the economy from social and religious life was perhaps the principal innovation of Western modernity. For most Islanders, however, economic activities could not be compartmentalised. Trobriand Island women continued to make skirts and bundles of banana-leaves and to distribute them at times of death as a means of maintaining social relationships and maintaining the dependence of men on them. No colonial officer took much notice, and the mortuary distributions were not affected by regulations. Yet the banana-leaves were fundamental to the true 'economy' of the Trobriands.[46] The Samoans' elaborate ceremonies for distributing 'ie toga reaffirmed social relationships of central importance. Despite colonial discouragement, these ceremonies, too, can be seen as part of the 'economy' in the Samoan sense. Between the world wars the people of Lomaiwai in Nadroga, Fiji, exchanged cylinders of salt for mats from Kadavu, yaqona from Colo, bark cloth from Vatulele, and Rewa pots; and Enga clans in the Highlands of New Guinea assembled lines of pigs for tee exchanges. The project of economic modernisation was, at best, inconclusive.

Finally, colonialism was an ideological moderniser, both because it assisted the spread of Christianity and because Western economics changed people's ideas. In contrast to older systems of exchange, the logic of modernity was to replace personal social relations with impersonal market ones; to favour status based on expertise and education over status founded in kinship and rank; to undermine the power of the group over the individual; to subvert traditional political orders; and to change the way people thought about their individual fate. That general

---

46 Weiner, *The Trobrianders of Papua New Guinea*, 27–31, 162–3.

thrust was compromised, however, by the ideology of the Native (and its extension, the Native Mother), which validated and promoted collectivist thinking and behaviour. The intended outcome of colonial policy was not modernity itself but the ambivalent vision of the Modern Native.

BIBLIOGRAPHIC ESSAY

The sources for Papuan colonial administration include West (ed.), *Selected Letters of Hubert Murray*; Lewis, *Plantation Dream*; and Weiner, *The Trobrianders of Papua New Guinea*. For New Guinea administration, O'Neill, *Up From South*; Cooke, *Working in Papua New Guinea*, and McSwain, *The Past and Future People*. Jinks, 'Policy, Planning and Administration in Papua New Guinea, 1942–52', surveys pre-war as well as war-time and post-war government policies; so does Mair, *Australia in New Guinea*; and Bulbeck, *Australian Women in Papua New Guinea*. The decisive roles of indigenous policemen are analysed by Kituai, 'My Gun, My Brother'; Gammage, 'The Rabaul Strike'; Kituai, 'Innovation and Intrusion'; and Gammage, 'Police and Power'.

Bennett, *Wealth of the Solomons*, is the source of much insight into Solomon Island colonialism, together with Keesing and Corris, *Lightning Meets the West Wind*. For the New Hebrides Condominium, see Bonnemaison, *The Tree and the Canoe*. For New Caledonia, Connell, *New Caledonia or Kanaky?*; and Merle, *Expériences coloniales: la Nouvelle-Calédonie, 1853–1920*. Meleisea, *The Making of Modern Samoa*, analyses German and New Zealand colonialism. For the Japanese period in Micronesia, see Peattie, *Nan'yo*. Macdonald, *Cinderellas of the Empire*, throws clear light on colonial administration in the Gilbert and Ellice group (now Kiribati and Tuvalu); and so does Grimble, *Tungaru Traditions*. The two poles of interpretations of Fijian colonialism are represented by Scarr, *Fiji: A Short History*, and Lal, *Broken Waves*. Other sources used here are Young, 'Lau; a Windward Perspective'; Macnaught, *Fijian Colonial Experience*; and Gillion, *The Fiji Indians*.

The letters from New Guinea Lutheran evangelists are in the Christian Keysser Papers, Lutheran Archives, Neuendettelsau, Bavaria. On the role of evangelists, see also Lātūkefu, 'The Impact of South Sea Islands Missionaries on Melanesia', in Boutilier, Hughes and Tiffany (eds), *Mission, Church and Sect in Oceania*; and Garrett, *Footsteps in the Sea*.

The section on the Native Mother is drawn from Vicki Lukere's PhD thesis, 'Mothers of the Taukei: Fijian Women and the Decrease of the Race', ANU, 1997; and Jolly, 'Other Mothers: Maternal "Insouciance" and the Depopulation Debate in Fiji and Vanuatu, 1890–1930'.

On colonial health practices and policies, see Davies, *Public Health and Colonialism: German New Guinea*; and Denoon, Dugan and Marshall, *Public Health in Papua New Guinea, 1884–1984*; on colonial and mission education, see Smith, *Education and Colonial Control in Papua New Guinea*.

THE PACIFIC SINCE 1941

CHAPTER 9

THE WAR IN THE PACIFIC

A WORLD AT WAR

In the Pacific Islands, World War II came first as a reverberation of distant events. As Adolf Hitler ascended the Eiffel Tower in June 1940 to survey the boulevards of German Paris, the administrators of France's colonies turned to shortwave radio for news. What they heard posed a dilemma. France had fallen and a pro-German government had reached an armistice with Hitler. Should they follow General de Gaulle and rally behind Free France, or was their loyalty owed to the new collaborationist government of Marshal Pétain? The BBC proclaimed the Free French cause, Radio Saigon backed Pétain, and the French colonists were divided. The few Islanders with opinions on the matter, such as the Tahitian Princess Teri'i Nui O Tahiti, favoured de Gaulle. The French Resident in the New Hebrides, a hybrid colony administered jointly by France and Britain, quickly opted for the Allies, but for months the governors of French territories prevaricated. Then in September 1940 settlers in Noumea and Tahiti resolved the issue by staging *coups d'état* against their governors and installing Free French governments. In New Caledonia the coup was supported by Australia, which sent a cruiser to Noumea with the Free French leader. As a consequence of these events, a few hundred men from the French colonies—Polynesians, *demis* and Kanaks—became the first Islanders to fight in World War II when they arrived in the Middle East in mid-1941 as volunteers in France's Pacific Battalion.

From 1939 until December 1941 when Japan and the United States opened hostilities, war raged only through Europe and the Mediterranean. Australia and New Zealand, as British dominions, sent armies to aid Britain, including a Maori battalion which saw action in Greece in 1942. For most Islanders, however, war was a remote prospect. People near Rabaul, the little capital of New Guinea, were glad to sell baskets and drums to the 900 soldiers who arrived early that year in Lark Force, sent by Australia to strengthen Rabaul's defences against German submarines and in case Japan entered the war. More soldiers came later—friendlier, more relaxed Australians than the villagers were used to—and their camp offered opportunities to New Guineans for work cutting grass or as 'cook-boys'. Many Australian settlers had left

Map 17   Maximum expansion of Japanese control

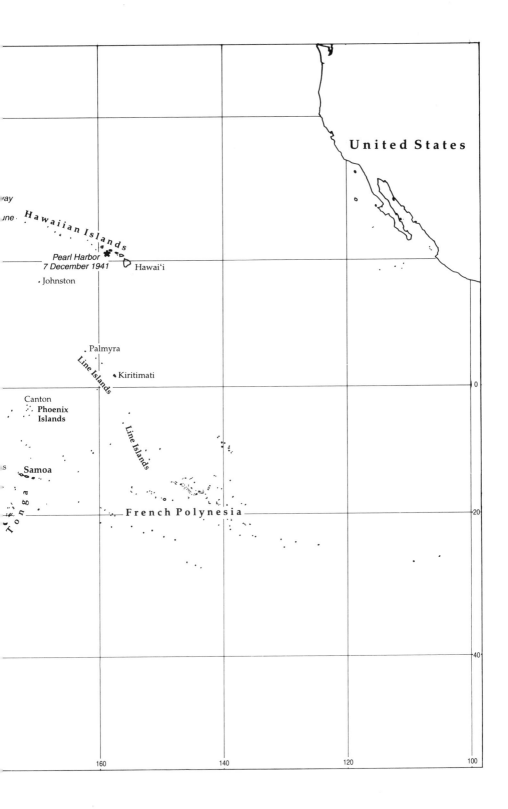

way

une

Hawaiian Islands

Pearl Harbor
7 December 1941   ▽ Hawai'i

• Johnston

. Palmyra

Line Islands   ▴ Kiritimati

United States

Canton
∴ **Phoenix
Islands**

Line Islands

s   **Samoa**

Tonga   **French Polynesia**

0

20

40

160   140   120   100

New Guinea to enlist. Nobody imagined how swiftly a far more numerous set of foreigners would occupy Rabaul. In the other Australian territory, Papua, the government's newspaper explained in 1941 who these foreigners were: not white men, and a 'strange thing about them' was 'the way their eyes slant upwards at the outer corners'.[1] Throughout the Islands the war was little more than talk. The British in Fiji arranged for news of invasion to be signalled from village to village by the beating of drums, and drilled the people of Suva in blackout procedure. Queen Sālote in Tonga threw her support behind Britain, and Tongans, like Fijians, raised funds generously for the war effort. Tongan contributions paid for three Spitfires for the Royal Air Force. Only in Japanese Micronesia did the pace of life quicken enough after 1939 to suggest a great conflict. Korean conscripts arrived in 1939 to work on fortifications. They were followed by 2000 convicts from Yokohama, and the Islanders themselves were compelled to leave home and chip away in the hot sun building coral runways on remote atolls.

When it finally came, war burst over the Islands like a thunderclap. The air strike against the United States fleet at Pearl Harbor on 7 December 1941 initiated a blitzkrieg against other targets in the Pacific and South-East Asia, all rapidly taken. Allied war planners proved grievously wrong. They expected Japan to attack one place at a time, but with devastating effect the Japanese mounted simultaneous offensives. The day after Pearl Harbor, 192 Japanese naval planes attacked the bombers and fighters of the United States Army Air Forces on the ground at Clark Airfield near Manila, opening the campaign which drove the Americans from most of the Philippines by Christmas. Three days after Pearl Harbor, the Japanese Special Naval Landing Force did brief battle with Americans and Chamorros before accepting the United States surrender and raising the Rising Sun over Government House in Guam. By then the Japanese had blockaded Hong Kong, bombed Singapore and landed in British Malaya, driving the British before them as they pushed southward. In the Pacific they had a foothold with a small garrison in the British Gilbert Islands at Butaritari. The speed was breathtaking.

Japan mounted assaults from bases stretching from one end of its Micronesian territory to the other, from Saipan to Kwajalein. For the first six months operations went precisely as planned. After Guam and Butaritari, the Japanese turned south and bombed Rabaul on 4 January. Escorted by aircraft carriers, the South Seas Detachment left Guam on 16 January and landed more than 5000 troops in the Gazelle Peninsula of New Britain, to capture Rabaul a week later. Other troops moved on to occupy Kavieng in New Ireland and, by early March, the mainland New Guinea towns of Lae and Salamaua. As Australians fled south, leaving thousands of plantation and mine labourers unpaid and unrepatriated, the Japanese brushed aside the colony's feeble defences and within a few months controlled all coastal New Guinea from the Dutch border to Milne Bay. Other forces moved east into Bougainville and the

---

1 Inglis, 'War, Race and Loyalty in New Guinea, 1939–1945', 508.

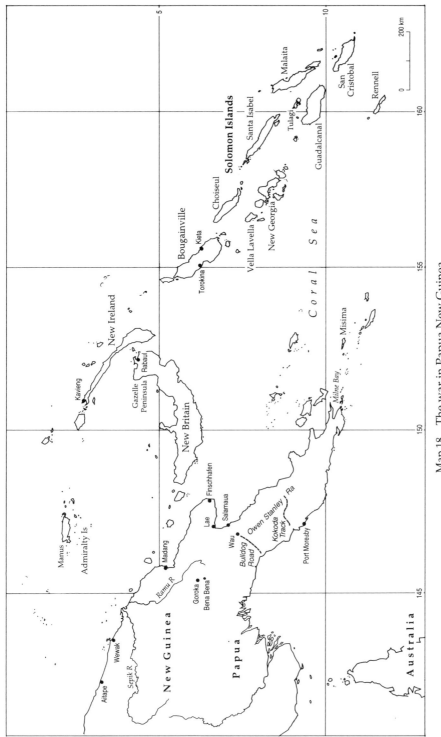

Map 18 The war in Papua New Guinea

Solomons and west to Manus and Hollandia, the capital of Dutch New Guinea, commanding a swathe of territory that could serve as the springboard to Papua and complete control of the island of New Guinea. After that, Japan planned to occupy Samoa, Fiji and New Caledonia.

The Pacific War can be visualised as a sudden thrust outwards from Micronesia for the first half-year, extending control south and south-east—over Guam, the Gilberts, New Guinea and parts of the Solomons, including the capital at Tulagi and Guadalcanal Island. Until May 1942 the invaders encountered no effective resistance. Japan's Greater East Asia Co-Prosperity Sphere, now vastly extended, encompassed not only most of South-East Asia but also the Gilbert Islands, the Solomons, Australian New Guinea and parts of Papua. The Japanese were poised to capture Port Moresby by sea. Then, in early May, they were turned back from a seaborne invasion of central Papua by carriers and aircraft of the United States fleet in the Battle of the Coral Sea. A month later, at the Battle of Midway, the Americans repelled the combined Japanese Fleet under Admiral Yamamoto and retained a vital submarine refuelling base, Midway Atoll north-west of Hawai'i. For a short time Japan continued to gain territory, two small islands in the Aleutian chain of Alaska in June 1942 and the phosphate islands of Nauru and Banaba in August; but the highwater mark had been reached. After that, though much fighting was to come, Japan suffered only reverses.

The Allied reoccupation of territory was relentless, leaving Japanese on many Islands isolated from supplies as the Americans leapfrogged north and north-west towards Japan. From January 1944 the Americans were not only reclaiming Allied territory but taking Japanese islands, beginning with Majuro Atoll in the Marshalls, and by the end of the war all of Japanese Micronesia was theirs. Unlike the Germans, who had hardly bothered to defend Micronesia in World War I, the Japanese fought tenaciously, and the Island sites of bloody battles have passed into American and Japanese folklore.

Of all the Pacific theatres, hostilities lasted longest in New Guinea and most soldiers died there. Of 300,000 Japanese who landed in New Guinea and the Solomons, only 127,000 survived. More died from sickness than in battle, and most died in New Guinea. General Hatazo Adachi of the XVIIIth Army committed suicide at Rabaul at the end of the war, wishing to remain 'as a clod of earth in the South Seas' with the officers and men of his army. Perhaps 90,000 men of the XVIIIth Army succumbed to malnutrition, disease and Allied bullets along the New Guinea coast and its hinterland between Milne Bay and Aitape.

Failing to reach Port Moresby by sea, the Japanese were also turned back from an advance across the Owen Stanley Ranges in November 1942 when they lost Kokoda government station. By February 1943 they had been forced to retreat from the goldfields town of Wau and for the next two and a half years the XVIIIth Army fell back westward along the New Guinea coast, from Salamaua, Lae, Finschhafen and Madang, its remnants pinned in the east Sepik area inland from Wewak. At the end of 1943 Allied forces landed in west New Britain and over the next eighteen months they fought the Japanese all the way to their heavily defended stronghold in the Gazelle Peninsula. There about 100,000 men, including 20,000 civilian workers, surrendered at the end of the war, releasing the people of east New Britain from almost four years of occupation, longer than anywhere else in the Pacific except neighbouring New Ireland. Outnumbered by the Japanese whom they had to feed, and with agriculture interrupted by daily bombing raids, the Tolai population fell by at least one-quarter. On Bougainville, United States Marines established a beachhead at Torokina at the end of 1943 and from October 1944 Australians replaced them and spent the rest of the war attacking the dwindling, isolated and desperate XVIIth Army.

The war in the Solomons was over more quickly. Having taken the western Solomons and northern Guadalcanal in the first half of 1942, the Japanese faced stubborn United States resistance and then a massive counter-attack, which drove them from most of the archipelago within a year and left Guadalcanal as an American base for further assaults. Towards the end of 1943, the Americans began their westward onslaught from the central Pacific, beginning with the bloody battles at Butaritari and Tarawa against heavily fortified atolls in the Gilberts, and transforming Japanese bases into American bases. The people of the Gilberts saw one military occupation after another as thousands of Japanese were killed and replaced by Americans. The Americans bypassed one island however: and Banaba endured some of the most appalling atrocities of the war. Of 160 Islanders still there in mid-1943, only two survived.

The Americans bypassed fortified Japanese bases with brilliant results. In March 1944 the Japanese still held four of their six bases in the Marshall Islands, yet the group was already effectively in United States hands. The Japanese had Wotje, Jaluit, Mili and Maloelap, but with their supply lines cut by American submarines the bases were worse than useless. The Americans rained bombs on whatever they did not occupy, so the bases became merely targets for endless bombing raids and outposts of slow starvation. After the Marshalls and central Carolines the Japanese expected the next American attack to be made on Palau in the western Carolines; Obata Hideyoshi, in charge of the XXXIst Army in Saipan, certainly expected it there, far to the south of his own command. Instead, in the northern summer of 1944, the Americans struck at the economic heart of Japanese Micronesia in the northern Marianas, taking Saipan and Tinian in battles of annihilation, and establishing forward positions well within Japan's inner defence perimeter. Soon afterwards American Marines stormed the beaches of Guam.

That left Palau. Here the most effective Japanese defence in Micronesia was still to come in the prolonged and costly battle waged over more than two months for the islet of Peleliu, where a maze of coral caves, rocks, peaks and gullies honeycombed with tunnels became the best-defended Japanese position in the entire war. More than 10,000 Japanese died in the battle for an island 10 kilometres by 3. Stranded on the main island of Babeldaob from then until the surrender in

September 1945, in what is still remembered by Palauans as the year of famine, 50,000 Japanese troops competed with 5000 Palauans for food and survival. When the war ended, there remained the massive task of repatriating combatants and military labourers. The Americans decided to clear Micronesia of all Japanese, Okinawans, Koreans and Taiwanese—147,000 in all—whether or not they were combatants. Among other things, that meant moving the entire Okinawan population of the Marianas back to Japan, a task not completed until the end of 1947. Almost to the last person, non-Micronesians were deported.

EVACUATIONS

Like all wars, the Pacific War caused civilian evacuations. The first to flee before the Japanese were Europeans who had bolstered their authority by claiming to be invincible. They were now shown to be vulnerable. The 1400 men of Lark Force fought for only a few hours before they were captured or scattered in the massive Japanese landing of 23 January 1942. Of those who fled into the jungles, about 400 escaped from New Britain. Others surrendered after a few weeks of malaria and hunger. The Australians' departure from Kieta on Bougainville was an even greater blow to white prestige. At the first sight of a Japanese aircraft the Australians decamped, leaving the town to be looted by villagers. Missionaries, planters and officials in the Solomons jostled to board the last steamer out of Tulagi in February 1942, abandoning converts and unpaid labourers—who did not forget the betrayal. All the Seventh Day Adventist missionaries fled south from the Solomons. Those Methodist missionaries who remained at their posts in Rabaul and New Ireland died as a result. In Papua, Anglicans and Catholics stayed at their posts while the Methodists evacuated in January 1942. The European Methodists left behind ten families of Samoan, Fijian, Tongan and Rotuman missionaries. Henry Williams assured them sanctimoniously and implausibly that 'our flesh may depart from you but our spirit will abide in Papua, for we have truly yielded ourselves for your benefit'. Isikeli Hau'ofa, the long-serving Tongan missionary, told his pastors and teachers on Misima Island that it was 'the kind of situation that Jesus referred to when he said that when the wolf comes the hireling runs away'. The South Sea Island missionaries felt forsaken. Like their counterparts in New Guinea, they had no pay and had to face the Japanese and care for their congregations in the most difficult circumstances. In Papua, however, the difficulty was compounded by abandonment.

When the bombs fell, villagers fled too. The people of Port Moresby fled in canoes and overland soon after the first Japanese bombings. 'The harbour was full of canoes', Rarua Tau recalled, 'sailing and some rowing with people crying and calling.' Korobosea, Kila Kila and Vabukori villagers went to coastal settlements to the south-east. Hanuabadans were settled west along the coast at Manumanu and nearby, almost 4000 living there by May 1942. The Australians put them to work making thousands of palm-frond sheets for houses in Port Moresby, in exchange for rations and some cash. Fires destroyed their homes while they were away, but children in the evacuee villages continued to go to the mission school, and a number of men served in the Papuan Infantry Battalion, or worked as medical orderlies or clerks. After the war their village on stilts over the sea was rebuilt—after long delays—as part of war compensation. While some Hanuabadans grew bitter about their treatment, above all for the lack of Australian recognition of their feats as soldiers and carriers, their sufferings pale by comparison with those of Islanders evacuated behind Japanese lines.

Japanese forces occupied Nauru and Banaba in August 1942, eager to resume the mining of phosphate. Within six months the tide of war was turning and American bombers severed the shipping lanes linking Japan with its Co-Prosperity Sphere. Like Japanese-occupied islands elsewhere, Nauru and Banaba were blockaded, their garrisons desperate for food on grossly over-populated islands. In the midst of this crisis the Japanese began moving Islanders around, 1200 from Nauru to Chuuk Atoll and 300 from Banaba to Tarawa and, inexplicably, another 400 from Banaba back to Nauru, where there was already privation.[2] Chuuk Atoll, then known as Truk, was Japan's Pearl Harbor. With high islands in a huge lagoon, its magnificent harbour was ideal for Admiral Yamamoto's Combined Fleet that was supposed to engage the Americans in the decisive naval battle that never came. Chuuk for the Japanese in the early stages of the war was like Tonga for the Americans, a base far from the war zone where officers and men could relax with sport, beer, good food and Island women. By the time the Nauruans reached Chuuk, however, the situation was deteriorating and, apart from a meagre ration of rice, their food was whatever they could grow or catch in competition with the Chuukese. Then came the American bombing attack of 17 and 18 February 1944, two days of terror that annihilated 270 aircraft and left ten warships and thirty-one merchant vessels at the bottom of the lagoon or in the deep waters beyond Chuuk's fringing reef. The Americans then moved on without landing, leaving the inhabitants to eke out a miserable existence until the end of the war, by which time more than one in three Nauruans there had died. The better option for Nauruans was to stay on Nauru. There was enough to eat, pumpkins and fish especially, even after the last transport left the island in September 1944. But to stay on Banaba, the other phosphate island, was fatal. More than 100 Banabans and other Gilbert and Ellice Islanders were still on Banaba in August 1945. The Japanese commander told them the war was over, then lined them up on a cliff the following day and had them shot or bayoneted. A survivor, Kabunare, fell over the cliff as if dead and hid in caves for months until he was sure the war had ended.

The Japanese evacuated entire populations as the American threat loomed. The people of Peleliu and Angaur found refuge on the main Palauan island of Babeldaob, where the chief of Ngaraard offered to

2 Viviani, *Nauru: Phosphate and Political Progress*, 81; Macdonald, *Cinderellas of the Empire*, 148.

take them in with his community who were surviving the bombing by hiding in the jungle. Many sickened, some died and all endured months of privation before American pilots began waving from their planes instead of releasing bombs, indicating that the war was over. A Palauan who lived close to the Japanese encampments at Aimeliik remembered the daily arrival of American bombers from Guam at about eleven o'clock: they came in threes, so often during the day that fishing and gardening had to be done at night. Islanders elsewhere were left to survive as best they could while bombs fell and Marines stormed ashore. At Enewetak Atoll, the westernmost of the Marshalls, bombs fell for weeks before the mighty assault of the Marines against Japanese positions. An Enewetakese said of the bombers: 'Sometimes it was like night, the sky was so dark, and then red and white when the bombs exploded, reflective, so bright you would never see properly.'[3]

On Guam, the Japanese knew that Chamorro sympathies lay with the Americans, and as the threat of invasion grew after the fall of Saipan in July 1944, they undertook a massive evacuation. Almost the entire population of 20,000 was force-marched across the island to internment camps. When the Japanese rounded up the 800 villagers of Merizo, they selected two groups of thirty each, put them in caves and massacred them with sabres and hand grenades. Altogether they executed about 700 Guamanians during the war, some by beheading. Jesus Reyes Quinene, who organised a Chamorro contingent in the days before liberation, entered these words in his diary for 30 July 1944:

> Hearing that yesterday our young boys found on one of the Japanese trenches 30 men dead, so I arranged to go out and investigated. We found according to the clothes worn by the boys that they were the 30 chamorros boys from Merizo who were killed. Investigation convinced us that they were killed by hand grenade. We returned to our hideout in the evening. At about 7 o'clock this evening 3 of our boys and [two] americans reaches our hideout and boy are we happy. Good nite and sweet dreams.[4]

In an extraordinary postscript, a lone Japanese soldier, Corporal Yokoi Shoichi, walked out of the jungle in Guam to surrender in January 1972.

ISLANDERS IN THE ARMED FORCES

More than 3500 Papuans and New Guineans fought in the Pacific Islands Regiment, which was in Bougainville, New Britain and north of the Sepik River when the war ended. Another 3137 Papuan and New Guinean police saw action, and 955 served as medical orderlies. More than 2000 Fijians served as soldiers in the Solomon Islands campaign, and 680 Solomon Islanders enlisted in the Solomon Islands Defence Force. The Tongan Defence Force—2700 men at peak strength—was formed solely to defend Tonga itself but about 50 Tongans served in the

---

3   White and Lindstrom (eds), *The Pacific Theater*, 126–7.
4   Farrell, *Liberation – 1944*, 53.

Solomons by joining the Fiji Military Forces. The Fitafita guard and First Samoan Battalion, Marine Corps Reserves, were units of 500 men each raised for the defence of American Samoa and did not see service abroad. Small numbers of Islanders from Pohnpei and Palau joined the *teishintai* or volunteer units of the Japanese forces and served as non-combatants in New Guinea. One of them—the 104th Construction Detachment from Palau—was abandoned at the end of the war and took years to get home. Most of the 300 volunteers who fought in North Africa, Italy and Provence in the Tahitian company of the French Battalion of the Pacific were Polynesians and *demis*, and their comrades-in-arms included Melanesians from New Caledonia.

Before the war, prominent settlers disapproved Australia's plans for Papuan and New Guinean police and volunteers to form the nucleus of a New Guinea Field Force. 'Natives' might be useful as cheap labour but they would run at the first sound of bombardment, it was thought, and could not be trusted with firearms.[5] As Australian government officers fled from Rabaul in January 1942, they tried to disarm the New Guinea police. Despite such doubts, one of the last acts of the ageing lieutenant-governor of Papua, Sir Hubert Murray, was to approve the establishment of the Papuan Infantry Battalion. Three hundred men were in the battalion when Japanese bombs fell on Port Moresby in February 1942. The force expanded over the next two years, to be joined in March 1944 by the first of the New Guinea Infantry Battalions. Together, they became the Pacific Islands Regiment, formed in October 1944 to do more of the fighting and lighten the load of Australian troops. By then the image of Papua New Guinean troops, at least among senior Australian officers, was far more positive. They were now seen as fighters skilled in stealth and surprise attack, men whose knowledge of the bush and experience in tribal warfare could advance the Allied cause. This assessment is borne out by the record of the Pacific Islands Regiment, which accounted for the deaths of 2209 Japanese for the loss of just 63 Australians and Papua New Guineans. Altogether, 85 Papuan and New Guinean soldiers and police were killed in action and 201 were wounded.[6] Many more villagers, especially in disputed areas of New Guinea, were *de facto* soldiers acting as scouts and spies for both sides and using traditional techniques of warfare. Years later, a man from Mambuk village in the east Sepik remembered giving the Australians a lesson in tactics: '"Your European way of fighting should be thrown out, and you must follow the native way . . . Put black paint on the face, or cover it up with mud. Surround the place to be attacked at five o'clock in the morning, then at six o'clock, attack." They said this was a better way to fight.'[7] Some, perhaps many, Papua New Guineans and Solomon Islanders believed that their knowledge of magic protected them from enemy bullets and assured them of victory. They proved expert guerrillas. On Bougainville in the last year of the war, Japanese soldiers came to fear Bougainvilleans above all. 'The Nip puts

5 Nelson, 'As Bilong Soldia', 20–1.
6 Griffin, Nelson and Firth, *Papua New Guinea*, 98; Long, *Final Campaigns*, 634.
7 Curtain, 'Labour Migration from the Sepik', 61.

the rifle down and gets a few feet away from it and he is a dead Nip', the Australian coastwatcher Paul Mason reported. 'The natives are certainly giving the Nips the shits. They are more frightened of the natives than they are of our troops.'[8]

World War II was not the only war in New Guinea. Papuan and New Guinean soldiers often found themselves in the lands of traditional enemies and used the cover of the wider war to pursue vendettas, or found themselves under attack from villagers who had formed alliances with the Japanese. One corporal was said to have killed his own guards with an axe because they were related to his people's enemies. And the war changed the soldiers' view of themselves: they were not ignorant Kanakas who could be ordered about, but had proved themselves the equals of white men. They deserved respect. They should not be ordered, as they were in February 1945, to wear bars on their laplaps instead of stripes on their arms like white soldiers (the order, said a sergeant, was like telling him to wear stripes 'on his arse'). They should be paid far more; and they should not be fobbed off with false promises. Resentment smouldered, then flared in incidents that took Australian officers by surprise. On three separate occasions they battered down detention centres to liberate fellow soldiers from imprisonment, angry that soldiers should be gaoled at all. He was not just a Kanaka any more, Corporal Buraura said, but now 'Savvied plenty and could stand up and talk'.[9] An Army report concluded that the soldiers took exception to the differences between their treatment and that of Australians. The commander of the Ist Army in New Guinea signalled that the soldiers of the Pacific Islands Regiment 'are natural experts in jungle warfare and few Australians ever reach their individual standards. All this fully realised by native soldiers who feel that their pay of 4d per day and no compensations or pensions most unfair.'[10] In response to the unrest, and just days before the Japanese surrender, the Army increased pay rates and provided for post-war compensation (albeit at a niggardly level). Discharged with portraits of King George VI or kept on during 1946 to serve as cheap stevedores for the Army, the men of the Pacific Islands Regiment remembered the war with both pride and bitterness and waited in vain for recognition they knew they deserved.

Fijians enlisted in large numbers, trained eagerly for jungle warfare and served with distinction in the Solomons. But World War II divided Fiji. For a variety of reasons the Indians did little for the war effort. Only one, a doctor, served with the Fiji Military Forces in the Solomons Campaign, and only a few hundred were persuaded to join the Fiji Labour Corps. In the inopportune year of 1943, when the British and Americans were praising Fijians for their patriotism and loyalty, Indian cane farmers held a prolonged strike against the Colonial Sugar Refining Company (CSR) and left tens of thousands of tons of sugar unharvested. The memory of who fought and who did not, who helped and who hindered, has haunted Fijian politics ever since.

8 Griffin, 'Paul Mason', 157.
9 Nelson, 'Hold the Good Name of the Soldier', 202–16.
10 Long, *Final Campaigns*, 262–4.

Recruiting from the villages was simple. British authorities had only to ask the *Roko* (or paramount chief) in each province. He then asked the chiefs beneath him, and a plentiful supply of recruits appeared, each eager to uphold the honour of his people. The Buli Nadi (chief of the Nadi district) told Solomone Vesaukula of Nasavu and Opeti Balenaisa of Nasolo, for example, to join the army. They did so, proud to represent their *vanua*. To miss such an opportunity was shameful, especially as the call for recruits came as well from the most respected of Fiji's chiefs, Ratu Lala Sukuna, who saw the war as a chance for Fijians to prove themselves. Recruiting appealed to respect for superiors, pride in soldiering and attachment to the community of one's ancestors, sentiments that were rooted in the past and fortified by the separate administration of Fijians. By August 1943, a total of 6371 Fijians were in the Fiji Military Forces, including the Labour Corps, alongside 808 New Zealanders and 264 Indians. In the Solomons 42 Fijians died and 2029 came home. One who did not come home won a Victoria Cross for heroism.[11]

Indo-Fijian enlistment was much less straightforward. Indians had fewer reasons than Fijians to fight for the Empire, if any. They had endured the humiliations of indentured labour and now endured the oppression of working under contract to CSR. India itself was convulsed by nationalist agitation against British rule. Indo-Fijians would fight to save Fiji, but if required to fight for the Empire elsewhere they deserved equal pay and conditions with Europeans in the military forces. That was the position adopted by leaders such as A. D. Patel and Vishnu Deo. Rather than accept such demands, the authorities disbanded the only Indian platoon of the Fiji Military Forces. After that, the government did not welcome Indian offers to enlist and turned them down repeatedly. The British doubted if Indians would 'obey unquestioningly' and feared arming men who might foster sedition. Instead, in a bungled recruiting exercise that was opposed by the CSR, the government called for 1000 Indians to join the Fiji Labour Corps. CSR wanted Indians to stay on their tenant farms producing sugar, and its contracts prevented farmers from leaving home for more than two months. Only 331 Indians joined up, confirming the opinion of Europeans and Fijians that they could not be trusted. 'Fijians are becoming increasingly resentful of the fact that Fijians are serving in large numbers in the war and Indians are not', the government reported in 1943. 'Economic fear enters here also when Indians are seen to be trying to buy land with war profits or to lease land left vacant because the native owners are in uniform.'[12]

The war confirmed the alliance between Europeans and Fijians. Having arrived in Fiji with a message to the chiefs that the 'business of brave men in time of danger is to fight, to suffer, to die if need be', Governor Sir Philip Mitchell came to regard the Fijians as a 'noble people' with an 'innate sincerity and simplicity of purpose and sense of

11 Lal, *Broken Waves*, 110; Ravuvu, *Fijians at War*, 53.
12 Gillion, *The Fiji Indians*, 179.

duty which are wholly admirable'.[13] The British regarded Fijians as a model colonial people—patriotic, devoted to duty and ready to lay down their lives for the Empire—whereas they blamed Indians for most of the trouble in the colony. Fijians offered loyalty and obedience, while Indians demanded equality and a place in the political life of Fiji. Hardly surprisingly, many British officials professed a deep love of the Fijian people.

Their performance on the battlefield was certainly meritorious, earned high praise from American and New Zealand commanders, and remains a source of pride half a century later. Fijian commandos, in some cases accompanied by Tongans, saw action in Guadalcanal, New Georgia and Vella Lavella in the Solomon Islands. An American naval commander who watched Fijians unload at a beach on Guadalcanal, breaking the record set by American Marines, thought they were the finest troops his ships had carried in the South Pacific. Everywhere they went, the Fijians were praised for their spirit, bravery and skill, in part because these things were true and in part to serve the purposes of Allied propaganda stereotypes of the loyal native. Later accounts by servicemen show that, like all soldiers, they were afraid, homesick and uncertain. Corporal Aisake Tanadrala recalled his reaction when asked by his sergeant to check a Japanese soldier who had been shot:

> I crawled down to where the dead Japanese was lying and crouched near him. I felt so squeamish at the ghastly sight that I could not touch the man. I sat there silent, so bewildered that I did not know what to do. Some Americans arrived and grabbed the man's watch, took his pistol, and anything they found as souvenirs. I stood quietly and murmured to myself, 'So, this is it.'

For Fijians who served in the war zones, the hero was another Fijian, the missionary Usaia Sotutu, who stayed on Bougainville during the Japanese occupation and whose knowledge enabled the Fijian 1st Battalion to escape from the Japanese by following a secret jungle path. Staff Sergeant Luke Vuidreketi wrote:

> the Fijians never had any hope of survival, having been informed from air reconnaissance that the enemy was closing in again with greater numbers from all sides. Our Battalion Commander, G. T. Upton, asked the coast-watchers if they knew of any way out. Sotutu's reply that day has been re-echoed through all these years by the men of the First Battalion: 'there are 99 tracks on Bougainville known to the Japanese, I know the 100th. Follow me!'[14]

ISLANDERS AS LABOURERS

While some Islanders fought, many more laboured for the military forces. Micronesians were the first labour conscripts when Japanese officials, acting under the authority of Japan's Military Manpower Mobilisation Law of 1939, began compelling them—together with

13 Macnaught, *Fijian Colonial Experience*, 150; Ravuvu, *Fijians at War*, 55.
14 Ravuvu, *Fijians at War*, 31, 47.

conscripts from Korea and from Japanese prisons—to work to fortify Japan's South Seas Mandate. The Japanese lagged far behind the United States technologically and depended on hordes of labourers with primitive tools to construct airstrips and naval bases. From 1941, under martial law, Micronesians could be ordered to work anywhere. On Pohnpei labourers from the Mortlocks worked alongside men from Chuuk, Pingelap and Sapwuafik. The lure of patriotic adventure soured fast for those Pohnpei men who volunteered for service in non-combatant colonial units. They fetched, carried, and died. Of 20 who landed in New Guinea in 1942, 17 died at Buna. Another 179 men from Kitti chiefdom in Pohnpei were relocated to Kosrae to build an airstrip in 1943, only to be stranded for the rest of the war and left to compete for the meagre food. As the war progressed, the authorities took more men from Micronesian communities and pressed harder on them to work, losing whatever legitimacy Japan had commanded. Nan'yo-cho, once a flourishing tropical possession, ended as a forced labour camp.

In Papua New Guinea too, military authorities treated labour recruiting as a matter of life and death. Labourers were mobilised on a much larger scale here than elsewhere and often compelled to work, with 37,000 labourers working for the Australians in mid-1944, for example, compared with 1000 employed by Americans earlier on Efate, 1500 in Noumea, and a peak strength of 2500 in the Solomon Islands Labour Corps.

In those parts of Papua and New Guinea not occupied by the Japanese, civil government was handled by the Australian New Guinea Administrative Unit (Angau). Its task was to conscript labour for the army and plantations, build roads, airstrips and camps, and maintain control by patrolling villages, extending patrols as the Allies advanced. Angau officers were instructed to meet the requirements of the military forces 'even if a temporary sacrifice of native interests is involved'. Many officers had been in New Guinea before the war, and tended to treat villagers in a colonial way. Papuans bore the brunt of work for the Australians in the early stages. Fighting in the second half of 1942 was concentrated around Milne Bay, on the Kokoda Track in the Owen Stanley Mountains to the north-east of Port Moresby, and on the Buna–Gona coast of northern Papua. From June 1942 Angau was authorised to conscript men for army service anywhere in the two territories. An Angau officer explained, 'If the natives do not wish to volunteer they are to be conscripted to work for twelve months anywhere in the Territory.' Another patrol officer was commanded to recruit for Kokoda all able-bodied men under his control. 'Kokoda Road has priority over all labour demanded. The need for carriers is urgent, therefore recruiting must be carried out forthwith.' The tropical rainforest and precipitous ridges of the bush track from Kokoda to Ower's Corner were the terrain into which conscripted Papuan labourers were sent with forty-pound packs, which might be 600 rounds of rifle ammunition or a man's rations for twelve days or three small mortar bombs.[15]

15 Robinson, *Villagers at War*, 16 ff.

The Japanese thought the crossing of Papua would be simple. They would rise to the highest point in the Owen Stanleys and descend on the southern side to Port Moresby. The instructions to the colonel who reconnoitred the area were to advance to the 'mountain pass south of Kokoda' and make the track usable for horses. The Japanese found no mountain pass but a succession of high ridges and deep gorges linked by a tortuous jungle path so steep that troops struggled to move. The Australians entering the track from the south met the same problems. They were soaked by constant rain, their feet grew pulpy, they quickly became exhausted, and the wounded had to be carried from the front line along the slippery mud and tangled roots of the forest floor. Carriers became a lifeline for Australians, and photographs of Papuans bearing wounded soldiers on stretchers across the mud made the Australian public aware that they depended on the Papuans. Carrying on the Kokoda Track was arduous for the hardiest labourer. 'The condition of our carriers at Eora Creek', an Australian officer wrote,

> caused me more concern than that of the wounded . . . Overwork, over-loading (principally by soldiers who dumped their packs and even rifles on top of the carriers' own burdens), exposure, cold and underfeeding were the common lot. Every evening scores of carriers came in, slung their loads down and lay exhausted on the ground; the immediate prospect before them was grim, a meal that consisted only of rice and none too much of that, and a night of shivering discomfort for most as there were only enough blankets to issue one to every two men.[16]

The Australian press and newsreels sentimentalised carriers as faithful native bearers. They became 'Fuzzy-Wuzzy Angels', a phrase from the pen of an Australian soldier on the Kokoda Track, Bert Beros:

> Using leaves to keep the rain off
>   And as gentle as a nurse
> Slow and careful in bad places
>   On the awful mountain track,
> The look upon their faces
>   Would make you think that Christ was black.[17]

A group of Australians in Brisbane calling themselves 'Friends of the Fuzzies' raised money and sent Christmas parcels for the carriers. Patronising and romanticised as the Australian reaction was, it expressed the reality of the carriers' achievements. They carried rations and ammunition to the front, and—with skill and care—carried the wounded back safely along slippery rock ledges, past waterfalls and over precipitous ridges. When they had to stop for the night, they sheltered and fed the wounded without thought for themselves, then slept four on each side. Many Australians would have agreed with the sergeant who thought no tribute too high for carriers who had saved the lives of two of his men.

16 McCarthy, *Kokoda to Wau*, 1959, 132.
17 Inglis, 'War, Race and Loyalty', 503.

Those carriers had little choice about working. A patrol officer described what happened when he asked for a hundred men:

> There was no response and all had to be selected by me and sent off under escort, even then some escaped. After that there was an order sent out from this office [Kerema] that all natives of this district would have to go to work, somewhere or other and that they should be prepared for this. A month or so later, patrols went out and within a period of two weeks recruited almost one thousand natives for work at Lakekamu. This confirms my belief that these natives will respond to force and command, but they will not be coaxed.[18]

Villagers signed contracts as they had before the war—but under the gaze of a policeman carrying a rifle and bayonet.

The war intensified demands on villagers in coastal Papua beyond anything in their experience. Village constables were to ensure that every able-bodied man was made available to the Army, determine why any man was at home, enforce obedience and arrest deserters. One patrol officer told villager constables in 1943 'to arrest any boy who could not prove he wasn't a deserter'. Before the war indentured labourers had mostly been strong young men, but now entire villages were drafted. Men were classified according to their strength. A-class labourers went to the front line: they were the Fuzzy-Wuzzy Angels. B-class usually went to Angau's plantations to tap rubber and make copra, while C-class stayed at home to grow food. Women were not categorised, but they too made sago for the carriers and wove palm fronds for building material. Villagers grew sweet potato, cleared jungle tracks, cleaned reoccupied villages as the Japanese retreated, buried the dead and—armed with spears, axes and old rifles—accompanied the troops as irregulars. In a mountainous country without roads, villagers carried the war on their backs. Everything armies needed was moved by porterage, from arms and ammunition to food, mail and medicines. Mingisin from New Guinea said, 'The policemen carried nothing, the soldiers carried nothing, kiaps too did not carry any cargo. We had to carry the food supplies and ammunition.'[19]

Highlanders, though they never saw Japanese, were also caught up as labourers, at least in the eastern Highlands. The Japanese bombed Bena Bena and the airstrips at Goroka and Asaroka in May 1943, and the raids intensified as the Australians in Bena Force responded by clearing airstrips. Thousands of Chimbu tribesmen came east across the mountains to the Asaro valley to cut the grass and stamp the Goroka airstrip to an acceptable compactness. The people of Bena Bena were put to work growing sweet potato for the Chimbu labourers. Some of the airstrip clearing was a feint to deceive the Japanese into over-estimating Allied strength and attract them into useless raids. By one account, the villagers 'thought it was all a huge joke and when the Japs put on an attack they would roll around on the ground with laughter'.[20] But

18 Robinson, *Villagers at War*, 51.
19 Curtain, 'Labour Migration', 67.
20 Dexter, *The New Guinea Offensives*, 239.

Highlanders drew the line at carrying down across the mountains as far as the Ramu River, where they were susceptible to malaria. They had not forgotten the deaths of kinsmen some years before when taken below the high ground. Indeed, the most important effect of the war on the eastern Highlanders was a dysentery epidemic in August 1943.

Carriers who performed miracles in getting the wounded out of battle zones and worked with fortitude often took the opportunity to desert. A major air raid was, understandably, enough to send most labourers into the bush. When four American Beaufighters strafed an Australian command post by mistake in June 1943, for example, 300 carriers fled, sending Angau officers in pursuit of their precious labour force. Carriers absconded in large numbers from the Bulldog Line of Communication, a track which linked the Lakekamu River in Papua with the goldfields town of Wau in New Guinea. Carved out of hillsides in high mountain country, with passes as high as 10,000 feet and rainfall up to 200 inches a year, the Bulldog Road cost men from the coastal Toaripi villages much hard labour and a great deal of abuse from desperate Angau officers. While 1000 carriers were walking the track, a further 480 were assigned to making it into a road good enough for jeeps, a task that took eight months and had lost its military usefulness when completed.

Toaripi remembered the war as a time when they were compelled to work on the Bulldog Road. Men accustomed to the warmth of the coast hated the dank cold of the mountains, and they resented a regime of carrying that frequently had them on the move before they could eat. When blankets and rations were short, or when Australians conducted searches and confiscated money, or when Japanese planes dropped bombs, many headed home. 'Apprehension of deserters' became one of Angau's main tasks in the area, and patrol officers were asked to find out why desertions were so numerous. Some deserters were gaoled, though gaol failed to deter when the alternative was carrying a 45-pound load along a muddy track with only a flannel shirt for warmth. So, on the orders of the Australians or with their connivance, police caned a deserter on the spot, sometimes with his hands and legs held as he stretched over a 44-gallon drum; or they gave him pack-drill, carrying a load at a running pace for up to six hours; or they kept him in the sun all day. Carriers who refused to lift loads could expect a punch on the ear. Angau were helped by informers happy to denounce deserters who did not belong to their own people. One Papuan pastor was honoured with a loyal service medal at least in part for his achievements in capturing deserters.

THE QUESTION OF LOYALTY

Like the carrying of the wounded, the rescue of crashed fliers was the stuff of legend, with villagers cast as angels of mercy; and like the image of the Fuzzy-Wuzzy Angels, it was based on fact. An Australian soldier who survived a crash in the mountains north of the Markham valley in 1943 sent back this message by runner: 'To 24 Aust Inf Bn Badly burnt both legs, broken jaw, 2 bad eyes. Picked up by party of natives. Pilot killed and buried. Boy starting 4 day trip Sunday. Might make it.' Villagers found the body of the pilot first. They washed it before burial, built a hut over the grave with his possessions inside, and planted flowers. Then they found the survivor, washed him, tended his injuries and carried him out of the mountains on a stretcher.[21] The people of the Polynesian outlier of Sikaiana in the Solomons welcomed three American airmen who came ashore in August 1942, provided a house, and cared for the one who was injured. Forty years later the injured American attributed his survival to the fact that 'two older men were constantly with me washing the wounds, etc.'.[22] On the home fronts in the United States, New Zealand and Australia people were led to believe that loyalty inspired Islanders to carry the wounded and rescue airmen. In fact, as many soldiers knew, villagers also carried wounded Japanese and rescued pilots from the wrecks of Zero fighters. For the Islanders loyalty was situational.

In Lae the Japanese proved less oppressive than the returning Australians. The Japanese wanted people to stay in the village growing food, whereas the Australians wanted them to carry. Further west and in the New Guinea islands, where the Japanese stayed longer and grew desperate, their welcome soon ran out. Michael Somare, later Prime Minister of Papua New Guinea, recalled the celebration in his east Sepik village when the Australians left, and said his people found the Japanese 'extremely friendly'. As a boy, Somare learned to count and sing in Japanese at a village school.[23] In the Sepik area many villagers welcomed the Japanese. The XVIIIth Army recruited villagers, entrusted some with responsibilities and briefly built a following among the people. 'I helped the Japanese', a former *luluai* said. 'I was made a Captain. I was like a policeman in charge of people. I was given a shot gun and hand grenades. I was in charge of men who were to guard the road in the Yangoru area. We were also to guard important Japanese officers.' Another villager in the Japanese police said he had the job of 'guarding the women of the Japanese who were behind a wire fence on a hillside' and remembered that the Japanese only had a few words of Tok Pisin such as *sindaun, sanap* and *maski* (sit down; stand up; never mind). But in the last eighteen months of the war, the Americans' campaign against enemy shipping severed supply lines to most Japanese units. Whole armies were left in isolated pockets to fend for themselves. The soldiers in the Sepik region had to live off the land, and that meant stealing food from villages, shooting pigs and even cannibalism: 'If a man would not quickly provide yams, taro or *saksak* [sago] on demand, the soldiers would hang him upside down by a rope around his legs in the centre of the village, and then ransack his gardens and kill his pigs. When they had finished they would untie their captive.'[24] The Japanese shot so many young men of Timbunke for suspected

21 *Ibid.*, 409–11.
22 White and Lindstrom, *The Pacific Theater*, 162.
23 Somare, *Sana*, 4–5.
24 Curtain, 'Labour Migration', 31, 42, 47.

collaboration that initiation ceremonies were suspended there for many years.[25] Japanese and villagers fell out elsewhere for the same reason. In the beginning, people from the Kaliai area of west New Britain did not object to working as carriers and general labourers. The Australians had demanded the same, after all, and the Japanese took care of villagers by giving medical aid and warning of American air raids. But as the Japanese retreated in 1944, they shot pigs and took food indiscriminately. Villagers especially resented the loss of pigs, the heart of systems of exchange and ceremonial life. Without them, ceremonies had to be cancelled or curtailed. Explaining why he had tortured a Japanese, a New Guinean said his belly was hot when he thought of the pigs they had killed in his village.[26] Villagers' accounts of cannibalism by the Japanese are numerous and consistent enough to establish that it occurred, at least in the Sepik. An eyewitness said that people in one village were lined up, machine-gunned and cut up for food and that he saw their flesh being cooked for starving soldiers.[27]

People near Lae were among the first in New Guinea to see the Japanese both come and go. For them, as for others, the question of loyalty was tactical and depended on the outcome of the war. The sheer number of Japanese at first suggested they would win and be the new masters. 'We thought the Japanese could beat you when you left these places', a *luluai* told a patrol officer, 'so we went their way. Afterwards when you bombed and bombed we were doubtful, so we made up our mind to sit in the middle but when you hunt them from these places we will know that you are the stronger.' Everywhere villagers had little choice. Their gardens and pigs were spared only for as long as they carried and spied for whoever was more powerful. Survival demanded co-operation.

Japanese propaganda stressed a new equality. Were they ever invited to sit at the same table as Australians and eat with them?, villagers were asked. Of course not. Japanese and New Guineans, by contrast, were brothers who would eat together, and in future Japan would bring factories with all the goods people wanted. The message promised cargo and it tapped villagers' resentment about a powerful symbol of exclusion—being prevented from sharing food with Europeans.

Allied propaganda for New Guinea was in the hands of the Far Eastern Liaison Office, which prepared the leaflets—23 million—dropped on Japanese positions and New Guinea villages. The office took Papuans and New Guineans to Australia and sent them back with gramophones and records to impress their fellows with the superiority of the Australian cause. They also organised radio broadcasts, usually a mixture of advice and threats, like this from H. L. R. 'Horrie' Niall to the people of the Morobe district:

> This is Master Niall. I'm still here at Wau. Now we are winning the war, there's a temporary setback. In the meantime be neutral. Don't go and actively assist the Japs. We know the Japs have got command of your part of

25 Roscoe and Scaglion, 'Male Initiation and European Intrusion into the Sepik', 420.
26 Read, 'Effects of the Pacific War in the Markham Valley', 103.
27 Curtain, 'Labour Migration', 52.

the country but don't assist them or we'll be very annoyed later on. We're going to win the war.

Angau sent a message to village leaders in the Markham area warning that the actions of those who had 'willingly helped the enemy' had been noted and would be avenged. An Australian involved in propaganda work, former District Officer G. W. L. 'Kassa' Townsend, thought that the 23 million leaflets had saved the faith of the New Guineans in their government, an absurdly optimistic view. Villagers appear to have appreciated leaflets that gave warning of hostilities, offering them time to escape, and treated the rest with scepticism. What mattered, as villagers pointed out to an Angau officer, was whether or not the Japanese were stronger than the Allies.

Villagers who held positions of trust with the Japanese had to decide when to make a prudent retreat to the Allies. Apo Amala, from Butibam village near Lae, worked first for the Japanese, whom he considered 'kind and just', then went over to the Allies and won a medal in the New Guinea Infantry Battalion. In the fighting for Bobdubi Ridge, villagers carried for both sides in turn. Such were the rapid adjustments that the war demanded, and more and more villagers switched sides as the outcome became obvious. Australians nevertheless conducted witch-hunts against 'collaborators'. In February 1944, before a crowd of more than a thousand villagers, they hanged a man called Tuya for leading a Japanese patrol to a party of Australians and helping to kill one of them. Tuya said he shot the master under orders, afraid that he would be killed if he did not.[28] Another man offered a similar defence and survived:

> The government had deserted us (*mi nogat king, mi nogat gauman*). What else could we do when the Japanese came? We did not have any weapons to fight them. We were just like women. And so when the Japanese came we had to obey. We have been like wives first to the Germans, then to the Australians and finally to the Japanese. We had to submit to the Japanese.[29]

The Japanese response to 'treason' in their own island territories was far more severe. As conditions worsened in the Marshalls, whole villages escaped to the Americans, stealing boats and guns and bringing intelligence. The Japanese responded by killing hundreds of Marshallese with machine-guns and swords, and subjecting many more to torture.[30]

ISLANDERS AND THE NEW FOREIGNERS

Armed conflict did not reach Fiji, Vanuatu, Western Samoa, American Samoa, Tonga, the Cook Islands or the three French territories, but American forces used them as staging areas and recruited thousands of labourers. Tuvalu was bombed but remained out of the war zone. In the

28 Robinson, *Villagers at War*, 140, 150, 151, 160.
29 Curtain, 'Labour Migration', 32.
30 Peattie, *Nan'yo*, 302.

emergency of early 1942, the American Joint Chiefs of Staff determined that United States forces should be deployed to secure 'the British antipodes and the islands and sea lanes between them and our West Coast and Panama'. This meant building a chain of air-fields from Hawai'i to Australia on islands such as Johnston, Palmyra, Canton, Christmas, Viti Levu, Efate and the main island of New Caledonia. It meant supplementing Marine forces in the Samoas, strengthening the naval fuelling station at Bora Bora in French Polynesia, constructing an advanced base on Espiritu Santo, and despatching a task force to Tonga. The Americans came suddenly and in thousands. By mid-1942 about 3500 were stationed at Bora Bora, 8000 in American Samoa, 5000 in Western Samoa, 2600 on Wallis, 8700 in Tonga, 5800 on Efate, 500 on Santo and 22,000 in New Caledonia, with an entire infantry division in Fiji. And this was only the beginning. By the end of the war a million Americans had passed through Manus in the Admiralty Islands, where at night the naval base in Seeadler Harbour could be seen from far out to sea. The Americans swept Islanders into a world of quonset huts, jeeps, open-air picture shows, baseball fields, ice boxes, and condoms. Above all, they had money and spent it extravagantly.

In the territories behind Allied lines, many Islanders found the war years exhilarating. They enjoyed the novelty, excitement, equality, money and sense of purpose. 'There was a great big *fa'alavelave'*, an American Samoan said, using the metaphor of a task on which the whole extended family had to work together. 'Samoans in World War II were willing to do more than they were asked. Look at all these people coming to our islands; there must be a big *fa'alavelave*. We must help these people; this is our country; we are Americans. The money was wonderful.'[31] Where New Zealanders had paid Tongans $56,000 to build most of Fua'amotu air-field, the Americans spent $498,000 to finish what little remained of the job, with much of the money ending in Tongan hands. Tongans stopped planting taro and began selling souvenirs, washing uniforms, shifting cargo, hiring out horses and carts, and meeting the American sailors' insistent demand for sex. Young Tongans still joke about what their grandmothers did in the 1940s. The girlfriends of United States Navy officers and men were the conduits for a stream of goods, from cases of beer and cigarettes to generators and radios, to the villages of Tongatapu from the naval station at Ma'ufanga. One officer deployed military labour to have an entire house built for his girlfriend. It was a heady time for many Tongans, blemished only by the 'Great Cigarette Raid' of 1944 when Tongans stole Navy stores and the Americans retaliated by combing the island for suspects, setting up roadblocks, arresting forty men and beating them until they revealed the cigarettes. Navy men forced their way into the home of Premier Solomone Ata and stood him up against the wall while they conducted a search. But in the wider context of the war, the affair hardly mattered.[32]

The outside world—above all the American military machine—came to the Pacific in prodigious proportions, dwarfing anything that had

31 White and Lindstrom, *The Pacific Theater*, 384.
32 Weeks, 'United States Occupation of Tonga', 399–426.

ever come before. A Samoan recalled the coming of American troops after the attack on Pearl Harbor: 'The pouring of American troops into Samoa is something I will never forget. The ships kept coming in, ships moving around the island, and ships anchored at the mouth of the harbor ready to come in. As soon as they finish unloading, they moved out, the next one came in, dropping off marines and supplies.'[33] Scenes like this, repeated across the Pacific, left lasting impressions of inexhaustible wealth and technical prowess. The people of Funafuti in Tuvalu had never before seen vessels as large as those of the United States Navy that sailed into their harbour in October 1942. 'All of a sudden the American soldiers arrived', Isaac Gafu from Malaita recalled of the situation on Guadalcanal, 'and, my goodness, it was difficult to count how many of them were disembarking from the ships.' The American naval construction battalions, or Seabees, composed of hundreds of tradesmen and surveyors, transformed the landscapes of Islands within weeks of coming ashore. If coconut palms were in the way, they blew them up. If coral was needed for runways, they dug it up with excavators, collected it with bulldozers and transported it in dump trucks. Almost half of the coconut palms of Nanumea in Tuvalu were destroyed to make way for an air-field that occupied one-sixth of the atoll. The Seabees covered runways with Marston matting, lengths of perforated metal that found endless uses in the Islands for decades after the war. In west New Britain, reached by the Americans at the end of 1943, villagers remember them possessing so many armoured vehicles that they could afford to drive them into a swamp and leave them. From their barges came endless tins of food—'those Americans, everything they had came in tins'—and the food was freely shared with villagers until their houses were stacked. The enduring image of Americans for a generation of Islanders was of a people both wealthy and generous, unlike the Japanese or any of the colonial Europeans.[34]

Having no stake in colonial rule, and consisting of black as well as white troops, Americans were a new kind of outsider. They came, built air-fields in a week, gave away so much food that it could not be eaten, and just as quickly departed, their place taken by colonial officials who were determined to put the 'natives' back in their place and who often seized the goods they had just been given. 'When America was here', a villager from Erakor village on Efate, Vanuatu, recalled, 'no problems with food, cigarettes, and money. There were a lot of them all the time . . . You did not have to pay anything . . . You did not ask for these things, they wanted to give them to you.' A Palauan woman who emerged from hiding to join the Americans was astonished by their generosity:

> And they offered us food, and candy. And we took the candy, but didn't eat it. We put it aside in our purses to give to our children. And so they gave us more, and again more. Soon we had a pile of food in our baskets, and we finally ate some ourselves. All different kinds of food, and food we hadn't had before. Bread, cheese. Good food.[35]

33 White and Lindstrom, *The Pacific Theater*, 386.
34 *Ibid.*, 174, 361.
35 *Ibid.*, 304–5, 131.

Men from the Toaripi area of Papua remembered Americans taking their side and objecting to Australians calling them boys: 'They should not call you boys, you are men already.'[36] People from north Malaita and Nggela collected money and presented it to American commanders to induce them to stay and replace the British as rulers.

Some people, like the Santa Cruz Islanders who worked at the main American base on Guadalcanal, observed that the US military forces segregated black troops and treated them as inferiors. Most Islanders were more impressed by the fact that black Americans wore the same uniforms as whites, ate the same foods, carried the same guns and drove the same jeeps. By comparison with their own colonial subordination, the position of black Americans appeared as one of equality with whites. Asked about the Americans decades later, the Solomon Islands leader Jonathan Fifi'i could recall 'no difference between white and black. They had the same jobs, they sat down together, they were equal.'[37] For Fifi'i the American armed forces were a model of social relations. After the war, inspired by the possibility of such apparent equality, he opposed the British and spent three years in prison for sedition. The Toaripi villagers who worked for Angau were amazed to observe black men, Americans, openly disagreeing with white Australian army officers. With their apparent lack of deference to white authority and ready access to white wealth, black American servicemen put the subservient position of Melanesians into sharp relief and undermined the legitimacy of the colonial order.

The Americans were not the only new outsiders. New kinds of Australians appeared too, men in uniforms who ignored the Army's tedious rules against fraternisation between 'service personnel and natives'. The Army did not like Australian soldiers sharing taps with Papuans and New Guineans, stopping jeeps to give them a lift, allowing them to address soldiers by Christian names and committing other violations such as 'frolicking together in the water'. While some soldiers accepted the rules, many more ignored them. One villager caught in a Japanese air raid was surprised to find himself welcomed into a trench by Australian soldiers rather than ordered to leave as he would have been by colonial Australians. Informal, egalitarian and disrespectful of authority, the soldiers seemed to Ngarawapum villagers in the Markham valley to be a different people from the pre-war Australians or those in Angau. They were not the 'English', who ordered everyone about, but 'Australians', who sat down with people and shared a tin of bully beef or a packet of cigarettes.[38]

All colonial authorities struggled to keep the colonial social code intact and maintain their hold over conditions of labour. They wanted to keep wages low and prevent troops from spreading anti-colonial ideas. The simplest interactions, it was feared, could undermine Islanders' faith in their colonial masters. By inviting Islanders into their tents, drinking with them out of the same glasses and eating from the

36 Robinson, *Villagers at War*, 80.
37 'Setting the Record Straight on "Marching Rule" and a 1927 Murder'.
38 Read, 'Effects of the Pacific War in the Markham Valley', 106–11.

same plates, soldiers were eroding the strict social codes meant to maintain the prestige of the white man. The sharing of food, in particular, was a universal Pacific symbol of equal and reciprocal relationships, and had been systematically denied. 'The test of colour feelings', an Anglican missionary wrote of the Solomons, 'is whether a man will eat with another or not. That is the Melanesian test. No Government official or trader will allow Melanesians to eat with him or even drink a cup of tea with him, for the sake of British prestige.'[39] While soldiers often ignored orders to keep Islanders at a distance and Islanders relished the new equality, American military commanders chafed at having to do the bidding of the British and French. In Noumea the Americans eventually assumed control of labour so as to ensure that labourers would be paid, accommodated and fed well enough to do a good job. On Efate an overseer from Tanna called Thomas Nouar took the food his labour line were getting from the colonial authorities—rotten meat and inedible taro—and presented it to an American officer, who immediately organised decent food and clothing. He later remembered that the Americans had wanted to pay higher wages but 'the French and the British stood in the way. They paid us badly . . . They blocked, they prevented.' The men of Tanna who worked on Efate were eager to work for these new foreigners, who not only offered unprecedented working conditions—good food, transport, clothes, and even entertainment—but also appeared to be the saviours promised by the mythical John Frum (see chapter 12). Followers of John Frum gathered on Tanna in 1943 to build an airstrip for American planes and offer America and its wealth a direct link with their island.[40]

The political mood changed even in Islands lightly touched by the war. Islanders at Aitutaki, the site of an American army air force facility in the Cook Islands, encountered friendly foreigners who paid high wages, gave things away, offered excellent health care, and thought the Islanders had had a raw deal from New Zealand. The Aitutakians became sharp critics of New Zealand, and Albert Henry was to lead political protest after the war.[41] Pouvanaa A Oopa, the man from Huahine who became a symbol of Polynesian nationalist sentiment, also emerged as a political figure. After being detained on his home island by the French, he sailed 900 kilometres in a canoe to the United States naval base at Bora Bora to bypass the local authorities and send a Polynesian petition to General de Gaulle. For his trouble he was detained again by the French authorities, who disliked Polynesians turning to Americans for assistance. Dissatisfied veterans of the war later joined Pouvanaa in demands for greater political autonomy (see chapter 10).

The history of the war for Island women can be reconstructed only from the most fragmentary evidence. We should remember, however, that like all wars the Pacific War was a time of rape. According to Angau officers, hardly a village between Lae and the mouth of the Sepik River

39 Laracy (ed.), *The Maasina Rule Movement*, 5.
40 White and Lindstrom, *The Pacific Theater*, 406, 411.
41 Gilson, *Cook Islands*, 192–8.

was spared from rape by the Pacific Islands Regiment. At Monakasat on the Huon Peninsula, soldiers of the Pacific Islands Regiment were said to have left a thirteen-year-old girl bleeding after their attack on her, and with a packet of biscuits to pay for the trouble. Nearby a village woman was raped three days after her confinement, and the assault was thought to have contributed to her death. Senior Australian Army officers were concerned, but not greatly. After all, said one, 'the marys "raped" very easily'. Towards the end of the war on Guam, groups of Chamorro girls were taken to caves and systematically raped by Japanese troops, and similar incidents may well have occurred elsewhere as military discipline disintegrated.[42]

PROPHECY, DELIVERANCE AND SUBVERSION

For some people the coming of Japan or America fulfilled prophecies. Whereas the Islanders of Tanna in Vanuatu and Malaita in the Solomons welcomed the Americans, villagers in the Madang area of New Guinea identified the Japanese as their saviours. In all three cases, deliverance was from the oppression of colonial governments. Tannese came to believe that John Frum had prophesied the arrival of the Americans: 'We were ignorant of planes, but he was the first to say that planes would arrive. We were ignorant of many things, but he said that trucks for us would arrive; there were no trucks on Tanna, but John said that they would come.'[43]

In 1939 a Malaitan prophet correctly predicted the coming of the Americans, who were welcomed as offering a superior way of life. Tagarab, Kaut and other cult leaders in the Madang area of New Guinea believed the Japanese were spirits of the dead or special people who had come to open the road of the cargo and deserved help to drive every white person out of New Guinea. By the time the Allies regained Madang in April 1944, Tagarab had been shot dead by the Japanese after he turned against them. The Allies then arrested Kaut as a collaborator. But the belief that the cargo would come and that the Japanese would help to bring it lived on in the mountains of the Bagasin area, west of Madang. Here an extraordinary rebellion erupted in 1944, when a man called Kaum seized weapons from the retreating Japanese and assembled perhaps 2000 people in a stockaded settlement. Kaum said the guns had come directly from a deity called God-Kilibob, to whom prayers must be said and offerings made. When God-Kilibob was happy with them—once they abandoned sorcery and arguing over women—He would turn them white and send cargo directly by aircraft so that Europeans could not intercept it. In the end He would send an army of Japanese to join Kaum and his people in attacking Madang. Meanwhile, Kaum drilled his troops for the day of salvation. His movement collapsed in November 1944 when troops invaded his stockade and arrested him.[44]

42 Nelson, 'Hold the Good Name of the Soldier', 208; and Farrell, *Liberation – 1944*, 43.
43 White and Lindstrom, *The Pacific Theater*, 405.
44 Lawrence, *Road Belong Cargo*, 98–115.

The war was a startling event, undermining old assumptions about the colonial order and inspiring numerous beliefs of this kind. A villager from the Yangoru area of New Guinea described a pre-war prophet who made magic so that another country would replace Australia: 'Why are we wild, raw bushmen (*buskanaka*) while the *waitman* has a comfortable life (*sindaun gutpela*)? You come with me friend, we will work some magic and you will become the same as the *waitman*.' The prophet danced and said: 'a new country will come and fight Australia'.[45] On Misima Island the sudden departure of most Europeans in 1942 prompted Bulega from Siagara village to prophesy. St James and Ezekiel had come to his house, he said, sent by Adolf Hitler, who had ordered the people of Misima to clean the mound of earth traditionally believed to be the resting place of their ancestors. That accomplished, a new world could come, they would be rich and would not have to work. Later that year a party of police, led by an Australian Army officer, was killed on an expedition to arrest Bulega. In the wake of these murders Bulega fled, was arrested and committed suicide, and the Australians hanged another eight men at Misima in February 1944. The hangings took all day, and Angau invited villagers to watch. According to a missionary, the event 'left a very bad effect on the people and brought us as a race into contempt'.[46] At the end of the war, prophets were proclaiming their messages of instant change in many other parts of New Guinea and Papua. In Madang the former police sergeant Yali, proclaimed by many as supernatural, inaugurated his own Rehabilitation Scheme in which followers modelled their lives on army camp routines.

'Cargoism', drawing on Melanesian notions of religious ritual as a technology for producing wealth, was the intellectual framework within which many villagers sought to explain the extraordinary gap between their poverty and the wealth of the whites, and from which they drew hope of improvement. The experience of war, and of vast wealth suddenly on their shores, became part of the cargoists' explanation. Missionaries condemned such movements, which competed with their own message of salvation. Colonial administrators suppressed them as threats to government authority. Anthropologists have disagreed in interpreting them (see chapter 12), some discerning forerunners of anti-colonial nationalism, others claiming that they can be understood only in local terms, still others saying the term 'cargo movements' is misleading and demeaning. Some movements, like the attempt by Tommy Kabu to reorganise the village economies of the Purari delta, did not await a magical transformation but simply called upon people to abandon old ways in favour of doing business in the European fashion. In Manus, the ex-soldier Paliau Maloat also combined a new cosmology with a program of social transformation, which has survived for nearly fifty years, despite the suspicion of the colonial and the independent governments. Kabu and others like him failed or enjoyed only small success principally because they lacked the technical knowledge and accounting experience to run a business.[47] However such movements are

45 Curtain, 'Labour Migration', 37.
46 Mackay, 'The War Years: Methodists in Papua, 1942–1945', 29–43.
47 Maher, *New Men of Papua*.

interpreted, they all drew inspiration from the new ways of living and organisation so dramatically displayed during the war.

Nowhere in Melanesia was subversive sentiment so effectively stimulated as in the Solomons. Men who joined the Solomon Islands Labour Corps received one pound a month for heavy and unremitting work building airfields, carrying equipment and moving cargo behind American lines. They were employed by the British but worked for the Americans, whose casual generosity made one pound a month seem niggardly, especially as the Americans pointed out they were being exploited. In 1943 and 1944 dissatisfaction crystallised into a movement centred on 'Are'are in south Malaita. Known as Maasina Rule, the movement was sufficiently organised to collect a head tax and reinstitute a version of customary law by 1946. It was boosted by the post-war British attitude towards Islanders' wealth. Numerous Islanders lost the booty of war when they were shipped home from Guadalcanal and compelled to hand over their newly acquired goods to colonial authorities, who thought people with plenty of food and possessions would be less likely to work on plantations. Ariel Sisili, a Malaita mission teacher later gaoled by the British for treason, compared the 'new dawn' that broke upon the Solomon Islands when the Americans arrived with the re-establishment of the old regime after the war. Almost everything 'the natives got from the Americans during war times in exchange or payment for the things they worked or made as souvenirs as war clubs, inlaid walking sticks or platted grass skirts etc.', he wrote in his manifesto of 1949, 'either were burned up by British Officials or took away for themselves good things as they pleased . . . The wages paid by America for Natives labour during war-times the Br. Govt held for themselves.'[48] Arnon Ngwadili of the Solomon Islands Defence Force said the British burnt some goods and bulldozed others into pits, forbidding him and his friends from taking food home. The memory outraged him even thirty-five years later.[49]

As Maasina Rule spread through the eastern and central Solomons in 1946 and 1947, the British became alarmed and arrested leaders on Malaita, Guadalcanal and San Cristobal, incarcerating hundreds who refused to pay tax. In Operation De-Louse, the first of the mass arrests, they used police exclusively from the western Solomons where people did not support Maasina Rule, and westerners in the Armed Constabulary—the 'Black Army'—became the core of the special force deployed against dissidents. Two years later, as rumours spread that the Americans were coming back to replace the British, villagers piled beacons to burn for the ships, and built stores for the cargo.[50] The British did not retrieve their position on Malaita until the 1950s. Like other Melanesian movements of the time, Maasina Rule drew on a mixture of ideological elements, Christian, pagan, cargoist and labourist. Its ideas

48 Laracy (ed.), *The Maasina Rule Movement*, 170–1.
49 White and Lindstrom, *The Pacific Theater*, 366.
50 Allen, 'The Post-War Scene in the Western Solomons and Marching Rule', 89–99;
      Laracy (ed.), *The Maasina Rule Movement*, 29.

were not new in the Solomons, but the war inspired a new formulation of them and the most effective anti-colonial movement in the entire period of British rule.

ASSESSMENTS

Colonial rule would not be the same again. Islanders had been changed by the war, and so had international opinion. Colonies were now seen not as permanent additions to the imperial realms but as territories set upon paths of development that would ultimately lead to self-government or independence. Trusteeship arrangements under the United Nations replaced the old League of Nations mandates. That meant a new political status for the former Japanese islands held by the United States Navy, and for New Guinea, Nauru and Western Samoa. In New Guinea and Micronesia the transition proceeded smoothly and without reference to Islanders' opinion. New Guinea became a trusteeship territory under Australia and was administered jointly with Papua. The Micronesian islands entered American trusteeship in 1947 under a unique and fateful provision that it was a 'strategic trust' in which the administering authority could conduct military experiments. When Nauru became a trusteeship territory under Australia, however, the Council of Chiefs complained directly to the United Nations that they 'still had no voice in the formulation of general administration policies or in the control of the finances of the island'. Under pressure from Australia, the Nauruans withdrew the petition, but it was evidence of new confidence.[51] Much the same happened in Western Samoa, where leaders such as Tupua Tamasese Mea'ole feared that a trusteeship agreement might frustrate the long-standing Samoan desire for independence and break the promise of the Atlantic Charter. A Fono of all Samoa in November 1946 brought together the political elite to discuss trusteeship. Many of them—like Islanders everywhere—argued that their country would be better off under the Americans, who had money, rather than their own set of foreigners, who did not. According to Tamasese, 90 per cent of participants began the meeting with that view and called for Western Samoa to unite with American Samoa. In the end they decided to stick with New Zealand but to petition the United Nations for self-government and a political status like that of Tonga.[52]

The end of the war brought constitutional changes to the French territories as well. They ceased to be colonies and became overseas territories of the French Union, their interests supposedly represented by a deputy and a senator each in the National Assembly in Paris. Everyone became a French citizen and suffrage became universal. As the 30,000 Kanaks of New Caledonia discovered, these changes made a difference but not a revolution. Kanaks were no longer confined to

51 Viviani, *Nauru*, 94.
52 Davidson, *Samoa mo Samoa*, 164–6.

reserves or subject to special native regulations. They could live and work in Noumea without seeking permission. They could be paid the same wages as Europeans. Yet they remained marginalised, living on a fraction of the land that had been theirs, free to compete in the capitalist economy and without the resources and education to do so effectively.

Australia, with a sense of gratitude to the people of Papua and New Guinea, offered a New Deal. It was limited. The planters returned and plantations took the labour that might conceivably have enriched village life under a different policy of development. Yet in one respect the New Deal made a striking difference, at least temporarily. Against all bureaucratic advice, the Minister for External Territories, Eddie Ward, ordered that all labour contracts be cancelled from 15 October 1945. To the disgust of employers, who never forgave Ward for undermining their authority, the labourers heard the news first in a radio broadcast in the Motu language. The response of almost all 35,000 indentured men was to go home immediately, leaving rubber trees untapped, coconuts rotting, ships unloaded and hotels unstaffed. They gathered at wharves awaiting repatriation, and took to the tracks in the direction of their villages. The Minister's remarks were reported:

> Our soldiers were being allowed to go home, after years of war; the Government was determined that the natives should have the same post-war privilege, and return to their villages if they wished. He had been told repeatedly that the natives did not object to indentured labour—that they would sign on again and again. Well, this was the test. Would they demonstrate their liking for the contract system by signing on again after October 15? Most of them had gone home . . .[53]

The effect of this dramatic measure was to halt the production of copra and rubber, but Australia had not transformed colonial policy. It had merely given labourers a break from a system that soon resumed. Rather than focusing on village cash crops, the administration assisted planters to return, and Australia's New Deal proved to be a reassertion of white dominance modified by initiatives in health, education, war compensation and agricultural extension. Not until the end of 1950 did Australians finally abolish the indentured labour system that had sustained their plantations in peace and their armies in war.

Like the Australians in New Guinea, the British in the Solomons and in the Gilbert and Ellice Islands delivered far less than they promised. Britain's plans, conceived in the spirit of the *Colonial Development and Welfare Act* of 1940, would have rapidly improved communications, education and health if they had been realised. There was even a proposal to place plantations in the hands of Solomon Islanders. But the war had laid waste the infrastructure of these economies at a time when Britain itself was on its knees. Wharves were in ruins, water supplies unconnected, towns reduced to rubble, plantations overgrown, and these things did not change fast. Colonial officials on the spot improvised for years with materials left over from the war while waiting

53 *Pacific Islands Monthly*, December 1945.

for funds and equipment. The British did not begin building their new headquarters at Tarawa until 1952, for example, and in the decade after the war they spent about one-third of what they had originally intended to spend on development in the Solomons.

In Fiji the war had the effect of fortifying Fijian tradition. One British official could not think of 'a finer native in the Empire, physically and morally, than the Fijian' and certainly none more loyal.[54] The Fijians' eager rush to arms strengthened the case for a separate Fijian administration. But the government went further. In the reforms of 1944 it put control of the Fijian administration in the hands of the chiefs to an extent not known since 1915. At the head of a new Fijian Affairs Board sat Ratu Lala Sukuna who, with the help of his fellow chiefs, now possessed centralised control over the affairs of every Fijian village and the behaviour of its people. Even in the post-war world the Fijian villager could be required to grow food, build houses and make *tapa* cloth for the chiefs in accordance with traditional obligations. Sukuna's vision of a revitalised hierarchical order was an explicit rejection of Western individualism, and could not last indefinitely against the pressures of modernity. As an official in London warned, it could 'only tend to the strengthening of communal separateness and the intensification of communal problems for the future'.[55] In this way World War II served as a crucible of Fiji's later political problems.

The war fought over their beaches, islets, lagoons, mountains and swamps had a profound impact on many people. Armies brought destruction, disorder and massive loss of life. The military forces needed Islanders to grow food, cut grass, load and unload bombs and other military equipment from ships and aircraft, maintain stores, do the washing, carry rations and munitions over jungle tracks, build roads and air-fields, spy on the enemy and, in some cases, fight. In forward areas such as Guam, Papua, New Guinea, the Solomons, the Gilberts and Japanese Micronesia, foreign armies replaced civilian administrations, subjecting Islanders to forms of martial law. Islanders were caught in a vast conflict that was not of their making. They were mobilised in the cause of one side or the other or, as the war progressed, by both in succession, each imposing its own idea of loyalty. Some people became evacuees, most fatefully on Nauru and Banaba and in the Japanese mandate, but in Guam and Papua and New Guinea as well. The war brought money, equipment, technology, new ideas, different kinds of foreigners, and new ways of behaving towards foreigners— all on a scale which was new to most Islanders and for which somnolent pre-war administrations had not prepared them. In New Guinea, Papua and the Solomons the war and its foreign wealth inspired some communities to seek new explanations for their subordination and, in movements that drew upon Melanesian epistemologies, to challenge the colonial order.

Just as the war brought Islanders into unprecedented contact with

---

54 Lal, *Broken Waves*, 135.
55 Gillion, *Fiji Indians*, 194.

outsiders, so it left many communities in fresh isolation. Hundreds of thousands of people in New Guinea and the Solomons, lightly touched by the fighting, experienced the war as a withdrawal of government. Except in a few areas such as east New Britain, Japan's administration of New Guinea and the Solomons—as distinct from its military presence—was either brief or absent altogether. The people of Vanatinai, an island in eastern Papua, remember the 'fighting' of the early 1940s, but this was the fighting which they resumed among themselves after the Australians left, compelling many villagers to seek refuge on the high ridges of the island's mountain range.[56] Much the same happened at Aitape in New Guinea, where coastal villagers looted the town and attacked inland people.[57] On the northern Santa Cruz Islands of the Solomon group, people revitalised trade links between islands, built more canoes, and revived the use of red feathers as a form of money. Isolation, a product of war, briefly reinvigorated Santa Cruz custom. People also reconsidered custom as government and mission authority disappeared. On Nidu in the Santa Cruz group, almost half the population adopted a 'New Law' that allowed men to have sexual relations with unmarried women without restriction.[58] The Ibiaga of the Markham valley in New Guinea took the opportunity of leaving their village, where they had been assembled only for administrative convenience, and returned to the scattered households they preferred; they liked being away from the government.[59]

The war was a turning-point in the history of colonial rule, though not in the direction of armed struggles for independence as in parts of South-East Asia. The war's influence on the Pacific was more modest. War-time experiences undermined the mystique of white supremacy (or, for that matter, Japanese supremacy). Islanders had seen Europeans afraid, fleeing in panic. 'Several native platoons', an Australian colonel reported, 'had experienced occasions in action when green Australian infantry had not shown up particularly well . . . These occurrences were the subject of much unfavourable comment by the natives.'[60] They had seen Europeans steal and loot. They had seen Europeans dependent upon villagers for survival in the direst circumstances. They had witnessed the collapse of colonial authority. They had enjoyed a taste of the American way of life. And while Europeans easily re-established authority during and after the war, many people did not accept it readily because they now knew how different things could be. The war also changed colonial administration in scale and direction. Everything governments did after the war was on a vastly greater scale, and some of what they did was meant to prepare Islanders for independence in the remote future. The war heralded the coming of developmental colonisation.

56 White and Lindstrom, *The Pacific Theater*, 215.
57 Allen, 'The Importance of Being Equal', 189.
58 White and Lindstrom, *The Pacific Theater*, 266–70.
59 Read, 'Effects of the Pacific War in the Markham Valley', 98.
60 Long, *Final Campaigns*, 264.

BIBLIOGRAPHIC ESSAY

In many Island groups the Pacific War is so central in remembered history that it looms large in the general histories cited in the Introduction to Pacific Islands Bibliography at the end of chapter 1. Soon after the war, its military history was researched for official publications through the Australian War Memorial in Canberra. Works cited include three volumes from *Australia in the War of 1939–1945*: McCarthy, *South-West Pacific Area—First Year. Kokoda to Wau*; Dexter, *The New Guinea Offensives*; and Long, *The Final Campaigns*. A parallel project in the United States, *History of United States Naval Operations in World War II*, sponsored Morison's *The Struggle for Guadalcanal, August 1942 – February 1943*, and *Coral Sea, Midway and Submarine Actions May 1942 – August 1942*. These works concentrate on Australian and United States citizens respectively, and throw only incidental light on the experience of Islanders.

The experience of Islanders was researched much later than the experience of soldiers. The most useful accounts include Robinson, *Villagers at War*; Read, 'Effects of the Pacific War in the Markham Valley, New Guinea'; Weeks, 'The United States Occupation of Tonga, 1942–1945'; Laracy (ed.), *The Maasina Rule Movement*; Ravuvu, *Fijians at War, 1939–1945*; and most comprehensively White and Lindstrom, *The Pacific Theater*. Many ex-soldiers published reminiscences, for example Townsend, *District Officer*; and Fifi'i, 'Setting the Record Straight on "Marching Rule" and a 1927 Murder'. Most military formations had chroniclers. Using these, and archival information, Nelson has published 'The Troops, the Town and the Battle: Rabaul 1942'; 'As Bilong Soldia: The Raising of the Papuan Infantry Battalion'; 'Taim Bilong Pait: The Impact of the Second World War on Papua New Guinea'; and 'Hold the Good Name of the Soldier: The Discipline of Papuan and New Guinea Infantry Battalions, 1940–1946'. Other useful works cited here include Griffin, 'Paul Mason: Planter and Coastwatcher'; Mackay, 'The War Years: Methodists in Papua 1942–1945'; Oram, *Colonial Town to Melanesian City: Port Moresby, 1884–1974*; Viviani, *Nauru: Phosphate and Political Progress*; and Farrell, *Liberation – 1944*.

Studies of post-war consequences include Laracy (ed.), *The Maasina Rule Movement*; Maher, *New Men of Papua: A Study in Culture Change*; and Allen, 'The Post-War Scene in the Western Solomons and Marching Rule'.

A NUCLEAR PACIFIC

THE DAWN OF THE NUCLEAR AGE

When the atomic bomb ended the war in the Pacific, President Harry Truman noted in his diary: 'It is a good thing that Hitler's crowd or Stalin's did not discover this atomic bomb.' Truman's satisfaction was brief. For a few years the United States alone possessed the technology; then the Soviet Union, Britain and France also armed themselves with nuclear weapons. The Soviets tested their bombs, however contaminating, within their own borders. The Americans, British and French resorted to distant colonies where populations were sparse and the political costs minimal. Several Pacific Islands met these criteria: Bikini and Enewetak atolls in the Marshall Islands for the United States, Christmas and Malden in the Northern Line Islands for Britain, and Moruroa and Fangataufa atolls in the Tuamotu Archipelago for France.

The nuclear history of the Pacific begins with two central facts. The test sites were on Islands remote from Western population, and Islanders were politically subordinated to the nuclear powers. To these colonial sites Britain added remote islands and desert country in Australia, made available by a government which was eager to help and little concerned about the consequences for Aboriginal people. At different times and in different places, nuclear devices were tested almost continuously from 1946 to 1996. The Americans conducted atmospheric tests of atomic (and later hydrogen) bombs in the Marshall Islands between 1946 and 1958, paused, then returned to the Pacific for a final series at Johnston Atoll and Christmas Island in 1962. The British tested weapons in the Australian atmosphere from 1952 to 1957, with minor trials continuing until 1963, and detonated hydrogen bombs at Christmas and Malden Islands in 1957 and 1958. The French tested at Moruroa and Fangataufa from 1966 to 1992, in the atmosphere until 1975, then underground. Amid intense regional and global opposition, France conducted a final series of nuclear explosions in 1995 and 1996.

Long-term consequences were becoming evident before the testing ended. The American tests contaminated and destroyed land, and left physical injury and psychological disturbance among groups of Marshall Islanders whose lives have revolved around the bomb since the 1940s. These effects have been public issues in the Marshall Islands

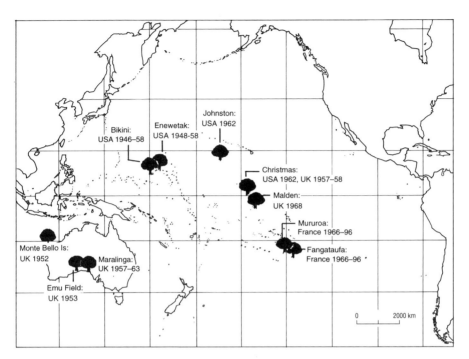

Map 19   Nuclear test sites

and the United States for many years, and form the basis of compensation. An Australian inquiry in 1985 found that Britain's bombs had contaminated land and exposed people to fallout, but could not quantify radiation injuries nor say who had suffered them. Much is suspected but almost nothing proved about the radioactive effects of British H-bomb tests in the Pacific. As for French testing, tight security blanketed the program. The government could not deny global fallout from atmospheric testing—on this issue there was independent monitoring—but on almost every other count they have claimed a perfect safety record. No comprehensive and independent study of contamination has ever taken place, although the authorities have permitted other studies under strict supervision.

Contamination and injury were only parts of the aftermath. Just as significant were political and social effects. During the 1970s more and more Island peoples embraced the idea of a nuclear-free Pacific. French testing was denounced by newly independent governments and by the South Pacific Forum, and evoked an anti-nuclear sentiment which found expression in the forum's South Pacific Nuclear-Free Zone Treaty of 1985. Political leaders in Palau wrote a nuclear-free constitution which brought down upon them years of conflict with the United States, and among themselves. In the Marshall Islands and in French Polynesia, years of military spending bequeathed a legacy of pronounced economic dependence, and critically influenced political agendas.

MICRONESIA

Towards the end of the war in the Pacific, the Americans expelled Japan from the scattered islands of Micronesia in a series of bloody battles. They then established themselves as rulers over territory which they regarded as vital to United States security. For some Micronesians peace proved more destructive than war. The United States exploded sixty-six nuclear weapons in the northern Marshall Islands between 1946 and 1958, including the most powerful and contaminating bombs in the history of American testing.

The Marshall Islands

To begin with, American testing affected two atolls in the Ralik chain, Bikini and Enewetak, whose populations were evacuated in 1946 and 1947. The 166 people of Bikini, moved east to the smaller atoll of Rongerik, were asking to go home within months, only to be told that repatriation was out of the question. The bombs which exploded over a flotilla of discarded battleships, cruisers and destroyers in Bikini lagoon made fish, crabs, plants and even the mud dangerously radioactive. 'We tried to explain', a scientist recalled, 'how the trees and the village had been pretty well destroyed and how the water and the fish were still unsafe and might be for years and months to come. Of such things, these people could understand nothing, but their feelings were unmistakable.'[1]

The 142 people of Enewetak were moved to Ujelang Atoll on 21 December 1946, as recorded in an Enewetakese song:

> On the day of the twenty-first all of the people came to this atoll.
> But we do not worry for it is the will of the Lord.
> We are very sad, we miss the islands from which we are separated,
> But we do not worry for it is the will of the Lord.[2]

The Americans were happy to encourage their belief that forced migrations were God's will and that nuclear tests would benefit all humankind; and the Marshallese accepted much of what was done without open complaint. Islanders, used to obeying chiefs, adapted to the Americans—the 'chiefs of the earth'—with apparent equanimity and a desire to please. Many Americans, expecting people to say forthrightly what they thought, mistook compliance for agreement and support. Yet behind the politeness lay a determination to be compensated and a fierce attachment to the lands of their lineages. Chiefs, after all, were obliged to care for their people. As time passed, the atoll peoples became dogged negotiators for compensation, decontamination, and repatriation.

Before that happened, two more groups of atoll dwellers joined the Bikinians and Enewetakese as casualties of American tests—the people of Rongelap and Utrik. In a seven-minute meeting in January 1950,

---

1 Bradley, *No Place to Hide*, 162–3.
2 Tobin, 'The Resettlement of the Enewetak People', 231.

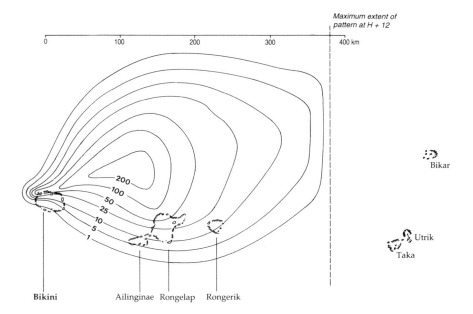

Map 20   Fallout from Bikini

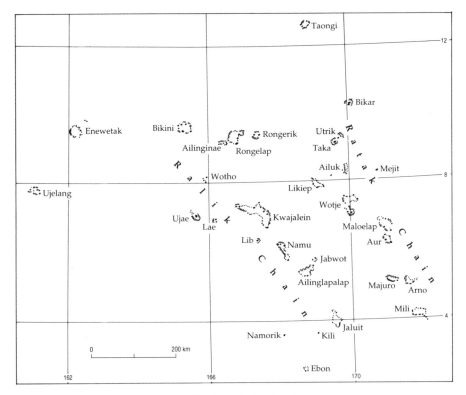

Map 21   Marshall Islands

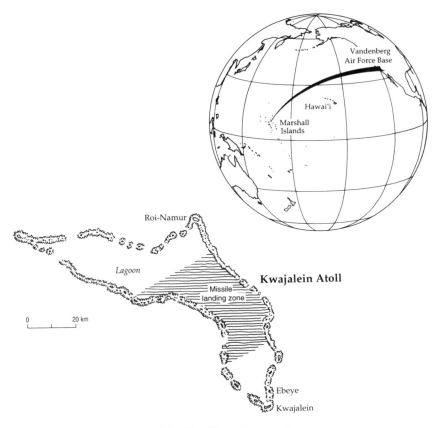

Map 22   Kwajalein Atoll

President Truman decided that the United States would proceed with the 'Super', the hydrogen or thermonuclear bomb, capable of an explosion hundreds of times more powerful than the atomic bomb. Within three years the Americans had detonated their first thermonuclear device, MIKE, with an explosive force equivalent to 500 Hiroshimas. MIKE completely removed an island from Enewetak Atoll and left a hole more than a kilometre wide in the fringing reef. Yet even MIKE was less destructive than the Americans' first test: in the 1954 series in the Marshall Islands, the BRAVO shot created a mushroom cloud of unprecedented magnitude and spread radioactive fallout over a vast area.

On the day BRAVO exploded, John Anjain was awake early on an island of his home atoll, Rongelap, 300 kilometres east of the test site at Bikini:

I thought I saw what appeared to be the sunrise, but it was in the west. It was truly beautiful with many colors—red, green and yellow—and I was surprised. A little while later the sun rose in the east. Then sometime later something like smoke filled the entire sky and shortly after that a strong and warm wind—as in a typhoon—swept across Rongelap. Then all of the people heard the great sound of the explosion. Some people began to cry with fright. Several hours later the powder began to fall on Rongelap, which covered our island and stuck to our bodies.[3]

Radioactive ash fell gently throughout the day, forming a thin white layer over trees, houses and sand; and afternoon rain carried the particles into water tanks. Ships of the American Joint Task Force passed near Rongelap and Ailinginae that night without stopping to evacuate their inhabitants and the following day RadSafe crews landed an amphibious plane in Rongelap lagoon. They ran Geiger counters over sand, soil and plants. They told the people 'Don't drink the water', then departed. For reasons that remain disputed, the Americans did not evacuate the Islanders until the morning of the third day after the blast. The people of Utrik Atoll further east, also exposed to fallout, were not evacuated for a further day.

The Americans took the people to Kwajalein Atoll further south, where they could be cared for and examined. People's skin and eyes itched, they vomited and suffered from diarrhoea, and they were burnt on necks, shoulders, arms and feet—radiation injuries which are meticulously recorded in official photographs, each person wearing a number such as 'RONG No. 39' for scientific analysis. Having apparently made a complete recovery within a few months, the people wished to go home, but they could not be permitted to do so. Fallout had contaminated their homeland and for the next three years they were required to live on an island in Kwajalein Atoll.

BRAVO briefly brought the 11,000 Marshallese to world attention. In the week after BRAVO a group of Island leaders including Kabua Kabua and Dwight Heine petitioned the Trusteeship Council of the United Nations. They pointed out that the people of Rongelap and Utrik were 'now suffering in various degrees from "lowering of the blood count", burns, nausea and the falling off of hair from the head', and that the Americans had moved people from their homes to make way for the tests. Loss of land was a particular concern:

> Land . . . means more than just a place where you can plant your food crops and build your houses; or a place where you can bury your dead. It is the very life of the people. Take away their land and their spirits go also . . . Kwajalein Island is being kept for military use. Bikini and Eniwetak were taken away for Atomic bomb tests and their inhabitants were moved to Kili Islands and Ujelang Atoll respectively. Because Rongelab and Uterik are now radio-active, their inhabitants are being kept on Kwajalein for an indeterminate length of time. 'Where next?' is the big question which looms large in all of our minds.[4]

The Marshallese called for an immediate end to all nuclear experiments in their islands. Their petition produced no result. The Trusteeship Council merely expressed regret, noted with satisfaction that the health

3 'Nuclear Specter in the Marshalls', *Asian Action: Newsletter of the Asian Cultural Forum on Development* (July–August 1982).
4 United Nations Trusteeship Council, T/PET.10/28, 6 May 1954.

of the Islanders was now said to be restored, and welcomed American assurances that no one would be permanently displaced from their homes. A similar petition two years later was equally ineffective. When the people of Rongelap brought a civil suit against the United States for damages of $8.5 million in 1960, the American Chief Justice of the Trust Territory dismissed it, arguing that the United States as a sovereign power was 'immune from suit without its own consent'.

Protests multiplied as the long-term effects of radiation exposure became evident and the colonial authority of the Americans weakened. Some Marshallese contested the official argument that the winds had unexpectedly shifted after the BRAVO test and came to believe that they were guinea pigs, deliberately exposed to fallout so that the United States would have a group of irradiated human beings for long-term study. The issues raised in the 1954 petition—radioactive injury, loss of land, removal of people from their homelands—later became central to negotiations over compensation which accompanied the transition of the Marshalls to a new political status.

Driven by the arms race with the Soviet Union, the pace of American nuclear testing quickened during the 1950s. As many bombs were exploded at Bikini and Enewetak in 1958 as in all previous Pacific tests. The American megaton range tests of the 1950s created what the US Department of Energy later called 'intermediate range fallout' on a further eleven atolls or single islands.

A bizarre disjunction of power and attitudes divided Americans from Micronesians. On one side, defence intellectuals in the Rand Corporation concocted apocalyptic plans for America's arsenal. On the other, Micronesians on remote islands worried about stillbirths, poisoned fish and contaminated land, and were powerless to do much about them. The nuclear war plan presented to the Kennedy administration in 1961 called for a cataclysmic first strike against the Soviet Union, Eastern Europe and China as a response even to the threat of a Soviet invasion of Western Europe, and accepted the deaths of 285 million Russians and Chinese as the price to be paid for freedom. One general joked to the Defense Secretary Robert McNamara: 'I hope you don't have any friends or relations in Albania, because we're just going to have to wipe it out.' By no means all Americans thought this way, of course— McNamara himself was horrified—but such views were widespread in the American military and betrayed an arrogance which carried over into the military's approach to the testing program. For soldiers who contemplated hundreds of millions of deaths, a few hundred displaced or exposed Islanders hardly mattered.

The Islanders' concern was with loss of land and with feeling safe and well again. The people of Rongelap told a United Nations Visiting Mission in 1961 of miscarriages, abnormal births, stomach disorders and fatigue, and said that fish from the lagoon gave them boils in the mouth. They wanted to know if the fallout from BRAVO still lingered. Questioned by the United Nations team, the US High Commissioner described these problems as 'more psychological than real' and suggested that some were feigning illness to attract compensation. This difference of views restarted the debate, with the Marshallese claiming the worst and the United States authorities suspecting ulterior motives and making light of what had happened.

The truth about the health effects of fallout, while shocking enough, lies between these extremes. Beginning in 1963, the exposed Rongelapese developed a clear pattern of long-term injury attributable to the bomb, and the people of Utrik followed them in this pattern in 1976. The most common effects were thyroid growths or nodules, which by 1979 had been found in 77 per cent of those Rongelapese under ten years of age at the time of BRAVO. A sizeable number of people underwent thyroid operations in the United States. After initial scepticism, American doctors accepted that tumours on the thyroid gland and some cases of stunted growth were long-term consequences of exposure to radiation. Questioned in 1973, the Rongelapese named seventeen people whose deaths they attributed to the bomb, a figure disputed by American doctors who would concede only that one death—that of Lekoj Anjain of leukemia—was probably caused by fallout. One long-term effect was indisputable: the experience of the 1950s induced long-term anxiety among Islanders, most of whom were still afraid to eat local food twenty years later. People on Rongelap and Utrik told members of the Micronesian Congress in 1972, 'Whenever we have a cold, or some other kind of sickness, we think of the bomb.' The distinction between 'psychological' and 'real' was false. American doctors still visit the Marshall Islands twice a year to examine and treat the 160 remaining fallout victims, who are thought to be 'at increased risk for malignant diseases as late complications of radiation exposure'.

At the same time, the people of the radiation atolls had much to gain from embellishing the story of their sufferings and, from many accounts, did so. By this means—perhaps only by this means—they could elicit public and Congressional sympathy and eventually compensation in the terms of the Compact of Free Association between the Marshall Islands and the United States. Under this Compact (discussed more fully in chapter 11) in 1986, the United States established a once-for-all trust fund of $150 million to distribute through a nuclear claims tribunal in the islands, while at the same time blocking any future claims.

The people of Bikini and Enewetak never abandoned hope of going home to decontaminated atolls, free of radioactive debris. At a cost of $100 million, the United States cleaned up Enewetak in the late 1970s, shovelling tens of thousands of cubic metres of radioactive soil and test equipment on to Runit Island and capping the debris with a huge concrete dome. When hundreds of Islanders returned to Enewetak in 1980, they could live on only three of the atoll's forty islands. The others were too radioactive. Total decontamination is impossible. For the Bikinians there was a false start in the 1970s. After an inadequate clean-up, more than 100 resettled on Bikini, only to be moved off again in 1978 when scientists discovered that they were absorbing unsafe levels of strontium and cesium. A far more thorough clean-up of Bikini, funded by the US Congress, began in 1988. Since then clean-up teams have covered the island of Eneu with potassium fertiliser in an attempt to stop radioactive cesium-137 from entering coconuts and other plants. Meanwhile the Rongelap people left their home atoll, fearing its radioactivity, for an isolated island at the western end of Kwajalein Atoll. Greenpeace activists moved them there in 1985 in the *Rainbow Warrior*. A radiological reassessment of Rongelap completed in 1988 found the atoll safe for adults so long as they did not eat food from its northern islands, and it reached no firm conclusions on the position of children. While the Rongelap people remained elsewhere, mainly surviving on American food aid, the United States Congress appropriated $1,950,000 in 1991 for the resettlement of Rongelap.

By April 1992 the people of the four recognised 'radiation atolls' had received $US67 million in direct compensation, and a further $21 million had been paid for a health-care program, scientific surveys and damages claims. The Nuclear Claims Tribunal established by the Marshall Islands government recognised twenty-five medical conditions presumed to result from radiation exposure, and specified compensation in each case: $75,000 for recurrent cancer of the thyroid, for example, $125,000 for cancer of the ovary, and $100,000 for 'severe mental retardation (provided born between May and September 1954, inclusive, and mother was present on Rongelap and Utrik Atolls at any time in March 1954)'.[5] A total of 345 individuals had been compensated for such conditions by March 1992. Making the most of the opportunity, no fewer than 9544 people from Rongelap, Utrik, Enewetak and Bikini had enrolled in the Four Atoll Health-Care Program.

The most significant legacy for the affected people was the loss of independence itself. The US Department of Agriculture supplied food aid to the four atolls and will do so until at least 1997. To a greater extent even than their fellow Marshallese, the people of the radiation atolls depended on American white rice, white flour, canned fish, pancakes and doughnuts. Some suffered from diabetes and obesity. Their lives were organised around compensation moneys, medical care and welfare entitlements. In a cultural transition effected by the bomb, they had become nuclear dependants.

People on Enewetak tell a revealing version of the mythic story of Etao, the trickster god of the Marshalls. After adventures throughout the island chain, Etao sails for Kiribati and Fiji with the beautiful daughters of a chief from the atoll of Mili. Then he is taken to the island of 'America', where he is seized and put in a bottle. 'He is only allowed to secure his release if he agrees to help the government with its experiments on planes, rockets, bombs, and spacecraft.'[6] Kwajalein Atoll was still being used for missile experiments in the 1990s, and a bargain of the kind that applies to Etao seems to have been at the heart of relations between the Marshall Islands and the United States since 1946.

5 US General Accounting Office, *Marshall Islands: Status of the Nuclear Claims*, Washington DC, 25 September, 1992, 19.
6 Laurence Carucci, 'The Source of the Force in Marshallese Cosmology', in White and Lindstrom, *The Pacific Theater*, 92.

Palau

Other Micronesians became increasingly aware of the experiences of Marshall Islanders. The Congress of Micronesia, formed in 1965, assembled representatives from all districts and provided intensive political training. A cross-section of Micronesians served on the congress's Special Joint Committee Concerning Rongelap and Utirik Atolls, set up in 1972, and travelled to the atolls to speak to the people. Among them were Palauans who already feared for the future of their islands in the western Carolines after the Americans announced plans in 1971 for the possible military use of large parts of Palau. Before allowing Palauans to enter a less dependent political status, the Americans wanted a cast-iron guarantee that certain lands would be available on short notice for military training, air-fields and port facilities, amounting to 28 per cent of the islands' area. This guarantee, the Americans insisted, should be part of the Compact of Free Association then being negotiated between the United States and Micronesia.

In Palau, as elsewhere, land was 'the very life of the people', the source of security, identity and status, and of their perpetuation. Palauan landowners had vainly been seeking the return of vast tracts of public lands from the United States administration since the 1950s. Now Palauans confronted possible demands for more land from the Department of Defense, whose practice in the Marshall Islands had been to seize islands first and compensate afterwards. The reaction of Palauan legislators and chiefs was first to reject outright any military installations, and then to tie the American demand for land options to the issue of returning public lands to their owners. The United States later agreed to restore public lands, but remained adamant on military land options.

During the 1970s negotiations over Micronesian decolonisation attracted little interest in the outside world. For the United States military, however, continued access to the islands and atolls was strategically vital, and for that reason the Americans did not want Micronesia to gain full independence. Henry Kissinger, Assistant to President Nixon for National Security Affairs, permitted the CIA in 1973 'to assess the possibility of exerting covert influence on key elements of the Micronesian independence movement and on those other elements in the area where necessary to promote and support United States strategic objectives', and the Ford administration authorised the CIA to conduct a clandestine intelligence collection operation from early 1975 until December 1976.

The CIA's influence was meagre, if not counterproductive. In 1979 the Palauans, having decided to seek an independent future, wrote a constitution which alarmed the American authorities and made Palau an international issue. The Americans warned them that 'any prohibition against nuclear or conventional weapons . . . would create problems of the utmost gravity for the US'.[7] The warning was ignored.

---

7 Smith, *Micronesia: Decolonisation and US Military Interests*, 46.

The Palau constitution provided that 'Harmful substances such as nuclear, chemical, gas or biological weapons intended for use in warfare, nuclear power plants and waste materials therefrom, shall not be used, tested, stored or disposed of within the territorial jurisdiction of Palau without the express approval of not less than three-fourths (3/4) of the votes cast in a referendum . . .' Another section, anticipating a decolonisation agreement, required a similar referendum to approve any such agreement 'which authorizes use, testing, storage or disposal of nuclear, toxic, chemical, gas or biological weapons intended for use in warfare'.

In the strictest sense, the constitution did not make Palau nuclear-free. Instead, it required 75 per cent approval at a referendum before nuclear-related activities could take place. Given the difficulty of surmounting such an impediment, however, the constitution was nuclear-free in effect. Palauans overwhelmingly approved it in July 1979 and again a year later. The constitution with its 75-per-cent hurdle was the basis upon which they became self-governing in 1981, though still under American control as part of the Trust Territory. The tortuous subsequent history of Palau revolved around a simple pattern of opposing interests. On one side was the United States, determined to retain military access after the Stars and Stripes was lowered. The Americans were willing to give large volumes of aid to a decolonised Palau, but only under conditions which were incompatible with the nuclear-free character of Palau's constitution. On the other side, Palauans aspired to a status free of supervision, yet they had grown accustomed to the standard of living created by Trust Territory subsidies and welfare programs. From the Americans' point of view, the Palauans had to choose between aid and anti-nuclearism. They need only abandon the nuclear-free idea and aid would flow.

Palauans were divided along traditional as well as ideological lines, with government leaders mostly supporting a change to the constitution in accord with American wishes. In 1983, 1984, four times in 1986 and 1987, and again in 1990, with American encouragement, Palauan leaders took their people to plebiscites attempting to reconcile the agreement over aid—the Compact of Free Association—with the constitution. On no occasion was the required majority of 75 per cent reached. By increasing the political stakes, the dispute exacerbated political divisions and contributed to corruption, intimidation and assassination. One president was gunned down in 1985, his successor killed himself in 1988, and the father of a pro-constitution activist was shot dead in a political murder. Rather than spending political education funds on an even-handed basis, the Palau government used money to favour the Compact cause. In the heat of the dispute in 1987, threats of violence were common. At the same time some Palauan political leaders began to let contracts in return for favours and to spend official funds in unaccountable ways. A United States investigation revealed, among other things, that five Palauan officials and businessmen had received 'questionable payments' of $775,000 from IPSECO International Power Systems, which had built an extraordinarily expensive electric power plant.

To the outside world, especially to anti-nuclear activists in Western countries, Palau attracted sympathy and support as a nuclear-free David menaced by a nuclear-armed Goliath. The reality was more complex. Some Palauans were playing politics, fighting traditional factional battles, or attempting to exploit Palau's strategic value to get more money. For others, perhaps for most, the issue was not directly nuclear but revolved around land, a continuing source of dispute since World War II. This sentiment found expression in a statement by Compact opponents in 1992:

> As you are well aware, the political climate around the world is changing; we watch the CNN and we know that: the cold war is over; the Soviet Union is no longer a threat; the European community is talking about uniting; apartheid is history in South Africa; and the United States is reducing 140,000 reservists by 1993, and more by 1996. The strategic value of Palau as perceived ten years ago is now obsolete . . . We are concerned that under the Compact every inch of Palauan land is vulnerable to United States military use . . . We do not want our land to be someone else's 'contingency plan'.[8]

Under the Compact, the Americans had options on land for military use for fifty years, although financial assistance was promised for only fifteen. Aware of this, Palauans inserted a section in their constitution—of much less interest to outside sympathisers than the nuclear clauses, yet potentially of great significance—forbidding the taking of land from landowners 'for the benefit of a foreign entity'. Since the United States is 'a foreign entity' according to a later judgement by the Palau Supreme Court, any attempt by an independent Palau government to requisition land for the use of the American military could be ruled unconstitutional.

The writers of the constitution were also inspired by memories of the privation, hunger and destruction of the last year of World War II, and of the wholesale deportation of Japanese. Five of the eleven Palauan delegates who drafted the nuclear-free provisions were either part-Japanese or had been named by their parents in honour of Japanese friends. The constitution was as much anti-war as anti-nuclear.

The impasse was always the 75-per-cent hurdle. Palauans went to the polls on this issue as well, in 1987 and again in 1992, to change the 75 per cent to 50 per cent plus one. On the first occasion a group of women elders who intended to challenge this decision in court were intimidated into withdrawing their case, and a delegation from the International Commission of Jurists claimed that violence had prevented due process of law. When the case came to the Supreme Court of Palau in 1988, it ruled that the amendment of 1987 was 'null, void and of no effect'. The 1992 referendum finally cut the Gordian knot. By a margin of six to four, the Palauans amended their constitution so that a simple majority would be enough to approve the Compact. The amendment was upheld and—assured by the Clinton administration that the United States would exercise its rights 'to train and manoeuvre in Palau' only at times of 'crisis or hostilities'—the people of Palau

8 *Pacific News Bulletin* (October 1992), 2.

voted in 1993 for free association. Palau became independent on 1 October 1994.

Palau is small even by Pacific standards: the population is 15,000. Its independence was achieved on United States terms. The dispute was about the terms of a limited decolonisation: what they are to be, and who is to dictate them. Given Palau's size and economic dependence, it will inevitably remain within the American orbit. But a sizeable—and constitutionally decisive—minority resisted the idea of conceding too much for the sake of aid, in particular of leaving open the possibility of an American military presence on their land.

AUSTRALIA AND CHRISTMAS ISLAND

In World War II Britain defeated its enemies but ceased to be a Great Power. Unable to accept this ineluctable fact, political leaders embraced the nuclear bomb as a new source of status and influence. 'If we are unable to make the bomb ourselves and have to rely entirely on the United States for this vital weapon', wrote Lord Cherwell, 'we shall sink to the rank of a second-class nation, only permitted to supply second-class troops, like the native levies who were allowed small arms but not artillery.'[9] From 1947 Britain developed its own nuclear deterrent. Some advisers and ministers would have preferred to co-operate directly with the United States, but the latter was not keen to help. The *McMahon Act* of 1946 specifically debarred American scientists from sharing nuclear information with foreigners, and when Britain requested the use of Enewetak Atoll for tests in the early 1950s, the Americans refused. Not until 1958 was the *McMahon Act* amended to permit Anglo-American nuclear weapons co-operation, and by then the British had gone elsewhere—first to Australia for atomic tests with yields in the kiloton range, then for H-bomb tests to two islands in the Gilbert and Ellice Islands Colony, Christmas and Malden. In what was known as the Maralinga Experimental Programme, kept secret until the 1980s, the British continued with a series of minor trials in South Australia until 1963. British bombs contributed only 4 per cent of global nuclear fallout up to 1980; their last atmospheric explosion took place in 1958 and, forswearing such tests, Britain signed the Partial Test Ban Treaty in 1963. Yet British experiments contaminated land and exposed some Aboriginal people, and possibly some Gilbertese, to unknown amounts of radioactivity.

Access to sites was the least of Britain's problems. The Australian Prime Minister Robert Menzies readily agreed to the site suggested by the British Admiralty for the first test in 1952—the uninhabited Monte Bello Islands off Western Australia—and just as willingly co-operated in making other sites available in the arid west of South Australia, first Emu Field and later Maralinga. Menzies decided first and told his Cabinet afterwards, believing it an honour to help Britain in this way.

9 Arnold, *A Very Special Relationship*, 5.

Alan Butement, the Australian government scientist who recommended Maralinga, believed that the country was empty: the track which crossed Maralinga was no longer in use 'except by one or two elderly blacks and then on rare occasions'. But even in the 1950s groups of Aboriginal people were leading traditional lives in South Australia, visiting white settlements only occasionally. The Yankunytjatjara and Pitjantjatjara were continuing to move over the desert country which became the Maralinga Prohibited Zone, in search of hunting grounds, food and water, to reassert social connections, and for ceremonial purposes. Groups of people were 'constantly forming and re-forming, splitting and recombining'.

The authorities also failed to ensure that no Aborigines were within the prohibited zone when bombs were detonated. Ground patrols were hampered by lack of vehicles, equipment and official support and had an impossible task in seeking Aborigines in an area of over 100,000 square kilometres. The reality of air patrols, as one pilot admitted later, was that the plane 'really just flew up the road and not over the country . . . I took the view that the country was too vast to cover on a grid basis.' In any case, Aboriginal people hid from the planes in fear, and some were living well within the Maralinga Prohibited Zone throughout the test period. The one government officer who knew the country well and tried to alert the authorities to the inadequacy of the search program was accused of 'apparently placing the affairs of a handful of natives above those of the British Commonwealth of Nations'. This was Walter MacDougall who, trying to stop people from moving across the prohibited area, resorted to warning the Yankunytjatjara and Pitjantjatjara 'that malevolent spiritual forces were active in the south, and that the poison of the bombs was linked to the traditional "poison" of *mamu*'. One Pitjantjatjara man recalled 'being turned back from a ceremonial strip towards the south-west, by MacDougall's warning that there was a poison there . . . so strong it would kill people who breathed it'.[10]

When researchers for the Australian Royal Commission asked the desert peoples what had happened to them in the 1950s, they received unexpected replies. The Yankunytjatjara and Pitjantjatjara at Ernabella wanted to talk about catastrophes that had befallen them, about desperate illness, suffering and death. Prompted by researchers who wanted to know about clouds of fallout and flashes in the sky, many people wove references to such events into a single explanation of the sudden and numerous deaths that occurred among children and adults in 1948 and 1957, on the second occasion coinciding with nuclear testing. They were describing epidemics of measles, perhaps their first exposure to it. By asking about one disaster, researchers stumbled on another, less catastrophic in Western eyes but far more so for the Ernabella people, who saw measles and fallout as part of a continuous process of death and destruction brought by white people.

Other Aboriginal people were physically affected by fallout. At Wallatinna, 173 kilometres from Emu Field, they told the Royal

10 Goodall, ' "The Whole Truth and Nothing But . . ." ', 116–17.

Commission of the 'black mist' that enveloped them after a test in 1953. The nuclear explosion generated fallout in a north-easterly direction, partly in a strange cloud described as 'wide . . . fairly low on the ground and it looked black and spreading out . . . it was coming slow with the wind pushing it'. After the cloud had passed, people vomited and developed sore eyes, skin rashes and fevers. The Royal Commission concluded that fallout had covered people at Wallatinna and made some temporarily ill, but drew no further conclusions, pointing to the 'lack of historical records on death and illness among Aboriginal people'.

A survey of the South Australian test sites found that the secret trials conducted in the 1960s had dispersed about 22 kilograms of plutonium-239 and a similar amount of uranium-235. Both elements remain radioactive for thousands of years, and plutonium-239 represents a particular threat if inhaled in contaminated dust, ingested in food, or absorbed in wounds. The desert people would be especially susceptible because of the dust raised by their normal activities. Dust is often on food, and many suffer from open sores, cuts and burns. After procrastinating for almost a decade, Britain finally agreed in 1993 to pay £20 million, less than half the sum required to clean up the contaminated lands of the Maralinga Tjaruta people, and work began on removing topsoil, encasing radioactive material in glass underground, and fencing off the most dangerous areas.

Christmas Island (now Kiritimati) was the site of British H-bomb tests in 1957 and 1958, and was made available to the United States in 1962 for Operation Dominic, its final atmospheric tests. A few hundred Gilbertese were working on copra plantations on the island when the British forces arrived, and some were employed by them. Toakau Takoro, interviewed in 1992, recalled being taken offshore on to a vessel where he and other Gilbertese labourers were shown cartoons below decks while the blasts took place. Similar temporary evacuations were made in 1962, though, as the tests continued, fewer people bothered to leave. The radioactive effects remain disputed. Almost all were 'clean' explosions high above the ground and therefore created almost no fallout. On the other hand, rain-outs after the blasts could have carried radioactive particles to the ground and sea where they became concentrated in food chains. For this reason, some say that there might be radioactive pollution on Kiritimati Island.

FRENCH POLYNESIA

As in Kiribati and the Marshall Islands, colonialism and nuclear testing have gone together in French Polynesia. France would not have tested there if the islands had been independent, and, once it was detonating bombs suspended from balloons over the Tuamotu Archipelago, the government feared that an active independence movement would cripple its strategic interests. The answer was to combine the carrots of French funds and the sticks of prohibition directed at local political opponents. It proved a successful combination.

Over the years of bomb testing from 1966 to 1996, military spending turned French Polynesia into a nuclear dependency, where people relied on the testing centre to supply the cash, capital investment and jobs that underpin modernisation in the territory. As a consequence, two themes recur in the political life of French Polynesia. The first is that the majority of indigenous Maohi people have not rallied behind a nationalist movement. The second is a system of patronage, in which jobs, services and property change hands in return for votes, and which is ultimately underwritten by financial transfers from France. Ever since the building boom of the mid-1960s, when thousands of army personnel arrived in Tahiti to initiate the testing program, French Polynesia has had an economy of transfer, where money comes from the other side of the world in return for the provision of strategic services. An artificial economy, built upon the patronage of an external power, has become the conduit for patronage at lower levels, territorial and municipal. The modern history of French Polynesia then is a 'nuclear history' in the sense that nothing of importance in its recent politics and economics can be understood without reference to the overwhelming presence of the Commission d'Energie Atomique (Atomic Energy Commission) and the Centre d'Expérimentation du Pacifique (CEP, Pacific Experimentation Centre).

The Établissements français d'Océanie (the colonial title for French Polynesia), comprising the Austral, Gambier, Marquesas, Society and Tuamotu groups, were administered from Pape'ete in Tahiti. Once annexation was completed in 1880, French Polynesia became a backwater of little significance to metropolitan France. After World War II France, like other imperial powers, was inclined towards self-determination for its colonies. The 1946 constitution for the first time recognised 'peoples and nations' in overseas France and their right to develop their civilisation and manage their affairs. Overseas inhabitants were accorded the status of French citizens and allowed to establish political parties. Until the 1950s the territory made slow but steady moves towards greater autonomy, and independence seemed a distinct possibility. The process of devolution culminated in the Defferre Law, whereby French Polynesia was granted partial autonomy, in 1957. According to its architect, the law was designed to prepare for a transition to independence. The Territorial Assembly gained many powers, especially in the economic domain.

French reforms were paralleled by the growth of a Tahitian nationalist movement under the charismatic leadership of Pouvanaa a Oopa. Pouvanaa had enlisted in the Pacific Battalion in World War I and rallied behind de Gaulle's Free French in World War II. His bitterness was therefore intense when the Governor exiled him to Huahine Island in 1942 because he had petitioned for social reform. After his release, he was arrested three more times as a result of non-violent political activities. Pouvanaa quoted these experiences as a reason for his entry into politics. Following his election to the French National Assembly in 1949, he established a political party, the Rassemblement Démocratique des Populations Tahitiennes (RDPT, Democratic Rally for the Tahitian People), with a wide-ranging agenda of political and social reform. In particular, the party sought expanded access to education and public-sector jobs, better provision of services and social security, land reform, and economic development; all in favour of the Maohi people. To achieve these ends, RDPT wanted to expand the powers of the Territorial Assembly and reduce the role of the Governor. Pouvanaa envisaged autonomy in close association with France, and made no reference to independence.

The popularity of the RDPT's vision and of Pouvanaa personally were evident in the party's electoral victories from 1949 until 1957. The party's supporters were overwhelmingly poor, rural Maohi, attracted by the program and by Pouvanaa's religious, populist oratory. Pouvanaa was re-elected to the National Assembly in 1951 and 1953; his colleagues Dr Florisson and Jean-Baptiste Céran-Jerusalémy won seats as National Senator and Councillor to the French Union; and the RDPT won clear majorities and formed governments following the 1953 and 1957 territorial elections. The main opposition party, the anti-autonomist Union Tahitienne Démocratique (UTD) had to be content with winning Pape'ete's municipal government. However, the RDPT had difficulty realising its agenda, which was blocked by the Governor and by the bureaucracy. The territorial government's powers were finally expanded in 1957, but the following year was marked by crisis and little was achieved before a new statute came into force in 1958.

The RDPT government also faced resistance in the Territorial Assembly. The Opposition (the UTD and independents combined) had attracted 55 per cent of the popular vote, mainly in urban areas. The crisis came to a head in April 1958 over the RDPT's plan to introduce income tax. A large crowd besieged the Assembly with a bulldozer and a truck-load of stones. French police looked on while the Assembly building was stoned. The Governor supported the Opposition's demand that the income tax law be suppressed. A motion to that effect was passed in the absence of the RDPT, which boycotted the session. The coalition which frustrated the RDPT's agenda included local business interests, the Governor (who controlled the police) and Gaullist politicians and officials in metropolitan France. The RDPT's troubles were compounded by rivalry between Pouvanaa and his second-in-command, Céran. An open split led to the expulsion of Céran, whose faction then created a splinter party, RDPT–Aratai.

Meanwhile in Paris the Fourth Republic was crumbling. When it collapsed in May 1958, General de Gaulle resumed power and viewed developments in Tahiti with concern. Popular support for the RDPT did not bode well for his strategic plans for the territory, which required social stability and an acquiescent local government. Advances towards autonomy were reversed. On 28 September 1958 France submitted a referendum to its overseas territories to ratify the Fifth Republic Constitution. One of its purposes was to determine whether the colonies wished to remain a part of France or become independent. De Gaulle offered only two options: 'If you say YES in this referendum, it means that you are willing to follow the same road as France, for better or for worse . . . If you say NO . . . France will not hold you back. She will wish you luck and let you lead your own life, without giving you any further moral or material help.'[11] France wanted a strong Yes vote to legitimise a strong role in territorial affairs—French Polynesia was under consideration as a site for nuclear testing. A resounding Yes vote would minimise opposition and discredit the RDPT which campaigned for independence. As it transpired, 64 per cent voted Yes—less than an overwhelming mandate. The nationalist movement therefore still posed a threat to French control.

Pouvanaa campaigned for independence, although he had previously advocated autonomy within the Republic. His switch was probably a response to the slow pace of statutory reform and the obstructive behaviour of the Governor. This is not to say that independence was ever absent from Pouvanaa's agenda and, given his nationalist record, it was not surprising that he seized the opportunity of the referendum to hasten independence.

More surprising was the RDPT's inability to muster a majority. The recent split was not fully understood by party rank and file, particularly in the outer islands which accounted for about half of the population and formed the core of RDPT support. Two factors made it virtually impossible for RDPT and Pouvanaa to communicate their new platform. The French administration and private interests obstructed access to the outer islands; and the administration denied the RDPT access to the radio station, which was instead made available to loyalists. Governor Bailly toured the islands for the Yes campaign and made good use of the station. Independence, he warned, would mean 'disorder in your daily life and in your spirits, for many it will mean days without food and nights in anguish of tomorrow, fear in the eyes of your children, anarchy with its whole cortege of misfortune, sickness and famine'. The Yes campaign was promoted by the Catholic Church, traditionally loyalist, and the Protestant Church, which had hitherto tolerated Pouvanaa. In view of the weight behind the Yes campaign, it was surprising that the No campaign garnered one-third of the vote.

A month later Governor Bailly dissolved the Territorial Assembly, alleging that it had lost its mandate. Within days Pouvanaa and many of his followers were arrested on dubious charges of arson. They languished in prison for a year before trial. Pouvanaa was sentenced to eight years' gaol and fifteen in exile. Arson was merely the pretext for Pouvanaa's arrest. The political motives were revealed when the Governor asserted that 'those who remain on the road to discord would have no more right either to pardon or to pity'. This hardly implied disinterested justice.

The Territorial Assembly then addressed the territory's position within the Republic and, after much debate, requested a reduction in the powers devolved to the territory a year earlier. The French state not only adopted these proposals but added further restrictions. The statute was modified by a French ordinance in December 1958. The statute concentrated enormous powers in the Governor, who retrieved his

---

11 Danielsson and Danielsson, *Poisoned Reign*, 36.

position as chief executive of the territory. The Territorial Assembly and government could make no decisions without his prior approval. He could also dismiss individual government members or even the whole government.

The Territorial Assembly's choice did not necessarily reflect public opinion. The electorate which gave the RDPT an absolute majority the previous year had endorsed its platform for full autonomy. At the next opportunity in 1960, Pouvanaa's son, Marcel Oopa, was elected to the National Assembly. He died in office and was replaced by the RDPT's John Teariki who retained the seat in the 1962 election. Territorial elections that year reduced support for the RDPT but it remained the largest party, winning fourteen of the thirty seats, and formed a coalition government.

Support for the nationalists was viewed with apprehension in Paris. The French Atomic Energy Commission, initiated in 1954, had identified two possible sites for nuclear tests—the Sahara Desert in Algeria and the Tuamotu Islands. Four atmospheric and thirteen underground tests were carried out in the Sahara between 1960 and 1962, before testing ceased with Algeria's independence. French politicians would not consider mainland France, so the Tuamotu group became the only option. Located in a far-flung, sparsely populated and little-known corner of the empire, its selection was unlikely to provoke protest in France. Moreover, the proposed sites were well out of the way of major maritime and air routes, and were uninhabited. The high cost of building and maintaining such a remote site was offset by its physical and political isolation. When the National Council of Defence announced the creation of the CEP in July 1962, there had been no consultation with territorial representatives. Indeed, they were not advised of the decision until January 1963 when President de Gaulle informed a delegation of Tahitian politicians in Paris, and assured them that 'There will be no danger . . . We shall make the tests only when the wind blows in the right direction . . . [and the CEP will provide] a new source of revenue and employment.' Construction began in 1963, while testing commenced in 1966.

One reason for French secrecy was the hope that the 1962 territorial election would vote the RDPT out of office, but the return of Teariki and the RDPT-dominated assembly and coalition government showed that the nationalist party was far from spent. Not only did the RDPT revive its campaign for autonomy, but Teariki was a fervent critic of the test program. The RDPT was a vocal opponent of French strategic interests, and France found this intolerable. In 1963, when Pouvanaa (from prison) encouraged the RDPT to place the question of independence on the agenda of its next congress, de Gaulle invoked an archaic law which provided for the dissolution of groups or parties which threatened 'national integrity'. The RDPT had no legal recourse. Its elected representatives, led by Teariki, reconstituted themselves as Here Ai'a (Patriots' Party) in 1965 and removed independence from the party's platform. A decade passed before another party formally advocated independence.

Meanwhile France acquired sovereign rights to Moruroa, Fangataufa and a military base in Faa'a in February 1964 via a Treaty of Cession. Bypassing the Territorial Assembly, the decision was referred to the Governor's Permanent Commission, where it was approved by three votes to two. The treaty granted the atolls to France free of charge for as long as they were needed for the test program, after which they would be returned without any obligation for rehabilitation or compensation. All parties at first opposed the CEP, through concern for its impacts on health, environment and society. Gaullist protests were quickly silenced by an appreciation of the economic benefits, but the autonomists maintained their vigilance throughout the 1960s and 1970s.

The inaugural congress of Here Ai'a in July 1966 coincided with the first nuclear explosion at Moruroa. Teariki used the occasion to launch a concerted campaign against the CEP. Earlier, he had protested that seven inhabited atolls lay within the defined danger zone which was closed to maritime and air traffic. The CEP responded by reducing the radius of the zone, but Tureia's sixty inhabitants remained within the danger area. CEP authorities claimed there was no danger to Maohi people in the vicinity of Moruroa, but this was hardly convincing given that European personnel were evacuated. Later, Islanders were advised of precautions to take when radioactive clouds passed overhead. Suspicion mounted when the publication of statistics on causes of death ceased a month after the first test, and the main hospital in Pape'ete was placed under military control. Analyses of the effects of radiation undertaken by military laboratories were deemed state secrets and only selected data were published. A nuclear explosion on 11 September 1966, hurried so that President de Gaulle himself could observe it, generated fallout that was caught in winds blowing west across the rest of the Pacific. In an official protest, New Zealand noted 'high levels of radioactivity in the air and in rainouts in various Pacific Islands, including the Cook Islands, Western Samoa and Fiji'. New Zealand's monitoring stations recorded significant fallout from every atmospheric test, sometimes blown back but more often carried around the earth and deposited throughout the southern hemisphere.

Teariki's anti-nuclear campaign was strengthened by an unexpected ally in September 1965. E'a Api, led by Francis Sanford, had its support base in the Faa'a municipal council. Sanford contested Teariki's seat in the National Assembly in 1967. Having made no public statement on the CEP, he gained the support of the Governor and defeated Teariki by the narrowest of margins. Only then did he denounce testing. Now two significant parties campaigned for autonomy and opposed the CEP. The autonomists regained a majority in the Territorial Assembly in 1967. Their first act was to vote for internal autonomy. This motion was ignored by Paris, but fresh National Assembly elections in 1968 gave Sanford the opportunity to campaign explicitly on the issue of autonomy within the French Republic, and to win an outright majority against the anti-autonomist, Gaullist candidate. The autonomist parties passed several resolutions on the tests. From its inception the autonomists had asked that the CEP's presence be subject to a territorial referendum. This demand was often repeated, but the concerns of territorial councillors fell on deaf ears in Paris and a response was rarely forthcoming. Whenever the Governor did respond, it was only to say that, as a matter of national defence, nuclear testing was outside the Territorial Assembly's jurisdiction. In spite of opposition by many politicians, it proved impossible to create a bipartisan front on the issue. It also proved difficult to mobilise mass action.

The nationalist cause was strengthened when Pouvanaa was granted a Presidential pardon and returned to a hero's welcome in November 1968. A year later his civic rights were restored, and he won the National Senate election of 1971 with two-thirds of the popular vote. When he was re-elected to the Territorial Assembly in 1972, and became its president, he delivered his inaugural speech in Tahitian. This was unprecedented, and the autonomist parties vigorously endorsed his campaign to grant Tahitian the status of an official language. At seventy-seven, Pouvanaa was still setting the nationalist agenda.

Far from conceding autonomist demands, France further diluted the territorial government's powers. In 1972, forty-four new municipalities were created where there had been only four. The municipalities obtained substantial powers and budgets, to which the territorial government was obliged to contribute. Yet the territory exercised minimal oversight over municipal authorities, which reported direct to the Governor or to the Minister for the Interior. Now forty-eight mayors enjoyed patronage. Henceforth electors increasingly voted on the basis of municipal patron–client relations, personal loyalties, and parochial concerns. The autonomists lost their majority in the 1972 election, largely because they had opposed the creation of additional local authorities and thus incurred the ire of municipal power-brokers. The Gaullists negotiated a very shaky coalition with a small new party and independents.

Despite these losses, the autonomists' campaign against atmospheric nuclear testing reached fever pitch in the early 1970s, fuelled in part by knowledge of the Marshallese experience and by evidence from New Zealand radiologists on the French tests. Territorial protests grew as morale was bolstered by international protests. Chile, Ecuador, Colombia, Venezuela and Argentina called on France to stop testing. Australia and New Zealand took France to the International Court of Justice, where they argued that French fallout infringed national sovereignty and exposed their peoples to insidious poison. New Zealand sent a naval frigate to the Tuamotus to relay photographs of mushroom clouds. Anti-nuclear activists sailed yachts into the test zone and dared the authorities to arrest them. The best known was the Canadian David McTaggart, who was beaten by French marines as they boarded his *Greenpeace III* in 1973. Photographs of the incident, smuggled out of French Polynesia, dramatised the issue world-wide.

Sanford, still a deputy to the French National Assembly, tirelessly lobbied the French and international peace movements and the United Nations against the tests, in tandem with his campaign for autonomy. He and Pouvanaa jointly sent an open letter to the people of metropolitan France, asking that they urge their government to desist from nuclear tests in Polynesia: 'Since 1963, French Polynesia has expressed, through the voice of its elected representatives . . . incessant protests accompanied by demands for international control over radioactive contamination in our natural environment.' Sanford's greatest publicity coup resulted from an alliance with a metropolitan liberal politician, Jean-Jacques Servan-Schreiber, who led a 'Battalion of Peace' to Tahiti in June 1973. This high-profile delegation lent support to the biggest-ever anti-nuclear demonstration in the territory. Sanford then issued an ultimatum to President Pompidou to stop the tests or risk a referendum on independence. This was, however, an empty threat from an isolated deputy. Conflicting messages were emanating from Tahiti. Sanford and his party E'a Api, together with Teariki's Here Ai'a and the peace movement, were campaigning against the tests. The president of the Territorial Assembly, Gaston Flosse, was asking the CEP to remain as long as possible; and trade union leaders were angered by the impact of the regional anti-nuclear boycott on trade and communications.

France was still conducting atmospheric tests ten years after the United States, Britain and the Soviet Union had signed a Partial Test Ban Treaty and moved their tests underground. Ultimately, France succumbed to pressure and in August 1973 announced a shift to underground testing. Nevertheless, a final series of powerful atmospheric explosions took place in 1974 before testing began below the coral atoll in 1975 and, when they ran out of space, under the lagoon. The decision was influenced by trade and diplomatic sanctions which outweighed any technological benefits from atmospheric tests. Tahitians had also sent a strong message during the Presidential elections in 1973 when 51 per cent voted for the ostensibly anti-nuclear and pro-autonomy candidate François Mitterrand. Although Mitterrand lost to Giscard d'Estaing, the latter took note of Tahitian sentiment. Two months later he announced the shift to underground testing. Early the following year he initiated negotiations for reform of the territory's political status.

When negotiations began, the autonomists had their demands ready, while the Gaullists (still opposed to autonomy) made a moderate request for self-management. Negotiations dragged on for two years. One obstacle was the fact that the French government withdrew from its original negotiating stance and offered extremely limited interpretations of autonomy. The other was a series of defections (and counter-defections) in the Territorial Assembly which paralysed its operations. The autonomists demanded fresh elections, which they believed they would win. The Governor instead ordered the Assembly to meet. At dawn on 10 June 1976, autonomist militants and their elected leaders occupied the Assembly building and locked the doors. The occupation lasted for ten months. Sanford further forced the issue by resigning from the National Assembly and winning the by-election, again on the platform of autonomy. At this point France reopened negotiations with Sanford's more moderate allies, and with the Gaullists. The resulting statute of 1977 bore a closer resemblance to the UTD's limited self-management than to autonomy, but the autonomists accepted the compromise since it included an agreement to hold fresh elections. They won a majority of seats, but this was a hollow victory given the restrictiveness of the new statute to which they were now committed.

Although the autonomists and some marginal anti-nuclear groups continued to campaign against the CEP, they lost much of their external support once the tests moved underground. However, if not for the pressure of the autonomists, their consistent electoral support, and the final desperate strategy of paralysing the Territorial Assembly, even Giscard's minimal reform might not have occurred. France had manipulated negotiations to exclude the more radical autonomists and retained wide powers. However, several new *indépendantiste* parties founded in the mid-1970s were highly critical of the 1977 statute. There was no honeymoon before clamour arose for internal autonomy on one hand, and independence on the other. The new parties initially had few members and won neither Assembly seats nor municipal councils in 1977, yet they acquired considerable influence in debates.

Charlie Ching, a nephew of Pouvanaa, formed the Te Taata Tahiti Tiama (Free Tahitian) party in 1975, dedicated to immediate and total independence by any means—including armed struggle. The party formed a covert paramilitary wing, Toto Tupuna (Blood of our Ancestors), to attack military targets relating to CEP operations. In November 1977 four members of Toto Tupuna turned instead to civilian targets, detonating a bomb in the Pape'ete telephone exchange and murdering a French businessman. The militants were arrested, along with Ching and two other party members, and brought to trial in January 1979 after several procedural irregularities. The sentences ranged from twenty years for the self-confessed commandos to ten years for Ching, although no evidence implicated him directly. French lawyers were brought in for the defence, and the trials were thrown out and sent to the Court of Appeals in Versailles, where the sentences were greatly reduced. The lawyers also won the right for the accused to be tried in their own language. These proceedings attracted unprecedented publicity. A *Le Monde* journalist observed that 'a trial of terrorism has become the trial of French colonialism'. Toto Tupuna was generally condemned for its violence, but (from a prison cell) Ching received 5.6 per cent of the vote for one of the two territorial seats in the National Assembly, a surprising show of support for a new party with a radical agenda and a militant strategy.

Disillusioned Maohi found more durable representation in two other new parties, Ia Mana Te Nunaa (Power to the People) and Tavini Huiraatira No Te Ao Maohi (Rally to the Service of the Maohi People). These parties caused much greater concern to France than Te Taata Tahiti Tiama because they advocated non-violent and democratic methods for promoting independence and opposing the tests. More-over, they provoked the mainstream parties to broaden their conception of autonomy. Both parties opposed nuclear testing. Ia Mana was concerned about the economy and society, whereas Tavini focused on the environment and the health of CEP workers and Islanders. Ia Mana was an explicitly socialist party which—in a devoutly religious electorate which harboured a deep antipathy to the left—nevertheless won three Territorial Assembly seats in 1982. However, Ia Mana's leader, Jacqui Drollet, failed to be elected mayor. Tavini gained its first electoral success in the 1983 municipal elections when it took control of Faa'a, the most populous municipality, and its leader, Oscar Temaru, became mayor. Tavini won its first two Territorial Assembly seats in 1986.

Mass protests against the CEP dwindled after the tests went underground, but the autonomist politicians maintained their opposition and the campaign received a boost under the influence of the new parties and in response to a series of accidents at the test site. One involved an explosion and fire, releasing radiation which killed two workers and injured four other personnel. Another in July 1979 was caused by a bomb which the French detonated half-way down a shaft, producing a subterranean landslide and a tidal wave through the Tuamotu Archipelago. These incidents led the Territorial Assembly unanimously to demand immediate suspension and an independent commission of inquiry into site safety. France rejected both demands. In 1981, further accidents occurred at Moruroa in which storms caused plutonium residues from the atmospheric tests to traverse the lagoon. The conservative Tahoeraa leader, Gaston Flosse, requested a mission of international experts. Here Ai'a followed with another call for suspension. Both proposals passed the Territorial Assembly but were again refused by France.

In the early 1980s the anti-nuclear campaign was thus for a time bipartisan and demonstrations increased in size and frequency. This was in part because hopes that President Mitterrand and the new Socialist government would end the tests were dashed when testing resumed after a brief suspension. France directed greater efforts into public relations. This campaign to reassure the population, and to silence external critics, included three much lauded visits by independent missions to ascertain the safety of the site: Tazieff in 1982, Atkinson in 1983, and Cousteau in 1987. Their reports were presented by France as proof that the tests posed no immediate risk to health or the environment. However, the missions were brief, restricted in their sampling, and—denied access to the most heavily contaminated sections of the atoll—produced no long-term conclusions.

French governments—socialist or conservative—were adamantly opposed to a national, much less territorial, referendum on the CEP, despite numerous proposals by the Territorial Assembly. In 1989, Socialist Prime Minister Rocard again ruled out the prospect: 'The presidential election [of 1988] including French Polynesia, has confirmed national support for the politics of defence. This is sufficient.' He reiterated a long-standing policy, that France's defence would not be decided by consulting districts or territories. On the other hand, the government was prepared to consider concessions to autonomy. For three decades the conservative Tahitian parties had opposed expanded autonomy. Surprisingly then, in March 1980 the Tahoeraa leader, Gaston Flosse, made a complete volte-face and presented himself as the foremost proponent of internal autonomy. He recognised that the concept had gained respectability in France and locally. The established autonomists were never able to regain the ground they lost to Flosse's high-profile campaign. When territorial elections were held in 1982, Teariki's Here Ai'a won only six seats, and Sanford held the only seat won by E'a Api, whereas Tahoeraa won thirteen, and was able to govern with the erratic support of minor parties and independents. Ironically Flosse, the Gaullist and once fervent opponent of autonomy, led negotiations for internal autonomy with the formerly autonomist Socialists in France. In the new statute of 1984, some powers were devolved, but the territory's authority was still largely restricted to local affairs. Paris retained a vast domain, including foreign relations, the 200-mile exclusive economic zone, immigration, law and order, defence, and the public service.

France's essential interests were protected. It is less obvious why territorial representatives accepted the statute. Oscar Temaru dismissed it as 'a rubbish bin where one can put anything one wants', but Alexandre Léontieff, in Flosse's camp, described it as offering 'the benefits of independence without the inconveniences'. Temaru's comment reflects his party's perception that the statute makes symbolic and insubstantial concessions, whereas Léontieff expressed the mainstream view that this statute was the best option available. The upper limits of self-government were attained within a framework acceptable to France. Territorial representatives were constrained by the need for French approval, for without it they could not rely on financial support for French Polynesia's extreme economic dependence.

In 1981, President Mitterrand observed that 'the absence of real economic development means that French Polynesia has never been so dependent on France'. The CEP played a central role in producing this outcome. Throughout the 1950s French Polynesia had enjoyed a reasonable trade balance, with exports covering 90 per cent of imports, and was relatively independent of subsidies. At the end of the decade the economy took a turn for the worse. The cash economy, based on only five major exports, was vulnerable to fluctuating demand. Prices for copra and coffee declined, pearl-shell was being displaced by plastic buttons, and the vanilla plantations were struck by disease. The Makatea mine ran out of phosphate and closed in 1966. At the same time, population growth and urbanisation increased the demand for imports. When a territorial delegation went to Paris to ask for assistance in 1963, de Gaulle announced the imminent installation of the CEP and an economic aid package in virtually the same breath. The offer was impossible to refuse.

The CEP had brought prosperity through massive investment in infrastructure, customs revenue, local expenditure and employment. Direct employment was significant in the 1960s construction period. It peaked at 5400 locally recruited workers in 1967 but rapidly receded in the 1970s. Like CEP expenditure, the program's demand for labour fluctuated, causing havoc in employment and migration. The erratic patterns ceased and jobs became scarce. The evolution of technology, and the gradual reduction in tests, meant almost no new recruitment after 1986. Since then the CEP has employed only a few hundred local people on a permanent basis, although employment in related sectors remained high.

Military and civil spending, and the drive to recruit Maohi labourers, diminished the incentive for new ventures in the primary sector. On many outer islands the majority of adult men left to work for good CEP wages. At the same time the public sector expanded exponentially and public-service salaries increased, attracting people from agriculture and fishing, and from other private-sector activities. The territory had been essentially self-sufficient in food in the 1950s. By the late 1960s more than half of commercially sold food was imported. In the early 1990s the territory was producing merely a quarter of its food. The wages of 15,000 French workers for the CEP contributed to this outcome, and so did the expanding public service. A similar development occurred in the Marshall Islands under the impact of American nuclear testing and the Kwajalein military base: by the late 1980s the Marshalls were importing 90 per cent of their food. The escalation in imports and the drop in exports blew out the trade deficit. Whereas 1960 exports covered 75 per cent of imports, by 1965 this fell to 9 per cent and never recovered. The only productive sectors of the economy to experience real growth were tourism and black pearls; but such growth had little impact on the trade imbalance. The principal obstacles to manufacturing and other industry are distance, high costs of production, and a limited domestic market.

The CEP's impact was greatest during its establishment in the mid-1960s when its contribution to gross domestic product peaked at 76 per cent. Once construction was completed there was a marked decrease in the CEP's economic role. When atmospheric testing ended in 1975, CEP expenditure fell to 26 per cent of gross domestic product. France compensated with increased civil spending, mainly on public works and the civil service. As a result of these external transfers, the 1960s and 1970s were marked by rapid economic growth. However, apparent prosperity masked deteriorating conditions in the domestic economy. By the 1980s, French Polynesia's economy was severely imbalanced, with a top-heavy public sector and little development or diversification of primary and secondary activities. From 1986 economic growth stagnated, consumer spending declined, and capital took flight. The economy was not helped by a further scaling down of CEP activities and expenditure with the shift to offshore testing and a reduction in the number of tests. The territorial government resorted to borrowing. By 1993 the government was spending as much on debt servicing as it was gaining in new loans. The suspension of tests in 1992 was the last straw: the government turned again to France for short-term relief and funds for a long-term development strategy.

French Polynesia is not unusual in the Pacific for its extreme economic dependence. What does distinguish the territory is the extent of its aid dependence, the high cost (and standard) of living, and the withering away of the subsistence safety net. In most respects French Polynesia's economic evolution has resembled that of other overseas territories and departments, which also enjoy higher standards of living than their independent neighbours. However, metropolitan transfers have been much higher than in other overseas dependencies because of military spending. The timing of the expenditure from the early 1960s onwards suggests that it was designed to buy acquiescence in the French presence and the CEP. French policy was very effective in achieving this objective. By 1990, the territory depended on France for 75 per cent of its external income (35 per cent from the military). French Polynesia was earning a mere 25 per cent of external receipts from its own resources, principally black pearls and tourism. Five years after Internal Autonomy was granted, France's grip was bluntly explained by Prime Minister Rocard: 'Who pays, controls.'

In April 1992 the pro-independence and anti-nuclear parties welcomed the nuclear test moratorium; but the mainstream parties had come to accept or support nuclear testing for fiscal reasons. The CEP also served as a lever for local politicians to extract further financial aid from France. Finally, the territorial government could not be sure that high levels of civil aid would continue in a post-nuclear era, since the CEP had been France's primary strategic interest. Ironically then, the government opposed the CEP's departure because the territory had become dependent on the transfers and economic activity which it generated. A local magazine's headline 'Tests Stop: Apocalypse Now!' reflected the panic in the government and the business community. The moratorium precipitated a budget deficit of crisis proportions.

The territory experienced difficulties even during a temporary suspension, when the site was kept operational. The Territorial Institute of Statistics estimated that the CEP's departure, without compensation, would incur a 23 per cent decrease in gross domestic product and a 17 per cent fall in employment. By contrast tourism, the biggest foreign-exchange earner (after state transfers) accounts for only 7 per cent of gross domestic product and 6 per cent of jobs. The difficulties would be exacerbated if a permanent test ban were accompanied by an abrupt reduction in civil services and subsidies. However, this is unlikely in the short term. In all its other overseas territories, France has subsidised standards of living to retain loyalty. France will presumably maintain high rates of expenditure due to broader perceptions of French Polynesia's strategic significance, the potential wealth of the exclusive economic zone, and as an outpost for projecting French culture and language.

In the wake of the test suspension, a Polynesian delegation to France called for national solidarity on the grounds that, 'having provided the nuclear test site free of charge to the nation's disposal, the territory has, for nearly thirty years, contributed continuously to the national defence'. To reassure French Polynesia, France agreed to a ten-year development plan entitled 'Pact for Progress'. France agreed to continue civil transfers at current levels for at least another decade. Plans were also put in train to promote development projects. However, even if existing commitments are fulfilled, the 'Pact for Progress' could not compensate fully for military transfers.

Legal and economic constraints alone do not account for the wide-spread acceptance of the French presence. Equally significant were the intensity and speed of social change in the identity and life-style of the Maohi people. The CEP played a significant role in accelerating assimilation. Its installation coincided with an abrupt and pervasive influx of French culture, combined with the development of a modern economy. The rapid absorption of Maohi people into the urban economy coincided with a disintegration of traditional society and culture.

A French-only language policy was imposed in 1860 and remained in force until 1971. All state education was in French. One French official felt that the single-language policy probably expressed fear that any expression of indigenous identity could be linked to nationalism and aspirations for independence.[12] Until its recent revival in political discourse, the Tahitian language was rendered virtually irrelevant in public life. Tahitian did gain status as an official language of the territory in 1980, but French continued to dominate as the language of education, the media, courts, commerce and the professions. In an oral culture, preservation of the language has enormous importance for interpreting and preserving culture and history. A linguist and theologian, Duro Raapoto, believes that oral proficiency in Tahitian is limited. In 1992 he estimated that in Tahiti, where the majority of the population lives, only the older generation had competency in Tahitian while those under thirty had a fragile knowledge and teenagers were hard pressed to speak Tahitian without substantial additions of French. In extended families, young children who speak only French cannot communicate with their grandparents. 'To achieve a reconciliation with our land and culture it is necessary not to pass by the language. The language for me is fundamental. The young people have to speak the language in order to be able to speak about culture, about theology, and many other things.'[13]

The electronic media radiated French language and culture. France established a special television service to all its overseas territories. The Maohi are particularly susceptible as they come from an oral culture and because there is widespread semi-literacy. The introduction of television coincided with the CEP, and later transmission was extended to the outer islands via satellite. By the 1990s television reached roughly 90 per cent of the population, and 81 per cent of households owned sets. French Overseas Television (RFO) is beamed direct from Paris with only a small percentage of programs in Tahitian and about Tahiti. This infrastructure is enormously expensive. Significantly, France did not devolve control over electronic media to the territorial government. It is hard to gauge the full impact of television, but it has had a major influence on Maohi attitudes and life-style. Television viewing has usurped time formerly devoted to the family meal, one of few opportunities for children to speak in Tahitian and pick up cultural values from their parents and grandparents. Similarly, programs and advertising raise expectations and shape tastes for consumer goods.

---

12 Lionel Rimoux, Assistant High Commissioner, personal communication, 1992.
13 Duro Raapoto, personal communication, 1992.

The education system has given little emphasis to Maohi history and culture. Jean-Marc Pambrun, a cultural researcher, noted that courses on Maohi culture are woefully inadequate: 'There is a need to describe and write Polynesian history right from its origins and great founding myths up to the present . . . It is impossible to give the Polynesian his identity, to forge a national identity with the present state of the curriculum.'[14] Since Internal Autonomy in 1984, the absence of a commitment to increase knowledge of Maohi language and culture can be attributed to the territorial government. However, this observation needs to be qualified by acknowledging the entrenched nature of institutions and processes which perpetuated assimilation even after direct French control lapsed. French Polynesia's experience of assimilation is mirrored in the Marshall Islands, where the people have been subjected to an English-language policy and American-based schooling. The Marshallese have also been inundated with American television and radio broadcasting and Western consumer culture.

Until the 1960s French settlement was negligible. The CEP brought an influx of military and civilian personnel, raising the French population from several hundred to several thousand. Later, rapid economic growth attracted investors and French people in general. In 1988, the proportion of European residents (over 90 per cent French) had stabilised at 12 per cent. CEP also promoted tourism, because Faa'a airport which serviced CEP facilitated tourist access. The number of tourists leaped from 4000 in 1960 to a peak of 161,000 by 1986. The combined impact of French residents, transient military and public-service personnel and tourists in such a small community reinforced assimilation.

A related trend was the emergence of a *demi* mixed-race category. The *demis* are distinguished by the extent to which they have assimilated French language, culture, attitudes to education, work and life-style. Being part-Maohi, they have also acted as a conduit for French culture to the wider population. Successful *demis* act as role models for a locally born person in the modern economy and French political system. In the public sphere they removed the need for direct oversight by metropolitan personnel and provided an appearance of governance by the people. Furthermore, loyalist parties and French media use allegations of racism to undermine support for pro-independence parties. This is not difficult, given that the pro-independence parties seek to remove the French state and their policies automatically alienate the ethnic French and, to a lesser extent, those who are part-French.

The relatively low rate of immigration has shaped attitudes in other ways. In comparison to New Caledonia, where the Kanaks have been outnumbered by immigrants, the Maohi have never been a minority, and their proportion has been increasing. Maohi have larger families than other groups and a very low rate of emigration. In 1988, ethnic Maohi constituted 66.5 per cent of the population, and together with

---

14 Jean-Marc Pambrun, Director of Department of Traditions at the Musée des Îles, personal communication, 1992.

part-Maohis reached 83 per cent. People do not feel under threat like Kanaks in New Caledonia.

Before the CEP, there was already a gradual drift to the capital. The rural exodus escalated in response to the demand for labour. The population share of Tahiti and its sister island, Moorea, rose from 59 per cent in 1962 to 74 per cent in 1967, with more than half in Pape'ete. The life-style, culture and community of the outer islands was quickly replaced by an urban and proletarian form of work and society. These changes were to a large extent consequences of the modernisation and economic growth which accompanied the CEP. They were not state policies designed to acculturate the people, but this was their effect.

The rapid changes of the 1960s brought about increasing stratification along class and racial lines. *Demis* dominated the political arena and the administration while *demis*, Chinese and metropolitan French controlled commerce, industry and the professions. Since the 1960s the vast majority of Maohi have become concentrated at the bottom of the hierarchy as low-paid workers, small farmers, or the unemployed. Despite the low status of the Maohi and their economic marginalisation, enormous material benefits flowed from France's commitment to remain. The CEP and French civil transfers brought unprecedented infrastructural development. Economic growth offered the Maohi opportunities for fast money in the urban labour force. The expansion in services included rapid growth of schools and hospitals. Although the territory does not provide unemployment benefits, a wide range of benefits are available to families, old-age and invalid pensioners. Similarly, the almost universal provision of running water, electrification and telecommunications would have been unthinkable, especially in the outer islands, without financial assistance.

As the French government frequently emphasised, in contrast to independent Island countries, the Maohi have obtained high standards of living in a material sense. Social change shaped and raised expectations, but economic growth and social services satisfied them. The nationalists' appeal for a sacrifice in living standards after independence has hardly been persuasive. Nor have *indépendantistes* been able to capitalise on the stark inequalities between ethnic groups. Maohi awareness of inequality has not galvanised them into a nationalist conception of 'us' Maohi versus 'them'. Satisfaction is not absolute, especially among young Maohi. Several years of recession have swollen the number of unemployed and disaffection is rising, as evidenced in the destructive riots of October 1987, lesser riots in the early 1990s, and the widespread rioting which accompanied the resumption of testing in 1995. Nevertheless, most people continue to perceive France as a guarantor of their well-being, and the growing number of disillusioned Maohi has not strengthened the pro-independence parties.

Electoral trends since 1984 indicate consistent voter support for parties which would maintain close links with France and work within the current statute. Support for pro-independence parties is restricted to a minority. Ia Mana finally lost its place in territorial politics after the 1991 elections, whereas Tavini enjoyed a modest increase from two to four in the 41-seat assembly. Tavini benefited from Ia Mana's demise and from the effects of the recession which added to the pool of poor and unemployed Maohi. But Tavini's support was still largely restricted to its municipal power-base in Faa'a. Between 1982 and 1991 the pro-independence share of the vote fell slightly from 14.6 to 13.8 per cent. Elections to the French National Assembly provide another measure of popular opinion. The March 1993 national elections confirmed the conservative trend of territorial elections. Flosse won the eastern division in the first round. His coalition partner, Jean Juventin, had more difficulty in the densely populated western division which he took on the second round. His principal challenger, Oscar Temaru, scored 44.3 per cent. The 1993 elections gave the highest tally ever received by a pro-independence party, but Temaru's popularity was probably due to his personal integrity and a protest against Juventin (recently implicated in corruption) rather than a vote for independence.

Since Internal Autonomy in 1984, policy differences between the established parties have virtually disappeared, replaced by a gradual convergence. Although no party has obtained sufficient electoral support to govern in its own right, one party stands out from the others. For over a decade, up to and including the territorial election of 1996, Tahoeraa received the largest share of seats and dominated five of the six coalitions. The personal appeal of its leader, Gaston Flosse, outer islands conservatism, and the backing of non-Maohi ethnic groups, have been major elements in support for the party with the strongest and longest commitment to ties with France.

Personalisation of politics and parochial voting have also helped to determine the success of parties. This process impedes the development of a territory-wide Maohi movement. The tendency to vote for incumbent mayors and territorial representatives (often the same person) is pronounced. All the principal players, notably Flosse, Juventin and Temaru, are mayors of Tahiti's largest municipalities. Flosse has served three terms as President, three terms as National Deputy, and served as Mayor of Pirae since 1963. He has held all three offices simultaneously since 1993.

Limited devolution has paradoxically strengthened France's hold. Internal Autonomy protected France's strategic objectives; yet it offered enough concessions and symbols to satisfy mainstream politicians. Meanwhile the inability of pro-independence parties to rally Maohi undermined their external support. Unlike the Kanak campaign in New Caledonia, Maohi *indépendantistes* have not gained patronage from the South Pacific Forum, nor have they reinscribed the territory on the decolonisation list at the United Nations. The rest of the world was largely unaware of the Maohi independence movement until the dramatic anti-nuclear riots of 1995.

The territorial government of French Polynesia would like extra powers. It would like greater control over immigration, a larger role in the regional affairs of the South Pacific and jurisdiction over the 200-mile economic zone. But those who decide will be the politicians in Paris rather than those in Pape'ete. The years of nuclear testing have left a legacy not only of contaminated atolls but, more significantly, of economic, political and cultural absorption of the territory into France itself.

THE IDEA OF A NUCLEAR-FREE PACIFIC

So long as the Islands were colonies, Islanders' objections to nuclear tests could be dismissed by the authorities. But in the 1970s, as more territories gained independence and French atmospheric testing offered a rallying point for nuclear-free sentiment, popular opposition became more organised and began to influence the foreign policies of new states. 'A nuclear-free Pacific', defined radically by some and moderately by others, was the universal goal of independent states by the early 1980s.

The Conference for a Nuclear-Free Pacific in Fiji in 1975 initiated an organised movement for a nuclear-free and independent Pacific. The conference, composed of delegates from all over the Pacific, declared that the Pacific people were 'sick and tired of being treated like dogs', and called for a treaty to establish a comprehensive nuclear-free zone in the Islands. In the following years the movement embraced other campaigns against large-scale military manoeuvres, the testing of intercontinental ballistic missiles at Kwajalein, the practice bombing of Kaho'olawe Island in Hawai'i, the mining of uranium in Australia, and the dumping of radioactive waste by Japan. It supported the constitution of Palau, the independence movements in the French territories, and the guerrilla resistance in East Timor and Irian Jaya; and its members regularly demonstrated against French testing. The movement failed to reach many of its objectives, which by their nature affected the security interests of the United States and France. Yet it popularised an idea and gave expression to widespread sentiment.

The leaders of newly independent Island countries had been quick to raise the nuclear issue. Heads of government at the first South Pacific Forum meeting in 1971 appealed to France to make its current test series the last in the Pacific, and in 1972 they called for an end to all atmospheric testing. The 1975 forum accepted New Zealand's idea of a South Pacific Nuclear-Free Zone in principle. In the early 1980s the idea of a nuclear-free Pacific began to find its way into the foreign policies and constitutions of Island states. Papua New Guinea and Vanuatu endorsed the concept of a South Pacific Nuclear-Free Zone in 1981; Vanuatu declared itself nuclear-free; and Palau and the Federated States of Micronesia, in advance of independence, adopted constitutions with nuclear-restrictive provisions. In New Zealand the Labour Party, still in opposition, vowed to make New Zealand nuclear-free when it won office.

The Australian Prime Minister Bob Hawke, elected in March 1983, sensed that nuclear-free sentiment had to be taken seriously. If it were not, he feared that some South Pacific countries, frustrated by lack of action to stop nuclear testing at Moruroa, would begin to impede the free movement of United States naval vessels and aircraft. Nuclear-free sentiment provoked by France would be directed at the United States and would undermine its strategic position in the South Pacific. So it was Australia, not an Island nation, that proposed a South Pacific Nuclear-Free Zone Treaty at the 1983 South Pacific Forum meeting and then chaired the forum working group on the treaty. Over the next two years Australia exercised its influence over the Island states to ensure that the final treaty would be moderate, directed at French bomb testing rather than United States nuclear ship visits or missile testing. Papua New Guinea, Solomon Islands and Vanuatu wanted stronger provisions, such as a ban on missile testing and time limits on port visits by nuclear-armed vessels. But the last thing Australia wanted was to harm United States strategic interests, and Australia's initiative can be seen as a policy of curbing the enthusiasm of Island states. As a US Congressional report on 'Problems in Paradise' pointed out in 1989, 'the issue of transitory ship visits was left to the individual discretion of each Treaty signatory. Thus, on this important issue, the Treaty has no adverse impact on the interests of the United States, since we are not precluded from doing anything we had been doing or were planning to do.' Twelve of the sixteen forum countries had signed the treaty by 1996. Whereas Western countries regarded the nuclear-free zone as an arms-control measure, Islanders without influence in world politics tended to see it as environmental protection. The treaty's protocols were presented to the five declared nuclear weapons states for signature, but only China and the former Soviet Union had signed by 1993. France refused, and so did the United States and Britain.

The end of the Cold War and the suspension of French testing removed the urgency from nuclear issues in the regional politics of the South Pacific. But one of the first acts of Jacques Chirac on becoming President in 1995 was to announce that France would test more bombs. In a stroke, he put the nuclear issue back at the centre of regional politics, sparking outrage in South Pacific countries and protests world-wide. Ieremaia Tabai, Secretary-General of the South Pacific Forum, called the decision provocative and predicted that it would damage France's relations with the region. Within days a forum delegation protested formally to the government in Paris, and within weeks thousands of people in French Polynesia took to the streets of Pape'ete in a demonstration larger than any since 1973. They marched behind anti-nuclear banners to welcome Greenpeace's *Rainbow Warrior*, and their dissent showed that the independence movement was far from defunct. Keen to make a symbolic point, Greenpeace sailed the *Rainbow Warrior* into the exclusion zone around Moruroa Atoll on 10 July 1995, ten years to the day since French secret service agents had sunk its namesake in Auckland harbour. French naval commandos stormed the vessel, smashed windows and overpowered the protesters with teargas, provoking further opposition to French testing world-wide.

Tensions rose as the first test approached. France seized Greenpeace protest vessels near Moruroa. Parliamentarians from Australia, New Zealand, Japan and Europe marched alongside Polynesians in another demonstration in Tahiti. And when the bomb exploded on 5 September, Pape'ete erupted in a major riot. Demonstrators stormed the international airport terminal with bricks, iron bars and a bulldozer. As police responded with stun grenades and teargas, the rioters moved on Pape'ete itself, where they rampaged through the streets, looted shops, overturned cars and set part of the town ablaze. International media images suggested a colony on the point of revolt, but the true significance of the riot remained to be seen. Many rioters were from the poorest parts of Pape'ete, unemployed youth who would lose little if France left French Polynesia. Other Polynesians who wanted France to stop nuclear tests nevertheless valued the French as generous patrons of their standards of living: they were anti-nuclear but pro-French. Independence remained a minority cause, as the 1996 territorial election revealed. While the independence representatives expanded from six to eleven members in an assembly of forty-one, Gaston Flosse's pro-French Tahoeraa party easily won a majority and continued to control the territorial government.

In one sense the nuclear era in the Pacific ended in 1996, when France bowed to international opinion and finished its test program ahead of schedule. Almost everyone in the Pacific had long wanted the islands and the ocean to be free of all things nuclear. The idea that the Pacific should be nuclear-free had become part of the region's identity and now, at last, that aspiration seemed to be fulfilled. Fifty years after the first nuclear blast at Bikini Atoll, France began to dismantle the Pacific test facilities and joined the United States and Britain in signing the South Pacific Nuclear-Free Zone Treaty. All five nuclear powers had agreed that the days of testing in the Pacific were over. But in another sense the nuclear era would not be closed now, or for centuries to come. The legacy of half a century of nuclear blasts remained in the bodies of people exposed to radiation, in the natural environment of the test atolls, and in the risk of future contamination.

BIBLIOGRAPHIC ESSAY

An introduction to Pacific nuclear issues is provided by Firth, *Nuclear Playground*. Leading sources for American testing and Micronesian consequences are Kiste, *The Bikinians*; Weisgall, *Operation Crossroads: The Atomic Tests at Bikini Atoll*; Bradley, *No Place to Hide, 1946–1984*; Tobin, 'The Resettlement of the Enewetak People'; Smith, *Micronesia: Decolonisation and US Military Interests in the Trust Territories of the Pacific Islands*; Wood, 'Prelude to an Anti-War Constitution'; Carucci, 'The Source of the Force in Marshallese Cosmology', in White and Lindstrom, *The Pacific Theater*. Government reports may be found in Fifth Congress of Micronesia, First Regular Session, *A Report on the People of Rongelap and Utirik Relative to Medical Aspects of the March 1, 1954, Incident: Injury, Examination, and Treatment*, February 1973; Second Regular Session, *Compensation for the People of Rongelap and Utirik*, February 1974; United Nations Trusteeship Council reports; US Department of Energy,

Radiological Survey Plan for the Northern Marshall Islands, 22 August, 1978; and two publications from the US General Accounting Office: *Marshall Islands: Status of the Nuclear Claims Trust Fund*, Washington, DC, 25 September 1992; and *U.S. Trust Territory. Issues Associated with Palau's Transition to Self-Government*, Washington, DC, 1989.

British nuclear testing and Australian and Island consequences are treated by Arnold, *A Very Special Relationship; Report of the Royal Commission into British Nuclear Tests in Australia*, Canberra, 1985; Goodall, '"The Whole Truth and Nothing But . . ."'; Department of Primary Industries and Energy, *Rehabilitation of Former Nuclear Test Sites in Australia*, Canberra, 1990; and Meyenn, 'Only One Babai Pit in a Lifetime'.

The leading source on French testing and French Polynesian consequences is von Strokirch, 'Tahitian Autonomy: Illusion or Reality?'. See also von Strokirch, 'The Impact of Nuclear Testing on Politics in French Polynesia'; Grand, 'Pouvanaa a Oopa et Nationalisme à Tahiti'; Finney, 'French Polynesia: A Nuclear Dependency'; Danielsson and Danielsson, *Poisoned Reign*; Tagupa, *Politics in French Polynesia, 1945–1975*; International Physicians for the Prevention of Nuclear War, *Radioactive Heaven and Earth*; l'Association des français contre la bombe, *Le Bataillon de la Paix*; Mazellier, *Tahiti Autonome*; Thual, *Equations Polynésiennes*; Blanchet, *A Survey of the Economy of French Polynesia: 1960 to 1990*; Delegation Polynésienne, *Pacte de Progrès*; Poirine, *Tahiti: Stratégie pour l'après-nucléaire*; Shineberg, 'The Image of France'; Finney, *Polynesian Peasants and Proletariat*; and Lextreyt, 'De la chute de Pouvanaa au retour en arrière des institutions'.

THE MATERIAL WORLD REMADE

The movement for a nuclear-free Pacific recast itself in terms of a Nuclear-Free and Independent Pacific, recognising that national sovereignty is a pre-condition of reasserting control over the environments. Resource bases had been ravaged by the extraction of resources and capital. As new governments struggled to build economic bases and coherent states, issues critical to the management of resources were often compromised. Nor are the issues contained within the nation-states, for Pacific peoples live in ecosystems dramatically affected by global processes, and have created regional organisations to negotiate their interests in the international arena.

CONTEMPORARY POLITIES

The last major region of the globe to be colonised by Europeans was also the last to be decolonised, a process not yet complete. France maintains sovereignty over French Polynesia, Wallis and Futuna, and New Caledonia. The United States maintains the territories of American Samoa and Guam, the latter claiming the right to United States commonwealth status, like its culturally similar neighbour, the Northern Mariana Islands. Tokelau remains a self-governing territory of New Zealand. After the Pacific War, the Netherlands tried to govern West Papua despite the claim of Indonesian nationalists to the whole of the former Dutch East Indies. In 1962 the province's fate was determined when the United Nations endorsed an 'act of free choice' organised by the Indonesian interim administration. Since then Irian Jaya has been a province of Indonesia, despite sporadic resistance in the name of the Oposisi Papua Merdeka (OPM, Free Papua Movement) who insist that it was merely transferred from one colonial power to another. Since the OPM is poorly disciplined and lacks significant external support, Irianese are likely to remain encapsulated, like the Hawaiian nation in the United States' fiftieth state, the Maori nation in New Zealand, and Aboriginal Australians.

To be credible as successor governments, anti-colonial movements had to overcome localism and tribalism and forge political unity on an unprecedented scale. In Irian Jaya, the OPM's failure to transcend parochial interests has limited its effectiveness. At the other extreme, the kingdom of Tonga shed its British protectorate without fuss and without modification to its constitution. Equally, long before colonial annexation Samoans shared a cultural identity—indexed by *fa'aSamoa*—and a vision of unified rule under the Tafa'ifā. Once New Zealand conceded defeat and enlisted supporters of the Mau in the new Fono of Faipule (chapter 8), Samoans worked with the government and waited for independence. In 1948, government was restructured as a two-party parliamentary democracy, and debated the form of future government. The constitution largely confirmed customary modes of authority and land-holding in a parliamentary democracy with a head of state embodying ceremonial authority, the modern version of the Tafa'ifā. Until 1990 only *matai* could vote, and about 96 per cent are male. At independence in 1962, the question of the head of state was resolved by alternating between the Tupua and Malietoa families—a model that harks back to Steinberger (see chapter 6).

Britain, with little continuing interest in the Pacific, ceded independence as soon as credible political movements were available to administer successor-states: Fiji in 1970, the same year in which Tonga regained independence, the Solomon Islands and Tuvalu in 1978, followed by Kiribati in 1979 (with which Tuvalu had been administered as the Gilbert and Ellice Islands). In 1980 the Anglo-French Condominium of the New Hebrides became the republic of Vanuatu, despite French obstruction and secessionist movements (see chapter 12).

In the Australian sphere, Nauru achieved independence in 1968, but the prospects for Papua New Guinea remained ambivalent until 1972, when a conservative government in Australia decided to press towards decolonisation. Later that year, Australians elected the Labor Party to office. Prime Minister Whitlam was embarrassed that Australia was one of the last colonial powers, and determined to decolonise within three years. That goal required the co-operation of Papua New Guinea's first fully elected House of Assembly, elected earlier that year. The largest grouping in the House, the United Party, represented the undeveloped Highlands and resisted rapid change which might transfer power to the better-developed coastal regions. Michael Somare's Pangu Pati took the opposite view, and built a fragile coalition government whose agenda included many issues, any one of which could subvert the drive for independence. The most urgent were the drafting of a constitution, secessionist movements in Bougainville, Papua and the Highlands, incipient violence around Rabaul, a trickle of refugees across the unmarked border with Irian Jaya, finding citizens to replace Australians in the public service, negotiating an aid package with Australia, and renegotiating the mining agreement for Bougainville. To complicate matters, parliamentarians had no experience of government, no tradition of party solidarity, and minimal formal education.

The government's handling of these fateful issues was stunningly successful. A Constitutional Planning Committee favoured drastic decentralisation of power: provincial governments were created and entrenched, meeting the demands of Bougainville. The government renegotiated the mining agreement (see below), and reached agreement on a gradual phasing out of Australian budgetary support. Somare proved a skilful conciliator, and Tei Abal a constructive leader of the Opposition, so that several tensions abated. The localisation of the public service caused much less disruption than had been expected. Highlanders' anxieties about educated coastal people gradually subsided, and so did the fears of coastal Papuans about uneducated Highlanders coming to Port Moresby. With immense skill and a little luck, the country reached independence in September 1975 with a functioning public service, a guaranteed income, and an agreed constitution.

During these epic years, several issues were side-stepped. Decentralised decision-making meant, for example, that landowners negotiated directly with timber companies, expecting them to build the roads, schools and hospitals which the government could not afford. The consequences included opportunities for corruption, and the clear-felling of large tracts. Similarly, income-generating projects from road construction to mining entailed protracted negotiations to compensate landowners for inconvenience or loss.

These difficulties were compounded by the democratic provisions of the constitution, reacting against the extreme centralisation of the late-colonial administration. Members of Parliament were elected for their parochial popularity, to go to Port Moresby and bring services and projects. Their party loyalty was elastic. A government which lost its parliamentary majority could not call an early election, nor could members be disciplined by the threat of expulsion from their party. Ambitious backbenchers could readily cross the floor to create a new (and equally unstable) majority. No government has retained office throughout the five-year term of each Parliament, as the executive fell hostage to the aspirations of legislators. During the 1980s especially, members could demand services and projects for their constituencies, whether or not these conformed with national priorities or budget constraints. In funding these local projects, some departments lost the resources to carry out their national functions. Backbenchers also won massive increases in salaries, privileges, and 500,000 Kina ($500,000) each per annum to spend on constituency projects. In short, the executive lost control over the legislators, and the government lost control over the budget. Civilian control over the Defence Force was also thrown into question by ill-discipline, even before the Bougainville crisis (see below, and chapter 12).

Governance was uneven in the nineteen provinces. The more affluent, with qualified staff and money to pay them, often worked well; but poorer provinces could not carry out their functions, and several were suspended. Some national politicians (including Paias Wingti, Prime Minister in 1992) could see no valid role for provincial governments, and the national government (under his successor, Sir Julius Chan) moved to restructure them. Some provincial politicians, especially in the island provinces of Manus, New Ireland, East and West New Britain, began to ask if they needed a national government. In 1994 matters nearly came to a head, when a meeting of New Guinea Islands premiers, in Rabaul, presented an ultimatum to Port Moresby: abandon the threat to provincial governments, or they would consider collective secession. The crisis was literally overshadowed by the volcanic eruption a few days later, which destroyed Rabaul and required relief efforts on a national scale. If the crisis was deferred, however, it was not resolved. Mismanagement also attracted criticism from the Australian government as chief aid donor, and from the World Bank. Since 1995, when Prime Minister Chan disclosed the country's empty treasury, Australia has offered short-term assistance only on condition that Papua New Guinea meets the demands of the World Bank to restructure its finances. Acrimonious negotiations have revealed that the government's difficulties in controlling backbenchers are matched by the World Bank's troubles in imposing its programs on a reluctant government.

France was determined to retain sovereignty, not only in Tahiti (see chapter 10) but equally in New Caledonia. There, Melanesian dispossession had been thorough: Islanders retained their land in the Loyalty Islands, but on the main island they were confined to crowded reserves, whence they were recruited to work in mining and agriculture. Their standards of living and life expectancy were markedly inferior to those of the settlers who (with Wallisians and other immigrants) outnumbered them. With little access to higher education, they were largely absent from the professions and management. A nationalist position was first articulated by university students in the late 1960s, inspired partly by the tumultuous events of 1968 in Paris, and equally by memories of the 1878 rebellion in New Caledonia (chapter 7). They struck a resounding blow in reclaiming the pejorative term 'Canaque' as Kanak, a term of ethnic pride, and insisting on Kanaky as the name for New Caledonia. The agitation struck a chord among older Melanesians, and several political parties sprang up to represent the drive for independence, varying only in tactics and commitment to socialist objectives.

Like Tahitians, Kanak nationalists confronted an intransigent government in Paris, then pinned their hopes on the Socialist President Mitterrand (1981–95), and were grievously disappointed. As in Tahiti, municipal governments created local patronage networks to divide the nationalists and undercut the authority of the territorial assembly. Kanak nationalists were also assailed by a settler majority, who aspired to become a settler society like Australia or New Zealand, and whose loathing of 'Kanak Socialist Independence' led to violence. Despite these discouragements, Kanak intellectuals quarried their history for inspiration, and (in the Front de Libération Nationale Kanake et Socialiste, FLNKS) drew the parties together behind the astute leadership of Jean-Marie Tjibaou. Although two of his brothers, along with other Kanaks, were killed by white and mixed-race farmers in 1984, Tjibaou persisted in negotiating for a peaceful transition to independence. Since the loyalist majority remained intransigent, and Paris ambivalent, there was too little progress to arrest another drift to violence. The climax was reached on the outer island of 'Uvea, where

Kanak militants captured several gendarmes. On 5 May 1988 French troops stormed the cave where the hostages were held. Three soldiers died, and nineteen Kanaks—three of them killed after they had surrendered.

That tragedy shocked Paris into negotiations, from which emerged the Matignon Accord. New Caledonia was divided into three provinces, two of which (the Loyalty Islands and the north of the main island) elected Kanak governments who set about land reform and other measures to redress the Kanaks' historic disadvantages. The territory's destiny would be determined in 1998, by referendum, on a restricted franchise likely to yield a majority of Kanak voters. If they held together, therefore, they could achieve independence or some form of association with France. Some militants, outraged by the massacre, felt that the accord conceded altogether too much to France. In May 1989, extremists assassinated Tjibaou and his deputy Yeiwene Yeiwene, but the Matignon Accord survived as the medium-term framework of politics.

Some Islanders in small and isolated territories did not wish to sever ties completely. The Cook Islands were the first to negotiate an intermediate status: free association. Under this arrangement with New Zealand in 1965, which can be terminated unilaterally, Cook Islanders hold dual citizenship, and enter and work freely in New Zealand. The Cook Islands rely on New Zealand for aid and assistance in foreign affairs (although they sometimes differ from New Zealand policy). This was the model for the free association between Niue and New Zealand from 1974. More loosely, it was the model for the arrangement agreed upon for several island groups in the United States Trust Territory of the Pacific Islands. Negotiations between the United States and representatives from the Marianas (except Guam, a US territory since 1898), the Caroline and Marshall Islands, were always difficult. The Islanders preferred independence, but selected free association as more achievable. The US team was instructed not to discuss independence. By the second round, the US advocated commonwealth status for the whole Territory: at issue was access to nuclear and strategic facilities (see chapter 10), and prohibiting the islands from unilateral termination of any agreement. When negotiations stalled in 1975, the US finally accepted the separation of the islands. The Northern Marianas, willing to permit the use of one island for US military purposes, achieved separate commonwealth status (and high *per capita* payments) in 1976. Palau and the Marshall Islands, which held strong bargaining positions because of US strategic interests, opted for separate republics. Yap, Chuuk, Pohnpei and Kosrae formed the Federated States of Micronesia (FSM). The FSM and the Marshalls entered into 'free association' with the US in 1986. Once its constitution was amended to meet US demands, Palau also became a freely associated state in 1994. Citizens of associated states retain free access to the US, but maintain their own citizenship. They are self-governing and control their foreign affairs (unless contrary to US defence interests), but the association can only be terminated bilaterally, an anomaly which delayed the entry of the Marshalls and the FSM into the United Nations until 1991.

THE TRANSFORMED MATERIAL WORLD

Once independent, Island governments could begin to redistribute resources—or to redefine them. Pacific peoples have always reshaped environments to suit their purposes (chapter 2) and early European, Asian and American colonists made similar mistakes, with one critical difference. They could afford to over-exploit the Islands since they did not need to live there. They could displace or minimally employ local residents, and recognised no obligation to manage resources towards long-term sustainability, nor to recognise environmental controls. Some of the lands and seas had been ravaged by their absentee owners. Fifty years after World War II, some islands are still littered by tanks and landing craft rusting on the beaches, the occasional mine washing ashore, or forgotten but live munitions. Several nuclear atolls remain off-limits. The phosphate islands, their pocked landscapes resembling the moon once their soils were strip-mined, are suing their former trustees for the considerable costs of rehabilitation. Angaur, in Palau, was doubly affected: phosphate mining degraded the interior of the island (chapter 7), which after severe bombing was covered in concrete air-fields as a United States base to attack the Japanese strongholds on Peleliu and Babeldaob (chapter 9). The nickel and gold mines of New Caledonia, Irian Jaya and Bougainville removed mountains, polluting rivers and watersheds, reaching international waters and affecting sea resources. The degradation of ecological systems is well documented, and species extinction rates are among the highest in the world.

Colonial governments introduced concepts of national—as opposed to village or clan—control of certain lands for the common good, and expectations that roads, education and health should be provided by the government—expectations that increased after independence. Elected governments were expected to understand local meanings of land and sea tenure, despite their colonial transformation. Thus independent governments complicated the struggles to define the material world, and allocate and exploit its resources. The struggle is ideological as well as material, and involves not only Islanders and transnational corporations, but also governments and communities. How shall the concerns of landowners be balanced against the provision of services for the whole population? Whose laws shall prevail? Do landowners control the body of the land (sub-surface mineral rights), or just its 'skin'? The Purari River seemed to offer a prospect of hydro-electric power to the government of Papua New Guinea, provoking this reflection from a pastor to a community in the Purari delta:

> Sometimes I wonder how the whiteman will be able to close our river to make power for Papua New Guinea. Many of us believe that they will not be able to succeed in their attempt to close the river. To us it is a sacred place . . . because that is where our ancestors came from. The trees, animals, birds, and even rivers are the product of our ancestors. If the whitemen close the river it will be only a short period of time before our ancestors will spoil their work and open the river once more. How can our Black government ignore our beliefs? What is more important, is it money or is it our traditional

beliefs and values? [Around Port Moresby] Motuans can no longer hunt or dig the soil for gardens. Instead they have turned to the government for work in office buildings. I do not want this to happen here or to our children . . .

I would like my children to know that the river is part of our life. What will happen to us when the clever men close the river?[1]

Pacific ecosystems are dramatically affected by global processes. Global warming places atolls at the greatest risk, yet farming practices, industrial pollution, forestry and mining in other countries contribute most to these threats. Even small sea-level rises could submerge entire island chains in the Marshalls, Carolines, Kiribati, Tuvalu, the Tuamotus, Cook Islands, and much of Tonga. Concern over environmental issues, and the need for a regional forum, encouraged the creation of Islander-controlled regional institutions. When the South Pacific Commission (created by colonial powers after World War II) refused to debate French nuclear testing, the self-governing countries formed the South Pacific Forum in 1971. (It expanded north of the equator in the 1980s.) The forum took the lead in creating institutions, both economic (Forum Fisheries Agency) and environmental (South Pacific Regional Environment Program).

Although transformations of the sea and land environment are the most apparent changes, the small, cumulative changes in styles of living, together with technical developments in airlines, communications and medical services, may have broader consequences. New foods, materials, technologies and religions are interwoven into life patterns. Atoll dwellers continue links to the high islands which supply many necessities and amenities. High islands continue to give aid during crises, such as the droughts associated with the 1980s El Niños, and super-typhoons and hurricanes of the early 1990s. As shipping services to the outer islands decline and populations increase, more people choose urban living on the high islands or metropolitan centres, or build cement-block houses to withstand the storms. Televisions and videos, satellite communications allowing radio and telephone conversations with family members abroad, metropolitan news services, convenience foods such as rice, canned fish and meat, gasoline-powered motorboats and canoes, aeroplanes have become integral to Island living.

Island structures, physical and metaphoric, are constantly transformed, each creating the other. Changes in trade networks, incorporating new materials and technologies, ramify into the selection of marriage partners, who then affect the management of disputes between groups. Resettlement in urban centres and transformations of housing styles affect relationships within and between households. Schooling of children affects work patterns, and so do men's and women's wage labour. As household food production yields to wage employment, and rice and tinned meat replace taro and fresh fish, nutritional and health standards sometimes decline even faster than the

1   'Purari, Overpowering Papua New Guinea?' in Moody (ed.), *The Indigenous Voice*, 196.

balance of payments. Altered economic flows and the inter-generational transmission of knowledge in turn feed back into demographic transitions. At the household level, material transformations are daily experienced and often creatively adapted. It is also at the household and individual levels that dislocations are first felt.

This chapter addresses issues which Islanders face as they interact with the environment which must sustain future generations, symbolically and materially. It raises questions, for there is no agreed framework through which to understand relations between economies, cultures and environments. At the most basic level economists and Islanders struggle to understand the relationship of subsistence food production to national economies and international labour markets. Then analysts divide over whether to consider national economies as separable, or intrinsic parts of a regional economy. These arguments raise basic issues—are the new nation-states the world's richest, or among its poorest? Bonnemaison captures the significance of this debate for understanding the perspectives of those Tannese who turned their backs on Christianity (chapters 7 and 12):

> A visitor is immediately struck by the beauty and multiplicity of traditional food gardens with their yam and taro root crops. The gardens have evolved on brown humus soils which are continually renewed and fertilised by volcanic ash. Unless there is a hurricane or severe drought, these gardens provide subsistence food in varied and sufficient quantities for large surpluses to be exchanged among local groups in the course of alliance rituals. Modern resources that would allow for cash earnings are conspicuously absent, however. Therefore Tanna is both rich and poor. From the standpoint of a traditional way of life, the island population lives in abundance to some extent, yet it is a modern 'proletariat' when considered in the context of an imported socioeconomic framework . . . The Tannese are aware of their remoteness from today's consumer world, a world to which they barely have access. They involve themselves all the more in production and traditional ritual exchanges. Devoid of cash, the islanders are rich in pigs, kava, and giant tubers, which they trade off with pomp and ostentation from one ceremony to the next. Poor in relation to the outside world, they endeavour to remain rich in their own context, in order to be generous among themselves.[2]

Tanna is unique in its cosmologies, but many other societies share the anomaly of being at once rich and poor—and generous. A different conundrum puzzles scholars who analyse governments: many seem to live far beyond their means, and wealth flows from the metropolitan powers far outweigh Islander contributions. Reading balance sheets, with their stark contrasts between puny exports and burgeoning imports, they propose terms such as 'dependent development' or 'welfare capitalism' to delineate a paradox. Yet the Pacific nations defy economic theories which described a very different 'dependency' of landless Latin American peasants dependent on wage labour for their very subsistence.

---

2 Bonnemaison, *The Tree and the Canoe*, 108–9.

Problems of translation and comprehension occur when Western terms are applied to Pacific economies, as demonstrated by Baré's essay on Tahitian economic terms.[3] The primary distinction in Tahitian understandings is between 'outside' and 'inside'—an opposition also critical to Hawaiian understandings, yet one that maps poorly onto Western geographical distinctions. Mismatched semantic categories confound analyses of the meanings of 'dependence' on the 'outside'. The contrast between 'outside' and 'inside' in Tahitian does not rest entirely on geography or place of origin, but equally on ways of thinking. Long-standing 'foreign' institutions such as the church are now internalised, as are locally built hotels (even if they are owned 'externally'). Copra, the quintessential colonial crop for export, has been thoroughly indigenised as a 'root' activity since it is fundamentally connected with the earth. Ambiguities abound. The semantic fields associated with salaried employment, loans, and debt, expressed in Tahitian, relate more directly to Tahitian models of a cycle of exchange, involving reciprocity not normally part of Western contractual terms. For instance *tarahu* is generally glossed as 'to employ', but in Tahitian it connotes borrowing someone (which will require a reciprocal payment). The phrase *aufaura'a 'ava'e*, used today for wages, reverses the usual Western asymmetry between employer and employee, for it originally described the tribute paid to the chiefs, and was later extended to 'voluntary' contributions to churches. Payments which we would call wages, dues and taxes are all contained in the one phrase. More important in macro-economic terms, no indigenous concept approximates capital, and any attempt to discuss 'national wealth' (Gross Domestic Product) would speak about the adequacy of the land (*rava'ira'a fenua*) and its usefulness, not concepts of added value. The reversal of Western expectations is found elsewhere as well: Carolinians expect resources to flow mainly from the resource-rich high islands (and by extension from the United States) to the coral atolls.[4]

Pacific intellectuals differ in their perceptions of the inter-relatedness of islands. Epeli Hau'ofa's conclusion for the South Pacific could easily include the Northern Pacific, and integration of the entire area into a wider Pacific Rim economy and society. He maintains that there already exists

> a single regional economy upon which has emerged a South Pacific society, the privileged groups of which share a single dominant culture with increasingly marginalised local sub-cultures shared by the poorer classes. The regional society is emerging from the process of decolonisation which, contrary to stated intentions, has integrated the Pacific islands into the Australian/New Zealand economy and society to the extent that the islands cannot or will not disentangle themselves. In view of the integration, we must re-examine many of the assumptions that we have about development in our region.[5]

The economist Te'o Fairbairn sees the Island nations as separable, their economies equally (but separately) based on frail foundations: 'their

3 Baré, 'Talking Economics in Tahitian'.
4 Alkire, *Lamotrek Atoll and Inter-island Socioeconomic Ties*.
5 Hau'ofa, 'The New South Pacific Society', 1.

economies remain fragile because of severely restricted resource bases, geographic isolation and dispersal, and small domestic markets set against rapid population increase. In addition, they have become heavily dependent on world markets and are vulnerable to the instability associated with these.'[6] These statements summarise two analytical frameworks. The economist's view undoubtedly prevails, particularly among development experts and agencies. This perspective emphasises land-based resources and visible exports, citing remote export markets and small local markets as constraints.

REDEFINING RESOURCES

To view the Islands in order of land size is to privilege those which rise from the western Pacific continental shelf. This land-based model is based on the continental perspectives of orthodox analysis—but alternative portrayals deserve equal attention. The first is a navigator's view of islands, each surrounded by an arc of signs telling the alert sailor that an island is near—floating debris, the movements of frigate birds and boobies, the deflection of ocean swells, reflections on the clouds. In this view, the ocean is not a barrier, but a bridge. This view is radically different from the usual Western representation—black dots, many not even named, roughly related to land size, scattered and isolated on an expanse of blue ocean.

Independent Island nations could assert alternative perceptions of resource definition and control, beginning with the ocean. The 1970s Law of the Sea negotiations had centred around definitions: were a nation's resources limited to its land base and a 3-mile (or 12-mile) distance from shore, or should other cultural and economic definitions of land and sea tenure be considered (an argument developed primarily by island nations)? Should the sea be considered a resource in common? Only independent nations were party to the negotiations, with one exception. Since the land-based position of the United States ran counter to the interests of the Micronesians for whom it was trustee, these islands were accorded observer status in negotiations, which culminated in the protocols of the 1982 United Nations Convention of the Law of the Sea (UNCLOS III). These allow nations to declare a 200-mile exclusive economic zone around their lands, in which each maintains sovereign rights over resources but allows free air and sea transit. The matter of highly pelagic species, such as tuna, was contested finally only by the United States.[7]

Resource bases change considerably once the exclusive economic zones are included (Table 11.1). The map showing 200-mile economic zones turns full circle to approximate the island navigator's map. Except for Papua New Guinea, the large islands lose their dominance,

6   'Subsistence Economy and Policy Options for Small Island Economies', in Hooper *et al.* (eds), *Class and Culture in the South Pacific*, 56.
7   Jon Van Dyke and Carolyn Nicol, 'U.S. Tuna Policy: A Reluctant Acceptance of the International Norm', in Doulman (ed.), *Tuna Issues and Perspectives*, 105–32.

TABLE 11.1
PACIFIC NATIONS INCLUDING EXCLUSIVE ECONOMIC ZONES

Island polity	Resident population (1994)	Land area (km²)	Density by land area	Exclusive economic zone (km²)	Overall density
American Samoa	54,600	197	277.16	390,000	0.14
Cook Islands	19,100	240	79.58	1,830,000	0.01
Federated States of Micronesia	105,900	701	151.07	2,978,000	0.04
Fiji	777,700	18,272	42.56	1,290,000	0.60
French Polynesia	218,000	3,265	66.77	5,030,000	0.04
Guam	146,700	541	271.16	218,000	0.67
Irian Jaya	1,400,000	420,000	3.33	n.a.	n.a.
Kiribati	78,300	690	113.48	3,550,000	0.02
Marshall Islands	54,069	176	307.21	2,131,000	0.03
Nauru	10,600	21	504.76	320,000	0.03
New Caledonia	182,200	19,103	9.54	1,740,000	0.10
Niue	2,100	259	8.11	390,000	0.01
Northern Marianas	56,600	471	120.17	1,823,000	0.03
Palau	16,500	494	33.40	629,000	0.03
Papua New Guinea	3,951,500	462,243	8.55	3,120,000	1.27
Solomon Islands	367,400	28,369	12.95	1,340,000	0.27
Tokelau	1,500	10	150.00	290,000	0.01
Tonga	98,300	747	131.59	677,021	0.15
Tuvalu	9,500	26	365.38	900,000	0.01
Vanuatu	164,100	12,190	13.46	680,000	0.24
Wallis & Futuna	14,400	255	56.47	300,000	0.05
Western Samoa	163,500	2,820	57.98	95,800	1.71
	7,892,570	971,093	8.13	29,721,824	

Source: Exclusive economic zones are based on South Pacific Commission figures compiled by Doulman, updated from SPREP action strategies for Tonga and Western Samoa: David Doulman, 'Distant-Water Fleet Operations and Regional Fisheries Cooperation', in Doulman (ed.), *The Development of the Tuna Industry*; South Pacific Regional Environment Program, *The Kingdom of Tonga: Action Strategy for Managing the Environment*; and *Western Samoa: National Environment and Development Management Strategies*.

and ratios between populations and resources equalise. Some of the smallest states—French Polynesia, Kiribati, FSM, the Marshall Islands—join Papua New Guinea as key players in the international resource stakes.

The new nations largely continued the economic linkages established by their colonial predecessors in order to fund the now essential education, medical and public safety services. Unless resources were already depleted (as in Banaba and Angaur) the governments continued to allow mining and other projects, in return for an increasing share of the profits. Colonial governments had rarely covered costs, and the new nations were no more successful. Most maintained primary trade relations with their former colonial administrators, and relied heavily on them for aid and governmental support.

Economies are political, and so are the analytical constructs which we employ to understand them. Islander perceptions of the world as arcs of linked units, rather than isolates, are becoming the lived reality. These linkages run counter to the self-contained nation-state models on which Table 11.1 is based, arguing instead for models which emphasise interdependence.

The 1996 Cook Islands 'Winebox' scandal (allegations that officials conspired in a fraudulent accounting) demonstrates the interpenetrations of Island and Pacific Rim economies, and the ways in which Island nation policies affect the reputations of their former colonisers and aid donors. As an integral part of New Zealand before the establishment of free association, Cook Islander small farmers provided tropical juices, fruits and vegetables for the New Zealand winter market. As New Zealand opened its market to outside vendors, Cook Islanders lost their small, but secure niche, and many more joined the migration stream to New Zealand. Nearly 70 per cent of all Cook Islanders now live in New Zealand, creating interests among both New Zealand and Cook Islander politicians to maintain a small stable homeland community, at present maintained by a large public sector supported by New Zealand aid which pays higher wages than private-sector employment. Eventually the Cook Islands government turned to offshore banking to create a more independent financial base. The legal issues concern allegations that a 15 per cent withholding tax certified as having been paid to the Cook Islands by Japanese, Australian and New Zealand investors was returned to the firms, less a fee, thus defrauding the taxpayers of the investors' nations. New Zealand has particular vested interests in the issue, as former administrator of the Cook Islands and current 'free associate' and major aid donor, and as the New Zealand investors include national corporations. More clearly at stake, however, is New Zealand's international reputation, and the potential ramifications of such an alleged fraud on New Zealand's economy and monetary reputation. The public inquiry and court cases are being heard in New Zealand—the first major public inquiry into the secret nature of tax-free havens, with grave implications for Pacific politicians in their homelands and in New Zealand.

In this context the 1995–6 turmoil in Vanuatu may be instructive. At independence in 1980 the anglophone Vanua'aku Pati held government with a large majority of votes and seats. By 1991 Vanua'aku had splintered, and lost the general election to a coalition led by Maxime Carlot Korman and the leading francophone party. When that party also split, in 1995–6, following general elections, political stability collapsed, parliamentary rules and conventions were placed under stress, and some politicians were accused of improperly issuing colossal bank guarantees. As in Papua New Guinea and the Solomon Islands, strenuous political competition seemed to erode the principles with which political parties first took office, and the procedures enshrined in the independence constitutions.

Considered in Western terms, the imbalance between exports and imports in many Island nations is so pronounced that one must ask how it is sustained. Do the differences result in interest-generating loans? Do Pacific nations benefit equally? Why do metropolitan powers continue their subsidies? Are such transfers 'aid'? The answers (like the questions) are political. How do we evaluate the role of Island nations in defining the power of metropolitan states, and serving as political, economic and environmental buffers in international relations? Do Islanders receive a fair return for their timber, minerals, and fish? What is the role of 'invisible' exports such as tourism and overseas banking?

Table 11.2 presents a perspective based on the gross domestic product and the proportion of official development assistance. Nauru retains its primacy, but its phosphates will soon be exhausted. Considered according to *per capita* gross domestic product, the next five polities are territories of metropolitan countries, followed by freely associated states, and last by those which are independent. Of the independent nations, only Fiji boasts high *per capita* income. Polities which embody free association or incorporation with metropolitan powers enjoy the highest gross domestic products.

Such broad indicators fail to capture the essence of Pacific economies: to what extent is subsistence wealth added into the domestic product, or the contributions of overseas family members? What is the distribution within the country?—the 31 per cent of Nauru's population who are non-Nauruan, primarily phosphate workers, cannot expect to share

TABLE 11.2
ECONOMIC STATISTICS OF PACIFIC NATIONS

Island polity	Year	Gross domestic product ($A'000s)	Per capita gross domestic product	Per capita official development assistance
American Samoa	1985	260,417	6,660	2,117
Cook Islands	1993	89,866	5,195	912
FSM	1993	315,399	3,400	
Fiji	1993	2,077,830	2,716	64
French Polynesia	1992	4,106,108	19,622	
Guam	1990	1,513,369	12,356	878
Kiribati	1990	43,430	600	421
Marshall Islands	1991	95,815	1,995	1,386
Nauru	1989	206,250	22,418	27
New Caledonia	1990	3,053,988	17,970	1,901
Niue	1991	8,835	3,946	4,034
Northern Marianas	1994	732,432	12,941	
Palau	1988	63,291	4,163	907
Papua New Guinea	1993	7,269,565	1,882	127
Solomon Islands	1993	336,572	947	174
Tokelau	1990	800	478	3,750
Tonga	1992	176,968	1,815	389
Tuvalu	1990	12,265	1,256	694
Vanuatu	1993	267,793	1,678	337
Wallis & Futuna				75
Western Samoa	1992	212,674	1,305	160

Source: These figures are compiled by the author from a broad range of official sources. For future updates, consult the South Pacific Economic and Social Database, maintained by the National Centre for Development Studies, ANU.

equally. The issues, of course, are more complex than any econometric analysis. What is the cost of strategic denial, or of open sea and air routes? What are the costs to Islanders, to the biosphere and to all peoples, of marine and land degradation? Geopolitical concerns explain why France and the United States support mainly the islands under their influence, and these polities top the listings of gross domestic product in proportion to their degree of incorporation. Strategic concerns affect funding, and certain Island nations, or their elites, would better be considered 'rentier' than 'dependent'. Yet this analysis is not widely accepted, for it acknowledges that some transfers are rental payments rather than aid. Similarly, the United States and Japan refuse to negotiate solely for 'payments' for licensing rights to harvest tuna, but insist on labelling part of the transfers as economic or technical assistance—although 85 per cent of these payments are directly linked to the fisheries' catch locations.[8] Metropolitan as well as Pacific nations redefine economic terms bearing in mind the implications of the labels. As long as transfers are termed aid, they mask political and economic realities.

These practices also make it difficult to track debt ratios. The World Bank monitors only Fiji, Papua New Guinea, the Solomons, Tonga, Vanuatu and Western Samoa. In 1990 to 1991 most held their own, with roughly equal ratios of external debt to gross domestic product, and maintained steady levels on interest payment. Tonga reduced both its absolute debt and its debt ratio from 52.9 to 37.8 per cent. Only Papua New Guinea is on the World Bank's cautionary list. However, Western Samoa endured a disastrous year, moving from 50 per cent in 1990 to 93 per cent in 1991 due to plummeting exports and soaring imports, and since 1991 the situation has worsened. Pacific economies are extremely vulnerable to weather and commodity prices, and the early 1990s experienced a series of devastating typhoons, affecting food and export crops for decades.

A high figure for gross domestic product does not equate to a high quality of life—sometimes the reverse. Nauru has one of the lowest life expectancy rates (55 years) and high rates of diseases associated with changing eating habits, obesity and lack of exercise: diabetes (the highest prevalence in the world), hypertension, heart attacks, stroke, and gout. A more nuanced measure of quality of life has therefore been developed, as shown in Table 11.3. The wide variation in *per capita* gross domestic product for the same nations in Tables 11.2 and 11.3, derived from different sources, further illustrates the limits of such measures.

It is difficult to quantify quality of life, and to relate these indicators to gross domestic product, but one unfortunate correlation is suggested by Table 11.3: the largest independent nations fare badly in education. Comparing the Cook Islands and the Solomon Islands, Crocombe and Crocombe conclude that smaller countries are better able to tap resources from donors, since grants are made on a national, rather than *per capita*, basis; there is a negative correlation between sovereignty and

---

8 Van Dyke and Nicol, 'U.S. Tuna Policy', in Doulman (ed.), *Tuna Issues and Perspectives*,
   121. See especially Secretary of State Schultz's message to Pacific island delegations,
   appendix 4, 130–1.

TABLE 11.3
HUMAN DEVELOPMENT INDICATORS

Country	Life expectancy at birth	Adult literacy	Mean years of schooling	GDP (US$ per capita)	Index
Cook Islands	69.8	99	8.4	3,416	985
Palau	67.0	98	9.6	3,289	939
Niue	66.0	99	8.3	3,051	879
Tonga	69.0	99	7.1	1,396	723
Fiji	63.1	87	6.8	1,991	652
Tuvalu	67.2	99	6.8	1,068	652
Marshall Islands	61.1	91	8.5	1,576	611
FSM	64.1	81	7.6	1,474	604
Western Samoa	63.1	98	9.1	722	578
Kiribati	60.2	93	6.1	461	439
Vanuatu	62.8	64	4.0	1,020	424
Solomon Islands	60.7	23	2.8	529	191
Papua New Guinea	49.6	52	2.1	999	138

Source: UNDP, Pacific Human Development Report, Suva, 1994.

education; a strong correlation between high *per capita* income and high levels of foreign investment with access to all levels of education; benefits are concentrated in urban areas; and education and training facilities outside conventional institutions (provided by businesses, international agencies and non-government organisations) are also concentrated in urban areas.[9]

This may be the greatest lesson revealed by Western economic indicators. Regardless of their levels of 'subsistence affluence', all Islanders participate in the world economy to the extent that education, health, roads, power and water must be provided by governments, or by resource corporations in return for access. A government's access to funds depends on the products it can sell and the terms of trade it can negotiate, and the levels of aid. These relate in part to the country's importance to donors and agencies and its degree of autonomy. The ability of Pacific nations to amend definitions of control of resources to include the exclusive economic zones, for instance, and the ability to obtain a high rate of return for these resources and regulate poaching, relate directly to the funds available for vital services. Islanders' desire for roads, electricity and education contributes to their tolerance of forestry and mining projects whose sponsors promise such benefits.

Certain kinds of degradation are general—deforestation, pollution of water supplies and the marine environment, the loss of marine species—but Island experiences vary according to location, habitat, size, population, political structure, and external links. The case studies that follow describe interactions between Pacific populations in the frameworks of their resources, suggest alternative perspectives, and consider the roles of international organisations and national aid programs in defining and managing the island habitat.

9   Crocombe and Crocombe, 'Scale, Sovereignty, Wealth and Enterprise'.

THE DAILY WORLDS OF CORAL ISLANDERS

Perhaps the most elusive concept for continental people is that Islanders' lived-in world continues beyond the beach into, through, and over the seas, the underwater terrain of the lagoon and sea-routes to neighbouring islands as familiar to a Pacific fisher as fields and roads to a farmer. Our consideration of the Islanders' material world begins with the seas and smallest islands.

To a visitor arriving one morning by government field-ship on one of the Carolinian atolls of the FSM, the first impression is continuity with past life-ways, blended with a very modern life-style. The voyaging canoe and thatched canoe houses along the shore are the first images to meet the eye, then men in loincloths, gathered in the canoe-houses for the formal exchange of greetings. The visitors may then disperse to the houses of their kin, any strangers being taken under the care of individuals designated by the chief. Women in hand-woven lava-lavas join in the greetings outside thatched homes on coral rubble platforms, as toddlers peep shyly at the visitors. One man wears a T-shirt heralding the regional Catholic high school, while one of the women wears a T-shirt blazoned with a Nuclear-Free Pacific slogan, above her lava-lava.

Life on a Carolinian atoll is interwoven in myriad ways with lives elsewhere. The visiting canoe came from the neighbouring island to which several young men moved after marrying there; they were returning with children to visit parents and relatives. The bright orange sail of the canoe is made of sailcloth which has replaced pandanus matting. Although the canoe retains its importance for visits and fishing, most travellers arrive on the field-ship which visits on a monthly schedule. Visitors bring information and presents. Young people seek news of friends studying in Guam, Hawai'i and California or (if there are outsiders) practise the English they learn at school. Passengers return from jobs, school or the hospital in the state capital. The ship unloads rice, sugar, flour, coffee, tinned fish and meat, fuel, cigarettes and perhaps beer, as well as supplies for the teacher and nurse, and any other state projects. The field-ship also brings bright cotton threads with which women weave lava-lavas on backstrap looms. Depending on world prices, the ship may load copra to tranship through the capital. But even with a national subsidy, copra prices are usually too low to repay the time spent, especially since children abroad send packages and building supplies. As the ship heads on to the next atoll, it carries new passengers and smoked and dried fish, coconuts, fresh reef fish and turtle eggs and finely woven cloths, for passengers and kin abroad.

When the ship departs, life returns to normal until punctuated by a rare tourist dive boat or yacht, or a tuna seiner far out at sea. In the morning women and children head down to the lagoon for baths, then some women return to weave, while others go inland to their taro patches. The women also make fine banana-fibre lava-lavas for personal wear and as tributary offerings to the chiefs, and through them in a hierarchy of gifts culminating in the village of Gagil on Yap. Men repair boats or head out beyond the reef to fish, if the season and weather are right, near a seamount or islet within their customary fishing rights. Children accompany their parents and grandparents to the taro patches and navigation houses, unless they are old enough to study with the teacher in an airy schoolhouse. The island nurse dispenses medicine, perhaps consulting the state hospital, sharing radio time with the magistrate. On some islands in the evenings, people gather around a television set which plays games, videos of Japanese and American movies, or the video of a recent cultural event showing friends and relatives dancing or making speeches. Depending on the season, men and women join in dance practice to prepare for a graduation or other event. The people worship at the local Catholic church, at services conducted mainly by local deacons under the Chuukese bishop based on Weno.

Fishing is more than a living. Throughout the Pacific, fishing for skipjack tuna has long been one of the most exhilarating sports, communal activities, and chiefly pastimes. In the Caroline and Tokelau Islands, where master fishers still use specialised canoes and pearl-shell lures, a successful trip provokes celebration and ritual performance.[10] Infectious excitement is generated by a communal fishing drive when tuna enter a Carolinian lagoon, or when canoes return from a successful fishing expedition and favourite reef and pelagic fish are available in communal and familial distributions. There have been few studies of the contribution of local fisheries to consumption, and those studies have focused on regions like the Carolines and Tokelau where traditional fishing practices are still followed. Offshore fishing nations are interested in the pelagic species, especially skipjack and yellow-fin tuna, and international estimates of subsistence fishing focus on local consumption of pelagic species. Despite the symbolic importance of these fish, however, reef fish provide the foundation for local consumption. In Tokelau, about 85 per cent of animal food consumed is local, predominantly fish and sea products (89 per cent); 19 per cent of total consumption is from tuna and similar species, while 65 per cent is from inshore fish.[11] A two-to-one ratio of reliance on lagoon to pelagic species would probably be normal throughout the region, but urbanisation affects inshore fisheries through overfishing and pollution. Regardless of the craft and fishing equipment used, fishermen continue to rely on lagoon and offshore fishing. Wage labourers continue to go on fishing expeditions for sport and sustenance, incorporating motorboats, spear-fishing and new line-fishing techniques among their technology. For Tongan fishermen, especially those without agricultural land rights, fishing is a major source of protein, for obligatory non-market transfers (fetokoni'aki), and for sale to earn cash.[12]

The material world encompasses new materials, new foods, instant radio and satellite communication, and new religions, yet each is incorporated in Island ways. The cotton threads or banana fibres are

10 Robert Gillett and Foua Toloa, 'The Importance of Small-Scale Tuna Fishing: A Tokelau Case Study', in Doulman, Tuna Issues and Perspectives.
11 See Gillett, Satawal; Gillett and Toloa, 'Small-Scale Tuna Fishing'.
12 Sitiveni Halapua, Fishermen of Tonga, 66–73.

woven into lava-lavas in patterns conserved for centuries and still part of an exchange system which distributes resources across the high islands and atolls. The favoured purple dye now comes from duplicating machines—a by-product of American bureaucracy. In addition to local foods, people eat imported rice and tinned fish, augmenting a diet that was at times too restricted. Barring typhoons or droughts, local foods are generally sufficient, and apparent 'dependence' on Western goods is partly a matter of convenience and preference. Surprisingly, the number of navigators has remained constant, and so has the number of residents, since population growth syphoned off to the urban centres of the new nation and its metropolitan ally. Despite a strong subsistence base, cash is integral to Island living—to purchase kerosene for cooking, staple imported foods, cloths, and goods, fuel for outboard engines, school fees of children abroad, and government services—to pay the magistrate, nurse and teacher, and the inter-island ship's fuel. The Islanders have few 'visible' exports. According to models which equate visible exports with development, the Islands are 'dependent' on the outside world.

But are they? This scenario could equally apply to many atoll groups (in French Polynesia, the Cook Islands, Tuvalu, Kiribati) with simple substitutions. In most cases at least a quarter of the island population live abroad, I-Kiribati and Tuvaluans primarily in their own capitals, but other Islanders as far away as Auckland or Noumea. Much of the cash income is remitted by these people. The perceived dependence depends partly on the unit considered—Island nation-state, or the family, many of which include overseas members. Islanders have incorporated new resources, so that the remotest atoll can have daily radio communication with the capital on health issues, emergencies, or to monitor shipping. As low-lying islands begin to experience the intense storms predicted as early effects of global warming, satellite networks report and arrange relief.

Transformations are more visible in the capitals—international news services, hospitals, schools and colleges. Academies prepare sailors to join international fleets. Colleges, often linked by satellite to distance education courses and overseas conferences, prepare students for government positions, or for education abroad. In these centres tourist resorts may be found—the latest 'clean' development. It is also here that development projects are centred, for here are the limited infrastructural supports: airports, ports for transhipment, and (in American Samoa and the Solomons) a cannery.

THE INTERNATIONAL FISHING INDUSTRY

UNCLOS III set the stage for the current political economy of the region. Sea resources constitute a primary subsistence base and they provide up to 25 per cent of the gross receipts of some nations. Local populations, however, consume only a fraction of the pelagic fish passing through their waters—perhaps only 10,000 tonnes annually, compared to a 1984 international harvest in excess of 650,000 tonnes. Accurate statistics are elusive, but the scale of this transformation can be seen in the Japanese industry. In 1977, 48 per cent of all Japanese tuna was obtained within 200 miles of other nations, and the UNCLOS declaration depressed the tuna industry for years. After UNCLOS the Islands could at last negotiate with metropolitan powers for payment for resources harvested from their exclusive economic zones. In 1982 the FSM joined Kiribati, the Marshall Islands, Nauru, Palau, Papua New Guinea and the Solomon Islands to establish the Nauru Group. These contiguous countries cover about 14 million square kilometres, including the waters of the FSM and Papua New Guinea in which up to three-quarters of all the reported tuna are caught by purse-seiners from the deep-water fishing nations. Through concerted action, creating a Regional Register of Fishing Vessels, and providing basic licensing terms and conditions, the Nauru Group reduced administrative costs and helped to prevent the deep-water fishing nations from playing off one against the others.[13]

The UNCLOS agreement coincided with the development of purse-seiners. Beginning with eight in the Pacific in 1976, by 1982 Japan had thirty-three. The United States followed the Japanese lead. By 1984 more than 120 purse-seiners were operating in Pacific waters, and by 1985 the Forum Fisheries Agency registered the maximum (158) that could legally operate in its member countries. The United States licensed 60 vessels, Japan 33, and the Philippines and Soviet Union 13 each. The average daily tonnage varies from 30–35 and 40–45 for single seiners, and 17–20 for group seiners. The importance of Pacific fisheries rose proportionately: the US catch in the western Pacific rose from 6 per cent of the total in 1980 to 66 per cent in 1984. Of the world's canned tuna, 60 per cent is taken in the region.

Despite the establishment of international property rights through the exclusive economic zones, fair payment proved elusive. When Papua New Guinea seized the US vessel *Danica* in 1982 the US threatened trade sanctions, and it did retaliate against the Solomon Islands when it seized the American tuna seiner *Jeanette Diana* in 1984. Shortly thereafter the Soviet Union entered the tuna boat wars, offering a lucrative fee to Kiribati in return for a five-year fishing licence. This agreement was followed by another with Vanuatu. To repair its plummeting Pacific image, the US finally signed an agreement with sixteen members of the Forum Fisheries Agency in early 1987. In this first multi-lateral agreement brokered by the agency, the US agreed to pay a minimum of $60 million over five years—approximately 9 per cent of the value of the catch.[14]

Here the connection between licensing fees and aid becomes clear. As the American Tunaboat Association refused to pay more than a small proportion of the commercial rate, the United States provided the

---

13 Introduction, 'The Case of the Nauru Group', and Yoshiaka Matsuda, 'Postwar Development and Expansion of Japan's Tuna Fishery', in Doulman (ed.), *Tuna Issues and Perspectives*.
14 Grynberg, 'The Tuna Dilemma'.

balance—from its aid budget. Aid and access rights are linked for other countries as well, despite official denials and Island nations' attempts to disentangle the two. Japan is a major donor, supporting fisheries projects in countries with which it has licensing agreements. Since that sixteen-nation agreement, it has been impossible either to conclude more agreements or even to retain the modest 9 per cent fee. The dissolution of the Soviet Union and the end of the Cold War weakened the Islands' leverage. Unlike some mining agreements which have been renegotiated upwards (see below), Pacific nations now are lucky to obtain about 5 per cent of the market value of fish reported caught within their waters. Most Pacific nations rely on both fisheries and aid, and it has been difficult for them to hold a unified position.

Nor is the percentage the only problem. The Forum Fisheries Agency estimated the 1991 tuna catch at more than 1 million tonnes. Considering just the purse-seiner catch, the South Pacific Commission estimated that three major deep-water fishing nations reported less than 20 per cent of their catch. While Japan and the United States apparently report relatively accurately, economists doubt the figures for South Korea and Taiwan. In the 1980s and 1990s a major sport was to try to catch poaching vessels fishing and collecting clams in territorial waters. This unequal battle offered prizes—confiscation of the vessel, or payment of a fine. Drawbacks quickly emerged. Even if the island avoided confronting a superpower, some vessels were so marginal that their home countries refused to pay the fine or to repatriate the crew, leaving the host country to support them until they could earn their way home. Islanders pursue multiple strategies to manage and obtain payment: surveillance, on-board monitors and reporting devices, and increased participation in commercial fishing. Australia, New Zealand and the United States provided aid to buy and operate high-speed patrol boats, and to facilitate air monitoring. The Japanese joined them in providing aid for freezing and chilling facilities, port and airport services. As infrastructure became available, the FSM fisheries authority negotiated for transhipment at FSM ports, rather than the deep-sea mother ships which are difficult to monitor. Local leaders now question whether the fees paid for transhipment cover the pollution and other costs of having the vessels in port, which also permits Islanders to see the tons of fish taken, and the wastage associated with large-scale exploitation—and to experience depression when markets are glutted by local gifting and sale of fish.

Many Pacific nations seek joint ventures with foreign companies, and purchase fishing vessels outright. As they expand their fleets and port services, they may increase their share of revenues and obtain more accurate data. The FSM acquired purse-seiners in joint venture, and the Marshalls acquired long-liners; both seek partners to operate shore facilities, processing plants, and canneries. However, Palau's experience was discouraging—the Van Camp processing plant shut in 1979, unable to compete in the world market. More recently, two cargo planes regularly flew fresh tuna from Palau to the high-end Japanese *sashimi* market, but this trade was discontinued. Tuna canneries in American

Samoa survive partly because of its favoured trade status with the United States.

The Solomon Islands presents the best case history of the possibilities and problems of joint ventures. Since 1971 the Solomons developed its fisheries industry in conjunction with the Japanese Taiyo Fishery Company. The joint venture, Solomon Taiyo Ltd, has operated since 1973, opening a cannery at Tulagi and operating pole and line vessels in the Solomon Islands' economic zone, most of which was protected from use by other nations. In the late 1970s a second tuna-fishing company, National Fisheries Development Ltd, opened, which incorporated local ferro-cement shipbuilding and training of crews. The national Fisheries Division developed expertise in establishing a management plan. In 1986 Solomon Taiyo ordered two purse-seiners, and made plans for a second cannery. By 1987 the industry provided about 7 per cent of all formal employment, and has consistently contributed between 30 and 40 per cent of the nation's total exports and 25 per cent of its cash national product. The Solomon Islands has enjoyed close working relations with its Japanese partners, and for the most part the agreement has provided market data on catches and sales otherwise difficult to obtain. Nevertheless the venture has had difficulties responding to fluctuations in international finance, various world market factors, and the human failures of communication and localisation of fishing crews. Gradually the crews are acquiring experience and professionalism, but most build upon poor education. The expansion of Solomon Taiyo into group purse-seining expanded catches, still within the limits allowed by the government, and increased productivity, but at the cost of continued reliance on Japanese managers. This joint venture has allowed the Solomon Islands to expand its fisheries and enjoy a high return (estimated at 9 per cent of Solomon Taiyo's gross earnings), as well as substantial secondary benefits. Compared with licensing fees, which rarely reach that percentage even when combined with aid, the Solomon Islands fisheries provide substantial employment in fishing and canning. Yet Hughes concludes that 'human resources rather than fish, boats, or shore bases are likely to be the limiting factor, and increased attention will have to focus on training, motivation, retention, and efficiency'.[15] In a nation with the lowest literacy rates in the region, this is critical.

By 1993, fishing revenues still provided 23 per cent of total exports and 8 per cent of formal domestic employment in the Solomons. Fish provided a substantial benefit to citizens, 80 per cent of whom are farmers and fishers. But revenues could be much higher: Japanese pole and line vessels operating in the exclusive economic zone pay 4 per cent of the value of their catch, and other payment schemes are used for other countries and methods of fishing. Only 10 per cent of the Solomons zone is open to vessels under the US multi-lateral treaty; the rest is fished by joint-venture operations directly negotiated with provincial

---

15 Anthony Hughes, 'High Speed on an Unmade Road: Solomon Islands' Joint-Venture Route to a Tuna Fishery', in Doulman (ed.), *Tuna Issues and Perspectives*, 203–24.

governments, and few details of these agreements are known: 90 per cent of the zone is in practice managed by provincial governments, few of whom have the experience and knowledge to maximise returns. Throughout the region, only multi-lateral action enables countries to maximise both fees, based on the percentage of the value of the catch taken, and accurate reporting (estimated at between 15 and 21 per cent of catches, by South Pacific Commission and Marine Resource Assessment Group studies in 1990 and 1991). The Forum Fisheries Agency is negotiating a new agreement on behalf of the Solomon Islands, Kiribati, the FSM, the Marshall Islands, Tuvalu, Nauru, Papua New Guinea and Palau, based on low-cost access for operations based in these countries. This may provide some necessary solutions.[16]

If fishing yields are to be maintained, host nations and deep-water fishing nations must find ways to co-operate. After years of pressure, the Pacific nations managed to outlaw a highly destructive practice: in 1989 the Wellington Convention prohibited drift-net fishing within national exclusive economic zones and a defined area of the high seas. Pacific nations led United Nations discussions for a global moratorium, but the fishing industry and major powers have been unresponsive. In 1994 a United Nations conference met to implement UNCLOS III and regulate fishing on the high seas, to protect endangered stocks. The increased participation of Islanders in regional and international agencies supports the establishment of guidelines for pelagic species. Without controls in the exclusive economic zones, however, such treaties may be worthless.

Indigenous marine conservation practices involve concepts of property, laws and personal relationships qualitatively different from Western practices. However, indigenous practices should not be romanticised: they did not extend to all resources currently exploited, nor do the wider social relationships operate in the ways that they once did. More important, many resources previously managed have been over-exploited, such as the hawksbill sea turtles which supported European 'tortoiseshell' fashions. Similarly poachers, seeking only the abductor muscle, decimated the giant clams (*Tridachna gigus*) in Palau's waters, one of the few areas where the animal survived. In such cases extraordinary measures are needed to re-establish and protect populations as their breeding habitats are taken over by expanding populations, and chiefly taboos no longer function. The Micronesian Mariculture Research Centre in Palau created a successful research and development program, collecting eggs from the wild, then growing the turtles until large enough to survive on their own, achieving survival rates of 75 to 80 per cent over a natural survival rate of 1 or 2 per cent. The centre's most successful project has been a giant clam hatchery, creating a seeding population of five species.

More important, the biological and social contexts for managing inshore resources have been transformed, and recording past practices

16 Australian Agency for International Development, *The Solomon Islands Economy: Achieving Sustainable Economic Development*, Canberra, 1994, 37–41.

would be insufficient, even if it were possible. Many management practices used in the past—restricting seasons, size, gear, species taken, and protecting breeding habitats—coincide well with Western techniques. Two constraints militate against their application: resolving the degree of centralisation of management responsibilities (and national co-ordination if control is returned to local levels), and integrating modern and traditional knowledge.

> The introduction of commercial fishing, the rise of trochus, bêche-de-mer, green snail, lobsters, pearl-shell as important exportable resources, the introduction of new fishing gear and faster boats all brought new management challenges that traditional management was not designed to cope with. Then there are the subtler but no less important impacts of Westernised political, economic, and religious systems on local authority and management. The question of how best to accomplish this transfer of knowledge to assist villagers to handle these new challenges seems to be the single most important subject that emerged during our discussions [at the South Pacific Commission Technical Meeting on Fisheries].[17]

As Islanders achieved increased recognition of their land rights, they sought recognition of sea rights as well. Under the Waitangi Tribunal, Maori resource rights are being reassessed (see chapter 12). Yet even as Maori fisheries rights were established, international problems of allocation were recreated domestically. Should fisheries payments go to the iwi (tribal groups) based on their percentage of the shoreline, to all Maori equally, or in some combination? The confrontation resulted in a High Court recognition of an urban Maori group, which does not claim land as its basis of membership, as an iwi, providing for urban Maori participation. In Australia Aboriginal people and Torres Strait Islanders seek judicial recognition of property ownership and offshore hunting rights. Their case was strengthened by the High Court's landmark Mabo decision on native title in 1992, which opens the way for a major restructuring of native land and sea claims.

URBANISATION AND THE ENVIRONMENT

While the Solomon Islands has been quite successful at managing its offshore resources, it has expressed concern at the probability that in-shore marine resources are being over-exploited through both commercial and subsistence practices in urban areas, and the effects of siltation and pollution in coastal and lagoon areas. Despite the high profile given to the multi-national exploitation of forest reserves, in its National Environment Management Strategy the Solomon Islands gave higher priority to issues of 'integrating environmental considerations in economic development, improving environmental education and awareness',[18] and specific policies on waste management and pollution.

17 Robert Johannes, 'Workshop Focus: Decentralised Nearshore Fisheries Management in Oceania', typescript, n.d. [1991].
18 Solomon Islands, National Environment Management Strategy, Apia, 1993, vii.

All issues are, of course, inter-related—as people move to urban areas or are forced off their lands by development projects, urban areas become overcrowded and unable to provide either subsistence through reef fishing and house gardens, or water and sewer services to support the population and protect the environment.

> Apart from overcrowded and sub-standard housing, and the prevalence of diseases related to poor and insanitary living conditions and polluted water supply . . . there are also the related issues of industrial pollution and its impact on the poor, and worsening nutrition as people depend increasingly on store-bought food. In addition, sensitive issues such as land tenure and political representation for urban people, and widening . . . social and economic disparities are major issues in the Pacific today.[19]

In many Islands the most severe threats to lagoon resources are due to pollution. Siltation and run-off from road construction damage the reefs on which such marine life depends. Ground water sources are polluted, and there are problems of waste disposal, and faecal contamination of urban waters and shellfish. In many localities, near-shore marine resources are over-exploited. The root causes are rapidly expanding populations and urbanisation. Population issues are highly contentious. Many countries have only recently re-established their pre-contact population levels. In other regions Catholicism is strongly embraced, and many people reject birth-control measures. For many Islanders, a large family is desired for economic security and in hopes that one child may break into the educated elite. Many Islanders have access to living in the lands of their former coloniser. Due to emigration, some Islands continue to experience high population growth but stable (Palau) or decreasing local populations (Tokelau, Niue). Growth rates are high. The regional average of 2.2 is second only to Africa at 2.9—a growth rate experienced by Vanuatu, and exceeded by the Marshall Islands, FSM, American Samoa, and the Solomon Islands. Only emigration offsets declining mortality and high fertility. High dependency ratios introduce problems of child-care and the provision of health and educational services, at high cost to governments. The standard of schooling is often low, limiting the success of students in tertiary education and forcing the employment of expatriates. Poor training also requires high expenditures in health and education services and limits the potential of some economic enterprises.

Many Islanders have moved to urban centres where services are clustered. At one extreme is the Commonwealth of the Northern Mariana Islands (CNMI). The most Americanised of the Micronesian island groups and headquarters for the US administration after World War II, Saipan had also experienced a high standard of living under the Japanese. As a US commonwealth in 1976 the CNMI pursued development through tourism and garment factories. The CNMI enjoyed privileged access to US markets; it is close to low-cost East Asian workers, and to high-paying Japanese tourists. But the few Chamorros and Carolinians alone could not construct resort hotels, nor were they

---

19 Bryant, *Urban Poverty and the Environment*, 48.

attracted to unskilled labour when they could sell or lease their lands at skyrocketing values. Today many enjoy new homes and cars, free education and health services, and many travel to the United States where they may own second homes and educate their children. Professional and unskilled workers are imported from Asia and other Micronesian islands. But the cultural costs of affluence are high. Within a decade, the indigenous peoples became a minority on their own island. In the workforce foreigners outnumber locals four to one. Exempted from US minimum wages and immigration restrictions, it is easy for families to employ Filipina maids, who know little of the culture and language (a problem shared by Palau). Most teachers are also foreign. This economic underpinning is vulnerable. Working and living conditions for the temporary workers are poor and overcrowded. The US government has investigated some foreign-owned garment factories for labour violations, and might withdraw the provision under which the garments enter the country without quota. Labour leaders there have attacked the industry whose 'US' product is not produced in conformity with US labour laws.

For many urban Islanders, especially those unable to obtain land rights, urban living resembles Lua's description of Haveluloto, Nuku'alofa:

> Haveluloto is no longer a peaceful village. By day, dust and smoke rise continuously and the noise from the engines of vehicles and from the Construction Company factory and the Copra Board fills the air. By night, there is the noise of instruments from the dance hall and singing from clubs that goes on until daybreak, and two movie theatres screen pictures six nights a week. Crime has become commonplace in the area. Land disputes are also on the increase. All of these problems have arisen because of the population influx . . .
>
> [T]hese new experiences demand a high price. Coconuts and fish can no longer be grown or gathered and must be bought, along with manioc, taro, yam, bread, tea, tinned meat and fish. Accommodation has to be found, often in a room with relatives or friends. Jobs are scarce and go to the more highly qualified. The temptation is strong to spend the day's pay on beer and entertainment . . .
>
> [There] are obvious disadvantages also in the difficulty of organising so many people coming from different backgrounds and all walks of life. Social disorganisation usually results in crime. The lives and needs of the Haveluloto residents are now becoming more sophisticated, but many do not know how to handle the new style and this creates frustration, disappointment and discouragement. Overcrowding has also given rise to pollution and poor health.[20]

REDEFINING MINERAL RESOURCES

Independent governments had few useful precedents to guide them in negotiating with landowners on one hand, and mining corporations on the other. Phosphate companies for example (see chapter 7) had paid derisory compensation to Islanders for the absolute loss of their

20 Lua, 'Migration into Haveluloto, Nuku'alofa'.

livelihood. In Australian territories and New Caledonia, land had simply been appropriated, and Fijian landowners were side-stepped when gold was discovered. Democratic governments could hardly treat landowning groups so casually. Equally, by the 1960s most mines were vastly larger and more expensive than during the 1930s. Their size made them vulnerable, and many independent governments were nationalising operations (Zambia, Chile and Malaysia) or insisting on joint ventures. In this environment governments could impose heavier royalties and stricter environmental controls, and agreements were commonly renegotiated once production began and governments were better informed of their value.

These trends made their way slowly into the Pacific. In the twilight of the colonial era, Conzinc Riotinto (CRA) began to prospect in Bougainville, and in 1967 Bougainville Copper Pty Ltd was floated. The geology of the site resembles several prospects in Irian Jaya and Papua New Guinea: colossal deposits of low-grade copper, capped by gold and laced with silver, requiring immense capital and skilled engineering. The government took a minority share, and some shares were sold to 'bona fide residents'. Bougainville Copper came into production in 1972 at a time of high copper prices. Profits in 1973 (in Australian dollars) amounted to $38.3 million (on earnings of $98.1 million) and the government earned $1.1 million in royalties, together with $10.4 million from dividends. Just in time for self-government, Papua New Guinea had a significant source of domestic revenue. However, the disruptive effects of mining fanned Bougainville secessionist sentiment which had smouldered through the colonial era. To hold the country together, Michael Somare's government took two critical steps. Bougainvilleans gained extensive autonomy through a provincial government, and the mining agreement was renegotiated. The new agreement secured for the national government larger revenues and an increased share of the venture. The more explosive issue was the distribution of revenues between national and provincial governments and landowners. The national government—starved of income and committed to 'equal development' throughout the country—was reluctant to treat Bougainvilleans differently, but did allocate some revenue to the provincial government. Less concern was given to Nasioi landowners who bore the environmental costs, including over 100,000 tonnes of tailings each day. In the 1980s, after much menacing rhetoric, a more assertive generation demanded huge compensation and sweeping changes in the distribution of benefits. When negotiations collapsed in 1989, the Bougainville Republican Army (BRA) stepped in, forced the closure of the mine, and launched insurrection (see chapter 12).

Meanwhile in 1967 the Indonesian government authorised the New Orleans-based Freeport company to mine copper and gold at Ertsberg in Irian Jaya. The Minister for Mines, keen to promote the first mineral venture since independence, 'accepted the draft written by the company as [the] basis for negotiations'.[21] Impressive engineering bulldozed

21 Lenny Siegel, 'Freeport Mines Indonesian Copper', *Pacific Research and World Empire Telegram*, 7:2 (1976), 8–11.

100 kilometres of road to the coast; 1600 metres of aerial tramway linked the mine to the mill; and a pipeline carried slurry to Amamapare port. Production began in 1972, and two years later the government re-negotiated the agreement to take advantage of improved copper prices. As in the first Bougainville negotiations, only the government and the company took part.

The Indonesian constitution identifies minerals as state property, and the Agrarian Law acknowledges farmers' rights only to land under cultivation. These provisions disadvantage the Damal and Amungme people who practised swidden farming above the ore, and denied them any claim for compensation. Freeport employed a few Amungme workers but judged that they were 'community types . . . They didn't understand working for their own profit. They just thought that when they worked it belonged to everybody and they weren't very energetic.'[22] The government and the company wanted them to depart. Local workers' huts were razed once their employment ceased, to discourage lingering, and a coastal village was built to draw people away from the site. Relations worsened until 1977, when rebellion flared across much of Irian Jaya in the name of the secessionist Oposisi Papua Merdeka (OPM, Free Papua Movement). In June, when two police were ejected from Akimuga, the army strafed the village. The people retaliated with an assault on the pipeline and oil tanks, and in August the army again strafed Akimuga, killing about thirty people. Armed resistance was snuffed out, and attempts at resettlement renewed. Since the coastal lands are malarious, however, few people co-operated. Environmental consequences were equally radical. The mill has a daily capacity of 115,000 tonnes—more than the largest aircraft carrier. As it is difficult to build tailings dams in unstable ground, the company deposits tailings into the rivers—one miner described this as 'speeding up geological time'.[23]

In the late 1980s, when Ertsberg mountain had been demolished, Freeport signed an agreement to develop the nearby Grasberg deposit. The reserves of gold, silver and copper—valued at $50 billion—make Grasberg one of the world's richest ventures. Jim-Bob Moffatt, then head of Freeport, described its role as 'thrusting a spear of economic development in to the heartland of Irian Jaya'.[24] In the view of the Indonesian government, development means assimilating the province into the national economy and society. Government policy envisages close settlement by rice farmers, and a new orientation to the land, making Irian Jaya more like the rest of Indonesia, rather than directing benefits towards the Amungme or the province. Endorsing this strategy, for many years the World Bank funded Indonesia's Transmigration Program through which people from densely populated central Indonesia were resettled in Irian Jaya (and other sparsely populated provinces). Between 1984 and 1989 the government opened at least 3 million hectares of Irianese forest to transmigration. Since many

22 Craven, 'Mineral Resources: A Discussion about an Irian Jaya Experience'.
23 Far Eastern Economic Review, 1994.
24 Adam Shwarz, Far Eastern Economic Review, 4 July 1991; Greg Earl, 'Indonesia: The Miners Who Dug up a Conscience', Reuters New Service, 3 May 1995.

projects were poorly planned, many disillusioned families quit. In 1986 the World Bank reversed its policy, but in 1987 invested in *Perkebunan Inti Rakyat*, or People's Nucleus Plantations, designed to establish state-owned estates. These transmigrant settlements continue to displace indigenous people, creating a supply of now landless, cheap labour.[25]

The Papua New Guinea government had nothing like the coercive power of the Indonesian state, so its next resource project—at Ok Tedi—generated radically different relationships with landowners. In this border area, its soaring mountains shrouded in forests and rain, colonial administration had arrived only in the 1950s (see chapter 4) and provided virtually no services. When the Kennecott company began testing on Mount Fubilan in the 1960s, it offered hospitals and schools, and sought the approval of landowners. The Wopkaimin welcomed their only prospect of 'modern' benefits from Mount Fubilan, which had always been a source of wealth and was the quarry for stone adzes (*fubi*). In the event, Kennecott withdrew, but interest revived in 1981, and a consortium of Australian, British, German and American interests with its new 20 per cent partner—the Papua New Guinea government —again proposed a mine. Again the landowners agreed. When it began work in 1982, Ok Tedi Mining Limited had an agenda which included social as well as environmental issues, recognising primary owners and other Min people living near by with more diffuse interests, as well as unrelated peoples affected by tailings downstream. It had to deal with two provinces and an unknown number of landowners, as well as the national government. When the tailings dam collapsed, the national government did not insist on rebuilding. Tailings find their way into the Fly River, which discharges into Torres Strait—with international ramifications. During the first decade, the interests of the company, landowners, provincial and national governments were renegotiated: the local share of royalties increased from 5 to 20 per cent in 1989 and recent policy provides for local equity. Ok Tedi Mining is also expected to provide services usually provided by a provincial government.

The government and mine managers expected the people to graduate from 'traditional' isolation into the 'modern' economy; but actual responses were less orderly. Many northern Ok people responded to a Christian revivalist movement (*rebaibal* in Tok Pisin), destroying cult houses, revealing sacred knowledge, and abolishing male initiation: the traditional male cult seemed irrelevant to contemporary problems. '*Rebaibal* ideology legitimates household autonomy in opposition to community reciprocity in the use of cash.' The neighbouring Wopkaimin, contrarily, had been ignored by mission workers, and built new ideas on the foundation of their male cult, rebuilding their cult house in 1981, and starting initiations in 1983. 'In rejecting *rebaibal* for decentralisation the Wopkaimin are reinstating old patterns of inter-hamlet reciprocity . . . Many value decentralisation as a way of preventing loss of cultural knowledge and ensuring the initiation of boys.'[26]

25 Kiddell-Monroe and Kiddell-Monroe, 'Indonesia: Land Rights and Development'.
26 Hyndman, 'A Sacred Mountain of Gold'.

Mount Fubilan was so inhospitable, so thinly populated, and contained such marginal ores that only high-technology engineering could mine it. Mount Kare was very different. CRA prospectors discovered alluvial gold north of Tari in the Southern Highlands province. This discovery provoked a classic rush in 1987. Clans on the fringes of the Tari basin claimed direct rights over the land. Other people based claims on kinship, marriage or even friendship. Large-scale battles between 1986 and 1988 'more or less split the basin in two'. By 1990 more than 100 million Kina ($100 million) worth of gold had been removed. Neither the company nor the government could control thousands of prospectors, acting out a scenario which might have been scripted in Hollywood:

> Refuse was scattered haphazardly around the houses, there were no sanitary facilities, and clean water was difficult to obtain. Settlements were based around a makeshift heli-pad which provided the only means of access (apart from foot), and high transportation costs were the main reason for the exorbitant price of food . . . Housing . . . was of two main styles—traditional, with timber slab walls and a roof of wild pandanus leaves; and 'modern' (ie plastic-clad and roofed) . . .
> Its bywords, among the people of Tari at least, were instant riches, sickness, immorality and waste.

The benefits were uneven and mainly ephemeral. Those who prospected benefited more than those who stayed at home—but wage earners fared best of all. Many women relished their first chance to earn cash. However, most of the wealth was quickly dissipated. 'Prospectors said that the gold seemed to run through their fingers—it was even said that there was a force "pulling back" the gold as fast as they found it.' Offsetting these benefits were large-scale fighting, diseases which flourished in unsanitary conditions, prostitution, alcohol abuse and gambling. This survey concluded that 'people will have to readjust to a subsistence lifestyle in a deteriorating physical environment and amid a steadily rising population'.[27]

Once CRA had endured the removal of a fortune in gold, company operations began in a joint venture with landowners. CRA was then harassed by small Australia-based companies 'prospecting by litigation', in alliance with landowners whose claims had been rejected. In the absence of a functioning provincial government, they were also beset by demands for roads, bridges, a high school and a hospital. As company managers mourned the old colonial days, so did the government, which could neither prevent the rush, nor harness its profits. From the landowners' point of view, the government could not provide schools and hospitals, so the mining company must. Eventually CRA quit altogether.

A prospecting boom during the 1980s (for oil as well as gold and copper) produced several new mines, and forewarned many rural communities of their once-only prospect of mineral rent—as resource-owners rather than citizens. Islanders on Lihir (off the coast of New Ireland) negotiated for several years before they conceded that the

27 Vail, 'The Impact of the Mt Kare Goldrush'.

Papua New Guinea government (which they first dismissed as 'merely a concept') was entitled to share 'their' royalties. The final agreement gave Lihirians broad powers over the entry or the employment of other Papua New Guineans. The agreement also provided that tailings would be dumped in deep water. Meanwhile the issues of tailings and compensation for resource-owners bedevilled negotiations in Porgera (in the western Highlands), and especially Ok Tedi. Some landowners along the lower reaches of the Fly River, represented by Australian lawyers, brought suit successfully against Broken Hill Proprietary Ltd as the controller of Ok Tedi Mining. What made this a landmark was that the suit was brought not in Papua New Guinea but in Melbourne (the centre of the company's operations). Mining companies and their workforces had long been transnational, and their range was now matched by environmental organisations, and by villagers themselves.

The government of Indonesia deploys ample power to ignore or disperse landowners; but the cumulative effects of mining and transmigration include the dispossession of scattered populations, the formation of squatter settlements around the towns, and general anxiety among any Irianese whose lands could be appropriated. Urban riots have reflected tensions between Irianese and other Indonesians, and between Irianese and the authorities. In February 1996, a group of OPM activists restored their cause to the world's spotlight by kidnapping European and Indonesian naturalists, and eluding the Indonesian army for three months in the broken and forested country of the interior, before they were tracked down and overwhelmed. Freeport's management was now under attack from American environmentalists, and from Indonesian human rights activists: when rioting closed the mine for two days, it was no longer possible to ignore either the communities on the mine site or the mayhem elsewhere in the province. Echoing the earlier moves made by companies across the border in Papua New Guinea, Freeport undertook to provide a range of services and employment, and to pay 1 per cent of profits to people of the province. And in another echo of Papua New Guinea scenarios, in May 1996 Tom Beanal lodged a $6 billion class action on behalf of the Amungme. The case was brought in New Orleans, and alleged environmental and cultural destruction. The affairs of a remote Indonesian province had become a global cause.

The redefinition of mineral resources depends crucially on political context. Powerful governments derive immense benefits, as France does in New Caledonia and Indonesia in Irian Jaya. The government of Papua New Guinea had mixed fortunes. Michael Somare's newly independent government inherited a large bureaucracy financed mainly by Australian aid. They could dismantle services and strive for self-reliance, or try to maintain them. 'By choosing to improve and extend services, the new government was bound to seek an accommodation with foreign governments on long-term aid and with foreign companies on major resource investments.'[28] The government intended to treat

28 Ross Garnaut, quoted in Amarshi, Good and Mortimer (eds), *Development and Dependency*, 215–16.

mineral projects as tax cows, to fund services on a national basis. That strategy failed to reconcile the Nasioi landowners to the Bougainville mine, and all other negotiations have taken care to compensate landowners, and increasingly involve them directly in negotiations, as happened on Lihir and in other contemporary projects.

These disputes illustrate regional and even global redefinitions of mineral resources, and the problems of distributing their costs and benefits. On the face of it, mining companies lost political power with decolonisation. Satellite land-mapping also reveals the physical impact of large-scale mining in the most remote places, so that destructive practices are more difficult to conceal. On the other hand, as 'bonanza' finds become rare, mining requires hugely expensive technology, which only large syndicates can afford. The vast capital, the hopes of land-owners, and the financial anxieties of host governments, all favour the interests of mining companies. Wherever the national government is weak, the company may be required to assume quasi-governmental powers, and the distinction between state and capital is very difficult to draw. The relationship is especially intimate when a government chooses to take up shares in mining operations, since the state becomes an ambivalent regulator of the environmental and social impacts of projects in which it holds financial interests.

Since the earliest modern projects were initiated in the 1960s, land-owners have come to wield increasing power, whether their claims have a legal basis or (as in Irian Jaya) rest on moral considerations. Land-owners, rather than well-paid mining workers or governments, have prevented some projects from beginning, just as they have extracted compensation and services from companies and governments, and in extreme cases brought operations to a standstill. Companies, projects, provincial and even national governments are transient: people's attachment to the land is well-nigh eternal. Their interests can only be accommodated at the expense of national revenues and the national services which depend upon this income. For this complex of reasons, therefore, mineral resources have generated as many political problems as fiscal solutions. In Papua New Guinea, agriculture has stagnated, and the lack of rural opportunities has fuelled urban drift. Dubious entrepreneurs descend on Port Moresby to seek corrupt partners. As law and order, and respect for government institutions, have been damaged, battles have broken out on mining fields on either side of the border. Meanwhile Papua New Guinea's financial problems mounted, until 1995 when the government had to come to terms with the World Bank. For a weak government, minerals proved a very mixed blessing.

LOGGING

Deforestation is a global problem: it affects the habitat and its species for generations, and contributes to global warming and to the pollution of waterways from runoff and soil erosion. Most of the clear-cutting is done by multi-national corporations who have limited long-term interests in any site. Although few Islands have sufficient timber to attract their attention, Melanesia holds vast forest reserves that, unlike the fish and sub-surface minerals, are integral to subsistence. The boom hit in the 1990s; government and local communities and researchers had little time to adjust to this volatile industry. In 1991 the Solomon Islands exported $SI54 million worth of logs, compared to $SI110 million in 1992. When export prices doubled in 1993, exports jumped to $SI230 million and suddenly accounted for 55 per cent of all exports, over-shadowing fisheries and contributing 25 per cent of government revenues. The situations in Papua New Guinea, Irian Jaya and Vanuatu were comparable—windfall profits to the companies and cash pay-ments to a few Islanders and provinces, from clear-cutting large tracts. The logging industry faced problems of prices, tax evasion, and under-reporting of export volumes, similar to those encountered in fisheries. The short- and long-term costs were staggering. Logging rates far surpass sustainable levels, and little reforestation is carried out, despite plans and promises. At the national levels charges of corruption have played into changes of governments and their ministers. Each new government announces policy changes to bring the industry under control and to obtain greater revenues, or reverses policies of the pre-vious administration. Regional inequalities have been exacerbated, providing some landholders and provinces with new revenues. But these revenues are used for private consumption and to import the machinery and other infrastructure for logging. There are strong demands for more government services in health and education, but the flow of income into recurrent expenditure and the volatile nature of this income have resulted in larger budget deficits despite geometrically increasing exports. While fisheries and logging and income boom in the largest and resource-richest Islands, the Solomon Islands, Vanuatu and Papua New Guinea are concomitantly losing productive capacity and increasing public deficits, and face severe and complex political and economic challenges.

The pre-independence British government in the Solomon Islands set up an economic portfolio to support independence, buying lands to create a forest reserve, and calling for reforestation. Immediate conflicts arose over land and resource ownership: under customary law, who-ever reforested could claim ownership of the trees. Partly to avoid colonial paternalism, politicians supported direct negotiations between landowners and companies, but few landholders had the experience to negotiate with multi-nationals. Predictably the national and provincial governments lost both control and revenues. As landholders experi-enced increasing difficulties with loggers, who failed to provide benefits any longer than their logging operation required, they increasingly turned to the Forestry Division for assistance. At the present rate of extraction the forests could be depleted by the year 2000, with little reforestation achieved.

Problems are not limited to the forest environment and sustainable development, but deeply affect personal relations. The high payments achieved by a few have focused attention on landownership rights and increased divisive litigation. Kwara'ae David Gegeo describes the disputes during his return visits to Malaita in the 1990s:

> The diverse ways in which the Kwara'ae regard land to be all life-sustaining are evident in their traditional myths, legends, music, religion, language, and of course, theory of food . . .
>
> [T]he last 20 years or so have seen a monumental escalation in the number of disputes and in their degree of intensity. Rightful ownership has become the dominant theme . . .
>
> Being a Kwara'ae myself, I am deeply concerned about the escalating disputes within and between clans. The extended family, traditionally the primary tool for mediating and resolving conflicts, is being threatened by capitalist transformation. If this cultural source of peacemaking is obliterated or even weakened, the problems—land related and otherwise—that will occur in Kwara'ae as capitalist transformation intensifies will be extremely difficult to control. Children growing up in the villages today will have seen and learned more about how to initiate disputes and how to break up families than about how to solve conflicts and unite households . . .[29]

Nor are foreigners alone in cutting the forests. Land tenure systems constantly respond to transformations in the ownership and use of resources, and often conflict with systems imposed by colonial governments. At least two tenure systems operate in Samoa, and under the new system individual ownership may be claimed over land newly cleared and planted. Upland forests are being cleared, less for the value of the timber than for the land rights established by clearing the land, rights concentrated among those who can hire workers to cut trees. Islanders are increasingly discriminating against distant kin, and use clan lands for commercial purposes.

RECONSTRUCTING AND MANAGING THE ENVIRONMENT

A few Pacific Islands managed considerable changes at independence. Throughout the US administration of the Trust Territory of the Pacific Islands the coral islet of Ebeye was a social and environmental disaster, home to Marshallese and other Islanders drawn to the high wages of the missile base at Kwajalein (chapter 9). Americans lived in comfort on Kwajalein, with ample housing, medical and recreational services (including a golf course). Islanders had to reside on Ebeye, 5 kilometres away, less than 180 hectares in area, where more than 9000 people crowded into housing supported by water and sewage systems designed for 3000. Medical and school services were minimal, and administrators feared that better services would lure more migrants. In the early 1980s some Kwajalein landowners reoccupied their island, halting missile tests and forcing a renegotiation of payments. The first mayor of Kwajalein after independence in 1986 used these funds and his new political control to transform the island: a desalination plant

29 Gegeo, 'Tribes in Agony'.

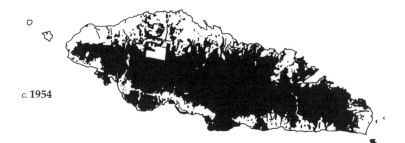

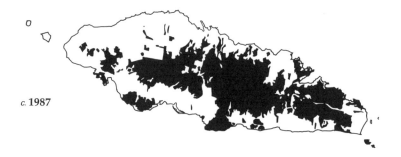

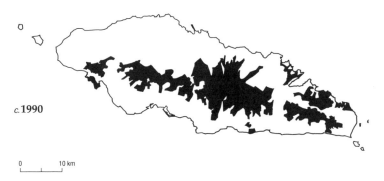

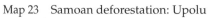

Map 23   Samoan deforestation: Upolu

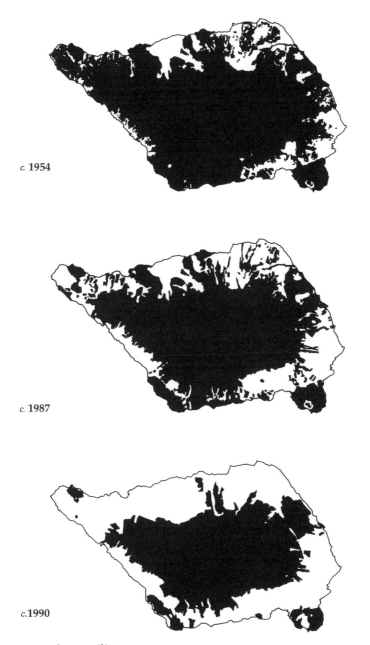

Map 23 contd   Samoan deforestation: Savaii

provided water, and housing and sanitation and public facilities improved. But the social and ecological balance is fragile. Such political leaders must contend with natural and man-made disasters while negotiating with members of disparate indigenous strata as well as outside agents. The more common Pacific experience is that which Hau'ofa describes: the new elite turning their skills into personal wealth, increasing disparities between themselves and a marginalised subculture. Monetary settlements can fuel as many problems as they solve.

INTERNATIONAL AID AND INTERNATIONAL CONSERVATION ORGANISATIONS

International organisations have played contradictory roles: the World Bank funded Indonesia's Transmigration Program (see above). Between 1984 and 1989 the government opened at least 3 million hectares of Irianese forest to transmigration, and forests were cut and lands appropriated for transmigrants. The damage to the peoples and forests— erosion, flooding, loss of flora and fauna—cannot be repaired. Original intentions to redistribute plantations and rationalise land use, positive responses to poverty and landlessness, may have very different outcomes, and international funding agencies are constantly caught between intentions and results.

National parks and nature reserves, unless carefully planned with community participation, can also alienate people from their habitats. While some Palauans welcomed the International Union for the Conservancy of Nature, the World Wildlife Fund, and the US-based Sierra Club and Oceanic Society in their battle against a proposed supertanker port in the 1970s, the proposal to establish Palau as an international nature reserve, in order to protect it from development, understandably raised questions of how local peoples would live and the degree of control they would exercise. Nature Conservancy and other organisations indigenised local offices and research, seeking to fund projects to protect the environment within the framework of maintaining indigenous direction. Nature Conservancy, the Asian Development Bank, and United Nations Development Program joined the South Pacific Regional Environment Program in funding the preparation of National Environment Management Strategies throughout the region.[30]

Even in areas not affected by mining and forestry, rising populations threaten upland forests. While the nineteenth-century depopulation of most Islands reduced population pressures, demographic resurgence has again placed forests at risk from those seeking homesteads and land. Even to manage Island ecosystems to support subsistence, following changing systems of food production, requires vigilance. When in 1983 the US Department of Agriculture sponsored a vegetation survey of Pohnpei, the researchers estimated that Pohnpei's forest areas were

30 NEMS reports were prepared for the Cook Islands, FSM, Marshall Islands, Western Samoa and Tonga in 1993 (available through South Pacific Regional Environment Program, Apia).

reduced from 70 to 55 per cent of the island's area. Watershed protection legislation was introduced in 1987, but local communities had been insufficiently involved and rejected regulations which failed to recognise traditional practices. Local and international agencies combined to form and fund the Watershed Steering Committee of local and state government agencies, the College of Micronesia, the Department of Agriculture, and Nature Conservancy. In 1991 the US Forest Service funded a pilot project on watershed management, which coincided with the initiative of four Kitti villages in forming a non-government organisation which worked with the state Forestry Division to create a local management group, a process that has now spread into other communities. This co-management approach, directed locally and buttressed by international funding and expertise, provides models for international involvement. The approach recognises that government funds will be insufficient to manage the forest resources; that the forest is not considered common property but has been regulated by traditional authorities; that communities have a greater stake than government managers, and therefore may be more effective in detecting infractions. Most important, the forest area that requires management is much larger than any that could practically be enclosed in reserves, and requires the participation of local communities in providing for sustainable land practices.

TWO LAWS TOGETHER

Wenten Rubuntja and Chips Mackinolty's painting, *Two Laws Together*, contrasts the depths of the divisions between Western and indigenous perceptions of place, while uniting them in the common cause of focusing attention on the landscape and its protection for future generations. It is this conjunction that presents the greatest challenge. The Western half of the landscape is a straightforward presentation of the land in European perspective: in the background is an easily recognisable representation of a mountain, in the foreground a large gum tree. To one who is not trained to see within Aboriginal perspectives, the Aboriginal half appears to be simply geometric forms without meaning. It takes special training even to begin to read the circles to represent waterholes or mountains, the arcs as people, the wavy lines as tracks laid down by ancestors during the Dreaming. Once such discovery is begun, however, it reveals a richness of knowledge of the landscape and the ways it is directly interconnected with ancestral, contemporary, and future generations. For it takes special knowledge to know where to find water in this desert environment, and to know the plants to harvest.

The past few decades have marked the beginnings of communications across paradigms of resource management in pursuit of a common goal, for it is clear that environmental degradation is the most critical issue facing the Islands. International political and economic considerations allowed a major restructuring of resource definition in the Law of the Sea negotiations in the 1970s; today metropolitan powers at times join international conservation organisations and indigenous peoples in attempts to mediate solutions, but the multiplicity of interests makes it difficult to bridge the gulfs of understanding. As the Ok Tedi and agro-forestry case histories confirm, good intentions and hard work may be insufficient.

BIBLIOGRAPHIC ESSAY

Decolonisation is well considered in Howe, Kiste and Lal, *Tides of History*; by Connell, *New Caledonia or Kanaky?*; Henningham, *France and the South Pacific: A Contemporary History*; and McHenry, *Micronesia: Trust Betrayed*. Current politics are recorded and analysed every year in *JPH* and *TCP*. Hau'ofa, 'The New South Pacific Society: Integration and Independence', is published in Hooper *et al.*, *Class and Culture in the South Pacific*.

The leading sources on Pacific fisheries issues are Doulman (ed.), *Tuna Issues and Perspectives in the Pacific Islands Region*; Gillett, *Traditional Tuna Fishing: A Study at Satawal, Central Caroline Islands*; Morauta, Pernetta and Heaney (eds), *Traditional Conservation in Papua New Guinea*; and Hyndman, 'Sea Tenure and the Management of Living Marine Resources in Papua New Guinea', which provides a bibliography of recent studies.

Mining is analysed on a regional scale by Howard, *Mining, Politics, and Development in the South Pacific*; and specific studies have been made by Jackson, *Ok Tedi: Pot of Gold?*; Emberson-Bain, *Labour and Gold in Fiji*; and Hyndman, 'A Sacred Mountain of Gold'. Vail's report on a gold rush is presented in 'The Impact of the Mt Kare Goldrush on the People of the Tari District'. Denoon *et al.* (eds), *Mining and Mineral Resource Policy Issues in Asia-Pacific*, contains several papers on current issues in Irian Jaya and Papua New Guinea, especially Ballard, 'Citizens and Landowners: The Contest over Land and Mineral Resources in Eastern Indonesia and Papua New Guinea', and Filer, 'Participation, Governance and Social Impact: The Planning of the Lihir Gold Mine'.

Forest issues are described and analysed by Park, *Tropical Rainforests*; Lamb, *Exploiting the Tropical Rain Forest*; and Colchester and Lohmann, *The Struggle for Land and the Fate of the Forests*. See also Australian Agency for International Development, *The Solomon Islands Economy*; Bennett, 'Forestry, Public Land, and the Colonial Legacy in Solomon Islands'; O'Meara, *Samoan Planters*; Falanruw, 'Food Production and Ecosystem Management on Yap'; and Raynor, 'Resource Management in Upland Forests of Pohnpei'. Bryant, *Urban Poverty and the Environment in the South Pacific*, traces the connections between economic and environmental problems. *Isla* 2: 1 (1994) is devoted to studies of Micronesian cultural ecology.

THE IDEOLOGICAL WORLD REMADE

CULTURES AND IDENTITIES

Central to many political and constitutional disputes in the Pacific Islands is the fact that cultural and national identities—and categories such as 'indigenous'—are ambiguous and contested. People who once identified themselves with a tribal group, a locality, or a particular leader have been asked to accept over-arching affinities with strangers and former enemies. Particularly in Melanesia, the rhetoric of national unity is vulnerable to assertions of cultural uniqueness and the priority of local custom. Even in more homogeneous societies, national governments must contend with district and village demands for autonomy. In the post-colonial era as never before, 'culture' is an arena of argument. Political debate is largely about culture and the nature of indigenous institutions: whether a change has traditional precedent, or betrays tradition.

Political transformation in the Islands has been a creative, negotiated process, in which Western models of 'kingship', 'nation' and even 'democracy' have been refashioned. Polynesian chiefs, for example, have readily made the transition to politicians and statesmen, although the justice of their continued authority has been challenged in Fiji and Tonga. The Tongan scholar Epeli Hau'ofa argues that democratic change is inevitable. Commoners, church leaders, emigrés, and intellectuals drive the democracy movement in Tonga:

> Forcing people with [these] backgrounds to remain in the ascribed subordinate place into which they were born, as some people have tried to do, is indulging in self-delusion, because that is another place, another time . . .
>
> In the three remaining truly aristocratic societies of the South Pacific (Tonga, Fiji, and Samoa), Tongan chiefs have the least control of and influence on the daily life of their people. The only area where the aristocracy exerts any meaningful control at all is at the apex of the state structure. Although Tonga has an absolute monarchical form of government, its population has developed a democratic culture to the extent that commensurate changes in the political institutions are but a matter of time, because the walls of Jericho are already shaken.[1]

After peaceful decolonisation, Melanesian nations, encompassing many different languages and cultural groups, faced perhaps the most

---

1 Hau'ofa, 'Thy Kingdom Come', 423–5.

difficult task of nation-building. The emergence of criminal 'raskols' in Papua New Guinea's towns from the 1970s onwards suggested a drastic decline in respect for the authorities, as well as a crisis in law enforcement. Some observers represent 'raskols' as victims of social inequality or as modern Melanesian Robin Hoods. In practice they are not necessarily unemployed, but come from a wide range of backgrounds, 'and many of those engaged in the more spectacular forms of crime have graduated through a range of minor criminal activities that victimize the poor'. Many have adopted a Robin Hood rhetoric, however, representing politicians and other power-holders as the 'real' criminals of Papua New Guinea society.[2]

Despite these difficulties, respected leaders could build a sense of national unity on the basis of celebratory multi-culturalism and broad regional affinities phrased in such terms as 'the Melanesian way'. Respect for human rights appeared to be a basic tenet of post-colonial governments, but recent years have seen some convergence towards the style of conflicts elsewhere. In 1987 Fiji became the first Pacific Island to experience a military coup, and soon afterwards the bloody Bougainville rebellion erupted. A president of Palau was killed in 1985 and his successor killed himself in 1988 (chapter 10). The 'Uvea massacre in New Caledonia in 1988 is described in chapter 11. Papua New Guinea's economic, social, and political problems had seemingly reached a crisis by the 1990s. Faced with multiple and overlapping crises, the national government focused on seeking a military solution to the Bougainville crisis, and amending structures of provincial governance (chapter 11). Some of the debate about the Bougainville rebellion suggests that the global context of micro-nationalism has begun to influence Melanesian perceptions of cultural difference. On the other hand, the ethnic rhetoric may be aimed at international public opinion, representing a federal–state conflict as a battle over indigenous cultural survival. The globalisation of political discourse and popular culture has intensified dilemmas of affiliation and self-definition, particularly for Islanders who have worked or been educated overseas. Life abroad may intensify self-consciousness about one's past and current life-style, but the apparent rise of a global metropolitan culture has not necessarily resulted in homogenisation, even among the intelligentsia. Cultural diversity is reproduced even as it is reinvented. Local identities, however they are reconstructed in the present, are not superseded so much as augmented by national and international affiliations.

Like emerging nations elsewhere, Island countries seek to create state-level identities that transcend regional and cultural differences. National symbols and emblems may be more effective than political rhetoric in marshalling citizens' loyalties, but the selection of symbols is fraught with divisive issues: whose symbols are to be chosen, how will they be represented, and who selects them? (Analogous questions have forestalled agreement on a national language, for example, in Papua New Guinea.) In Vanuatu, the government adopted a composite of

2   Goddard, 'The Rascal Road'.

customary (*kastom*) cultural symbols as emblematic of the nation—slit-gong drums, pigs' teeth, leaves.[3] The design of Papua New Guinea's new parliament house illustrates some of the hazards of crafting national symbols. One critic claims that regional rivalries and favouritism were played out in the design competition. Because the winning design emulates the dramatic soaring roof of a *haus tambaran* and incorporates other Sepik features, it can be criticised as 'Sepik-centric'. A Papua New Guinean who judged the competition called the building a 'cultural abortion' precisely because it combined diverse symbolic elements taken out of their cultural context. But such creative recombination seems a graphic representation of multi-ethnic nation-building.[4]

This chapter addresses the transformation of cultural systems and ideologies from the colonial era through decolonisation. The focus is on political ideas, cultural and local identities, and changing forms of group action. We also address the implications of decolonisation and economic transformation for women. Scholars suggest various causes for increasing political and other violence, such as foreign education, the frustration of young people, power disparities between ethnic groups, conflicts between region and nation over resources, and a growing gap between rich and poor. Engagement with the wider world also brings new behavioural models. As in Tahiti and throughout Micronesia (chapter 10) mass communications and consumerism offer an exotic array of life-styles and persuasions. Increasingly, Islanders feel free to choose individually. This may be the most profound way in which Pacific ideologies are 'remade'. In Western Samoa, for example, individualism threatens such *fa'aSamoa* ideals as family selection of *matai*, and *matai* custody of family lands. More *matai* attempt to name their children as their successors, and more land is acquired and transferred privately. The Lands and Titles Court is a frequent recourse for families contesting title decisions and land transfers. Most Samoans uphold customary ideals in the abstract, although they manipulate and even violate them in practice. Customary precedent is stretched and redefined to accommodate today's contingencies.

We ask whether Islanders' ideological worlds were 'remade' by foreign contact and colonisation and, if so, in what sense. Nationalist discourse and anti-colonial scholarship properly criticise many Western introductions, but some critiques propagate a simplistic dichotomy between traditional and modern. A visit to any Island (see chapter 11) confounds that distinction. Messy syncretisms and blurred boundaries are as common in the Islands as in popular culture anywhere, since Islanders have attempted to bend foreigners and their scenarios to their own agendas, 'indigenising' Christianity and other institutions. Except on Tanna and among the Kwaio of the Solomons, Christian affiliation became integral to daily life; but Islanders 'remade' ideologies, reinterpreting and reconstructing their cultures in interaction with foreigners. Lindstrom (below) describes this as a tradition of reinventing tradition.

3   Joan Larcom, 'Legitimation Crisis in Vanuatu', in Linnekin and Poyer (eds), *Cultural Identity and Ethnicity in the Pacific*, 176.
4   Rosi, 'Papua New Guinea's New Parliament House', 311.

For most Pacific peoples under colonial rule, the independent nation was a self-evident political goal; but the dichotomy of colony-or-nation may be too rigid to capture the range of Island experiences. First, the invasiveness of foreign colonial rule varied widely, due to geography, administrative competence and military support, the nature of indigenous authority, and the degree of local resistance. Foreign rule did not always and everywhere threaten cultural integrity and local self-determination. Colonial authorities and their laws were often a distant presence requiring interaction only over predictable matters such as tax. Confronted by tax collection and law enforcement, Islanders developed strategies of avoidance and resistance, testing the will of colonial administrators to force compliance. Colonial administration was less effective than schools or churches in reaching into local communities. In the meantime, Islanders under colonial rule gained access to metropolitan centres in Australia, New Zealand, and Hawai'i. Island goods had a favourable trade status in such markets and many Islanders saw migration as an opportunity for education and economic advantage.

Unsystematic resistance sometimes grew into organised anti-colonial movements, like the Tahitian RDPT (chapter 10), the Mau in Western Samoa or FLNKS in New Caledonia (chapter 11), or the Vanua'aku Pati in the New Hebrides (see below). For Fourth World peoples such as Maori and Hawaiians, however, colonial hegemony was inescapable. The trajectory, the rhetoric, and the dynamics of their political and cultural struggles are therefore very different and often more intense.

ENCAPSULATED COMMUNITIES

The Treaty of Waitangi Reconsidered

Chapter 7 proposed that social and economic changes in Maoridom at the beginning of this century were limited. For one thing the beginning of land development coincided with the Great Depression, and many Maori were forced back to subsistence agriculture and barter. Some abandoned the countryside, and were persuaded to move to cities and work in industries, as part of a deliberate government policy to create cheap labour. About 70 per cent of Maori now live in urban areas, locked into a vicious cycle of poor social conditions, low educational achievements, lower participation in skilled jobs, high unemployment, lower incomes than *pakeha*, and high crime rates, as well as low self-esteem and poor health. In 1994–5 the film *Once Were Warriors*, based on Alan Duff's controversial novel, brought Maori history and social problems to the attention of a world-wide audience. The film graphically depicts dysfunctional relationships, alcoholism, and brutal domestic violence in an urban Maori family. Although Duff's portrayal was criticised as extreme, few deny that Maori people are systematically disadvantaged.

In these circumstances the acknowledgment of Maori rights guaranteed in the Treaty of Waitangi resurfaced as a major political issue. As a result of the increasing politicisation of Maori in the 1960s, partly inspired by the American civil rights movement, the New Zealand government responded in 1975 with the *Treaty of Waitangi Act* establishing the Waitangi Tribunal. The Act allowed any Maori to submit a claim to the tribunal on grounds of being 'prejudicially affected' by any policy or practice of the Crown which was 'inconsistent with the principles of the Treaty'. The tribunal could not address issues originating before the Act, nor could it redress grievances. It was only authorised to recommend that government 'compensate for or remove the prejudice'. The Act was criticised for having no teeth, but in 1983 it vindicated Maori faith in the moral force of the treaty. In respect to the claim of Te Ati Awa of Taranaki against the discharge of sewage and industrial waste from the proposed Motunui Syngas plant onto their traditional fishing grounds and reefs, the tribunal concluded that the treaty obliged the Crown to protect Maori from the consequences of land development and settlement. It is worth noting that Maori tribal structure has facilitated negotiations with and claims against the New Zealand national government. Without an effective land-based local organisation, other indigenous peoples—from Hawaiians to Aboriginal Australians—have had difficulties presenting a united front to federal administrations. Only in 1992 did the *Mabo* judgement set aside the doctrine of *terra nullius* in Australia, forcing the national government to negotiate Aboriginal land rights.

Maori protests increased during the annual celebrations at Waitangi. During the days before 6 February 1984 more than 3000 people, representing tribes from across the country, marched to Waitangi and demanded that the celebrations be discontinued until the Crown fulfilled its treaty obligations. A national gathering then brought together opinions about the treaty. One resolution induced a radical change in the policy of the Labour government, which had been elected in 1984. It recommended giving the Waitangi Tribunal retrospective jurisdiction to examine grievances from the date of the treaty. To show its willingness to improve Maori–European relations, the Lange government amended the Act in 1985, extending the tribunal's jurisdiction back to 6 February 1840. It goes without saying that this clause opened up an important avenue for the redress of grievances, although the tribunal still makes only recommendations to the Crown, which retains sole authority to compensate for or remove the prejudices.

Queen Te Atairangikaahu is the first woman to lead the King Movement. The schism between the original, non-Tainui supporters of the King Movement and Potatau's own tribes (chapter 5) has never been repaired. Although Queen Te Ata is widely respected as ceremonial head of the Kingitanga, she is recognised as Queen only by her own confederation of tribes. For that reason too, most tribes have operated independently when lodging their claims. The decision of the Labour government in the 1980s to enable Maori people to seek redress of historic grievances has changed public opinion on Maori matters so much that the conservative National Party (re-elected to government in 1990 and again in 1993) has had no option but to try to settle Maori claims on the basis of the treaty. The first major deal which it negotiated concerned the use of New Zealand's fisheries, which is one of the most complex subjects in Maori colonial history.[5] The 'Sealord deal' was struck in 1992, providing that the government would pay the Maori $NZ150 million over three years as part of Sealord Products Ltd, the largest fishing and fish-processing company in the country. In addition, 20 per cent of fish species which were not yet part of New Zealand's quota system would be allocated to Maori tribes. In return, Maori people would discontinue all court actions and claims to the tribunal concerning commercial fisheries, and extinguish all Maori commercial fishing rights. The deal was agreed to be the 'full and final settlement' of Maori fishing claims. These final clauses, however, make the Sealord deal extremely controversial, especially as Maori tribes have not been able to reach agreement on the division of the fisheries among their organisations.

The second major deal negotiated by the government of Prime Minister Jim Bolger concerns the land claim by the Tainui tribes, the Maori Queen's main supporters. The government was forced to enter into these negotiations after the Tainui people won a historic case in the Appeal Court in 1989, concerning the sale of the New Zealand Coal Corporation. The court ruled that the government could not sell the corporation to private owners without a system of safeguards for Tainui's claim on the land and its resources, which had all been confiscated in the nineteenth century. Ultimately, a comprehensive settlement of the Tainui people's land grievances was signed by the government and the Maori Queen in May 1995, on the eve of the twenty-ninth anniversary of her coronation. The agreement included a formal apology from the Crown, acknowledging that it dealt unjustly with the King Movement in 1863, and it provides for the return of 15,790 hectares of Crown land. This amounts to about 2 per cent of the lands originally confiscated, to be returned over a period of five years, usually excluding all buildings. The value of the restored lands is estimated to be about $NZ170 million, and rents and leases might generate as much as $NZ14 million per annum. The settlement of the Tainui confiscations will support the King Movement's struggle to re-establish an economic base independent of the New Zealand state. The Tainui claim, however, is merely the tip of the iceberg of Maori claims. Only the future will tell whether these will be settled to the satisfaction of the Maori population, and to what extent the settlements will help to solve the problems arising from their disadvantaged position. In the 1950s *pakeha* scholars predicted that the Maori tribe was an anachronism and would gradually cease to have any effective function. The trend has been quite the opposite. Continually evolving and adapting to the national context, the tribe has become more active and solidary in politics and even in urban social organisation—a phenomenon that Roger Maaka describes as 're-tribalisation'. Maaka documents how some urban Maori living outside their tribal lands have established 'socially active tribal satellites in another tribe's territory'—an innovation that enhances their political clout while also providing a network for social support.[6]

5   'Muriwhenua Fishing Report', Waitangi Tribunal, Wellington, 1988.
6   Maaka, 'The New Tribe'.

Repression and Renaissance in Hawai'i

After annexation by the United States in 1900 (chapter 7) Hawai'i underwent traumatic changes affecting every aspect of life. Appointed territorial Governor, the conspirator Sanford Dole provided positions and contracts for friends and associates. The 'Big Five' corporations came to control business, the media, and politics. The *kama'āina* [long-resident] *haoles* who ran them were linked by kinship, marriage and interlocking directorships. Convinced of the superiority of the Anglo-Saxon 'race', they associated primarily with one another. White, Protestant, Republican and missionary-descended, this elite exerted tremendous power over Hawaiians and Asian immigrants. Beginning with the sugar industry, they gained control over transport, hotels, utilities, banks, insurance agencies and many small businesses. Monopolies developed in shipping, finance and communications. Land alienation and Asian workers enabled plantations to thrive, and many of the elite grew rich.

A massive program of assimilation and acculturation tried to convince Hawaiians that the United States was the legitimate ruler and that they were no longer Hawaiians but Americans. The term Hawaiian was redefined as racial rather than national. Citizens and residents of the former monarchy were identified no longer as Hawaiians but as Chinese, Korean, Japanese, Portuguese or Filipino. The divisive tactic was employed even among the Hawaiian people, when in the 1920 *Hawaiian Homes Act* the federal Congress mandated that 'native Hawaiians'—possessing at least 50 per cent aboriginal blood—should be entitled to special land privileges, while depriving others of lesser 'blood'.

The public schools were crucial. Mainland teachers were brought in to Americanise children who had to attend American schools where they were taught to pledge their allegiance to the United States. They were trained in foreign laws, told to adopt foreign morality, to speak only English, and to adopt an American life-style. In the schools and on the college campus, the native language was found only in foreign-language departments. The customs and traditions and even the people's names were suppressed. The great *makahiki* celebrations honouring Lono were never observed nor mentioned in the schools. Instead, Christmas was celebrated with plays and pageants. People were coaxed into giving children American names having no ties with the ancestors: names which described no physical substance, spiritual sense or human mood; names which could not call upon the winds or waters, the soil or heat; names totally irrelevant to the surroundings. Hawaiian arts and sciences were driven near to extinction. The practices of healing through plants, water or massage, or simply the uttered words, were driven into the back country. Predicting the future through animal behaviour, cloud colour, or the formations of leaves on trees was ridiculed. Hawaiian culture was being ground to extinction.

Tidal waves of Americans brought cultural, moral, religious and political concepts. Hawaiians were 'persuaded' to mimic their ways, idolise their heroes, and adopt their living styles. Americans took choice jobs with government agencies and management positions in business, and bought up many of the resources not already controlled by the Big Five. Though looked down upon by the *kama'āina haoles*, the *malihini* 'newcomer' *haoles* were equally self-assured, and found or created their own niches in commerce, real estate, labour unions, land development and the media. Most of the Asian sugar workers adopted the 'American dream', and many of their descendants have lived that scenario. The indigenous people, however, have mainly been left out of the success story.

The American military turned Hawai'i into a fortress, and Pearl Harbor into a major naval port. The Navy bombed valleys for artillery practice and took Kaho'olawe Island for a target range. The military tossed families out of homes, and eventually brought nuclear weapons to the Islands. Martial law could be declared at will, and conscription was imposed on Hawaiian citizens. Finally, after three generations of American control, 'Hawaiians' were given the opportunity to be equal Americans. The United States placed the following question to 'qualified' voters in Hawai'i: Shall Hawai'i immediately be admitted into the Union as a state? 'Qualified' voters were Americans resident in Hawai'i. Those who resisted US nationality and insisted on their Hawaiian citizenship could not vote. The US government offered only two choices: continued territorial status, or statehood within the union. The question, 'Should Hawai'i be free?' was of course not asked, and the 'Americans' overwhelmingly chose statehood.

Since 1946, under the charter of the United Nations, the United States has been obliged to report annually on its 'non-self-governing territories'. Hawai'i was listed as such a territory, along with Puerto Rico and others. Self-government was reached when a territory became a sovereign independent state, freely associated with an independent state, or integrated into an independent state. After the statehood vote the General Assembly accepted that Hawai'i had freely exercised the right to self-determination, and relieved the United States of responsibility to report.

Since then, however, there has been a dramatic shift in international opinion on national identity and sovereignty rights. As the 1960s began, the movement towards decolonisation had a major boost. The United Nations adopted the Declaration on the Granting of Independence to Colonial Countries and Peoples, which declared that all peoples have the right to self-determination: all peoples should be able freely to determine their political status and freely pursue their economic, social and cultural development. The United Nations mandated that immediate steps be taken to decolonise non-self-governing territories and transfer power to their peoples. The United Nations also established a special committee to oversee decolonisation. In the 1980s, that committee received reports that the United States had committed a fraud when it reported that the Puerto Ricans had freely chosen association, while tens of thousands who supported independence had been victimised. In 1984, 1985, 1986 and 1987, the special committee reaffirmed the inalienable right of Puerto Ricans to self-determination and inde-

pendence. The emergence of independent island nations and the pro-
motion of decolonisation by the United Nations have enhanced
Hawaiian awareness of indigenous rights. The international momentum challenges the assumption that no state may secede, once it has
become a member of the United States.

During the 1960s, Hawaiians witnessed the African-American
struggle for equality. The American Indian Movement's activities also
caught their attention. These movements were, however, overshadowed
by the Vietnam War. Many in Hawai'i acquired greater sensitivity to
racial identity and cultural pride, and a greater willingness to challenge
governments. Hawaiian music was taking on new vigour. Hula *halau*
(training schools and repositories of Hawaiian dance) gained prestige
and members, canoe clubs flourished, Hawaiian language-classes
burgeoned, as did interest in the natural medicines of Hawai'i and
Hawai'i's history. Hawaiian names came to be used assertively in public
contexts. This cultural rejuvenation was joined by people of many
different races.

Land became another focus of contention. The eviction of farmers
from Kalama valley on O'ahu sparked challenges to the land oligopoly.
The movement to save Kaho'olawe from bombing practice expanded
the target of protest to the previously sacrosanct military establishment,
and a plethora of Hawaiian organisations came into being in the 1970s.
The issue of sovereignty and self-determination was a natural out-
growth of disenchantment with social and economic conditions. By the
latter 1970s the sovereignty challenges were becoming more explicit. In
a highly publicised trial of a reputed underworld leader, the jurisdiction
of the state courts to sit in judgement over a Hawaiian citizen was
raised as a defence. The Blount Report, Cleveland's address to Congress, the Newlands Resolution and other historical documents were
made part of the case record. The attorney then challenged the authority
of the District Court to force him to participate as a juror, on the
argument that he was not a US citizen but a Hawaiian. Soon after, the
evictions of predominantly native Hawaiians from Sand Island, followed by evictions at Makua Beach and Waimanalo, all challenged the
jurisdiction of the courts to try Hawaiian citizens. The eviction cases
reflected another direction of activism: the Ceded Lands were characterised as stolen. During the Makua Beach eviction case, the state's expert
witness, when asked to trace the title of the Ceded Lands, stated that it
was state policy that no such tracing was necessary for those lands. The
court ruled that the Republic of Hawai'i had indeed the proper title to
cede those lands to the United States.

The awakening of Hawai'i to historic injustice had a significant
impact on the 1978 State Constitutional Convention, which created the
Office of Hawaiian Affairs to represent native Hawaiians. The trustees
of the office are elected by the indigenous people, and they are at least
in theory answerable only to them. It was expected that the United
States would soon acknowledge culpability for the overthrow of the
monarchy, and the office was envisioned as a repository for reparation
funds. The establishment of the Native Hawaiians Study Commission

by Congress during the Carter administration fuelled hopes that at last there would be some compensation for the loss of lands and sovereignty. The federal law establishing the commission also set a precedent by defining 'Hawaiians' as all persons descended from the aboriginal inhabitants, regardless of blood quantum.

Partisan politics derailed the Study Commission. The Carter government appointed the original nine members, six from Hawai'i and three from the mainland. The Reagan administration took office before the commission began work, however, and summarily dismissed the Carter appointees. The replacements were six mainlanders, including a Navy lawyer, and three Hawaiians. The commission held hearings, conducted research, and produced a thorough report on the cultural, social, economic and health status of Hawaiians. But the draft report in 1982 provoked outrage among native Hawaiians. The chapter addressing the overthrow of the monarchy wholly absolved the United States from guilt or responsibility. Written by the Navy lawyer, the chapter concluded that the United States bore no legal or moral responsibility for the loss of Hawaiian lands or sovereignty. The federal government owed Hawaiians nothing. The majority report acknowledged the disadvantaged social condition of native Hawaiians, but referred them to state agencies, private corporations and federal programs for Native Americans. No new programs were warranted, the majority concluded, and no money was due.

The final report was released in 1983. Predictably Volume 1, the majority report, was signed by the six mainland appointees. Volume 2, 'Claims of Conscience', is the dissenting report by the Hawaiian Commissioners. Volume 1 is a comprehensive source-book; Volume 2 rebuts the government's case on culpability. The issue of reparations was dead for the time being, although Hawai'i's Senators and Representatives continue to press Congress to reconsider.

The Office of Hawaiian Affairs operated on meagre funding—20 per cent of the revenues from the Ceded Lands. Many lucrative state facilities rest on Ceded Lands, but state agencies have been reluctant to pay. Amid growing public outcry over the state's conduct, the Office of Hawaiian Affairs threatened to sue. Its funds were increased in the late 1980s when Governor John Waihee, a Hawaiian, agreed to a pay-out to settle the fiscal claims. It is still seen as an organisation of limited scope, however, because its existence depends on the colonial constitution. Furthermore, since its constituency is racially defined, it cannot include all potential citizens of the Hawaiian nation. Its position on sovereignty espouses the model of a tribal nation similar to that of Native American nations. Today there is a growing vision of Hawai'i as an independent nation, in which the question of citizenship and residence would be settled not by racial extraction but by one's 'relationship' to Hawai'i, measured by some standard of acculturation, a vow of singular loyalty, ancestry from Hawaiian citizens prior to the American invasion, or other criteria.

More challenges to American rule are emerging: some school-children refuse to pledge allegiance to the United States; Hawaiian citizens refuse to file tax returns; more people deny the jurisdiction of

American courts. In 1993 weeks of public mourning, demonstrations, debate and re-enactments marked the centenary of Lili'uokalani's overthrow. In a radical move for an elected official, Governor Waihee ordered the US flag taken down and the Hawai'i state flag (the flag of the monarchy) to fly alone over state buildings. The action provoked counter-demonstrations and a stormy exchange of letters in newspapers. The houses of the state legislature used unusually strong language in a joint resolution recognising the anniversary:

> ... the United States military committed the first overt act to overthrow the independent nation of Hawai'i ... an overt act of military aggression against a peaceful and independent nation ...
>
> the Legislature believes that the proper status of Hawai'i's indigenous people within the political regime of the State of Hawai'i and the United States of America has still not reached its final stage and is still in the process of evolution; ...
>
> BE IT RESOLVED ... that the Legislature encourages the promotion of debate revolving around the future of Hawai'i as a Pacific Island society, within or without the United States of America.

In November 1993 President Clinton signed a joint resolution of the Congress (Public Law 103-150, 107 Stat. 1510) apologising to the native Hawaiian people for the complicity of the United States in the overthrow of the Hawaiian nation. While this legislation is extremely significant for native Hawaiian rights, it is limited to native Hawaiian people, appearing to foreshadow future treatment of Hawaiians as a dependent nation, like native American Indians. The question 'Shall the Hawaiian people elect delegates to propose a native Hawaiian government?' was put to a referendum of native Hawaiians in September 1996, when 73 per cent of voters approved the proposal. The administering entity was the Hawaiian Sovereignty Elections Council, created by state legislation but given broad discretion in determining the question, the voters' qualifications and the election rules.

POST-COLONIAL CHALLENGES

Custom Remade

During the colonial period, Melanesian 'tradition' became conspicuous and contentious in two arenas. Debate about local beliefs and practices escalated in association with cargo cults, that well-known form of Melanesian millenarianism. More recently, national independence movements again accentuated local consciousness of tradition. In the Pidgin Englishes of Melanesia, politicised tradition has come to be called *kastom* (or *kastam*, or *kastomu*). As they had during earlier cargo movements, Islanders again struggled to redefine and revalue their 'custom' in terms of how these practices might serve, or subvert, the new imperatives of national identity and unity. Melanesians reworked certain customs in service of nationalist rhetoric and purpose.

The gradual incorporation of Melanesia into global political, economic and communication networks has motivated transformations
within Island ideological worlds. Melanesians have long been remaking
those worlds: they have a tradition of remaking tradition. Given tradition's economic and political uses, large areas of culture have become
targets of political rhetoric. Custom is neither fixed nor unconsciously
experienced: its definitions and evaluations are constantly debated. A
person may build renown by introducing some cultural innovation.
Innovators include the leaders of popular movements, such as Paliau
Maloat on Manus in the 1950s (chapter 9) and Jimmy Moli Stevens on
Espiritu Santo in the 1970s, as well as ambitious village men such as Eric
Tari of Ambae Island in Vanuatu, who made a name in the late 1940s by
despatching in novel fashion sacrificial pigs. Dressed in a combination
of European and traditional clothing, at his ceremonial ground lit with
pressure lanterns, he killed the tethered pigs while driving by in his
war-surplus jeep.

Specific cultural forms identify local groups. Repertories of song,
archives of myth, community-linked dialects, catalogues of artistic
motifs and bodies of ritual etiquette distinguish kin group from kin
group, and village from village. Differentiated cultural forms possess
economic as well as political value. There are widespread Melanesian
systems of copyright, which maintain distinctive claims to cultural
resources. A dance, a new song, a new carving motif are all prestige
goods which bring a family just as much honour as the ubiquitous pig,
or the armbands and necklaces of the *kula* exchange ring. Local custom
heralds identity and social distinction, and groups can also trade and
exchange custom, selling a new song here, or buying a novel initiation
ritual there.

The borrowing of custom undermines any notion of primordial
tradition. An emblematic relationship exists between cultural practice
and social identity, but the identifying practices vary as people acquire
new custom and abandon old. It makes better sense to talk about a
broad, regional cultural heritage, rather than the traditions of single
community. A village or lineage's repertory at any time reflects the
selections they (and their neighbours, typically in opposition) have
made from the regional fund. Alongside their agenda of interests and
demands, European traders, officials and missionaries imported a fund
of cultural resources. They purposefully promoted much of this culture:
by the 1960s, 4500 missionaries were stalking souls in the Pacific—one
for every 600 Islanders.

Islanders were often willing consumers of Christianity, given their
valuation of new cultural forms. The sudden, stunning success of
Christian conversion in many communities typically followed the
appropriation of Christian dogma by ambitious brokers who repack-
aged beliefs and practices for an Island audience. John Goldie, a
Methodist missionary posted in 1902 to New Georgia, Solomon Islands,
counted more than 7500 converts in ten years. In 1910, he reported that
'not a single day passes that does not see some souls brought to Christ.
Some of the very pick of the young men have definitely given

themselves up to him, and are doing their best to lead others to him'.[7] Missionaries might have acknowledged Melanesian propensities to convert cultural forms into prestige exchange tokens, as well as the ambitions of the very pick of the young men.

Melanesians, like all subject peoples, had to accommodate or resist the overlapping political, economic and symbolic inequalities which colonialism imposed. Issues of incorporation and resistance were particularly acute given the character of Melanesian societies and cultures. Their assimilation within a global commodities market unsettled local gift economies. In contrast to Polynesian societies, Melanesians often had to deal directly with colonial powers, unmediated by local political authorities. The exigencies of colonialism ignited a panoply of efforts both to resist and to accommodate European demands. Many efforts centred in the domain of culture: people took a hard look at their institutions, practices and belief systems. Many attempted to borrow European custom, as they had purchased other cultural forms. By the turn of the century on Tanna (see also chapter 11), books, cloth and blankets had become prestige exchange items—and people continue to give each other cloth and blankets, along with pigs, garden foods and *kava* at ritual exchanges. The Tannese also remade some dances which celebrate these exchanges. Islanders re-evaluated their life-ways, sometimes positively but more often critically. They tinkered with marriage and exchange customs; they redesigned village architecture and the whole cultural landscape; they adopted new calendars and daily schedules punctuated with bells and alarms; they sought out new sources of supernatural assistance, sometimes welcoming Americans as a type of local ancestors or other munificent spirits; they instituted new regimes of the body, reworking customs of sexuality, bathing, and dress. And some put to work existing traditions of trance, drug use and dream interpretation in order to divine knowledge of a different future.

Not all resistance was confined to the cultural world, but warfare, strike or assassination was rare. A more regular cultural resistance was played out in new sorts of sorcery fears and in dream interpretation through which people constructed narrative critiques of colonial inequalities. The best-organised attempts to redesign everyday and ritual practices are movements that have been known as 'cargo cults' since the Pacific War. This term, first appearing in print in November 1945, became a generic label for a range of political organisations, movements, charismatic sects, and crusades. Scholars have applied this term to movements ranging from the early days of European contact (e.g. the Mansren cult of Biak, Irian Jaya, first described in 1857) to post-colonial organisations (e.g. the Bougainville Revolutionary Army). A lowest common denominator uniting this melange was reliance on ritual action and supernatural appeal to attain cult goals. These goals

7   Quoted in C. W. Forman, 'Foreign Missionaries in the Pacific Islands during the Twentieth Century', in Boutilier, Hughes and Tiffany (eds), *Mission, Church and Sect in Oceania*, 36.

often included the acquisition of Western industrial goods (*cargo* in Tok Pisin) and the establishment of a new harmonious order within village society, and between Melanesian and European communities. The term 'cargo cult' implicitly derided those efforts. Similar motives and parallel programs animated many of those who converted to Christianity as much as they did cargo cultists. Peter Worsley proposed that these were proto-nationalist responses to colonialism. Prophets articulated a message of resistance to European powers and created political alliances which pulled together atomised villages and lineages. Worsley supposed that resistance took this religious form because of rudimentary political and economic infrastructure. Modern political institutions would only develop in time. In future, he wrote, 'nationalist developments will probably be less and less under the aegis of millenarian cult leadership . . . the activist millenarian movement is typical only of a certain phase in the political and economic development of this region, and . . . is destined to disappear or become a minor form of political expression among backward elements'.[8]

There were, however, other reasons behind the Melanesian penchant for cultural reconstruction and religious innovation. Peter Lawrence and others have argued that the cargo cult was a normal, creative Melanesian form of cultural dynamism. Lawrence's analysis of the Yali movement near Madang, Papua New Guinea, located the roots of the movement within the bounds of Melanesian culture. He made sense of two puzzling features—why cargo, and why cult—in terms of indigenous cultural horizons. To explain a seemingly irrational appetite for 'cargo' which never arrived, Lawrence argued that cultists desired European commodities because of the social significance of goods within gift-based economies. Acquiring Western material culture was seen as a means of attaining economic and social equality with foreigners. For Islanders, Lawrence wrote, 'the cargo has become the symbol of the political power of the Europeans, and this power they feel they must combat'.[9] Lawrence also explained the organisation of these movements in cultural terms. Cults are not desperate reactions of people pushed around by powerful Europeans; rather, they are dynamic and creative enterprises with precedents in Melanesian tradition.

Cultic organisation and ritual innovation are normal political practice, given four widespread conditions. First, Melanesian religion is a technology with practical benefits. Islanders do not share Western distinctions between religion/economy and ritual/technology, and they ordinarily seek economic advantage through ritual action. Agricultural technology, for example, includes both techniques of soil preparation and spells to ensure fertility. Second, Melanesian epistemology presumes that knowledge is revealed and that the wise, therefore, have been inspired. Melanesians give little credit to individual creativity. Social activists are necessarily prophets who must present and legitimate their designs as ancestral revelations. Prophetic dreams,

---

8 Worsley, *The Trumpet Shall Sound*, 255.
9 Lawrence, 'Cargo Cult and Religious Beliefs among the Garia', 30.

mass hysteria, and cultic trance are normal devices to legitimate social change, not reactionary responses to intolerable conditions. Third, the Melanesian Big Man parallels the cult prophet: 'secular skill alone was inadequate. What counted was mastery of ritual by which men could ensure success. The leaders were men who "really knew" and who could direct the activities of others—those who did not "really know"— to the best advantage.'[10] Cults are, Lawrence argues, a variety of routine Melanesian politicking that has been coloured by the colonial encounter. As leaders, Big Men and prophets share similar political goals and strategies, and cargo is an especially promising new field for enterprising men. Finally, Melanesian notions of time expect social change to be abrupt, total and disjunctive. Melanesians normally organise cults when they seek to change their lives: 'What we call "cult" or "movement" is nothing less than the ordinary form of ritual and interpretive innovation in Melanesian societies.'[11]

This explanation perhaps understates the cults' novelty and detaches them from the particular questions which they address. Cargo cults served as a crucible of late-colonial cultural discourse, encompassing a critique of tradition and a recasting of convention. Many participants worried about powerful outsiders—but also worried about the condition and value of their own life-ways. The public, political reestablishment of tradition, or the invention of novel ritual within cultic contexts, solidified and fortified notions of local custom in general.

In some cults, such as the John Frum Movement on Tanna (chapter 9), a revised sense of identity solidified as people turned to tradition to oppose outsiders. Here *kastom* received a positive interpretation to counterbalance negative, Christian readings of Melanesian culture. People revived customs of reciprocal exchange, dance, and the *kava* ritual which they had abandoned on conversion to Christianity. Some, however, embraced Christianity but in a creatively revised form. Silas Eto on New Georgia and Jimmy Stevens on Espiritu Santo established independent churches based on readings of scripture which empowered Melanesian economic and political demands. In other movements, such as Maasina Rule in the Solomons (see chapter 9), people's attention focused on creating new political and leadership structures to oppose renewed European controls after the war. Alternatively, as in the early years of the Paliau Movement on Manus Island, cultists elaborated new regimes of hygiene, village design and work schedules to replace local ways which seemed inferior and disorderly.

The heyday of the cargo cult was the aftermath of the Pacific War. Word of John Frum—a spiritual middleman who links Tanna with the outside world, particularly America—reached the British District Agent in early 1940. The most successful and long-lasting cults resolved problems of leadership succession, maintained a vision of their policies and goals, and transformed themselves into composite political parties and churches. The John Frum Movement has supported candidates for

10 Lawrence, *Road Belong Cargo*, 31.
11 Wagner, 'The Talk of Koriki', 164.

local and national office in Vanuatu. It has also instituted a liturgical calendar of regular Friday meetings and annual holidays, including 15 February, which celebrates the day in 1957 when movement leaders raised their first flags. A body of exegesis has developed about the name. Is it derived from John the Baptist? John Broom—to sweep the whites off Tanna? John From America, or John Brown the emancipator? Is Frum related to *urumun*, a word for spirit medium? Whatever his source, John Frum has taken his place among the didactic ancestors and culture heroes.

In his first appearances near Green Point on Tanna's south-west coast, John Frum stated the need to revive knowledge which had been devalued during a period of Presbyterian mission control. He also talked of a coming cosmic inversion of relations between land and sea, mountain and valley, and black and white. Cargo elements played a part in his early messages, which predicted the arrival of the United States military bringing political freedom and economic largesse. Many Islanders abandoned the Presbyterian, Catholic and Seventh Day Adventist missions. In 1941 only a handful of Christians attended Sunday services; church membership did not recover until the 1950s and 1960s. Many men resumed drinking *kava*, thereby honouring their ancestors, and revived ritual exchanges and dance festivities. They also abandoned Christian coastal villages for garden and village sites which their families had deserted a generation before. Some, moreover, rejected money and challenged the presence of European traders.

Government and mission authorities tried to reassert control. Beginning in mid-1941, colonial agent James Nicol arrested and deported leaders. The first arrested was Manehevi, who was charged with impersonating John Frum and exiled to prison in Port Vila, in June 1941. Repression did not extinguish enthusiasm, and by 1943 new centres of activity had developed at Green Hill in the north and Sulphur Bay in the east. Enthusiasm was quickened by the arrival of thousands of Americans. Many Tannese men joined native labour corps to work at the United States base on Efate. Some John Frum talk in 1941 had already predicted an American arrival, and the United States quickly acquired first place in movement ideology as the primary source of foreign wisdom and goods.

The colonial government continued to arrest and deport leaders until 1956. Pressured by anthropologist Jean Guiart and others, the administration then freed leaders and reframed the movement as a religious cult rather than a subversive cabal. Thomas Nampas, Mwelis, Nakomaha, Poita and other returning leaders seized the opportunity to institutionalise a John Frum organisation *cum* church *cum* political party. They instituted periodic rituals and developed political programs in accordance with doctrinal tenets. They adopted symbols from their wartime experience—American flags, red crosses, military uniforms and drill. They also borrowed from Presbyterian ritual and organisation, instituting regular Friday night ritual dances, flower offerings, and John Frum altars and prayers. Since 1956, leaders have recruited police forces and guards and have convened courts to try people who offend cult discipline. Presently, about half of Tanna's population actively supports or welcomes John Frum ideology, affiliated either with the headquarters at Sulphur Bay or with other groups which propound competing interpretations of John Frum knowledge.

The establishment of national political parties in the early 1970s accentuated divisions among Tannese. Nearly all Presbyterians joined the Vanua'aku Pati, which took power as the first independent government in 1980. This party, founded by Peter Taurakoto, Donald Kalpokas, Walter Lini, and other British-educated religious and civic leaders, demanded early independence and land reform. French *colons* and francophone Islanders founded competing parties. Supported by the French establishment, these united under different names but came to be called 'the Moderates'.

Moderate leaders courted the John Frum organisation, who already opposed the Vanua'aku Presbyterians. Leaders eventually agreed to found a national John Frum party, and supported candidates who have won seats in the national parliament in every election since 1975. After several years of negotiation, all parties and the two colonial governments agreed to Vanuatu's independence in 1980. The success of Vanua'aku in elections preceding independence precipitated a minor revolt by John Frum and others on Tanna, and by Nagriamel Movement supporters on Espiritu Santo, led by Jimmy Moli Stevens. The rebels attracted assistance from French *colons* fearful of Vanua'aku rule, from elements in the French administration, and from the Phoenix Foundation (an organisation seeking a new nation in which to enact the principles of libertarian economics). The revolt on Tanna fizzled after Alexis Ioulou led a John Frum army in an assault on the government station at Isangel, and was shot and killed. The government, aided by Papua New Guinea troops, also put down the secession on Espiritu Santo.

During the 1980s, with Vanua'aku in power, John Frum people lowered their profile, but by the end of that decade they once again flew US flags and marched in US uniforms as part of the 15 February celebrations. In 1991, the Moderates emerged as the leading partner in a new coalition government and John Frum people remained an important component of Moderate support on Tanna. By then the Sulphur Bay branch was headed by a third generation of leaders who maintained the political structures and rituals from the 1950s but continued to rephrase ideology and programs to respond to circumstances. One constant theme has been the positive revaluation and reaffirmation of Island custom.

During the 1970s, the period leading to the independence of the Melanesian colonies, people again began reconsidering and remaking cultural practices. In particular, the term *kastom* spread throughout the region. Constructions of *kastom* contributed to broader political rhetorics such as 'Melanesian socialism', Fijian *vakavanua* (the 'way of the land'), and 'the Melanesian Way'. This latter concept developed in lawyer Bernard Narokobi's Papua New Guinea *Post-Courier* newspaper column 'The Melanesian Voice', between 1976 and 1978. Narokobi amplified an earlier rhetoric of 'the Pacific Way' which had emerged largely in the University of the South Pacific community in Suva, Fiji. Narokobi argued: 'I am convinced Melanesians are guided by a common cultural and spiritual unity. Though diverse in many cultural practices, including languages, still we are united, and are different from Asians and Europeans. Our ways are not so varied and contradictory as many have claimed . . . We are a united people because of our common vision.'[12] These concerns with custom cut somewhat differently than they had during cargo movements. Whereas people once worried about how to transcend backward tradition in order to accommodate to the colonial order, or how to revive tradition to resist this order, the problem in the 1970s and 1980s was to deploy *kastom* to oppose Melanesian ways to those of departing colonial powers, and then to create a sense of national identity and unity of national purpose. There are notable commonalities: leaders of both must rouse group solidarity, articulate credible visions of the future, and preserve their sometimes delicate authority. Politicians must build legitimacy for their administrations and fashion a sense of shared identity and political consensus among culturally diverse peoples. Once again, but on a larger scale, *kastom* provided a rhetoric to define the national community for its citizens. People could be defined as Papua New Guineans, Solomon Islanders, or ni-Vanuatu because they had, and sometimes shared, *kastom*:

> Political self-determination could not be achieved without first of all determining cultural identity. The cultural traits of the Papua New Guinean make him what he is . . . and not a Fijian or even an Australian. He has to identity himself first in order to determine what he wants for his society and to define the path or direction to take in the fast changing world of today.[13]

The proper role of tradition in search of economic development emerged as particularly worrisome. Debates about the utility of custom have focused on the consonance of tradition and democracy and on the position of women. Some cite *kastom* to reduce women's public role; others denounce *kastom* as an inadequate primer of modern gender relations. Others imagine a *kastom* heritage of gender equality, blaming the discount of women's capacities on European colonial practice. Constitution writers, politicians and educators have worked *kastom* in various ways into national institutions, particularly into legal, political and educational systems. Politicians also encouraged other aspects of emerging national cultures. In Vanuatu, this includes the use of Bislama, a local genre of string-band music, or the drinking of *kava*—Vanuatu's 'national drug'. Vanuatu's constitution declares the state to be 'founded on traditional Melanesian values' and established a National Council of Chiefs, charged with advising on matters concerning custom. Similar provisions exist in the constitution of Papua New Guinea, and the Solomon Islands in the 1980s also recognised Island councils of chiefs.

12 Narokobi, *The Melanesian Way*, 7.
13 Wari, 'The Function of the National Cultural Council', 110.

In Vanuatu, there has been self-conscious discussion about traditional consensus in decision-making bodies, the value of vernacular education, and reliance on customs of land tenure and dispute settlement. State leaders have attempted to remake indigenous mechanisms of decision-making and reconciliation to allay conflict over land occasioned by mining, plantations and logging. They have explored ways of reinforcing the authority of chiefs, Big Men, and other local leaders to resolve such disputes. After his election in 1989, President Fred Timakata pledged to strengthen the powers of village leaders: 'I should work with the traditional leaders who live with the grassroots people and get them to use their influence to get the people together . . . Nowadays if we really want to keep the unity of the country and maintain harmony then the chiefs will have to revert back to their old ways.'[14]

Kastom is therefore more than an agglutinative language of national affinity. Its twinned meanings of the 'customary' as well as the normatively 'traditional' not only describe who one is but prescribe how one should act. *Kastom* is a powerful idiom for organising and managing individual behaviour, promising social order alongside national unity. It can evoke new solidarities of action as well as identity. A national community of individuals with variant understandings and practices can all be 'customised'. Leaders concerned to alter people's everyday habits, or who hope to harmonise social behaviour, can find *kastom* a forceful rhetorical device for defining the nation and shaping its agenda.

This rhetoric smiles with promises of cultural identity and social regulation, but Vanuatu and Papua New Guinea have felt the teeth of *kastom*. Encapsulated communities may also cite cultural differences to challenge the legitimacy of the state. Where state discourse over-inflates shared *kastom* as a rhetorical adhesive, people may point to unshared custom to reject and withdraw from that state. Vanuatu in the 1980s and Papua New Guinea have already had to deal with rebellions phrased partly in an idiom of unshared *kastom*. The richness of local constructions of *kastom* supports tradition's multiple, and contradictory, capacities to sustain and to subvert national communities. *Kastom* can serve as an idiom of national identity and as a mechanism of state regularisation and control; but it may enunciate opposition and resistance with equal facility.

Coups in Fiji

Democracy is a foreign flower unsuited to the Fijian soil. So argued many nationalist-minded Fijians in the populist Taukei Movement, reflecting on the events of 1987. Democracy and the values of equal opportunity and individual rights were being used to deprive Fijians of their 'inherited rights', argued Asesela Ravuvu: 'Majority rule can turn into the rule of prejudice and the power of many to violate the rights of the few. Democratic decision-making procedures by no means guarantee the best decisions. In some circumstances the best decisions

---

14 J. Moala, 'Vanuatu's Chief', *Pacific Islands Business* 15: 2 (1989), 24.
15 Ravuvu, *Facade of Democracy*, x.

come from . . . a few well-meaning and knowledgeable people.'[15] Since Independence in 1970, Fiji had been ruled by the Alliance Party whose electoral victories seemed inevitable and whose leader, Prime Minister Ratu Sir Kamisese Mara, was the doyen of Pacific statesmen. In April 1987 the unthinkable occurred: the Alliance lost an election to a coalition of the new Fiji Labour Party (whose leader, Dr Timoci Bavadra, became Prime Minister) and the (Indian) National Federation Party (NFP). Bavadra's coalition, nominally left-leaning, was dominated neither by chiefs nor by the Fijian 'establishment'. The new government therefore threatened the foundations of a hierarchy: the unity of *turaga* (chiefs) and *vanua* (people), bound indivisibly by the chiefly system, and always returning the Alliance Party to office. Bavadra was one of the self-made Fijian middle class, typical of many who rose through the professions after independence. He was no radical. 'The chiefly system is a time-honoured and sacred institution of the *taukei* [the Fijian people]', he observed, for which he had 'the highest respect'. But democracy was a separate issue. 'The individual's democratic right to vote in our political system does not mean that he has to vote for a chief. It is an absolutely free choice.'[16]

His government was overthrown within a month, on 14 May, by Colonel Sitiveni Rabuka and the Royal Fiji Military Forces. A second coup in September ushered in an interim government (essentially the old Alliance Party, with Ratu Mara as interim Prime Minister), pending a new constitution. That constitution, promulgated in June 1990, enshrines Fijian paramountcy in the political system, and contains provisions which prevented Fiji's return to the Commonwealth. The Great Council of Chiefs, or Bose levu Vakaturaga, exercises a watchdog role in Fijian affairs, and appoints the president, who must be someone of chiefly rank from one of the three confederacies. It also nominates 24 of the 34 members of the Upper House. In the Lower House, 37 of the 70 seats are reserved for ethnic Fijians, 27 for Fijian Indians, five for General Voters (of mixed descent), and one for the Council of Rotuma, all elected from racially segregated rolls. Of the 37 Fijian seats, 32 are elected from 14 multi-member rural provinces.

When elections were held under this arrangement in May 1992, the outcome was astonishing. The Bose levu Vakaturaga sponsored the major Fijian party, Soqosoqo ni Vakavulewa ni Taukei (SVT). It should remain above electoral politics, argued many Fijians: it should be 'at the pinnacle of Fijian society, totally removed from the taint of ordinary politicking', said Apisai Tora, a leader of the Taukei Movement and founder of the All Nationals Congress. In the event, the SVT won 30 Fijian seats but only two-thirds of Fijian votes, provoking calls for the Bose levu Vakaturaga to withdraw its sponsorship; otherwise, Tora said, its 'reason for existence will be questioned in an increasingly hostile manner'.[17] The other Fijian seats were divided among minor parties. In the Indian constituencies, the old coalition collapsed between Labour (which lost most of its Fijian supporters and won only Indian seats) and the NFP. Labour won 13, and NFP 14.

16 *Fiji Times*, 22 March 1987.
17 *Fiji Times*, 10 October 1991, and 11 January 1993.

Equally arresting was the contest to become Prime Minister. Both candidates were members of the SVT: Josefata Kamikamica, a protégé of Ratu Mara, and Rabuka, the soldier turned politician. Rabuka enjoyed massive support within the SVT, but Kamikamica was backed by opposition members, including the NFP. The support of Labour tipped the scales to Rabuka, in exchange for assurances of a constitutional review, and several matters concerning agricultural tenancy, industrial relations and taxation. A constitution intended to promote the unity of Fijians had divided them; Ratu Mara's nominee had lost; a commoner was Prime Minister, by the grace of the party which he overthrew in the first coup; and he had conceded a constitutional review.

The government was hamstrung by dependence on factions and personalities. Rabuka and Ratu Mara—who became President on the death of Ratu Sir Penaia Ganilau—sniped at each other. In 1993 the government was defeated during a budget debate, and called a snap election. Kamikamica created his own party, the Fijian Association, and Rabuka's defeat seemed certain. In the event, however, the Fijian Association won only in Lau, Mara's paramountcy, and in Naitasiri. Rabuka's SVT polled fewer votes than before, but enough to capture most Fijian seats, and to form a coalition with the General Voters. Labour—paying the price for supporting Rabuka—lost many Indian votes to the NFP.

The coups and the constitution were intended to unify and defend Fijian power from a perceived threat from the Indian community, now some 43 per cent of the population. Their numbers have fallen in recent years due to emigration and a lower birthrate. Their main parties, NFP and Labour, divided over ideology and strategy, making any Indian threat increasingly implausible. On the other side, Fijian unity crumbled, partly on provincial lines. Why, many Fijians ask, should Ba Province, with a population of more than 55,000, be allocated as many seats (three) as Lau with 14,000? The main reason was to win the support of rural Fijians likely to support the traditionalist ideology. The allocation of seats by provinces also hinders governance. Parliamentarians' first loyalty is to their provinces, which expect representation in cabinet as a matter of right. Ministers, demoted for incompetence or fraud, portray their plight as a rebuke to their provinces. In a submission to the Constitutional Inquiry and Advisory Committee, a delegation of western Fijians criticised the constitution for discriminating against the 'progressively productive, better educated, forward thinking Fiji citizens of all races in favour of that minority segment of the community that represents (and seeks to reserve for itself) the aristocratic, undemocratic, privileged pattern of colonial life'.[18]

Bavadra's victory came when the social and ideological foundations of Fijian society were coming under strain. Modern education was opening up opportunities for individual talent. Migration and urbanisation—more than one-third of Fijians live in urban areas—were inducing changes in values and perspectives. The growing importance

18 Sutherland, *Beyond the Politics of Race*, 190.

of cash crops was changing the pattern of work and the use and distribution of resources. 'The combined introduction of new skills, new technology and money have weakened the functional cement which binds Fijian village society', wrote R. G. Ward, echoing Oskar Spate a generation earlier. 'This does not mean the structure has collapsed, or will do so in the near future. It does mean that the risk of disintegration exists if other factors shake the edifice.'[19] Many Fijians acknowledge these changes. Rabuka, for example, observed that 'the role of merit chiefs will eventually overcome those of traditional chiefs: the replacement of traditional aristocracy with meritocracy'.[20]

To consolidate its ethnic Fijian base, the Rabuka government promulgated a number of pro-Fijian policies. These included increasing scholarships for Fijian students; a small-business agency to advise Fijians; financial assistance to provincial councils and Rotuma to buy shares in the exclusively Fijian investment company, Fijian Holdings; funds to *mataqali* to purchase land; exempting Fijian businesses from income tax for twenty years; and transferring the management of 73,841 hectares of state land to the Native Land Trust Board. Well-connected civil servants and politicians have often taken advantage of these initiatives. Even then, the results have been discouraging, especially in the commercial sector. As Labour leader Mahendra Chaudhary put it, 'There must be something wrong within the system itself that with all these resources, the results are not forthcoming.'[21] Meanwhile Indian leaders complain of discrimination in the public sector, in statutory bodies, and in aid programs. Of 9572 civil servants in 1992, 61.4 per cent were ethnic Fijians and only 33.2 per cent Indians. There was not one Indian on the boards of the Reserve Bank, the Broadcasting Commission or, incredibly, the Sugar Corporation.

Two critical problems must be resolved. First, the *Agricultural Landlord and Tenant Act*, which regulates the leasing of Fijian land to some 12,000 Indian tenants, expired in 1996, and leases are renewed case by case. Some Fijian leaders want to link the renewal of leases to the Indian acceptance of Fijian political dominance. Some landowners want share-cropping to become an integral part of lease arrangements. Western landowners want to curb the Native Land Trust Board, and to negotiate directly with tenants. Others oppose all renewals because they themselves want to enter farming. Meanwhile Indian tenants want to escape the tyranny of short-term leases. If leases are renewed, on what basis will rents be assessed? If not, will tenants be resettled, or receive compensation for their improvements? Should Indians move away from the land altogether into small business?

Second, the constitution is again under review. The present arrangements reduce Indians to second-class citizenship, and government policies limit their opportunities in the public sector. Those who can, emigrate—some 30,000 since 1987. Those who cannot, hope that the new Constitution Review Commission will recommend changes to

19 Ward, 'Native Fijian Villages: A Questionable Future', 36.
20 *Fiji Times*, 29 August 1991.
21 *Islands Business*, August 1993.

allow them to participate once again in national decision-making. The fate of those recommendations will be determined by powerful segments of Fijian society and by the attitude of the international community. Ratu William Toganivalu, a long-time Alliance politician, once said: 'We, the indigenous people of the country, should not be tempted into the notion that by suppressing the Indian people, it would enhance our lot. If you do that, we all are suppressed.' But his is the minority voice among Fijians; most would prefer to see Fijians in control of the national political process.

Analyses of the Fiji crisis vary, but opinions cluster at two poles. Indigenous nationalists tend to applaud Rabuka's takeover as the only way to prevent 'foreign' (Indo-Fijian) domination and protect native sovereignty. They see the racially weighted constitution as a model for indigenous peoples who have become minorities in their own land. Members of the Taukei Movement publicly defined themselves as 'the indigenous owners of the land', and claimed that an Indian-dominated government would have dispossessed Fijians of their communal lands. This threat appears remote in light of the legal protection afforded to Fijian customary land, but the rhetoric played well to foreign audiences and to some Fijians. Liberal scholars counter that Fijian sovereignty was never at risk and that the new constitution is undemocratic and racist. They argue that the coup leaders have used inflammatory and simplistic racial rhetoric to mask the real issues of class, rank, and customary authority. In either case, Rabuka's rhetoric has had a potent appeal. The question for his supporters is whether democracy must necessarily be abridged in order for indigenous populations to enjoy self-determination. And those who believe that multi-ethnic democracy is not only possible but desirable are wondering whether, in the present global political climate, every cultural group needs its own ethnically bounded nation to preserve its heritage and political rights.

The Civil War in Bougainville

The government of Papua New Guinea did not fully resolve the question of Bougainville's autonomy, nor the distribution of costs and benefits of large-scale mining (see chapter 11). Tensions therefore accumulated until full-blown civil war erupted in 1989, when rebels closed the mine. A year later the national government withdrew the Defence Force (PNGDF) and imposed a blockade that prevented food and medical supplies from reaching Bougainville. The crisis has been exacerbated by an apparent failure of civilian control over the PNGDF and by acute internal divisions—generational and ethnic—among Bougainvilleans. Negotiations and foreign-brokered attempts at resolution have foundered in part because neither side has been able to articulate a position based on consensus. The rebels declared a 'Republic of Bougainville' in May 1990 and formed the Bougainville Interim Government. But the Bougainville Revolutionary Army (BRA) has always held the real power on the rebel side, and Francis Ona, self-styled Supreme Commander, also describes himself as President and

Father of the Nation. Though allied in their political objectives, relations between the older civilian leaders and the BRA have always been uneasy, and politicians who advocated moderation were either killed or driven from the island. A guerrilla force composed largely of young men, the BRA has been minimally controlled by the provisional government or by its own command structures. Given Bougainville's ethnic diversity, some BRA units are seen as little better than an occupying army in parts of the province.

PNG forces took control of Buka Island north of Bougainville in September 1990. Some Buka leaders allied themselves with PNG and publicly rejected secession. Buka Islanders claimed that they were suffering because of a dispute that primarily concerned landowners around the Panguna mine. The PNGDF armed a militia, the Buka Liberation Front, to combat the BRA and the result was civil war on Buka. More than 12,000 residents were relocated into refugee camps as ill-disciplined forces traded atrocities. The excesses on Buka were followed by an 'unauthorised' reoccupation of northern Bougainville by the PNGDF, raising questions about the government's control of the military.

By early 1992, the PNGDF had re-established control over northern Bougainville, and the BRA destroyed several villages in an effort to stall the advance. BRA raids also alienated Siwai people in the south-western part of the island and allowed the PNGDF to gain a foothold there. On the basis of a presence in the north and the south, the Papua New Guinea government claimed that Bougainvilleans were free to participate in the 1992 national elections. Only pro-government candidates had the temerity to stand, however, and in South Bougainville only 240 of a possible 30,000 voters cast their ballots. Of all voters, 90 per cent came from government-secured North Bougainville, undermining the credibility of the island-wide regional seat.

Australia, which supplies arms to Papua New Guinea, has also come under criticism for failing to protest human rights abuses in Bougainville and for allowing the PNGDF to outfit helicopters as 'gunships' (in technical terms, firing platforms), in violation of an agreement between the two governments. The PNGDF has re-established some level of control over much of the island, with the crucial support of anti-BRA militias, called 'the Resistance'. The mine and adjacent mountainous areas remain firmly in BRA hands, and something of a stalemate has been reached, with the BRA still able to mount military operations as far afield as the northern tip of the island. Following abortive peace talks in the former provincial capital of Arawa during October 1994, non-BRA groups made an agreement with the central government (the Mirigini Accord) which led to the creation of a province-wide body, the Bougainville Transitional Government to replace the long-suspended North Solomons Provincial Government. Its leader and Premier of the province is Theodore Miriung, formerly a prominent lawyer and acting PNG High Court judge, who sided with the rebels in 1990. He broke away from the BRA leadership in October 1994 when they refused to attend the Arawa peace talks. At the insistence of (but with continuing interference from) the PNG Prime Minister, Sir Julius Chan, exploratory peace talks started between the Bougainville Transitional Government on the one hand, and the Bougainville Interim Government and the BRA on the other. The first round was held in the Australian town of Cairns in August 1995. The ambition was to find a consensus position to put to Papua New Guinea concerning Bougainville's future status.

Despite their factional divisions, many Bougainvilleans desire a greater degree of autonomy for the province, and are sympathetic to the longer-term goal of an independent Bougainville. It is not clear that Papua New Guinea authorities realise how deep-seated this desire is. Nor is it clear whether they will be able to respond in such a way as to alleviate rather than exacerbate the current crisis. The Bougainville secession has been called an example of ethnic 'nationalism', but clearly this term inadequately describes the roots and dimensions of the conflict. The rebellion has divided Bougainville, setting language groups, regions, and generations against one another and creating a pervasive atmosphere of feuding and distrust.

Can Women Make a Difference?

The BRA at first comprised the mine landowners, but drew in young men of the rest of the island. The unrest could have been avoided had the Papua New Guinea government attended to the landowners' years of grievances over inadequate royalties, destruction of their environment, and related social problems. In their last attempt to raise grievances and demands, the landowners blew up electricity pylons along the road linking the port and the mine, and blocked the road. The government hastily sent a police riot squad, who, instead of controlling the conflict, behaved appallingly, burning houses, raping women, and shooting civilians and animals at will. This behaviour led young men to arm themselves to defend their land, women and children. The government reinforced the riot squad with soldiers, and lit a bitter fire throughout the island and especially among the young men who decided to help the landowners. By now the objective of the struggle had already changed to Bougainville independence. The fight was not new: long before 1962 (when copper was discovered in Panguna) the Bougainville people had demanded their independence. Yet the government was unprepared for the speed with which Bougainvilleans worked, even declaring their separate independence two weeks before Papua New Guinea achieved independence from Australia. The government of Papua New Guinea put the Bougainville people on hold: unfortunately this state of affairs has not changed.

The civil war, which began in 1989, has caused misery and devastated the people of the island as well as many Papua New Guineans. What began as a local expression of grievances has engulfed the whole North Solomons Province. Things have again reached a stalemate: there is no willingness to lay down arms by all parties, nor is there much improvement in the services provided by the Papua New Guinea government. That government has stated that Bougainville independence is inconceivable, while the BRA and the Bougainville Interim Government believe otherwise. In its effort to maintain the status quo, the Papua New Guinea government has put in place reconstruction, rehabilitation and reconciliation programs: some schools have reopened, and with the help of international organisations and the Red Cross, medicines have been brought in but not in adequate amounts; and the PNGDF is deployed over much of the island in an effort to re-establish peace and normality.

Can women collectively make a difference in finding a resolution? Women have been the backbone: maintaining some degree of peace and order, sustaining the cohesiveness of families, gathering food, and providing security for their children. Yet they have become victims, together with children and the elderly, of a guerrilla war which was not of their making. Typical of their suffering at the hands of both sides is Sister Elizabeth Ropoke's experience as one of five nuns, prisoners of the BRA:

> We continued our ministry among the people in the camps, where almost half the population was concentrated . . . Day and night we were taunted and threatened, but we never stopped speaking for what we thought should be done. On some occasions we were on the point of being killed, but divine providence always rescued us . . . Until that point in my life I had taken everything for granted, but during the crisis I saw and felt the real suffering of the crucified Christ . . . We sat and cried when everything went haywire . . . seeing people killed in front of us, some being hanged. These executions were mostly carried out by the cultists who believe in no future and seek only to return to the ancestral way of living.[22]

In 1994, at the Bougainville peace talks in Arawa, women—mothers, church organisation representatives, the president of the North Solomons Women's Council (Agnes Titus) and scores of young women in the Kieta area—came out of their bush dwellings and attended. With one voice they called for peace, demanded peace, wept for peace, talked and sang about peace, and prayed for peace in Bougainville. Agnes Titus demanded peace in her radio talk with Joseph Kabui. Since then the cry for peace rings in the mind and heart of every Bougainvillean.

Workshop after workshop on peace, conflict resolution and reconciliation have been held by non-government organisations, Australian and Bougainville Catholics, the Australian Quakers, and individuals representing Australian non-governmental organisations. Meanwhile, cultural peace and reconciliation activities have been organised by women as well as men and children. In 1994, small-scale business workshops for women were held on Buka by Australian women driven by the impulse of women's solidarity. Care Australia has set up an office in Port Moresby staffed by a Bougainvillean woman whose task is to identify the areas which Care Australia can best serve.

The issues include health, education, security, peace-making, and generating income. Bougainvillean women have travelled overseas

---

22 Elizabeth Ropoke, in *South Pacific Journal of Mission Studies*, xiv (1992), quoted in Griffin, *Bougainville: A Challenge for the Churches*.

from Geneva to Bangkok and Beijing, to tell the world of their plight, destitution, lack of medical facilities, loss of lives—the sad tales of the people of Bougainville. Four conferences have been held at the Australian National University since 1990. Women have described terrible experiences, the lack of essential services and goods, and the national government's efforts in reconstruction and rehabilitation. No criticism is intended, but women have been confined to the sphere of telling the world of Bougainville's misery, marginal to the main arena of the politics. If women are confined to that level of participation, they will continue to be afraid that they will be accused of collaboration, resulting in fear of being harassed, fear of rape, fear of the unknown, and even death. Should women still be passive observers of fights between the Papua New Guinea government, the Bougainville Transitional Government, the Bougainville Interim Government, the BRA, the PNGDF, and the police? 'Yes, darling, yes mother, yes sister, yes aunty, feed our children and continue to maintain peace in the village, and when you tell the world about our plight, just tell them of the misery and destruction of our environment. Leave politics to us men!' Is this the whole of women's capability? I hope not!

In 1992, I went to Bougainville to visit my family, and the first thing my brothers reminded me about was the land. There is a phrase in my Teop language (spoken on the north-east coast of Bougainville) regarding landownership: '*a moon to sinana ni na bono kasuana*' ('a woman mothers the land' or 'a woman is the mother of the land'). This concept encompasses several meanings, and not only in the Teop area. In Nagovisi, in the south-west of the island, 'the authority figure of a lineage is a senior female, called "tumeli"'. Lineage matters, such as apportioning rights to land, are referred to her. 'Should a married man ask for the right to plant permanent crops for his wife and children on his own matrilineage land, he will be refused on the grounds that married men may not make permanent use of their matrilineage grounds ... unless his wife's people vow to maintain connections through deaths, shell money, or assistance in fighting or mortuary rites.'[23] In the Teop–Tinputz area, when a married man wants land from his clan for his family, he must approach the woman. There are three possibilities: the woman gives permission only to cultivate but not to own, or he may be allowed to buy the land with traditional currency, or he is not granted permission either to use or to purchase. With the third option, the man can take his family to his wife's land and do the right thing, work on his wife's land.

Another phrase in Teop depicts this power: '*a moon to sinana ni na bona rivuhu*' ('a woman mothers the treasury' or 'a woman is the mother of the treasury'). The treasury contains traditional currency and other valuables used in major transactions, marriages, and in settling disputes. This degree of authority and power is found throughout most of the island. In the Halia and Haku language areas (a large section of Buka Island) high-ranking women are given the title *Te Tahol*, often

23 Mitchell, *Land and Agriculture in Nagovisi*, 10, 22.

glossed as 'queen'. At her marriage ceremony, the bride is carried on a wooden platform by men of her clan, proudly parading her to her would-be in-laws and to the general public. She embodies fertility, life, continuation of the clan, power and authority over land and the traditional treasury. Men do have rights and roles in these matters but women have the power to veto decisions. Men are simply custodians and guardians of these things.

Building on this authority and power, women should be more involved in the higher levels of decision-making. This would not be tokenism, but recognition of the power women hold. After all, it is land that the fight is all about. Francis Ona is not going to make a lone decision on reopening the mine, nor are the male relatives. Women as landowners will have to be consulted, after which the nuts and bolts of the decision will follow. There may be a need to translate these powers into the terms of the modern political world. How are they to exploit their status as landowners and treasurers in order to influence decisions in relation to Bougainville's political status? But perhaps there is also a need to draw and define areas of participation in the political arena. Who is to draw and define them? Women themselves should do so, on the basis of their existing authority and powers. Is it a question of time, or overcoming ignorance, before their sphere of influence is recognised and they can make a change in the modern politics of Bougainville?

REMAKING GENDER IDEOLOGIES?

We have argued that Islanders adapted Western political models. In gender relations too, a dynamic conjunction linked indigenous precedents and foreign ideas and institutions. Marxist scholars assert that women's standing necessarily declines in the wake of Western contact, but this assertion is difficult to sustain if we consider the cultural diversity of the Pacific. Women's standing varied greatly, from the sacred chiefesses and strong-willed older kinswomen of Hawai'i to the publicly devalued wives of New Guinea men's cultists. A simple contrast between Melanesia and Polynesia is also inadequate; Melanesian women of matrilineal societies were both culturally valued and socially significant. Many Polynesian women were seen as receptacles of a certain sacred power, but in most societies they were clearly secondary to men in public and political affairs.

Early Western-influenced legal changes tended to subordinate and marginalise women. Cash cropping and wage labour have also been cited as producing women's oppression and the 'commoditisation' of their work and products. But many Island feminists believe that indigenous men used introduced ideologies to reinforce their position vis-à-vis women. Some Melanesian women criticise kastom as a male tool used to subordinate women, and Maori women have asked whether the exclusion of female voices from public speaking on the marae is really 'traditional'. Late colonial laws—such as were instituted in Micronesia under the Trust Territory—may have given women more civil and legal rights than they had previously. In other words, there is no consensus on women's 'status' either before or after contact. Put another way, there is and was tremendous diversity in gender roles and ideologies.

Gender relations can be seen as a politics in which men and women vie for interpersonal leverage and decision-making authority. Women's cultural standing and social position are often ambiguous and contested. Colonial ideologies and institutions were profoundly male-centred, but women developed unpredictable responses to institutionalised male dominance. They not only sought to influence male public leaders, but formed their own organisations to apply political leverage. Even in societies where they are explicitly denigrated, women found ways to press their men to give up drinking, gambling, and squandering money. In some areas women also took advantage of new modes which, in Marxist theory, should have victimised them.

Because of wage labour and new crops, the trend in Melanesia has been for men to do less work (and women more) in food production. Men have come to rely increasingly on women's work for their subsistence and prestige activities, and this has correlated with women's public devaluation. Among the matrilineal Nagovisi of Bougainville, however, economic changes and cash cropping did not undermine women's importance. Nagovisi garden land is passed down from mothers to daughters. Married men can use the land only if their kinswomen approve. When taro was the staple crop, men did the heavy clearing and women did most of the planting and day-to-day management. After World War II, however, a taro blight throughout and beyond the Solomons resulted in a shift to sweet potato. Men's work shrank and women's management became more complex. Nevertheless 'the overall relationships of women to men do not appear to have changed significantly'.[24] The Nagovisi do not bear out the expectation that the less men work in comparison to women, the more women will be devalued.

In cash cropping too, the implications for Nagovisi gender relations were unexpected. The Department of Agriculture encouraged Nagovisi to grow cocoa. Families planted cocoa on the wife's land, and men and women had regular tasks in its cultivation. Cocoa land and trees are inherited by a woman's daughters, but the money earned is kept in the household rather than shared with the woman's matrilineage. The government favoured men when it disseminated knowledge about cash cropping, and encouraged men to register cash crops individually and pass them on to their sons. Cocoa was processed and marketed by the local Producers' Cooperative Society, which had an all-male membership and staff. 'Women take little interest in the affairs of the Society and rarely attend meetings.' While this scenario seems predisposed to strengthen men's position *vis-à-vis* women, Nash reported that

24 Jill Nash, 'Women, Work, and Change in Nagovisi', in O'Brien and Tiffany (eds), *Rethinking Women's Roles*, 98.

'matrilineal institutions have actually been strengthened', and uxori-local residence became the dominant pattern.

In Highland Papua New Guinea, a patrilineal area famed for 'sexual antagonism', women developed a novel system to arrest the erosion of their economic rights. Entrepreneurial *bisnis* and opportunities to amass cash—notably coffee sales and wage labour—have been skewed towards men. But from about 1960, women in Simbu and Goroka initiated a savings and exchange system called Wok Meri (women's work). Women formed Wok Meri groups by pooling some of their earnings from coffee or vegetable growing. They carried on ceremonial exchanges with other Wok Meri groups and acted as local banks, giving small loans to women. The rationale was simple: 'Wok Meri began because women disapprove of men's expenditure of money for playing cards and drinking beer.'[25]

Wok Meri exchanges mirrored male ceremonial exchanges, but the movement also used Western banking models to advance women's enterprises—and this system developed without national intervention or exhortations from foreigners. One ritual was a symbolic marriage, which raised money through 'bride-price' payments. When they had raised enough capital, the Wok Meri groups invested in much the same businesses as men—trucking, storekeeping, and coffee plantations. The leaders (*vena namba* 'Big Women'—a new title) networked with other Wok Meri groups, organised ceremonies, exhorted their followers to save and contribute to exchanges, and competed with other 'Big Women': 'The reputation of a "big woman" . . . depends not only on her personal wealth but also on the group's successful completion of a cycle of exchanges and on the amount of money controlled by the group.' Women combined indigenous and foreign models to reverse their exclusion from the cash economy and to claim jural rights denied them in their own societies. Women had engaged in collective action in earlier decades, but the immediate precursors of Wok Meri groups were church organisations—Lutheran women's fellowships in Simbu, and fund-raising work groups in Chuave—in which 'Women learned how to sustain and work in all-female groups for non-traditional purposes.'[26] But men also supported Wok Meri activities. Each group employed young men as bookkeepers and 'chairmen', spokesmen and monetary advisers. More importantly, women called on coffee income belonging to their husbands. Men, in other words, believed that they had an interest in women's prestige activities.

The Wok Meri movement illustrates women's response to a gender asymmetry which was both old and new. Women's economic marginal-isation was indigenous to a degree, but exacerbated by developments after World War II. The prohibition movement in Chuuk (formerly Truk) mobilised women in a collective attempt to deal with alcohol abuse. In parts of Micronesia and Papua New Guinea, men are expected to become uncontrollably violent when they drink and, in effect, acquire

25 Lorraine Dusak Sexton, 'Pigs, Pearlshells, and "Women's Work" ', in O'Brien and Tiffany (eds), *Rethinking Women's Roles*, 121.
26 *Ibid.*, 124, 150.

a licence for aggression and random violence. Early colonial regimes imposed prohibition because of racist assumptions that the 'natives' had a weakness for drink. In the era of decolonisation the legal right to drink was seen as a form of emancipation. Ironically, some Pacific nations have considered reimposing prohibition to cope with the rise of alcoholism and alcohol-related violence, notably among young men.

In Island societies men are the main consumers of alcohol; when women drink, they rarely do so in public. In Chuukese ideology women were expected to be submissive, and relegated to the domestic domain. Before 1970, very few girls continued their education beyond elementary school because of parental resistance. Collective activism and public leadership by women were unprecedented, and the women of Chuuk had virtually no role in the decision to legalise alcohol in 1959. Legalisation occurred when the subsistence economy was being supplanted by wage labour, and Moen was experiencing rapid urbanisation. By the 1970s alcohol use among young men was associated with disruptive public behaviour, sometimes leading to homicide, suicide, or automobile accidents. When the District Legislature failed to pass effective controls in 1976, church women and their male allies presented their own bills, which produced a prohibition law for Moen in 1977. At least in part, American colonial innovations laid the groundwork for women to play a greater public role. At the end of World War II, women in the Trust Territory were enfranchised and legally protected from gender discrimination. A small cohort of elite, educated women emerged. On the local level, women's organisations evolved from religious groups to service clubs working to improve child-care, family welfare, and education. Since 1970 more women have enrolled in secondary education, although a disparity persists. By the 1970s women's occupations and economic activities had diversified, and some women had attained responsible public positions. In 1977 church women and their supporters launched a petition for a referendum on alcohol; 93 per cent of those who voted supported prohibition. In 1979, when legislators were considering legalisation, women organised a demonstration—'something theretofore unheard of in Truk'.[27] Defying men's ideas of appropriate feminine behaviour, they marched with picket signs, surrounded the legislature, and staged a sit-in. In all, women thwarted three attempts to repeal prohibition. Their victory is qualified by the flourishing black market and the variable police commitment to enforcement, but public drunkenness and violence have been reduced, and women insist that domestic life has become more peaceful.

These accounts do not deny that colonialism diminished women's social and cultural standing; but we should temper such sweeping statements. By introducing economic modes and institutionalising ideologies of male dominance, colonialism often diminished women's standing, but not always. The argument has been made, for example, that women's status was diminished when Western cloth replaced the

27 Marshall and Marshall, *Silent Voices Speak*, 72.

native cloth that women manufactured in most Island societies. But Pacific women were not only makers of cloth, and their social and cultural value did not necessarily hinge on what they produced materially. In Tonga, Pohnpei, and Hawai'i, women retained considerable personal authority and cultural esteem as senior kinswomen. Any evaluation must be informed by understanding the cultural estimation of women's work, women's products, and women themselves. Many examples would support Jill Nash's conclusion:

> importing a new crop or production method involves many complex factors. A bundle of Western cultural patterns are simultaneously imported as well . . . imported cultural baggage gives priority to men. However, we must give indigenous peoples some credit; they do not always accept what is offered in the form in which it has been exported. There is a reinterpretation that makes it difficult to predict what the ultimate effects will be.[28]

The coups in Fiji and the Bougainville rebellion challenge the notion that Islanders are culturally predisposed towards inter-racial and multicultural harmony. Those who believe in Oceanic Edens may interpret these crises as the result of ideological and political contamination. Anthropologists have found that most Pacific ideologies of belonging lack the biogenetic essentialism found in Western models. Pacific Islanders welcomed, married, adopted, and employed foreigners with little apparent regard for ethnic difference. Therefore, ideas of ethnic or racial superiority and exclusion must surely originate elsewhere; their proponents must have learned them in study or service abroad. Liberal scholars tend to attribute such nastiness only to Western societies. Such a dichotomy is, of course, simplistic and stereotypic. Rabuka's racial rhetoric may not be rooted in Fijian cultural ideology, but neither is he a pawn in a scenario of Western 'impact' or a hapless victim of 'intellectual colonisation'. In public discourse Island political actors deploy racialist and nationalist ideas against established authorities. But underlying and feeding the rhetoric are more basic structural issues and intersecting interests—individual, local, factional, generational, and class.

PACIFIC CULTURAL IDENTITIES[29]

Literature and art express modern Pacific cultural identities, embodying their creators' visions of who they were, are, and could be. These visions encompass ethnicity, geographical context, gender, and politics. Although foreign scholars tend to view these as discrete, Islanders regard all aspects of life as inseparable parts of who they are, and our views as Islanders may not coincide with other people's views of us. Our cultural identities are always in a state of becoming, a journey in which we never arrive; who we are is not a rock that is passed on from generation to generation, fixed and unchanging. Cultural identity is

28 Nash, 'Women, Work, and Change', in O'Brien and Tiffany (eds), *Rethinking Women's Roles*, 119.
29 An earlier version appeared in Howe, Kiste and Lal, *Tides of History*.

process, not product. The oral histories, imaginative literature, and the visual and performing arts of the Islands indicate significant moments in the evolution of cultural identities. Because national ruling elites can impose on the people their versions of national identity, their views affect national policies and influence international thought. Besides, the educated elite in urban areas or in metropolitan countries are becoming increasingly influential in shaping cultural identities in their home islands through remittances. Most of the sources used here, then, are views of the elite.

A Rotuman model similar to those of other Pacific peoples divides history into three phases: *ao maksul ta* (time of darkness), *ao taf ta* (time of light), and *ao fo'ou ta* (new time), corresponding to the Euro-American categories of pre-colonial, colonial and post-colonial. The Rotuman and Western modes of history both use European intrusion as the basis for chronology, but with the essential difference that the Rotuman highlights Christianity in shaping cultural identities. In a nutshell, cultural identity was contested during the time of darkness, was transformed (with certain elements suppressed) during the time of light, and is negotiable in the new time.

In the time of darkness, Islanders shared a circular view of life. Donna Awatere has written of Maori notions in which 'past and present merge in the cyclic rhythm of nature and the ancestors' rhythm of life and death'.[30] Albert Wendt referred to this period as the time of *Pouliuli*, 'the Great Darkness out of which we came and to which we must all return'.[31] This circle of life has no beginning and no end, and each living thing is part of it. At the centre are the gods of the ancestors, who maintain the unity of the circle from within, and attract attention from the periphery. This view contrasts with the Western linear view of evolution, marked by development and progress. Using this yardstick, the *papālagi* (sky bursters) regarded the Islanders as 'primitive' or 'uncivilised'. This linear perspective also designated the time of darkness as static and simple. Such a view is not shared in the oral histories of the Islands.

Darkness in Polynesian conception was fluid and ambiguous: Hine Nui te Po (literally, the Lady of Darkness) was originally the Lady of Light, an embodiment of double identities, whose vagina is the site of birth and of death. Such ambivalence is evident in many creation myths, including the Hawaiian Kumulipo (see chapter 2). Further, many myths, legends, chants and songs recount sea exploits and navigational feats which suggest a dynamic period of contact between Islands, conflict, and settlement. For example, the oral history of Pohnpei reveals conquest by successive outsiders, with accompanying changes in social practice and new skills and knowledge. 'Polynesians' in Pohnpei and Kosrae in perhaps the twelfth or thirteenth century produced enormous changes in social structures, introducing *kava* and other elements, and leaving massive stone ruins.

---

30 Awatere, *Maori Sovereignty*, 62.
31 Wendt, *Pouliuli*, 145.

This phase produced some of the most dynamic and imaginative art forms, testimony to fervent attempts to understand the universe, religious preoccupation, and territorial expansion. Witness, for example, the elaborate and magnificent war clubs, spears, canoes, carvings and statues in museums and private collections around the world. This artistic excellence was most marked in the larger islands of Melanesia and Polynesia, where internal conflict was dominant. Instead of hindering artistic production, political rivalry and conflict acted as catalysts. Contemporary developments indicate that during times of conflict, artists and the arts become a focal point for cultural and spiritual sustenance. Drawing from their surroundings, artists created objects or songs and dances which served practical or religious purposes. The weaving of fine mats, the carving of ritual objects, the building of spirit houses, the preparation of costumes for dramatic performances—these and many more activities embodied images and visions not just of the immediate environment, but of islands and peoples beyond the seas.

The arrival of Europeans was not a complete surprise. A seer in Tahiti predicted the arrival of foreigners who would possess the land and put an end to existing customs; a prophet in Hawai'i recounted a revelation from heaven and the subversion of *kapu*. A prophet from Kwaio and John Frum of Tanna also foretold the arrival of Americans. Reactions to early Europeans ranged from fascination to indifference, from fear to adulation, from envy to contempt. The missionaries who followed found many of their compatriots revelling with the 'natives' in the 'darkness'. In the *ao taf ta*, time of light, many practices were relegated by missionaries to the time of darkness and marked for eradication. As missionaries steered Islanders along the path of 'civilisation' and 'progress', a linear perception of history replaced the cyclic view. In time, Islanders came to think of their history in terms of 'darkness' and 'enlightenment'.

Christianity and capitalism almost succeeded in reducing Islanders in the eastern Pacific to caricatures of the colonisers. From the arrival of the missionaries until World War II, Islanders were taught to emulate their dress, language, behaviour and customs. However, along the rocky road to piety, many Islanders satirised Europeans and the new religion even as they appropriated and refashioned it. The Samoans had *fale 'aitu*, 'houses of spirits', comic sketches which parodied European behaviour. Richard Henry Dana described *oli* (lyric utterances) by a noted Hawaiian improviser which derided Americans and Englishmen.[32] A visitor to Rarotonga described young men parodying military manoeuvres and engaging in drunken orgies to flout the church. In both Samoa and Tonga, buffoonery has made its way into church-related activities as both entertainment and a means of criticising the church and its clergy. In the Cook Islands, *nuku* (Biblical pageant) day is held once a year. Hundreds of children dressed in colourful costumes perform pageants, march with banners, and sing. Christianity's impact

32 Dana, *Two Years Before the Mast*, 117.

varied: Islanders accommodated what the colonisers imposed yet resisted it by infusing it with cultural elements which made it an indigenous institution. In short, Islanders recognised the malleability of Christianity and the need to modify Christian practices to suit their cultures.

Christianity propagated values and beliefs which were supposed to prepare Islanders for a modern world. Although Islanders often appeared to have totally rejected certain ancestral beliefs which came under censure, this mask was often thin. At times of crisis, many reverted to the ancestral spirits. Albert Maori Kiki's observation in 1968 that many Orokolo people are 'Christian and churchgoers, but they put the Bible aside on week-days'[33] is still valid, though the degree of reliance on the old gods and remedies varies, depending on the effectiveness of missionisation and Christian faith.

From the eighteenth century to the 1980s, representations of Pacific Islanders were the domain of Europeans whose views were ethnocentric at best and racist at worst. World War II did much to transform these views, although Islanders occasionally exploited stereotypes of the 'native' or 'savage' to their advantage: war narratives on Santa Isabel contain 'an ironic mixture of humorous self-deprecation and superior cunning . . . the image of "savage" is accepted on one level to be denied on another, establishing an ironic counterpoint characteristic of much of the war's oral literature'.[34] The foreign soldiers were ill prepared for the tropics. As Papua New Guineans, Fijians and Solomon Islanders helped them as soldiers, carriers, stretcher-bearers or guides, and as human beings struggled together against a common enemy, 'Fuzzy-Wuzzy Devils' became 'Fuzzy-Wuzzy Angels' (chapter 9). The success of the Maori Battalion during the same war also enhanced Maori prestige and pride. First-hand experience with Islanders helped in a small way to dispel ignorance, fear and prejudice, at least among Western soldiers.

Whether positive or negative, however, stereotypic representations reduced Islanders to two-dimensional figures, and Islanders have had to contend with ascribed identities. As Western-style education expanded, young Islanders increasingly came to assert their right to define and represent their own identities. The University of Papua New Guinea opened its doors in 1966, and its students started writing imaginative literature with the encouragement of Ulli and Georgina Beier. Soon poems, stories, plays and novels were being written in English. No longer were Islanders content to allow representations to be the preserve of foreigners. Many saw it as their mission to restore full humanity to their people. The brightest students often studied abroad, particularly in Australia or New Zealand; but this experience often resulted in alienation from the land and the community. Many Islanders educated overseas discover on their return the need to learn or relearn traditional skills in order to rejoin a community and regain an indigenous identity.

33 Kiki, *Ten Thousand Years in a Lifetime*, 168.
34 Lamont Lindstrom and Geoffrey White, 'War Stories', in White and Lindstrom, *The Pacific Theater*, 8.

The era of decolonisation saw a cultural reawakening in literature and art. In their attempts to mould nation-states, Island leaders organised national art and craft festivals to revive suppressed art forms. The tourism industry also took a keen interest in the revival of dances and crafts. Artists gained access to new tools, materials and ideas, and improved transport allowed them to meet each other more easily than before. The culmination of this renaissance was the first South Pacific Festival of Arts (now the Festival of Pacific Arts) in Suva in 1972. The Suva festival was a turning point in restoring dignity and pride to all Pacific countries, except Guam and Tahiti which did not participate until the second festival four years later in Rotorua, New Zealand. Isolated attempts to revive art forms—particularly in the visual and performing arts—were brought together and celebrated. The result was a cultural explosion on a scale previously unheard of in the Pacific. Islanders became aware of differences as well as commonalities between themselves and their neighbours. The success of the first festival reverberated far and wide; since then, this festival has brought together artists every four years—to dance, sing, laugh, learn from one another, and celebrate their Pacific identities.

Christianity has shed its 'light' on the Islands for more than a hundred years; cultural elements which are revived are therefore usually those which can be reconciled with Christian beliefs. These reconstituted forms that fuse selected elements from the 'time of darkness' and the 'time of light' have become, over the years, traditional. Pacific cultures and arts are continually taking on elements from European, Asian, American and other Pacific cultures. The final mix is therefore quite different from pre-European ways. Nevertheless these identities are valid and necessary, as Islanders struggle towards self-determination in all spheres of their lives. A selected and politicised synthesis of past and present characterises contemporary expressions of identity in the *ao fo'ou ta*, 'new time'. The term post-colonial does not accurately describe this period, for there are neo-colonial practices even in independent nations. In the French colonies, New Zealand and Hawai'i, where indigenous people still struggle for sovereignty, the term is meaningless. The Rotuman word *fo'ou* is more accurate: it means 'new', suggesting strangeness and unfamiliarity. In Rotuma, it is usually used in the context of shifting allegiances between foreign and local ways. Someone who behaves in an 'un-Rotuman' fashion may be mocked for having 'sold out' to foreign ways. Sometimes the same term is used to justify certain kinds of dress or behaviour, to impress on others the realities of living in the present and the evolutionary nature of culture. These uses of the word *fo'ou* to censure or to justify dress or behaviour suggest that cultural identity has become negotiable.

Attempts to preserve traditional cultures in a context of profound social change have led to charges of 'invented traditions' and 'inauthenticity' by Western scholars. As may be expected, these views provoke counter-arguments from Island and other scholars. Often the focus of these arguments is blurred, for the wrong questions are asked and the answers are muddled and unhelpful. Increasingly, indigenous scholars prefer that outsiders refrain from pontificating about indigenous identities. It is unlikely, however, that non-indigenous scholars will stop writing about the constructions of identity; a more realistic approach would be for all concerned to focus on issues that will lead to the restoration of equality and human dignity. The question of 'authenticity' is far less important than understanding the cultural, historical and political reasons for the essentialist stance adopted by some present-day political movements. Seeming inconsistencies or contradictions in the way Islanders symbolically express their identities are symptoms of the multiplicity of competing cultures and ideologies in contemporary society.

In the name of progress, education continues in the language of the coloniser while lip-service is paid to the teaching of native languages. The literature taught in schools and universities is still predominantly European or American. Shakespeare is forced on Fijian and Indian students destined to work in sugar fields or cassava plantations. Many parents, teachers and influential figures still believe that what is foreign is best. Thus indigenous literature, oral and written, and Pacific visual and performing arts are either absent or trivialised in curricula. Those who graduate from foreign-style institutions know more about the history, geography and cultures of the West than about their own heritage or that of other Islands.

In its early stages the University of the South Pacific showed great promise in restoring Island pride. Yet a generation later its Literature and Language Department has yet to teach any Pacific language. Few of the university's largely expatriate (or even local) staff are seen at cultural events, and students who spend time preparing for cultural presentations often resent the fact that their contributions make no difference to their grades. Those who benefit most academically are those who choose not to participate in cultural activities, which they view as a hindrance to their studies. The trend towards a more relevant and Islander-designed education develops slowly. The valorisation of the 'Pacific Way' has yet to filter into education, which holds the key to a mental revolution. Unless politicians and teachers introduce sweeping changes in curricula, true decolonisation of the mind will remain a dream.

Islanders in urban centres holding white-collar jobs face similar cultural conflicts. They feel Pacific in their love of laughter and generosity of spirit, in their emphasis on people rather than possessions, yet they speak English, wear Western clothing, and pay rent or mortgages. Torn between being traditional and being 'realistic' in the modern setting, they are often unable to reconcile these notions of identity. There is, of course, nothing shameful about having two or more identities, or an identity that is composite: the bilingual or bicultural individual has a distinct advantage. The secret is the ability to adjust to circumstances, as Rotumans are prone to do. A Rotuman male usually answers the question 'Who are you?' by mentioning his name, parents, and village. Rarely is the question of identity asked directly because it is considered rude. Instead, people whisper, 'Who is that person?' Since Rotumans do not customarily take their father's name as their surname (though many now follow the European custom), a person's name seldom reveals anything unless both parents' names are mentioned. Sometimes this is adequate; otherwise mention of the village suffices. This 'consocial' identity reflects the value of kinship and the importance of the extended family. This view of personhood is true of other Pacific Islands as well. Outside one's island of birth, identity becomes variable and more susceptible to manipulation. If asked 'Who are you?' in Hawai'i, the same Rotuman may say he is Fijian, since constitutionally Rotuma is part of Fiji. If asked the same question in England, he may claim the Pacific Islands as his place of origin. The answer, in other words, depends on the context and the respondent's motives. In general the Rotuman tries to be inclusive, particularly if it is desirable to forge a common background. No Rotuman wants to be identified as Fijian if the association will not bring credit.

However, a sense of shared identity rarely extends to whites, whose physical appearance and values, in addition to their membership of the colonising group, make Islanders only too aware of difference. Instead of a better appreciation of Euro-American values, Western-style education seems to breed alienation and critique, as evidenced by the number of educated Islanders in colleges and universities who vigorously assert a cultural identity rooted in the past. These Islanders may work in professions which are rooted in Western middle-class culture, but they cultivate symbols which express their own cultural roots. In these situations, symbols of cultural identity signify resistance to certain values of Euro-American culture. Whites are often politically useful to Islanders, however, and there are contexts where both indigenous Islanders and 'white Islanders' stand to gain from co-operation and alliance.

Educated urban Islanders often experience alienation when they return to their villages. However, some Islanders can switch from a 'white' way of behaving to a localised Pacific one. Some return to their home islands regularly, and establish links with migrant communities wherever they find themselves. These dual or multiple identities, deliberately cultivated, are best suited to life in the contemporary Pacific. Unfortunately, few Islanders today have a clear vision of their identity and their place in modern society; few are committed to political action to unite their people and restore their pride. They pay lip-service to a Pacific identity but have only a vague idea of how such an identity translates into action. European or American culture and its methods, perspectives and technology have to be harnessed creatively to suit changing circumstances even as the individual remains grounded in a cultural centre and is not afraid to criticise and resist institutions or ideologies that perpetuate oppression. Only then can Islanders successfully confront the legacies and challenges imposed by the dominant Western cultures.

National unity is problematic for many Island states. Colonial policy was frequently one of divide and rule; in many Island societies kin, faction, and linguistic differences, as well as geography, make it difficult to forge a national identity. The quest for national unity often involves the selection of cultural symbols of the dominant political group. A small Western-educated elite usually defines these symbols, which may or may not be acceptable to the majority. Whether these symbols are slit-gongs, pigs' teeth, and decorative leaves as in Vanuatu, the bird of paradise of Papua New Guinea, or the flag of the Federated States of Micronesia, the intention is to create a feeling of identification and pride in one's nation. In the best of times, such symbols are accepted by the population; at other times, rumblings of resentment surface. The architecture of public buildings is one way in which Pacific elites have attempted to define a distinct national identity. The rebuilding of Maori meeting houses and the design of parliament buildings in Samoa and Papua New Guinea are good examples of national architecture using modern tools to construct a distinctly local design. These magnificent buildings draw on the best in foreign and local cultures. However, they are sometimes criticised for favouring a particular group at the expense of others.

After the 1987 coups in Fiji, there were rushed attempts to establish a distinctly Fijian presence in the civil service and commerce. The most powerful symbol of this assertion is the new parliament building modelled on a Fijian *bure*, to replace the British-style buildings of the colonial government. Other examples of symbolism designed to affirm a cultural identity rooted in ethnicity include the wearing of gourd helmets by Hawaiians in front of the Honolulu Federal Court Building in 1976, the revival of the *heiva* and tattoo in Tahiti, and the practice of rituals such as the Maori *tangi* (funeral ceremonies) which assert indigenous practices in the face of *pakeha* hegemony. Perhaps the most potent symbol in the quest for self-determination is the revival of languages. In New Zealand, Maori is now taught in a number of schools. 'Language nests' where pre-school children can be immersed in a Maori-speaking environment are also beginning to effect changes at the national level. The language nest (*punana leo*) model was adopted by Hawaiians seeking to restore their language to public education, and some Hawaiian children now have the option of being taught in Hawaiian in State-supported primary schools. A significant victory was achieved in February 1992 when the Board of Education approved 'a policy allowing public school students to be taught almost entirely in the Hawaiian language through high school'.[35]

National representations aimed at outsiders, such as arts festivals, tend to project images of a static, 'traditional' culture. Arts festivals typically emphasise earlier creative forms rather than those of the hybrid present. Vigorous attempts to revive canoe-building skills in preparation for the 1992 Festival of Pacific Arts constitute one such example. These representations tend to minimise change, perhaps partly because of an indigenous cyclical view of history, but also because of the need to symbolise cultural autonomy, real or imagined.

---

35 *Ka Leo o Hawai'i: The Voice of Hawaii* (University of Hawai'i student newspaper) 10 February 1992, 1.

In the matter of religion, however, most Islanders have no intention of resurrecting their ancestors' gods. Instead, Christianity and its practice are regarded as traditional. Important ceremonies therefore include Christian prayers and hymns in the native languages. At a 1991 tourism conference held at the Sheraton Waikiki in Honolulu, Tongans living in Honolulu sang Christian hymns as their contribution to the cultural program. When a visiting intellectual learned that hymns were planned, she responded: 'That's good. Keep the culture alive!' This statement was interpreted literally by her fellow Tongan, though the respondent, who shared this 'joke' with me, was being ironic. Not all Islanders hold identical views on appropriate representations of culture or tradition; and this incident highlights the co-optation and indigenisation of Christianity.

The emergence of a regional identity is slow, and largely confined to the educated elite. Students at the University of the South Pacific tend to eat, play, dance, and sing with students from their own islands, but they are also exposed to other Pacific cultures. When the university was established its member countries were confined to Melanesia (except Papua New Guinea), Micronesia (Kiribati, Nauru), and Polynesia (excluding the French territories and Hawai'i). Now, however, the Federated States of Micronesia and the Marshall Islands contribute to the university financially and a handful of their students are enrolled. The invocation of regional cultural affinities and historical common-alities is sometimes dismissed as opportunistic, but these Islanders are building lasting friendships and social networks which will shape the destinies of Pacific countries. Islanders in regional institutions such as the South Pacific Commission, the Forum Secretariat, the Pacific Conference of Churches, and the University of the South Pacific tend to see themselves as 'pan-Pacific' or international persons with a commit-ment to the region, although they may still strongly identify with a specific group. Educated overseas and accustomed to a cosmopolitan atmosphere, they are attracted to regional institutions where there is more tolerance of different values and opinions than in their home villages. The South Pacific Games, which include the French territories and Micronesia, also promote regional feeling although athletes com-pete for their island nations. Like the Festival of Arts, the games are rare opportunities for Islanders to meet, share, and compete in a friendly atmosphere. They provide an economic boon for the host country and avenues for fostering co-operation.

For both independent and Fourth World Islanders, participating in white colonial society or Western international institutions has required a cultural synthesis, or at least an ability to 'switch codes'. Euro-American elements have been incorporated into evolving constructions of identity. Many Pacific women have embraced Western feminism in their search for a cultural and gender identity which is free of both foreign colonialism and indigenous male oppression. Some activist Maori women reject the authority of male elders who claim that women, and particularly young women, are devalued in Maori culture and, for example, have no right to speak publicly on the *marae*. The same trend is noticeable among Island women in Hawai'i, Fiji, and Guam. On the other hand, in Tonga and Samoa there appears to be a strong anti-feminist movement among women intellectuals, or at least a tendency to reject established feminism because of its primary association with white, Western, middle-class women. Regardless of the different positions, Island women are increasingly forging regional organisations based on gender, circumventing the hierarchies of race, nation, and patriarchy.

The *ao maksul ta* (time of darkness) was a period of contested identities, marked by exploration and trade. Then came the *ao taf ta* (time of light), when missionisation transformed cultural identities by converting Islanders to a new religious order while suppressing certain cultural practices. However, as Islanders embraced Christianity, they infused it with their own symbols and ways of worshipping. Since World War II, in their quest for personal, national and regional identities, Islanders have sought ways to reconcile indigenous culture, Christianity, and Euro-American values of materialism and progress. A wide range of fusions ensued, creating different identities from which to choose and multiple ways of symbolising them. In the contemporary phase, the *ao fo'ou ta*, Pacific cultural identities are indeed negotiable.

BIBLIOGRAPHIC ESSAY

Urban crime in Papua New Guinea has been analysed in Morauta (ed.), *Law and Order in a Changing Society*; and by Goddard, 'The Rascal Road: Crime, Prestige, and Development in Papua New Guinea'.

The leading analyses of millenarian movements (or 'cargo cults') are Worsley, *The Trumpet Shall Sound*; and Lawrence, *Road Belong Cargo*. Other case studies include Guiart, *Un Siècle et Demi de Contacts Culturels*; Mead, *New Lives for Old*; Schwartz, *The Paliau Movement*; Burridge, *Mambu*; Gesch, *Initiative and Initiation*; Laracy, *Pacific Protest*; and Rimoldi and Rimoldi, *Hahalis and the Labour of Love*. Recent overviews include Burridge, *New Heaven, New Earth*; Christiansen, *The Melanesian Cargo Cult*; and Steinbauer, *Melanesian Cargo Cults*. Kilani, *Les Cultes du Cargo Melanesiens*, and Buck, *Cargo-cult Discourse*, apply a more standard Marxist theoretical perspective. Jarvie, *The Revolution in Anthropology*, reviews explanations of cargo cult to criticise anthropological interpretations in general. May, *Micronationalist Movements in Papua New Guinea*; Hempenstall and Rutherford, *Protest and Dissent in the Colonial Pacific*; and Loeliger and Trompf, *New Religious Movements in Melanesia*, discuss other sorts of political and religious movements. Trompf, *Cargo Cults and Millenarian Movements*, and Lattas, *Alienating Mirrors*, return to cargo cults, exploring new applications of the term. McDowell, 'A Note on Cargo Cults', and Lindstrom, *Cargo Cult*, question uses of cargo cult within and beyond Anthropology.

Discussion of cultural politics is widespread. Three special issues of journals have addressed this topic: Keesing and Tonkinson edited a special issue of *Mankind* (13) in 1982; Jolly and Thomas edited a special issue of *Oceania* (62) in 1992; and White and Lindstrom did the same for *Anthropological Forum* (6) in 1993. Melanesian *kastom* and the 'invention' or remaking of tradition are also addressed by Babadzan, 'Kastom and Nation-building in the South Pacific', and by Keesing, 'Creating the Past' and 'Reply to Trask'. Responses include Trask, 'Natives and Anthropologists', and Linnekin, 'Text Bites and the R-word'. For parallel debates outside Melanesia, see Hanson, 'The Making of the Maori'; Linnekin, 'Defining Tradition'; and Linnekin and Poyer, *Cultural Identity and Ethnicity in the Pacific*. The most articulate protagonist of Melanesian cultural distinctiveness is Narokobi, *The Melanesian Way*. The Fiji coups have provoked substantial scholarship, including Ravuvu, *The Facade of Democracy*; Scarr, *Fiji: Politics of Illusion*; Sutherland, *Beyond the Politics of Race*; and Lal, *Power and Prejudice*. Updates on Bougainville have been published by ANU since 1990.

13

THE END OF INSULARITY

ISLANDER PARADIGMS FOR THE PACIFIC CENTURY

Nineteenth-century imperialism erected boundaries that led to the contraction of Oceania, transforming a once boundless world into the Pacific Island states and territories that we know today. People were confined to their tiny spaces, isolated from each other. No longer could they travel freely to do what they had done for centuries. They were cut off from their relatives abroad, from their far-flung sources of wealth and cultural enrichment. This is the historical basis of the view that our countries are small, poor and isolated . . . This assumption, however, is no longer tenable as far as the countries of central and western Polynesia are concerned, and may be untenable also of Micronesia. The rapid expansion of the world economy since World War II . . . had a liberating effect on the lives of ordinary people . . . The new economic reality made nonsense of artificial boundaries, enabling the people to shake off their confinement and they have since moved, by the tens of thousands, doing what their ancestors had done before them . . . [T]hey strike roots in new resource areas, securing employment and overseas family property, expanding kinship networks through which they circulate themselves, their relatives, their material goods, and their stories all across their ocean, and the ocean is theirs because it has always been their home.[1]

Pacific Islands, and their inhabitants, were always more inter-related than the literature about them recognised. The End of Insularity, then, signifies the end of colonial perceptions of insularity that belied reality. It also denotes the empirical reality of contemporary lives as Islanders renew and expand linkages across the Pacific. In conclusion, we again 'envision a continuum of human movements and transactions across the Pacific', looking to Islanders for paradigms through which to understand the region. As demonstrated throughout this book, the histories of Islanders are histories of movement—into the Pacific to settle; sailing between islands to maintain links; marrying, trading and warring. Even after Europeans tried to contain them, they continued to travel, as missionaries, as workers, fighting and being displaced by the Pacific War and nuclear testing, establishing and staffing regional institutions. Islanders continue to maintain mobility as they take part in new Pacific life-styles, religions, economies and political regimes.

1   Hau'ofa, 'Our Sea of Islands'.

Webs of relationships span Pacific and continental societies. For many, these relationships included marriages with members of other societies. As poignantly described by Hereniko (chapter 12), Pacific cultures are constantly incorporating elements from their joint heritages. For members of newly established nations, as well as for Islanders living outside their islands of birth, ethnic self-identification may be contextual and multiple, requiring sophisticated syntheses, balances, and code-switching. Peoples living in Pacific societies are descended primarily from the peoples of the Islands, but also from colonial adventurers and traders, indentured labourers from other islands and continents, men and women who sought employment and adventure abroad, as well as those exiled by natural and unnatural disasters. A common factor of Islanders' recent experiences has been increased mobility—from hamlets and villages to towns and regional centres and beyond. Including indigenous peoples, over a million Islanders live and work in New Zealand, the United States and Australia.

One of the furthest-reaching effects of the decolonisation of the Islands is the deconstruction of colonial paradigms. Pacific Islands are increasingly perceived as interdependent units joined by ship and aeroplane, even if these connections rely on ever-changing schedules. Today's air routes reunite the Pacific, linking Guam with Australia, the Marshall Islands and Nauru with Kiribati, Tuvalu and Fiji, Hawai'i with Tahiti. Islanders constantly traverse these routes, establishing multinational families and communities. The world's last major colonial division is bridged as the new nations of the northern Pacific join larger organisations, both regional (Pacific Forum) and international (United Nations). While Europeans are splitting into fractious ethnic nations, new nation-states in the Pacific not only combine multiple ethnic groups within a single polity, but combine into effective regional organisations.

As we conclude this study by examining the dispersal of Islanders and the settlers to whom the Islands are host and home, we come full circle to the issues of ethnicity, and the core relationships of Islanders with the land and the sea. Our shifting paradigms—isolates, dependencies, interdependencies—impact also on the ways in which we perceive people traversing national boundaries. Do they remain integral members of their home societies? Are they seeking adventure and resources, following ancient patterns of oceanic voyaging, or migrant workers, accumulating money to remit home? Are they integral members of their new societies, or unwelcome guest-workers? How are issues of ethnicity, identity and race determined? How many generations of residence achieve 'indigenous' status, or is this concept restricted to bloodlines? If the latter, are the mother's line and the father's equally valued? Is adoption allowed? These issues are negotiated both according to customary practices and within the legal frameworks of governments, generating answers based on local histories and international circumstances.

PACIFIC PARADIGMS

> If we look at the myths, legends and oral traditions, and the cosmologies of
> the peoples of Oceania, it will become evident that . . . their universe com-
> prised not only land surfaces, but the surrounding ocean as far as they could
> traverse and exploit it, the underworld with its fire-controlling and earth-
> shaking denizens, and the heavens above with their hierarchies of powerful
> gods and named stars and constellations that people could count on to guide
> their ways across the seas. Their world was anything but tiny . . .
>   There is a gulf of difference between viewing the Pacific as 'islands in a
> far sea' and as 'a sea of islands'. The first emphasises dry surfaces in a vast
> ocean far from the centres of power . . . The second is a more holistic per-
> spective in which things are seen in the totality of their relationships.[2]

Epeli Hau'ofa's essay, 'Our Sea of Islands', spurred debates by his
colleagues at the University of the South Pacific on its twenty-fifth
anniversary. Hau'ofa is himself a traveller: he grew up in Papua, son of
Tongan missionaries, and lives and teaches in Fiji. In his earlier works
Hau'ofa, like other scholars, embraced the 'dependency theory' perspectives of a single regional economy articulating relations between
European-controlled metropoles and Pacific peripheries. Transnational
interests permitted the emergence of privileged classes in the Islands
and an international Pacific elite. He relied upon academic models
which focus on small nations dependent on powerful Pacific Rim
nations. From the perspective of international donors, the Islands were
too small, too poor in resources, and too isolated ever to support the
metropolitan style of life to which most Islanders aspired. Even after the
recognition of exclusive economic zones (see chapter 11), Islanders
depended on international aid and remittances from relatives abroad.
This Pacific could never again be self-reliant, not because it lacks
resources, but because it was locked into an economy 'that will not
allow them to be'.[3] The migration of Islanders offered poor people
access to international resources, yet perpetuated unequal economic
relations and served this regional integration, following a MIRAB model
of small island nations characterised by dependency on MIgration,
Remittances, and Aid which sustained a Bureaucracy, trapped in international dependency at the mercy of metropolitan benefactors.

Two economists coined the term MIRAB to describe the dependent
economies of Kiribati, Tuvalu, the Cook Islands, Niue and Tokelau. It
could also be applied to Tahiti, American Samoa, and throughout the
former United States Trust Territory of Micronesia. As an analytic
model, MIRAB has been vehemently rejected by Pacific politicians, for it
flies in the face of national sovereignty and self-sufficiency. Relative to
independent Western Samoa, American Samoa is rich in cash and jobs,
in part due to United States aid and the large territorial bureaucracy.
Although Western Samoa is widely viewed as the bastion of *fa'aSamoa*

2   *Ibid.*, 7.
3   Hau'ofa, 'The New South Pacific Society', 10.

tradition, many of its citizens work in the tuna canneries of Pago Pago. Although the United States minimum wage does not apply in American Samoa, wages are still greater than could be earned in Western Samoa. American Samoa is also the site of a new national park. Under an unprecedented lease arrangement with the federal government, the *matai* of the villages concerned will receive tens of thousands of dollars for lands that are little used.

The MIRAB model, while hotly contested, continues to inform analyses (even for the Marshall Islands where remittances flow out from Marshallese at home to students and others abroad). The urban dimension of the contemporary Pacific was highlighted by Munro, who renamed the model as MURAB.[4] Brookfield proposed the term MIRAGE, since the bureaucracy comprises aid-funded Government Employment. In all MIRAB variants, a sustainable economy is unachievable—a mirage —and is replaced by development through international largesse. As agricultural and fisheries production is lost along with the emigrants, MIRAB becomes the economy itself, not just its support:

> Overseas dependent territories are no longer the classic colonies that once generated a wealth of literature on the evils of unequal exchange, colonialism, dependence, exploitation, and uneven development. By contrast they are recipients of considerable largesse . . . political incorporation has led to the construction of a welfare state . . . [and] migration to the metropolitan country is a right that is jealously guarded.[5]

Those countries with close relations with a former coloniser enjoy better living standards than others, but whether such standards are based on philanthropy is largely a matter of definition (see chapter 11). This is underscored by Hau'ofa: 'when the flows of resources within the region are added up, Australia and New Zealand still come out well ahead. For what they give you in aid they receive in return a great deal more in the forms of export earnings and repatriation of profits on investments.'[6] Hau'ofa draws attention to the lived experiences and perceptions of ordinary people. The disjunction between elite and ordinary experiences creates the tension which compels us to re-examine our models. But neither are these simple dichotomies—the transnational elite against the ordinary farmers and fishers, or subsistence opposed to monetary economies, or even centres against peripheries.

The resources of Islanders were never restricted to their land areas, but included their relatives abroad and the seas between them. Today's resource areas have expanded into Pacific Rim nations. It is not charity but the labour of family members abroad—elite and working class— that produces remittances. To label this 'dependency' is belittling, and masks relationships of dominance. Rarely considered is the dependency of the host community on inexpensive imported labourers, for whom it need not pay the costs of schooling and retirement: in 1961, when

4   Munro, 'Migration and the Shift to Dependence in Tuvalu', in Connell, *Migration and Development*.
5   Connell, 'Island Microstate', 272.
6   Hau'ofa, 'The New South Pacific Society', 9.

Wallisian and Futunan chiefs proposed to recall their workers, the French government granted an indemnity to the chiefs to avoid 'a shortage of workers in New Caledonia and in the New Hebrides that might create a crisis in those islands' economies where French interests were at stake'.[7] Nor are Islanders any more willing to recognise the contributions of foreign workers to their own economies, especially when these workers are Asian. Once the people native to the land become a minority, it matters little whether this resulted from colonial labour practices or the choices of post-colonial governments. The multi-ethnic composition of Pacific nations and multi-national residence of Pacific families require that we rethink our models.

Settlers now eclipse the indigenous peoples in Australia, New Zealand, Hawai'i, Guam and New Caledonia. Among these settlers are other Pacific Islanders who moved in response to colonial land and labour requirements, further complicating notions of who may be called 'indigenes'. Some Islands have been affiliated into metropolitan nations, without plebiscite—the Torres Strait Islands to Australia; Hawai'i, American Samoa and Guam to the United States; Rapanui to Chile; Irian Jaya to Indonesia; Tokelau to New Zealand; New Caledonia, Wallis and Futuna, and Tahiti to France. Other peoples have chosen lesser degrees of incorporation (see chapter 11).

Islanders previously spread throughout their islands; today many crowd into urban centres at home and abroad. Auckland is the largest Polynesian city, home to over 103,000 Islanders and over 104,000 Maori, together comprising more than 22 per cent of Auckland's population. The Islanders are youthful and sustain the nation's highest fertility rates: one-third of Auckland's population under the age of twenty-five is Maori and Pacific Islander. Throughout the sea of islands much life centres around urban concerns and relationships to home communities. Yet the next level of abstraction, wherein Pacific Rim nations serve as 'metropolitan centres' to the 'peripheral' states of the Pacific, is less persuasive. To any Islander, it is the Pacific that is centre to the peripheral nations. This is lucidly stated by Witi Ihimaera and his colleagues:

> The concepts of centre and margin are challenging ones for any minority culture. English post-colonial and post-modern methodologies have defined the centre in majority terms as that which is mainstream. Maori literature, like many indigenous literatures, is, by this definition, not the centre. From our perspective Maori literature is the centre—for if you are Maori and looking out, you do so from your own centre. This is the subversive view-point we have taken. We wish to look at things our way, from the inside out, not from the outside in.
>
> The centre for all minority cultures must be where language, customs, laws and traditions continue to make a construct which establishes that 'this is what makes us who we are'.

For Maori, the physical centres are the *marae* and the elder custodians of knowledge. Throughout the Pacific similar cultural institutions and

7 A. Likuvalu, 'History and Migrations of Wallis and Futuna People', in Pollock and Crocombe (eds), *French Polynesia*, 222–3.

elders hold centre stage. But this recentred view also dissolves upon closer scrutiny:

> While the marae and the custodians of our literature still remain our centre, we ourselves have shifted from it. We are an urbanised, articulate population on the move. Over 80 percent of us now live in urban areas, the majority in the Auckland region. We have not only become absorbed into the wider New Zealand culture—a monocultural Pakeha society in the process of becoming more bicultural and multicultural—but also, in a world of rapid communications, we are part of the global village. Sixty percent of us are under the age of 25 and our lives are as affected by international politics, economics and cultural trends as is the rest of the world's population. Some margin, ne?[8]

A key metaphor in Pacific societies is the path that records the roads travelled by the ancestors who explored the lands and seas, and the relations they established. For the Walpiri in Australia the path is the Dreamtime track laid down by the ancestors, moving across, above, and into the landscape, through nodes where entry may still be made into this ancestral world of Aboriginal cosmology.[9] Contemporary Walpiri are connected to the landscape, their ancestors and future progeny through their travels along this dreamline, rooted in the landscape by interacting with it. By retracing the passage, relationships are maintained. Similarly Islanders arriving at a new place search their genealogies and histories to establish connections with the people of this land, to establish the channel through which relationships already exist or may be recreated. For Palauans the roads connecting a visitor with the host determine the types of foods and services to be offered, while for Tannese such paths delineate possibilities of exchange and refuge.

Exchange systems comprise nodes connected by networks reaching out to distant lands. Among the best-known are those of the early Lapita obsidian trade, the Yapese Empire, the Vitiaz Straits, the Kula, and the Tongan Empire. Today's voyagers journey to the next node where family members and friends provide support, eventually moving on, perhaps establishing new nodes in a journey of initiation and challenge. For many, the initial paths and safe havens of expanding networks have been travelled for centuries. Social scientists call this 'step migration', and the routes from Lamotrek to Ulithi, Yap and Guam are familiar ones, expanded today to include Honolulu and Los Angeles. A well-worn north-eastern route runs from Apia and Tongatapu to Pago Pago and on to Honolulu, San Diego and Salt Lake City: a southern route runs to Apia, Auckland and Sydney. Other routes trace passages from Tanna to Port Vila, Sydney and Brisbane, and from Pape'ete, Wallis and Futuna to Noumea.

Instead of the common centre–periphery model, let us imagine a network model based on Pacific modes of interaction. This would demonstrate the linked networks of population movements along well-established paths, and their Pacific centre.

8 Ihimaera *et al.*, *Te Ao Marama*, 15–16.
9 Nancy Munn, 'The Spatial Presentation of Cosmic Order in Walbiri Iconography', in A. Forge (ed.), *Primitive Art and Society*, New York, 1973, 212.

Cultural identity in Melanesia is a geographical identity that flows from the memories and values attached to places. Membership in a clan or social group, individual or collective identity, is inherited through a network of places, the sum total of which constitutes a territory. Each local group is thus a kind of 'geographic society', defined in relation to the space within which it resides, or a 'territorial society', deriving its identity through appropriation of a common territory but also from identification with that homeland.[10]

How do Islanders abroad maintain a sense of cultural identity which is rooted in the landscapes of their home islands? Bonnemaison poses the conundrum: how can we reconcile the tree and canoe? His image arises from a metaphor of identity in Vanuatu, in which the canoe offers lines of movement while the tree represents root and stability. Tannese believe that these images are not contradictory, that man is the tree taking root, while the local group is the canoe exploring the world along established 'roads'. Bonnemaison discovers a model of place as a basis of social identity that may apply throughout the Pacific, for everywhere origin myths trace the paths of apical ancestors, the land and seascapes traversed, that today provide a network of alliances allowing safe passage.

It is from the juncture of stasis and mobility that Tannese identity is expressed, by maintaining and expanding the social canoe's network. Mobility in Vanuatu is not free wandering, but travel along organised networks. Order is established through this law of space. Each geo-political unit in Tanna is conceived as a particular canoe, organised around a network of strongholds. The mobility of the canoes demonstrates the field of alliances that define the safe space for movement. A network of routes radiates from each port, and allied groups in the wake of the canoe form a second level of security and foothold in neighbouring islands. In the past Tannese voyaged for initiation, exchange, refuge, or shame and exile. Individuals and groups travelled through networks of places and routes and, through their passage and the gifts they bore, maintained the route and the strength of ancestral connections. 'The routes followed over land or sea are appropriated by social groups as if they were an extension of their own territories. Men define themselves as much by their roads as by their places.' To have roads is to possess power, for mobility permits exchange, and provides the possibility of refuge.

Today's voyages take Tannese as far as Australia and beyond. Yesterday's journeys to work in Queensland, to enter into exchange and allow the traveller to obtain Western goods, did not always have the desired ends, for Europeans saw Tannese merely as impersonal and interchangeable plantation labourers, not as reciprocating human beings. At the same time the landscapes of sacred dwelling sites were abandoned to Christianity. A century and a half of coconut plantations and labour mobility transformed both the voyagers and their landscape. Nearly half the people on Tanna reside outside their traditional use rights. Land tenure systems, based on shifting agriculture, were flexible to meet changing needs: identifications between land and

10 Bonnemaison, 'The Tree and the Canoe', 30 ff.

people are today being reconstituted, and connected with continued mobility. The circular mobility so characteristic of Melanesian migrants may constitute, not contradict, this identity of place, and today's journeys for education and employment may be analogous to historical journeys of initiation.

CITIZENSHIP, IDENTITY AND ESSENTIALISING NOTIONS

Tuimaleali'ifano describes how a Samoan community settled in Fiji:

> In forming a community, the Samoan language became the common medium of communication in addition to a working knowledge of varying degrees of Fijian, Rotuman, Wallisian, Futunan and Gilbertese. According to most Samoan accounts, the Wallisians and Futunans were the first arrivals in Navesi and gradually moved to Vila-Maria in Tamavua. Because of the comparably larger number of Samoan couples with their greater inter-marriages to Europeans, Rotumans, Tongans, Tuvaluans, Wallis/Futunans, Chinese, I-Kiribati, Fijians, and Indians, a distinctive 'fruit salad' community on a Samoan base emerged in Navesi Sefulu Maila.[11]

Who can be labelled Pacific Islander, and by what criteria? Racial purity may be a more Western than Pacific manner of conceptualising membership. On a personal level Islanders may draw upon multiple heritages, for example 'a Fiji citizen of Chinese/Samoan/Cook Islander/Danish ancestry adopted by a Fiji-born Gujarati–South Indian man and his Fiji-born Samoan wife' has a wide range of ethnicities that may be selected or ascribed. Familial and dynastic marriages contracted to establish relationships with newcomers or neighbours are important at all levels of society, most marked perhaps among members of the elite. It is a long-established practice among elite clans of Koror in Palau to marry into powerful outside groups. Marriages were contracted with other elite clans of Palau and even on Yap—the offspring of the latter were especially favoured as they could own lands and titles in Palau through the maternal line, and on Yap through the father. Both para-mount clans of Palau trace their descent from Portuguese shipwrecked on the now-submerged northern atoll of Ngeruangel. Koror marriages have been contracted with early ship captains, the German colonial administrator (a singularly successful mode of incorporating foreign power!), Japanese and Chinese traders, a United States spy (during the Japanese regime), American businessmen, and other Pacific Islanders. Adoption also figures prominently in such dynasties: in a previous generation a girl was adopted from a neighbouring island, became a beloved member and was granted its highest female title, which she held until her death. While some Palauan communities pride them-selves on Palauan bloodlines, Koror prides itself on incorporating outsiders through marriage and adoption. The descendants of dynastic marriages are true people of Koror; their strength is that they may also draw upon powerful external links.

11 Tuimaleali'ifano, *Samoans in Fiji*, 52–3.

Governments prefer discrete entities—the island nation and legalist definitions of citizenship. When Koror crafted its constitution in 1983, definitions of citizenship and levels of political participation according to traditional status were hotly debated. Although by tradition nearly any Palauan could become a person of Koror, Koror's strength and weakness was that two-thirds of the population of Palau had moved to this capital and many residents held primary allegiances to home communities—a problem common wherever a sense of community is complicated by immigration. According to Palau's national constitution, only individuals able to trace Palauan heritage through at least one parent may become Palauan citizens; birthright citizenship does not apply to children born in Palau to foreigners. This clause was approved to forestall the processes whereby the Chamorros of Guam have become a minority on their own island. Such provisions solve the immediate problem, but their continuation and the use of foreign workers could create a new category of stateless individuals after a generation or two.

The pace of demographic transition is accelerating: Chamorros became a minority on Guam over several hundred years of colonial administration. On the neighbouring island of Saipan, Chamorros and Carolinians of the Northern Mariana Islands became a minority after only a decade of self-government. Eager to take advantage of the economic boom of the 1980s, the Marianas government negotiated exemptions from United States laws regulating foreign workers, and imported thousands of Korean, Chinese, Japanese and Filipinos to build hotels and work in the tourism and garment industries. Nor were all immigrants labourers; investors from these nations and the United States established businesses that were subject only to local taxes. The 1980 population of the Northern Marianas was 16,780. By 1990 the population had nearly trebled to 43,345, of whom only 46 per cent are citizens or nationals. The indigenous Chamorros (14,194) and Carolinians (2987—descended from Islanders resettled on Saipan by the Germans) and all other Micronesians and Islanders number fewer than the Asian workers—Filipinos alone nearly outnumber the Chamorros. Previously the Chamorros and Carolinians were at times in competition. Today they band together to form a single unit against outsiders, and a new ethnic term 'Chamolinian' is sometimes heard. Such minority status is likely to persist as some local people, newly wealthy after leasing their lands to foreign businesses, move on to the United States.

Fiji's attempts to protect the rights of indigenous citizens, treated in chapter 11, have had uneven results for individuals of mixed heritage. The 1970 constitution defined three qualifications for citizenship: those who traced their ethnicity in the father's line from 'indigenous inhabitants of Fiji or any island in Melanesia, Micronesia or Polynesia'; Indians; and others, including those granted citizenship by application. Under those regulations, children of a Fijian woman and a Samoan man were citizens. By the 1976 census only those descended from inhabitants of the islands in 1874 and eligible to be included in the Registry of Native Lands were considered Fijian. Children of a Fijian woman and a Samoan man were now excluded from full privileges. While still able to vote, many Pacific Island residents lost recognition 'in terms of land, education sponsorships, and commercial opportunities'.[12]

Pacific constitutions vary in the degree to which they recognise other Islanders as citizens, and the extent to which such requirements are followed. While not allowed full landholding privileges, descendants of Indian and other Pacific Islander labourers and migrants may vote in Fiji. In contrast, Fijian and Solomon Islander descendants of indentured labourers in Tonga are considered alien unless naturalised. Residence and incorporation into community life may be considered more important than bloodlines. For instance, in practice although not by law, Palau treats as full citizens the few Japanese children fostered in Palau at the end of World War II.

For many years most Pacific censuses enumerated only residents, despite the significant numbers of Islanders living abroad who participate in home affairs. Palauans abroad continue to vote in home elections, sometimes providing the deciding votes; Cook Islanders in New Zealand elect their own representative to the Cook Islands Parliament. Some recent censuses have tried to obtain estimates of citizens living abroad. In 1994 Kosrae, one of the Federated States of Micronesia (FSM), conducted a census including all residents and those citizens living abroad for five years or less, assuming that these citizens were more likely to be returning from schooling or temporary employment. There was no attempt to tabulate long-term emigrants, whether or not they might return to claim land and residence rights. In contrast, Nauru enumerates all Nauruans *de jure* in their household whether resident or not, and all non-Nauruans on a *de facto* basis. The Nauruan census also enumerates resident Pacific Islanders from other nations—approximately 24 per cent of the population.

Issues of indigenous identity are critical in Island contexts; in Australia, New Zealand and the United States, Islanders are such a minor component of the population that until recently few attempts were made to identify them. Until the 1990 United States census all Pacific Islanders were amalgamated with 'Asians' in a composite category of Asia–Pacific Islander. Islander organisations are campaigning to persuade more of their constituents to participate in censuses, and for separate designation (granted in 1990) since census numbers are linked to access to community services. Yet multiple ethnicities elude attempts to categorise them, even when the questions are asked. Is ethnicity based on place of birth, nationality or birthplace of one or both parents, language spoken at home, or self-ascription? How many levels of self-ascription are requested, and tabulated? A common feature of metropolitan censuses is the recognition that Islanders are undercounted. This is only partly attributable to propensities to stay longer than visas allow—only a small fraction of over-stayers are Islanders. Others simply avoid the census officers and the forms. The extent of under-counting is impossible to gauge, but a 1992 health survey in South Auckland found 32 per cent more Pacific Islanders than were

12 *Ibid.*, 10.

counted in the 1991 census, but only a 3–6 per cent discrepancy for New Zealanders of Maori and European heritage.[13]

Beginning in 1990, the United States census allowed a range of Islander ethnic identifications, and requested information for all individuals over five years of age concerning birthplace, year of entry, place of residence five years previously, primary language at home, and nationality of both parents, making it possible to discern certain broad movements between the United States, its territories and former territories. However since 1986 citizens of the United States freely associated states have free entry, so entry and departure data are no longer collected. The staggered census years in the region compound the difficulties of comparing data from before and after the Compact.

No community better exemplifies the damaging effects of essentialising notions of identity, mixed heritage, and international mobility than the Chamorros of Guam, as discussed by the Chamorro scholar Robert Underwood. The first colonised in the Pacific, the indigenous peoples of the Mariana Islands were reduced to 5 per cent of their precontact numbers by diseases and wars with Spain. Finally vanquished by 1700, a mere 3000 survivors were resettled on Guam, where they began reconstructing their lives. They became Catholic, married members of the Spanish, Philippine and Mexican ruling class, and incorporated many elements from these cultures. From their own heritage they maintained their language, the strength of the extended family with its matrilineal bias, and a preference for hierarchies in which status is demonstrated by generosity. Members of the elite emphasised their Spanish heritage, and 'many Chamorros were left with a strong sense of inauthenticity about their origins as a Pacific people . . . best captured in a children's book on the history of Guam, which labelled the precontact culture as Chamorro and the hybrid successor as Guamanian'.[14]

In the nineteenth century some Chamorros resettled on Saipan, with Spanish encouragement, while others travelled to Hawai'i and the United States as whalers. In 1886 the Governor of Hawai'i reported 800 Chamorro workers in Honolulu (a significant proportion of the Chamorro population), but in 1899 when Guam was claimed by the United States after the Spanish–American war, the Chamorros on Guam were separated from those on Saipan. The other Mariana Islands and the Carolines became a territory of Germany, then of Japan, and many Chamorros were relocated throughout the Carolines and Marshalls, while those residing on Guam looked towards the United States and began joining US military forces.

By 1978 the Federation of Guamanian Associations of America estimated that 55,000 Chamorros lived in California—a possibly inflated estimate, but in comparison to the 47,000 estimated to reside on Guam, the estimate again raised questions of what comprised Chamorro, or Guamanian, identity. Being an American was increasingly a part of this identity, especially after the 1950 passage of the *Organic Act* through

13 Bathgate *et al.*, *The Health of Pacific Islands People in New Zealand*.
14 Underwood, 'Excursions into Inauthenticity', 161.

which Chamorros became US citizens, and a US system of education was established. Higher education in America became common not only for children of elite families, but also for military families. With increased affluence during the tourism boom of the mid-1970s, more families settled in California where they created substantial populations close to military bases. Compared with other California immigrants, the Chamorros were few in number and quite assimilated to American life-styles, so they did not form recognisable neighbourhoods or enclaves. Relatively anonymous in America, they strove to create a Chamorro culture by constructing pseudo-extended families and Chamorro clubs. Underwood relates this sense of cultural loss directly to an increased political activism, both on Chamorro issues and in wider California Pacific Islander coalition politics.

New layers of inauthenticity then became apparent—home island Guamanians' private doubts about the authenticity of Chamorro festivals in California, and the degree to which other Islanders recognised Chamorros at home or in the United States as having a unique Pacific culture. This was nowhere more apparent than in the Festivals of Pacific Arts discussed in chapter 12. Although organised for Islanders, not tourists, festival representations of identity are directed towards outsiders and have tended towards the traditional past, not the hybrid present. At the 1980 festival in Port Moresby, Islander participants had difficulty crediting the modern dance performances offered by the Guamanian troupe as authentically 'Pacific'. By the 1988 festival, however, other nations started moving beyond the strict constraints of traditional pasts. In large part it was due to Chamorro activist and educator Laura Torres Souder's capable explanations that Pacific audiences began to appreciate Guam's syncretic offering of dances as speaking to the shared histories of many Pacific peoples. Participants began to recognise that the ability to incorporate and benefit from newcomers is a strength of Pacific cultures.

Debates on tradition and custom have elevated the issue to a pan-Pacific concern. Contrasts between 'true' and 'invented' traditions, lived realities and rhetorical representations, imply that only unself-conscious 'culture' is authentic, so that self-consciousness itself must be inauthentic. Such Western dichotomisation of dialectically integrated processes inevitably leads to serious distortions and untenable conclusions. Pacific cultures are anything but unitary. Pivotal academic authors have argued that

> Pacific self-awareness precipitated out of the colonial encounter, consciousness attained through wrestling with the other. The arrival of Europeans no doubt pushed a sense of cultural difference and of cultural alternatives in qualitatively new directions ... but is anyone, anywhere, anytime 'simply living their culture' without an awareness of cultural alternatives? Perhaps it is another Western myth to credit Westerners with the knowledge of difference, and others with the lack of such knowledge. The diversity and insularity of the precolonial Pacific did not imply cultural insularity ... Linguistic and cultural differences were precipitated out of contrast as much as separate development ... Trade and ritual exchange in

the Pacific often depending on amplifying differences of ecological niche, productive specialism, and cultural styles.[15]

Vicente Diaz documents the history of outsider laments on the demise of the Chamorro people, arguing that

> Guam's history does not have to be understood as the definitive Euro-Americanization of the Chamorro people at the tragic expense of indigenous culture. Nor does Chamorro culture need to be understood in terms of an immutably bounded, neatly contained thing that was once upon a time characterised by essential qualities, pure and untainted, as Chamorro culture has (a)historically been conceived and represented.

Diaz does not underestimate the crisis facing Chamorros. Although they demonstrably maintained considerable control over their identity and lands until World War II, since 1960 they have been engulfed by foreign residents:

> An unprecedented political and cultural predicament faces the Chamorros today: there are many non-Chamorros in the land while many Chamorros no longer have access to land. There are also more Chamorros in other lands than there are Chamorros in Guam. And there are many Chamorros, in Guam and elsewhere, who are not fluent in the Chamorro language. Chamorro survival appears especially urgent, and the stakes appear even greater today than ever before in Guam's long colonial history.
>
> This twentieth-century cultural crisis makes it even more important to rethink the reigning ideas of culture, politics, and history in places like Guam.[16]

EXILES AND ASSISTED MIGRANTS

Just as some Islanders are engulfed by foreigners, others became minorities in new islands through resettlement by colonial administrations, either for the perceived welfare of the Islanders after a natural disaster, or to answer colonial needs for labourers or land. Even apparently altruistic reasons often had political and unexpected outcomes. The Germans relocated Carolinians from atolls devastated by typhoons, and in the process provided workers for the colonial economy on Saipan. In extreme cases, entire Island populations were moved, such as the transfer of Banabans to Rabi Island in Fiji to facilitate phosphate mining, and the evacuation of Bikini Atoll (chapter 10).

The scale of nineteenth-century population movement is poorly documented, as well as the degree of compulsion involved. Today most movement involves individuals or households who enjoy relative freedom of movement within the political constraints discussed below. Not all Islanders enjoy free entry to other Pacific or Pacific Rim nations, but migration for employment, education, and family reunion allows significant possibilities. Qualitative differences between migrant

15 Jolly, 'Specters of Inauthenticity', 58.
16 Diaz, 'Simply Chamorro', 53.

communities, and those relocated with the assistance of some outside agency, warrant separate consideration. We need to consider whether their special circumstances were due to colonialism directly, or to the structural relationships of these communities within their societies and to the agency that resettled them.

In the 1960s Homer Barnett co-ordinated a study of displaced communities in the Pacific. These groups included entire societies that were forced to move, sub-groups who began as satellites of a home community, new communities formed by people who had not previously lived together, and immigrants from one island who chose to live apart and not form a new community. For some immigrants the relocation was part of older patterns of regional movement: for others the experience had no precedent. One of the most important factors that explained community differences was whether members of the community chose to move (a migrant community) or did so at the instigation of an outside agency (a relocated community). The settlement of both types of migrants was constrained by the structures and cultural expectations of migrant and host communities. Settlement in the political systems that characterise most Pacific polities mediated towards gradual incorporation over several generations. In contrast, settlement in a hierarchical state or colonial system typically resulted in the maintenance of ethnic boundaries. During the nineteenth and twentieth centuries any relocation was mediated by colonial administrations, which supported the maintenance of ethnic boundaries even in non-hierarchical societies if the community's primary relationship was to the colonial agency.

This special relationship to the agency in most cases transformed the relationship of the relocated community to its hosts, even when both were members of one culture, such as the Bikinians who resettled within the Marshall Islands. The power differential between colonial administration and the community, the nationality of the colonial power, and the community's desired ends all affected outcomes. Bikinians wanted the United States administration to take responsibility for them, thereby establishing dependence upon a wealthy, powerful, but largely absent foreign government. In the process the Bikinians were able to bypass their relationship with their paramount chief. By contrast, Tikopians who resettled Nukufero did not want the administration to be involved in their affairs. Cultural premises interacted with politics and economics.

To this day some relocated communities retain, or have established, a special relationship with their former colonial government that affects their economic options. The Bikinians negotiated a direct relationship with the United States, and maintain a separate status within the independent Marshall Islands, of which the paramount chief is now President. Along with the peoples of Utrik, Enewetak, and Rongelap, they comprise the 'Atomic Atolls' which receive separate income from trust funds, and foodstuffs to compensate for their removal from their subsistence base. Banabans have had to master more complicated relationships. When they were resettled on Rabi in 1945 (having already been relocated to Tarawa, Nauru and Kosrae during the Japanese occupation), Banaba was part of the Gilbert and Ellice Islands colony. By agreeing to move to Rabi Island in Fiji, the Banabans were strategically moving closer to the British High Commissioner for the Western Pacific (the Governor of Fiji) so that they could state their grievances to him, and claim proper compensation for phosphate mining. In the 1960s they forced the departure of their colonial adviser on Rabi, and in 1970s instigated successful litigation against the British Crown. During the 1978 constitutional conference Banabans argued in vain for a status independent from Kiribati, like its sister phosphate island of Nauru. Today they maintain special representation within both the Kiribati and Fijian governments.

Although safe migration and assistance routes are an integral part of Pacific land-based identities, mobility alone has proved an inadequate substitute for the land, even when augmented by financial payments. Resettled in turn to Rongerik to Kwajalein to Kili, the Bikini community tried to use part of its financial settlement to buy land on the big island of Hawai'i, but was rejected by the local community. Today most live on one of the islets of Majuro Atoll. For both Bikinians and Banabans, even substantial payments cannot replace the islands, and may even divide the community. The Banaban situation demonstrates the complexity of relationships mediated through land. In part the dilemma revolves around a conflict between individual rights, based on individual land-ownership on Banaba, and the collective needs of Banabans in confrontation with the British Phosphate Commissioners; and on Rabi, which had none of the infrastructure that had been developed by the commission and colonial government on Banaba. The commissioners maintained that royalties should be paid to the collectivity, since custom did not cover sub-surface mining rights. Banabans held that the phosphate was taken from Banaban lands owned individually, so that royalty payments should be made individually. But collective action (in support of individual payments) was required in order to confront the British Phosphate Commissioners. Banabans also believed that Rabi should be autonomous and owned by Banabans, since it had been purchased with phosphate money. Nor did they expect to do manual work on Rabi that required less skill and responsibility than positions they had held with the mining company on Banaba. 'We did not come to Rabi to be workers on the land . . . We did not come here for work, but for freedom on our money.' Conflict continues—reaching collective decisions on individual or collective uses of the money, and the rights of future generations, has become no easier with large sums of money now to be managed.

The transformation of the Banaban economy from one dominated by subsistence fishing into one based on royalty payments has deeply affected the Banaban mentality. The peculiar nature of this monetary income has not given the Banabans, as a group, much experience with working for money. The rising expectations of a steadily growing number of Banabans have mainly been satisfied by their leaders' fighting for a large share of phosphate income and distributing this to the community . . . That the Banabans equate development, Westernisation, or progress, or whatever other meaning they attached to the process of change, with control of money is not surprising. One of their more important native categories, land, became a source of direct monetary income.[17]

Nevertheless Banabans have land rights on Rabi, and Banaba is habitable. Any lasting resettlement of Bikini is uncertain; and in the process of shifting between radically different atolls, the Bikinians, over strong internal opposition, have also transformed their land tenure system, creating conflicting rights to land and resources. Increasingly frequent out-marriage and population growth also affect vested rights, which must be constructed in terms of money, not land, in circumstances that separate Bikini and other atomic atolls from the rest of the country. Banaba and Bikini exemplify the issues facing the peoples of Moruroa, and other Pacific peoples displaced or otherwise separated from land-based identity and subsistence base. Access to cash settlements has affected the demography of Banaba and Bikini. In 1945 1003 individuals were settled on Rabi, of whom 30 per cent were I-Kiribati. In 1985 there were 4064 members of the Banaban community on Rabi. Since anyone descended from a Banaban is considered Banaban—there is no such thing as a part-Banaban, and there are high levels of inter-marriage with I-Kiribati—92 per cent of the community is now considered Banaban. They differ from the communities formed of migrants, who depend primarily on individual and community relationships with their home communities, and maintain the option of returning home. To a lesser extent transformations of subsistence to royalty payment economies have also occurred for the peoples of Angaur, Nauru, and the displaced communities of Bougainville, Ok Tedi, Freeport and the like (see chapter 11).

Population pressures and environmental risks contribute to the need for relocation or migration. Environmental risks, such as the volcanic eruption that destroyed Rabaul, more commonly affect the high islands on the western Pacific Rim. These islands are less likely to suffer population pressures and more able to absorb immigrants from disasters. But small coral atolls such as Tuvalu, the Tuamotus, Tokelau, Kiribati, and the Marshalls, are at risk both from population pressure and from any rise in sea levels. The South Pacific Regional Environmental Program co-ordinates regional assessments and action plans to deal with these risks. The Marshall Islands government has highlighted the potential impact of global warming at the United Nations and by providing leadership in attempts by the Alliance of Small Island States to raise public awareness. A scientific station has been established to monitor sea-level changes. Since numerous Pacific nations are composed solely of atolls, any population shifts will necessarily involve international agencies.

The Marshallese have considerable experience with migrant and relocated communities. The government formally recognised a migrant community established in southern California over the past twenty

17 Martin Silverman, 'A Study of a Banaban Meeting', in M. Lieber (ed.), *Exiles and Migrants*; and H. Dagmar, 'Banabans in Fiji'.

years—in 1993 the Marshallese opened a consulate in Newport Beach. This community, which has found an employment niche and established a strong community group, church, and relationships with local schools, could form the basis for a larger community. Whereas several hundred Marshallese on Hawai'i form a large ethnic group, an even larger group in southern California would scarcely be noticed in this region of high immigration.[18]

Kiribati also has experience with resettlement, and is in the midst of an experimental resettlement to the Line Islands,[19] impelled by population densities exceeding 5000 per square kilometre in urban Tarawa. In the 1930s the Gilbert and Ellice Islands colonial authorities had attempted to resettle part of the Phoenix group, including Sydney Island. Considerable care was given to selecting immigrants who agreed to relocate and to give up all property rights on their home atolls. Although the migrants were taken from throughout the southern Gilberts, which have slightly differing customs, it was anticipated that the relocated community would replicate a Gilbertese style of life, but constant compromises and adaptations were required. Seating places in the community meeting place had to be created for the joining families, and both farming and fishing resources differed, requiring shifts in the ways labour was organised. A schism developed between 'collectivists' and 'individualists'[20] (mirroring the dialectics of Banaban confrontations). For the first decade the resettlement seemed successful, but by the 1950s the island group experienced prolonged droughts, and representatives petitioned the government to find them a new home. Resettlement in the Gilberts was impossible and there were no other suitable unpopulated islands. Eventually the colonial administration arranged for a new settlement in the (British) Solomon Islands. Settlers were sent from both the Gilberts and Sydney Island, under a Gilbertese director, to Titiana Point on Ghizo Island in the western Solomons. Again culture change was not anticipated, although Ghizo is not a coral atoll and the new site differed in both subsistence and wage possibilities, and in its heterogeneous population of Solomon Islanders, Polynesians from Rennell, Sikaiana, Ontong Java, as well as Chinese, Fijians, and Japanese. Eventually the entire Sydney Island population was transferred to the Solomons, and some lands were made available to the Gilbertese on the Shortland Islands 250 kilometres to the north, on the border with Bougainville. By 1963 the government made a land allocation to each Gilbertese household, but since insufficient lands were available in Titiana, the offshore island purchased by the government and previously used communally and lands in the Shortlands were included. The allocation created further problems: first because the allotments were all below minimum requirements for household subsistence; then because they were dispersed and depended on contested definitions of

18 Jim Hess, 'Migration, Networks, Resources, and Households: The Formation of a Marshallese Community in Orange County', typescript, 1993.
19 B. Tonganibeia, 'Kiribati: Development and Internal Migration', in McCall and Connell, *A World Perspective on Pacific Islander Migration*.
20 Silverman, 'A Study of a Banaban Meeting,' 211.

household and household head; and finally because they created future problems on how land would be reallocated once a household head died. By 1963 the entire Phoenix resettlement program was terminated and the remaining settlers transferred to the western Solomons, Titiana serving as an entry point. By the mid-1970s the timber industry in the western Solomons attracted Gilbertese employees, who shifted their families to another community at Ringgi Cove.

The current attempt to shift surplus population from the Tungaru to the Line Islands may not succeed, but the Kiribati government sees few alternatives. In 1985 only 3.5 per cent of all I-Kiribati were known to have been abroad, mainly working on Nauru or as seamen. When mining ceases on Nauru in the late 1990s Kiribati must anticipate the return of the I-Kiribati employed there and the cessation of their remittances ($A187,00 in 1987). This repatriation follows and parallels the return of I-Kiribati workers from Banaba in 1979 and 1980, when mining ceased there. The conclusion of employment on Nauru therefore closes the major I-Kiribati migration route. Kiribati and Tuvalu in 1994 petitioned Australia and New Zealand for an additional thousand workers' permits, but these were denied. In consequence, both nations face population pressures, with limited land areas on dispersed atolls. It is to accommodate this pressure that the Kiribati government is trying to resettle the Line Islands and once again to develop the Phoenix Islands. One of the persistent structural problems is the high cost of providing services over such a vast area. The governments of Kiribati, Tuvalu, and the Marshalls Islands in 1995 agreed to combine air and shipping services, to cut these costs.

CONTEMPORARY VOYAGING

We know more about population movements between Pacific Islands and their former colonial administrators than we do about island groups long linked by intermarriage and trade but separated by nineteenth-century colonialism—I-Kiribati in the Marshall Islands, or Rotumans in Kosrae. The colonial experience fragmented some wider linkages, and continues to shape present relationships. The history and nature of links to Pacific Rim countries significantly affect migration possibilities. Most contemporary migrants follow paths previously established by workers abroad, and corresponding to legal access generally provided only by former colonisers. Migration outside nation-states is predominantly a Polynesian and Micronesian phenomenon. While much migration occurs within Papua New Guinea, few citizens live abroad—a similar situation for the Solomon Islands, New Caledonia, and Vanuatu, none of whom enjoy free entry to overseas countries. (Some Indo-Fijians emigrated to Canada beginning in the 1960s, and more have migrated to Canada, the United States, Australia, and New Zealand since the 1987 coups. These resettlements are possible because the migrants' individual skills are in demand in the countries of settlement.) French Polynesians, Wallisians and Futunans, Kanaks of

New Caledonia, and those formerly under the French government of the New Hebrides, rarely emigrate to distant France, but travel within the French Pacific, most especially to New Caledonia. The peoples of Kiribati and Tuvalu, discussed above, have even fewer options. By contrast, citizens of Guam, American Samoa, Rapanui, and Tokelau, and citizens of the Pacific's freely associated states and the Commonwealth of the Northern Marianas, all enjoy free access to their former metropoles. Western Samoans enjoy relatively free access to New Zealand through a negotiated quota system and family reunion.

Maori and Pacific Islanders together comprise 11 per cent of the population of New Zealand. Pacific Islanders alone comprise 4.9 per cent of the population. New Zealand hosts the largest populations of Islanders abroad, both in proportion to the general population, in sheer numbers (167,073 in 1991), and rate of growth (60.2 per cent in the last decade). Islanders form the fastest-growing component of New Zealand's population, due to their fertility rate and numbers of immigrants (50.8 per cent of the total). Samoans form the majority of this community, at 85,743.[21] In proportion to their home populations, however, the people of Niue, Tokelau, and the Cook Islands maintain the largest expatriate communities: 85, 70, and 69 per cent of their total populations reside in New Zealand. Although Tongans do not enjoy free entry to any Pacific Rim nation, they have successfully settled abroad mainly through family reunion programs; they are third to the Cook Islanders into New Zealand, and third to Guamanians into the United States.

The United States is the second most important destination. In addition to 211,014 Hawaiians, the 1990 census counted 154,010 Pacific Islanders, nearly half of whom had been born in the United States. Starting from a large population base in 1980, Islanders increased at 41.5 per cent in the decade to 1990, an impressive rate compared to an overall average of 9.8 per cent growth. Samoans form the largest Islander immigrant group, at 62,964. Although Tongans and Fijians showed very high rates of growth, this was due to their smaller 1980 base and numbers of Indo-Fijians who moved after the coups. Guamanians increased at 61 per cent from 1980 to 1990, to just under 50,000. All figures are estimates, because of the difficulties of attributing ethnicity. High rates of growth among Hawaiians and Guamanians may also indicate reidentification rather than population growth.

It is difficult to identify Islanders living in Australia, as data from the 1986 census is questionable and the 1991 census asked no questions about ancestry or ethnicity. Based on the 1986 ancestry data, there were about 65,000 persons with at least one Islander ancestor, living predominantly in New South Wales. New Zealand Maori, at 26,000, comprised 40 per cent of the Islanders in Australia. They enter freely through the Trans-Tasman Agreement, also used by some other Islanders. The long-term presence of Maori in Australia has hardly been noticed, primarily since statistics were compiled in the first instance

21 Bathgate *et al.*, *The Health of Pacific Islands People in New Zealand*, 38.

according to birthplace, and New Zealand was not included among the Pacific Islands. The other major groups had Fijian, Tongan, Papua New Guinean, Western Samoan, Cook Island, and Nauruan ancestries.

The primary node of transfer between Pacific Rim countries is Samoa. American Samoa serves as both destination and stepping-stone into the United States for Western Samoans and Tongans, although destination choices fluctuate along with the economies of New Zealand and the US. During New Zealand's 1970s recession Islanders turned towards American Samoa and the US. By 1980 one-third of American Samoa's population had been born in Western Samoa or Tonga, and of the Samoans living in the US nearly one and a half times as many had been born in Western Samoa as American Samoa. In the late 1980s, as the New Zealand economy strengthened and the US economy declined (especially in Hawai'i, California, Washington and Utah), the flow again shifted. By 1990 the increase in Samoans in the US comprised only persons born in American Samoa. Apparently those born in Western Samoa were following the southern route into New Zealand, which experienced an even higher rate of growth. Nearly half of the peoples of the two Samoas now reside abroad.

American Samoans and Chamorros from Guam have enjoyed free access to the United States since 1951 and 1950 respectively; since World War II many followed military service options. Guam and Saipan demonstrate the complicated issues created by both US and local policies. In the two decades beginning with free entry to the US, the majority of Chamorros moved in search of better education and employment, while Palauans began moving to Guam to take advantage of the relatively strong employment opportunities. With the transfer of the Trust Territory government to Saipan in the 1960s, Islanders from throughout the territory, but predominantly Palauans, were hired by the territorial government. These population shifts created bases from which later communities could grow, as leaders created strong community organisations, built a meeting house on Guam, and provided the assistance and security normally offered by extended family members in Micronesian societies. Also in the 1960s Micronesian citizens of the Trust Territory became eligible for financial supports to pursue higher education in the US, but had limited entry for employment until the termination of the trusteeship in 1986 (or 1994 for Palau). Palauan populations on Guam in the 1980s were estimated at 2000, with a smaller number on Saipan. With the establishment of new Micronesian governments in the late 1970s and early 1980s, most of the territorial migrants moved home, but other migrants joined those already established.

The Compacts of Free Association created the possibility of free entry to the United States. FSM citizens moved primarily to Guam, while Marshallese moved to the US. (Palauans continued to be restricted primarily to short-term educational entry until 1994.) FSM citizens were quick to take advantage of Guam's booming economy. In the first year approximately 1600 moved to Guam, and by the end of 1991 the number exceeded 6000. Another stream moved north to Saipan at a lower and more stable rate. In both cases, the majority were from

Chuuk, the largest and most densely populated state of the federation. This extraordinary impact of US policies on the demography of Guam has been debated by American and Micronesian leaders, and the US has provided mitigation funding to assist local institutions. For many, Guam was an intermediate stop to Hawai'i and the continental US. For others, it was an exciting new home, close enough to maintain contact while becoming more independent of family members. On both Guam and Saipan, post-Compact migration was augmented by Asian immigration. Micronesians, Filipinos and other Asians provide teachers and medical professionals throughout the region, as well as semi-skilled and unskilled labourers for the construction industry, garment factories, and tourism. Indigenous leaders decry the loss of majority status due to emigration, but acknowledge that a majority of their people have chosen to reside in the US. The overlapping populations no longer conform to island boundaries.

Gender is always a complicating factor in overseas communities, and it is difficult to generalise patterns; but a striking feature of Palauan migration to Guam is the predominance of women who migrated for tertiary education, marriage, and jobs. Palauan women migrants to Guam outnumber men and have a higher school completion rate than Palauan men (though men slightly outnumber women in degree completion).[22] In the early years a number of Micronesian women married Americans and moved to the United States, creating bases where student migrants gathered. It appears that similar strategies of female out-marriage are followed by I-Kiribati women moving to the Marshalls. In this context the Marshallese community in Orange County, California, presents interesting gender patterns: although there are roughly equal numbers of men and women, there are slightly more women than men in their twenties, and again in the age groups over forty. This seems to reflect a practice of senior women moving to California to run the households of young immigrants and students. In all other age groups men slightly outnumber women.[23] By contrast the initial post-Compact Chuukese migration to Guam, at least, has been primarily male, a pattern followed historically throughout the Carolinian atolls where men were expected to travel and often married outside the home atoll, and women ideally stayed home to protect continued matrilineal land rights. During the past two decades, however, expectations and migration patterns have been transformed, mainly due to the value attached to secondary education, which is not available on the atolls. A nearly equal number of young women from Pollap, for instance, now leave the island for higher education, and the establishment of a Pollapese community on Weno (in Chuuk) is creating a bi-local Pollapese community.[24] And as the Chuukese community becomes more established on Guam, gender ratios have equalised and living arrangements shifted from single male to family-oriented households.[25]

22 DeVerne Smith, 'The Palauans on Guam', typescript.
23 Hess, 'Migration, Networks, Resources, and Households'.
24   Flinn, 'From Sea and Garden to School and Town'.
25 Rubinstein and Levin, 'Micronesian Migration to Guam', 350–5.

Another potential node between Pacific Rim destinations is the FSM and the Marshall Islands. Marshallese and I-Kiribati have a history of intermarriages (as do Kosraeans with Nauruans or Rotumans). Thus it is possible for Nauruans and I-Kiribati to migrate to the United States through the FSM and the Marshalls, but it does not appear that either route is often used. Not all oceanic travellers settle new lands. Thirty per cent of I-Kiribati men abroad work as seamen—a percentage similar to that of Tuvalu. Kiribati, Tuvalu and the FSM maintain maritime academies which train Islanders as navigators, captains, port captains, and seamen for national, regional, and European shipping lines.

While shifts between the FSM and Palau to Saipan are deemed international, they are equally well understood as part of the general movement of people from rural to urban centres. This shift is the primary characteristic of migration within Papua New Guinea, Vanuatu, and the Solomon Islands. Cultural differences between migrant and home communities in this region are at least as great as those between the Micronesian islands. It is rather due to the configuration of post-colonial nation-states that population shifts are labelled either international, or rural-to-urban.

In colonial Melanesia, towns were the preserve of Europeans: Melanesian and other workers were permitted only under labour contracts, and their housing was provided, regulated, and segregated. The considerable urbanisation of Melanesian populations is therefore a very recent development, and colonial influences continue to affect contemporary cities.[26] One of the most disturbing phenomena, in the absence of effective housing policies by either colonial or post-colonial governments, is the development of squatter settlements in Port Moresby, Lae, Suva and Luganville. The problem is not confined to Melanesia, but also exists to a lesser extent in Apia and Rarotonga, and south Tarawa: only aggressive development of leaseholds by the American administration in Micronesia prevented its occurrence there. Until World War II most workers in Papua New Guinea lived during brief contracts in employers' housing; after the war increasing numbers of migrants brought wives and children to Port Moresby. As housing provided by employers was inadequate, they sought permission to build on Motu and Koita land, or squatted on government lands. Experiences of the urban migrants varied by cultural group, related to their educational and employment levels and modes of entry. By 1965 the Hula had established a stable population in Port Moresby with generally secure housing and employment, while over two-thirds of the Toaripi lived in scrap-iron houses in squatter settlements, the men working in low-paying jobs with little security.[27] To this day, land titles have not been regularised for those living on government lands, despite the increasing permanence of a number of such settlements, now characterised by cement houses and regular water supplies, that resemble rural villages and comprise wantoks from the same village or region. Many of those

26 Connell and Lea, 'Cities of Parts, Cities Apart?'
27 Nigel Oram, 'The Hula in Port Moresby', and Dawn Ryan, 'Toaripi in Port Moresby and Lae', both in May (ed.), *Change and Movement*.

living on Motu and Koita lands have established relations of kinship and exchange that assure continuity of tenure, and the possibility of building permanent homes.

Urban centres continue to be sites of exploration and excitement throughout the Pacific, particularly in French Polynesia and the Micronesian nations, which are predominantly urban, but also in Papua New Guinea and the Solomons where exploratory visits to the cities may lay the basis for long-term movement. Frazer, studying To'ambaita migrants to Honiara in the 1970s, describes the predominantly young male practice of *liliu* (*wokabaot*, or walkabout), both in terms of general spatial mobility within the region, the movement towards wage labour in town, and walkabout within Honiara, especially by the unemployed and new arrivals. Such moving is far from aimless, as young men seek strategic contacts and sustain group cohesion and support. In the process some succeed in a range of jobs, and perhaps start a small business.[28]

It is difficult to reduce any phenomenon so multi-faceted as overseas migration to one explanation. Economic factors, including employment, are primary in drawing Islanders abroad, closely related to better educational opportunities. Those who complete advanced and professional degrees are highly sought after by home communities, but may remain abroad where salaries or prospects may be greater. Others may remain either to complete their schooling or to avoid the embarrassment of failure. Marriage also affects decisions to return home. While Islanders may expect an overseas stay to be temporary, in the long term and as the centre of gravity of a family shifts through further migration, settlement may become permanent. Of Western Samoan-born migrants to the US, 60 per cent became naturalised citizens, and this rate was a probable outcome for all Island-born immigrants to the United States.[29]

There clearly are several different trajectories for Islanders abroad. As described by Hau'ofa, there is an international elite, employed in regional organisations, institutions and the private sector. In many ways these highly educated Islanders replaced colonial expatriate business people, bureaucrats, educators and health officials, and many educate their children in the international schools once reserved for children of colonial officials. Marcus's description of Tongan elite families as transnational corporations may unduly emphasise central control over dispersed resources, but it is not uncommon for families to have three or four interacting nodes, owning land, houses and businesses, and channelling youngsters through secondary schools and universities and in family businesses throughout the region. Others, less affluent, still manage to maintain transnational life-styles combining international travel with travel and training opportunities through home island employment, or to manage international trade.[30]

There are obvious parallels, but it is misleading to equate the new Pacific elite with their colonial predecessors. Konai Thaman contrasts

28 Frazer, 'Walkabout and Urban Movement'.
29 Ahlburg and Levin, *The North-East Passage*, 47.
30 Marcus, 'Power on the Extreme Periphery'.

her shifting world-views as she moved through the nodes of Tongan migration: to Auckland for grammar school and university, back to Tonga as a teacher, on to the University of California for advanced studies, then to the University of the South Pacific at Suva. At home in Tonga her world was tied up with the legacy and commitments of family and kin, while her sojourn in Auckland permitted the development of a personal identity. After the initial shock at the pace of California, she learned to appreciate diversity and experimentation, and to develop her creativity as a poet and writer. Her studies in remote sensing and international education developed a global view, and awareness of the finite nature of world resources and the impact of high technology. Now at home in Suva with teaching and administrative duties at the university, she is an example of the new regional leader who works with, teaches and counsels Islanders from throughout the region. Her pan-Pacific experiences and identity are critical to her success in this regional institution.[31]

Initial migration constraints, as well as the size, location, and time depth of the immigrant populations, have affected populations. While Samoans and Chamorros enjoyed free entry, a larger percentage of Chamorros moved to California; both Chamorros and Samoans in California had higher educational and employment levels than those in Hawai'i. For nearly thirty years, the primary way Micronesians from the Trust Territory could enter the United States was higher education. As a result, in 1990 they had levels of education well above the national average. Length of residence as well as educational and skill levels affect an immigrant's earning power. Because most of the Micronesians were recent immigrants (perhaps still in school), they also had a high proportion of individuals living below poverty levels. It is too early to tell whether their educational attainment will provide the early Micronesian immigrants with greater economic mobility. Guamanian citizens in California have been characterised as economically and socially comfortable members of the middle class, although this has been questioned by the Chamorro scholar Faye Muñoz.[32]

The life-style of most Islanders abroad is less affluent than the population at large, and too many live in dire poverty, with poor educational and technical skills and limited access to employment. Although migrants might enjoy a higher standard of living than family members on the home island, whom they assist through remittances, they live at the lower end of the spectrum in their new communities, where they experience high unemployment rates, lower income levels, lower disposable incomes because of larger family size and reliance on part-time employment, and low levels of home ownership. In 1991 in New Zealand, 80 per cent of the employed Islanders earned less than $20,000 per annum, compared to 64 per cent for the general population. Islanders were twice as likely to be unemployed, with rates ranging from 20.0 to 30.6 per cent for one quarter in 1991. High unemployment

---

31 Thaman, 'The Defining Distance'.
32 Muñoz, 'Pacific Islanders: A Perplexed, Neglected Minority'.

rates were directly linked to the low school qualifications. A similar situation affects migrants to the United States. These constraints take a heavy toll on the migrants' health.

A rare longitudinal analysis can be found in the Tokelau Islands Migrant Study, which studied home and migrant communities and collected epidemiological data from 1968 to 1986. Tokelau experience is atypical, due to the extreme isolation of the home atolls and Tokelau's close relationship to New Zealand, but there are strong parallels in many other atoll societies. Although Tokelau has experienced rapid population growth and a majority of its people now reside abroad, the numbers on the home atoll remained roughly the same over the twenty-year study. The communities at home and abroad interact closely, with home societies experiencing transformations, although not at the same rate as emigrants. During New Zealand's economic downturns of the 1970s some families returned to Tokelau, moved on to Australia, or spread out in New Zealand. The New Zealand-born generation is now reaching adulthood, allowing us to see second- and third-generation effects of migration.[33] Language and schooling problems are easing, and there has been steady progress in home ownership and access to material goods, but dispersal has resulted in an increasing number of Tokelauans, especially the young, partially dissociating from community events. A key focus of the study was health. Despite a quite homogeneous genetic base, and a blurring of migrants and non-migrants because of constant moving back and forth, 'the incidence and prevalence of a number of chronic diseases—such as diabetes, gout, chronic lung disease, asthma, hypertension, and possibly coronary heart disease—were higher among the migrants than among the non-migrants. . . . correlates of these diseases are factors associated with life in the cosmopolitan culture of New Zealand'. Obesity, dietary changes, environment, and increased stress were all factors. Nevertheless, few migrants considered that their health had declined, and 86 per cent reported that their life in New Zealand was 'better' than it had been in Tokelau: those interviewed explained this improvement in terms of 'improved living standards, more independence, and better educational and cultural opportunities'.[34] In his study of a Samoan community in California, Janes found similar factors, highlighting structural stresses due to poor economic conditions, family stressors especially for women, and acute stressors, all related to national and world economic changes.[35] The larger body size of Samoan immigrants, positively correlated with high social status in Samoan culture, contributed to higher rates of cardiovascular and metabolic diseases but did not result in higher mortality rates, as an American medical model would predict. The positive effects of Samoan social institutions apparently buffer certain of the negative effects. 'What overwhelmingly irresistible force can make a people voluntarily leave their country at a rate where, in

33 C. Macpherson, 'Public and Private Views of Home'; and 'I Don't Go There So Often Now'.
34 Wessen *et al.*, *Migration and Health in a Small Society*, 383, 287.
35 Janes, *Migration, Social Change and Health*.

20 years or so, the population is depleted by almost 50 per cent? Why are the Niueans abandoning in such large numbers an island which they and their ancestors have inhabited for over a thousand years?'[36]

Niue presents a provoking example of the cultural and demographic risks of free association. This large raised coral island for centuries operated under a system of strong familial autonomy, without hereditary chiefs. Migration to New Zealand was steady after World War II, but peaked in 1974 when internal self-government and free association were granted: more than half of all Niueans then decided to move to New Zealand. Today fewer than 2500 people live on the island, while 14,500 (85 per cent) live in New Zealand. Commonly, second- and third-generation Niueans have never visited Niue. While Niueans might cherish an ideal of returning home, the gulf between elite bureaucrats and the have-nots at home continues to fuel emigration. Independence might have closed this migration door and resulted in greater development at home, but Niueans were unwilling to give up the benefits of association, nor did the New Zealand government, careful of its international image, seriously consider forcing such a solution. Who is the constituency of the Niuean government: only those residing on the island, or the entire population—and are the interests of the two populations compatible?

One critical concern is the rising proportion of elderly and extreme elderly (over 8 per cent) living on Niue, resulting in an aged dependency ratio three times that commonly found in Third World nations.[37] This is a pattern long identified in islands experiencing heavy emigration. While the numbers of individuals remaining in the home community may remain stable, the age distribution often favours the elderly and the young; the 15–29 age group moves first, seeking higher education and employment. (This process is equally true for hinterland populations on the larger islands, and atolls.) Eventually a proportion of the young adults return home, but increased out-marriage and the greater distances of spousal origins often incline people to remain abroad. In the home communities the households most at risk are those of the elders, especially if their children are absent. Even if they receive remittances of money and foodstuffs, these may be irregular, nor do they make up for routine assistance with household tasks and sociality.[38]

In Tokelau and other remote atolls such as Namoluk, although the majority of the people reside abroad, the population on the atoll has remained stable and there has been no migration of workers. Throughout the Pacific, most notably in those areas with higher living standards and relatively great employment possibilities, workers are often drawn in to replace those abroad. These include islands within the American sphere of influence: Saipan, Guam, Palau, Kwajalein in the Marshalls,

36 H. Douglas, 'Niue: The Silent Village Green', in Hooper *et al.* (eds), *Class and Culture in the South Pacific*, 186.
37 Barker, 'Home Alone'.
38 Marshall, 'Education and Depopulation on a Micronesian Atoll', and 'Beyond the Reef'; Louise Morauta, 'Urban Movement and Rural Identity'; and Ryan, 'Toaripi in Port Moresby and Lae', and 'Home Ties in Town: Toaripi in Port Moresby'.

American Samoa, but also Nauru, New Caledonia, and the mining areas of Papua New Guinea and New Caledonia. The common factor is development projects that employ large numbers of unskilled and semi-skilled workers—mining, construction, tourism, and canning or garment industries. Since the decolonisation of most of the Pacific and repatriation of Chinese and Vietnamese workers from Western Samoa and Vanuatu, most of these migrant workers are themselves Pacific Islanders, often of the same or similar culture as the host community.[39] For example, Western Samoans are employed in the tuna canneries of Pago Pago, or provide household labour within their kin-group households. Nauru employs predominantly I-Kiribati as phosphate miners, alongside a small proportion of Asians. Skilled and unskilled workers from throughout the Pacific are drawn to Ebeye, where Islanders working on the Kwajalein missile base live.

Filipinos, Japanese, Chinese, Koreans and other Asians are drawn into employment in the contexts of long histories of colonial relations. For Filipinos working on Guam and Saipan, prehistoric relations were transformed when both areas came under Spanish colonisation in the 1600s, and in the 1700s when Filipinos were brought in to rejuvenate the decimated population. After World War II Filipino labour migrants are perceived as threatening, despite their contributions to building amenities. Partly at issue is the degree to which immigration might be short- or long-term, especially on Guam where birth confers United States citizenship. Current possibilities of capitalising on cheap Asian labour override common interests against economic exploitation.[40]

THE CHALLENGE

Making sense of multi-cultural heritages and kin relationships is a challenge faced creatively, perhaps nowhere more evident than in Auckland. In the schools children deal constantly with positive and negative images of being Samoan, Tongan, Niuean. Clearly not *pakeha*, neither are they members of the *tanga te whenua*, the Maori people of the land. But neither are the majority of Maori in Auckland, away from their *iwi* and *marae*. Reaching out to representations of global culture, the youth may select the colours of the Black LA gangs of Los Angeles, transforming these meanings as well in the process. In 1993 'The Contest', staged by a mainly Samoan theatre company, drew upon images of a mythical past to pose a multi-generational challenge between orators representing two families. The son of the man overcome in the first contest moves back and forth between the timeless scene of the challenge and a contemporary Auckland, accompanied by his mother who, in turn, alternates between roles as a very contemporary Samoan mother and the supportive wife of the deceased orator, assisting her son in strategies to overcome the usurper. The son must

39 Tom, *The Chinese in Western Samoa*; G. Haberkorn, 'Paamese in Port Vila', in Connell (ed.), *Migration and Development*, 155.
40 Diaz, 'Bye Bye Ms. American Pie'.

find an appropriate, but new, oratorical challenge to avenge the death of his father. When finally he succeeded in vanquishing the elder orator with the rhythms and speed of rap, the entire audience erupted in cheers and laughter.

The next theatrical presentation, *F.O.B.* (the slang acronym for Fresh Off the Boat), enjoyed an extended run at the Aotea Centre, with sell-out crowds. This serious comedy deals with the challenge and new definitions of leadership—what is the role of the mother's brother, the elder *matai*, in today's overseas community? Newly arrived from Samoa, offering cultural knowledge but also demanding the respect due to the mother's elder brother, he found his role as leader had less meaning in Auckland and within the household his sister had established, as she learnt how to live and raise her children in the new environment.

This is a challenge throughout the Pacific, played differently by different communities. In most of the societies of Micronesia, where titles are more directly tied to, and speak for, the lands they represent, titleholders are contained within their home communities. Even at home their roles are eroded by new forms of government. While members of elite clans may take more active roles in community leadership abroad, they do so without benefit of chiefly titles. By contrast, many Samoan *matai* titles are split, with several representatives, some of whom commute between overseas and home to maintain leadership of their lineages in multiple sites. Issues of leadership, balances between land-based and new economic prestige systems, and between individual and community interests, continue to challenge Pacific communities in their homes that today span the contemporary Pacific.

A more serious challenge faces Pacific leaders. Returning to the metaphor of the tree and the canoe, Pacific societies have always combined stasis and mobility along shared exchange routes, but the societies were centred. The century of colonialism transformed Pacific economies, creating states and relative differences of economy and power between them. Yet these new states do not coincide with the nations (or societies) they attempt to contain. In Papua New Guinea or the Solomon Islands, many societies are contained within one state; Samoa is split between two. More important, people expand across boundaries creating new canoes, new centred and interacting communities spanning the post-colonial polities. New pan-state societies are created as Islanders tap new resources, facilitated by the ease of air transport and satellite communications. Previous dichotomies between North and South, Rim and Basin, even Pacific and Asia, have dissolved.

Contemporary Pacific societies bridge state boundaries in ways that few colonial officers and their imported labourers did. Samoans span not only the two Samoas, but Auckland, Hawai'i, and California. Palauans connect Palau, Guam, Saipan, Hawai'i and California. Tongans have once again expanded their sphere of influence into Samoa and on to Auckland, California and Sydney. Papua New Guineans move within their country and on to Australia, while the various communities of Vanuatu move to Port Vila and beyond. Filipinos and a few island Indonesians traverse the narrow distance to Palau, Guam and Saipan, reconnecting the western Austronesians across academic and colonial divides. Pacific heads of state, and the trans-Pacific leaders who direct regional organisations and teach at regional institutions, have a trans-Pacific constituency. How will they meet the challenge of leading this new transnational Pacific?

BIBLIOGRAPHIC ESSAY

Works on migration cited here include Hooper *et al.*, *Class and Culture in the South Pacific*; Connell (ed.), *Migration and Development in the South Pacific*; Bonnemaison, 'The Tree and the Canoe: Roots and Mobility in Vanuatu Societies'; Tuimaleali'ifano, *Samoans in Fiji*; Lieber (ed.), *Exiles and Migrants in Oceania*; McCall and Connell (eds), *A World Perspective on Pacific Islander Migration*; Barringer *et al.*, *Asians and Pacific Islanders in the United States*; Baudchon, 'Movement in the French Pacific: Recent Situation and Prospects'; and May (ed.), *Change and Movement: Readings on Internal Migration in Papua New Guinea*. The literature on MIRAB includes Watters, 'Mirab Societies and Bureaucratic Elites' in Hooper *et al.*, *Class and Culture in the South Pacific*; Ogden, 'MIRAB and the Marshall Islands'; Munro, 'Migration and the Shift to Dependence in Tuvalu' in Connell (ed.), *Migration and Development in the South Pacific*; and Connell, 'Island Microstate'. For the health of Islanders abroad, and the interacting effects of health, education and employment, see Bathgate *et al.*, *The Health of Pacific Islands People in New Zealand*.

Reports on migrants in host communities include US Department of Commerce, *1990 Census: Commonwealth of the Northern Mariana Islands*; Dagmar, 'Banabans in Fiji'; Crawford, *Republic of the Marshall Islands, National Environment Management Strategy*; Republic of Kiribati, *Statistical Year Books*; Price, 'The Asian and Pacific Island Peoples of Australia'; Lowe, 'Maori in Australia: A Statistical Summary', in McCall and Connell, *A World Perspective on Pacific Islander Migration*; Ahlburg and Levin, *The North-East Passage*; Franco, *Samoans in Hawai'i*; Janes, *Migration, Social Change and Health: A Samoan Community in Urban California*; and Va'a, 'Effects of Migration on Western Samoa'.

GLOSSARY

'afakasi (Samoan) : half-caste; cf. *demi, hapa-haole*

ali'i (Hawaiian, Samoan) : chief(s)

arii nui (Tahitian) : authority

aufaura'a 'ava'e (Tahitian) : tribute to chiefs, hence 'voluntary' church contributions

bêche-de-mer : trepang, sea slugs

bisnis (Tok Pisin) : business

Bose levu Vakaturaga : Fijian Great Council of Chiefs

buli (Fijian) : lower-level chief

bure (Fijian) : house

caldoches (French) : settlers in New Caledonia

cantonnements (French) : in New Caledonia, the policy of confining Melanesians to reserves

colons (French) : settlers

dama : Tari ambiguous spirit beings

demis : In French Polynesia, the population with mixed Polynesian and European or Chinese ancestry

fāgogo (Samoan) : fables, family storytelling form

fetokoni'aki (Tongan) : obligatory non-market transfer

gafa (Samoan) : genealogies

gau : strings of shell crafted from *Spondylus*

gauman (gavman) (Tok Pisin) : government

girmit (Indian) : contract of indenture; hence *girmitiyas*, indentured labourers

haka (Maori) : war chant

haole (Hawaiian) : white person; *hapa-haole*, half-caste

haus tambaran (Tok Pisin) : spirit house

heiau (Hawaiian) : structure dedicated to Lono

hiri (Tok Pisin) : trading network in the Gulf of Papua

Ibedul : paramount chiefly title of Koror, Palau

'ie toga (Samoan) : fine mats, the principal form of woman-made wealth

iwi (Maori) : tribal group(s)

kama'āina (Hawaiian) : children of the land

kamokim : Wopkaimin leader

kapu (Hawaiian) : taboo system

kastom (Melanesian) : tradition
kaukau (Tok Pisin) : sweet potato (*Ipomea batatas*)
kava : a mild narcotic made from the root of *Piper nethysticum*
kawanatanga (Maori) : translation of 'governorship'
kesame : Onabasulu spirit people
kiaps (New Guinea colonial) : patrol officers
Kingitanga (Maori) : kingship
kotahitanga (Maori) : oneness
kula : exchange network in Milne Bay, Papua
kula iwi (Hawaiian) : 'plain of one's bones', ancestral lands
kumara (Maori) : sweet potato (*Ipomea batatas*)
lakatoi (Motu) : sailing vessel in the Gulf of Papua
lotu : church, congregation, hence '*lotu* Tonga', '*lotu* Taiti' etc.
luluai (New Guinea colonial) : village constable or headman
mahu (Tahitian) : transsexual
malaga (Samoan) : 'travelling parties', exchanging fine mats at
  ceremonial events
Malaiya : legendary origin place of Onabasulu
mamaia : religious movement in nineteenth-century Tahiti
mana (Polynesian) : spiritual authority, hence sovereignty
marae (Maori) : tribal meeting place
matai (Samoan) : titled person
mataqali (Fijian) : descent group, landowning community
me'ae : Marquesan stone structures
mere (Maori) : spears
moka (Melpa) : formal gift-giving, usually of pigs (cf. *tee*)
Nahnken : second-ranked chief in Pohnpei
Nahnmwarki : paramount chief of Madolenihmw
'oloa (Samoan) : food, canoes and tools produced by men
pa (Maori) : fort
pakeha (Maori) : white person
papālagi (Samoan) : 'sky bursters', hence foreigners
pule (Samoan) : authority
raay (Yap) : calcium carbonate discs
rava'ira'a fenua (Tahitian) : the adequacy of the land, or national
  wealth
rebaibal (Tok Pisin) : spiritual or religious revival
Roko Tui (Fijian) : governors of provinces, appointed by the
  Governor, supervising *buli* or local chiefs, e.g. Roko Tui Bau
ruunanga (Maori) : inter-tribal councils
santo kokumin (Japanese) : 'third-class people', hence Micronesians
  during the Japanese period
siapo (Samoan) : bark cloth
tabu : type of shell
tabua (Fijian) : whale's teeth
taeao o le atunu'u (Samoan) : 'mornings of the country', or notable
  events
Tafa'ifā : supreme authority in Samoa, holder of the four leading
  titles

tala fa'aanamua (Samoan) : stories in ancient style
tala fa'asolopito (Samoan) : 'tales told in succession', i.e. sequential narratives
tala o le vavau (Samoan) : 'oldtime stories'
tee (Enga) : formal gift presentation (cf. *moka*)
tambu (Tolai) : shell wealth
tanga te whenua (Maori) : people of the land
tapa (**kapa**) (Polynesian) : bark cloth
tapu tarahu (Tahitian) : borrowing someone's services, hence to employ
taukei (Fijian) : common people, indigenous people
Tok Pisin : language widely spoken in Papua New Guinea; cf. Bislama in Vanuatu, Solomons Pijin
tulāfale (Samoan) : orators
tupu (Samoan) : would-be kings
tupua (Maori) : strange beings or goblins
turaga (Fijian) : chiefs: *turaga ni koro*, village headmen
utu (Maori) : 'return', hence revenge
vakamisioneri (originally Fijian, now widespread) : contributions towards overseas missions
vanua : land, with cognate physical, social and cultural dimensions; also people
Vunivalu (Fijian) : war king of Bau
waka (Maori) : canoes
wantok (Tok Pisin) : a speaker of one's own language, hence kin
yaqona (Fijian) : see *kava*

BIBLIOGRAPHY

Abbreviations

ANU   Research School of Pacific and Asian Studies, Australian National University, Canberra

IPS   Institute of Pacific Studies, University of the South Pacific, Suva

JPH   *Journal of Pacific History*

JPS   *Journal of the Polynesian Society*

TCP   *The Contemporary Pacific*

UHP   University of Hawai'i Press

Adams, Ron, *In the Land of Strangers: A Century of European Contact with Tanna*, ANU, 1984.
Ahlburg, D., and Levin, M., *The North-East Passage: A Study of Pacific Islander Migration to American Samoa and the United States*, ANU, 1990.
Aldrich, Robert, and Connell, John, *France's Overseas Frontier: Départements et Territoires d'Outre-mer*, Melbourne, 1992.
Alkire, William, *Lamotrek Atoll and Inter-island Socioeconomic Ties*, Urbana, 1965.
Allen, Bryant, 'A Bomb or a Bullet or the Bloody Flux? Population Change in the Aitape Inland, Papua New Guinea, 1941–1945', *JPH* xviii: 3–4 (1983).
Allen, Bryant, 'The Importance of Being Equal: The Colonial and Postcolonial Experience in the Toricelli Foothills', in Nancy Lutkehaus *et al.*, *Sepik Heritage: Tradition and Change in Papua New Guinea*, Bathurst, 1990.
Allen, Colin H., 'The Post-War Scene in the Western Solomons and Marching Rule: A Memoir', *JPH* xxiv: 1 (1989).
Allen, Jim, 'When Did Humans First Colonise Australia?', *Search* xx (1989).
Allen, Jim, Gosden, Chris, and White, J. Peter, 'Human Pleistocene Adaptations in the Tropic Island Pacific: Recent Evidence from New Ireland, a Greater Australian Outlier', *Antiquity* 63 (1989).

Allen, Jim, and Gosden, Chris, *Report of the Lapita Homeland Project*, ANU Prehistory Occasional Paper 20, 1991.

Allen, Jim, *et al.* (eds), *Sunda and Sahul: Prehistoric Studies in Southeast Asia, Melanesia and Australia*, London, 1977.

Allen, Michael, 'The Establishment of Christianity and Cash-Cropping in a New Hebridean Community', *JPH* iii (1968).

Amarshi, A., Good, K., and Mortimer, R. (eds), *Development and Dependency: The Political Economy of Papua New Guinea*, Melbourne, 1979.

Andaya, Leonard Y., *The World of Maluku: Eastern Indonesia in the Early Modern Period*, UHP, 1993.

Anderson, Athol (ed.), *Traditional Fishing in the Pacific: Ethnographic and Archaeological Papers from the 1st Pacific Science Congress*, Bernice P. Bishop Museum, 1986.

Arnold, Lorna, *A Very Special Relationship: British Atomic Weapon Trials in Australia*, London, 1987.

l'Association des Français contre la bombe, *Le Bataillon de la Paix*, Editions Buchet/Chastel, Paris.

Awatere, Donna, *Maori Sovereignty*, Auckland, 1984.

Babadzan, A., 'Kastom and Nation-building in the South Pacific', in R. Guidieri, F. Fellizzi and S. J. Tambiah (eds), *Ethnicities and Nations: Processes of Interethnic Relations in Latin America, Southeast Asia and the Pacific*, Houston, 1988.

Ballard, Chris, '"The Centre Cannot Hold": Trade Networks and Sacred Geography in the Papua New Guinea Highlands', *Archaeology in Oceania* xxix: 3 (1994).

Ballard, Chris, 'The Death of a Great Land: Ritual, History and Subsistence Revolution in the Southern Highlands of Papua New Guinea', PhD thesis, ANU, 1995.

Baré, Jean-François, 'Talking Economics in Tahitian: A Few Comments', *Pacific Studies* 15: 3 (1992).

Bargatsky, Thomas, 'Beachcombers and Castaways as Innovators', *JPH* xv: 1 (1980).

Barker, J., 'Home Alone: The Effects of Out-Migration on Niuean Elders' Living Arrangements and Social Supports', *Pacific Studies* 17: 3 (1994).

Barringer, Herbert, Gardner, R. W., Levin, M. J. (eds), *Asians and Pacific Islanders in the United States*, New York, 1993.

Barwick, G. F., *New Light on the Discovery of Australia as Revealed by the Journal of Captain Don Diego de Prado y Tovar*, H. N. Stevens (ed.), Hakluyt Society Works, London, 1930, vol. 64, series 2.

Bateson, Gregory, *Naven*, Stanford, 1958.

Bathgate, Murray, *et al.*, *The Health of Pacific Islands People in New Zealand*, Wellington, 1994.

Baudchon, Gerard, 'Movement in the French Pacific: Recent Situation and Prospects', *Asian and Pacific Migration Journal* 1:2 (1992).

Beaglehole, J. C. (ed.), *The Journals of Captain James Cook on his Voyages of Discovery*, 3 vols, Cambridge for the Hakluyt Society, 1955–74.

Beaglehole, J. C., *The Exploration of the Pacific*, Stanford, 1966.

Beaglehole, J. C., *The Life of Captain James Cook*, London, 1974.

Becket, Jeremy, 'Politics in the Torres Strait Islands', PhD thesis, ANU, 1963.

Beckwith, Martha (trans. and ed.), *The Kumulipo: A Hawaiian Creation Chant*, Honolulu, 1972 (first published 1951).

Beechert, Edward, *Working in Hawai'i: A Labor History*, Honolulu, 1985.

Bell, Clive (ed.), *The Diseases and Health Services of Papua New Guinea*, Port Moresby, 1973.

Bellwood, Peter, *The Polynesians: Prehistory of an Island People*, London, 1987.

Bellwood, Peter, Fox, James, and Tryon, Darrell (eds), *The Austronesians: Historical and Comparative Perspectives*, Canberra, 1995.

Bennett, Judith, *Wealth of the Solomons: A History of a Pacific Archipelago, 1800–1978*, UHP, 1987.

Bennett, Judith, 'Forestry, Public Land, and the Colonial Legacy in Solomon Islands', *TCP* 7:2 (1995).

Blanchet, G., *L'Economie de la Polynésie française de 1960 à 1980: un aperçu de son evolution*, Paris, 1985; translated as *A Survey of the Economy of French Polynesia: 1960 to 1990*, ANU, 1991.

Bonnemaison, Joel, 'The Tree and the Canoe: Roots and Mobility in Vanuatu Societies', *Pacific Viewpoint* 26 (1985).

Bonnemaison, Joel, *The Tree and the Canoe: History and Ethnogeography of Tanna*, UHP, 1994.

Boutilier, James, Hughes, Daniel, and Tiffany, Sharon (eds), *Mission, Church and Sect in Oceania*, Lanham, Md, 1978.

Bowdler, Sandra, '50,000-year-old Site in Australia—Is It Really That Old?', *Australian Archaeology* 31 (1990).

Bowdler, Sandra, 'Some Sort of Dates at Malakunanja II: A Reply to Roberts *et al.*', *Australian Archaeology* 32 (1991).

Bowdler, Sandra, '*Homo sapiens* in Southeast Asia and the Antipodes: Archaeological vs Biological Interpretations', in T. Akazawa, K. Aoki and T. Kimura (eds), *The Evolution and Dispersal of Modern Humans in Asia*, Tokyo, 1992.

Bowdler, Sandra, 'Sunda and Sahul: A 30K Yr Culture Area?', in Smith, Spriggs and Fankhauser (eds), *Sahul in Review*.

Bowdler, Sandra, 'Offshore Islands and Maritime Explorations in Australian Prehistory', *Antiquity* 69 (1995).

Boyd, Mary, 'The Military Administration of Western Samoa, 1914–1919', *New Zealand Journal of History* 2 (1968).

Bradley, David, *No Place to Hide, 1946–1984*, Hanover, University of New England, 1983.

Brass, Tom, 'The Return of "Merrie Melanesia": A Comment on a Review of a Review', *JPH* xxxi: 2 (1996).

Brauer, Gunter, and Smith, Fred (eds), *Continuity or Replacement: Controversies in* Homo sapiens *Evolution*, Rotterdam, 1992.

Brown, Paula, 'Gender and Social Change: New Forms of Independence for Simbu Women', *Oceania* xix (1988).

Bryant, Jenny, *Urban Poverty and the Environment in the South Pacific*, Armidale, NSW, 1993.

Buck, P., 'Cargo-cult Discourse: Myth and the Rationalization of Labor Relations in Papua New Guinea', *Dialectical Anthropology* 13 (1989).

Buckley, Ken and Klugman, Kris, *The History of Burns Philp*, Sydney, 2 vols, 1981 and 1983.

Bulbeck, Chilla, *Australian Women in Papua New Guinea: Colonial Passages 1920–1960*, Cambridge, 1992.

Burridge, K. O. L., *Mambu: A Melanesian Millennium*, London, 1960.

Burridge, K. O. L., *New Heaven, New Earth: A Study of Millenarian Activities*, Oxford, 1969.

Burton, John, 'Axe Makers of the Wahgi', PhD thesis, ANU, 1984.

Bushnell, Andrew, '"The Horror" Reconsidered: An Evaluation of the Historical Evidence for Population Decline in Hawai'i, 1778–1803', *Pacific Studies* xvi: 3 (1993).

Campbell, Archibald, *A Voyage round the World from 1806 to 1812*, 1822; reissued by UHP, 1967.

Campbell, Ian, 'European Transculturalists in Polynesia 1789–ca.1840', Ph.D thesis, University of Adelaide, 1976.

Campbell, Ian, 'The Historiography of Charlie Savage', *JPS* 89 (1980).

Campbell, Ian, *A History of the Pacific Islands*, Christchurch, 1989.

Campbell, Ian, *Island Kingdom: Tonga, Ancient and Modern*, Christchurch, 1992.

Campbell, Ian, 'European Polynesian Encounters: A Critique of the Pearson Thesis', *JPH* xxix: 2 (1994).

Chappell, David, 'Shipboard Relations between Pacific Island Women and Euroamerican Men, 1767–1887', *JPH* xxvii (1992).

Chappell, David, 'Secret Sharers: Indigenous Beachcombers in the Pacific Islands', *Pacific Studies* xvii: 2 (1994).

Chase, A., 'Which Way Now? Tradition, Continuity and Change in a North Queensland Aboriginal Community', PhD thesis, University of Queensland, 1980.

Christiansen, P., *The Melanesian Cargo Cult: Millenarianism as a Factor in Cultural Change*, Copenhagen, 1969.

Clifford, James, *Person and Myth: Maurice Leenhardt in the Melanesian World*, Berkeley, 1982.

Clunie, Fergus, *Fijian Weapons and Warfare*, Fiji Museum Bulletin 2, Suva, 1977.

Clunie, Fergus, 'The Fijian Flintlock', *Domodomo: Fiji Museum Quarterly* i (1983).

Clunie, Fergus, 'The Manila Brig', *Domodomo: Fiji Museum Quarterly* ii (1984).

Colchester, Marcus, and Lohmann, Larry, *The Struggle for Land and the Fate of the Forests*, Penang, 1993.

Connell, John, *New Caledonia or Kanaky? The Political History of a French Colony*, ANU, 1987.

Connell, John, 'Island Microstate: The Mirage of Development', *TCP* 3: 2 (1991).

Connell, John (ed.), *Migration and Development in the South Pacific*, ANU, 1990.

Connell, John, and Lea, J., 'Cities of Parts, Cities Apart? Changing Places in Modern Melanesia', *TCP* 6: 2 (1994).

Connolly, Bob, and Anderson, Robin, *First Contact: New Guinea's Highlanders Encounter the Outside World*, New York, 1988.

Cooke, John, *Working in Papua New Guinea, 1931–1946*, Brisbane, 1983.

Cooper, Matthew, 'Economic Context of Shell Money Production in Malaita', *Oceania* xli: 4 (1971).

Corris, Peter, *Passage, Port and Plantation: A History of Solomon Islands Labour Migration*, Melbourne, 1973.

Craven, Edward, 'Mineral Resources: A Discussion about an Irian Jaya Experience', in B. Farrell (ed.), *Views of Economic Development in the Pacific*, University of California, Santa Cruz, 1975.

Crawford, Martha, *Republic of the Marshall Islands, National Environment Management Strategy*, Apia, 1993.

Crocombe, R. G., *Land Tenure in the Cook Islands*, Melbourne, 1964.

Crocombe, R. G. (ed.), *Land Tenure in the Atolls: Cook Islands, Kiribati, Marshall Islands, Tokelau, Tuvalu*, IPS, 1987.

Crocombe, Ron, and Crocombe, Marjorie Tuainekore, 'Scale, Sovereignty, Wealth and Enterprise: Social and Educational Comparisons between the Cook Islands and the Solomon Islands', *Comparative Education* 29: 3.

Curtain, Richard, 'Labour Migration from the Sepik', *Oral History* vi: 9 (1978).

Dagmar, Hans, 'Banabans in Fiji: Ethnicity, Change and Development', in Howard (ed.), *Ethnicity and Nation-building*.

Dana, Richard Henry, *Two Years Before the Mast*, New York, 1959.

Danielsson, Bengt, and Danielsson, Marie-Thérèse, *Poisoned Reign: French Nuclear Colonialism in the Pacific*, Harmondsworth, 1986.

Davidson, D. S., 'The Chronology of Australian Watercraft', *JPS* 44 (1935).

Davidson, James, 'Problems of Pacific History', *JPH* i (1966).

Davidson, James, *Samoa mo Samoa: The Emergence of the Independent State of Western Samoa*, Melbourne, 1967.

Davies, Margrit, *Public Health and Colonialism: The Case of German New Guinea, 1884–1914*, London, 1996.

Daws, Gavan, *Shoal of Time: A History of the Hawaiian Islands*, UHP, 1968.

Daws, Gavan, *Holy Man: Father Damien of Molokai*, New York, 1973.

Daws, Gavan, *A Dream of Islands: Voyages of Self-discovery in the South Seas*, Brisbane, 1980.

Delegation Polynésienne, *Pacte de Progrès: Economique, social et culturel de la Polynésie française*, Tahiti, January 1993.

Dening, Greg, 'Ethnohistory in Polynesia: The Value of Ethnohistorical Evidence', *JPH* i (1966).

Dening, Greg, *Islands and Beaches. Discourse on a Silent Land: Marquesas 1774–1880*, Chicago, 1980.

Dening, Greg, *Mr Bligh's Bad Language: Passion, Power and Theatre on the 'Bounty'*, Cambridge, 1992.

Dening, Greg, *The Death of William Gooch, A History's Anthropology*, Melbourne, 1995.

Denoon, Donald, 'Pacific Island Depopulation: Natural or Unnatural Causes?', in Linda Bryder and Derek Dow (eds), *New Countries and Old Medicines*, Auckland, 1995.

Denoon, Donald, Dugan, Kathleen, and Marshall, Leslie, *Public Health in Papua New Guinea, 1884–1984: Medical Possibility and Social Constraint*, Cambridge, 1989.

Denoon, Donald, and Snowden, Catherine (eds), *A History of Agriculture in Papua New Guinea*, Boroko, n.d. [1981].

Denoon, Donald, *et al.* (eds), *Mining and Mineral Resource Policy Issues in Asia-Pacific*, ANU, 1995.

Dexter, David, *The New Guinea Offensives, Australia in the War of 1939–1945*, series 1, vol. vi, Australian War Memorial, 1961.

Diaz, Vicente, 'Simply Chamorro: Telling Tales of Demise and Survival in Guam', *TCP* 6: 1 (1994).

Diaz, Vicente, 'Bye Bye Ms. American Pie: The Historical Relations between Chamorros and Filipinos and the American Dream', *Isla* 3: 1 (1995).

Dodson, J. (ed.), *The Naive Lands: Prehistory and Environmental Change in Australia and the South-West Pacific*, Melbourne, 1992.

Douglas, Bronwen, 'Discourses on Death in a Melanesian World', in Merwick (ed.), *Dangerous Liaisons*.

Doulman, C. (ed.), *The Development of the Tuna Industry in the Pacific Islands Region: An Analysis of Options*, East-West Center, Honolulu, 1987.

Doulman, David (ed.), *Tuna Issues and Perspectives in the Pacific Islands Region*, East-West Center, Honolulu, 1987.

Dunlop, Peggy, 'Samoan Writing: Searching for the Written Fāgogo', *Pacific Islands Communication Journal* 14: 1 (1985).

Dumont d'Urville, J. S. C., *Voyage de la Corvette L'Astrolabe . . . pendant les années 1826, 1827, 1828, 1829*, Paris, 1830.

Dunmore, John (trans. and ed.), *The Journal of Jean-François de Galaup de la Pérouse*, Hakluyt Society, London, 1994–95.

Emberson-Bain, 'Atu, *Labour and Gold in Fiji*, Cambridge, 1994.

Faaniu, Simati, *et al.*, *Tuvalu: A History*, IPS, 1983.

Falanruw, Marjorie, 'Food Production and Ecosystem Management on Yap', *Isla* 2: 1 (1994).

Farrell, Don, *Liberation – 1944*, Tamuning, Guam, 1984.

Feil, D. K., 'Women and Men in the Enga Tee', *American Ethnologist* v (1978).

Fifi'i, Jonathan, 'Setting the Record Straight on "Marching Rule" and a 1927 Murder', *Pacific Islands Monthly* (July 1982).

Fingleton, Jim, 'Pacific Values and Economic Development? How Melanesian Constitutions Deal with Land', in P. Sack (ed.), *Pacific Constitutions*, ANU, 1982.

Finney, Ben, *Polynesian Peasants and Proletarians*, Cambridge Mass., 1973.

Finney, Ben, 'French Polynesia: A Nuclear Dependency', in A. B. Robillard (ed.), *Social Change in the Pacific Islands*, London, 1992.

Firth, Stewart, 'Governors versus Settlers: The Dispute over German Labour in Samoa', *New Zealand Journal of History* 11 (1977).

Firth, Stewart, *New Guinea under the Germans*, Melbourne, 1983.

Firth, Stewart, *Nuclear Playground*, Sydney, 1987.

Fison, Lorimer, *Tales from Old Fiji*, London, 1904.

Fitzgerald, Thomas, *Education and Identity: A Study of the New Zealand Maori Graduate*, Wellington, 1977.

Flinn, Juliana, 'From Sea and Garden to School and Town: Changing Gender and Household Patterns among Pollap Atoll Migrants', *Pacific Studies* 17: 3 (1994).

Foley, William, *The Papuan Languages of New Guinea*, Cambridge, 1986.

Fortune, Reo, *Sorcerers of Dobu*, New York, 1963 (first published 1932).

Fosberg, F. R. (ed.), *Man's Place in the Island Ecosystem*, Honolulu, 1965.

Franco, Robert, *Samoans in Hawai'i: A Demographic Profile*, Honolulu, 1987.

Frankel, Stephen, *The Huli Response to Illness*, Cambridge, 1986.

Frankel, Stephen, and Lewis, Gilbert (eds), *A Continuing Trial of Treatment: Medical Pluralism in Papua New Guinea*, Boston, 1989.

Frazer, Ian, 'Walkabout and Urban Movement: A Melanesian Case Study', *Pacific Viewpoint* 26 (1985).

Frost, Alan, 'Towards Australia: the Coming of the Europeans 1400 to 1788', in Mulvaney and White (eds), *Australians to 1788*.

Fry, Greg, 'South Pacific Regionalism', MA thesis, ANU, 1979.

Gammage, Bill, 'The Rabaul Strike, 1929', *JPH* x (1975).

Gammage, Bill, 'Police and Power', in H. Levine and A. Ploeg (eds), *Work in Progress: Essays in Honour of Paula Brown Glick*, Frankfurt, 1995.

Ganter, Regina, *The Pearl-shellers of Torres Strait: Resource Use, Development and Decline, 1860s–1960s*, Melbourne, 1994.

Gardner, Robert, and Heider, Karl, *Gardens of War: Life and Death in the New Guinea Stone Age*, New York, 1968.

Garrett, John, *To Live Among the Stars: Christian Origins in Oceania*, IPS, 1982.

Garrett, John, *Footsteps in the Sea: Christianity in Oceania to World War II*, Geneva and Suva, 1992.

Gegeo, David, 'Tribes in Agony: Land, Development and Politics in Solomon Islands', *Cultural Survival Quarterly* 15: 2 (1991).

Gesch, P., *Initiative and Initiation: A Cargo Cult-type Movement in the Sepik Against its Background in Traditional Village Religion*, St Augustin, 1985.

Gillett, Robert, *Traditional Tuna Fishing: A Study at Satawal, Central Caroline Islands*, Honolulu, 1987.

Gillion, Ken, *The Fiji Indians: Challenge to European Dominance, 1920–1946*, ANU, 1977.

Gilson, Richard, *Samoa, 1830–1900: The Politics of a Multi-Cultural Community*, Melbourne, 1970.

Gilson, Richard, *The Cook Islands, 1820–1950*, ed. Ron Crocombe, Wellington, 1980.

Goddard, Michael, 'The Rascal Road: Crime, Prestige, and Development in Papua New Guinea', *TCP*, vii: 1, 1995.

Golson, Jack, 'Agriculture in New Guinea: the Long View', 'Agricultural Technology in New Guinea', and 'New Guinea Agricultural History: A Case Study', in Denoon and Snowden (eds), *A History of Agriculture in Papua New Guinea*.

Golson, Jack, and Gardner, Doug, 'Agriculture and Sociopolitical Organisation in New Guinea Highlands Prehistory', *Annual Review of Anthropology*, 1990.

Goodall, Heather, '"The Whole Truth and Nothing But...": Some Intersections of Western Law, Aboriginal History and Community Memory', in B. Attwood and J. Arnold (eds), *Power, Knowledge and Aborigines*, Bundoora, Vic., 1992.

Gotschalk, J., 'Sela Valley: An Ethnography of a Mek Society in the Eastern Highlands, Irian Jaya, Indonesia', PhD thesis, University of Amsterdam, 1993.

Grand, A. R., 'Pouvanaa a Oopa et Nationalisme à Tahiti', PhD thesis, University of Paris, 1981.

Graves, Adrian, *Cane and Labour: The Political Economy of the Queensland Sugar Industry*, Edinburgh, 1993.

Green, R. C., 'Near and Remote Oceania—Disestablishing "Melanesia" in Culture History', in A. Pawley (ed.), *Man and a Half: Essays in Pacific Anthropology and Ethnobiology in Honour of Ralph Bulmer*, Auckland, 1991.

Grezel, Isidore, *Dictionnaire Futunien-Français avec Notes Grammaticales*, Paris, 1878.

Griffin, James, 'Paul Mason: Planter and Coastwatcher', in J. T. Griffin (ed.), *Papua New Guinea Portraits: The Expatriate Experience*, ANU, 1979.

Griffin, James, *Bougainville: A Challenge for the Churches*, Sydney, 1995.

Griffin, James, Nelson, Hank, and Firth, Stewart, *Papua New Guinea: A Political History*, Melbourne, 1979.

Grimble, Arthur, *Tungaru Traditions: Writings in the Atoll Culture of the Gilbert Islands* (ed. H. E. Maude), Honolulu, 1989.

Groube, Les, 'Contradictions and Malaria in Melanesian and Australian Prehistory', in M. J. T. Spriggs *et al.*, *A Community of Culture: The People and Prehistory of the Pacific*, ANU, 1993.

Groube, Les, *et al.*, 'A 40,000-year-old Human Occupation Site at Huon Peninsula, Papua New Guinea', *Nature* 324 (1986).

Grynberg, Roman, 'The Tuna Dilemma', *Pacific Islands Monthly* (May 1993).

Guiart, Jean, *Un Siècle et Demi de Contacts Culturels Tanna, Nouvelles-Hebrides*, Paris, 1956.

Gunson, W. N., *Messengers of Grace: Evangelical Missionaries in the South Seas, 1797–1860*, Melbourne, 1978.

Haberkorn, Gerald, 'Paamese in Port Vila', in Connell, *Migration and Development*.

Halapua, Sitiveni, *Fishermen of Tonga: Their Means of Survival*, IPS, 1987.

Handy, E. S. C., *Polynesian Religion*, Bernice P. Bishop Museum, 1927.

Hanlon, David, *Upon a Stone Altar: A History of the Island of Pohnpei to 1890*, UHP, 1988.

Hanson, A., 'The Making of the Maori: Cultural Invention and its Logic', *American Anthropologist* 91 (1989).

Hau'ofa, Epeli, *Kisses in the Nederends*, Auckland, 1987.

Hau'ofa, Epeli, 'The New South Pacific Society: Integration and Independence', in Hooper *et al.*, *Class and Culture in the South Pacific*.

Hau'ofa, Epeli, 'Our Sea of Islands', in Eric Waddell, Vijay Naidu and Epeli Hau'ofa (eds), *A New Oceania: Rediscovering Our Sea of Islands*, Suva, 1993.

Hau'ofa, Epeli, 'Thy Kingdom Come', unpublished ms., 1993.

Hecht, Julia, 'The Culture of Gender in Pukapuka: Male, Female and the *Mayakitanga* "Sacred Maid"', *JPS* lxxxvi (1977)

Hempenstall, Peter, *Pacific Islanders under German Rule: A Study in the Meaning of Colonial Resistance*, ANU, 1978.

Hempenstall, Peter, and Rutherford, Noel, *Protest and Dissent in the Colonial Pacific*, IPS, 1984.

Henningham, Stephen, *France and the South Pacific: A Contemporary History*, Sydney, 1992.

Herr, Richard, 'Regionalism in the South Seas', PhD thesis, Duke University, 1976.

Hess, Jim, 'Migration, Networks, Resources, and Households: The Formation of a Marshallese Community in Orange County', 1993, typescript in possession of Karen Nero.

Hezel, Francis, *The First Taint of Civilization: A History of the Caroline and Marshall Islands in Pre-Colonial Days, 1521–1885*, UHP, 1983.

Hezel, Francis and Berg, Mark (eds), *Micronesia: Winds of Change*, Saipan, 1979.

Hill, A. V. S., and Serjeantson, S. W. (eds), *The Colonization of the Pacific: A Genetic Trail*, Oxford, 1989.

Hilliard, David, *God's Gentlemen: A History of the Melanesian Mission, 1849–1942*, St Lucia, Qld, 1978.

Hiscock, Peter, 'How Old are the Artefacts in Malakunanja II?', *Archaeology in Oceania* 25 (1990).

Hooper, A., *et al.* (eds), *Class and Culture in the South Pacific*, Auckland, 1987.

Hope, Geoff, and Golson, Jack, 'Late Quaternary Change in the Mountains of New Guinea', *Antiquity* 69 (special number 265), 1995.

Howard, Alan, and Borofsky, Robert (eds), *Developments in Polynesian Ethnology*, UHP, 1989.

Howard, Alan, and Kjellgren, Eric, 'Martyrs, Progress and Political Ambition: Re-examining Rotuma's "Religious Wars"', *JPH* xxix: 2 (1994).

Howard, Michael, *Mining, Politics, and Development in the South Pacific*, Boulder, 1994.

Howard, Michael (ed.), *Ethnicity and Nation-building in the Pacific*, Tokyo, 1989.

Howe, Kerry, *The Loyalty Islands: A History of Culture Contact, 1840–1900*, ANU, 1977.

Howe, Kerry, 'The Fate of the "Savage" in Pacific Historiography', *New Zealand Journal of History* xi (1977).

Howe, Kerry, *Where the Waves Fall: A New South Sea Islands History from First Settlement to Colonial Rule*, Sydney, 1984.

Howe, Kerry, Kiste, Robert, and Lal, Brij, *Tides of History: the Pacific Islands in the Twentieth Century*, UHP, 1994.

Hunt, E. E., Kidder, N. R., and Schneider, D. M., 'The Depopulation of Yap', *Human Biology* xxvi (1954).

Huntsman, Judith, and Hooper, Antony, 'Structures of Tokelau History', in *Transformations of Polynesian Culture*, Auckland, 1985.

Hviding, Edvard, *Guardians of Marovo Lagoon: Practice, Place and Politics in Maritime Melanesia*, UHP, 1996.

Hyndman, David, 'Sea Tenure and the Management of Living Marine Resources in Papua New Guinea', *Pacific Studies* 16: 4 (1993).

Hyndman, David, 'A Sacred Mountain of Gold: The Creation of a Mining Resource Frontier in Papua New Guinea', *JPH* xxix: 2 (1994).

Ihimaera, Witi, *et al.* (eds), *Te Ao Marama: Contemporary Maori Writing*, Auckland, 1993.

Inglis, Ken, 'War, Race and Loyalty in New Guinea, 1939–1945', in Inglis (ed.), *The History of Melanesia*, University of Papua New Guinea, 1969.

International Physicians for the Prevention of Nuclear War, *Radioactive Heaven and Earth*, New York, 1991.

Irwin, Geoffrey, 'The Emergence of Mailu', *Terra Australis* 10 (1985).

Irwin, Geoffrey, *The Prehistoric Exploration and Colonisation of the Pacific*, Cambridge, 1992.

Jaarsma, S. R., '"Your Work Is of No Use to Us . . .": Administrative Interests in Ethnographic Research (West New Guinea, 1950–1962)', *JPH* xxix: 2 (1994).

Jack-Hinton, Colin, *The Search for the Islands of Solomon, 1567–1838*, Oxford, 1969.

Jackson, Richard, *Ok Tedi: The Pot of Gold?*, Port Moresby, 1982.

Janes, Craig, *Migration, Social Change and Health: A Samoan Community in Urban California*, Stanford, 1990.

Jarvie, I., *The Revolution in Anthropology, Chicago*, 1964.

Jennings, J. D. (ed.), *The Prehistory of Polynesia*, Cambridge, 1979.

Jinks, Brian, 'Policy, planning and administration in Papua New Guinea, 1942–52', PhD thesis, University of Sydney, 1975.

Jolly, Margaret, 'Specters of Inauthenticity', *TCP* 4: 1 (1992).

Jolly, Margaret, '"Ill-Natured Comparisons"?: Racism and Relativism in European Representations of ni-Vanuatu from Cook's Second Voyage', *History and Anthropology* 5: 3 (1992).

Jolly, Margaret, *Women of the Place: Kastom, Colonialism and Gender in Vanuatu*, New York, 1994.

Jolly, Margaret, 'Other Mothers: Maternal "Insouciance" and the Depopulation Debate in Fiji and Vanuatu, 1890–1930', in M. Jolly and K. Ram (eds), *Maternities and Modernities: Colonial and Post-colonial Experiences in Asia and the Pacific*, Cambridge, 1997.

Jolly, Margaret, and Macintyre, Martha (eds), *Family and Gender in the Pacific: Domestic Contradictions and the Colonial Impact*, Cambridge, 1989.

Jolly, Margaret, and Thomas, Nicholas (eds), *The Politics of Tradition in the Pacific*, special issue 62 of *Oceania* (1993).

Jones, Pei Te Hurinui, *King Potatau: An Account of the Life of Potatau Te Wherowhero, the First Maori King*, Auckland, 1959.

Kamakau, Samuel, *Ruling Chiefs of Hawaii*, Honolulu, 1961.

Kawharu, I. H. (ed.), *Waitangi: Maaori and Paakehaa Perspectives of the Treaty of Waitangi*, Auckland, 1989.

Keesing, Roger, 'Creating the Past: Custom and Identity in the Contemporary Pacific', *TCP* 1–2 (1989).

Keesing, Roger, 'Colonial History as Contested Ground: The Bell Massacre in the Solomons', *History and Anthropology* 4 (1990).

Keesing, Roger, 'Reply to Trask', *TCP* 3 (1991).

Keesing, Roger, and Corris, Peter, *Lightning Meets the West Wind: The Malaita Massacre*, Melbourne, 1980.

Keesing, Roger, and Tonkinson, Robert (eds), *Reinventing Traditional Culture: The Politics of Kastom in Island Melanesia*, special issue 13 of *Mankind* (1982).

Kelly, Raymond, *Etoro Social Structure: A Study in Structural Contradiction*, Ann Arbor, 1974.

Kelsey, Jane, *A Question of Honour? Labour and the Treaty, 1984–1989*, Wellington, 1990.

Kennedy, Paul, *The Samoan Tangle: A Study in Anglo-German-American Relations*, St Lucia, Qld, 1974.

Kiddell-Monroe, Skephi, and Kiddell-Monroe, Rachel, 'Indonesia: Land Rights and Development', in Marcus Colchester and Larry Lohmann (eds), *The Struggle for Land and the Fate of the Forests*, London, 1993.

Kiki, Albert Maori, *Ten Thousand Years in a Lifetime*, Melbourne, 1968.

Kilani, M., *Les Cultes du Cargo Melanesiens: Mythe et Rationalité en Anthropologie*, Lausanne, 1983.

Kirch, Patrick, *The Evolution of the Polynesian Chiefdoms*, Cambridge, 1984.

Kirch, Patrick, *Feathered Gods and Fishhooks*, UHP, 1985.

Kirch, Patrick, 'Rethinking East Polynesian Prehistory', *JPS* 95: 1 (1986).

Kirch, Patrick, *The Wet and the Dry: Irrigation and Agriculture in Polynesia*, Chicago, 1994.

Kirch, Patrick, and Hunt, T. (eds), *Archaeology of the Lapita Cultural Complex: A Critical Review*, Seattle, 1988.

Kiste, Robert, *The Bikinians: A Study in Forced Migration*, Menlo Park, 1974.

Kituai, Augustin, 'Innovation and Intrusion: Villagers and Policemen in Papua New Guinea', *JPH* xxiii (1988).

Kituai, Augustin, 'My Gun, My Brother: Experiences of Papua New Guinea Policemen, 1920–1960', PhD thesis, ANU, 1994.

Knapman, Bruce, 'Capitalism's Economic Impact in Colonial Fiji, 1874–1939: Development or Underdevelopment', *JPH* xx (1985).

Knapman, Bruce, *Fiji's Economic History, 1874–1939: Studies of Capitalist Colonial Development*, ANU, 1987.

Knapman, Claudia, *White Women in Fiji, 1835–1930: The Ruin of Empire*, Sydney, 1986.

Kunitz, Stephen, *Disease and Social Diversity: The European Impact on the Health of Non-Europeans*, Oxford, 1994.

Kuykendall, Ralph, *The Hawaiian Kingdom*, Honolulu:
  vol. 1, *1778–1854: Foundation and Transformation*, 1938;
  vol. 2, *1854–1874: Twenty Critical Years*, 1953;
  vol. 3, *1874–1893: The Kalakaua Dynasty*, 1967.
Lal, Brij V., *Girmitiyas: The Origins of the Fiji Indians*, ANU, 1983.
Lal, Brij V., *Power and Prejudice: The Making of the Fiji Crisis*, Wellington, 1988.
Lal, Brij V., *Broken Waves: A History of the Fiji Islands in the Twentieth Century*, UHP, 1992.
Lal, Brij, Munro, Doug, and Beechert, Ed (eds), *Plantation Workers: Resistance and Accommodation*, UHP, 1994.
Lamb, David, *Exploiting the Tropical Rain Forest: An Account of Pulpwood Logging in Papua New Guinea*, UNESCO, Paris, 1990.
Lambert, S. M., *A Yankee Doctor in Paradise*, Boston, 1941.
Langdon, Robert, *The Lost Caravel*, Sydney, 1975.
Langdon, Robert, *The Lost Caravel Re-explored*, Canberra, 1988.
Langdon, Robert, 'When the Blue-egg Chickens Come Home to Roost: New Thoughts on the Prehistory of the Domestic Fowl in Asia, America and the Pacific Islands', *JPH* xxiv (1989).
Langdon, Robert, 'The Banana as a Key to Early American and Polynesian History', *JPH* xxviii (1993).
Langdon, Robert, 'The soapberry, a neglected clue to Polynesia's prehistoric past', *JPS* 105: 2 (1996).
Langmore, Diane, *Missionary Lives: Papua, 1874–1914*, UHP, 1989.
Laracy, Hugh, *Marists and Melanesians: A History of Catholic Missions in the Solomon Islands*, ANU, 1976.
Laracy, Hugh (ed.), *The Maasina Rule Movement: Solomon Islands, 1944–1952*, IPS, 1983.
Laracy, Hugh (ed.), *Tuvalu: A History*, IPS, 1983.
Laracy, Hugh (ed.), *Pacific Protest: The Maasina Rule Movement, Solomon Islands, 1944–1957*, IPS, 1983.
Latouche, Jean-Paul, *Mythistoire Tungaru*, Paris, 1984.
Lattas, A. (ed.), *Alienating Mirrors: Christianity, Cargo Cults and Colonialism in Melanesia*, special issue of *Oceania* 63: 1 (1992).
Lātūkefu, Sione, *Church and State in Tonga*, ANU, 1974.
Lātūkefu, Sione, 'Oral History and Pacific Island Missionaries', in D. Denoon and R. Lacey, *Oral Tradition in Melanesia*, Port Moresby, n.d. [1981].
Lawrence, Peter, 'Cargo Cult and Religious Beliefs among the Garia', *International Archives of Ethnography* 47 (1954).
Lawrence, Peter, *Road Belong Cargo: A Study of the Cargo Movement in the Southern Madang District*, Manchester, 1964.
Lessa, W., 'The Portuguese Discovery of the Isles of Sequeira', *Micronesica* xi (July 1975).
Lewis, David, *The Plantation Dream: Developing British New Guinea and Papua, 1884–1942*, ANU, 1996.
Lewthwaite, G. R., 'Geographical Knowledge of the Pacific Peoples', in H. R. Friis (ed.), *The Pacific Basin: a History of its Geographical Exploration*, New York, 1967.

Lextreyt, M., 'De la chute de Pouvanaa au retour en arrière des institutions', *Bulletin de la Société des Etudes Oceaniennes* 245, December 1988.

Lieber, Michael (ed.), *Exiles and Migrants in Oceania*, Honolulu, 1977.

Likuvalu, Albert, 'History and Migrations of Wallis and Futuna People', in Pollock and Crocombe, *French Polynesia*.

Lili'uokalani, *Hawai'i's Story by Hawai'i's Queen*, Rutland, Vt, n.d. [1964].

Lindstrom, Lamont, *Cargo Cult: Strange Stories of Desire from Melanesia and Beyond*, UHP, 1993.

Linnekin, Jocelyn, 'Defining Tradition: Variations on the Hawaiian Identity', *American Ethnologist* 10 (1983).

Linnekin, Jocelyn, 'Statistical Analysis of the Great *Mahele*: Some Preliminary Findings', *JPH* xxii (1987).

Linnekin, Jocelyn, *Sacred Queens and Women of Consequence: Rank, Gender, and Colonialism in the Hawaiian Islands*, Ann Arbor, 1990.

Linnekin, Jocelyn, 'Ignoble Savages and Other European Visions: The La Pérouse Affair in Samoan History', *JPH* xxvi: 1 (1991).

Linnekin, Jocelyn, 'Text Bites and the R-word: The Politics of Representing Scholarship', *TCP* 3 (1991).

Linnekin, Jocelyn, and Poyer, Lyn (eds), *Cultural Identity and Ethnicity in the Pacific*, UHP, 1990.

Loeliger, Carl, and Trompf, Gary (eds), *New Religious Movements in Melanesia*, IPS, 1985.

Long, Gavin, *The Final Campaigns: Australia in the War of 1939–1945*, series 1, vol. vii, Australian War Memorial, 1963.

Lua, Kisione, 'Migration into Haveluloto, Nuku'alofa', in *In Search of a Home*, IPS.

Lukere, Vicki, 'Mothers of the Taukei: Fijian Women and the Decrease of the Race', PhD thesis, ANU, 1997.

Maaka, Roger, 'The New Tribe: Conflicts and Continuities in the Social Organization of Urban Maori', *TCP* 6 (1994).

McArthur, Norma, *Island Populations of the Pacific*, ANU, 1967.

McCall, Grant, and Connell, John (eds), *A World Perspective on Pacific Islander Migration: Australia, New Zealand and the USA*, Sydney, 1993.

McCarthy, Dudley, *South-West Pacific Area—First Year. Kokoda to Wau: Australia in the War of 1939–1945*, series 1, vol. v, Australian War Memorial, 1959.

Macdonald, Barrie, *Cinderellas of the Empire: Towards a History of Kiribati and Tuvalu*, ANU, 1982.

McDowell, N., 'A Note on Cargo Cults and Cultural Constructions of Change', *Pacific Studies* 11 (1988).

McGee, W. A., and Henning, G. R., 'Investment in Lode Mining, Papua, 1878–1920', *JPH* xxv (1990).

McHenry, Donald F., *Micronesia: Trust Betrayed*, New York, 1975.

Mackay, Ross, 'The War Years: Methodists in Papua, 1942–1945', *JPH* xxvii: 1 (1992).

Macnaught, Timothy, *The Fijian Colonial Experience: A Study of the Neotraditional Order under British Colonial Rule prior to World War II*, ANU, 1982.

Macpherson, C., 'Public and Private Views of Home: Will Western Samoan Migrants Return?' *Pacific Viewpoint* 26 (1985).

Macpherson, C., 'I Don't Go There So Often Now: Changing Patterns of Commitment to Island Homelands among Some Migrants and Their Children', *Pacific Studies* 17: 3 (1994).

McSwain, Romola, *The Past and Future People: Tradition and Change on a New Guinea Island*, Melbourne, 1977.

Maddocks, Ian, 'Venereal Diseases', in Bell (ed.), *The Diseases and Health Services of Papua New Guinea*.

Maddocks, Ian, 'Medicine and Colonialism', *Australian and New Zealand Journal of Sociology* 11: 3 (1975).

Maher, Robert F., *New Men of Papua: A Study in Culture Change*, Madison, 1961.

Mair, Lucy, *Australia in New Guinea*, 2nd edn, Melbourne, 1970.

Malinowski, Bronislaw, *Argonauts of the Western Pacific: An Account of Native Enterprise and Adventure in the Archipelagoes of Melanesian New Guinea*, London, 1992.

Malo, David, 'Decrease of Population', *Hawaiian Spectator* 2 (1839).

Malo, David, *Hawaiian Antiquities*, 1839; 2nd edn, Bernice P. Bishop Museum, 1951.

Marcus, G. E., 'Power on the Extreme Periphery: The Perspective of Tongan Elites in the Modern World System', *Pacific Viewpoint* 22 (1981).

Marshall, Mac, 'Education and Depopulation on a Micronesian Atoll', *Micronesica* 15: 1–2 (1979).

Marshall, Mac, 'Beyond the Reef: Circular, Step, and "Permanent" Migration from Namoluk Atoll, FSM', typescript, 1992.

Marshall, Mac, and Marshall, Leslie B., *Silent Voices Speak: Women and Prohibition in Truk*, Belmont, Calif., 1990.

Martin, John, *Tonga Islands: William Mariner's Account (An Account of the Natives of the Tonga Islands, in the South Pacific Ocean . . .)*, 5th edn, Tonga, 1991.

Masterman, Sylvia, 'The Origins of International Rivalry in Samoa', MA thesis, University of London, 1934; published under the same title, London, 1934.

Maude, Harry, *Of Islands and Men: Studies in Pacific History*, Melbourne, 1968.

Maude, Harry, *Slavers in Paradise: The Peruvian Slave Trade in Polynesia, 1862–1864*, ANU, 1981.

May, R. J. (ed.), *Change and Movement: Readings on Internal Migration in Papua New Guinea*, ANU, 1977.

May, R. J. (ed.), *Micronationalist Movements in Papua New Guinea*, ANU, 1982.

Mazellier, P., *Tahiti Autonome*, Pape'ete, 1990.

Mead, Margaret, *New Lives for Old: Cultural Transformation—Manus, 1938–1953*, New York, 1956.

Meggitt, M. J., 'Male–female Relationships in the Highlands of Australian New Guinea', *American Anthropologist* lxvi (1964).

Meggitt, Mervyn, '"Pigs are Our Hearts": The Te Exchange Cycle among the Mae Enga of New Guinea', *Oceania* xliv: 3 (1974).

Meleisea, Malama, *The Making of Modern Samoa: Traditional Authority and Colonial Administration in the Modern History of Western Samoa*, IPS, 1987.

Meleisea, Malama, *et al.*, *Lagaga: A Short History of Western Samoa*, IPS, 1987.

Mellars, Paul, and Stringer, Chris (eds), *The Human Revolution: Behavioural and Biological Perspectives on the Origins of Modern Humans*, Edinburgh, 1989.

Mercer, Patricia, *White Australia Defied: Pacific Islander Settlements in North Queensland*, Townsville, 1995.

Merle, Isabelle, 'The Foundation of Voh', *JPH* xxvi (1991).

Merle, Isabelle, *Expériences coloniales: la Nouvelle-Calédonie, 1853–1920*, Paris, 1995.

Merwick, Donna (ed.), *Dangerous Liaisons: Essays in Honour of Greg Dening*, Melbourne, 1994.

Meyenn, Natalie, 'Only One Babai Pit in a Lifetime: Gilbertese Migration in the Pacific, 1938 and 1963/1964', BA Honours thesis, ANU, 1992.

Mitchell, Donald, *Land and Agriculture in Nagovisi*, Madang, 1976.

Moody, Roger (ed.), *The Indigenous Voice: Visions and Realities*, 2 vols, London, 1988.

Moore, Clive, *Kanaka: A History of Melanesian Mackay*, Port Moresby, 1985.

Moore, Clive, Leckie, Jacqueline, and Munro, Doug (eds), *Labour in the South Pacific*, Townsville, 1990.

Moorehead, Alan, *The Fatal Impact: An Account of the Invasion of the South Pacific 1767–1840*, London, 1966.

Morauta, Louise, 'Urban Movement and Rural Identity: A Papua New Guinea Example', *Pacific Viewpoint* 26 (1985).

Morauta, Louise (ed.), *Law and Order in a Changing Society*, ANU, 1986.

Morauta, Louise, Pernetta, John, and Heaney, William (eds), *Traditional Conservation in Papua New Guinea*, Port Moresby, 1982.

Morison, S. E., *The Struggle for Guadalcanal, August 1942 – February 1943: History of United States Naval Operations in World War II*, Boston, 1966.

Morison, S. E., *Coral Sea, Midway and Submarine Actions, May 1942 – August 1942: History of United States Naval Operations in World War II*, Boston, 1967.

Moyle, Richard, *The Samoan Journals of John Williams, 1830 and 1832*, ANU, 1984.

Moynagh, Michael, *Brown or White? A History of the Fiji Sugar Industry, 1873–1973*, ANU, 1981.

Mulvaney, D. J., and White, J. Peter (eds), *Australians to 1788*, Sydney, 1988.

Munn, Nancy, 'The Spatial Presentation of Cosmic Order in Walbiri Iconography', in A. Forge (ed.), *Primitive Art and Society*, New York, 1973.

Muñoz, Faye, 'Pacific Islanders: A Perplexed, Neglected Minority', *Social Casework* (March 1976).

Munro, Doug, 'Migration and the Shift to Development in Tuvalu', in Connell, *Migration and Development*.

Munro, Doug, 'Revisionism and its Enemies: Debating the Queensland Labour Trade', *JPH* xxx (1995).

Narokobi, Bernard, *The Melanesian Way*, Boroko and Suva, 1980.

Nelson, Hank, *Black, White and Gold: Gold Mining in Papua New Guinea, 1878–1930*, ANU, 1976;

Nelson, Hank, 'As Bilong Soldia: The Raising of the Papuan Infantry Battalion', *Yagl-Ambu* 7 (1980).

Nelson, Hank, 'Taim Bilong Pait: The Impact of the Second World War on Papua New Guinea', in W. McCoy (ed.), *Southeast Asia under Japanese Occupation*, Yale, 1980.

Nelson, Hank, 'Hold the Good Name of the Soldier: The Discipline of Papuan and New Guinea Infantry Battalions, 1940–1946', *JPH* xv: 4 (1980).

Nelson, Hank, *Taim Bilong Masta: The Australian Involvement with Papua New Guinea*, Sydney, 1982.

Nelson, Hank, 'The Troops, the Town and the Battle: Rabaul 1942', *JPH* xxvii: 2 (1992).

Neumann, Klaus, *Not the Way It Really Was: Constructing the Tolai Past*, UHP, 1992.

Newbury, Colin, 'The Makatea Phosphate Concession', in R. G. Ward (ed.), *Man in the Pacific Islands*, Oxford, 1972.

Newbury, Colin, *Tahiti Nui: Change and Survival in French Polynesia 1767–1945*, UHP, 1980.

Obeyesekere, Gananath, *The Apotheosis of Captain Cook: European Myth-making in the Pacific*, Bernice P. Bishop Museum, 1992.

O'Brien, Denise, and Tiffany, Sharon (eds), *Rethinking Women's Roles: Perspectives from the Pacific*, Berkeley, 1984.

O'Faircheallaigh, Ciaran, *Mining in the Papua New Guinea Economy, 1880–1980*, UPNG, 1982.

Ogden, Michael, 'MIRAB and The Marshall Islands', *Isla* ii (1994).

Oliver, Douglas, *Ancient Tahitian Society*, 3 vols, ANU, 1974.

Oliver, W. H., and Williams, B. R. (eds), *The Oxford History of New Zealand*, Oxford, 1981.

O'Meara, Tim, *Samoan Planters: Tradition and Economic Development in Polynesia*, New York, 1990.

O'Neill, Jack, *Up From South: A Prospector in New Guinea, 1931–1937*, Melbourne, 1971.

Ongka: A Self-account by a New Guinea Big-man, trans. Andrew Strathern, London, 1979.

Oram, Nigel, *Colonial Town to Melanesian City: Port Moresby 1884–1974*, ANU, 1976.

Ottino, P., *Rangiroa*, Editions Cujas, Paris, 1972.

Panoff, Michel, 'Maenge Labourers on European Plantations, 1915–42', *JPH* iv (1969).

Panoff, Michel, 'The French Way in Plantation Systems', *JPH* xxvi (1991).

Park, Chris, *Tropical Rainforests*, London, 1992.

Parmentier, Richard, *The Sacred Remains: Myth, History, and Polity in Belau*, Chicago, 1987.

Parry, John, *Ring-Ditch Fortifications in the Rewa Delta, Fiji: Air Photo Interpretation and Analysis*, Fiji Museum, Bulletin 3, 1977.

Parsonson, G. S., 'The Settlement of Oceania: An Examination of the Accidental Voyage Theory', in J. Golson (ed.), *Polynesian Navigation*, Wellington, 1963.

Paton, John G., *John G. Paton, Missionary to the New Hebrides: An Autobiography*, London, 1891.

Pawley, Andrew, and Ross, Malcolm, 'Austronesian Historical Linguistics and Culture History', *Annual Review of Anthropology*, 1993.

Pearson, Richard, 'Trade and the Rise of the Okinawan State', *Bulletin of the Indo-Pacific Prehistory Association* x (1991).

Pearson, W. H., 'The Reception of European Voyagers on Polynesian Islands, 1568–1797', *Journal de la Société des Océanistes* 26 (1970).

Peattie, Mark, *Nan'yo: The Rise and Fall of the Japanese in Micronesia, 1885–1945*, UHP, 1988.

Ploeg, Anton, 'First Contact in the Highlands of Irian Jaya', *JPH* xxx: 2 (1995).

Poirine, Bernard, *Tahiti: Stratégie pour l'après-nucléaire*, Tahiti, 1992.

Pollock, Nancy, and Crocombe, R. G. (eds), *French Polynesia: A book of selected readings*, IPS, 1988.

Pool, Ian, *Te Iwi Maori: A New Zealand Population Past, Present and Projected*, Auckland, 1991.

Powdermaker, Hortense, *Stranger and Friend: The Way of an Anthropologist*, London, 1967.

Pratt, George, 'The Genealogy of the Sun: A Samoan Legend', *Australian Association for the Advancement of Science* 1 (1888).

Price, Charles, 'The Asian and Pacific Island Peoples of Australia', in J. T. Fawcett and B. V. Cario (eds), *Pacific Bridges: The New Immigration from Asia and the Pacific Islands*, New York, 1987.

Rallu, J. L., 'Population of the French Overseas Territories in the Pacific: Past, Present and Projected', *JPH* xxvi (1991).

Ravuvu, Asesela, *Fijians at War, 1939–1945*, IPS, 1974.

Ravuvu, Asesela, *Vaka i Taukei: The Fijian Way of Life*, IPS, 1983.

Ravuvu, Asesela, *The Fijian Ethos*, IPS, 1987.

Ravuvu, Asesela, *The Facade of Democracy: Fijian Struggles for Political Control, 1930–1987*, Suva, 1991.

Raynor, Bill, 'Resource Management in Upland Forests of Pohnpei: Past Practices and Future Possibilities', *Isla* 2: 1 (1994).

Read, K. E., 'Effects of the Pacific War in the Markham Valley, New Guinea', *Oceania* xviii: 2 (1947).

Rimoldi, M., and Rimoldi, E., *Hahalis and the Labour of Love: A Social Movement on Buka Island*, Oxford, 1992.

Ritter, Philip, 'The Population of Kosrae at Contact', *Micronesica* xvii: 1–2 (1981).

Rivers, W. H. R. (ed.), *Essays on the Depopulation of Melanesia*, Cambridge, 1922.

Roberts, R. G., *et al.*, 'Thermoluminescence Dating of a 50,000-year-old Human Occupation Site in Northern Australia', *Nature* 345 (1990).

Robinson, Neville, *Villagers at War: Some Papua New Guinean Experiences of World War II*, ANU, 1981.

Roscoe, Paul, and Scaglion, Richard, 'Male Initiation and European Intrusion into the Sepik: A Preliminary Analysis', in Nancy Lutkehaus *et al.*, *Sepik Heritage: Tradition and Change in Papua New Guinea*, Bathurst, 1990.

Rosi, 'Papua New Guinea's New Parliament House: A Contested National Symbol', *TCP* 3: 2 (1991).

Routledge, David, 'Pacific History as Seen from the Pacific Islands', *Pacific Studies* 8: 2 (1985).

Roux, J. C., 'Traditional Melanesian Agriculture in New Caledonia and Pre-contact Population Distribution' in Yen and Mummery, *Pacific Production Systems*.

Rowland, M. J., 'The Distribution of Aboriginal Watercraft on the East Coast of Queensland: Implications for Culture Contact', *Australian Aboriginal Studies* 2 (1987).

Rubinstein, Donald, and Levin, Michael, 'Micronesian Migration to Guam: Social and Economic Characteristics', *Asian and Pacific Migration Journal* 1: 2 (1992).

Ryan, Dawn, 'Toaripi in Port Moresby and Lae', in May (ed.), *Change and Movement*.

Ryan, Dawn, 'Home Ties in Town: Toaripi in Port Moresby', *Canberra Anthropology* 12 (1989).

Sahlins, Marshall, *Moala: Culture and Nature on a Fijian Island*, Ann Arbor, 1962.

Sahlins, Marshall, *Historical Metaphors and Mythical Realities: Structure in the Early History of the Sandwich Islands Kingdom*, Ann Arbor, 1981.

Sahlins, Marshall, 'The Stranger-King, or Dumezil among the Fijians', *JPH* xvi (1981).

Sahlins, Marshall, *Islands of History*, Chicago, 1985.

Sahlins, Marshall, *Anahulu: Historical Ethnography*, vol. 1 of P. V. Kirch and M. D. Sahlins (eds), *Anahulu: The Anthropology of History in the Kingdom of Hawaii*, Chicago, 1992.

Sahlins, Marshall, 'The Discovery of the True Savage', in Merwick (ed.), *Dangerous Liaisons*.

Sahlins, Marshall, *How 'Natives' Think—About Captain Cook for Example*, Chicago, 1995.

Salisbury, Richard, *From Stone to Steel: Economic Consequences of a Technological Change in New Guinea*, Melbourne, 1962.

Salmond, Anne, *Two Worlds: First Meetings between Maori and Europeans, 1642–1772*, Auckland, 1993.

Saunders, Kay, *Workers in Bondage: The Origins and Bases of Unfree Labour in Queensland, 1824-1916*, Brisbane, 1982.

Scarr, Deryck, 'Creditors and the House of Hennings', *JPH* vii (1972).

Scarr, Deryck, *I, The Very Bayonet*, vol. 1 of *The Majesty of Colour: A Life of Sir John Bates Thurston*, ANU, 1973.

Scarr, Deryck, 'Recruits and Recruiters: A Portrait of the Pacific Islands Labour Trade', in J. W. Davidson and Deryck Scarr (eds), *Pacific Islands Portraits*, ANU, 1973.

Scarr, Deryck, *Fiji: A Short History*, Sydney, 1984.

Scarr, Deryck, *Fiji: Politics of Illusion*, Sydney, 1988.

Scarr, Deryck, *The History of the Pacific Islands: Kingdoms of the Reefs*, Melbourne, 1990.

Schieffelin, E., and Crittenden, R. (eds), *Like People You See in a Dream: First Contact in Six Papuan Societies*, Stanford, 1991.

Schieffelin, E., and Gewertz, D., *History and Ethnohistory in Papua New Guinea*, Oceania Monographs 28, University of Sydney, 1985.

Schwartz, T., *The Paliau Movement in the Admiralty Islands, 1946–1954*, New York, 1962.

Schwimmer, Erik (ed.), *The Maori People in the Nineteen-Sixties*, Auckland, 1968.

Scragg, Roy F. R., 'Lemankoa: 1920–1980', typescript.

Serpenti, L. M., *Cultivators in the Swamps: Social Structure and Horticulture in a New Guinea Society*, Assen, 1965.

Sharp, Andrew, *The Discovery of Australia*, Oxford, 1963.

Sharp, Andrew, *The Voyages of Abel Janszoon Tasman*, Oxford, 1968.

Shineberg, Barry, 'The Image of France: Recent Developments in French Polynesia', *JPH* xxi (1986).

Shineberg, Dorothy, *They Came for Sandalwood: A Study of the Sandalwood Trade in the Southwest Pacific, 1830–1865*, Melbourne, 1967.

Shineberg, Dorothy, 'Guns and Men in Melanesia', *JPH* vi (1971).

Shineberg, Dorothy, '"Noumea No Good, Noumea No Pay": New Hebridean Indentured Labour in New Caledonia, 1865–1925', *JPH* xxvi: 2 (1991).

Shineberg, Dorothy, '"The New Hebridean is Everywhere": The Oceanian Labor Trade to New Caledonia, 1865–1930', *Pacific Studies* 18: 2 (1995).

Shineberg, Dorothy (ed.), *The Trading Voyages of Andrew Cheyne*, UHP, 1971.

Sinclair, Keith, *The Origins of the Maori Wars*, Wellington, 1957.

Sinoto, Yosihiko H. (ed.), *Caroline Islands Archaeology: Investigations on Fefan, Faraulep, Woleai and Lamotrek*, Bernice P. Bishop Museum Pacific Anthropological Records, 35, 1984.

Smith, Bernard, *European Vision and the South Pacific*, 2nd edn, Sydney, 1985 (first published, 1960).

Smith, De Verne, 'The Palauans on Guam', typescript.

Smith, Gary, *Micronesia: Decolonisation and US Military Interests in the Trust Territories of the Pacific Islands*, Canberra, 1991.

Smith, M. A., Spriggs, M. J. T., and Fankhauser, B. (eds), *Sahul in Review*, ANU Prehistory Occasional Paper 24, 1993.

Smith, Peter, *Education and Colonial Control in Papua New Guinea: A Documentary History*, Melbourne, 1987.

Smith, T. R., *South Pacific Commission: An Analysis after Twenty-five Years*, Wellington, 1972.

Somare, Michael, *Sana*, Port Moresby, 1975.

Spate, Oskar, *The Pacific Since Magellan*, ANU:
    vol. 1, *The Spanish Lake*, 1979;
    vol. 2, *Monopolists and Freebooters*, 1983;
    vol. 3, *Paradise Found and Lost*, 1988.
Spriggs, M. J. T., 'Vegetable Kingdoms, Taro Irrigation and Pacific Prehistory', PhD thesis, ANU, 1981.
Spriggs, M. J. T., 'Dating Lapita: Another View', in M. J. T. Spriggs (ed.), *Lapita Design, Form and Composition*, ANU Prehistory Occasional Paper 19, 1990.
Spriggs, M. J. T., 'What is Southeast Asian about Lapita?', in T. Azakawa and E. Szathmary (eds), *Prehistoric Mongoloid Dispersals*, Oxford, 1996.
Spriggs, M. J. T., and Anderson, Athol, 'Late Colonization of East Polynesia', *Antiquity* 67 (1993).
Stannard, David, *Before the Horror: The Population of Hawai'i on the Eve of Western Contact*, UHP, 1989.
Steinbauer, F., *Melanesian Cargo Cults: New Salvation Movements in the South Pacific*, St Lucia, Qld, 1979.
Strathern, Marilyn (ed.), *Dealing with Inequality*, Cambridge, 1987.
Sutherland, William, *Beyond the Politics of Race: An Alternative History of Fiji to 1992*, Canberra, 1992.
Tagupa, William, *Politics in French Polynesia, 1945–1975*, Wellington, New Zealand Institute of International Affairs, 1976.
Takaki, Ronald, *Pau Hana: Plantation Life and Labor in Hawai'i, 1835–1920*, UHP, 1985.
Thakur, Ramesh (ed.), *The South Pacific: Problems, Issues and Prospects*, London, 1991.
Thaman, Konai, 'The Defining Distance: People, Places, and World-view', *Pacific Viewpoint* 26: 1 (1985).
Thomas, Nicholas, 'The Force of Ethnology: Origins and Significance of the Melanesia/Polynesia Division', *Current Anthropology* 30 (1989).
Thomas, Nicholas, *Marquesan Societies: Inequality and Political Transformation in Eastern Polynesia*, Oxford, 1990.
Thomas, Nicholas, 'Partial Texts: Representation, Colonialism and Agency in Pacific History', in *JPH* xxv (1990).
Thompson, V., and Adloff, R., *The French Pacific Islands: French Polynesia and New Caledonia*, Berkeley, 1971.
Thual, F., *Equations Polynésiennes*, Paris, Groupe de l'union centriste, Senat, 1992.
Tobin, Jack, 'The Resettlement of the Enewetak People: A Study of a Displaced Community in the Marshall Islands', PhD thesis, University of California, Berkeley, 1967.
Tom, Nancy, *The Chinese in Western Samoa 1875–1985*, Apia, 1986.
Townsend, G. W. L., *District Officer: From Untamed New Guinea to Lake Success, 1921–46*, Sydney, 1968.
Trask, H.-K., 'Natives and Anthropologists: The Colonial Struggle', *TCP* 3 (1991).
Trompf, Gary (ed.), *Cargo Cults and Millenarian Movements: Transoceanic Comparisons of New Religious Movements*, Berlin, 1990.

Tryon, Darrell (ed.), *Comparative Austronesian Dictionary*, 5 vols, Mouton de Gruyter, Berlin, 1995.

Tuimaleali'ifano, Morgan, *Samoans in Fiji: Migration, Identity and Communication*, Suva, 1990.

Underwood, Robert, 'Excursions into Inauthenticity: The Chamorros of Guam', *Pacific Viewpoint* 26 (1985).

Uriam, Kambati, *In Their Own Words: History and Society in Gilbertese Oral Tradition*, Canberra, 1995.

Va'a, L. F., 'Effects of Migration on Western Samoa: An Island Viewpoint', in G. McCall and J. Connell (eds), *A World Perspective on Pacific Islander Migration: Australia, New Zealand and the USA*, Sydney, 1993.

Vail, John, 'The Impact of the Mt Kare Goldrush on the People of the Tari District', in T. Taufa and C. Bass (eds), *Population, Family Health and Development*, UPNG, 1993.

Viviani, Nancy, *Nauru: Phosphate and Political Progress*, ANU, 1970.

von Strokirch, Karin, 'The Impact of Nuclear Testing on Politics in French Polynesia', *JPH* xxvi (1991).

von Strokirch, Karin, 'Tahitian Autonomy: Illusion or Reality?', PhD thesis, La Trobe University, 1993.

Wagner, Roy, 'The Talk of Koriki: A Daribi Contact Cult', *Social Analysis* 46 (1979).

Waiko, John, 'Be Jijimo: A History According to the Traditions of the Binandere People of Papua New Guinea', PhD thesis, ANU, 1982.

Waiko, John, *A Short History of Papua New Guinea*, Melbourne, 1993.

Ward, Alan, *A Show of Justice: Racial 'Amalgamation' in Nineteenth-Century New Zealand*, Canberra, 1974.

Ward, R. Gerard, *Land Use and Population in Fiji: A Geographic Study*, 1965.

Ward, R. Gerard, 'Native Fijian Villages: A Questionable Future', in M. Taylor (ed.), *Fiji: Future Imperfect*, Sydney, 1987.

Ward, R. Gerard, 'Contract Labor Recruitment from the Highlands of Papua New Guinea, 1950–1974', *International Migration Review* xxiv: 2 (1990).

Ward, R. Gerard, and Kingdon, Elizabeth (eds), *Land, Custom and Practice in the South Pacific*, Cambridge, 1995.

Wari, K. R., 'The Function of the National Cultural Council in Co-ordinating Cultural Development in Papua New Guinea', in R. Edwards and J. Stewart (eds), *Preserving Indigenous Cultures: A New Role for Museums*, Canberra, 1980.

Watters, R., 'Mirab Societies and Bureaucratic Elites', in Hooper *et al.*, *Class and Culture in the South Pacific*.

Weeks, Charles J. Jr, 'The United States Occupation of Tonga, 1942–1945: The Social and Economic Impact', *Pacific Historical Review* 56 (1987).

Weiner, Annette, *Women of Value, Men of Renown: New Perspectives in Trobriand Exchange*, Austin, 1976.

Weiner, Annette, *The Trobrianders of Papua New Guinea*, New York, 1987.

Weiner, Annette, and Schneider, J. (eds), *Cloth and Human Experience*, Washington, DC, 1989.

Weisgall, Jonathan, *Operation Crossroads: The Atomic Tests at Bikini Atoll*, Annapolis, 1994.

Wendt, Albert, 'Guardians and Wards: A Study of the Origins, Causes and First Two Years of the Mau Movement in Western Samoa', M.A. thesis, Victoria University of Wellington, 1965.

Wendt, Albert, *Pouliuli*, Auckland, 1977.

Wessen, A., *et al.*, *Migration and Health in a Small Society: The Case of Tokelau*, Oxford, 1992.

West, Francis, *Selected Letters of Hubert Murray*, Melbourne, 1970.

Wetherell, David, *Reluctant Mission: The Anglican Church in Papua New Guinea, 1891–1942*, Brisbane, 1977.

White, Geoffrey, *Identity Through History: Living Stories in a Solomons Island Society*, Cambridge, 1991.

White, Geoffrey, and Lindstrom, Lamont (eds), *The Pacific Theater: Island Representations of World War II*, UHP, 1989.

White, Geoffrey, *et al.* (eds), *The Big Death: Solomon Islanders Remember World War II*, Honiara and Suva, 1988.

White, Geoffrey, and Lindstrom, Lamont (eds), *Custom Today*, special issue 6 of *Anthropological Forum* (1993).

Whittaker, J. L., *et al.* (eds), *Documents and Readings in New Guinea History: Prehistory to 1889*, Brisbane, 1975.

Williams, John, *Missionary Enterprises in the South-Sea Islands*, Philadelphia, 1888.

Williams, John A., *Politics of the New Zealand Maori: Protest and Cooperation, 1891–1909*, Auckland, 1969.

Williams, Maslyn, and Macdonald, Barrie, *The Phosphateers: A History of the British Phosphate Commissioners and the Christmas Island Phosphate Commission*, Melbourne, 1985.

Wood, Ellen, 'Prelude to an Anti-War Constitution', *JPH* xxviii (1993).

Worsley, Peter, *The Trumpet Shall Sound*, New York, 1968.

Wurm, S. A., *Papuan Languages of Oceania*, Gunter Narr Verlag, Tubingen, 1982.

Yamakazi Tomoko, 'Sandakan No. 8 Brothel', in *Bulletin of Concerned Asian Scholars*, October–December 1975.

Yen, D. E., 'The Development of Sahul Agriculture with Australia as Bystander', *Antiquity* 69, special number 265 (1995).

Yen, D. E., and Mummery, J. M. J. (eds), *Pacific Production Systems: Approaches to Economic Prehistory*, ANU, 1990.

Young, John, 'Lau: A Windward Perspective', *JPH* xxviii (1993).

Young, Michael, '"Our Name is Women: We Are Bought with Lime-sticks and Limepots": an Analysis of the Autobiographical Narrative of a Kalauna Woman,' *Man* n.s. xviii (1983).

Young, Michael W., *Fighting with Food: Leadership, Values and Social Control in Massim Society*, Cambridge, 1971.

FILMS

Aoki, Diane (ed.), *Moving Images of the Pacific Islands: A Guide to Films and Videos*. University of Hawai'i, 1994, is an essential catalogue. Several excellent film and television documentaries are cited in this volume, or have shaped the authors' perceptions. These are listed by directors, titles, medium and date of production, consultant (if any), and name of distributor.

Andrews, George, *Auckland Fa'aSamoa*, TV, 1982, consultant Albert Wendt, Television New Zealand.

Buckley, Anthony, *Man on the Rim*, 13 TV films, 1988, consultant Alan Thorne, New South Wales State Library.

Connolly, Bob, and Anderson, Robin, *First Contact*, 16mm and video, 1983, Ronin Films.

Connolly, Bob, and Anderson, Robin, *Joe Leahy's Neighbours*, 16mm and video, 1988, Ronin Films.

Connolly, Bob, and Anderson, Robin, *Black Harvest*, 16mm and video, 1992, Film Australia.

McGraw–Hill, *Dead Birds*, 16mm and video, 1963, CRM.

Nairn, Charlie, *Ongka's Big Moka* (Granada Disappearing World Series), 16mm and video, 1974, consultant Andrew Strathern, Granada TV; known in the USA as *The Kawelka: Ongka's Big Moka*.

O'Rourke, Dennis, *Yap: How Did You Know We'd Like TV?*, 16mm and video, 1982, Film Australia.

O'Rourke, Dennis, *Half Life: A Parable for the Nuclear Age*, 16mm and video, 1986, Film Australia.

Owen, Chris, *Man Without Pigs*, 16mm and video, 1990, consultant John Waiko, Ronin Films.

Papua New Guinea Office of Information, *Trobriand Cricket: An Indigenous Response to Colonialism*, 16mm and video, 1976, consultant Gerry Leach, Ronin Films.

Pike, Andrew, Nelson, Hank, and Daws, Gavan, *Angels of War*, 16mm and video, 1983, Ronin Films.

Sekiguchi, Noriko, *Senso Daughters: Senjo no Onnatachi*, 16mm and video, 1990, Ronin Films.

INDEX

The entry for a country includes the people of that country, e.g. Tonga includes Tongans.

China

Japan

N o r t h   P a c i f i c   O c e a n

Midway Is.

Ryukyu Islands

Bonin Is

Wake

Johnston

Philippines

Mariana
Islands

Guam

Yap

Caroline Islands

Marshall
Islands

Palau

Federated States of Micronesia

Howland Baker

Kiribati

K i r i b a t i

Nauru

Banaba

Phoenix

Papua
New Guinea

Solomon
Islands

Tuvalu

Tokelau

Indonesia

Santa Cruz

Rotuma

Wallis
Futuna

San

Vanuatu

Fiji

T o n g a

Northern
Territory

Queensland

New
Caledonia

Western Australia

A u s t r a l i a

Norfolk

Kermadec
Islands

South
Australia

New South Wales

Lord Howe

Victoria

New
Zealand

Tasmania

Chatham
Islands

United States

Mexico

Hawai'i

Colombia

Galapagos
Islands

Ecuador

Peru

...Islands

Line Islands

Marquesas

k

F r e n c h

Tuamotu Archipelago

Society Islands

P o l y n e s i a

Tahiti

...nds

Austral Islands

Pitcairn

Chile

Rapanui ·
(Easter)

S o u t h   P a c i f i c
O c e a n